SHAREHOLDER PROTECTION IN CLOSE CORPORATIONS

Close corporations, which are legal forms popular with small and medium enterprises, are crucial to every major economy's private sector. However, unlike their 'public' corporation counterparts, close corporation minority shareholders have limited exit options, and are structurally vulnerable in conflicts with majority or controlling shareholders. 'Withdrawal remedies' – legal mechanisms enabling aggrieved shareholders to exit companies with monetary claims – are potent minority shareholder protection mechanisms.

This book critically examines the theory and operation of withdrawal remedies in four jurisdictions: the United States, the United Kingdom, Germany, and Japan. Developing and applying a theoretical and comparative framework to the analysis of these jurisdictions' withdrawal remedies, this book proposes a model withdrawal remedy that is potentially applicable to any jurisdiction. With its international, functional, and comparative analysis of withdrawal remedies, it challenges preconceptions about shareholder remedies and offers a methodology for comparative corporate law in both scholarship and practice.

Alan K Koh is Assistant Professor of Business Law at Nanyang Business School, Nanyang Technological University (Singapore), where he teaches corporate law and governance. He earned his Dr jur at Goethe University Frankfurt and is an Advocate and Solicitor of the Supreme Court of Singapore. His research focuses on comparative law and corporate law and governance in Asia. He is an elected member of the International Academy of Comparative Law.

INTERNATIONAL CORPORATE LAW AND FINANCIAL MARKET REGULATION

Corporate law and financial market regulation have major implications for how the modern economy is organized and regulated and for how risk is managed and distributed – domestically, regionally and internationally. This Series seeks to inform and lead the vibrant scholarly and policy debate in this highly dynamic area by publishing cutting-edge, timely and critical examinations of the most pressing and important questions in the field.

Shareholder Protection in Close Corporations

THEORY, OPERATION, AND APPLICATION OF SHAREHOLDER WITHDRAWAL

ALAN K. KOH
Nanyang Technological University

CAMBRIDGE
UNIVERSITY PRESS

CAMBRIDGE
UNIVERSITY PRESS

Shaftesbury Road, Cambridge CB2 8EA, United Kingdom

One Liberty Plaza, 20th Floor, New York, NY 10006, USA

477 Williamstown Road, Port Melbourne, VIC 3207, Australia

314–321, 3rd Floor, Plot 3, Splendor Forum, Jasola District Centre, New Delhi – 110025, India

103 Penang Road, #05–06/07, Visioncrest Commercial, Singapore 238467

Cambridge University Press is part of Cambridge University Press & Assessment, a department of the University of Cambridge.

We share the University's mission to contribute to society through the pursuit of education, learning and research at the highest international levels of excellence.

www.cambridge.org
Information on this title: www.cambridge.org/9781009545754

DOI: 10.1017/9781108634618

First published 2022
First paperback edition 2024

A catalogue record for this publication is available from the British Library

ISBN 978-1-108-49666-7 Hardback
ISBN 978-1-009-54575-4 Paperback

To my father, who taught me how (and how not) to learn, teach, and live

Contents

Figures and Tables

Preface

In close relationships, oppression, discord, and injustice are ubiquitous. Regrettably, no one person, much less a single book, can address that. This Book's goal is necessarily modest: to show how shareholder oppression and conflict in close corporations may be resolved by withdrawal. My substantive arguments and proposals are aimed primarily at persons working in corporate law (whether scholars, practitioners, or policymakers). But this Book's very form itself is an argument about comparative law methodology. It shows how comparative law – shorn of the interminable debates plaguing it – may be used as a *practical* tool for a first serious and coherent scholarly project on a classic legal problem that is executable by a single, determined jurist armed with time and the necessary language proficiencies. In other words, this Book is also intended as a working model of how to do comparative law seriously – and hopefully, to its intended audience, reasonably well – in English.

Acknowledgements

Every scholar begins their career heavily in scholarly debt. Happily, publishing a Book – and writing this section – is a way to acknowledge this, even if such debts only keep mounting. This Book began life as a scholarly project sparked by professional tribulations shortly after earning my first degree at the Faculty of Law, National University of Singapore (NUS Law). Along the way, it became a dissertation that was accepted for the award of the degree of Dr jur (Doctor of Law) (*summa cum laude*) by the Goethe University Faculty of Law in July 2019. I am deeply in debt to my *Betreuer*, Professor Moritz Bälz, for accepting me as *Doktorand* that blazing summer day in 2015, for his patience and candid feedback over the four years and three jobs it took to finish, and (together with Frau Marion Lewald) for shepherding me through an unfamiliar if rational and efficient administrative process. I am also grateful to Professor Tobias Tröger for graciously committing to act as *Zweitgutachter* (examiner) for a foreigner of strange background and for his critical comments on key parts of the dissertation, and to Professor Andreas Cahn for chairing my *Disputation* and for his feedback.

Next, I am deeply grateful to my commissioning editor, Joe Ng of Cambridge University Press, for his support and understanding (not least for the inevitable delays), to the anonymous referees who provided constructive feedback, to the *International Corporate Law and Financial Market Regulation* series editors for accepting this Book, and to Gemma Smith for her assistance on many matters. I would also like to thank James Baker, Helen Kitto, Maureen MacGlashan, Lee Xin Li, and many others without whom a book would be just a manuscript.

No thanks would suffice for Dan Puchniak, who has looked out for me since my undergraduate days at NUS Law, launched my fledgling scholarly career not once but twice, and who will always be the leading role model in my life as a teacher, scholar, and deeply decent human being. Kevin Tan, Takahashi Eiji, Harald Baum, Nakahigashi Masafumi, Philipp Maume, Ernest Lim, Teo Keang Sood, Mike Klausner, Gary Bell, and Tan Cheng Han have too at critical times offered their encouragement and support, for which I will always be grateful.

Scholarly colleagues who have kindly provided feedback on parts of this Book or other works based on the project material include, in no particular order, Christian Hofmann, Wakita Masanori, Goto Gen, Kim Kon-Sik, Curtis Milhaupt, Shishido Zenichi, Matsumoto Nobuko, Tokutsu Akira, Harata Hisashi, Chen Jianlin, Marc Dernauer, Stacey Steele, Vivien Chen, Akshaya Kamalnath, Chun Kyung-hoon, Robert Thompson, Martin Gelter, Afra Afsharipour, Robert Merkin, and Takahashi Eiji. I am grateful to Kato Akemi, Goto Kiwamu, and Katayama Shino for their kind assistance with obtaining access to Japanese legal materials, to Ng Wei Siang and Lim Jia Ren for their assistance with proofreading, and to Chong Shouyu for able research assistance.

To my contemporaries and erstwhile NUS Law colleagues Tan Zhong Xing, Justin Tan, and Kenneth Khoo: my thanks for the comradeship, despite our political and scholarly differences, in both good times and bad. My former Centre of Asian Legal Studies (CALS) colleagues Ayesha Wijayalath, Chong Siew Men, Shazny Ramlan, Dian Shah, Bo Tiojanco, Margaret Ang, Alexandria Chan, Shirley Mak, Finna Wong, and others also provided a sense of community that kept me going during hard times. The long-suffering librarians of NUS Law's C.J. Koh Law Library also deserve thanks for their patient support. I am also grateful to the senior scholars who, out of concern for me, tried to dissuade me from writing this Book at all – happily, their fears did not come to pass. My apologies to anyone whom I have inadvertently omitted to acknowledge.

Parts of the research for this Book could not have been performed without the support of institutions across the world. I acknowledge – with gratitude – the generous financial support from my previous employers CALS (Ad Hoc Grants) and NUS Law (Faculty Research and Conference Fund/Faculty Conference Fund) that funded in whole or part research visits, presentations, or conferences at the University of Tokyo, Max Planck Institute for International and Comparative Private Law (MPI-Privatrecht), University of New South Wales, Osaka City University (now Osaka Metropolitan University), La Trobe University, Case Western Reserve University, Seoul National University, Hitotsubashi University, the University of Melbourne, and Goethe University Frankfurt. I also thank the Max Planck Society for funding my Visiting Fellowship at MPI-Privatrecht in summer 2016, and Seoul National University for arranging and funding my visit in November 2019. I also benefited from presenting and discussing this work in Japanese at the 428th Meeting of the Kansai Business Law Study Group in February 2021.

To my current employer, the Division of Business Law, Nanyang Business School (NBS), Nanyang Technological University (NTU), the Head of Division Anil Samtani, and my colleagues (especially my fellow AC2302 Company Law and Corporate Governance instructors Joyce Lee and Fernandez Navprakash), I am grateful for a largely peaceful and supportive work environment (except for the disruptive COVID-19 pandemic) in which I could complete this Book. My NBS AC2302 students, who are a joy to teach, have been patiently understanding of – and even amused by – my oddly specific and inexplicable enthusiasm for shareholder oppression as a topic. Research funding from the NTU Start-Up Grant 04INS000773C300 is gratefully acknowledged for, inter alia, supporting my attendance at a conference at Monash Business School, purchase of scholarly resources, and employment of a research assistant. This research is also supported by the Ministry of Education, Singapore, under its Academic Research Fund Tier 1 (04MNP001989C300).

With one exception, my immediate family never quite understood what I was doing and why, but my parents tolerated with minimal complaint my constant presence at home before a screen surrounded by precariously balanced towers of paper. For their tolerance and patience I am grateful. An educator both inside and outside the public school system for most of his life, my late father Koh Joon Seng was also my first teacher, and in a roundabout way inspired me to take on the path of not just a scholar, but also an educator like he was. This Book, which was completed shortly after he left us, is dedicated to him. Among the living, my deepest gratitude is to my constant companion and now wife, Samantha, for everything – hugs, handcrafted caffeinated beverages, reading countless drafts of this Book in various stages of despair and completeness, supporting me and my mother through my father's final days, and the unshakeable belief that this Book would against all odds someday see the light of day. To her I owe everything.

This Book draws on papers that have received the American Society of Comparative Law Younger Comparativists Committee's Colin Picker Prize in Comparative Law (2018), the Asian Law Institute's Asian Law Junior Faculty Workshop Best Paper Prize (2019), and a commendation by the Governance Institute of Australia at the 2020 Corporate Law Teachers Association (now Society of Corporate Law Academics) Annual Conference. Parts of Chapters II and VII build on material originally published as Alan K. Koh, 'Shareholder Protection in Close Corporations and the Curious Case of Japan: The Enigmatic Past and Present of Withdrawal in a Leading Economy' (2020) 53(4) *Vanderbilt Journal of Transnational Law* 1207–64. I gratefully acknowledge Vanderbilt University Law School and the editors of the *Vanderbilt Journal of Transnational Law* for granting permission to incorporate published material into this Book.

I have attempted to state the laws of the various jurisdictions touched on as they were available to me as of the end of 2020 to early 2021, although (fittingly and usually unavoidably for most comparative works) due to limitations in accessibility to resources greatly exacerbated by the COVID-19 pandemic, the laws of Germany and Japan are mostly stated as of 2017–18 with only partial updates since. Errata and updates, if any, will be available at my website (www.alankkoh.com) or SSRN page (http://ssrn.com/author=1855690).

Abbreviations

A; A2d; A3d	Atlantic Reporter 1st/2nd/3rd series (West)
AB	Aktiebolag
AC	Appeal Cases
AD2d; AD3d	New York Reports Appellate Division, 2nd/3rd series
AG	Aktiengesellschaft
All ER	All England Law Reports
ann.	annotated
AnnCalCorpCode	West's Annotated California Corporations Code
AppCt	Court of Appeals; Appellate Court; Appeals Court
AppDiv	Appellate Division
BB	*Betriebs-Berater*
BCC	British Company Cases
BCLC	Butterworths Company Law Cases
BGB	Bürgerliches Gesetzbuch
BGBl	Bundesgesetzblatt
BGH	Bundesgerichtshof
BGHZ	Entscheidungen des Bundesgerichtshofes in Zivilsachen
BR	West's Bankruptcy Reporter
Bt	betéti társaság
BT-Drs	Bundestagdrucksache
BV	Besloten vennootschap
c.; ch.; Ch.	chapter of a book; a statute
CA	Court of Appeal (may differ by context but usually England and Wales)
CalApp4th; CalApp5th	California Appellate Reports, 4th/5th series
CalRptr2d; CalRptr3d	California Reporter, 2nd/3rd series
CB	Cumulative Bulletin
CDCal	United States District Court for the Central District of California

cf.	*confer/conferatur* (compare)
CFR	Code of Federal Regulations
Ch	The Law Reports, Chancery Division series (England and Wales); Chancery Division, High Court of Justice of England and Wales (as part of neutral citation)
ChD	Chancery Division, High Court of Justice of England and Wales
1st/2nd/ … Cir	United States Court of Appeals for the 1st/2nd/ … Circuit; (Louisiana) Court of Appeal, 1st Circuit
Co.	Company
Comp.	Compiled
Corp.	Corporation
CSOH	Outer House of the Court of Session (Scotland) (neutral citation)
Ct	Court
CtApp	Court of Appeals; Court of Appeal
Cth	Commonwealth (Australia – federal)
D__	District (United States District Court for ___ District)
DB	*Der Betrieb*
DC	District of Columbia
Del	Delaware
DelCh	Court of Chancery of Delaware
DGCL	Delaware General Corporation Law
Dist.	District
Div.	Division (of the Inner House of the Court of Session (Scotland))
DLLCA	Delaware Limited Liability Company Act
EBOR	*European Business Organization Law Review*
ECFR	*European Company & Financial Law Review*
ECR	European Court Reports
ed.; eds.	editor; editors
ed.	edition
… Edw 7	King Edward VIII (years of reign)
EEC	European Economic Community
e.g.	*exempli gratia* (for example)
et al.	and others
et seq.	and what follows
EU	European Union
EWCA Civ	Court of Appeal of England and Wales (Civil Division) (neutral citation)
EWHC … (Ch)	High Court of Justice of England and Wales (Chancery Division) (neutral citation)

EWHC ... (Comm)	High Court of Justice of England and Wales (Commercial Court) (neutral citation)
F; F2d; F3d	Federal Reporter 1st/2nd/3rd series (West)
f.; ff.	folio (on the (next) page(s))
fig.	figure
Fla	Florida
fn.; fns.	footnote(s) (usually referring to a footnote in the cross-referenced text)
FSupp	Federal Supplement (West)
Ga	Georgia
GenG	Genossenschaftsgesetz (Gesetz betreffend die Erwerbs- und Wirtschaftsgenossenschaften)
GK	Gōdō Kaisha
GmbH	Gesellschaft mit beschränkter Haftung
GmbHG	Gesetz betreffend die Gesellschaften mit beschränkter Haftung
GmbHR	*GmbH-Rundschau*
Hare	Hare's Reports (English Reports)
HB	House Bill
HGB	Handelsgesetzbuch
HKC	Hong Kong Cases
HKCA	Hong Kong Court of Appeal
HKCFA	Hong Kong Court of Final Appeal
HKLRD	Hong Kong Law Reports and Digest
HL	House of Lords (UK)
IH	Inner House of the Court of Session (Scotland)
Ill	Illinois
Ill2d	Illinois Reports, 2nd series
IllApp3d	Illinois Appellate Court Reports, 3rd series
Inc.	Incorporated
Ind	Indiana
IRC	Internal Revenue Code (US)
IRS	Internal Revenue Service
Ibid.	ibidem (in the same place)
i.e.	*id est* (in other words)
J	Judge/Justice (United States); Justice (common law jurisdictions generally)
JCLS	*Journal of Corporate Law Studies*
Kaishahō	*Kaisha Hō* [Companies Act] (Japan)
Kan	Kansas
KanApp2d	Kansas Court of Appeals Reports, 2nd series
kft	korlátolt felelősségű társaság

KG	Kommanditgesellschaft
KGaA	Kommanditgesellschaft auf Aktien
KK	Kabushiki Kaisha
KMU	kleine und mittlere Unternehmen
L	law; laws
La	Louisiana
LG	Landgericht
LJ	Lord Justice/Lady Justice; *Law Journal*
LLC	Limited Liability Company
LRev	*Law Review*
LMCLQ	*Lloyd's Maritime and Commercial Law Quarterly*
LQ	*Law Quarterly*
LQR	*Law Quarterly Review*
Ltd	Private Limited Company (UK); Public Limited Company (Singapore)
Mass	Massachusetts; Massachusetts Reports
MassLRptr	Massachusetts Law Reporter
MBCA	Model Business Corporation Act
Md	Maryland; Maryland Reports
Md App	Maryland Appellate Reports
MdSpecApp	Maryland Court of Special Appeals
Mich	Michigan; Michigan Reports
Minn	Minnesota
Minshū	Saikō Saibansho Minji Hanreishū
Misc 2d/3d	New York Miscellaneous Court Reports, 2nd/3rd series
MLR	*Modern Law Review*
Mo	Missouri
MoMiG	Gesetz zur Modernisierung des GmbH-Rechts und zur Bekämpfung von Missbräuchen
Mont	Montana; Montana Reports
n.; nn.	note(s) (usually referring to another footnote within this Book but also for sources using endnotes/non-footnotes)
NC	North Carolina
NCApp	North Carolina Court of Appeals Reports
NCCUSL	National Conference of Commissioners on Uniform State Laws
ND	North Dakota (state and neutral citation)
NE2d; NE3d	North Eastern Reporter, 2nd/3rd series (West)
Neb	Nebraska; Nebraska Reports
Nev	Nevada; Nevada Reports

NI	Northern Ireland
NJ	New Jersey; New Jersey Reports
NJSuper	New Jersey Superior Court Reports
NJW	*Neue Juristische Wochenschrift*
NJW-RR	*Neue Juristische Wochenschrift Rechtsprechungs-Report*
No.	number
NM	New Mexico; New Mexico Reports
NTA	Kokuzei-chō [National Tax Agency] (Japan)
NW; NW2d	North Western Reporter, 1st/2nd series (West)
NY; NY2d; NY3d	New York; New York Reports, 1st/2nd/3rd series
NYBCL	New York Business Corporation Law (McKinney)
NYLLCL	New York Limited Liability Company Law (McKinney)
NYS2d; NYS3d	West's New York Supplement, 2nd/3rd series
NZG	*Neue Zeitschrift für Gesellschaftsrecht*
NZLR	New Zealand Law Reports
OH	Outer House of the Court of Session (Scotland)
OHG	offene Handelsgesellschaft
OLG	Oberlandesgericht
Or	Oregon; Oregon Reports
OrApp	Oregon Reports, Court of Appeals
P; P2d; P3d	Pacific Reporter 1st/2nd/3rd series (West)
Pa	Pennsylvania
PA	Public Act (US)
para.	paragraph
PL	Public Law (US)
plc.	Public Limited Company (UK)
Pte Ltd	Private Limited Company (Singapore)
Pty Ltd	Proprietary Limited Company (Australia)
PULLCA	Prototype Limited Liability Company Act
QC	Queen's Counsel
r.; rr.	rule(s)
RSC	Revised Statutes of Canada
Rdn	Randnummer
Re. . . .	in the matter of . . . (common law cases)
Rev.	Revised
RG	Reichsgericht
RGBl	Reichsgesetzblatt
RGZ	Entscheidungen des Reichsgerichts in Zivilsachen
RI	Rhode Island
RULLCA	Revised Uniform Limited Liability Company Act
s.; ss.; §	section(s)
S	Seite

SB	Senate Bill
SC	South Carolina; South Carolina Reports
SCC	Supreme Court of Canada (neutral citation)
Scot	Scotland
SCR	Supreme Court Reports (Canada)
SE	Societas Europaea
SE2d	South Eastern Reporter (West), 2nd series
SGCA	Singapore Court of Appeal (neutral citation)
Shōhō	*Shōhō* [Commercial Code] (Japan)
SI	Statutory Instrument
SME	small and medium enterprise
SLR	Singapore Law Reports
SLT	*Scots Law Times*
So3d	Southern Reporter, 3rd series (West)
SpruchG	Spruchverfahrensgesetz (Gesetz über das gesellschaftsrechtliche Spruchverfahren)
Stat.	Statutes
SupCt	Supreme Court
Super	Superior Court
SW2d; SW3d	South Western Reporter, 2nd/3rd series (West)
tbl.	table
Tenn	Tennessee
Tex	Texas
UG	Unternehmergesellschaft
UK	United Kingdom of Great Britain and Northern Ireland
UKPC	Privy Council of the UK (neutral citation)
ULLCA	Uniform Limited Liability Company Act
USA/US	United States of America
US	United States Reports
US-CC	US-Close Corporation
USCA	United States Code Annotated (West)
. . . v. . . .	against (common law cases)
Va	Virginia; Virginia Reports
VC	Vice-Chancellor (England and Wales; Delaware)
. . . Vic	Queen Victoria (years of reign)
VLR	Victorian Law Reports (Victoria, Australia)
vol.	volume
Wash	Washington
Wash2d	Washington Reports, 2nd series
WashApp	Washington Appellate Reports
Wheat	Wheaton (volume of United States Reports by Henry Wheaton)

WL	Westlaw (document identifier)
WLR	Weekly Law Reports
WVa	West Virginia; West Virginia Reports
YK	Yūgen Kaisha
ZJapanR [JJapanL]	*Zeitschrift für Japanisches Recht* [*Journal of Japanese Law*]

I

Introduction

A OBJECTIVES OF THIS BOOK

Oppressed, outvoted, and outgunned minority shareholders have a seemingly obvious solution for their woes: vote with their feet, sell their shares, and leave the company. But this 'Wall Street walk' is only available to shareholders in public, listed corporations. What if selling your shares on the stock market is simply not an option – because there is no market for them?

Although the importance of shareholder exit is taken for granted by corporate governance scholars devoted to the study of *public corporations*, exit's equally essential role in *close corporations* – privately owned business entities from which shareholder exit might not be possible – is often overlooked. What close corporations need are legal solutions enabling, in appropriate circumstances, a shareholder to voluntarily exit a company with a monetary claim. 'Withdrawal remedies', a family of doctrinally distinct but functionally equivalent legal solutions, cater precisely to this demand.

Despite their presence in the world's leading corporate law jurisdictions, withdrawal remedies have received little recognition as a coherent category in the international comparative corporate law discourse. No international, functional, and comparative analysis on close corporation withdrawal remedies across leading economies addressing their nature, functions, and effectiveness as minority shareholder protection currently exists. This is a surprising gap in the literature, given that close corporations are generally the dominant business form in each economy, and that substantial domestic awareness of the importance of shareholder protection in close corporations exists in virtually every major jurisdiction.

This Book critically analyses withdrawal remedies in the world's four largest developed economies, namely the United States of America (US), Japan, the Federal Republic of Germany (Germany), and the United Kingdom of Great Britain and Northern Ireland (UK). These four jurisdictions not only exert strong influence on the world economy and legal thought, but also span both the common law/civil law and the East/West divides. Together, they constitute a rich sample of our world's immense legal diversity and heritage. Analysis of the four jurisdictions is conducted by applying a theoretical and comparative framework developed for this Book. Based on the insights garnered, I propose a model withdrawal remedy of general, potentially universal, application in legislative reform, judicial dispute resolution, and other areas.

Having set out the objectives of this Book, issues of methodology and terminology are clarified next.

B METHODOLOGY

1 *Why Look at Close Corporations?*

Small and medium enterprises (SMEs) are a dominating presence in the private sector of every economy, the vehicle for entrepreneurship, and a crucial engine of innovation and economic growth. The importance of SMEs holds true not only for the world's developed economies generally,[1] but also specifically in four world-leading economies in terms of economic and legal influence, namely, the US, the UK, Germany, and Japan.[2] SME firms often, if not usually, take legal form as unlisted, closely held business entities offering separate legal personality and limited liability.[3] These closely held business entities vastly outnumber widely held entities, and account for a significant share of economic output and employment in these four jurisdictions.

Considering the SME sector's economic importance and the fundamental differences between SMEs and the large, often multinational business conglomerates that easily dominate both popular imagination and academic writing, it is trite that SME-focused scholarship is both necessary and

[1] OECD: OECD (2010): 5; Asia: ADB (2015): 7. Minor jurisdictional differences in definitions of SME do not impede meaningful comparison.

[2] USTR (2021); EC (2019); BMWi (2021); METI (2016): 1.

[3] Bachmann et al. (2014): v.

TABLE 1.1 *SMEs in four leading jurisdictions*

Jurisdiction (Year of data)	Share of total number of business entities (%)	Share of private sector employment (%)	Economic contribution (%) [basis, year if different]	Dominant close corporation legal form(s)[1]
US (2017)[2]	99.6	48.1	41.9 [annual payroll][3]	US-close corporation/ LLC[4]
UK (2020)[5]	99.9[6]	52.1[7]	52.2[8] [private sector turnover]	Private limited company (Ltd)[9]
Germany (2018)[10]	99.5	78.4[11]	61.1[12] [enterprise net value added]	GmbH[13]
Japan[14] (2016)	99.3[15]	61.6[16]	52.9[17] [gross value added, 2015]	KK/GK[18]

1 Excluding sole proprietorships. See also I.B.4 below.

2 Computed based on 'Corporation', 'S-Corporation', 'Partnership', and 'Sole Proprietorship' category data from USCB (2020).

3 Cf Kobe (2012): 44 (non-farm sector SMEs contributed 44.6 per cent by GDP in 2010).

4 US close corporation (US-CCs) are reflected in economic statistics primarily as S-Corporations (with pass-through tax treatment), whereas LLCs are usually classified as partnerships; see VI.B.3, VI.D.3. Of the 5,553,337 private sector SME firms (defined as employing fewer than 500 employees, and excluding 'Nonprofit', 'Government', and 'Other' entities), 3,085,273 (55.6 per cent) are S-Corporations, and 700,127 (12.6 per cent) are partnerships. Partnerships are not further broken down into LLCs/LPs/LLPs/ LLLPs/general partnerships/etc., but it may be safely assumed that LLCs comprise the plurality if not majority. In contrast, C-Corporations (932,891) comprise 16.8 per cent, and sole proprietorships (835,046) just 15.0 per cent. Figures are computed based on USCB (2020).

5 BEIS (2020).

6 Calculated from BEIS (2020): 4 tbl. A.

7 Excluding the 4.568 million businesses without employees (comprising sole proprietorships, partnerships with one self-employed owner-manager, and companies with only one employee), employers employing up to 249 employees employed 11.870 million out of 22.766 million employees, or 52.14 per cent: ibid. 4 tbl A.

8 SMEs (including those with no employees) account for GBP 2,270,229 million out of the total turnover of 4,346,969 million for all businesses, or 52.23 per cent. If businesses without employees are excluded, 48.45 per cent (GBP 1,954,601 million out of GBP 4,034,341 million). Computed from figures in ibid.

9 Actively trading companies (including a small fraction that are limited liability partnerships, public companies, etc.) comprised 34 per cent of the total business population, while sole proprietorships comprised 59 per cent and partnerships 7 per cent: ibid. 5. Only a tiny fraction of all companies are non-Ltds: see V.B.3.

10 IfM (2021b).

11 Including apprenticeships; for employees subject to social insurance contributions only, 57.6 per cent: ibid.

12 By enterprise turnover, 34.4 per cent: ibid.

13 IV.B.3 tbl. 4.1. Many German limited partnerships (KG) are formed around a GmbH core: IV.B.3.

14 SMEA (2020). Figures are for non-primary industry corporates only.

15 Ibid. Appendix III-21.

16 Ibid. Appendix III-29.

17 Ibid. Appendix III-36.

18 KKs include ex-*Yūgen Kaisha* (YKs). On KKs and GKs see VII.B.1, VII.E.1 respectively.

desirable.[4] However, corporate law scholarship has not always given SMEs – or more specifically, the close corporation legal forms often adopted by multi-owner SMEs[5] – their due. Whereas shareholder (investor) protection issues in public, widely held companies has captivated high-level international academia for decades,[6] the same cannot be said for the close corporation, the 'orphan of corporate law'.[7] The fact that the close corporation seldom attracts the level of scholarly attention that would befit a subfield separate and distinct from the public corporation-dominated paradigm[8] is unfortunate. It should not be forgotten that the close corporation is the cradle of modern business; regardless of eventual size or scale, virtually all businesses begin life as a closely held business entity, most frequently as a corporation offering limited liability.[9]

As a (if not *the*) dominant business entity by the numbers in any economy and a key vehicle of entrepreneurship and economic growth, close corporations should be a topic of interest for regulators, policymakers, judges, legal practitioners, and scholars alike. This is underscored by the work of the United Nations Commission on International Trade Law (UNCITRAL)'s Working Group I on a draft 'legislative guide' on a new business organization form for SMEs.[10] No jurisdiction serious about corporate law and the SME sector can turn a blind eye to the legal issues faced by close corporations, especially the issue of shareholder protection.[11] Indeed, there is no shortage of high quality local scholarship from each of the world's leading jurisdictions on close corporation issues – but narrowly focused on domestic law.[12] There remains a considerable gap in the *international* corporate law literature on close corporations from a comparative perspective.[13]

4 Business and economics researchers recognise the study of SMEs as a separate and respectable academic subfield with its own speciality journals.

5 While SMEs do not necessarily take the close corporation form, it is fair to say that a significant proportion – perhaps even a majority – do. SMEs also take the form of sole proprietorships and partnerships in the narrow sense (i.e. firms with or without separate legal personality but in any event without full limited liability for the partners), although precise breakdowns for each jurisdiction are not freely available. These business forms are beyond the scope of this Book.

6 The literature is legion. See e.g. La Porta et al. (1997); La Porta et al. (1998); La Porta et al. (1999); La Porta et al. (2000); Easterbrook & Fischel (1991); Kraakman et al. (2004).

7 This memorable moniker is from Chayes (1960): 1532.

8 Germany is a happy exception to the rule – but only domestically.

9 Or closely related hybrid forms such as limited liability companies (LLCs) in the US. Even highly valued technology 'unicorns' that subsequently 'go public' or get acquired by incumbent giants often start as closely held start-ups.

10 UNCITRAL (2020).

11 Japan is a partial exception, at least historically. See VII.B.2.

12 Articles in periodicals are numerous; for sample book-length works, see e.g. O'Neal & Thompson (2020b) and Ribstein (2010) (the US); Hollington (2017) and Boyle (2002) (the UK); Fleischer & Goette (2018) and Goette (2014) (Germany); Kanda (2014) (Japan).

13 Exceptions include Bachmann et al. (2014); Roth & Kindler (2013); McCahery & Vermeulen (2008) (on non-listed firms generally).

2 Why Compare Four Jurisdictions – and How? Introducing the Tripartite Method

'Comparative law' is a discipline of considerable vintage, as well as great methodological diversity – and controversy.[14] It thus behoves the comparatist – apprentice and expert alike – to explain and defend their choices. I do so with reference to comparative law methodologies as specifically applied to influential corporate law works.[15]

An approach that has seized the field of comparative corporate law by storm[16] is 'leximetrics'[17] or 'numerical comparative law'.[18] Broadly speaking, these terms refer to a method that encompasses any 'quantitative measurement of law'[19] that 'translate[s] [statutes and cases] into numbers'.[20] While the leximetric movement has made tremendous strides relatively quickly and produced a substantial body of high-level literature,[21] the method is not without fundamental limitations. The first is lack of detail and precision.[22] Even in highly sophisticated projects, index construction, accurate coding of the variables, and the assignment of proper weights to each examined element pose formidable challenges for researchers seeking to minimize subjectivity and error in judgement.[23] Second, leximetrics work best when the necessary groundwork, such as clear definitions of the factors to be examined, terminology transcending the boundaries of individual jurisdictions, are in place.[24] In the case of withdrawal (the subject of this Book), there is yet to be any international, comparative, and functional terminology that is widely recognised or accepted,[25] which poses

14 For a sampling of various approaches, see Siems (2018b); Bussani & Mattei (2012).

15 Literature on comparative law theory and methodology is hopelessly voluminous, but helpful examples featuring concrete analysis of corporate law is uncommon. Selected exceptions are referenced below.

16 See e.g. Lele & Siems (2007); Armour et al. (2009a); Armour et al. (2009b); and Siems (2010).

17 As coined in Cooter & Ginsburg (2003).

18 As popularised by Siems (2005).

19 Siems (2008): 114.

20 Siems (2005): 523.

21 See e.g. sources in (n. 16) above.

22 Puchniak (2012): 28; Lele & Siems (2007): 19–21.

23 Siems (2018b): 211; see also Spamann (2010): 483.

24 For example, Katelouzou and Siems' ten variables in their 'shareholder protection index' rely on seemingly accepted concepts such as 'independent directors' and 'derivative suits': Katelouzou & Siems (2015): 130 tbl. 1. But even these cannot be taken for granted; as two studies on a range of Asian jurisdictions on derivative actions and independent directors (Puchniak et al. (2012); Puchniak et al. (2017)) show, different jurisdictions adopt very different versions of these corporate law institutions.

25 'Withdrawal' for the purposes of this Book is defined and distinguished from related concepts in II.C, II.D.1–2. Although the first edition of *The Anatomy of Corporate Law* introduced a concept of '*the right to withdraw* the value of one's investment', this referred primarily to the appraisal-type rights and remedies, and not 'withdrawal' within the sense of this Book: Kraakman et al. (2004): 25. Other than the UK unfair prejudice remedy, which is only mentioned briefly in a paragraph focusing on other types of exit rights, *Anatomy* did not discuss other 'withdrawal' remedies within the sense of this Book in other jurisdictions: see ibid. 123. The third edition demonstrates an improved awareness of withdrawal remedies, but again does not go into any significant depth: Armour & Enriques et al.

considerable difficulties for leximetrical analysis. Third, even a successful attempt to analyse withdrawal with an exhaustive, leximetrical study of up to hundreds of national and state/provincial-level jurisdictions[26] would not capture the detailed and nuanced jurisdiction-specific information necessary to produce a model remedy of general application[27] – which is an aim of this Book.

The more traditional approach adopted by serious, mainstream comparative works in corporate law would feature just one or at most two other jurisdictions, draw on primary sources from no more than two languages, and target any proposals at just one specific jurisdiction.[28] Although this is a popular approach well-suited to monographical projects, analytical depth and detail of the two or three jurisdictions under study is almost invariably achieved at a cost: the big picture. The resulting work may often be of value to a particular jurisdiction (often the author's own) as a source of ideas and law reform proposals. The downside: being of limited general application, the product is unlikely to draw interest from the broader international audience.

A third and more modern approach, exemplified by *The Anatomy of Corporate Law* and works in similar style,[29] is to create a broad framework of sorts into which individual legal elements from various jurisdictions – statutory provisions, judicial precedent, or scholarly doctrine[30] – are plugged. A variation of this method is to use hypothetical cases in place of a framework.[31] When this method is well-executed, the

(2017): 34 and fn. 25 (discussing a 'right to withdraw' but meaning again appraisal rights in corporations, withdrawal rights specific to partnerships, mutual funds (investment companies) in the US, or otherwise created expressly by contract), 88 (mentioning that 'corporate law sometimes does provide stronger exit rights, in particular for closely held companies, but usually only upon egregious abuse of power by a controlling shareholder or in conjunction with a major transformation of the enterprise' but citing only appraisal and the mandatory bid rule as examples), 152 and fns. 52–4 (generally discussing dissolution but not withdrawal remedies, with the interesting exception of Brazil), 188 (mentioning that unfair prejudice in the UK potentially offering minority shareholders exit at a fair price in the context of majority-minority shareholder conflict in mergers).

In leximetrical studies, withdrawal also receives scant attention. Shareholder withdrawal and exit rights and remedies are conspicuously absent in the 'shareholder protection index' in Katelouzou & Siems (2015). See also Lele & Siems (2007): 49 (including in the definition of 'right to exit' only exit rights that are typically available only in public, listed corporations).

26 When sub-national level entities such as Canadian provinces and US states are included, the total number of jurisdictions with corporate law regimes would comfortably exceed 200.

27 As an eminent American legal scholar responding to the LLSV phenomenon once colourfully put it: 'Orthodox comparative lawyers would have shrunk back from such an ambitious endeavor and if they had attempted, it would have wound up with a tome of 2000 pages and 6000 footnotes filled with caveats and qualifications that would have rendered it unreadable': Vagts (2002): 604.

28 Schindler (1999) (comparing Germany with France); Sakamaki (1973) (comparing Japan with the UK and US); Takahashi (1998) (comparing Japan and Germany); Hirota (2013) (comparing Japan with the UK and Canada); Boros (1995) (comparing the UK and Australia). A partial exception is de Vries (2010) (comparing the Netherlands with the UK and Germany but targeting its proposals towards only Dutch law).

29 Armour & Enriques et al. (2017); Bachmann et al. (2014); Roth & Kindler (2013); Siems (2007).

30 On 'legal formants', see Sacco (1991): 22.

31 Siems & Cabrelli (2013); see also LoPucki (2018).

product offers conceptual clarity, the potential of general application, and value to a broad audience. What is inevitably sacrificed is the opportunity to offer readers foreign to a particular jurisdiction an internally coherent view, from the perspective of a quasi-insider of that jurisdiction, of the legal regime or institution that is the subject of the comparative study. A reader seeking something other than a solution to a specific scenario – such as a reasonably concise overview of the legal principle or institution in question – in any particular jurisdiction would have to look elsewhere.

The fourth and increasingly popular approach is to combine elements of the second and third approaches to produce a long collection of essays featuring thematic or conceptual framework chapters (sometimes combined into a single lengthy 'general report'), as well as jurisdiction-specific chapters ('national reports' or '*Länderberichte*'). The core of the work is usually a questionnaire into which information from each individual jurisdiction would be fitted, with varying degrees of success, for the jurisdictional chapters.[32] While this two-part method is frequently employed in studies of listed corporations,[33] it has never been applied to an internationally well-regarded comparative study of close corporations.[34] Further, even when well-executed, a study of a large number of jurisdictions produces – at best – a 'loose taxonomy',[35] but not a detailed model capable of implementation.

The approach employed in this Book (which I coin, for convenience, the 'tripartite method') is intended to strike balances between breadth[36] and depth,[37] and between cross-jurisdictional conceptual coherence and intra-jurisdictional consistency. Building on recent developments in comparative corporate law scholarship, the tripartite method most closely tracks the fourth approach described above, while also adding to it.

The first part defines the problem and develops the theory. One conceptual chapter (Chapter II) defines the problem,[38] key terms, and critical concepts including 'withdrawal' itself. Part of another chapter (Chapter III) develops two distinct models of withdrawal and offers critical observations based on synthesis of the four jurisdictions analysed. The tripartite method's first part is performed both before and after the jurisdictional description and analysis in the second part; the two parts may be visualized together as a 'sandwich' with the first part's 'bread' around the second part's 'meat'.

32 E.g. Puchniak et al. (2012); Fleckner & Hopt (2013); Belcredi & Ferrarini (2013); Davies et al. (2013); Puchniak et al. (2017).

33 Examples include essay compilations on derivative actions in Asia, independent directors in Asia, boards of (predominantly) public companies in Europe, and corporate governance of public companies. A pattern is easily discernible.

34 A partial exception is McCahery et al. (2004), albeit with Asian jurisdictions entirely omitted.

35 E.g. Puchniak & Kim (2017).

36 Incorporating the 'historical comparative perspective' and 'functional comparison'; see Siems (2017): 13.

37 Applying a 'rule-based comparison'; see Siems (2017): 12–14.

38 'Functional comparison'; see Siems (2017): 14–16.

In the second part, the law and context of withdrawal in four jurisdictions, being a manageable but sufficient number for a nuanced and representative picture, are described and analysed individually in jurisdictional chapters (Chapters IV to VII). Focusing on primary and secondary sources in that jurisdiction's legal language, each jurisdictional study critically presents the institution of withdrawal from a quasi-insider's perspective, in a form recognizable to a jurist native to that jurisdiction,[39] while remaining approachable to readers trained elsewhere.[40] Part of the comparative chapter (Chapter III) offers the reader a bird's-eye view of withdrawal law by organising the findings of individual jurisdictional studies under a single analytical framework. It should be noted that in execution, Parts I and II of the method work iteratively.

The Book goes further than previous comparative corporate law works by crafting a concrete, detailed, and generalized model regime.[41] For the tripartite method's third and final part, a chapter (Chapter VIII) is dedicated to a proposed model solution which is – in contrast with conventional works – of general application, and not limited to any of the four jurisdictions analysed or any other single jurisdiction.[42] The model solution further doubles as an issue checklist for readers with interests beyond legislative reform.

Readers accustomed to different approaches to comparative analysis should find both the familiar and the new in the 'tripartite method' pioneered in this Book.

3 *Why Compare These Four Jurisdictions?*

The four jurisdictions – the US, the UK, Germany, and Japan – are chosen for their economic and legal significance. As four of the world's six largest economies by gross domestic product,[43] their economic importance is beyond reasonable doubt. Further, as mature, developed economies with established legal systems and legal cultures, and mostly functioning courts,[44] they are highly relevant to legal scholarly discourse at the international level, often serving as bases of reference for scholarly work and law reform

39 Bell (2011): 168. Bell also calls on the comparatist 'to be the voice of [foreign legal] system, albeit with a non-native accent': ibid.

40 Bell (2011): 171; see also Michaels (2019): 371 (functionalist comparative jurist's role is *interpreting*, rather than merely describing, foreign law). The tripartite method's first two parts roughly correspond to the first two steps of Michaels' interpretative functionalism; cf Michaels (2019): 386–8.

41 It is 'applied comparative law' with a normative orientation; see Siems (2017): 25.

42 The Book does not claim that any of the four target jurisdictions has the 'better law'; see Michaels (2019): 379–81 (on the limits of equivalence functionalism). However, the model remedy, which is developed based on the evaluative results of the four jurisdictions analysed and the two models of withdrawal constructed, does aspire to be a 'better law' that is both technically superior and better achieves the aim of shareholder protection. See Siems (2014): 120–2 (on 'better law' as a comparative law goal).

43 As of 2019, the US was first, Japan third, Germany fourth, and the UK sixth; in second place was China and fifth India: World Bank (2021b).

44 Developing or transition economies do not necessarily possess all three features; study and analysis of the judicial role and of legal reform in developing economies are therefore complicated by additional challenges. See e.g. Armour & Enriques et al. (2017): 269; Skeel (2004): 1570–3.

efforts in other jurisdictions.[45] Their importance is underscored by their inclusion as four of the 'core jurisdictions' analysed in the leading comparative corporate law text, *The Anatomy of Corporate Law*, continuously since its first edition.[46]

While no four jurisdictions can truly and adequately reflect the full spectrum of the world's several hundred jurisdictions, the four selected jurisdictions come close. Spanning the dominant divide between the common and civil law traditions; the three continents of Europe, North America, and the chronically underrepresented Asia; and three legal languages (English, German, and Japanese), the four jurisdictions constitute a reasonably representative slice of our planet's immense legal diversity.

4 *Close Corporation Statutory Forms in the Four Jurisdictions*

The 'close corporation' that is the subject of this Book is a functional concept, one that is implemented in slightly different ways in each of the jurisdictions examined in depth later. The specific legal entities adopted for the archetypical close corporation in each jurisdiction are introduced here.

The earliest popularized close corporation form clearly recognizable as such is arguably the ***Gesellschaft mit beschränkter Haftung*** ('Limited Liability Company', abbreviated **GmbH**) available since 1892. The GmbH is an entity established pursuant to and governed primarily by its own separate statute, the *Gesetz betreffend die Gesellschaften mit beschränkter Haftung* (Limited Liability Companies Act[47]), abbreviated GmbHG.[48] Described as the most important and most successful German legal export,[49] the GmbH has gone on to inspire similar close corporation forms in other jurisdictions, including Japan.

In the UK, the **private company limited by shares**, abbreviated variously as 'private limited company', 'private company',[50] or just '**Ltd**', is the classic close corporation form. Although currently regulated under the same Companies Act 2006 with its public cousin, the public limited company (abbreviated 'plc'), the UK Ltd is distinguishable from the plc by (1) its inability to offer its own securities to the public; and (2) lighter regulatory burdens.[51] Unlike the GmbH, the Ltd was not

45 It is trite that the US, UK, and Germany are extremely influential on the development of corporate law: Pistor et al. (2002): 799. However, Japan not only retains its traditional influence in Taiwan, but has also in recent years extended its influence into South-east Asia and Central Asia.

46 Kraakman et al. (2004). The first edition featured at least one author representing each of four jurisdictions; with the addition of Wolf-Georg Ringe (Germany) and Gen Goto (Japan), the third edition published in 2017 (Armour & Enriques et al. (2017)) now features at least two from each of the four.

47 Per the 'official' unofficial translation adopted by the German Ministry of Justice (Reusch (2019)).

48 Widely held or listed corporations adopt another form, the *Aktiengesellschaft* (stock corporation, abbreviated AG).

49 Lutter (1992): 49.

50 'Private company' can also include companies without limited liability for members, or companies limited by guarantee. These companies are extremely rare and beyond the scope of this Book.

51 Companies Act, s. 755; Davies (2020): 28–9.

legislatively designed from the get-go as a vehicle for closely held businesses; rather, it was developed organically by businesses and their legal advisers, and only later formally recognised by statute.[52]

Close corporations in the US are, as with all legal forms adopted by business, regulated under the laws of the individual states. As such, it is not technically accurate to speak of '*the* close corporation', but at best, 'close *corporations*' in the plural or as a category. US close corporations fall into two major types. The first and older type is the **Close Corporation** in the narrower, US sense (which I abbreviate '**US-CC**' for this Book), a category of corporations that is recognized as a distinct category by courts and legislatures, and which apply different rules at common law and in special legislation to this category.[53] The emergence of the US-CC as a distinct category at common law and in state incorporation statutes took place gradually over the twentieth century.[54] The second category is the **Limited Liability Company** ('**LLC**'). Strictly speaking not a corporation, and created by one state in 1975 in response to a firm's lobbying, the LLC quickly spread across the states during the late 1980s to early 1990s in a 'revolution' driven by favourable federal tax treatment.[55] There is awareness that US-CC-type problems manifest in LLCs and may require similar solutions.[56]

Japan's close corporations today are mostly organized as ***Kabushiki Kaisha*** ('Stock Corporation', abbreviated '**KK**'). Although originally intended to be the vehicle for large, publicly traded corporations, postwar Japan saw the widespread use of the KK by small businesses, including single-owner businesses.[57] Historically, however, the KK was not alone. From 1938 to 2006, the KK shared space with the 'proper' closed corporation form of Japan, the ***Yūgen Kaisha*** ('Limited Liability Corporation', abbreviated '**YK**'). Modelled on the German GmbH partly because of the former's success and influence across the world and partly because Japan's commercial law was based on Germany's,[58] the YK as a distinct entity came to an end after the *Kaishahō* (Companies Act of 2005) entered force in 2006, with the result that no new YKs could be established and all existing YKs were forcibly converted into KKs. The *Kaishahō* also created a new entity: the US LLC-inspired[59] ***Gōdō Kaisha*** (also translated 'Limited Liability Company', abbreviated '**GK**').

The legal entities described above are the main, but not the only forms adopted by close corporations. Although not necessarily 'corporations' in a strict doctrinal sense,[60]

52 V.B.1.

53 VI.B.2; Thompson (1993): 704.

54 VI.B.1; Wells (2008).

55 VI.D.1.

56 VI.E.3.i; VI.F.3; see also O'Neal & Thompson (2020b): ch. 6.

57 VII.B.1.

58 VII.B.1.

59 VII.C.1.

60 See Ribstein (2010): 1; Schmidt (2002): § 3 I 2 a (distinguishing between corporations (*Körperschaft*) and partnerships (*Personengesellschaft*)).

limited partnership forms such as the German *Kommanditgesellschaft*, the Japanese *Gōshi Kaisha*, the UK or US liability partnerships may also be adopted by SMEs. However, to keep things focused and brief, non-corporations and issues specific to corporate groups[61] are excluded from this Book's scope.

5 A *Note on Terminology*

Comparing jurisdictions using different languages and following different legal traditions creates serious terminological challenges.[62] To facilitate comparison of four jurisdictions using three languages – but four sets of legal terminology[63] – this Book strikes several compromises.

First, for convenience, 'corporation' and 'company' are used interchangeably. Second, I endeavour to use consistently, as far as possible, functional and jurisdiction-neutral versions when referring to US and UK legal terms and when translating from German and Japanese. This may deviate from what might otherwise be standard practice when writing about any one specific jurisdiction in English. 'Withdrawal'[64] is one example; another is the use of 'corporate constitution' or just 'constitution'[65] when referring to the *Satzung* (German GmbH);[66] *teikan* (Japanese KK or GK);[67] certificate of incorporation and by-laws (US close corporation); operating agreement (US LLC); or articles of association/company constitution (UK Ltd[68]).

A third and particularly delicate compromise concerns the terms 'shareholder' and 'member'. I use them interchangeably in the general chapters,[69] but not in the jurisdiction-specific chapters.[70] The reasons for this compromise are as follows. 'Shareholder' is widely, even universally adopted when referring to a variety of equity holders across the spectrum of corporate entities in legal and scholarly literature in English. By contrast, 'member' or its linguistic equivalents are principally used in formal, technical settings such as legislation. However, in the close corporation context, where jurisdictions other than the UK frequently use terms

61 There are striking similarities between the problems faced by minority shareholders of dominated subsidiaries in corporate groups and those of minority shareholders in classic close corporations. However, a proper treatment of the former would require at least its own volume.

62 Bachner (2009): 30.

63 As Chapters V and VI reveal, close corporation doctrine in the UK and US have developed independently (except for an early phase: see III.G.2.i) with different legal solutions and different jargon.

64 See II.C.

65 Although 'constitution' is now also the UK-specific term, prior to the Companies Act 2006 the technical term was 'memorandum and articles of association'.

66 More often translated 'articles of association'.

67 Commonly translated 'articles of incorporation'; see JLTC (2019):211.

68 See (n 66) above.

69 Chapters I, II, III, VIII, and IX

70 Chapters IV to VII.

in their respective languages different from those used when referring to public corporations, 'member' is generally more accurate and appropriate both conceptually and linguistically. I therefore deliberately use shareholder and member in their respective stricter meanings in jurisdiction-specific chapters: US-CC shareholders (or stockholders, depending on state) versus LLC members, German AG shareholders (*Aktionäre*) versus GmbH members (*Gesellschafter*), and Japanese KK shareholders (*kabunushi*) versus GK members (*sha'in*). The UK context is somewhat more complicated. As a matter of formal statutory law, the proper term for all UK companies – public or private – is 'member'.[71] However, 'shareholder' is widely used in lieu of or interchangeably with 'member' not just in the business context, but even in UK-centric legal scholarship.[72] To mirror the public versus private/close corporation distinction in the other three jurisdictions, I use 'member' exclusively in the UK Ltd context, thereby departing from popular usage but using the correct formal legal term.

A further compromise is the use of the direct if inelegant term 'membership interest' when referring to the equity and membership interests of members (but not shareholders) in the US-LLC (membership interest), German GmbH (*Geschäftsanteil*), and Japanese GK (*mochibun*). Conversely, I use 'shares' for the UK Ltd because that happens to be both the popular and legally proper terminology, and for the US-CC as a contrast to the US-LLC.

Finally, when referring to court decisions, the neutral term 'judicial precedent' is used mostly interchangeably with 'case law' or 'jurisprudence'.

The above attempts to balance conflicting considerations of generality versus specificity, and functional utility versus formal accuracy, result in terminological and translation choices that are unlikely to satisfy every reader. It is nonetheless hoped that they would be taken in the spirit in which they are made and perhaps inspire further and better scholarly attempts at tackling – if not overcoming – the fundamental terminological and translation challenges of multi-jurisdictional comparative legal scholarship.

C OVERVIEW OF THE BOOK

This Book is structured primarily around three Parts, each broadly corresponding to one part of the tripartite method.[73] Each of the three Parts is briefly summarised in the following subsections (I.C.1–3). The final Part, which contains the conclusions, contributions, and applications of this Book, is summarized in the final subsection below (I.C.4).

71 Companies Act 2006 (UK), s. 112.

72 Notably, the standard text in the UK (Davies & Worthington (2016)) uses the two terms interchangeably.

73 'Theory' falls under the tripartite method's part one, 'Operation' mostly under part two, and 'Application' under part three. However, although Chapter III is under the 'Operation' Part of the Book and mostly concerns part two, III.G belongs to part one.

1 *Theory*

The theoretical core of the Book, Chapter II centres on the two fundamental concepts: the close corporation and withdrawal. After explaining the close corporation's distinctive features in contrast with the archetypical corporation in the comparative corporate law literature, I set out the close corporation's cardinal problems: conflict between minority and majority shareholders, and the attendant enhanced risk of inter-shareholder exploitation. Over time, leading jurisdictions have converged upon shareholder exit as the ultimate solution to shareholder conflict. Shareholder exit is also a potent source of protection for minority shareholders, who are exceptionally vulnerable to exploitation in the close corporation context due to its distinctive features.

Withdrawal remedies, the sole category of exit strategies that adequately addresses the demand for shareholder protection, comes next. Consolidating what would appear at first glance to be different, but which upon closer examination reveal themselves to be functionally similar legal strategies in the four jurisdictions under study, I introduce and define the concept of 'withdrawal remedies' as legal mechanisms enabling voluntary shareholder exit from the corporation that is coupled with an enforceable monetary claim for the value of the withdrawing shareholder's membership interest. I also show how 'withdrawal' is to be distinguished from related concepts in shareholder protection and dispute resolution, and how it is the only mechanism that can put an end to intractable shareholder conflict that cannot be resolved amicably by the parties or through other legal mechanisms.

Withdrawal cannot escape the impact of contractarian thought on modern corporate law scholarship. A key question is *how* withdrawal should be implemented: should this be on a default or mandatory basis? To answer this, I analyse reasons why shareholders (minority and majority) might find access to withdrawal desirable – and why they might not. The analysis draws on insights from behavioural economics such as 'sticky defaults' and applies them to the specific context of withdrawal in close corporations. I explore alternatives to the 'pure' default and mandatory visions of withdrawal that can cater to the needs of not just those seeking access to withdrawal, but also of those who would willingly forgo or curtail it.

2 *Operation*

Chapters III to VII provide a comparative overview and jurisdiction-specific analyses of withdrawal remedies in four leading economies, namely Germany, the UK, the US, and Japan (collectively 'target jurisdictions').

This Part begins with Chapter III, which sets out the framework for the comparative analysis that will be applied to each of the jurisdiction-specific chapters. Each Chapter will examine the history, grounds, scope of protection, applicable parties, and the mandatory/default nature of the withdrawal remedy in that jurisdiction.

These are the salient features where the jurisdictions differ in their respective approaches to withdrawal. Chapter III also examines the legal actors involved in the creation and development of withdrawal regimes, and the phenomenon of spontaneous functional convergence of the four jurisdictions towards two distinct conceptual models of withdrawal. I draw on the comparative insights from these four jurisdictions to design a model withdrawal remedy, which I present in Chapter VIII.

Chapter IV examines the withdrawal remedy in Germany, arguably the earliest major jurisdiction to introduce a close corporation legal form – the GmbH. The history of German GmbH law, especially the law of member withdrawal, belies Germany's image and reputation as a 'civilian' jurisdiction. Despite the GmbH's beginnings as a revolutionary invention of the German legislator, GmbH law is since little touched by major legislative reform, and heavily shaped then and now through German judicial precedent and academic literature. Member withdrawal for 'good cause' (*Austritt aus wichtigem Grund*), developed in the absence of express statutory provision, is an example of this *par excellence*. The flexible core concept of '*wichtiger Grund*', which supports withdrawal in a wide variety of circumstances, powerfully demonstrates withdrawal's value in the close corporation context. Germany's experience illuminates the path for jurists of any jurisdiction interested in developing a functioning withdrawal regime of its own – even if politician-legislators accomplish and contribute nothing.

Chapter V turns to the UK, whose withdrawal remedy has served as the model for similar remedies across the Commonwealth. The UK's first attempt at legislating an 'oppression' remedy in 1948 was largely ineffectual before a second legislative reform creating an 'unfair prejudice' remedy was achieved in 1980. Although initially a great success that spawned a rapidly developing jurisprudence, the perception of an explosion in shareholder litigation in the courts and mushrooming costs against the backdrop of ongoing civil justice system reforms caused serious backlash in the 1990s. On the judicial front, Lord Hoffmann's seminal speech in the House of Lords case of *O'Neill* v. *Phillips* effectively became the last word on unfair prejudice. Contemporaneously, law reform attempts by both the Law Commission and the Department of Trade and Industry aimed at addressing the perceived problems of unfair prejudice ultimately led nowhere. The meteoric rise and gradual fall of the unfair prejudice remedy in the UK is a tale of the power of judges to obstruct, of how one decisive voice prevailed over many divided against themselves, and of the limits of legislative reform in close corporation law.

Chapter VI turns to the US, where various states developed diverse responses (through both judicial innovation and legislative reform) over different time periods, including withdrawal remedies, for over one hundred close corporation legal forms – one US-CC and one LLC for each of the over fifty states and territories. While many US states recognize withdrawal as a solution to majority-minority shareholder conflict in US-CCs, several states have resisted or even renounced withdrawal. The attitude towards LLCs, which are rapidly growing in popularity across the US, is more ambivalent, as state legislatures and judges have been slower to respond to the close corporation problem. While the contractarian-led scholarly debate on whether corporate law should be mandatory or default[74] is instructive in canvassing the full spectrum of possible positions, the reality that withdrawal is often missing from state LLC statutes is not attributable to state legislatures taking reasoned policy positions in response to the scholarly debate. Rather, withdrawal's lack of presence in LLCs is attributable to incentives created by federal taxation policy, and which are unrelated to the close corporation problem of majority-minority conflict. That said, there are signs that history moves in circles as withdrawal remedies reminiscent of US-CCs (re)emerge in LLCs.

Chapter VII begins by examining the intriguing puzzle of Japan. Chapter II establishes earlier that withdrawal is important for shareholder protection. However, until relatively recently, shareholders and members of Japan's close corporations had no access to withdrawal under the law, as neither of Japan's then-dominant close corporation forms offered this. A 1980s legislative reform attempt to introduce withdrawal also failed. By revealing how shareholders in Japan responded to the absence of withdrawal, I show how Japan's experience – unique among the four leading jurisdictions under study – serves as a historical counterfactual that powerfully demonstrates the demand for and importance of withdrawal remedies in practice. More recently, withdrawal remedies at law became available in Japan, for the first time and for a true close corporation form, with the watershed *Kaishahō* – and by semi-accident. The GK, the new and American-inspired close corporation form introduced by the *Kaishahō*, offers withdrawal remedies unprecedented even by comparative law standards, but numerous challenges lie ahead. While the GK's withdrawal regime has yet to establish itself as an integral part of the corporate law landscape, Japan stands as an instructive example of the potential pitfalls involved in introducing close corporation withdrawal by legislation.

3 *Model*

With the case for withdrawal remedies made and critical comparative analysis of several jurisdictional variants conducted earlier in the book, Chapter VIII integrates insights from the theoretical and comparative analyses into a model withdrawal solution. This 'Model Remedy' gives effect to private ordering arrangements and offers judicially administered solutions where contract is absent or otherwise defective. Chapter VIII also explains the Model Remedy's key features: a trichotomous classification of the grounds for withdrawal (fault, non-fault, and at will), and a combination of mandatory, sticky default, and default rules and standards differentiated by the grounds involved.

Drawing on and improving upon existing legal regimes, the Model Remedy provides practical guidance on the design and implementation of calibrated withdrawal solutions responsive to a broad range of scenarios. It will be useful for legislators and judges seeking to address intracorporate conflicts in close

74 On mandatory and default rules, see II.E.

corporations. Legal practitioners may also find the proposed framework useful for drafting close corporation constitutions and shareholder agreements.[75]

4 *Conclusion and Contributions*

Chapter IX summarises this Book's key findings and explores applications and extensions of the corporate law concepts and comparative law methodology developed in this Book.

This Book contributes to legal scholarship in three ways. First, I establish a coherent set of corporate law concepts and terminology[76] that clarifies and expands our understanding of some of corporate law's most fundamental and intractable problems as manifested across diverse jurisdictions.[77] By applying insights from behavioural law and economics such as 'sticky defaults', this Book both enriches our understanding of the problems and expands our range of potential solutions[78] to close corporation law's challenges.

Second, this Book contributes to comparative law scholarship by developing and applying a novel comparative law method which I call the 'tripartite method'.[79] My method combines richly textured jurisdictional studies[80] with a jurisdictionally neutral and theoretically informed comparative framework[81] to craft a model solution that is potentially generalisable and applicable in diverse jurisdictions.[82] The tripartite method is thus rigorous, structured, and useful not only for scholarly work but also law reform and other practical needs.[83]

Third, this Book contributes to comparative corporate law by identifying and analysing the phenomenon, which I call 'spontaneous functional convergence', in withdrawal law. This subtype of convergence occurs where jurisdictions appear to have – largely independently of other jurisdictions – developed legal regimes that are functionally similar but formally different using mostly, if not exclusively, *domestic* legal sources and inspirations. The spontaneous convergence observed in the withdrawal regimes of the target jurisdictions point to withdrawal as – if not quite the end of history – then at least an evolutionary milestone for close corporation law.[84]

75 See also IX.B–C.
76 II.C–D.
77 III.B–G.1.
78 II.E; VIII.B–C.
79 I.B.2.
80 Chapters IV to VII.
81 III.B–F.
82 Chapter VIII.
83 IX.B–C.
84 III.G.2–3.

PART 1

Theory

II

The Concept of Withdrawal

A INTRODUCTION

The 'cardinal problem' in close corporations is '[i]nternal conflicts between majority and minority shareholders'.[1] When a conflict – whether beginning as an act of majority opportunism against the minority, a good-faith disagreement over business affairs, or any other variation – escalates into an irreconcilable fallout and a breakdown in trust between the participants, the enterprise as a going concern with its pre-dispute membership is inevitably dead. Trust, once broken, is difficult to restore.[2] It is at best difficult, if not improbable, that the parties can go back to business as usual after experiencing the type of intractable conflict that requires resolution by a third-party arbiter such as a court.

Legal solutions purportedly aimed at resolving conflict, but which do not involve the exit of one or more of the parties, cannot repair a business relationship marred by broken trust and mutual acrimony. Unless the parties themselves reach and commit to a mutually acceptable arrangement, the only viable *legal* solution often is a permanent one: severance of the relationship, with at least one party exiting from the enterprise. Unsurprisingly, over time legislatures, courts, and scholars have come to the general agreement that the ultimate solution to shareholder conflict takes some form of shareholder exit by which the legal relationships between the shareholder and the company, and between the shareholder and their co-shareholders, are severed.[3] This form of exit is coined 'withdrawal' for this Book.

Functional, jurisdiction-neutral definitions of withdrawal and its variants – including 'at will', 'on grounds' ('fault' and 'non-fault') – are introduced in this Chapter.[4] By contrasting withdrawal with other options,[5] this Chapter makes the case for withdrawal as a necessary and usually superior legal solution to shareholder conflict.[6]

That said, withdrawal remedies are not free from the mandatory/default tension in corporate law. Close corporation participants have good and not-so-good reasons, often contingent on specific circumstances, to restrict or even eliminate access to withdrawal. These reasons are critically evaluated using concepts and insights from behavioural economics literature.[7] Concepts such as debiasing and insulating strategies, sticky defaults and altering norms, and 'mandatory core' are applied or introduced to illuminate paths for withdrawal between extreme visions of corporate law, and to balance the competing objectives of facilitating party autonomy and protection of the deserving.[8]

1 Fleischer (2014): 29.
2 Trust broken by mere untrustworthy behaviour can be restored, but not if deception was also involved: see Schweitzer et al. (2006).
3 The details of how each target jurisdiction (Germany, the USA, the UK, and Japan) implements withdrawal are explored in Chapters III to VII.
4 II.C.
5 II.D.1–2.
6 II.D.3.
7 II.E.2–3.
8 II.E.3.iii, II.E.4. These insights are implemented in Chapter VIII (Model Remedy).

II.B introduces the distinctive features of close corporations and the problem of majority–minority shareholder conflict. Withdrawal is defined in II.C. II.D distinguishes withdrawal from other related concepts, and considers their relative strengths and weaknesses vis-à-vis withdrawal. Weaving in insights from behavioural economics, II.E examines the balance between mandatory and default aspects in withdrawal design, and analyses arguments for and against access to withdrawal. II.F concludes.

B FEATURES OF CLOSE CORPORATIONS AND THE PROBLEM OF SHAREHOLDER CONFLICT

Close corporations, like all business corporations,[9] have standard corporate characteristics such as separate legal personality (entity shielding), and formal legal separation of share (or more precisely, equity[10]) ownership and management power.[11] Although 'close corporation' cannot be defined with certainty,[12] specific characteristics unique to close corporations are readily identifiable.

Restrictions on shareholder exit are one such feature. Although incorporated companies make it possible to freely transfer participant (shareholder) interests,[13] close corporation shares are typically subject to share transfer restrictions either as a matter of mandatory corporate law[14] or by agreement of the shareholders incorporated into the corporate constitution.[15] The lack of secondary markets for such shares also means that unhappy shareholders cannot simply follow the 'Wall Street Rule' and exit by selling their shares on the stock market.[16] Share transfer restrictions often translate into stable shareholding structures and majorities in close corporations.[17] When the majority–minority relationship breaks down, whether due to oppression of the minority by the majority, rent-seeking by the majority, or any other reason, the minority is at the risk of losing all prospect of return on their investment[18] – unless and until the majority consents to an exit. However, even if the

9 In other words, excluding other types of juridical persons such as local government bodies or non-profit organizations.

10 Encompassing shares, stock, membership interests, *Geschäftsanteil*, *mochibun*, etc.

11 Armour & Enriques et al. (2017): 5.

12 'Chester Rohrlich once described a close corporation as being like a spiral staircase: difficult to define, but you know one when you see it': Kessler (1985): 661.

13 Armour & Enriques et al. (2017): 10–11; Davies & Worthington (2016): paras. [2–24] to [2–25].

14 *Kaishahō*, Article 585 (Japan) (applying to 'membership companies' [*mochibun kaisha*] but not stock corporations [*kabushiki kaisha*]); Davies & Worthington (2016): para. [2–26] (formerly mandatory in the UK Ltd).

15 See, e,g. GmbHG, § 15(5) (Germany); *Kaishahō*, Article 107(2)(i) (Japan) (applying to stock corporations [*kabushiki kaisha*]); Companies Act 2006, s. 544 (UK); Davies & Worthington (2016): para [2–26]. For empirical data, see Kitazawa & Hamada (1983): 30 tbl. 12; Wedemann (2013): 20 tbl. 5. See also O'Neal & Thompson (2020a): § 2:6 text to fns. 33–5, § 7:2 text to fn. 9.

16 Fleischer (2018a): 682; Wells (2008): 275; Eidenmüller (2014): 6.

17 See Fleischer (2014): 34.

18 Thompson (1993): 703; Neville (2010): 260.

majority were to agree to buy the minority out, absent an external market for the minority's interest or any legal obligation to do so, the majority has little economic incentive to offer a fair price.[19]

Another distinctive characteristic of close corporations is informal management arrangements, which typically involve shareholders directly participating in management as directors, employees or both.[20] Shareholders who have invested substantial personal wealth in the close corporation have strong incentives to participate actively in management precisely because exit is difficult.[21] Instead of dividends from the corporation, a shareholder's salary or other compensation from employment, managerial positions, directorships, or a combination thereof may well be their main source of income and the return on their investment.[22]

The resulting absence of a separation between ownership and control is a defining feature of the close corporation,[23] and creates organisational and managerial problems distinct from public corporations. Overlap between management and shareholders and the small number of shareholders in a close corporation aligns the interests of the two classes.[24] This same overlap places shareholders in a better position to monitor and assert their interests against the (other) shareholder-directors.[25] Conflicts between directors and shareholders – which are the dominant agency problem in widely held corporations – are seldom the defining problem in the close corporation context.[26]

Rather, it is shareholder conflict, particularly between majority/controlling and minority shareholders, that poses the greatest challenge – memorably termed the 'Achilles heel'[27] – to close corporations.[28] The principle of majority rule usually grants majority shareholders substantial control over the majority–minority shareholder relationship. Only a simple majority of votes is required to pass an ordinary shareholder resolution or the equivalent,[29] which may generally be used to execute a vast number of corporate decisions.[30] Therefore, when majority and minority do not agree, absent special protection for the minority, the expected result is a fait

19 Andersson (2010): 197; see also Thompson (1993): 703–4; Fleischer (2014): 29–30.
20 Easterbrook & Fischel (1986): 274–5; Rock & Wachter (1999): 916.
21 Neville (2010): 279.
22 Moll (2004): 340; Wells (2008): 275.
23 Shishido (1990): 355; Wells (2008): 274.
24 Easterbrook & Fischel (1986): 274.
25 Ibid. 278; Eidenmüller (2014): 8.
26 Eidenmüller (2014): 8; see also Fleischer (2018a): 683 (observing that 'in a publicly listed corporation with a broad shareholder base, *vertical* governance problems predominate', whereas 'closely held corporations are far more troubled by *horizontal* governance issues') (italics original).
27 Neville (2010): 247.
28 Fleischer (2014): 29; Miller (1997): 383. Other forms of shareholder conflict exist, such as obstruction by minorities and deadlock (especially between 50 per cent-50 per cent two-shareholder corporations): see Wedemann (2013): 53–7.
29 Fleischer (2014): 33.
30 For example, by default, the appointment or removal of a director can be generally performed by an ordinary resolution in the UK, USA, Germany, and Japan.

accompli favouring the majority and often, although not necessarily, against the minority's interests.

As a leading commentator puts it, 'shareholder conflicts in close corporations are almost as diverse as real life'.[31] The first source of shareholder conflict is interpersonal relations. Strong personal relationships between co-shareholders are common in close corporations and offer considerable advantages to closely held businesses.[32] However, these relationships may break down and give rise to interpersonal conflicts that might spill over into the business,[33] with potentially devastating consequences for the corporation's operational health, or even its continued existence.[34]

Another source of majority–minority shareholder conflict is business disagreements.[35] When serious disagreements arise over the strategic direction of the corporation or mismanagement of the corporation, a locked-in and outvoted minority has little ability to pressure management or the majority to address minority concerns over business direction, efficiency, or profitability.[36] While disagreement may be part and parcel of life in business, what begins as bona fide business disagreements can escalate into open and eventually intractable conflict.[37]

The most serious type of conflict, known variously as 'freezeout', 'squeeze-out', or 'oppression',[38] arises when the minority's rights and interests – typically in terms of income or participation in the business – are disregarded or denied, or when the majority exercises its rights or powers in ways abusive or harmful to the minority. For example, particularly where majority shareholders also serve as directors, they may use their management and/or shareholder powers to extract benefits for themselves at the expense of the corporation and the minority shareholders.[39]

31 Wedemann (2013): 46 ("Gesellschafterkonflikte in der geschlossenen Kapitalgesellschaft „sind [...] fast so vielgestaltig wie das wirkliche Leben." ").

32 Neville (2010): 249; Fleischer (2014): 31; see also Mahoney (2000): 177.

33 Means (2009): 1208.

34 O'Neal & Thompson (2020b): § 1:4; see also Fleischer (2014): 31 ('differences at a *personal* level can complicate *professional* interactions and may even endanger the corporation's existence') (italics in original).

35 Neville (2013): 199.

36 Neville (2010): 276–7.

37 See Neville (2010): 258.

38 Moll & Ragazzo (2017): § 7.01[A] fns. 8–9 and text thereto (7–5); O'Neal & Thompson (2020b): § 1.1.

39 Although majority shareholders may also feel consequences from harm to the corporation caused by directors in the sense that their shares decrease in value, this may be more than offset by benefits derived in other capacities (e.g. directors, investors in another entity). As a result, *from a practical perspective*, the harm is primarily or exclusively felt by minority shareholders. Practitioners are particularly aware of this: see e.g. Koehnen (2004): 449 ('Corporate harm may be felt by only a minority of shareholders because the controlling shareholders have provided themselves with benefits or have otherwise insulated themselves from the harm. Alternatively, corporate harm in private corporations is often targeted at minority shareholders'). See also Eidenmüller (2014): 9–10. On phenomena such as 'tunnelling' and 'private benefits of control' more generally (i.e. not specifically in the close corporation), see Enriques & Tröger (2019).

Who wins in majority–minority conflicts? Oppression 'normally does not contemplate fair payment to the [minority] for the interests, rights, or powers which they lose'.[40] Close corporation minority shareholders are thus not only structurally vulnerable to opportunism from the majority,[41] but also – in the absence of an easy exit option – 'locked-in'.[42] Outvoted and thus without formal legal powers as of right with which to improve their situation or resolve conflicts in their own favour, minority shareholders without special protections stand in a particularly weak position vis-à-vis the majority. The risk that minority shareholders would be exploited by majority shareholders is therefore inherent and characteristic of the close corporation,[43] and inextricable from the lack of exit.[44]

To address shareholder conflict and resulting problems, some form of legal mechanism for the protection of minority shareholders is clearly necessary. Many of the world's jurisdictions – represented and exemplified by the four target jurisdictions covered in this Book – have independently developed responses to close corporation shareholder conflict. Although known by various names in different languages, a family of solutions – oppression, unfair prejudice, *Austritt aus wichtigem Grund*, *yamu wo enai jiyū ni yoru taisha* – coalesce around a single core idea: *withdrawal* from the close corporation. A precise definition of 'withdrawal' based on jurisdiction-neutral terminology and concepts is offered in the next section.

C 'WITHDRAWAL': ANATOMY OF A JURISDICTION-NEUTRAL, FUNCTIONAL CONCEPT

'Withdrawal' is this Book's umbrella term for a category of solutions developed by different jurisdictions to facilitate a shareholder's voluntary exit from the close corporation.[45] This Book analyses withdrawal regimes in four jurisdictions across three continents and which span the divide between the common and civil law traditions. As each of the four jurisdictions has its own history, legal framework,

40 O'Neal & Thompson (2020b): § 1.1.

41 The risk of majorities exploiting minorities through tunneling and other means is a problem common to concentrated ownership in general. However, when coupled with the absence of satisfactory or even readily available exit options, majority exploitation poses a uniquely problem in close corporations. See Thompson (1993): 699.

42 Fleischer (2014): 35.

43 Means (2009): 1209.

44 Ibid. 1218 ('in an immediate sense, shareholder oppression stems from lack of exit'); see also Rock & Wachter (1999): 916–7.

45 When I started working on this Book in 2015, I had not come across any English-language publication available at the time that consciously used 'withdrawal' in the same sense as I do here. Since I began working on and discussing the idea of withdrawal at various settings with other scholars, Fleischer has switched from 'exit' to 'withdrawal': cf. Fleischer (2014): 66–8 (using 'exit rights') with Fleischer (2018a): 700–3 ('withdrawal rights') (published online in 2016). UNCITRAL previously adopted 'withdrawal' together with the (presumably US-origin) 'dissociation' but later dropped 'dissociation' entirely: cf. UNCITRAL (2020a): 35–6 with UNCITRAL (2020b): 34 fn. 100.

nomenclature, and modes of academic legal discourse, the very definition of 'withdrawal' itself poses significant challenges.

Two considerations prevail when formulating a definition. First, to facilitate meaningful comparative analysis while conveying accurately in English – which is particularly challenging for Germany and Japan – the nuances of each jurisdiction's approach, adopting neutral and functional terminology free of the legal-doctrinal baggage of individual national regimes is essential. The word 'withdrawal' is thus a deliberate choice: it is not used as a legal term of art in any major English-language[46] jurisdiction.[47] Choosing the term 'withdrawal' is also a departure from the practice, which is adopted by other commentators performing multi-jurisdictional comparisons, of borrowing from existing legal terms of art.[48] Second, for the concept of 'withdrawal' (or 'withdrawal remedy' or 'withdrawal regime'[49]) to be workable, it must be both sufficiently broad for cross-jurisdictional comparison, and precise enough to be recognisable and useful to jurists from each jurisdiction.[50]

For this Book, I define withdrawal as follows:

> voluntary exit from a close corporation by a shareholder desirous of exit resulting in a monetary claim payable to the withdrawing shareholder in exchange for the latter's loss of status, rights, duties, and other interests in the close corporation.

Unless expressly modified or where the context clearly requires otherwise, withdrawal means *non-* or *extra-contractual* rights and remedies in *corporate law*.[51] In other words, withdrawal is an outcome that either results from, or is enforceable by, a direct suit.[52] The following five features are ordinarily present in a jurisdiction's withdrawal regime:

(1) the shareholder ('withdrawal seeker') voluntarily elects, with or without reasons, to terminate their legal relationships with the close corporation and with the other shareholders;

46 This includes not only common law, but also 'mixed' jurisdictions using English as an official legal language. To the best of my knowledge, no (major) jurisdiction with English as a legal language (except Louisiana) uses the word 'withdrawal' as the formal name of a legal right or remedy reminiscent of 'withdrawal' as defined in this Book.

47 I acknowledge my intellectual debts to Scogin (1993) (using 'withdrawal' in the context of comparing US and German law) and Goette (2014) (using the untranslated English word 'Exit' in a German-language study of different exit-type remedies in German law). See also n. 45 above.

48 The closest analogous comparative study, featuring UK, German, and Dutch law, uses the term 'oppression remedies': de Vries (2010): 443. Oppression is a term of art in the UK (and Anglo-Commonwealth) and USA.

49 I deliberately use 'remedy' or 'regime' instead of 'right'. Withdrawal 'right' would be inappropriate in the context of the UK's and USA's withdrawal regimes; there, the result (relief) of withdrawal is not as of (shareholder's) right, but rather as an exercise of judicial discretion.

50 Cf. Baum & Puchniak (2012): 7.

51 Although I refer to contractual complements or substitutes for withdrawal such as buyout clauses or agreements throughout the jurisdictional Chapters (IV to VII), I do so only in the context of examining whether and how far 'withdrawal', as I have defined it, may be modified or excluded by contractual arrangements.

52 See Koh & Tang (2021): 438.

(2) the termination of the legal relationship takes effect either
   (a) at the withdrawal seeker's election; or
   (b) by order of a third-party arbiter granted in response to an application by the shareholder;

(3) with the termination of the legal relationship, the shareholder ('withdrawing shareholder') bears the obligation to transfer their membership interest to another party, usually but not necessarily the corporation and/or other shareholder(s);

(4) the withdrawing shareholder gains the right to claim a monetary sum against the corporation, and/or other shareholder(s); and

(5) the withdrawing shareholder's duty to transfer their shares and their right to receive the monetary sum are enforceable through judicial or other legal proceedings ultimately supported by the coercive force of the state.

'Withdrawal' so defined is broad enough to encompass two major variants: 'at will', and what I call 'on grounds'.[53] *Legally*, the former may be triggered at the withdrawal seeker's mere whim, or for no reason whatsoever. The *practical* motive for triggering at-will withdrawal rights, however, may well arise from shareholder conflict. Withdrawal 'on grounds', on the other hand, is only available in specific situations verifiable by a third-party arbiter such as a court. Although not infrequently elided in the English-language close corporation literature and jurisprudence,[54] this distinction between 'at will' and 'grounds' is crucial to the analysis in this Chapter and the rest of the Book.

A second and closely related point is that withdrawal is both a 'rule' and a 'standard', which I collectively call 'norms' when not differentiating between the two. 'Rules' 'require or prohibit specific behaviors'; 'standards' on the other hand 'leave the precise determination of compliance to adjudicators after the fact'.[55] Withdrawal 'at will' is a rule; strictly speaking, withdrawal 'on grounds'

[53] I avoid the term 'for cause' because of its connotations in the employment law context, and because 'on grounds' is broader than what has been called 'cause' in a leading practitioner text. See e.g. Hewitt et al. (2016): paras. [13–11] to [13–12]. Note that concepts or language of 'fault' are not used here.

[54] For two illustrative examples, see Easterbrook & Fischel (1986): 285–9 (correctly grasping the concepts of 'right of dissolution at will', 'involuntary dissolution based on fault' and 'automatic buy-out right', but failing to demonstrate awareness of 'buy-out on "grounds"', which is the missing link and fundamental to the developing 'oppression' jurisprudence of that time); *O'Neill* v. *Phillips* [1999] 1 WLR 1092 (HL) 1104 (Lord Hoffmann) (conflating the concept of withdrawal 'at will' and withdrawal based on a breakdown of trust and confidence – the latter of which would fall within the concept of 'grounds'); see also Koh & Tang (2017): 375 (criticising the fundamental conceptual error in *O'Neill*) and further V.C.10. By contrast, German scholars do not seem to suffer from this problem: see IV.C.6 (summarising the careful debate over *ordentliche* ('ordinary', i.e. at will) and *außerordentliche* ('extraordinary', i.e. on grounds) *Austrittsrecht* (withdrawal)). For Japan, see VII.D.2–3 (discussing withdrawal at will and withdrawal on 'unavoidable grounds' separately).

[55] Armour & Enriques et al. (2017): 32; see also Eidenmüller (2014): 22–3; foundationally, see Kaplow (1992).

can be both a rule and a standard. For example, contractually or legally defined grounds such as death, resignation from employment or directorship, or bankruptcy are rule-like in their clarity; these are not the focus of this Book.[56]

By contrast, 'grounds' in the narrower sense hinge on either 'fault' of a party such as 'oppression' or 'unfairly prejudicial conduct', or 'non-fault' grounds such as 'breakdown of the relationship between shareholders'. Such grounds are standards because they are difficult for the parties themselves to agree upon, and ultimately require determination by a third-party arbiter considering the facts and circumstances. It is the latter (sub)category of grounds – those based on standards – that will take centre stage in this Book.[57]

How the two variants of withdrawal – in other words, withdrawal at will and withdrawal on standards-type grounds – respond to different reasons for and against withdrawal will be explored below.[58] How withdrawal's five features manifest in each of the target jurisdictions (i.e. Germany, the UK, the USA, and Japan) will be analysed in Chapter III.[59] The next section further clarifies what withdrawal *is* by distinguishing it from what it *is not*.

D DISTINGUISHING 'WITHDRAWAL' FROM RELATED MECHANISMS

As a relatively unfamiliar concept in shareholder protection, it is helpful to further clarify 'withdrawal' by contrasting it with other, possibly more familiar, mechanisms. In this section, I classify shareholder protection and conflict resolution mechanisms into two categories, exit (II.D.1) and non-exit (II.D.2); explain their scope and nature; and evaluate their strengths and weaknesses. The last part of this section (II.D.3) explains why 'withdrawal' is an indispensable component of shareholder protection that deserves the attention devoted to it in this Book.

1 *'Exit' and Its Variants*

The exit-type mechanisms discussed in this subsection are all specific legal remedies leading to a particular outcome: severing the exiting shareholder's relationships with the close corporation and other shareholders.

56 That is not to say that parties never dispute whether contractually stipulated grounds have been triggered. On the breach of a contractual agreement between shareholders see e.g. Hewitt et al. (2016): para. [13–12].

57 As will be clear in this Book's Part 2 ('Operation').

58 At II.E.

59 See III.C ('Types of Withdrawal Grounds').

i Exit

Shareholder 'exit' is a term not infrequently encountered in close corporation literature.[60] In line with general usage, 'exit' is defined in this Book more broadly than 'withdrawal', as:

> any legal mechanism by which a shareholder terminates their status as shareholder and the legal rights and obligations between the shareholder and the corporation and between the exiting shareholder and the other shareholders.

By this definition, 'exit' is broad enough to capture even the voluntary transfer of shares by a shareholder to another person. However, as this Book focuses on close corporations and conflicts between shareholders, I exclude from the scope of 'exit' voluntary transfers taking place in the absence of conflict, uncoerced by circumstances, and at a price satisfactory to the transferor.[61] 'Exit' in this subsection are all examples of direct suits.[62]

For this Book's purposes, the main subtypes of 'exit'[63] are 'withdrawal', 'dissolution', and 'appraisal'. 'Withdrawal' may thus be distinguished from 'exit' on the basis that the former is a subtype (subset) of the latter. I define 'dissolution' and 'appraisal' next.

ii Dissolution

In this Book, 'dissolution'[64] means:

> any legal mechanism by which a corporation's legal existence is terminated and its assets distributed to persons with legally-recognised claims against the assets in accordance with the applicable rules on priority and distribution.

Dissolution is the oldest, most obvious, and well-established method of exit from the close corporation.[65] For minority shareholders, who by definition do not command the requisite majority or supermajority control to dissolve the corporation voluntarily, dissolution as a form of exit usually takes the form of 'judicial' or sometimes 'involuntary' dissolution. For this Book's purposes, 'judicial dissolution' means:

> dissolution by judicial order granted in response to application by the aggrieved minority shareholder against the will of the majority shareholder.[66]

60 See e.g. Fleischer (2014): 66–8; de Vries (2010).

61 Ex ante contractual arrangements providing the minority a buyout mechanism – whether triggerable in times of conflict or otherwise – may be interpreted as pre-empting or taking precedence over the extracontractual regime; see III.F.

62 On direct suits see Koh & Tang (2021).

63 Cf. de Vries (2010): 7–10.

64 'dissolution' (US); 'winding up' (UK); '*Auflösung*' (Germany); '*kaisan*' (Japan).

65 Dissolution by judicial order is well-known since at least the nineteenth century: *Miner* v. *Belle Isle Ice Co* (1892) 93 Mich 97, 53 NW 218 (Mich); Joint Stock Companies Winding-up Act 1848, s. 5(8) ('just and equitable' winding-up) (now Insolvency Act 1986, s. 122(1)(g)); GmbHG, s. 61; *Kaishahō*, Article 833.

66 I do not discuss 'administrative' dissolution, which refers to dissolution either directly by a government authority, or upon application of a government authority to a court.

Upon a successful application resulting in a judicial order of dissolution, the corporation ceases its business activities, terminates its employees, liquidates its assets, pays off outstanding creditors, and distributes what is left of the corporation's assets to the shareholders pro rata according to their respective shareholdings. Dissolution causes all shareholders to 'exit' as it terminates all relationships between the corporation and the shareholders, and between the shareholders inter se.

Accordingly, dissolution is a form of exit, but differs from withdrawal on a single, fundamental point: dissolution leads to cessation of the corporation's existence; withdrawal does not. Dissolution is not a popular dispute resolution or shareholder protection mechanism in any jurisdiction for several reasons.[67]

First, the 'judicially-imposed death'[68] of the close corporation creates serious negative consequences for stakeholders and society. In liquidation, the value realized is often less than the business as a going concern,[69] meaning that distributions upon dissolution and liquidation to shareholders are often less than the value of their pro rata share of the business' going concern value. Dissolution of a profitable close corporation thus often causes loss not only to shareholders (regardless of whether they desire exit), but also employees, other corporate stakeholders, as well as the broader public interest.[70] This has led to general reluctance towards dissolution,[71] especially if the corporation remains profitable,[72] or if alternatives that permit one or more of the parties to continue operating the business – such as exit by withdrawal – are available.[73]

Second, dissolution may involve a transfer of value from the exit-seeking shareholder to other participants (e.g. co-shareholders or controllers). In a judicial sale of the business following dissolution, the defendant (majority) shareholder is often the only bidder and thus a person with monopsony power.[74] Since the only available purchaser for the corporation's assets may very well be the majority shareholder responsible for the circumstances causing the minority to seek exit in the first place,[75] this adds insult to injury to the minority. Instead of exerting a disciplinary effect on the majority and offering relief for the minority, dissolution could reward the majority for squeezing out the minority – thus creating perverse incentives.

Third, even a failed attempt at obtaining dissolution risks leaving the minority shareholder in a worse position than ever, and the underlying inter-shareholder dispute

67 de Vries (2010): 12.

68 *Re Radom & Neidorff, Inc* (1954) 307 NY 1, 7 (NY) (Desmond J).

69 Hillman (1982): 47–8; Bahls (1990): 332–3, fn. 275.

70 Bahls (1990): 296–7; Goette (2014): 26–7.

71 Easterbrook & Fischel (1991): 239; Hetherington & Dooley (1977): 18–19; BGHZ 9, 157, 158 (1953) (Germany); *Kaishahō*, Article 833(1) (Japan).

72 Thompson (1988): 204.

73 Haynsworth (1986): 50; see Insolvency Act 1986, s. 125(2) (UK).

74 Bahls (1990): 331.

75 Ibid.; Cohen (1945): para. 60.

unresolved. When dissolution is ordered, a majority shareholder desirous of continuing the enterprise would have at least some incentive to offer the minority a buyout on terms fair and acceptable to the minority.[76] By contrast, when dissolution is not ordered, there would be no pressure on the majority shareholder to offer terms acceptable to the minority when negotiating the latter's exit by non-dissolution means.[77]

Consequently, regardless of whether dissolution is readily or rarely available, it provides no solution to close corporation shareholder conflict that would consistently strike the right balance between minority and majority shareholders. Given dissolution's limited practical utility, I do not discuss it on its own terms[78] in this Book in any detail.

iii Appraisal

A form of exit that does not require termination of the corporation's existence is commonly known as 'appraisal' or sometimes 'dissenters' rights'. A classic definition of an appraisal right is:

> a statutory right to dissent from specified fundamental or structural changes in the life of their corporation [and] requires the corporation to facilitate the shareholders' withdrawal by buying back their shares for fair value, or its equivalent, as determined through appraisal proceedings.[79]

Available only in some jurisdictions,[80] exit by appraisal is triggered by clearly defined, statutorily enumerated grounds. These usually include fundamental corporate changes such as mergers, splits, conversion of the corporation into a different legal form, sale of the business or a substantial part thereof, or amendments to the corporate constitution.[81] Only shareholders who did not, or did not have the opportunity or right to, consent to the fundamental corporate change may 'perfect' their appraisal rights by complying with sometimes complex but necessary procedural formalities.[82] Exit is completed when the shareholder is paid for their shares by the corporation (and only the corporation) either voluntarily, or pursuant to

76 Hetherington & Dooley (1977): 27–8.

77 The same logic applies to withdrawal: if the minority shareholder fails to withdraw even with the legal process, what is there to stop a rational maximising majority shareholder from pressing home their advantage and force the minority shareholder out with a lowball offer?

78 Dissolution is closely linked to withdrawal in the US context and will be discussed in the context of withdrawal remedies in that jurisdiction (Chapter VI), albeit only where necessary. Other references to dissolution in the jurisdictional Chapters are almost exclusively in the context of history or enforcement mechanisms for withdrawal.

79 Kanda & Levmore (1985): 429. See also Koh & Tang (2021): 443–4.

80 National variants: 'appraisal right' (US); '*Abfindungsrecht*' (Germany); '[*hantai kabunushi*] *kabushiki kaitori seikyū-ken*' (Japan). Notably, the UK does not have an appraisal right recognizable as such, although there are arguably exceptions in contexts such as takeovers and schemes of arrangement; see Companies Act 2006, ss. 900(2)(e), 915A(5); 983, 986; Insolvency Act 1986, ss. 110–111.

81 See Koh (2014): 424–5; UmwG, § 29 et seq, § 36; Siegel (2011): 232–5.

82 See e.g. Koh (2014): 425–7; DGCL, §§ 262(a) & 262(b)(3), 262(d).

a judicial valuation proceeding.[83] Subject to exceptions prescribed by appraisal statutory provisions,[84] appraisal's availability turns on whether a triggering event has occurred, and not on characteristics such as shareholding structure or share transferability or tradability.

Appraisal's distinctive features are: (1) triggers clearly defined by reference to other corporate law provisions (e.g. did a merger etc. occur or not?); (2) extensive procedural formalities imposed upon shareholders seeking to exercise their rights; (3) liability to make payment for shares rests only with the corporation; and (4) applicability, in practice, to primarily widely held or listed corporations.

For length and scope reasons, appraisal will not be discussed further in this Book, but it is helpful for clarity to draw a conceptual distinction between 'withdrawal' and 'appraisal'. The first and most important concerns their scopes of application. In contrast with appraisal, withdrawal grounds are not defined narrowly or legalistically, and instead have a more open-ended character. Withdrawal is a 'standard' but appraisal is a 'rule'.[85] As Chapter III and the individual jurisdictional Chapters show, withdrawal can cover a wide range of circumstances relating to acts or conduct (or misconduct) of co-shareholders, personal circumstances of the withdrawal seeker, or the withdrawal seeker's mere whim.[86] Unlike appraisal, standing to commence withdrawal proceedings in court is not contingent on formal notice procedures or the like, even though the court plays a role in share valuation in both appraisal and withdrawal.[87] In appraisal, only the corporation is liable to pay the exiting shareholder; in withdrawal this may be either the close corporation itself or other parties such as co-shareholders.[88] Finally, appraisal triggers are not limited to close corporations, whereas withdrawal's availability – at least in the four target jurisdictions – is closely linked to close corporation intracorporate conflict.[89]

For the avoidance of doubt: this Book takes no position on the effectiveness of appraisal rights in resolving shareholder conflict *when appraisal is available*.[90] As

83 See e.g. DGCL, § 262(e)–(j); UmwG, § 34 and SpruchG, § 4.

84 For listed or unlisted but widely-held corporations, appraisal remedies may in some US jurisdictions be excluded by 'market out' exceptions, subject to further exceptions. See MBCA, §§ 13.02(b)(1)(i)–(ii), 13.02(b)(4); DGCL, §§ 262(b)(1), 262(b)(2); Siegel (2011): 245–50. By contrast, Japan's appraisal remedy has no 'market out' exception: Koh (2014): 424.

85 Cf de Vries (2010): 10.

86 III.C.

87 On valuation in withdrawal, see III.E.

88 See III.D.

89 Strictly speaking, there is a possibility that appraisal and withdrawal overlap in intracorporate conflict arising in response to fundamental corporate changes in close corporations, but I do not explore it in this Book.

90 See n. 89. The eclectic and incoherent nature of appraisal triggers *de lege lata* and the lack of a widely accepted overarching principle underlying appraisal are well-known and long-standing problems. For a canonical critique, see Manning (1962): 239–60; for a recent take see Iida (2013): 13–34, 223–33; for a more positive view, see Koh (2014): 456–8.

It is arguable, *de lege ferenda*, that appraisal grounds *should* be broadened or modified. However, this may well make appraisal in its expanded form indistinguishable from withdrawal. Hence, I draw

they stand, 'withdrawal' and 'appraisal' *de lege lata* are distinct concepts with different features and scopes of application. Due to length considerations and withdrawal's broader scope, withdrawal is this Book's exclusive subject.

2 'Non-Exit'

In contrast with the relatively well-defined 'exit' family of shareholder protection mechanisms, this subsection addresses other important, but less well-defined and relatively unfamiliar legal responses to shareholder conflict in close corporations.

i Expulsion

Expulsion[91] is withdrawal's mirror image; instead of exiting the close corporation themselves, the aggrieved shareholder forces the co-shareholder at fault to exit. Expulsion variants are available in all four target jurisdictions.[92]

Expulsion is a potent remedy usually granted only in exceptional situations. For an aggrieved minority shareholder to reach a satisfactory outcome through expulsion of a co-shareholder, the former must be prepared to remain with the close corporation, either by taking a more active role personally or relying on remaining co-shareholders to run the business. However, even if expulsion's relatively high legal threshold is met, expelling a majority shareholder is seldom a realistic solution for a minority shareholder unless at least one of the following applies: (1) the expelled defendant shareholder's monetary claim against the plaintiff shareholder or the close corporation is zero or very low compared to the value of the defendant's shares on a pro rata going concern basis;[93] (2) the plaintiff shareholder's resources are sufficient to finance the payment to the expelled shareholder;[94] (3) the close corporation's resources are sufficient to finance the payment within the limits of creditor protection rules. These conditions are not easily met. Thus, while expulsion may be viable in extreme cases and under the right conditions, it is by itself a seriously inadequate solution to the shareholder conflict problem in close corporations.

the line firmly between appraisal *de lege lata* and withdrawal, separating the two concepts for clarity of understanding and ease of discussion.

91 See generally Fleischer (2018a): 704–6.

92 Germany (*Ausschließung aus wichtigem Grund*): see generally Strohn (2018): Rdn 123–77. UK (unfair prejudice, buyout of majority by minority): *Re a Company (No 00789 of 1987), ex p Shooter* [1990] BCLC 384 (ChD); *Re Brenfield Squash Racquets Club Ltd* [1996] 2 BCLC 184 (ChD). US (US-CC close corporation in the narrow sense): see e.g. *Muellenberg* v. *Bikon Corp* (1996) 143 NJ 168, 182–3, 669 A2d 1382, 1389 (NJ) (ordering the oppressive majority shareholder to sell their shares to the oppressed minority shareholder). Japan: *Kaishahō*, Article 859 (*mochibun-gaisha no sha'in no jomei no uttae*).

93 The extent to which contractual clauses can reduce or eliminate payouts to expelled shareholders may be restricted by law; see Schmolke (2012) (Germany).

94 See e.g. *Muellenberg* v. *Bikon Corp* (1996) 143 NJ 168, 182, 669 A2d 1382, 1389 (NJ).

ii Voice

In his seminal work *Exit, Voice, and Loyalty*, Hirschman defines 'voice' as 'any attempt at all to change, rather than to escape from, an objectionable state of affairs'.[95] In contrast to the relatively clear-cut 'economic' concept of 'exit', 'voice' is 'messy' because it can manifest in a range of ways, and because it is an inherently political concept.[96] In the corporate law setting, 'voice' can manifest as voting or litigation.[97] The interaction between 'voice' and 'exit' (the latter in the broadest sense) is complex. Where exit is impossible, voice is the only way by which aggrieved members of an organization can react.[98] However, 'the decision whether to exit will often be taken *in the light of the prospects for the effective use of voice*', and 'in some situations, exit will therefore be a reaction of *last resort* after voice has failed'.[99] Thus, if one is 'sufficiently convinced that voice will be effective, then they may well *postpone* exit'.[100] Voice can therefore serve as both a substitute for and a complement to exit.[101]

In close corporations, voice rights, if sufficiently strong and well-designed, may prevent or resolve internally a range of shareholder conflicts without resorting to exit. For example, it is possible to specify ex ante that decisions shall be taken by a supermajority vote, or that a minority shareholder shall have a veto right over certain corporate decisions in which the minority shareholder particularly desires a say.[102] Litigation-type voice rights such as Germany's *Anfechtungsklage* (contestation action) may be useful against one-off majority decisions taken pursuant to defective procedures.[103] Even without voting, minor issues can be nipped in the bud through participation of both majority and minority in deliberative processes; even if decision-making power is ultimately vested in the majority, a minority who feels heard is more likely to consider the outcome to be fair.[104]

However, voice – and veto rights especially – are not without their risks and limitations. Excessively strong voting powers risk minority holdouts, obstruction of corporate decision-making, and inefficiencies in business management.[105] Ordinary voice rights, such as rights to attend and participate in shareholder meetings, may be breached, circumvented, or rendered un-exercisable by majority

95 Hirschman (1970): 30.
96 Ibid. 16.
97 Donald (2005): 306.
98 Hirschman (1970): 33.
99 Ibid. 37.
100 Ibid.
101 Ibid.
102 See generally Fleischer (2014): 42–5.
103 See Wertenbruch (2016): Rdn 120; Koh & Tang (2021): 445–7. Japan's Companies Act does not provide for a 'members' meeting' or 'resolution' for its close corporation form (*Gōdō Kaisha*), as business decisions may be taken (by default) by simple majority of the (executive) members: *Kaisha-hō*, Article 590 Paragraph 2, Article 591 Paragraph 1.
104 See Means (2009): 1229–31.
105 See ibid. 1251–2.

shareholders with impunity if the legal system does not adequately respond to and sanction such majority conduct.[106] Where majority infringement of minority voice is chronic, the minority would be forced either to tolerate or accept their diminishment in voice, or to seek judicial intervention to enforce their voice rights repeatedly at unacceptable cost. The first is no solution, and the second is too costly to be a viable solution. A third, theoretical response is seeking judicial intervention to police the affairs of the corporation prospectively for an indeterminate period of time. This, however, is unviable as courts are unlikely to have the authority or inclination to supervise close corporation affairs for the long term; enforcement of majority compliance with tailored, idiosyncratic court orders would also be costly.[107]

Ultimately, healthy operation of voice is possible and sustainable only in the absence of serious shareholder conflict. A credible threat of exit – to a point – strengthens voice,[108] and exit serves as the lasting solution to shareholder conflict where voice has tried and failed.

iii Duties

Binding itself voluntarily to stringent obligations is one way for the majority to make a credible commitment[109] to the minority that the latter's interests would be respected and protected.[110] A seemingly attractive solution to the close corporation problem therefore seems to be the concept of specific, special, or enhanced duties between majority and minority shareholders. The concept most often mentioned in the English-language literature is 'fiduciary duties' from US corporate law.[111] The German equivalent[112] in terms of importance – but substantially different in content – is the concept of a corporate law-specific 'duty of loyalty' (*gesellschaftsrechtliche Treuepflicht*) owed by the GmbH to members, by members to the GmbH, and between the members inter se.[113]

However, as a solution to shareholder conflict, enforcement of 'enhanced'[114] duties suffers from two limitations. The first is the existence and strength of the

106 See ibid. 1222–3.

107 Cf the criticism in n. 144 below and text thereto.

108 Cf Means (2009): 1253. While Means is not wrong that shareholder litigation may enhance voice, litigation that only supports voice without providing exit suffers from the defects discussed above. Even if we accept that exit 'on demand' (i.e. at will) is too much (Means (2009): 1253–4), exit in some form remains necessary.

109 On credible commitments see generally Williamson (1983).

110 Cf in different contexts, Rock (2002) and Tröger (2005): 40.

111 See e.g. *Donahue* v. *Rodd Electrotype Co* (1975) 328 NE2d 505, 515 (Mass); *G & N Aircraft, Inc* v. *Boehm* (2001) 743 NE2d 227 (Ind).

112 See Fleischer (2018a): 707–8.

113 Merkt (2018): Rdn 98. For the leading case, see BGH 05.06.1975 ('ITT'), BGHZ 65, 15.

114 I respectfully but firmly depart from the practice of comparative corporate law jurists in using 'fiduciary' as an umbrella term as it is misleading, not jurisdiction-neutral, and not infrequently

duties in question. Some target jurisdictions – particularly Germany and to a lesser extent the US – have well-established doctrine on shareholders' duties. That is not the case in the UK, where the reluctance to impose fiduciary or other status-based enhanced duties on majority/controlling shareholders inter se is well-entrenched.[115] Only in rare, fact-specific situations may shareholders make personal claims against directors or controlling shareholders,[116] and even then this may be thwarted by doctrinal obstacles.[117] In Japan, only executive members (*gyōmu wo shikkō suru sha'in*) who are empowered to manage the business owe substantial duties to the *Gōdo Kaisha*,[118] and are arguably liable for breach of those duties to other members personally only in exceptional circumstances.[119] Thus, the efficacy of shareholder duties varies considerably by target jurisdiction.

Second, even if there were duties applicable to the circumstances complained of, procedural obstacles and traps may make enforcement in practice difficult or illusory. In common law jurisdictions, minority shareholder attempts to enforce duties of majority shareholders (or directors that they support) are susceptible to tactics designed to delay and wear down the minority plaintiff. Requests or demands for information[120] may be stymied, and derivative suits are easily thwarted by procedural arguments and appeals that give abusive majorities ample time to enrich themselves and dissipate the corporation's assets.[121] Even in Germany, the *actio pro socio* is regarded by prevailing opinion to be a 'subsidiary emergency jurisdiction' (*subsidiäre Notzuständigkeit*),[122] the use of which is subject to onerous restrictions.[123]

Even if the plaintiff succeeds in establishing a breach of duty in court, the remedy may be of little value or comfort. It is one thing to be able to set aside a defective resolution or undo a particular act once; it is quite another to prevent the same conflict from reoccurring, or to heal the fracture in the majority-minority relationship.[124] Equitable or other discretionary judicial relief with the intention of prospectively regulating the majority-minority relationship suffers from the same

based on flawed understanding of fiduciary duties in Anglo-Commonwealth and US corporate law – which differ considerably.

115 Lim (2018): 115; see also *Re Coroin Ltd* [2012] EWHC 521 (Ch) [94]–[103]; Davies (2020): 152–4. For a Commonwealth common law perspective see generally Lim (2019).

116 See Hollington (2017): paras. [11–35] to [11–76]; Koh & Tang (2021): 442– 3.

117 See Koh (2016) (on reflective loss as an obstacle) and generally Koh & Tang (2021): 443.

118 *Kaisha-hō*, Articles 593 to 595. By default, all members are executive members unless provided otherwise by the corporate constitution (*teikan*): *Kaisha-hō*, Article 590 Paragraph 1.

119 *Kaisha-hō*, Article 597; see Ozeki (2014): 173. Ordinarily, the executive member is only liable to the company (*Kaisha-hō*, Article 596), but any member may represent the company through a derivative-action-like procedure (*Kaisha-hō*, Article 602).

120 Information rights vary considerably across the target jurisdictions. Cf GmbHG, § 51a (Germany); Koh & Takahashi (2015): 108 (UK); Geis (2019); O'Neal & Thompson (2020a): § 3:40, and ULLCA, §§ 410, 105(c)(8) (US); *Kaisha-hō*, Articles 592, 618 (Japan).

121 See O'Neal & Thompson (2020b): §§ 3:27, 7:7; Keay (2016).

122 Merkt (2018): Rdn 330; see also Barnert (2003): 120.

123 See Merkt (2018): Rdn 330; Koh & Tang (2021): 451–2.

124 See further below at II.D.3.

defects as voice discussed above.[125] Even if damages, the standard 'compensatory' remedy for breaches of duty,[126] were to be available[127] and awarded to the aggrieved minority shareholder,[128] this legal result, without more, does little to put an end to conflict so long as the minority cannot exit and is legally stuck in the status quo of being in business together with a now-unfriendly or actively hostile majority. In other words, non-exit-oriented legal reliefs cannot by themselves resolve the conflict with any finality save with the majority's willing cooperation.[129] Where relief for breach of enhanced duty comes in the form of minority exit from the corporation, it is indistinguishable from – and would for this Book's purposes be counted as – withdrawal.[130]

3 *Limitations of Non-Withdrawal Mechanisms*

It is theoretically possible that shareholder conflicts can be resolved, without exit, as between the shareholders themselves through dispute resolution mechanisms, or with the aid of temporary external intervention. Possible external interventions include provisional directors that can vote to break deadlocks,[131] or alternative dispute resolution mechanisms such as mediation.[132] However, the effectiveness of these non-exit mechanisms is limited to situations where the conflict is not yet intractable, and the parties are still committed to resolving their disputes consensually.[133] Temporary external intervention might even exacerbate the shareholder conflict it was supposed to resolve if the parties are unable to reach a mutually agreeable compromise over a prolonged period of time, and would constitute an unacceptable intrusion if administered over the long term.[134] Ultimately, there must come a parting of the ways in cases of shareholder conflict that cannot be resolved otherwise.[135] Judicial orders invalidating or restraining the execution of prejudicial acts[136]

125 See II.D.2.ii.

126 See e.g. *G & N Aircraft* (2001) 743 NE2d 227, 243.

127 Which cannot be taken for granted in Germany: see Merkt (2018): Rdn 200, 207–9.

128 Damages may, but are not necessarily, paid directly to the harmed aggrieved minority shareholder; in derivative actions, recovery is usually to the corporation. See Baum & Puchniak (2012): 7; Koh & Tang (2021): 435, 443.

129 While it is not inconceivable that the majority may voluntarily compromise and commit to acting in good faith towards the minority as part of a voluntary settlement, that depends on that particular majority shareholder's personal character or incentives rather than any ordered, intended, or predictable result of non-exit-oriented legal responses.

130 If the majority is forced to exit, that is 'expulsion': II.D.2.i.

131 Hetherington & Dooley (1977): 20–1.

132 See Goette (2014): 45–9.

133 See Hetherington & Dooley (1977): 21, 37; Goette (2014): 45, 50–2.

134 Hetherington & Dooley (1977): 21–5.

135 Neville (2010): 275–6.

136 See e.g. Koh & Tang (2021): 447.

have a role to play, but do not by themselves put an end to shareholder conflict. As one highest court pertinently observes:

> *[I]f the majority and minority cannot get along, litigation is not likely to improve matters between them. Anything short of a divorce is an invitation for repeat litigation in future.* Thus, although the court may 'direct or prohibit any act or cancel or vary any transaction or resolution' or 'regulate the conduct of the affairs of the company in future', such orders are likely to provide only temporary relief.[137]

In similar vein, a commentator identifies the following critical weakness of non-exit remedies in close corporations:

> Even if the deliberately wrongful conduct of a majority shareholder can be cured by other remedies, such as [suits to set aside resolutions], compulsory distributions or derivative actions, *nothing can ensure that the same misconduct will not occur again in the future if the relationship has deteriorated after the litigation, since the minority shareholder remains in a vulnerable position.*[138]

The court's imperative 'to bring[] to an end the matters complained of' was well-recognized, and in fact codified into statute in the UK as early as 1948.[139] Withdrawal's value as a means of putting an end to the conflict while facilitating a reasonable outcome for the minority shareholder is specifically acknowledged by the leading UK company law treatise:

> 'When business and, often, personal relations between quasi-partners have broken down and are incapable of reconstitution by a court, the only effective remedy is the minority's exit. A share purchase order gives the [minority plaintiff] an opportunity to exit from the company with the fair value of his or her investment, a result which is usually impossible in the absence of a court order, since often no potential purchasers of the shares are available or, even if they were, the purchase price a third party would be willing to pay would reflect, rather than remedy, the harm inflicted on the seller by the unfairly prejudicial conduct.'[140]

As the discussion above makes clear, even if it were theoretically possible in individual cases that the parties might reconcile after a duty/voice-based lawsuit, a legal system of rights and remedies cannot be solely based on the false hope that parties would always sort things out themselves. In a 'relationship[] characterized by an involvement that is personally intensive, broad in scope, and potentially long-lasting' such as that between participants in close corporations,[141] the law is

137 *Sembcorp Marine Ltd* v. *PPL Holdings Pte Ltd* [2013] SGCA 43; [2013] 4 SLR 193 [158] (Singapore Court of Appeal), quoting Wee (2009): para [5.97] (emphasis added by the Court).

138 Wang (2011): 3 (emphasis added).

139 Companies Act 1948 (c 38) (UK), s. 210(2). This statute's effectiveness (or lack thereof) as applied by the courts is a different story; see V.C.1.i.

140 Davies & Worthington (2016): para [20–19].

141 Eisenberg (1995): 251.

'not equipped to make rules that will hold a *relationship* together'.[142] Instead of 'try[ing] to enforce the contract [governing such relationships] and thereby keep the relationship together', the law should instead 'allow either party the right to easy exit on fair terms, even if easy exit is not written into the contract'.[143] Any remedy short of withdrawal (or dissolution) would be short-lived and likely lead to further litigation.[144]

E WITHDRAWAL DESIGN: THE DEFAULT/MANDATORY BALANCE

Withdrawal is essential to corporate law; *how* withdrawal should be implemented is thus also important. Should withdrawal be left to private ordering of the parties, or should it be a mandatory feature of close corporation law? Or somewhere in between? This section answers these questions. After introducing the mandatory/default tension that is the legacy of contractarian scholarship in corporate law (II.E.1), this section explores why shareholders – minority and majority – might find access to withdrawal desirable (II.E.2), and why they might not (II.E.3). In this process, insights from the emerging field of law and behavioural economics will be drawn on and applied to the specific context of withdrawal in close corporations. The last subsection (II.E.4) charts two paths between the 'pure' default and mandatory visions of withdrawal that would achieve the goals of both who seek access to withdrawal, and those who would forgo it.

1 *The Mandatory/Default Tension in Corporate Law*

Since the 1980s, corporate law has – especially in the US – become increasingly dominated by contractarians,[145] a loose group of scholars who 'view the corporation as a set of private contractual relationships among providers of capital and services'.[146] Central to contractarian thought is the division of legal norms into categories: 'default' norms that 'govern only if the parties do not explicitly provide for something different' and 'mandatory' norms that 'leav[e] parties no option but to conform to them'.[147] A third, related category is 'enabling' norms, which differ from 'default' norms in that the former requires 'conscious opt-in', whereas the latter

142 Ibid. 252.

143 Ibid. 253.

144 Molitor (2009): 561–2. See also nn. 2–3 above and text thereto.

145 For a critical assessment of the contractarians and their influence on corporate law, see Klausner (2006).

146 Butler & Ribstein (1990): 3; in similar vein, Coffee (1989): 1619. Modern corporate law contractarians trace their origin to Jensen & Meckling (1976), the seminal paper that entrenched the concept of the corporation as a 'nexus of contracts' in academic discourse. As of 5 March 2021, its Google Scholar citation count stands at 96,619: https://scholar.google.com.sg/scholar?cites=4986983958447029005 (accessed 5 March 2021).

147 Armour & Enriques et al. (2017): 18; see also Eidenmüller (2014): 18; Cheffins (1997): 217–19.

apply unless opted out of.[148] In other words, enabling norms are those you can say yes to ('opt-in'); default norms are those you can say no to ('opt-out'); and mandatory norms are those you cannot say no to.

The contractarian vision of corporate law is primarily that of default rules that parties seeking a customized bargain may opt out of.[149] Flowing naturally from the contractarian premise that corporate law is essentially contractual is the normative case that the law should not relieve shareholders from bad bargains using extra-contractual mechanisms.[150] To these contractarians, close corporation shareholders should be entitled to no further legal protection beyond what they have bargained for in contract.[151] Only as an exception do some contractarians tolerate extra-contractual, mandatory rules when there is market failure,[152] although even market failure might fail to sway the most hard-line contractarians committed to the motto 'Everything is negotiable'.[153]

In response to the danger of ex post opportunism by majority shareholders, a popular contractarian argument is that such a risk should have been obvious to minority shareholders, and prospective shareholders should account for this danger when bargaining over the founding documents of the corporation.[154] As the argument goes, shareholders join companies of their own free will, having first determined the advantages and disadvantages of doing so. While the terms of entry for public corporations may be standard and non-negotiable, close corporation shareholders may have had the latitude to negotiate for the terms of their entry. Such shareholders, being sophisticated enough to incorporate for the purpose of obtaining the benefits of limited liability and tax advantages,[155] should also be knowledgeable enough to protect the basic expectations that are fundamental to their involvement in business – including exit options. In any event, the shareholder's decision to accept close corporation membership is entirely voluntary. Inadequately protected minority shareholders have consented to the terms of their entry, and by extension, their disadvantaged position in the company.[156] If, for any reason, they have failed to provide for or dispensed with a certain method or degree of protection such as exit at a fair price, they should bear the consequences of such a decision.[157]

Regardless of the extent to which one is sympathetic to the contractarian perspective(s), their impact is such that it is normal for corporate law issues –

148 Eidenmüller (2014): 18–19. Early works (e.g. 1989 special issue of *Columbia Law Review*) do not consistently distinguish between 'default' and 'enabling', often using them synonymously. Cf Cheffins (1997): 217–18 (calling enabling rules 'permissive rules').

149 Easterbrook & Fischel (1991): 15. See also Bainbridge (2020): 554; Coffee (1989): 1618–19.

150 Riley (1992): 783.

151 Schmolke (2012): 409–10; Gillette (1985): 581; Dalley (2004): 221.

152 Klausner (1995): 769; Butler & Ribstein (1990): 64.

153 Clark (1989): 1705–6; Butler & Ribstein (1990): 58.

154 Bainbridge (2002): 830.

155 Easterbrook & Fischel (1991): 250.

156 Riley (1992): 783.

157 Means (2010): 1162.

including majority-minority shareholder conflict – to be first considered as problems to be solved wherever possible by express contract (with or without opt-in enabling rules), with corporate law norms – whether default or mandatory – playing only a supplementary role.[158] Put another way, the contractarian challenge to corporate law is essentially this: mandatory norms (existing or proposed) must be affirmatively justified, failing which they should be reduced to default or even mere enabling status.

The rest of this section responds to the contractarian challenge in the context of shareholder conflict in close corporations. Recall that II.C introduced two variants of withdrawal – 'at will' and 'on grounds', and that the discussion in II.D has established that a withdrawal regime is distinct from other legal mechanisms, and an essential component of a corporate law system's response to shareholder conflict in close corporations. Two questions are answered. First, should a withdrawal regime be default, mandatory, enabling, none of the above, or all of the above? Second, should the two variants of withdrawal – at will and on grounds – be treated differently, and if so, how?

2 *Reasons for Access to Withdrawal*

i Inevitability of Incomplete Contracting

Since withdrawal is a solution to shareholder conflict, the prevention or peaceful resolution of shareholder conflict would theoretically obviate the need for access to withdrawal. However, as the discussion below will show, it is impossible to eliminate ex ante any and all risk of shareholder conflict. Minority access to withdrawal is therefore a desirable counter to majority power that would otherwise usually prevail in a majority–minority conflict.

Intracorporate relationships have been characterized as 'contractual', as they are governed by the corporate constitution and other arrangements such as shareholder agreements. However, such intracorporate relationships differ from the classic, arms' length, one-off bargain-type transaction familiar to basic contract law in several aspects. First is the long-term nature of the intracorporate relationship. Second is the displacement of the ordinary rule in contracts that contractual entitlements and obligations may not be changed without unanimous consent of the parties. Instead, the general principle governing close corporations is majority or supermajority rule. These two aspects complicate and frustrate attempts to govern the relationship exhaustively by express contract.

The close corporation relationship[159] can essentially be characterized as a 'relational contract'[160] in which parties seek 'to formalize [their] relationship rather than commit

[158] Implicit in Fleischer (2014): 41, 46.

[159] Moll (2002): 754. See also Means (2010): 1195–6; Fleischer (2001): 4–5.

[160] Popularized by Macneil (1978).

to [] discrete transaction[s]'.[161] When incorporating a business, 'founding shareholders negotiate a long-term, open-ended relationship with each other for the general purpose of operating a profitable business'.[162] However, the longer the length of the relationship, the more circumstances change, and contingencies inevitably occur.[163] The relationship must necessarily be a flexible one to adapt to the business' changing needs over time, and the shareholders may be unable to reduce critical aspects of their relationship into concrete obligations.[164] It would be extremely costly,[165] if not (without the benefit of hindsight) impossible, to provide for every possible eventuality within a contract made ex ante – the well-known problem of contract incompleteness.[166] The sheer impossibility for humans to foresee and address ex ante future contingencies[167] inevitably dooms any attempt to stipulate exhaustively, in a contract, the situations and terms on which withdrawal would be available. Because contracts cannot be complete, allocation of power or residual control is important.

Further, the close corporation relationship clearly cannot be adequately governed by classical rules of contract. Instead, mechanisms under which the 'contract' can be renegotiated and amended, and disputes resolved flexibly are essential in such relationships.[168] In the context of close corporations – or corporations generally – the primary mechanism for resolving issues that have not been negotiated ex ante is majority rule.[169] While it works fine as a means of relatively efficient business self-governance when majority and minority are at peace,[170] the principle of majority rule allocates the risk of disagreement to the minority, thereby introducing further problems. Without a unanimity requirement, the majority or supermajority has substantial discretion to resolve post-incorporation matters in its own favour, and may make midstream changes to the close corporation relationship that benefits itself to the detriment of an outvoted minority.[171] The norm of majority rule prevailing in the absence of special minority rights – coupled with minority 'lock-in' that is an inherent feature of close corporations – creates the structural risk of oppression of minorities by majorities.

Even supposing that shareholders were hypothetically able ex ante to predict every conflict that could possibly arise given the facts and circumstances of their

161 Means (2010): 1195.
162 Ibid. 1196.
163 Eisenberg (1995): 252.
164 Means (2010): 1195–6.
165 Charny (1991): 1819.
166 Hart (1988): 123; Williamson (1979): 237–8, 241.
167 Hart (1995): 2.
168 Williamson (1979): 237–8, 241.
169 Means (2010): 1188; Bainbridge (2002): 824.
170 Majority rule is not inherently oppressive when the majority overrides the minority on a bona fide business decision. However, what begins as innocent, good-faith disagreement may progress into something more serious and sinister: see II.B.
171 Easterbrook & Fischel (1989): 1443. Appraisal rights may or may not, depending on the jurisdiction, offer an exit option to dissenting minorities; see II.D.1.iii above.

relationships and the business, this does not solve or prevent the problem of shareholder conflict. Even with perfect information, it is no more likely that the majority and minority can or would reach agreement about the 'fair' or 'correct' solution to each individual situation.[172] Thus, even if all conflict scenarios could be foreseen, they cannot be solved individually through ex ante bargaining and contracting. Some default norm would necessarily apply when parties cannot agree otherwise. Given the norm of majority rule as an overarching principle of corporate law and governance, the majority is likely to prevail as well – at least by default – unless majority rule itself is significantly abrogated, or an alternative norm exists.

Withdrawal offers a solution to both facets of the incomplete contracting problem. When majority–minority conflict of an unforeseen nature[173] breaks out, the presence of a withdrawal mechanism offers the minority an alternative outcome to that which would otherwise follow from majority rule.[174] If the minority possesses the option of voluntarily withdrawing from the company, the minority could effectively bring the conflict to an end unilaterally by exercising that option. Withdrawal has the advantage of not abrogating majority rule: the minority gets to withdraw with a monetary claim, but the result that the majority sought to achieve would not itself be invalid.[175]

However, permitting the minority to withdraw in any majority–minority conflict, big or small, real or perceived – that is, withdrawal at will or something close to it – creates its own set of serious problems.[176] An arrangement workable and acceptable to both majority and minority would probably fall somewhere in between the extremes of no withdrawal at all without majority consent, and withdrawal at will. In other words, withdrawal should be available in some situations but not others. This raises two questions: what are the situations that justify withdrawal? Who decides whether these situations have arisen on the facts?

Enter withdrawal 'on grounds'. As explained above,[177] withdrawal on grounds is only available in certain circumstances that are verifiable by a third-party arbiter such as a court or other dispute resolution body. The concept of grounds as a standard (i.e. not a rule), and which involves the involvement of a third-party arbiter, performs a valuable gap-filling function[178] by giving effect to the 'actual

172 Even if theoretically achievable, it is not necessarily realistic.

173 Or where the conflict was foreseen but the parties neglected to or were unable to reach a precise agreement on the consequences.

174 i.e. the general principle that losses lie where they fall – on the minority.

175 For example, if the majority refuses to issue dividends, withdrawal by the minority – in contrast with other broad discretionary powers that judges may exercise under some US or the UK statutes – does not result in majority's action being reversed; it is only that the majority or the corporation (as the case may be) must pay the minority its monetary claim. In this sense, the majority's decision stands, albeit at a price.

176 See e.g. Easterbrook & Fischel (1986): 288–90; Thompson (1988): 223. For reasons why shareholders may agree to forgo the widest possible withdrawal rights, see II.E.3.i below. Most target jurisdictions do not favour withdrawal at will; see III.C.4.

177 II.C.

178 O'Kelley (1992): 216, 247; see also Kraus & Scott (2009): 1025.

expectations' of the parties based on available evidence.[179] Examples of evidence useful to the third-party arbiter[180] include commercial practice;[181] the company's history,[182] structure, size, and nature;[183] the shareholders' past practice and conduct including informal communications;[184] and the relationship between the shareholders over time.[185] Categories of grounds recognized over a body of cases become part of the corpus of corporate law jurisprudence and doctrine,[186] and would become implied (either mandatorily or as a default unless expressly contracted out of)[187] into the shareholders' 'bargain', reducing transaction costs.

For parties who would have made provision for withdrawal had they considered the issue but ultimately omitted to do so, their intentions can be given effect via statutory or jurisprudential grounds. Grounds can be based on fault – which acts as a corrective to majority opportunism – or non-fault, which responds to a greater range of shareholder conflict where fault might not be clearly attributable.[188]

The next question is: who determines whether the grounds for withdrawal are established in each dispute? It is theoretically possible but improbable for the parties themselves to reach agreement on whether such grounds are made out, especially when a determination of 'fault' on one side or the other for the conflict is relevant to the availability and precise consequences of withdrawal. It is especially unlikely that a majority shareholder engaging in opportunistic conduct prejudicial to the minority's interest would voluntarily admit to being at fault and offer the minority an acceptable settlement.

A third-party arbiter that can make legally binding findings of fact and render a legally enforceable decision according to law is thus necessary; this means either a court or an arbitral tribunal.[189] Despite costs and drawbacks arising from the nature

179 Means (2010): 1190.

180 See generally *BCE Inc* v. *1976 Debenture Holders* 2008 SCC 69; [2008] 3 SCR 560 [73]–[84]. Although based on Canada's statutory oppression remedy and not without its detractors, *BCE* remains arguably the most comprehensive judicial statement on the subject in any language anywhere in the world. Koehnen's *Oppression and Related Remedies* (Koehnen (2004)) is endorsed at multiple points in the judgment, cementing its status as an authoritative text on shareholder oppression – at least in Canada. Koehnen is since 2017 a judge of the Ontario Superior Court of Justice.

181 Koehnen (2004): 88.

182 *Thomas* v. *HW Thomas Ltd* [1984] 1 NZLR 686 (New Zealand Court of Appeal) 694–5 (in the unfair prejudice context).

183 Koehnen (2004): 93. On how structure etc. affects withdrawal availability, see also II.E.3.i below (on technology start-ups and joint ventures). IV.C.2.ii (Germany) and V.C.4.iii.c (UK).

184 Charny (1991): 1872; Koehnen (2004): 94–5.

185 Eisenberg (1989): 1468, citing *Meiselman* v. *Meiselman* (1983) 309 NC 279, 298, 307 SE2d 551, 563 (NC).

186 See III.C for a comparative overview of the target jurisdictions.

187 On the varying degrees to which withdrawal grounds are mandatory or default, see III.F.

188 While there is some consensus that majority 'fault' should be grounds for withdrawal, jurisdictions vary considerably on the extent they recognise non-fault grounds. On this see III.C, III.G.3.

189 It is axiomatic that mediators, in contrast with judges and arbitrators, do not make determinations of fault.

of litigation,[190] the need for judicial intervention is especially strong in close corporations.[191] It is well-recognized that the feasibility of long-term relational contracts such as those between a corporation's shareholders[192] depends on the courts'[193] role in monitoring such agreements,[194] not least because there are areas in corporate law that are highly incomplete and therefore require delegation of residual 'lawmaking and law enforcement powers' to the courts.[195]

However, the effectiveness of withdrawal on grounds as a gap-filling regime would be completely undermined if it could be carelessly contracted out of by minority shareholders who are not fully informed of the consequences of doing so. I discuss below when shareholders might rationally and for good reason contract partly or completely out of withdrawal[196] – and when they might do so for suboptimal reasons.[197]

ii Fostering and Vindicating Trust

A fundamental assumption of contractarians is that shareholders are utility-maximizing rational participants[198] who consistently bargain for necessary protections prior to joining a close corporation business.[199] Under this *homo economicus* ('economic man')[200] model, prospective close corporation shareholders calmly evaluate the chances of success of the corporate endeavour, work out how much they (and the other participants) will be contributing to the enterprise, anticipate potential problems, and draft comprehensive contractual provisions governing different types of exit and when they are triggered, and complex clauses that would ensure a fair valuation for any party exiting the corporation.[201] However, for better or for worse, that is not how real people necessarily behave.

Suppose that our hypothetical minority shareholder is exceptionally well-informed and possessed of excellent cognitive abilities. Even this near-omniscient

190 Such as 'expense, time, uncertainty, and unpleasantness': Solomon & Solomon (1987): 111.
191 See Eisenberg (1989): 1464–6.
192 On the shareholders' relational contract see generally Whincop (2001): 122–6.
193 Even though arbitrators can resolve individual disputes, the nature of arbitration (beyond the highly idiosyncratic investor-state dispute resolution system) is that it generally does not create new law that would be helpful to future disputants. Only courts can make corporate law through resolving individual disputes; arbitrators – at best – apply (a simulacrum of) corporate law.
194 Coffee (1989): 1619–22.
195 Pistor & Xu (2003): 85 (in the context of enforcing fiduciary duties). On the substantial similarities and connections in the close corporation context between fiduciary duty breaches and shareholder withdrawal, see Thompson (1993): 699–700.
196 II.E.3.i.
197 II.E.3.iii.
198 See Bainbridge (2002): 23.
199 Means (2010): 1185–6.
200 Popularized by Thaler & Sunstein (2008): 6–7.
201 Some of the most well-known techniques used in joint ventures – in which participants bargain extensively – are summarised in Hewitt et al (2016): paras. [10–11] to [10–20].

being might not intend – or indeed, find it in their interests – to exercise those abilities in a manner predicted by the *homo economicus* model and bargain with the majority for special protections such as buyout rights. Equally if not even more important is the role of trust. A business endeavour usually commences amidst an atmosphere of optimism,[202] goodwill,[203] and – especially where the business venture is commenced by participants with a pre-existing personal relationship[204] – trust.[205] Participants therefore often desire to avoid discussion or bargaining over matters that might foster distrust[206] or lack of confidence[207] in each other. The very act of showing reluctance to trust may give others the impression of untrustworthiness.[208]

Formalising relations through the law itself creates distance between the parties, begins the process of eroding trust, and could escalate into increasing distrust.[209] Unsurprisingly, legal counsel to the parties – who we would ordinarily expect to be more familiar than the legally uninitiated client about the risks of shareholder conflict[210] – may face dilemmas over the extent to which they should raise possible issues to their clients for fear of 'spoiling the deal'.[211] Bargaining for minority protection without endangering the participants' relationship can be extremely difficult,[212] and even counterproductive.[213] Minority shareholders who wish to avoid signalling untrustworthiness may elect, notwithstanding misgivings, not to resist a proposal (by the majority or their advisors) for withdrawal to be limited or excluded. For the success of the enterprise, it may very well be the case that our hyperrational hypothetical shareholder would do well to keep their concerns to themselves and get on with the business of business.

This does not, however, mean that our minority shareholder can really be said to have made a conscious judgement call that withdrawal or other exit options are undesirable. It is merely that actively bargaining for them would be – in the law-and-economics terminology – too costly. Trusting – and therefore more likely trustworthy[214] – minority shareholders who eschew costly and trust-damaging legal

202 Murdock (1990): 426 ('From a relational standpoint, people enter closely-held businesses in the same manner as they enter marriage: optimistically and ill-prepared.'); Eisenberg (1995): 251–2; Thompson (1993): 705; Means (2010): 1163 ('founding a business is an inherently hopeful act').

203 O'Neal (1987): 124.

204 Illig (2006): 318; Hetherington & Dooley (1977): 2–3.

205 Moll (2005): 912 ('There is often an initial atmosphere of mutual trust that diminishes the sense that contractual protection is needed').

206 Cheffins (1997): 273–4.

207 Hetherington & Dooley (1977): 36–7.

208 Blair & Stout (2001): 1806.

209 Cross (2005): 1489–90; Sitkin & Roth (1993): 376. On 'bonding' as a means to increase trust, see II.E.2.iii below.

210 Lawyers, by contrast with their clients, tend to overstate risks; see generally Langevoort & Rasmussen (1997).

211 Solomon & Solomon (1987): 120.

212 Moll (2005): 914.

213 Blair & Stout (2001): 1807.

214 Blair & Stout (2001): 1806.

bargaining may decide not to actively bargain for withdrawal. The high transaction costs in this scenario make it attractive for corporate law to supply withdrawal mechanisms at least as a default, if not mandatory, feature. It is said that '[r]egulations may further trust by establishing a norm of behavior as a background and creating mutual understandings of trust'.[215]

By providing minority shareholders access to withdrawal when majority shareholders breach behavioural norms even when minority shareholders did not expressly bargain for withdrawal, corporate law can encourage and reward – or at least vindicate – minority shareholder trust in, and cooperative behaviour towards, majority shareholders. The imperative to vindicate the trust of minority shareholders is especially strong in the close corporation context given the minority's vulnerability from lack of exit. Trusting and trustworthy minority shareholders should be recognized for their socially beneficial behaviours; they deserve not the contempt of contractarian theorists for 'failing' to protect themselves by contract, but rather the fullest protection of (extra-contractual) corporate law.[216]

The foregoing also suggests that when parties have no reason to trust each other but nonetheless conclude that withdrawal may not be appropriate given their business' specific circumstances, or when the minority has alternative ways by which betrayal of trust by the majority can be sanctioned, they would have good reasons to agree to waive or limit access to withdrawal. These are discussed below.[217]

iii Voluntary, Binding Concessions by Majority to Minority

It is conceivable that majority shareholders may voluntarily offer some degree of access to withdrawal to minority shareholders for entirely rational purposes. By voluntarily 'bonding' themselves ex ante to withdrawal access for minority shareholders, the majority signals either its credible commitment[218] to behaving in a manner that would not be detrimental to the minority's interests, or at least its willingness to compensate the minority by ensuring that the minority can withdraw in such situations. Rational minorities that would have otherwise been unwilling to agree to invest and participate in the venture, or would have demanded a discounted price for shares, may be persuaded to join or contribute more capital because of the majority's credible commitment.

However, it is not so easy for the majority to make a credible commitment to the minority that the former would not take unfair advantage of the latter, not least

[215] Cross (2005): 1544; see also Levmore (2000): 2021. In the withdrawal context, while it is not necessarily advantageous for the minority to mention withdrawal before joining the business to avoid signalling distrust and untrustworthiness, it could be helpful for the parties to learn or be reminded after the fact that they (and especially majority shareholders) are held to certain behavioural standards by the applicable extracontractual withdrawal regime.

[216] Cf Means (2010): 1194.

[217] See respectively II.E.3.i and II.E.3.ii.

[218] Cf in the securities regulation context Rock (2002) and Licht (2003): 142.

because of the incomplete contracting problem.[219] Any contractual buyout provision triggered by contractually enumerated grounds beyond clear-cut cases such as death can, to a large extent, be circumvented by a majority shareholder careful enough to avoid creating the precise circumstances that would trigger it.[220] Take for example a generous buyback provision that could be exercised by the minority shareholder upon retirement or involuntary termination of employment. Such a provision could be circumvented by a majority shareholder careful enough to avoid terminating the minority outright, but otherwise intent on oppressing the minority in other ways before the minority gives up and 'retires'.[221] Difficult questions of interpretation as to the precise scope of any purely contractual withdrawal mechanism are likely to arise. Only full minority rights to withdraw at will are not susceptible to manipulation by the majority as to scope of application – but these come with their own set of drawbacks.[222]

The greater flexibility enjoyed by close corporation participants to structure their own affairs calls for more exacting judicial monitoring.[223] Without a mechanism premised on a gap-filling independent third-party arbiter who determines whether withdrawal should be accessible to the minority on the specific facts and circumstances, it is in practice difficult for majority shareholders to commit credibly ex ante to offering minority shareholders fair withdrawal options. The concept of withdrawal 'on grounds', as a standard premised on a third-party arbiter performing gap-filling and gatekeeping functions, thus offers an – if not the only – effective compromise making majority commitments credible without handing the minority sufficient power to tempt minority opportunism.[224]

3 *Reasons Why Shareholders Forgo or Limit Access to Withdrawal*

Withdrawal is useful in a wide range of situations as a response to shareholder conflict, but this does not mean that withdrawal in all its variants (i.e. at will and on grounds) is suitable for all situations. In this subsection, reasons for shareholders to expressly reject or limit withdrawal remedies are explored. An example of rejection of or limitation on access to withdrawal would include a valuation clause that would result in a monetary claim that is grossly disproportionate as compared to (i.e. much less than) the pro rata share of the business' going concern value, as this constitutes a de facto restraint on withdrawal.

219 Discussed above at II.E.2.i.

220 The majority shareholder may possibly engineer the death or incapacitation of the minority, but that is beyond the concerns of corporate law.

221 Constructive dismissal doctrine may be a possible safeguard only if the court interprets the buyback provision as incorporating constructive dismissal doctrine – which is extra-contractual labour law – into the contract.

222 See e.g. Easterbrook & Fischel (1986): 288–90; Thompson (1988): 223; see also II.E.3.i (on minority holdups).

223 Cf Coffee (1988): 940–1.

224 See Thompson (1988): 223–5.

i Conscious, Informed Agreement by Majority and Minority

Given the importance of private ordering to close corporations and their governance, it is beyond any serious doubt today that consensual arrangements entered into voluntarily by uncoerced parties based on relevant and adequate information should be generally given effect to by the law. Minority shareholders may wish to relinquish, reject, or limit their withdrawal rights for any number of good reasons; the examples discussed here are only indicative and by no means exhaustive.

Technology start-ups. Rock and Wachter famously described the technology start-up ('Silicon Valley start-up')[225] as an omelette that has yet to set: dissolution and sale of a start-up – which comprises 'match assets' or 'match investments' that 'have great value to insiders and little value to outsiders'[226] – midstream would be as disastrous as trying to sell a half-cooked omelette.[227] Given the high costs of easy dissolution, they argue that Silicon Valley start-ups should not offer easy exit.[228] They extend their argument to the close corporation form generally by arguing that firms should choose the close corporation only if they are heavy on match investments.[229] The problematic aspects and implications of their argument aside,[230] limiting or excluding access to withdrawal may, in specific situations, perhaps be desirable for both majority and minority shareholders.[231]

225 Defined at Rock & Wachter (1999): 918.

226 Ibid.

227 Ibid. 918–19. Unsurprisingly, the authors never considered anywhere in the article whether withdrawal 'on grounds' should also be excluded.

228 See ibid. 915, 920.

229 Ibid. 915, 920, 947–8. The authors do not, however, address the needs (such as of withdrawal) of the countless businesses that are not Silicon Valley start-ups, but which have taken close corporation forms (instead of partnership forms as they recommend) for various other reasons.

230 See n. 230 above. Their attempt to justify excluding judicial intervention in favour of non-legally enforceable norms in the close corporation is deeply problematic, non-generalisable, or both. First, part of their argument (in Rock & Wachter (1999): 925–9) hinges on the uniquely American idea that employees should be terminable at the will of the employer – a position that is far from universal in most of the developed world. Second, their account is premised on the Silicon Valley start-up: a creature that is not typical of close corporations in the rest of the world, or even in the USA beyond a few select regions such as the San Francisco Bay Area. It is unrealistic, as they implicitly do, to write off the majority, or even overwhelming majority, of businesses taking close corporation forms that do not have technology start-up-like characteristics. Another part of their argument, which attempts to justify *Wilkes* v. *Springside Nursing Home, Inc* (1976) 353 NE2d 657 (Mass), also hinges on assumptions inimical to rule of law. For example, Rock and Wachter point out that a minority shareholder squeezed out from employment, despite not having access to withdrawal, 'will be in a position to make [the majority shareholder's] life difficult by making requests for information and threats of litigation': Rock & Wachter (1999): 933. Rock and Wachter's by all accounts serious and sincere suggestion that 'threats of litigation' are a good substitute for – and should displace entirely – lawful withdrawal remedies should be repugnant to any jurist committed to the idea of rule of law. On other 'self-enforcement' techniques and their limits, see II.E.3.ii below. On threats as a partial functional substitute for withdrawal in Japan, see VII.B.2.i.

231 If the start-up goes public or is acquired by an incumbent giant *and* all shareholders gain the opportunity to exit (whether in whole or part), withdrawal may become less critical.

Corporate joint ventures. Although a subtype of close corporation,[232] corporate joint ventures in which parties are corporate entities instead of natural persons[233] differ in some respects from natural person-based close corporations such as family businesses or quasi-partnerships of equals. Joint venture parties are often large businesses with considerable economic resources, and which are less vulnerable than natural person-close corporation participants to the negative consequences of shareholder conflict.[234] Joint ventures are often structured with a 50–50 split in equity holdings or something close to it, and minority shareholders often bargain for and obtain extensive rights and powers.[235] Unlike some close corporation – especially family-controlled – businesses that can and are planned to go on almost indefinitely,[236] joint ventures between corporate entities have a 'life cycle' and mostly culminate in one or more parties exiting by selling their interests.[237] As such, careful planning for exit through contractual arrangements is of particular importance to corporates.[238] Withdrawal regimes applicable to close corporations more generally may, in the joint venture context, have their scope of application limited,[239] and be properly superseded by customized arrangements between two commercial legal entities usually made pursuant to legal advice.[240]

Minority hold-up. Shareholders may conceivably and rationally agree to eliminate minority protection such as exit rights at the time of entry due to the potential costs of such protection. Overly strong minority rights (or the threat to exercise those rights) might be used by minority shareholders to demand concessions, effect deadlock, commence abusive litigation, or otherwise engage in opportunistic behaviour at the majority's expense.[241] The risks include impeding efficient management by creating a de facto unanimity requirement for decision-making,[242] and

232 Insofar as the venture is conducted through a separate (corporate) entity; ie as an 'equity joint venture' rather than a 'non-equity alliance'; on terminology and possible structures in the UK/European context, see Hewitt et al (2016): para. [1–07], ch. 3.

233 Texts on joint ventures sometimes proceed on the assumption that the parties are corporates; see e.g. Shishido et al. (2015): 1 (premised on 'partner companies', i.e. corporate entities).

234 For example, with corporates as joint venture parties, a squeeze out does not have a similarly devastating economic impact as the loss of employment or other returns on investment might have for a natural person of modest means, as might often be the case in a family business or incorporated partnership-type close corporation.

235 The risk of deadlock is increased, but this is also partly countered by deadlock-breaking or exit mechanisms; see generally Hewitt et al. (2016): ch. 10.

236 See e.g. Economist (2004); Bennedsen (2014).

237 Hewitt et al. (2016): para. [1–10].

238 See generally Hewitt et al. (2016): ch. 13; Shishido et al. (2015): ch. 5.

239 See e.g. IV.C.2.ii (scope of *wichtiger Grund* depends on how capital-centric the GmbH is); Hewitt et al. (2016): paras. [11–21] to [11–22] (unfair prejudice in joint ventures); and VII.D.3.iii (on Shishido's views of the scope of 'unavoidable grounds' in the GK).

240 Although there will be exceptions, it is increasingly unlikely that multimillion (if not -billion) dollar joint ventures between corporates will be undertaken without presumptively competent legal advice.

241 Easterbrook & Fischel (1986): 289; Storm (2002): 437.

242 Cf Gordon (1989): 1583–4 (in the context of supermajority rules).

undermining the core principle of majority rule implicitly agreed upon by the shareholders at incorporation. It is therefore within the realm of reason that shareholders, in seeking to avoid such costs, may decide to do away with such protections, in particular buyout (i.e. withdrawal) rights that may be exercised by the minority at will.[243]

Special circumstances in connection with the minority's share acquisition. In some close corporations, minority shareholders do not invest both their own labour and capital. In family-owned and operated businesses, shares may be given by founder-majority shareholders to their family members as gifts. The 'bargain',[244] especially in family businesses run according to a strict hierarchy, is one where minority shareholders have no obligations and no voice, but may receive, by virtue of their shareholding, part of the benefits of the family business' success.[245] Another example would be schemes where employees are allotted or permitted to purchase shares according to pre-set terms, and where the shares must be relinquished or sold upon cessation of employment.[246] In both these situations, minority shareholders receive shares for free, or at prices that may be disproportionately low compared to what the pro rata percentage of the business' going concern value would be worth.[247] Under these circumstances, where the risk of ex post exploitation or detriment is already factored into the minority's investment ex ante,[248] forgoing access to withdrawal remedies, or valuation clauses severely limiting the value of the withdrawing shareholder's monetary claim, could be reasonable in light of the overall bargain.[249]

The discussion above shows that there are good reasons – premised on specific facts and arrangements – for minority shareholders to forgo or limit their own access to withdrawal in certain circumstances. However, this should not be confused with a general wish to exclude all prospect of legal[250] withdrawal (whether at will or on

243 Easterbrook & Fischel (1986): 285–6.

244 There might be no process of bargaining at all, especially when the shareholding and management structure is decided at the whim of the founder/controlling shareholder.

245 See Tang (2018): 24–6; see also e.g. *Thio Syn Kym Wendy* v. *Thio Syn Pyn* [2018] SGCA 46, [2018] 2 SLR 788 [6] (shares were given to plaintiff minority shareholders by founder-patriarch as a form of financial provision that could not be 'squandered'). However, this is not to say that junior members of family businesses always get to enjoy the benefits without burdens. Many get coerced into joining the business through emotional blackmail and other non- or extralegal sanctions, and are pressured to contribute labour in exchange for minimal contractual protection either as employee or minority shareholder. In such cases, withdrawal doctrine still has a role to play in facilitating just outcomes when intractable conflict occurs.

246 Although employee stock purchase plans (ESPPs) or employee stock ownership plans (ESOPs) are usually discussed in the context of listed companies, it is not impossible for simpler versions to be adopted in close corporations.

247 Typically, the corporation has either the obligation or right (option) to buy out the employee upon cessation of employment; see O'Neal & Thompson (2020a): §§ 7:4, 7:17–7:18.

248 Cf Illig (2006): 324–8.

249 See Schmolke (2012): 396, 416 (on membership interests received gratuitously).

250 A promise not to resort to non- or extralegal sanctions such as blackmail or violence is difficult if not impossible to enforce through legal means.

grounds). For conscious and informed consent by minority shareholders to the disadvantageous arrangement of forgoing or limiting access to withdrawal remedies to be meaningful, it should not be overly readily inferred by the third-party arbiter. Recent work has begun paying attention to the importance of 'altering rules' that regulate opt outs; in other words, how parties may contract around defaults (some of which may be 'sticky'). This theme is explored later.[251] For now, suffice it to say that ascertaining the scope of the minority's consent to curtailment of withdrawal access is important to ensure that conflict scenarios arising later would be precisely addressed. Finally, parties may resort to blanket opt-outs or waivers – which may be based on standard precedents and adopted without the benefit of independent legal advice for all parties – that do not precisely define their own scope of application. These should, in the absence of strong, compelling reasons, be narrowly construed or disregarded as not reflective of the parties' true intentions or reasonable expectations.

ii Self-Enforcement or Extralegal Sanctions

It is not inconceivable for economically or politically powerful individuals or entities to voluntarily take minority stakes in close corporations. In such cases, their power beyond that close corporation's confines may well be sufficient – and even more efficient than any official, legal enforcement regime – in ensuring that the majority gives due regard to their interests. It would be foolhardy for majority shareholders to trifle with minority shareholders backed by 'men with guns'.[252] The well-informed minority shareholder may also have access to blackmail as a method by which to safeguard their interests.[253] Alternatively, other non-legal mechanisms such as reputational sanctions may, under certain circumstances, be sufficient to regulate commercial relationships.[254] Thus, even when legal enforcement is available, non-legal sanctions may be preferred over legal sanctions when the former are no less accessible than the latter, or when the former clearly advantages one party over another.[255]

As applied to the close corporation conflict context, provided functional equivalents or substitutes to withdrawal or other conflict resolution mechanisms exist and perform adequately, withdrawal as a corporate law regime may not be strictly necessary if majority shareholders can be pressured to offer minority shareholders fair, 'voluntary' exit terms.[256] However, quite apart from doubts as to the effectiveness

[251] II.E.4.

[252] Cf Black & Kraakman (1996): 1940–2 (on the role of the mob in 'unofficial enforcement' of corporate law in Russia).

[253] Cf West (1999) (on institutionalised extortion of public listed corporations in Japan by organised crime operators (*sōkaiya*)).

[254] On reputational monitoring and enforcement, see generally Charny (1990): 408–20; see also Shapira (2015).

[255] Charny (1990): 425–6.

[256] On how functional substitutes developed in response to withdrawal's absence in Japanese corporate law, see IV.B.2.i.

of non-legal sanctions developed and studied in other contexts in deterring majority shareholder oppression in the close corporation setting specifically,[257] non- or extra-legal enforcement are in any event arguably beyond the scope of corporate law, or even the realm of law. Even though some persons have undeniably greater leverage or power over others, for any system of corporate law to take the view that reliance should be placed on extra- or non-legal mechanisms to the exclusion of legal ones would, however, be deeply problematic from the perspective of rule of law. Hence, this Book categorically rejects any suggestion that non- or extra-legal mechanisms are already – or should be considered – sufficient and satisfactory responses to the problem of shareholder conflict.[258]

iii Human Limitations

The analysis above in the previous subsection (II.E.2) and this (II.E.3.i–ii) is based on the premise that – as accepted by mainstream contractarian corporate law scholars –shareholders know what is best for themselves and take rational actions in accordance with their own interests. But is this *homo economicus* assumption reflective of reality? Modern behavioural economics paint a more nuanced picture of human capabilities. Humans are constrained by 'bounded rationality', in that

> The capacity of the human mind for formulating and solving complex problems is very small compared with the size of the problems whose solution is required for objectively rational behavior in the real world – or even for a reasonable approximation to such objective rationality.[259]

Affected by fundamental limitations in cognitive abilities such as computational skills and memory, humans resort to shortcuts and rules of thumb ('heuristics')[260] that may result in behaviour departing from what standard models would predict – even when it is rational to use such shortcuts.[261] Seemingly insignificant factors such as how questions are phrased and the starting points adopted in reasoning exert significant impact on decision-making, phenomena now called framing[262] and

257 It should not surprise that literature on nonlegal sanctions has hitherto focused largely on public listed corporations and their directors. To what extent can we expect reputational sanctions to have effect on majority shareholders of small firms if they have no interest in expanding the business or taking on additional board directorships?

258 To clarify: my discussion of the Japanese example at IV.B.2.i is not an endorsement.

259 Simon (1957): 198 (emphasis removed).

260 Heuristics 'reduce the complex tasks of assessing probabilities and predicting values to simpler judgmental operations ... In general [they] are quite useful, but sometimes they lead to severe and systematic errors': Tversky & Kahneman (1974): 1124; see also Gigerenzer (2007).

261 Jolls et al. (1998): 1477–8.

262 Tversky and Kahneman's classic study demonstrates that 'seemingly inconsequential changes in the formulation of choice problems caused significant shifts of preference'; in other words, people make decisions differently in response to the same problem 'framed' in different ways: Tversky & Kahneman (1981): 457.

anchoring.[263] As humans also behave with overconfidence[264] and over-optimism,[265] shareholders may underestimate the risks of unpleasant future events, such as shareholder conflict,[266] and overvalue the immediate cost outlays associated with legal advice and proper documentation.[267] Self-control problems[268] such as 'time-inconsistent preferences'[269] and 'projection bias'[270] are also human limitations that lead to contract incompleteness even for a shareholder who is fully informed and not overly trusting.[271]

Human limitations 'apply with special force to bargains concerning [close] corporations'.[272] There is empirical evidence showing that a significant proportion – or even a majority or supermajority – of close corporation shareholders fail to enter into shareholder agreements, make contractual provision for conflict resolution, or even educate themselves about the law before incorporation.[273] If even experienced legal advisors may not always be able to offer a satisfactory solution to a foreseen problem,[274] what chance do laymen shareholders have? As Carney succinctly puts it:[275] 'Investors in closely held enterprises are likely to be subject to conditions of bounded rationality, under which they either fail to perceive the complete set of problems that may occur later, or underestimate the probability of their occurrence'.

In the withdrawal context, parties may well underestimate the risk of shareholder conflict that cannot be resolved without the departure of one or the other from the business or overestimate their ability to reach a mutually acceptable settlement ex post without resort to extra-contractual norms or external intervention. Consequently, they may neglect to adopt customized withdrawal provisions, or voluntarily adopt precedents excluding or limiting access to withdrawal at general corporate law that may not be appropriate for their specific business context,[276] or both.

263 Sunstein & Thaler (2003): 1177–8. Anchoring as a concept was introduced in Tversky & Kahneman (1974): 1128.
264 See Mitchell (2002): 154–6. Interestingly, cross-country studies suggest that the Japanese (and Singaporeans) are least prone to overconfidence: ibid.
265 See e.g. Jolls (1998): 1659–62; Sunstein (2014): 44–8.
266 Means (2010): 1175.
267 Sneirson (2008): 916.
268 See generally Utset (2003).
269 Ibid. 1351–5, 1410 ('time-inconsistent preferences of transacting parties can lead the parties to repeatedly procrastinate adopting contractual provisions that they had a strict (long-term) preference to adopt').
270 Ibid. 1410 ('when trying to predict how their preferences may evolve during the transaction, parties will tend [to] project their current preference onto their future ones').
271 Ibid. 1335, 1410–11.
272 Eisenberg (1995): 1465.
273 See Neville (2010): 280–1.
274 Solomon & Solomon (1987): 120.
275 Carney (1987): 59–60.
276 The reverse – where excessively generous withdrawal mechanisms (such as at will) – are adopted routinely may also be possible. Cf Wedemann (2013): 80 (reporting that 67 per cent of constitutions of multi-member GmbHs provided for withdrawal rights).

Where the problem with minority shareholders is lack of awareness or information, there are different possible solutions. One school of thought proposes that paternalistic intervention should aim to accomplish what the decision-makers themselves wanted, but somehow failed in obtaining for themselves.[277] These 'libertarian paternalists' advocate regulatory solutions that reduce systematic errors but which allow parties to make substantive choices in accordance with their own preferences[278] – provided they have any.[279] Requirements as to form, disclosure, or cooling-off periods are examples of 'debiasing'[280] strategies preferred by libertarian paternalists. In the close corporation context, debiasing strategies advocated by scholars include warnings to incorporators of the dangers of shareholder oppression, exhortations to seek legal advice, or, as a more coercive manifestation, compelling incorporators to make an affirmative choice between different levels of minority shareholder protection.[281] As individuals are heterogeneous,[282] debiasing strategies have the advantage of improving the lot of people suffering from bounded rationality, while reserving maximum freedom of action to those who do not.[283] However, debiasing strategies risk creating distortions affecting those not previously acting under bounded rationality.[284] In other words, a possible approach would be to encourage shareholders to seriously consider, when forming their close corporation entities, whether and to what extent withdrawal mechanisms should be available for them. This could be facilitated through opt-in/permissive/enabling withdrawal options, instead of providing for a default or mandatory solution.

On the other hand, other regulatory interventions – insulating strategies[285] – go further to protect parties from the consequences of their own decisions. Insulating strategies are more overtly paternalistic and less readily justifiable, but nonetheless have a place especially when people are unable, have no incentive to, or cannot afford to learn how to make better decisions by themselves.[286] In other words, insulating strategies may be necessary when debiasing strategies are insufficient. The most straightforward and perhaps extreme example of an (ex ante) insulating strategy is a blanket ban on the use of a product.[287] An example of an ex post insulating strategy is judicial review of contractual valuation clauses,[288] which is

277 Thaler & Sunstein (2008): 5 ('In our understanding, a policy is "paternalistic" if it tries to influence choices in a way that will make choosers better off, *as judged by themselves*').

278 Ibid. 4–6.

279 Cf Sunstein & Thaler (2003): 1182 ('In unfamiliar situations, it is especially unlikely that well-formed preferences will exist').

280 See generally Jolls & Sunstein (2006) (giving concrete examples).

281 See Sneirson (2008): 919–20, 923–4; Molitor (2009): 574–8.

282 That is, people vary widely in how they rationally (or irrationally) act. See e.g. Mitchell (2002): 83–119, 139–67.

283 Jolls & Sunstein (2006): 206.

284 Ibid. 229–30.

285 Ibid. 200, 207–8, 226.

286 Rachlinski (2003): 1168, 1219–24.

287 Jolls & Sunstein (2006): 207–8.

288 Schmolke (2012): 409.

a mandatory standard (not rule).[289] More generally, withdrawal doctrines applicable as mandatory corporate law norms notwithstanding ill-advised attempts to opt out are also insulating strategies *par excellence*.

There is a major difference between the two types of strategies. In the context of withdrawal at least, debiasing strategies – such as educational measures and provision of information – require additional ex ante involvement of actors such as public officials and lawyers. This has upfront cost implications for the parties, the state, or both.[290] Depending on the legal system's particular features and institutions, a debiasing programme may or may not be fiscally or politically feasible.[291] In contrast, insulating strategies are essentially substantive law, which can be created relatively cheaply for subsequent use. Although not necessarily costless in application ex post, withdrawal litigation pursuant to substantive law not only resolves individual disputes with finality. They also potentially displace alternative (and no less costly) legal or extralegal mechanisms of conflict resolution and generate precedent – essential in a standard such as withdrawal 'on grounds' – that could over time increase predictability and reduce costs.

That said, debiasing and insulating strategies are not necessarily substitutes for each other,[292] nor is one necessarily superior to the other in all settings. For example, litigation-generated precedent could be packaged into content provided to shareholders ex ante as part of debiasing. Both strategies potentially have a place in a system of close corporation law.

4 *Striking the Default/Mandatory Balance in Withdrawal Design*

The analysis above shows that withdrawal can be sought or rejected for a wide range of reasons. Withdrawal at will as a default rule is, by itself, an inadequate response; a default rule could be too easily excluded carelessly or for the wrong reasons.[293] But if withdrawal at will were a mandatory rule, it would pose unacceptable risks to majority shareholders even if they have every intention of binding themselves to an acceptable standard of behaviour.[294] While certain events such as death or bankruptcy can be clearly defined (whether by contract or as a legal default) as grounds for withdrawal, transaction costs and incomplete contracting make it impossible for

289 'Heightened standards of products liability' are an insulating strategy based on a standard rather than a rule; see Jolls & Sunstein (2006): 207.

290 Cf Sneirson (2008): 925–31; Molitor (2009): 575–6.

291 For example, Germany requires notarization of GmbH corporate constitutions: GmbHG, § 2(1)–(1a). See also Noack & Beurskens (2008): 105–6. The mandatory involvement of German notaries charged with the duty of informing the parties about the consequences of a contemplated transaction thus serves as a unique debiasing strategy; see Schmolke (2012): 414.

292 See e.g. Molitor (2009): 582 (clarifying that his proposed debiasing-type solutions 'should not be used as to *replace* the current remedies in close business disputes; fiduciary-duty analysis and oppression statutes will still be needed') (italics original).

293 II.E.2.ii, II.E.3.i, II.E.3.iii.

294 II.E.2.iii.

the parties to address contractually the desired legal outcome in all possible shareholder conflict scenarios.[295]

In comparison, withdrawal on grounds as an open-ended standard (rather than a set of clear rules) with gap-filling functions to be performed by a third-party arbiter is a more useful mechanism that is more likely to be acceptable to both majority and minority shareholders.[296] However, as a standard, it cannot be effectively implemented only through contract as an enabling/permissive norm.[297] It might not occur to a trusting minority shareholder to bargain for an enabling standard, and even risky for one who wishes to signal trustworthiness to try.[298] While a default standard would be susceptible to exclusion or limitation for less-than-ideal reasons,[299] that is not to say that withdrawal 'on grounds' should necessarily be a mandatory standard. There are always circumstances where shareholders – majority and minority – may reasonably agree that it should be curtailed or even eliminated outright.[300]

Given that neither withdrawal at will nor withdrawal on grounds – whether as default, enabling, or mandatory rules/standards – are by themselves adequate solutions in light of the myriad considerations involved, we must look beyond the rigid default/mandatory dichotomy. To this end, this subsection explores two concepts: 'sticky defaults' and the 'mandatory core'.

i 'Sticky Defaults'

The concept of 'sticky defaults'[301] has been defined as follows:

> Sticky defaults . . . attempt to impede some parties who [would otherwise] have opted out of the default. . . . Under this conception, sticky defaults are metaphorically a kind of way station on the road to mandatory rules. They are quasi-mandatory rules that . . . [allow] a reduced number of contractors to opt for legal consequences that lawmakers disfavor.[302]

A key building block for the sticky default concept is 'altering rules', by which Ayres means 'the necessary and sufficient conditions for displacing a default legal

295 II.E.2.i.

296 II.E.2.i, II.E.2.iii.

297 While it is possible for parties to provide for standards in contract (e.g. 'best efforts' clauses), it is revealing that close corporation planning texts seldom if ever place any emphasis on standards – as opposed to rules – when designing exit options. The failure of enabling (i.e. opt-in) special close corporation legislation (some of which included withdrawal remedies on grounds that are standards) in the US further dashes any hope that withdrawal as a purely enabling standard would succeed. For general background on such legislation, see O'Neal & Thompson (2020a): § 1:25; on the failure of close corporation legislation, see e.g. Molitor (2009): 567–8.

298 II.E.2.ii. This also applies to bargaining for withdrawal at will as an enabling rule.

299 II.E.2.ii, II.E.3.i, II.E.3.iii.

300 II.E.3.i.

301 Although the term is first introduced in Ayres (1999): 907 fn. 37, the discussion that follows draws primarily on sticky defaults as developed in Ayres (2012).

302 Ayres (2012): 2087.

treatment with some particular other legal treatment'.[303] 'Impeding' altering rules 'selectively deter opt-out by artificially increasing its difficulty',[304] and are synonymous with 'sticky defaults' in Ayres' sense.[305] More conducive to private ordering than mandatory rules, but less so than normal defaults,[306] the goal of sticky defaults is 'to disproportionately block the more socially problematic opt-outs, while not blocking the less socially problematic opt-outs'.[307]

Implementing withdrawal on a sticky default basis alleviates the problem of contract incompleteness in a way that purely default or enabling norms (which can be displaced or neglected too easily) do not.[308] It further vindicates prosocial trusting and trustworthy behaviour of minority shareholders by obviating the need to proactively bargain for access to withdrawal and increasing the difficulty of opting out.[309]

Although unmistakable examples of sticky defaults are rare in the four target jurisdictions' withdrawal regimes,[310] one thing comes close: a model statute proposed by scholars. Hetherington and Dooley's provocative proposal for a 'mandatory' withdrawal at will statute (discussed later)[311] would permit 'waivers' of the proposed buyout right for not longer than two years at a time.[312] By stating how the consequence (a right to withdraw at will for the minority/50 per cent shareholder) may be altered (i.e. loss of that right), their proposal is not by today's terminology a mandatory rule. Their rationale for the two-year limit – to 'ensure that minority shareholders will not waive their statutory rights casually' and to 'prevent majority shareholders from taking undue advantage of the minority during the limited period the waiver is in effect'[313] – is clearly an intention to impede socially problematic opt-outs. As such, Hetherington and Dooley's proposal is a sticky default *par excellence*.

Theoretically speaking and *de lege ferenda*, sticky defaults could be designed to operate in the withdrawal context – specifically the limitation or exclusion of access thereto – by facilitating informed agreements[314] and remedying human limitations in contracting.[315] For example, before parties may displace the default legal consequence (withdrawal at will or on the full range of grounds, as the case may be) by

303 Ibid. 2036. Examples of altering rules include a statutory requirement that a [US] corporation opting into a provision that is not the default must do so by provision in its bylaws, and the use of 'as is' to displace implied warranties under the Uniform Commercial Code: ibid. 2052, 2054.

304 Ibid. 2084.

305 Ibid. 2086. Note that 'sticky defaults' have a different meaning in Ben-Shahar & Pottow (2006): 652.

306 Ayres (2012): 2087–8.

307 Ibid. 2088.

308 See II.E.2.i.

309 See II.E.2.ii.

310 Except perhaps the altering rule that contractual modification of the default withdrawal regime shall be via provision in the corporate constitution. Cf the first example in n. 303 above.

311 VI.C.7.

312 Hetherington & Dooley (1977): 52.

313 Ibid.

314 See II.E.3.i.

315 See II.E.3.iii.

curtailing/eliminating access to withdrawal, the parties could be made to satisfy certain requirements. These could be stipulations that majority shareholders must make disclosures,[316] or that minority shareholders must undergo debiasing by considering and acknowledging the risks associated with minority shareholding.[317] Careful design of altering rules or standards, such as requiring clear language in opting out of the default, may reduce the risk of party error by helping parties to choose what they really prefer.[318] For example, a preamble-like requirement that parties state expressly why they are placing limits on withdrawal (or excluding it outright and on what terms) would reduce judicial error by better communicating the parties' shared intent to the third-party arbiter.[319] This would be particularly helpful when signalling that the business is of the uncooked-omelette variety in which (temporary or contingent) restrictions on withdrawal are desirable or even essential.[320]

Sticky defaults involve trade-offs, particularly with transaction costs.[321] Extremely precise (and costly) altering rules may not be necessary for mild and easily justifiable restrictions on minority shareholder access to withdrawal. Hence, altering *standards*[322] (rather than one-size-fits-all rules) may be appropriate. An altering standard could involve proportional ex post review in which the precision required for the opting-out process (including clarity of contractual language, quality of disclosures by majority to minority, or level of minority understanding of conflict and oppression risk) increases with the withdrawal restriction's severity.[323] For example, simple language such as 'the minority shall not have the right under any circumstances to withdraw' may be sufficient to exclude withdrawal at will. Conversely, blanket opt-out by itself should not be sufficient to eliminate withdrawal on any ground outright; instead, the parties should include a preamble and proof of majority concession to minority (such as generous compensation)[324] if they wish to claim the certainty of a contractual 'safe harbour'.[325] In the valuation context, a valuation clause in which the withdrawing shareholder's monetary claim is grossly

316 Cf Ayres (2012): 2098–9 ('Information-forcing defaults will often be combined with necessary altering rules that require effective disclosure.'); Ayres (2003): 899 fn. 79 ('affirmative choice rule' defaults).

317 Cf Utset (2003): 1392–8; see also Molitor (2009): 574–8. An extension of this could be to require minority shareholders to sit and pass a test on shareholder oppression: cf Ayres (2012): 2076–80 (on 'train-and-test altering rules').

318 See Ayres (2012): 2044, 2061–2.

319 See ibid. 2061–3, 2073, 2082. Cf Molitor (2009): 583.

320 On start-ups and restrictions on exit see II.E.3.i above.

321 See Ayres (2012): 2044–5, 2061–3, 2066–8.

322 See Ayres (2012): 2037.

323 For conceptually similar examples, see e.g. Means (2009):1241–7; Illig (2006): 279–81, 324–50.

324 E.g. 'The Parties, having regard to the nature of the Business as a start-up built upon match-specific investments, and having regard to the Conditions of Employment of [the minority shareholder], agree that no Party may withdraw from [the close corporation] unless and until one of the following conditions ("Withdrawal Milestones"), whichever is first, is met: i) a period of three years having elapsed from the Effective Date of this Agreement; ii) receipt of Series B funding'.

325 See Ayres (2012): 2099–103. On the concept of safe harbours, see foundationally Swire (1993): 369–70.

disproportionately small compared to the fair value of their interest could be treated as presumptively invalid unless good, provable reasons exist to justify such treatment.[326]

To encourage opting-out in compliance with altering rules and standards, 'altering penalties'[327] could be part of the package. For example, a failed attempt to limit withdrawal grounds could result in several different possibilities.[328] One could be striking down all withdrawal restrictions in their entirely, restoring withdrawal at will as a 'default penalty'.[329] A less harsh result would be to read down the restriction to the extent supported by the parties' reasonable expectations,[330] or even further to allow the minority to withdraw with barely acceptable terms, such as a monetary claim on an unfavourable valuation basis.[331] It may be appropriate to calibrate the consequences of defective opt-out according to the sort of majority conduct that is sought to be rendered unactionable (i.e. excluded from withdrawal grounds). For example, attempts to exclude majority bad faith conduct from withdrawal's scope should be treated more harshly.[332]

We will return to these potential applications of sticky defaults and altering rules/standards later in this Book.[333] For now, the (mostly theoretical) sticky default analysis above presupposes that it is possible for any and all parts of the default withdrawal norms to be contractually modified or excluded provided that necessary procedures are complied with and the contractual language is sufficiently clear. But what about mandatory aspects of withdrawal?

ii Mandatory Core

Notwithstanding pervasive contractarian influence in modern corporate law scholarship, the notion of corporate law as a partly mandatory body of rules and standards persists. As explored in the next Chapter (III) and the subsequent four jurisdictional Chapters (IV to VII), withdrawal regimes in the four target jurisdictions – Germany, the US, the UK, and Japan – are partly default and partly mandatory in terms of both withdrawal grounds and valuation[334] as applied to most close corporation forms.[335] While the precise contours of the mandatory parts of withdrawal – not least because they are standards rather than rules – could be difficult to define and vary from

326 See Schmolke (2012): 417–18.

327 See Ayres (2012): 2044, 2046, 2096–103.

328 Cf Ben-Shahar (2011): 876–8.

329 See Ayres (2012): 2097–9; cf Ben-Shahar (2011): 877. If the default were withdrawal on grounds but not at will, restoring withdrawal at will would be an example of 'worse-than-default' treatment for defective opt-out attempts; cf Ayres (2012): 2099.

330 Cf Ben-Shahar (2011): 876–7.

331 See Schmolke (2012): 418; cf Ben-Shahar (2011): 877ff.

332 Cf Ben-Shahar (2011): 901–4.

333 See Chapter VIII (in Part 3 ('Application')).

334 See III.F and references therein.

335 The notable exception being the US LLC: ibid.

jurisdiction to jurisdiction, it is helpful to think of withdrawal regimes as layered: a largely default exterior with a 'mandatory core'.[336]

There is little cause for any concern that the mandatory parts of withdrawal would create any substantial risk of minority holdup.[337] Withdrawal at will is practically never a mandatory feature in any jurisdiction.[338] Even withdrawal on grounds is mostly default and can be curtailed substantially by contract either through safe harbour-type stipulations as to permissible majority conduct, or creation of alternative exit mechanisms that pre-empt the extracontractual withdrawal regime even if such mechanisms result in reduced monetary claims.[339] Despite weakening or even negating a withdrawal regime's minority protection function, valuation clauses – even those reducing monetary claims to zero – are not necessarily invalid so long as a legitimate reason exists.[340] Notwithstanding the mandatory core, private ordering is largely unfettered for majorities, even those acting and negotiating in less than good faith.[341] Far from being an alien and intrusive concept, the mandatory core of withdrawal is a well-established aspect of [close] corporation law *de lege lata* across leading jurisdictions, and – unsurprisingly – has echoes in other areas of law related to corporate law.[342]

F CONCLUSION

This Chapter has introduced the concept of withdrawal, a category of solutions responding to the problem of shareholder conflict in close corporations that have been developed or adopted by jurisdictions including Germany, the US, the UK, and Japan, and in two variants: 'at will' and 'on grounds'. It has also distinguished withdrawal from other forms of exit and non-exit rights and remedies and shown how withdrawal puts an end to intractable shareholder conflict when alternatives do not or can no longer work.

Despite its utility to minority shareholders, leaving withdrawal entirely to private ordering of the parties based only on enabling or simple default mechanisms is unsatisfactory due to incomplete contracting, complexities of human behaviour,

336 Coffee also used the term 'mandatory core' but in the context of corporate law as a system, rather than as an aspect of a particular remedy. Cf hereinafter Coffee (1989): 1619, 1621. To clarify, I also take the position that withdrawal as an institution should be recognized as the mandatory core – in Coffee's sense of the term – of close corporation law.

337 See II.E.3.i.

338 Fleischer (2018a): 704 (citing only Italy as an exceptional case offering withdrawal at will).

339 III.F.1.

340 III.F.2.

341 By which I mean negotiating with the intent of maintaining maximum latitude to engage in opportunistic conduct later.

342 Even contract law has its limits. Fraud is one of them: AmJur2d (2019): *Fraud and Deceit* § 17. Vitiation for fraud cannot be contracted out of: ibid. In civil law jurisdictions, general clauses of the civil code may serve as a mandatory core of private law. On how German unconscionability and good faith doctrines apply to close corporation law, see generally Schmolke (2012).

and other considerations. Neither is withdrawal on a completely mandatory basis acceptable or desirable given that business needs and considerations vary. Ways of striking a balance between default and mandatory extremes and goals such as vindicating socially beneficial behaviours (particularly trust and trustworthiness) of shareholders and deterring majority shareholder opportunism against minorities are explored.

Despite functional similarities, withdrawal remedies in the four target jurisdictions differ as to their respective legal origins and doctrinal foundations, when they are available, and the exact legal consequences that follow from withdrawal. In the next Part of this Book ('Operation'), I present my key findings and the comparative insights derived therefrom in the next Chapter (III), before taking a deep dive into each target jurisdiction's withdrawal regime over the four subsequent Chapters (IV to VII).

PART 2

Operation

III

Withdrawal in Comparative Perspective

A INTRODUCTION AND TERMINOLOGY

The previous Part (Chapter II) laid the theoretical foundations for this Book by setting out the close corporation problem, and by introducing, defining, and developing the concept of 'withdrawal remedies' (or just 'withdrawal') as a class of legal solutions to the problem. Part 2 (Operation) comprises five chapters exploring how withdrawal remedies manifest and operate in the four jurisdictions examined in this Book (collectively 'target jurisdictions'): Germany, the UK,[1] the US, and Japan.

This Chapter, the first in Part 2, has three aims. First, it highlights the findings of in-depth investigations of the target jurisdictions in the next four Chapters ('jurisdictional Chapters'). Second, it constructs a jurisdiction-neutral analytical framework based on – but separate from – each target jurisdiction's respective law. Using this framework, other (non-target) jurisdictions' withdrawal remedies may be analysed, and a model withdrawal remedy of general application (the subject of Chapter VIII in Part 3 ('Application')) may be constructed. Third, this Chapter identifies themes emerging from in-depth analyses of withdrawal's development in each target jurisdiction. Of note is how withdrawal demonstrates the phenomenon I call 'spontaneous functional convergence' in close corporation law towards two distinct yet connected models.

Given that the four target jurisdictions adopt rather different terminology – even in translation – some terminological clarifications and definitions are in order. The close corporation forms mentioned, namely Germany's GmbH, UK's Ltd, US' US-CC and LLC, and Japan's GK,[2] are referred to in this Chapter only in abbreviated form. 'Withdrawal' refers to, respectively, *Austritt aus wichtigem Grund* in Germany; the unfair prejudice remedy in the UK; oppression law and doctrine in the US (for both US-CC and LLC) and dissociation in the LLC; and *taisha* (encompassing both, unless the context otherwise indicates, *yokoku ni yoru taisha* and *yamu wo enai jiyū ni yoru taisha*) in Japan. Following Chapter II,[3] the shareholder/member that seeks to withdraw, regardless of reason (i.e. whether on grounds or at will), will be referred to as 'withdrawal seeker';[4] a shareholder that has lawfully or with proper grounds commenced the withdrawal process is a 'withdrawing shareholder'. Unless otherwise evident from context, 'shareholder' refers to both shareholders in the narrower sense (i.e. of Ltds, US-CCs) as well as members of GmbHs (*Gesellschafter*), LLCs, and GKs (*sha'in*).

III.B summarises the sources of withdrawal remedies in the target jurisdictions. III.C categorises withdrawal grounds – that is, the circumstances under which withdrawal would be available – into four types. The issue of who would be liable to pay the withdrawing shareholder the latter's monetary claim is the subject of III.D. The extent to which the target jurisdictions' withdrawal regimes protect, on a financial level, the

[1] References to 'Great Britain' or 'British' in this Chapter consciously exclude Northern Ireland, which before the Companies Act 2006 had its own corporate law legislation, the latest iteration of which was the Companies (Northern Ireland) Order 1986 (SI 1986/1032 (NI 6)).

[2] See respectively IV.B (Germany), V.B (UK), VI.B (US-CC) and VI.D (LLC) (US), and VII.C (Japan).

[3] II.C.

[4] Known, for procedural reasons, as 'petitioner' (UK) or 'plaintiff' or 'petitioner' (US), and often in the literature as 'minority shareholder' as it is usually minority shareholders who seek to withdraw.

withdrawing shareholder's interest will be summarised in III.E. III.F discusses the limits to which ex ante contractual arrangements are permitted to affect access to withdrawal and the quantum of the monetary claim – in other words, the default/mandatory balance of each regime. Finally, I draw together selected themes from the four jurisdictional Chapters in III.G, before concluding in III.H.

B LEGAL BASIS OF WITHDRAWAL

Withdrawal regimes in two target jurisdictions (the UK[5] and Japan[6]) are entirely statutory in origin; that is, withdrawal was not available at all until introduced by the relevant statute. Germany's withdrawal regime has no basis in the GmbH's organic statute, has resisted two codification attempts, and has from inception until present been a product of academic and judicial ingenuity and collaboration.[7] For the US-CC, withdrawal, depending on the state, may be either expressly and directly provided for by statute; direct and judicial in origin, whether as an extension of the power to order dissolution or as part of a court's discretionary powers in equity; available only indirectly; or completely unavailable.[8] By contrast, for the US LLC, withdrawal at will (in the states offering it) is based exclusively on clear statutory provision; withdrawal on grounds (oppression, 'not reasonably practicable', deadlock) may either be specifically provided for by statute, or exist as a possible option for a court statutorily vested with discretion to order an alternative to dissolution.[9]

What is striking, however, is the extent to which judicial precedent has been instrumental in creating or shaping withdrawal, either directly or through interpretation of statutory provisions across target jurisdictions. Japan, the target jurisdiction thinnest on judicial precedent, has the newest withdrawal statute, and arguably also the least scholarly literature offering guidance as to its application. The role of judges in shaping withdrawal law will be explored further below (at III.G.1).

C TYPES OF WITHDRAWAL GROUNDS ('WHEN CAN I WITHDRAW?')

As discussed in Chapter II, conceptually speaking withdrawal can be divided into two types: on 'grounds', or 'at will'.[10] The latter needs no reason to trigger other than the withdrawal seeker's whim, whereas withdrawal on 'grounds' is only available in certain circumstances that are verifiable by a third-party arbiter such as a court. By 'grounds' I refer to *wichtiger Grund* in Germany, 'unfair prejudice' in the UK, 'oppression' in the

5 V.C.1.i–ii.
6 VII.B.2, VII.D.1.
7 IV.C.1, IV.C.2.i, IV.D.
8 Respectively VI.C.2.i, VI.C.2.ii, VI.C.2.iii, and VI.C.2.iv.
9 VI.E.3.
10 II.C.

US, and *yamu wo enai jiyū* in Japan. This section presents three subclasses of withdrawal on grounds, before closing with withdrawal at will.

1 *Fault of Other Participants*

All target jurisdictions offer withdrawal on the ground that other participants – that is, co-members/co-shareholders in the close corporation – are at fault. In all target jurisdictions, fault is not a *rule* but a *standard*.[11] In Germany, the *wichtiger Grund* category of 'behaviour of other members' (*Verhalten der Mitgesellschafter*) largely corresponds to the concept of fault.[12] Unfairness is recognised under UK withdrawal law primarily in two scenarios – breach of formal written rules or of informal written expectations by other shareholders in control[13] – although the latter category makes up the bulk of UK case law. Oppression in US-CCs is primarily recognised for fault grounds, although individual states differ as to how egregious the conduct must be in order to be sufficient grounds for withdrawal relief.[14] The situation is similar for oppression in LLCs, although when compared to US-CCs fewer states seem to specify withdrawal as a possible form of relief from oppression.[15] There is virtually no jurisprudence at all in Japan on fault-based withdrawal, although scholars generally recognise squeeze-outs as *yamu wo enai jiyū* for the purposes of withdrawal.[16] On this issue the UK seems to be the most liberal of the target jurisdictions.

In Germany, the UK, and the US, the withdrawal seeker's acquiescence or consent to the circumstances or conduct later relied on as withdrawal grounds may lead to a denial of relief;[17] there is no Japanese authority on this point.

2 *Unclear or Both*

Sometimes, withdrawal seekers are not entirely innocent of poor conduct such as incompetence, greed, unreasonableness, or even sloth, which is seen to be especially problematic when withdrawal seekers played or were expected to play a more active role in the business than mere passive investors. Three of four target jurisdictions take a dim view of withdrawal seekers who are themselves not blameless in conduct. German law takes the withdrawal seeker's fault into consideration as part of the overall assessment of grounds, and the court may find a demand to withdraw unmeritorious or an abuse of right especially if the withdrawal seeker was primarily or solely at fault.[18] UK courts impose adverse consequences on withdrawal seekers at fault that range

11 On rules versus standards in withdrawal see II.C.
12 IV.C.2.iii.
13 Respectively V.C.4.ii, V.C.4.iii.
14 VI.C.3.i (trichotomous doctrinal classification), VI.C.3.ii (functional scholarly framework based on majority and minority perspectives).
15 Cf VI.E.3.i–ii, VI.F.3.
16 VII.D.3.iii.
17 Germany: IV.C.2.ii; UK: V.C.4.i.b; US: O'Neal & Thompson (2020b): § 7:32.
18 IV.C.2.ii–iii.

from costs consequences to denial of all unfair prejudice relief.[19] Withdrawal seekers at fault in US-CCs – except a handful of states such as New York – are generally unlikely to succeed.[20] Thus, fault is also a principle (and not a rule) in the sense that there is a balancing exercise involved between competing interests.[21]

Where the attribution of fault is unclear, Germany[22] and Japan[23] seem to make withdrawal at least possibly available. Where majority and minority (or equal) shareholders are both blameworthy in causing a deadlock, it may be possible to analyse this as a case of deadlock, which is discussed below.[24]

Conceptually, there is no way for a withdrawal seeker to rely only on circumstances attributable solely to their own fault; the only option in this situation is withdrawal at will, which has no requirement as to any party's fault.

3 *Non-Fault*

Non-fault grounds relate to circumstances arising either from voluntary action taken in good faith and with no ulterior motive, or circumstances not attributable at all to voluntary action of majority or minority shareholders. A classic example of the former is deadlock over corporate decision-making either at the board (if there is a board), or the shareholder level. The UK does not permit withdrawal on non-fault grounds at all.[25] Germany offers withdrawal if there is a complete breakdown in the relationship between members that threatens the viability of the GmbH as a going concern;[26] Japan seems to offer withdrawal for deadlock,[27] as do some US states.[28]

Unprofitability of the business over an extended time period gives rise to withdrawal (albeit with additional restrictions) in Germany,[29] and arguably Japan.[30] The US position is unknown. Germany recognises a change in the objects of the close corporation as a withdrawal ground,[31] but the position is unknown for the other target jurisdictions.

Finally, purely personal circumstances of the withdrawal seeker that are not objectively blameworthy conduct are recognised to some extent in Germany[32] and

19 V.C.4.i.b.

20 VI.C.3.ii. Only 'pure minority' perspective states may be amenable to granting relief: VI.C.3.ii.b. On the role of plaintiff's conduct see also O'Neal & Thompson (2020b): § 7:13.

21 See Eidenmüller (2014): 21–2.

22 IV.C.2.iii.

23 VII.D.3.i.

24 III.C.3.

25 V.C.10. However, dissolution may be available: see *Re Neath Rugby Ltd, Hawkes* v. *Cuddy* [2009] EWCA Civ 291; [2010] BCC 597 [104], [108] (winding-up (judicial dissolution) grounds do not overlap completely with unfair prejudice); French (2015): paras. [8.260]–[8.277] (dissolution for 'loss of substratum').

26 IV.C.2.iv.

27 VII.D.3.ii–iii.

28 VI.C.3.iii (US-CC), VI.E.3.iii (LLC); O'Neal & Thompson (2020b): §§ 7:16 fn. 22, 6:26.

29 IV.C.2.iv.

30 See Koide (2014a): 221–2 (discussing pre-Companies Act commentary).

31 IV.C.2.iv.

Japan,[33] but not the UK. There appears to have been no substantial discussion of this ground in the US.

4 *At Will*

Despite serious debates over withdrawal at will in three target jurisdictions (excepting the UK), withdrawal at will never caught on.[34] The only close corporation forms offering withdrawal at will – and only as a default – are the US LLC (some states)[35] and Japanese GKs.[36] However, withdrawal at will is an artefact of other considerations, and cannot be said to have been introduced consciously by legislators on shareholder protection grounds.[37]

D FINANCIALLY LIABLE PARTIES ('WHO PAYS WHEN I WITHDRAW?')

A core feature of withdrawal is the withdrawing shareholder's right to payment in exchange for their loss of status and rights as a shareholder.[38] It follows that the withdrawing shareholder's monetary claim must be satisfied by someone who is liable to pay, involuntarily if necessary. On this, the target jurisdictions differ considerably.

1 *Co-Shareholders at Fault*

In the UK, the parties most often ordered by the court to pay are the co-members whose acts or conduct caused the withdrawal seeker unfair prejudice,[39] although the share purchase order may theoretically be issued against non-members of the Ltd as well.[40] The picture is less certain in the US as to non-shareholders, but it is fair to say that shareholders responsible for oppressive conduct in US-CCs may be ordered to buy out the withdrawing shareholder, and the same arguably applies to a lesser extent in LLCs in the withdrawal for oppression context.[41]

32 IV.C.2.v.
33 VII.D.3.
34 IV.C.6 (Germany), V.C.10 (UK), VI.C.7 (US), VII.B.2.ii (Japan); Hamada (1974): 340–5.
35 VI.E.2 (US).
36 VII.D.2 (Japan).
37 VI.F.3 (US); VII.C.1, VII.D.1 (Japan).
38 II.C.
39 Hollington (2017): paras. [8–12], [8–44]; *Grace* v. *Biagioli* [2005] EWCA Civ 1222, [2006] 2 BCLC 70 [75].
40 V.C.6.
41 VI.C.2.i–ii (US-CC), VI.E.3.i–ii (LLC).

2 *'Innocent' Co-Shareholders*

In the UK and the US, the court usually has wide discretion to rule on the issue of who shall be liable to purchase the withdrawing shareholder's interest. Consequently, there is a theoretical possibility that an 'innocent' co-shareholder who was not responsible for the grounds on which withdrawal is sought may be on the hook. Although there is no statutory provision or line of jurisprudence clearly confirming this, there does not appear to be a single case in which a clearly innocent co-shareholder was made personally liable to the withdrawing shareholder.

3 *The Close Corporation Itself*

Under the German[42] and Japanese[43] withdrawal regimes, the GmbH/GK is the sole party that is liable, in the absence of other voluntary arrangements, to pay the withdrawing member. In the UK, the Ltd itself may be ordered to purchase the withdrawing shareholder's shares, but in the cases thus far the Ltd has not been the sole party required to make the purchase under the court order.[44] It is also possible for US-CCs in some states to purchase the withdrawing shareholder's shares pursuant to a court order or by voluntary election.[45] The US LLC is the party liable to pay the withdrawing member if the withdrawal was at will (i.e. dissociation etc.) and may also be liable in the case of withdrawal under oppression grounds.[46] Payment by the close corporation itself – an entity with limited liability – creates special problems and obstacles that are discussed below.[47]

E SCOPE OF PROTECTION ('HOW MUCH DOES WITHDRAWAL PROTECT ME?')

A withdrawal regime's effectiveness turns on the extent to which it protects the withdrawing shareholder's interests. To assess each withdrawal regime's scope of protection, I consider three aspects. The first two are connected to the quantum of the withdrawing shareholder's monetary claim upon withdrawal; in other words, the 'how much' question. The third aspect is the ease of enforcing the monetary claim against the party responsible for paying; that is, 'how easy is it to get paid?'

42 IV.C.3, IV.C.5.

43 VII.D.6.

44 *Re Edwardian Group Ltd, Estera Trust (Jersey) Ltd* v. *Singh* [2018] EWHC 1715 (Ch); [2019] 1 BCLC 171 [630]–[631] (making the share purchase order against both the defendant CEO and the company itself); *Shah* v. *Shah* [2011] EWHC 1902 (Ch) [57] (leaving the choice of purchaser between respondent shareholder and the company up to the agreement of the parties).

45 VI.C.2.i, VI.C.2.iii.

46 VI.E.3.

47 III.E.3.

1 *Valuation*

The primary component of the withdrawn shareholder's monetary claim is the amount corresponding to their equity interest in the close corporation.[48] The applicable valuation principles and discounts, if any, are critical to the final quantum awarded. In Germany,[49] the UK,[50] Japan,[51] and to some extent in the US,[52] the starting point is to value the withdrawing shareholder's interest as a pro rata share of the value of the whole business as a going concern – though not necessarily based on discounted cash flow (DCF). In general, minority discounts are not the norm in Germany or Japan,[53] but such discounts are applied with some regularity, although not consistently, in some US states[54] and to an even lesser extent and increasingly only under special circumstances in the UK.[55]

2 *Compensation Function*

The withdrawing shareholder's monetary claim can also include a second component: their 'share' of the loss suffered by the business attributable to the acts forming the basis for their withdrawal. Germany[56] and Japan do not recognise or discuss this in the literature at all. By contrast, courts in the UK[57] and some US states (for US-CCs)[58] may award the withdrawing shareholder this component at their discretion. The situation for US-LLCs is unknown.

3 *Enforcement and Obstacles*

The primary obstacle to enforcement of the monetary claim against the close corporation in Germany[59] and Japan[60] is onerous capital maintenance rules that either subject the process to creditor protection procedures or bar the claim outright. Although in Germany the withdrawing member may resort to judicial dissolution as

48 Known variously as 'compensation' (*Abfindung*) (Germany), purchase price (UK), buyout price (US-CC, LLC) or 'fair value' of the membership interest (LLC) (US), and 'refund' (*haraimodoshi*) (Japan).

49 IV.C.4.i.

50 V.C.7.i.

51 VII.D.5.i.

52 VI.C.5 (US-CC), VI.E.4 (LLC); Moll & Ragazzo (2017): § 8.02[B][3][a] (8–26 to 8–29); O'Neal & Thompson (2020b): § 7:20.

53 IV.C.4.i, VII.D.5.i.

54 VI.C.5 (US-CC), VI.E.4 (LLC).

55 V.C.7.i. Special circumstances include withdrawal seeker's fault and initial acquisition of shares at a discounted price.

56 de Vries (2010): 178.

57 V.C.7.iii; Koh (2016): 387–9.

58 VI.C.5.

59 IV.C.5.

60 VII.D.6.

ultimate enforcement,[61] it is unclear if this is permissible in Japan.[62] In the UK, the monetary claim is a claim for the purchase price of a court-ordered buyout. If the Ltd is the purchaser the court order may provide for the necessary capital reduction procedures; if it is another shareholder or a third party, the monetary claim can be enforced using ordinary civil processes against the purchaser.[63]

In US-CCs, the buyout is enforceable against the purchaser, which can be the US-CC or one or more shareholders, using ordinary means. Capital maintenance rules ('rules on distributions') apply if the US-CC is the purchaser, but it may be possible to enforce the claim by dissolution if necessary. At least one state provides for automatic dissolution of the US-CC if the purchaser defaults on the purchase price.[64] In some states, withdrawing LLC members used to have a right to dissolve the LLC to enforce payment upon withdrawal at will, although modern state LLC statutes seldom provide for withdrawal at will or any provisions on enforcement of monetary claims. In at least one state, the withdrawing member's claim is subordinated to other LLC creditors.[65]

The court usually has some flexibility to structure payment terms for the monetary claim in the UK[66] and the US.[67] In contrast, there is little discussion in Germany as to any flexible arrangements except in the context of ex ante arrangements in the corporate constitution,[68] and nothing in Japan.

F DEFAULT/MANDATORY BALANCE

It is beyond question that close corporations are free, to considerable albeit varying extents, under the laws of the target jurisdictions to organise themselves as their participants see fit. Withdrawal is one aspect on which parties not infrequently attempt to make their own arrangements that may deviate from the default position in corporate law. This section examines how such attempts are regulated in the target jurisdictions – mostly through a 'mandatory core'[69] approach in which access to withdrawal per se cannot be completely excluded by contract, but material aspects are otherwise largely amenable to contractual modification.

1 *Access to/Grounds for Withdrawal*

In all target jurisdictions, there is generally nothing to stop parties from making withdrawal more available (i.e. on more or wider grounds) through contractual

61 IV.C.5.
62 VII.D.6.
63 V.C.8.
64 VI.C.6.
65 VI.E.5.
66 V.C.8.
67 VI.C.6 (US-CC), VI.E.5 (LLC).
68 IV.C.5.
69 On this, see II.E.4.ii.

instruments than would otherwise be the case under their respective corporate laws.[70]

Under German law, withdrawal on *wichtiger Grund* is mandatory in the sense that it cannot be contracted out of entirely.[71] It is possible to restrict the scope of circumstances recognised as *wichtiger Grund* by excluding specific factual situations from its scope through provision in the corporate constitution, subject to the overall limitation that exercise of the withdrawal right may not be substantially curtailed or made more difficult.[72]

The UK unfair prejudice remedy is also mandatory and cannot be excluded entirely,[73] but withdrawal based on a breach of unwritten informal expectations is rarely possible in Ltds that are not structured as quasi-partnerships.[74] A further way of neutralising the unfair prejudice remedy is with a contractual exit mechanism. This eliminates the 'unfairness' that would arise from otherwise 'prejudicial' conduct[75] and further makes any findings of fact by a valuer practically unreviewable by the court, rendering the established legal grounds practically irrelevant.[76]

In the US, access to withdrawal on oppression grounds in US-CCs can be limited by contract by specifying permissible conduct (non-actionable) or reasonable expectations (actionable).[77] An alternative would be to implement contractual buyout provisions, but the extent to which they supersede oppression doctrine (and withdrawal via that route) depends on the scope of the contractual provisions.[78] For LLCs, withdrawal at will – either with a monetary claim or mere dissociation without payment – is almost universally default and may be eliminated entirely.[79] Withdrawal for oppression may be restricted by excluding certain acts or conduct from the scope of oppression, or by eliminating withdrawal as a remedy for oppression by provision in the corporate constitution (operating agreement).[80]

In Japan's GKs, withdrawal on unavoidable grounds (*yamu wo enai jiyū*) cannot be contracted out of entirely, but in the absence of guiding precedent, there is considerable scholarly controversy on the scope of the minimum core of unavoidable grounds.[81]

70 See IV.C.2.vii (Germany), V.C.9.i (UK), VI.C.3.iv (US). In Japan, the statutory default is withdrawal at will on notice, but it is uncertain whether the notice period can be shortened or waived: VII.D.2.ii. This is however subject to the limitations of contract incompleteness; see II.E.2.i.

71 IV.C.2.ii.

72 IV.C.2.vii.

73 V.C.9.

74 V.C.4.iii.d.

75 V.C.5.ii.

76 V.C.9.i.

77 VI.C.3.iv.

78 Ibid.

79 VI.E.2.i–ii.

80 VI.E.3. However, dissolution for oppression may not be eliminated: VI.E.3.i.

81 VII.D.3.iii.

2 *Valuation*

Shareholders of close corporations in all target jurisdictions may make arrangements as to valuation of a withdrawing shareholder's monetary claim that differ from the general position at law. In Germany, valuation methods may be stipulated by agreement; provisions that reduce the quantum of the withdrawing member's monetary claim are permitted to the extent that they do not eliminate or unduly restrict access to withdrawal. Provisions that eliminate payment outright or reduce it such that the quantum is disproportionately small compared to the full market value may be struck down as contrary to public policy unless special circumstances exist. If a valuation clause is struck down, the default legal principles will be applied.[82]

In the absence of precedent, scholars in Japan are divided on whether the statutory valuation provision applicable to GKs is mandatory or default, and on the extent to which parties' contractual arrangements are enforceable.[83]

In the UK, the recent trend is for courts to uphold valuation clauses regardless of context or content, and to intervene only when the clause cannot be procedurally operated as designed, such as when parties cannot agree on an independent valuer.[84] There is no indication that a UK court would be willing to override any substantive content.

States in the US take into consideration parties' agreements when performing valuations of shares of US-CCs, although states differ on whether or when they regard these agreements to be binding. Some states do not regard agreements premised on voluntary exit to be applicable to withdrawal for oppression, whereas at least one state does.[85] LLC parties are subject to very few, usually enumerated restrictions in private ordering. Although provisions eliminating payment entirely for withdrawal at will are technically permissible, they are discouraged.[86] There seems to be no authority on whether a contractual valuation clause can, in the context of withdrawal from an LLC on oppression grounds, reduce a payment to zero.

G THEMES IN WITHDRAWAL REGIMES

Although each telling a different story with different actors, conflicts, and resolutions (or not), threads from each jurisdictional Chapters can be woven into three major themes. This section explores each in turn.

82 IV.C.4.ii.
83 VII.D.5.
84 V.C.9.i.
85 VI.C.5.
86 VI.E.4.

1 *The Roles and Impact of Legislators, Judges, and Scholars in Shaping Withdrawal in Close Corporation Law*

Each target jurisdiction features the same legal actors – legislators, judges, and scholars – although the impact of each actor varies by jurisdiction, across time, and in intensity. As we shall see, the differences in their experiences, however, cannot be explained by the divide (perceived or real) between the civil and common law traditions. I round off this subsection with a few observations.

i Legislators

In terms of actual impact on the law of withdrawal, it is notable that neither of the two civil law target jurisdictions implemented any significant changes to pre-existing close corporation forms through legislation. The German legislator is perhaps the most conspicuous in their failure to exert any impact on the path of withdrawal on *wichtigem Grund* from the GmbH, as both reform attempts – one benign and one anything but – were thwarted by unrelated political events. However, it is perhaps precisely because of the legislator's absence that the other two constituencies were left sufficient room to develop withdrawal over the decades before it achieved recognisably modern form in 1991.[87] In similar vein, Japan's legislature – which is otherwise fairly active in corporate law reform – did not manage to implement a withdrawal regime in spite of considerable scholarly support when the moment came in the late 1980s.[88] But what it could not make better, it could unmake and start over. The legislature subsequently abolished Japan's venerable custom-designed close corporation form, created a simulacrum of the US LLC (as the GK), and implemented for the first time a system of withdrawal for close corporations in the country.[89]

By contrast, legislatures played decisive roles – for better or for worse – in the common law target jurisdictions. The 'unfair prejudice' remedy is perhaps the single greatest legislative achievement in UK corporate law since the advent of general incorporation. The tremendously open-ended nature of the statutory provision and the virtually unrestricted remedial discretion reflected the (partly unjustified) faith held by legislators and law reformers in the ability of British courts to solve close corporation conflicts using their discretionary powers.[90] The reform attempt that began in the 1990s (part of which led to the Companies Act 2006) did not, however, do credit to the law reform bodies involved insofar as unfair prejudice was concerned.[91]

87 IV.C.1, IV.D.
88 VII.B.2.ii.
89 VII.C, VII.D.1.
90 V.C.1.i.
91 V.C.1.ii–iii, V.D.2.

As to the UK's cousin across the pond, the over fifty state (and territorial) legislatures in the US cannot be described as a monolithic whole.[92] Suffice it to say that their involvement and impact on the law of withdrawal spans the spectrum. Although not without exceptions, state legislatures did an overall fair job in the US-CC content, either by introducing oppression statutes, providing in some statutes the textual basis for judicial discretion, or simply leaving judicial efforts at devising solutions – notwithstanding the absence of clear statutory authorisation – undisturbed and unchallenged.[93] For LLCs, however, legislatures were far more responsive to federal tax policy than the basic corporate law problem of intra-close corporation conflict, giving and taking away withdrawal at will without a care for the impact on close corporation conflict resolution. Apart from a few exceptions, it is difficult to say that state legislatures took corporate law legislation and their reform sufficiently seriously.[94]

ii Judges

As people ultimately responsible for the resolution – or non-resolution – of close corporation disputes according to law, it is obvious that they can exert decisive influence on the utility of withdrawal as a legal institution. However, the direction and size of that influence is determined by two factors: the amount of room for manoeuvre that is expressly created or left (intentionally or otherwise) by written legislation, and judicial attitudes.

Despite a somewhat inauspicious start under the Third Reich, withdrawal was in large part through the instrumental and progressive efforts of post-war Germany's judges – culminating in a 1991 judgment of unified Germany's Federal Court of Justice – developed and accepted as a part of the unwritten corpus of German GmbH law.[95]

The Japanese judiciary's track record is by comparison much thinner. Judicial reluctance to support a reform that would have granted judges significant discretion may have played a role in the failure in 1990 of the first and only serious attempt at introducing a withdrawal regime for the two then-dominant close corporation forms.[96] Since the advent of the GK, a new close corporation form, and its withdrawal regime in 2005, the courts have not yet had the opportunity to rule on the latter's operation.[97] However, with the number of GKs rising steadily, it is probably just a matter of time before close corporation disputes reach the courts[98] – but

92 On the fragmentation of US close corporation law, see VI.A, VI.F.

93 VI.C.2.

94 VI.F.3.

95 IV.C.1.i, IV.C.1.iii.

96 VII.B.2.ii.

97 The closest they have come is ruling on a case involving another type of legal entity that applies the GK's withdrawal regime *mutatis mutandis*: VII.D.3.i.

98 VII.E.1.

whether and how Japan's judges rise to the close corporation challenge remains to be seen.

Considering the vaunted reputation of the UK – and especially English – courts, it is difficult to conclude that the corporate law judges acquitted themselves admirably in the law of withdrawal. After thwarting the first legislative reform (which introduced the 'oppression' remedy) through their own intransigence by adopting an excessively narrow approach, a younger generation of judges in the 1980s through early 1990s seized the moment by applying their statutory powers under the restructured 'unfair prejudice' remedy progressively and to great success in solving close corporation disputes.[99] But all good things must come to an end. Widespread negative perception – in particular of ballooning litigation costs – prompted further reform attempts. These, in turn, were headed off by a fateful 1999 decision of the UK's apex court that halted the onward march of unfair prejudice law. Ever since then, unfair prejudice has remained an important feature of UK close corporation law, albeit in a state of relative stagnation.[100]

The US, again, has a mixed report card. In most states of the Union, judges led – or at least did not try or succeed in thwarting – the development of US-CC withdrawal regimes of varying strengths and utility.[101] In a few states such as Delaware and Texas, judges seemed to have rejected or renounced withdrawal remedies on ideological rather than practical or factual grounds.[102] It is anyone's guess whether and to what extent judges will play a similarly interventionist role in developing withdrawal on oppression grounds in LLCs – as they once did for US-CCs – in the future.

iii Scholars

Of the target jurisdictions, it was in Germany that scholars exerted the strongest influence on the development of withdrawal in the GmbH – a regime that has remained uncodified until present day.[103] The next is arguably the US, where scholarly treatises also exerted substantial influence on the development of oppression law in US-CCs in some states.[104] Interestingly, although contractarianism as a legal ideology pervades LLC law generally,[105] it is more difficult to conclude that legal scholars are responsible for the relatively unwelcoming legislative attitude to withdrawal at will specifically, or for the lukewarm judicial and legislative stances on withdrawal on grounds other than 'not reasonably practicable'/deadlock. In the UK,

99 V.C.1.i.
100 V.C.1.ii–iii, V.C.4.iii.b.
101 VI.C.2.i–iii.
102 VI.C.2.iv.
103 IV.D.
104 VI.C.3.i. Arguably the most influential and most cited (by courts) piece of scholarship is O'Neal & Thompson (2020b) and its forerunners; see Thompson (1988): 213–15.
105 VI.F.1, VI.F.3.

scholarly voices seemed to have done little good – or had much impact at all – during attempted legislative reforms of unfair prejudice at the turn of the century.[106] Although Japanese scholars were keenly aware of the imperative for withdrawal in close corporations in the 1980s, they did not succeed – perhaps in part due to their own limitations[107] – in seeing withdrawal implemented in the 1990 reforms.[108] After withdrawal was finally introduced as part of the new GK close corporation form, the paucity of Japanese jurisprudence on this new regime left a vacuum that is only partly filled by scholarly opinion. However, scholars have achieved little consensus on anything except perhaps that withdrawal on unavoidable grounds should be recognised in a squeeze out scenario;[109] it remains to be seen which direction(s) scholarship will take going forward, and how it would impact the work of the courts – if at all.

iv Observations

From the foregoing discussion, I make three observations. First, judicial attitudes make or break a legal system's withdrawal regime. In other words, judicial support for withdrawal is a *sine qua non* for its success. Although legislators can and, in some target jurisdictions (the UK, some US states, Japan), do play an important role in placing withdrawal on a firm footing in written law, the most they can do is to facilitate, but not compel, judicial flexibility and progressiveness. As is borne out by the British experience with the oppression remedy and Japan's ill-fated 1980s reform attempts, the proper legislation can be helpful – but without judicial will to implement it, even legislation that offers judges unlimited discretion will be useless.

Second, it is at least arguably acceptable and legitimate for judges to take the lead in creating or advancing withdrawal regimes, regardless of legal tradition or other considerations.[110] As we have seen, judges across the common/civil law divide have demonstrated a capacity and willingness to act independently and without legislative mandate to develop withdrawal on their own, relying on other parts of written law if they are available, or entirely as unwritten law if they are not. US judges in many states crafted withdrawal regimes in the shadow of dissolution provisions, or simply through the judicious exercise of their equitable powers. Even the usual 'civil law judges cannot/should not make law' objection falls flat in the face of Germany's example, which powerfully demonstrates how judges may confidently and legitimately develop withdrawal – with the support of the scholarly community – as an unwritten legal institution in the face of legislative

106 V.D.2.
107 See Egashira et al. (1990): 63 (Statement by Yamashita Tomonobu).
108 VII.B.2.ii.
109 VII.D.3.iii.
110 On the gap-filling function of judges in the withdrawal context, see II.E.2.i, II.E.2.iii, II.E.4.

inaction. Nor does the appeal to a supposed aversion to 'gouvernement des juges'[111] hold any water when *legislatures* expressly wish to vest judges with broad powers to resolve close corporation problems. In this regard, repeated refusal by British judges at critical periods in history to take a proactive stance on oppression/unfair prejudice and the Japanese judiciary's discomfort at the prospect of making judgment calls without extremely clear statutory guidance are, whatever their reasons, negative examples that likely set back close corporation minority shareholder protection for decades. Judicial passivity can no longer be justified today by appeals to lack of expertise or lack of guidance from non-statutory sources; advances in scholarship[112] and jurisprudence in the world's legally developed jurisdictions offer all the help a judge could ever need.[113] In close corporation law, a realm relatively free from the political and constitutional struggles between the judicial and political branches that plague other areas of law, there is no longer – if ever – good reason for judges to actively refuse to exercise their powers in furtherance of corporate law justice.[114]

Third, scholars in all target jurisdictions on the whole support withdrawal *on grounds*. Only in the US do we find a serious movement against withdrawal in any form in close corporations; even then, withdrawal's opponents do not command a majority.[115] While there may be justifiable concerns with excessively liberal rights to withdraw, withdrawal at will is not the consensus position *de lege lata*. The few scholars advocating for withdrawal at will as mandatory rules[116] may be provocative and influential, but they do not represent the mainstream opinion,[117] and thus

[111] Fleischer (2018a): 718 (suggesting this applies in the close corporation context, citing one Italian source touching on corporate law). With respect, Fleischer overestimates the true degree of aversion (outside of perhaps the highly charged environment of the US) among constituencies other than the courts themselves to vesting judges with discretion *in close corporation law*. Why judges themselves are reluctant to exercise statutorily granted powers *in close corporation law* is another question entirely – and may be a matter for future (possibly empirical) work; my point is that no *compelling reason justifying* judicial reluctance/abdication *in close corporation law* has ever been offered.

[112] To which this Book is but one contribution.

[113] Of course, it is up to the judge to make factual determinations, and this could possibly be difficult when a review of the 'relationship history' is called for. Cf Fleischer (2018a): 717 (suggesting mediation as a 'superior means of dispute resolution' in such situations). However, figuring out the facts is a basic, inherent aspect of judging that pervades every area of law in which facts are disputed. It would be unhelpful and indeed unbecoming if judges were to disclaim responsibility for making judgment calls just because doing so may be tedious and difficult. I assume that no scholar writing in good faith is actively trying to justify, much less advocate, judicial sloth.

[114] If the objection is that courts are overloaded, the fault almost certainly rests with underfunding and inefficiencies of the court system as a whole. If the objection concerns costs of litigation, that is a matter for attorneys' incentives and compensation structure, inefficiencies in legal processes such as outdated or non-existent technology and case management, or exorbitant court fees. In neither situation should broader legal system concerns be blamed on close corporation dispute resolution, nor should withdrawal seekers be made to bear the cost of denial of justice. Cf V.D.1 (unfair prejudice becoming the victim of England-wide problems with costs of civil litigation).

[115] See VI.F–G.

[116] IV.C.6.i (Germany); VI.C.7 (US).

[117] IV.C.6.ii (Germany); VI.C.7 (US).

should not be treated as straw men[118] by those who have an agenda against withdrawal in any form. The burden of persuasion is now firmly on those who would stand against withdrawal on grounds.

2 *Withdrawal As Spontaneous Functional Convergence in Close Corporation Law*

Having come this far, to the odd comparative corporate law jurist with the good fortune of taking a bird's eye view of the withdrawal scene, one fact stands out. It is this: each target jurisdiction seems to have – largely independently of each other and of other jurisdictions – developed their own respective withdrawal regimes using mostly, if not exclusively, *domestic* legal sources and inspirations. In so doing, the four target jurisdictions demonstrate a level of what might be aptly characterised as spontaneous convergence that points to withdrawal as an evolutionary milestone for close corporation law.

i Conspicuous Absence of Foreign Influence in Close Corporation Law and Jurisprudence

As a general point, the issue of shareholder protection in close corporation law has never been a centre of attention in the comparative corporate law literature. Existing work on comparative shareholder protection seldom focus on withdrawal[119] – if they even address it at all.[120] It should not surprise that existing comparative corporate law projects facilitating the transmission of ideas between various jurisdictions have had little effect on the actual law of close corporation withdrawal.

Turning now to each of the target jurisdictions, we begin with Germany. A product of the late nineteenth century, the GmbH is 'an artificial creation of the German legislator without precedent in history or in comparative

[118] Hansen (2018) ('the straw man fallacy . . . occurs when an opponent's point of view is distorted in order to make it easier to refute'). In other words, just because there are good arguments against withdrawal *at will* does not mean that a case against withdrawal *on grounds* can or has been made out.

[119] Works featuring more than one national law situating withdrawal remedies as one of several 'exit' remedies or within a broader piece on close corporations, and do not feature an overall comparative framework such as that presented in this Chapter include: de Vries (2010); Wang (2011); Goette (2014); Hirota (2013); Fleischer (2018a): 701–4; Fleischer (2014): 66–8. The few examples where withdrawal regimes in two jurisdictions are seriously compared (i.e. through citation to primary and secondary sources in the target jurisdiction's legal language) are not by leading or even mainstream academics: see e.g. Scogin (1993); Brinkman (2002). The only example I could identify wherein an analysis bearing a resemblance to this Chapter's was conducted is Veziroğlu (2018).

[120] See e.g. Djankov et al. (2008): 434 tbl. 1. This study, which is of great practical importance as it led the World Bank's *Doing Business* Report to assess the world's economies for related party transaction regulation, did not consider the remedy of withdrawal. *Quaere* if the *Doing Business* Report would have measured withdrawal's availability instead, had the Djankov et al study looked at withdrawal instead of just derivative actions. Another prominent example of a study claiming to study shareholder protection but completely omitting withdrawal (while including the derivative action) is Katelouzou & Siems (2015).

law',[121] and its *Austritt aus wichtigem Grund* can trace its roots to at least 1930,[122] long before any other major jurisdiction had seriously grappled with a withdrawal remedy. There is nothing to suggest that either of the two abortive state-led attempts – including one under the National Socialist regime – to codify the withdrawal regime was influenced by foreign law. Even if the only serious round of reforms that were ever implemented for the GmbH (MoMiG) may have been in part motivated by competition with the UK Ltd,[123] considering that withdrawal has till today never been codified or statutorily modified (including by MoMiG),[124] the case for foreign influence cannot be made.

Great Britain's oppression and the UK's unfair prejudice remedies have been similarly free from foreign influence, despite erroneous suggestion that the oppression remedy had antecedents in the laws of two US states.[125] There is no evidence from the Cohen Committee Report (1945), which laid the first foundations for what would become the UK's unfair prejudice remedy, that the Committee took into consideration any foreign law or practices before making its proposal for the oppression remedy.[126] In fact, given that the Report was produced during World War II, any suggestion that Germany or Japan provided inspiration would have been simply ludicrous.[127] Similarly, there is no evidence that the post-war Jenkins Committee (whose Report was submitted in 1962) took into account any foreign law when formulating its proposal to transform the statutory remedy for oppression into one addressing 'unfair prejudice'.[128] Although it is possible that corporate law judgments and scholarship from Anglo-Commonwealth jurisdictions (excluding those by sitting or former UK judges) might not have been completely ignored,[129] it is difficult to prove that they have had any serious influence or impact on the path of unfair prejudice law.

That is not to say that the 'two countries separated by a common language'[130] ignored each other completely.[131] The flow of legal ideas appears to be unidirectional –

[121] Fleischer (2018b): Rdn 50: 'Das GmbH-Gesetz ist eine Kunstschöpfung des deutschen Gesetzgebers ohne historisches oder rechtsvergleichendes Vorbild' (emphasis omitted).

[122] IV.C.1.i (to a judgment of the Imperial Court of Justice and a 1930 lecture by a prominent jurist).

[123] IV.B.1.

[124] See IV.C.2.i.

[125] Folk (1966): 954 fn. 441 (citing Californian and West Virginian statutes as 'vague antecedents'). This is unconvincing even on Folk's own terms, as what he describes resemble 'election' statutes that are at best indirect withdrawal remedies. See VI.C.2.iii.

[126] See Cohen (1945): paras 60, 152–3.

[127] The Committee was appointed on 26 June 1943 and made its Report in June 1945. There are references to the US and to Canada in the Report, albeit not on any issue relating to shareholder remedies.

[128] Jenkins (1962): paras. 199–205. Interestingly, evidence of US law was offered by a David Polk & Wardwell attorney for the Committee's consideration, but in the context of the derivative action, not withdrawal as such: see ibid. para. 207.

[129] See V.B.2.

[130] Often misattributed to George Bernard Shaw.

[131] It has been famously observed that '[i]n general, however, the American corporation lawyer seems to share the view of his English colleague about the iron curtain dividing their respective systems.': Gower (1956): 1401.

from the Old World to the New. Great Britain's oppression remedy, in particular, sparked considerable interest in the US. It notably served as the source of South Carolina's first withdrawal statute for US-CCs (1962),[132] and was at one time not an infrequent subject of discussion in US legal writing.[133] In particular, the development of 'reasonable expectations' as a basis for US-CC oppression relief in some US states has also been traced back to scholarly writing published in the US discussing the British oppression remedy.[134] Cases decided by British courts were also cited in several early US-CC oppression cases.[135] Be that as it may, whatever British influence there might have been in the early years, there is no evidence of any substantive influence from UK jurisprudence or literature in recent years,[136] nor could the hostility of certain states against any form of US-CC withdrawal[137] be explained by British/UK influence. As to the LLC, given that the entity's proliferation and the design of its withdrawal regimes are driven by the US' unique constitutional and policy environment,[138] except perhaps some possible murky antecedents in Latin American corporate law in its earliest days,[139] no influence of foreign law is likely – or indeed even possible.

Japan's first close corporation statute may have been inspired by the German GmbH-Gesetz,[140] but such a regime was never judicially developed or successfully implemented by legislative reform.[141] Even though the GK close corporation form – the first to offer withdrawal – was initially inspired by the US LLC, it cannot be said that the LLC was, in the result, 'transplanted' in any recognisable form. Instead, the final product as enacted is created by adapting legacy partnership forms for limited

[132] SCCodeAnn, § 12–22.23(a)(4) (1962); Folk (1966): 954 (observing that South Carolina 'adopt[ed] nearly verbatim . . . England's section 210 including the power to order buyout'); see also Afterman (1969): 1043.

[133] See e.g. O'Neal & Derwin (1961): 202–8; Folk (1966): 954–7; Afterman (1969).

[134] 'The widespread use in this country in the last few years of the reasonable expectations concept can be traced to impetus from abroad two decades ago': Thompson (1988): 211–12 (citing Afterman (1969)), 213–15 (citing the first edition of what became O'Neal & Thompson (2020b)). The first edition of what became O'Neal & Thompson (2020b) drew on material not only from Britain, but also from other Anglophone jurisdictions; see Sealy (1976). See also VI.C.3.i.

[135] See text in VI.C.3 before VI.C.3.i.

[136] Revealingly, the discussion in O'Neal and Thompson's treatise has not been updated to take into account post-1980 developments; see O'Neal & Thompson (2020b): § 10:14 (citing *O'Neill* v. *Phillips* [1999] 1 WLR 1092 (HL) as the sole post-1980 case and even then only cursorily). The only US case I could find in which the leading UK case *O'Neill* v. *Phillips* [1999] 1 WLR 1092 (HL) was cited concerned a Cayman Islands company, and *O'Neill* was cited as part of the court's consideration of foreign law: *Hayat* v. *Al-Mazeedi*, 10 January 2011, No 08–1004, 2011 WL 1532109, 28 MassLRptr 243 (MassSuper).

[137] VI.C.2.iv.

[138] See VI.F.3.

[139] VI.D.1.

[140] VII.B.1.

[141] VII.B.2.i–ii (discussing partial non-legal substitutes and the failed statutory reform attempt). Thus, although Japanese scholars advocating for withdrawal as a legal remedy were often familiar with and most probably influenced by the law of the other three target jurisdictions, such foreign influences did not ultimately manifest in legal change.

liability for all members,[142] and its withdrawal regime is built upon locally developed concepts (particularly *yamu wo enai jiyū* 'unavoidable grounds').[143] Although Japanese scholarly writing makes reference to foreign (and overwhelmingly US) close corporation law and literature not infrequently,[144] there is little evidence so far that such Japanese scholarly writing has had a substantial impact on the disposition of actual GK withdrawal cases – not least because there have been no cases. In any event, it would be extremely difficult to prove foreign influence given that Japanese judgments seldom, if ever, cite foreign legal sources.[145]

ii Why Does Convergence Matter?

We have observed that each target jurisdiction (for the US, a large part thereof) independently arrived at the conclusion that withdrawal is a desirable – and even necessary – feature of close corporations. That suggests that what we are observing here is nothing less than functional convergence (where corporate law systems achieve broadly similar results through different routes and legal norms[146]) in action – and at a concrete, observable, and meaningful level.

The theme of convergence was initially debated at the most macro level, such as between legal traditions or national legal systems.[147] When the theme of convergence entered the corporate law sphere, the focus has been largely on the notion that globalisation – and the competition this fosters – would lead national systems of corporate governance to converge on a single, efficient model.[148] According to the 'chauvinistic statement of the Americanocentric convergence thesis'[149] that is triumphantly titled 'The End of History for Corporate Law', this efficient model would, to no one's great surprise, be the US' so-called 'shareholder primacy' model.[150]

Be that as it may, the convergence debate in corporate law – carried out at the highest international levels between well-travelled American and European scholars of international repute – was almost exclusively about corporate *governance* of *public listed* corporations, and rarely concerned itself with the nuts and bolts of corporate

142 VII.C.1.

143 VII.D.1, VII.D.2.i (withdrawal at will) VII.D.3.i–ii (withdrawal on unavoidable grounds).

144 VII.E.2.

145 It is possible that expert opinions (*kanteisho*) drawing on foreign law and literature may influence a Japanese court's decision, but it would be extremely difficult to attribute any result or jurisprudential development to any specific foreign legal rule or idea.

146 For definitions of functional convergence, cf Siems (2007): 23–4 ('a comparable result is produced . . . but via different statutory paths'); Gilson (2001): 356 ('when existing governance institutions are flexible enough to respond to the demands of changed circumstances without altering the institutions' formal characteristics').

147 The literature is too legion to cite in full, but important texts include Merryman (1981); Legrand (1996).

148 For a handy summary of the debate, see Gordon & Roe (2004b). For a magisterial but difficult to follow treatise, see Siems (2007).

149 Terminology from Branson (2001): 330–1.

150 Hansmann & Kraakman (2001).

law in *close* corporations.[151] Indeed, all 'The End of History of Corporate Law' had to say substantively about close corporations was this:

> Closely held corporations, like publicly held corporations, operate most efficiently when the law helps assure that managers are primarily responsive to shareholder interests and that controlling shareholders do not opportunistically exploit noncontrolling shareholders.[152]

While Hansmann and Kraakman may have been premature in declaring victory of the so-called American 'shareholder primacy' model of corporate governance for large, listed corporations,[153] they might not be quite so off the mark on close corporations.

A compelling, if tentative, explanation for what I call the 'spontaneous convergence''[154] of the four target jurisdictions – in the absence of significant foreign influence or other usual convergence forces[155] – on withdrawal as a form of minority protection thus presents itself. Simply put, withdrawal is likely to be an *effective* solution. The effectiveness explanation for withdrawal's existence across legally and economically developed jurisdictions reinforces the remedy's centrality and practical importance to close corporations. An alternative explanation for convergence of this nature is that similar facts and problems would ordinarily result in similar law. Given the non-jurisdiction-specific nature of the problem of majority–minority shareholder conflict in close corporations,[156] it should not surprise that the four target jurisdictions have developed reasonably similar solutions to the same problem. But how far, and on which elements of withdrawal, have the target jurisdictions converged? Is there a 'end of history' for this phenomenon?

3 *Convergence in Withdrawal Design*

In the context of withdrawal from close corporations, the analysis in this Chapter (at III.C to III.E) has shown that substantial variation can be observed between the four

[151] See McCahery & Vermeulen (2004): 197 ('The common thread of this diverse body of work [on convergence] has been the effort to identify changes in capital market activity and regulation with the convergence of corporate governance institutions'); see also Hopt (2019): 1140 (dismissing comparative close corporation law as 'essentially part of comparative contract law', 1164–5 (not mentioning close corporations at all in the discussion on convergence); Armour & Enriques et al (2017): 51, 57–8, 68, 71, 76, 80 fn. 9, 120–1, 148–50, 157, 166–7, 264–6, 270–1 (same); Cabrelli & Siems (2015) (same). The leading volume on convergence in corporate law, Gordon & Roe (2004a), apart from a chapter version of Hansmann & Kraakman (2001), discusses closely held firms only in the context of disclosure and accounting requirements: Hertig (2004): 335–6.

[152] Hansmann & Kraakman (2001): 443.

[153] See generally Branson (2001); Puchniak (2007).

[154] I use 'spontaneous' to distinguish the withdrawal phenomenon from 'harmonisation', which connotes a deliberate effort to achieve a similar goal or uniformity of law. See Siems (2018b): 264.

[155] On convergence forces, see Siems (2018b): 265–7 and 266 tbl. 9.1 (in general), 271 (corporate law examples). None of the forces discussed apply to withdrawal in close corporations.

[156] See Fleischer (2014): 29–31. On shareholder conflict, see II.B.

target jurisdictions' withdrawal regimes at the level of individual elements (i.e. when, who, and how much). When these elements are assembled, however, a different picture emerges. Besides broad spontaneous functional convergence (i.e. at a meso-level) towards withdrawal as shareholder protection in each of the four target jurisdictions, spontaneous functional convergence also takes place on a micro-level within two pairs of two target jurisdictions each: Germany/Japan and the UK/US.

In this subsection, I offer a typology of withdrawal *on grounds* comprising two ideal-types or functional models and propose a way forward. For the avoidance of doubt, the discussion below[157] excludes withdrawal at will (which is available as a default in Japan for the GK and some US states for LLCs) as the weight of law and literature in the target jurisdictions is against it.[158]

i The Insurance Model: Germany and Japan

In terms of breadth of withdrawal grounds, Germany is the most liberal by far, closely followed by Japan. Withdrawal is permitted not only when fault of other participants is present, but also when the attribution of fault is unclear, when both withdrawal seeker and other participants are at fault, as well as non-fault scenarios such as relationship breakdown or deadlock, poor and irrecoverable business prospects, and even purely personal reasons on the part of the withdrawal seeker.[159] Withdrawal seekers in Germany and Japan who have fallen on hard times or fallen out with their co-venturers may take comfort in the fact that their corporate law regimes do not expect them to internalise their loss completely, nor to throw themselves at the complete mercy of corporate controllers.

However, what the law offers the withdrawal seeker may be lukewarm or cold comfort: a narrow remedy that is balanced against other interests and only weakly enforceable. The withdrawal seeker's monetary claim cannot include a compensation component in situations where withdrawal was prompted by the fault of others.[160] Both jurisdictions feature strong capital maintenance regimes for entities offering full limited liability for members and a strong creditor protection orientation.[161] As only the close corporation is liable to pay the withdrawing member's monetary claim, creditor protection considerations are triggered. The withdrawing member's interest in enforcing their monetary claim is thus subject to and dependent on the solvency of the GmbH/GK, subordinate to creditors' interests.[162]

157 At III.G.3.i–ii.
158 For exceptional examples of advocacy for unrestricted, mandatory withdrawal rights, see IV.C.6.i and VI.C.7.
159 III.C.
160 III.E.2.
161 See IV.C.5 (Germany), VII.D.6 (Japan).
162 III.E.3.

The German and Japanese withdrawal regimes may thus be characterised as inclusive but contingent forms of member protection. Functionally, the close corporation acts as a form of quasi-'insurance fund' for withdrawal seekers offering protection against part of the vicissitudes of life in a closely held business, but withdrawal's availability is naturally limited to the close corporation's assets and what the applicable capital maintenance and creditor protection regimes permit. Each close corporation member thus still bears the risk that is proper to their status as residual claimants with limited liability. Accordingly, I call this the 'insurance model' of withdrawal.

ii The Corrective Model: The UK and the US

Notwithstanding the seemingly generous 'reasonable expectations' grounds for withdrawal in selected states, the US also includes states that take a much narrower view of withdrawal grounds reminiscent of pre-unfair prejudice UK.[163] In any event, whichever the state, withdrawal grounds are essentially restricted to the fault of other shareholders, managers, or controllers of the corporation; the only and very limited exception to the fault standard is deadlock.[164] Similarly, in post-*O'Neill* UK, only independently unlawful acts or breach of 'equitable considerations' (the latter applicable only in the ill-defined subclass of Ltds known as 'quasi-partnerships')[165] by other participants in the close corporation are reliably actionable under its withdrawal regime. There is absolutely no allowance for non-fault withdrawal in UK law thanks to the *O'Neill* decision.[166] The two Anglophone jurisdictions are unsympathetic towards withdrawal seekers in situations where fault cannot be clearly attributed, and even less forgiving of withdrawal seekers at fault, although the UK is arguably slightly less vindictive on that front.[167]

Withdrawal seekers who satisfy the court that their suffering resulted solely (or overwhelmingly) from the fault of others may be few[168] – but the lucky few. If anyone were to be liable to pay the withdrawal seeker the latter's monetary claim, it would usually be the very parties at fault.[169] With the close corporation not usually on the hook,[170] business creditors' interests are not affected as a matter of corporate law, and

163 VI.C.3.i.

164 III.C.1–3.

165 V.C.4.iii.c.

166 III.C.3; V.C.10. The only possible withdrawal ground based on non-independently unlawful and non-representation/estoppel/promise-based conduct post-*O'Neill* seems to be 'objectively and commercially unreasonable standard for remuneration', which is also a fault ground; see V.C.4.iv.

167 III.C.2–3.

168 I make no claims about the absolute number or percentage of successful withdrawal seekers in the Anglophone jurisdictions versus the others; by 'few' I mean only in terms of the total (theoretical) pool of withdrawal seekers, including those who may wish to withdraw for reasons that are simply not actionable under the corporate law regimes in the US or UK.

169 III.D.1.

170 III.D.3.

thus pose no obstacle to the withdrawing shareholder's ability to enforce their monetary claim.[171] Not only would the withdrawing shareholder, as a starting point, reclaim the value of their membership interest,[172] they also stand a chance of being compensated for their 'share' of the loss caused to the close corporation by the party responsible for the grounds of withdrawal.[173]

The Anglo-American approach is more targeted by requiring clear attribution of fault, but also more powerful from the perspective of minority protection. It serves a compensatory function as the party at fault is liable to make the victim whole again. A potential positive side effect is deterrence: shareholders and other controllers whose acts and conduct can affect the fortunes of the close corporation and other shareholders would – on pain of substantial personal liability – do well not to use their powers in an abusive or prejudicial way without good justification. I adopt the terminology of 'corrective'[174] for this functional model in recognition of its underlying logic.

iii The Way Forward: Synthesis

With two models of withdrawal at hand, the temptation to adjudge one superior to the other arises. But this should be resisted. Both the insurance and corrective models of withdrawal are built on a single meta-principle: protecting shareholders desirous and deserving of exit, but not at the expense of innocent constituencies due to financial liability for the consequences of shareholder withdrawal. This fundamental tension, which animates withdrawal regimes in all target jurisdictions, may be called 'the golden thread' of withdrawal design. The golden thread has unravelled in two different paths because the forces tugging on the ends differ slightly under each model.

Under the insurance model of withdrawal, anyone who suffers serious hardship or prejudice that is not the result of their own voluntary acts is a 'deserving' shareholder. This explains why even shareholders who fall ill[175] may have access to withdrawal. The 'innocent' constituencies are primarily corporate creditors, as well as co-shareholders who might not be responsible for the withdrawal seeker's hardship. Their interests are accordingly protected by rules that limit enforcement of the withdrawing shareholder's monetary claim to the extent permitted by capital maintenance and creditor protection rules.

171 III.E.3. There is an exception whereby the withdrawing member's interest is subordinated to creditors' interests if the LLC proceeds to dissolution: ibid.

172 III.E.1.

173 III.E.2.

174 The similarity to tort law (or perhaps extracontractual liability more generally) is no coincidence. The choice of 'corrective' is nonetheless in homage to the basic corrective justice thesis in Weinrib (2012) while avoiding the doctrinal baggage of 'tort'. Note, however, that Weinrib's theory of corrective justice eschews deterrence: ibid. 43.

175 IV.C.2.v.

The corrective model is not about protecting shareholders from a wide range of risks, but only a specific sort: harms attributable to those in control of the close corporation. Only withdrawal seekers harmed personally by blameworthy conduct of other shareholders or controllers are considered 'deserving'. However, the close corporation, its business, and corporate creditors are presumptively innocent in such a scenario. To avoid causing prejudice to them, withdrawal is primarily in the form of compelling the party at fault to buy out the withdrawal seeker personally.

We thus observe that the two models, in making different constituencies their subjects on the two ends of the golden thread, do not contradict, but rather complement each other. Put another way, while corrective and insurance withdrawal models differ in micro-function, they are nonetheless meso-level *functional equivalents*. Their only weakness is that they are each but one half of the greater whole that is shareholder protection in close corporation law. The way forward – which will be paved in Chapter VIII – is simple: the synthesis of both models into a single, comprehensive model of withdrawal.

H CONCLUSION

This Chapter has constructed a jurisdiction-neutral framework of withdrawal based on the key findings from the withdrawal regimes of the world's four largest developed economies: Germany, the UK, the US, and Japan. It has also demonstrated the importance of the judicial role in the operation and development of withdrawal regimes, described the phenomenon of spontaneous convergence, and offered a typology of the withdrawal regimes studied that is built around two distinct but complementary models. The two models of withdrawal form the basis for this Book's proposed withdrawal remedy, which will be the subject of Part 3 ('Application') (Chapter VIII). The rest of this Part of the Book (Chapters IV to VII) comprises four self-contained jurisdictional Chapters, each providing an in-depth account of the target jurisdiction's withdrawal regime as contextualised within its system of close corporation law and written partly from the perspective of an insider of that jurisdiction. And with that, it seems fitting to begin our journey at the birthplace of the world's first custom-designed – and even having passed its quasquicentennial, still surprisingly modern – close corporation form: Germany.

IV

Germany

Judicial and Academic Development in the Shadow of Legislative Neglect

A INTRODUCTION

Notwithstanding the trauma of two World Wars, territorial losses, and the costs of reunification after more than four decades of partition, Germany has been for much of the past one and a half centuries – and remains today – a leader in innovation and the economic powerhouse of Europe.[1] It is uncontroversial that modern Germany's technological and economic achievements are considerable. Possibly less immediately obvious to the foreign jurist, especially one schooled only in the Anglo-American 'common law' tradition, is Germany's history of thought leadership in law and legal scholarship. German excellence extends beyond its vaunted Civil Code to the realm of corporate law[2] – and specifically, to the law of close corporations. The German ***Gesellschaft mit beschränkter Haftung*** ('Limited Liability Company', abbreviated '**GmbH**'), created by the German legislator in 1892 as the world's first and oldest close corporation form,[3] is 'one of [Germany's] most important and successful exports in law'.[4] Nevertheless, the relatively little attention accorded to the GmbH in English-language comparative corporate law literature belies GmbH's significance in corporate law scholarship and the modern German economy.[5]

Germany's experience with the GmbH is instructive for several reasons. Despite being nearly universally recognised as a 'civil law' or 'code' jurisdiction,[6] it is not legislative reforms, but rather jurisprudence and academic literature that have played the greater role in GmbH law's development.[7] This holds especially true in withdrawal's context: a distinctive feature of withdrawal's development in Germany's acclaimed GmbH is the fact that it took place entirely without legislative action or reform. The regime remains uncodified law;[8] through the process of development in an incremental and organic way, it has acquired unique features, chief of which is the extremely broad and flexible core concept of *wichtiger Grund* (good cause) underpinning the availability of withdrawal in each individual case.[9] Legal systems in which legislative reform is not feasible may find the German experience especially instructive in fashioning a judicial and academic response to the close corporation problem.

1 See Jamrisko et al. (2021) (Germany ranked world fourth on the 2021 Bloomberg Innovation Index, after South Korea, Singapore, and Switzerland); World Bank (2021b) (ranking Germany fourth in the world after the US, China, and Japan, and first in Europe, ahead of the UK and France).

2 Germany was among the five jurisdictions included in the very first edition of modern comparative corporate law's *magnum opus*, Kraakman et al. (2004).

3 The German enabling legislation preceded all other known legislative efforts, such as those of Portugal, Austria and Ecuador in 1906 and the UK's Companies Act 1907: Lutter (1992): 51. For a brief historical overview see IV.B.1 below.

4 Lutter (1992): 49.

5 See IV.B.3 below.

6 See Siems (2018b): 89 tbl. 4.1.

7 Schmidt (2002): § 33 II 2 a ('Man kann die Situation im Vergleich mit dem Aktienrecht dahin umschreiben, daß die *Aktienrechtsgeschichte* eine *Geschichte der Reformgesetze* ist, die *Geschichte des GmbH-Rechts* dagegen eine *Geschichte der Rechtsfortbildung*') (italics in original).

8 See IV.C.1.

9 See IV.C.2.

IV.B provides a concise overview of the GmbH that covers its history, legal features, and its importance to the modern German economy. IV.C follows with an in-depth, up-to-date examination of the withdrawal remedy in German GmbH law, beginning with a historical account of its development by scholarly commentary and judicial precedent in the absence of legislative reform. This section also analyses doctrinal and practical aspects such as enforcement and valuation. The sheer range of situations that can form the basis for withdrawal rights deserves special note. IV.D presents key takeaways from Germany's long and rich experience with the withdrawal remedy for comparative corporate law, and IV.E concludes.

B THE *GESELLSCHAFT MIT BESCHRÄNKTER HAFTUNG* (GMBH)

1 *History*

Germany's GmbH is a distinct business entity with its own enabling legislation (*Gesetz betreffend die Gesellschaften mit beschränkter Haftung* [Limited Liability Companies Act],[10] abbreviated GmbHG) and a long pedigree tracing back to the late nineteenth century. Unlike legislation governing most other organisational forms in German private law,[11] the GmbHG was 'an artificial creation of the German legislator without model in history of comparative law'.[12] Its prototype, 'commercial companies with limited liability' (*Handelsgesellschaften mit beschränkter Haftbarkeit*) was first proposed in 1884 by Wilhelm Oechelhäuser, a member of the Imperial Diet.[13] Although Oechelhäuser's proposal was rejected at the time, the idea did not die. After the Prussian Ministry of Commerce's consultations with merchant representatives revealed commercial demand for a new corporate form,[14] the Imperial Ministry of Justice prepared a draft that was quickly passed with minimal amendment.[15] Promulgated on 26 April 1892, the GmbHG entered force on 10 May 1892.[16] It would stand virtually unchanged for over one century.[17]

10 Per the 'official' unofficial translation adopted by the German Ministry of Justice; see Reusch (2019).

11 Other forms such as the association (*Verein*), stock corporation (*Aktiengesellschaft*), cooperative (*Genossenschaft*), and partnerships (*Personengesellschaft*) exist independently of written law and only retrospectively received from the legislator a finished legal form: Schmidt (2002): § 33 II 1 a.

12 Fleischer (2018b): Rdn 50 ('Das GmbH-Gesetz ist eine *Kunstschöpfung des deutschen Gesetzgebers ohne historisches oder rechtsvergleichendes Vorbild*') (emphasis in original).

13 The text of his proposal can be found in Fleischer (2018b): Rdn 55.

14 Fleischer (2018b): Rdn 61–3.

15 Fleischer (2018b): Rdn 64–6. With the legislative process lasting only about four months, the exceptional speed with which the GmbHG became law is due primarily to the imminent end of the Diet session with little enthusiasm for postponing deliberations on the bill to the next session: Fleischer (2018b): Rdn 67.

16 Fleischer (2018b): Rdn 66.

17 Schmidt (2002): § 33 II 2 a (observing that the only serious reform effort in 1980 was relatively modest). On the 1980 reforms ('GmbH-Novelle'), see Fleischer (2018b): Rdn 108–15. The GmbHG has remained until today a standalone statute, unabsorbed into any of Germany's great law codes.

Pressure for change would eventually come externally, from the European Court of Justice (ECJ). Its landmark decisions on the freedom of establishment[18] would unleash the forces of regulatory competition,[19] and specifically the UK private limited company (Ltd) upon the German legal and business world.[20] Compared to the cheap and flexible UK Ltd, the GmbH's disadvantages, such as its relatively cumbersome incorporation procedures and high minimum registered capital of EUR 25,000, began to draw serious concern amongst academics and pundits.[21] Within a few short years, over 40,000 UK Ltds were incorporated for the purpose of operating businesses primarily, if not exclusively, in Germany.[22] Notwithstanding the conservative German academy's unwillingness to endorse bold reform,[23] the German legislator ultimately did respond, and decisively. The result was the *Gesetz zur Modernisierung des GmbH-Rechts und zur Bekämpfung von Missbräuchen* [Act to Modernise the Law on the GmbH and to Combat Its Abuse] (universally abbreviated 'MoMiG'),[24] the first serious set of reforms to the GmbHG in its long, illustrious history.

MoMiG answered the English Ltd threat by introducing a new subvariant of the GmbH,[25] the 'entrepreneurial company (with limited liability)' (*Unternehme rgesellschaft (haftungsbeschränkt)*; abbreviated 'UG'[26]).[27] Within two short years of MoMiG entering force on 1 November 2008,[28] over 40,000 UGs were incorporated as of 1 November 2010.[29] MoMiG's seeming instant success made it possible for the Secretary of State for Justice[30] to declare 'victory' of German corporate law over UK

18 Case C-212/97 *Centros Ltd* v. *Erhvervs- og Selskabsstyrelsen* [1999] ECR I-1459; Case C-208/00 *Überseering BV* v. *Nordic Construction Company Baumanagement GmbH* [2002] ECR I-9919; Case C-167/01 *Kamer van Koophandel en Fabrieken voor Amsterdam* v. *Inspire Art Ltd* [2003] ECR I-10155; Case C-210/06 *Cartesio Oktató és Szolgáltató bt* [2008] ECR I-9641; Case C-378/10 *VALE Építési kft* ECLI:EU:C:2012:440. See further e.g. Wiśniewski & Opalski (2009); Borg-Barthet (2013).

19 Armour & Enriques et al. (2017): 21–2, 196–7. For a pre-*Centros* view, see Cheffins (1997): ch. 9.

20 See e.g. sources cited in Bachner (2009): 12 fn. 49.

21 Bachmann (2008): 1066–7; Beurskens & Noack (2008): 1073–5, 1083–4.

22 From 2004, the first year after the *Inspire Art* decision, to 2006 alone, I calculate that a total of 40,429 English Ltds in which the majority of the directors resided in Germany were incorporated; for raw data see Becht et al. (2008): 244, 248 tbl. 3.

23 The *Deutscher Juristentag* ['Association of German Jurists' as per its website (DJT (2020))], a prestigious private association of jurists from both academia and practice with a history of influence on German law reform, holds a biennial *Deutscher Juristentag* [when referring to the event, the official translation is 'German Jurists Forum']). The 66th German Jurists Forum held in Stuttgart in 2006 voted 166 to 14 to retain a minimum share capital as a condition of limited liability and 112 to 58 to reject reducing the minimum share capital of the GmbH from EUR 25,000: Bachner (2009): 14–15.

24 Enacted 23.10.2008, BGBl I, S 2026, in force from 01.11.2008.

25 GmbHG, § 5a.

26 For legal purposes, however, the firm name must include the slightly awkward '*Unternehmergesellschaft (haftungsbeschränkt)*' or 'UG (*haftungsbeschränkt*)' in full: GmbHG, § 5a, Paragraph 1.

27 For the purposes of this Chapter, the UG will not be discussed in any detail, but interested readers should see Schmidt (2008).

28 MoMiG, article 25, BGBl I, S 2043.

29 Takahashi (2012b): 320. See also Table 4.1 below.

30 Dr Birgit Grundmann held this position (*Staatssekretärin im Bundesministerium der Justiz*), which is equivalent to a Permanent Secretary in the UK system, from 2009 to 2014.

corporate law (at least in Germany) on 2 September 2010.[31] It remains unclear, however, as to what extent responsibility for the decline of the UK Ltd in Germany[32] may be attributed to MoMiG and German corporate law. Other factors, such as growing awareness in Germany of the regulatory and disclosure costs involved in operating foreign-registered entities and closing of legal loopholes, may have played no less important roles.[33]

2 *Legal Aspects*

The GmbH is arguably the first 'modern' close corporation form deliberately designed as such. The five fundamental characteristics of a business corporation recognised in the prevailing comparative corporate law literature are legal personality, limited liability, transferable shares, centralised management under a board structure, and shared ownership by contributors of equity capital.[34] The GmbH diverges from the comparative corporate law paradigm of the business corporation – which is based on public, as opposed to close corporations[35] – in significant ways. Of the five core features, only legal personality[36] and limited liability[37] are fundamental to the GmbH. As to transferability, GmbH membership interests (*not* 'shares'[38]) are transferable by default,[39] but in any event cannot be listed on a stock exchange.[40] As to management structures, although the GmbH is represented by a *Geschäftsführer*[41]

31 In a speech during the Symposium 'Aktuelle Fragen des gewerblichen Rechtsschutzes und des Unternehmensrechts im deutsch-japanischen Rechtsverkehr' held at the Westin Grand in Frankfurt am Main, from 1 to 3 September 2010, as noted by Takahashi (2012b): 321 fn. 45.

32 The number of German branches registered by UK companies from 2011 to 2016 declined steadily from a high of 17,551 in 2010 to 8,968 in 2016: Armour et al. (2017): 232 tbl. 3. The number of branches registered is an imperfect proxy for measuring the number of UK-incorporated businesses that have primary operations in Germany, as not all foreign-incorporated firms comply with the legal requirement to register a branch.

33 Loopholes permitting foreign-registered companies to avoid some onerous German insolvency rules and circumvent the German system of director disqualification were among those closed over the 2000s: Ringe (2013).

34 Armour & Enriques et al. (2017): 5.

35 The authors of *The Anatomy of Corporate Law* were careful to note that '[t]he analysis we offer in this book extends to all these special [i.e. close corporation forms such as the GmbH] and quasi-corporate forms insofar as they display most or all of the core corporate characteristics': Armour & Enriques et al (2017): 16.

36 The GmbH is a juridical (legal) person: GmbHG, § 13, Paragraph 1; Fastrich (2013a): Rdn 4.

37 GmbHG, § 13, Paragraph 2; Fastrich (2013a): Rdn 4.

38 On terminology see I.B.5.

39 By notarial deed: GmbHG, § 15, Paragraph 3.

40 In this respect, GmbH membership interests (*Geschäftsanteile*) are different from shares of an AG (*Aktien*). See Windbichler (2013): § 20 Rdn 3. GmbH membership interests cannot be evidenced by a security instrument (*Wertpapier*): ibid. § 20 Rdn 7.

41 The *Geschäftsführer* may, but need not be a member: GmbHG, § 6, Paragraphs 2–3. The GmbH *Geschäftsführer* must be distinguished from the two types of 'boards'/ 'directors', i.e. managing board/board member (*Vorstand/Vorstandsmitglieder*) and supervisory board/board member (*Aufsichtsrat/Aufsichtsratsmitglieder*), which are mandatory in the 'two-tier' AG. The supervisory board is an optional organ for GmbHs in general: GmbHG, § 52, Paragraph 1. Supervisory boards are mandatory for GmbHs subject to co-determination. See Windbichler (2013): §22 Rdn 19.

(often translated as 'director' or 'managing director') who acts for and on behalf of the GmbH,[42] there is flexibility as to the division of powers between the members as a whole acting in general meeting (*Gesellschafterversammlung*) and the *Geschäftsführer*.[43] It is also common for GmbH members to serve as *Geschäftsführer*.[44] Thus, a GmbH may – but need not – be structured as an entity with centralised management under a board structure. Investor ownership[45] is also not an essential feature as membership status or 'ownership' of the GmbH can be made contingent on a member's continued performance of their additional *personal* obligations (*Nebenleistung*).[46]

Much of the GmbHG comprises default rules that members may deviate from via provision in the corporate constitution (*Satzung*). This feature further differentiates the GmbH from its 'public' counterpart, the stock corporation (*Aktiengesellschaft*, abbreviated 'AG'), which is governed almost exclusively by mandatory rules.[47] As GmbH members enjoy the freedom of private ordering (*Gestaltungsfreiheit* or *Satzungsautonomie*), transferability of GmbH membership interests – a default feature – can be restricted by provision in the corporate constitution.[48]

For readers interested in understanding the GmbH on its own terms, a nodding acquaintance with basic German corporate law concepts and terminology is helpful. The GmbH is an association (*Verein*) and corporation (*Körperschaft*) in the Civil Code sense,[49] and a commercial company (*Handelsgesellschaft*) in the Commercial Code sense.[50] It is classified (together with the AG) as a 'capital-based company' (*Kapital gesellschaft*),[51] as distinguished from the 'person-based company' (*Personengesellschaft*) category which includes the civil law partnership (*Gesellschaft bürgerlichen Rechts*),

42 Windbichler (2013): §22 Rdn 4.

43 The members may by provision in the corporate constitution limit the powers of the *Geschäftsführer*, or even issue binding instructions to the *Geschäftsführer*: GmbHG, § 37, Paragraph 1; Windbichler (2013): §22 Rdn 11. There are some mandatory duties of the *Geschäftsführer*, such as those concerning book-keeping (GmbHG, § 41), observing capital maintenance rules when making distributions (GmbHG, § 43, Paragraph 3), etc.: Windbichler (2013): § 22 Rdn 11.

44 Wedemann (2013): 17–18.

45 As described in Armour & Enriques et al. (2017): 13–15.

46 See (n. 71) below.

47 See GmbHG, § 45 (establishing the freedom of members to make arrangements as to the GmbH's affairs via the corporate constitution); Fastrich (2013a): Rdn 4; Raiser & Veil (2015): § 37 Rdn 1; Windbichler (2013): § 20 Rdn 3. The AG is regulated primarily by the *Aktiengesetz* [AktG], which is an entirely separate statute that establishes, in principle, mandatory rules: AktG, § 23, Paragraph 5.

48 GmbHG, § 15, Paragraph 5.

49 Fastrich (2013a): Rdn 4; Windbichler (2013): § 20 Rdn 2. An 'association' means an entity formed by persons (whether legal or natural), as opposed to property, which would be a foundation (*Stiftung*). See also Schmidt (2002): § 3 I 2 a (using association in the wide sense and corporation synonymously to refer to the category of legal forms that includes but is not limited to associations in the narrow sense, i.e. associations or registered associations).

50 GmbHG, § 13, Paragraph 3; Fastrich (2013a): Rdn 4. This means that the more general Civil Code and Commercial Code provisions and concepts apply to the GmbH where they do not conflict with provisions of the more specific GmbHG or other legislation.

51 Schmidt (2002): § 3 I 2 a. This category also includes the *Societas Europaea* (European Company) (SE) and the *Kommanditgesellschaft auf Aktien* (KGaA): Raiser & Veil (2015): § 1 Rdn 1.

silent partnership (*stille Gesellschaft*), commercial partnership with unlimited liability (*offene Handelsgesellschaft*, abbreviated 'OHG'), and limited partnership (*Kommanditgesellschaft*, abbreviated 'KG').[52]

3 *Economic Importance*

The GmbH is by far the most popular for-profit corporate entity in Germany. As of 1 January 2015, there are 73.58 times as many GmbHs (1,156,434) as AGs (15,716). The GmbH also outnumbers the AG, OHG, and KG combined. While the numbers for both AGs and OHGs have declined, the GmbH experienced moderate growth, with the UG subvariant showing double-digit growth (13.42 per cent) and reaching the 100,000 milestone[53] in 2014. Growth in GmbHs and UGs also translate into growth of KGs, which are commonly structured[54] as a hybrid entity with a corporation (often a GmbH) as the general partner with unlimited liability (*Komplementär*) and styled 'GmbH & Co. KG'.[55] Such a hybrid combines tax transparency and limited liability for natural persons participating in the entity.[56] The KG's growth is attributable to the continued popularity of hybrid forms, and the growth in the corporations that become the general partners in the KG, particularly the GmbH and its 'Mini-Version', the UG.[57]

The GmbH's popularity extends beyond commercial registers. It is also the favourite corporate form for Germany's vaunted SME sector,[59] and strongly associated with

TABLE 4.1 *Selected registered legal entities in Germany*

Entity	GmbH (total)	UG	GmbH (ex. UG)	AG	OHG	KG[1]
2014	1,127,620	92,874	1,034,746	16,005	24,991	249,372
2015	1,156,434	105,341	1,051,093	15,716	24,534	254,013
Growth	2.56%	13.42%	1.58%	1.81%	1.83%	1.86%

Source: based on Kornblum (2015)[58] with figures for GmbH (ex. UG) and growth rates computed
The figure for 2015 is as of 1 January 2015; for 2014, 1 January 2014.
Legend: UG – *Unternehmergesellschaft* (a GmbH subvariant); AG – *Aktiengesellschaft* (stock corporation); OHG – *offene Handelsgesellschaft* (commercial partnership with unlimited liability; KG – *Kommanditgesellschaft* (limited partnership)

[1] The KG figures include '[Corporation] & Co KG' hybrid forms in which the unlimited partner (*Komplementär*) is a corporation: Kornblum (2015): 693. Examples include 'GmbH & Co KG', 'UG & Co KG', and 'AG & Co KG'.

52 Schmidt (2012): § 3 I 2 a.
53 Kornblum (2015): 687.
54 Schulz & Wasmeier (2012): 28–9.
55 On the concept, see Raiser & Veil (2015): § 1 Rdn 5–7. For a comparative analysis of the KG (and GmbH & Co KG) with other limited partnership forms, see Röder (2014).
56 Röder (2014): 153.
57 Kornblum (2015): 688 tbl. 2, 693.
58 Kornblum (2015): 688 tbl. 1.
59 See Fleischer (2016): 24–5; Schulz & Wasmeier (2012): 11. On Germany's SME sector see BMWi (2021).

closely held companies known as *Mittelstand* in the business and economics literature.[60] German SMEs (*kleine und mittlere Unternehmen*, abbreviated 'KMU') occupy a central position in the German economy, accounting for 99.5 per cent of the total number of companies, 78.4 per cent of employees and apprentices, and 61.1 per cent of the net value added by enterprises.[61] Although the average GmbH is much smaller compared to the average AG,[62] the GmbH's overall dominance over the AG in terms of economic impact shows up clearly in the tax statistics. In 2018, the total turnover of the 544,738 GmbHs subject to value-added tax (*Umsatzsteuer*) is, at EUR 2,613.1 billion, 2.845 times that of the 7,777 AGs at EUR 918.5 billion.[63]

With its sheer numbers, status as the favoured business vehicle of Germany's vaunted SME sector, and dominance on multiple economic indicators, it is beyond doubt that the GmbH plays a leading role in the modern German economy, and occupies a pre-eminent position amongst Germany's myriad business entities.

C WITHDRAWAL FOR 'GOOD CAUSE' (*AUSTRITT AUS WICHTIGEM GRUND*)

1 *History*

i Early Judicial Initiatives

The development of member exit by expulsion (*Ausschluss* or *Ausschließung*)[64] and withdrawal (*Austritt*) in the GmbH ran counter to the expectations of the legislator.

60 Lutter (1992): 76 (linking the success of the GmbH to its popularity amongst *mittelständischen Unternehmer* [medium-sized enterprise]); Schulz & Wasmeier (2012): 116 (noting that few German enterprises are listed companies, and most of these, which include the *Mittelstand* companies, are organised as GmbHs). For a historical overview of the *Mittelstand*, see Berghoff (2006).

Strictly speaking, while *Mittelstand* and SMEs (in German: *KMU*) largely overlap, they are defined differently. *Mittelstand* as a concept captures the overlap between management and share ownership, whereas SMEs are defined in terms of employee headcount and turnover. Compare IfM (2021c) (defining a 'mittelständischen Unternehmen' [Mittelstand enterprise] as one in which two or fewer natural persons and their family members hold directly or indirectly at least 50 per cent of the interest in the enterprise, and considering *Mittelstand*, family companies ('*Familienunternehmen*'), and family-run companies ('*familiengeführte Unternehmen*') to be synonymous) with IfM (2021a) (defining SMEs (KMU) as enterprises with fewer than 500 employees and a turnover of up to EUR 50 million, with further definitions for 'small' and 'micro' enterprises).

61 IfM (2021b).

62 There are exceptions. For example, Robert Bosch GmbH is the main entity of a leading industrial conglomerate but takes the GmbH form and is majority owned (92 per cent) by a charitable foundation (the Robert Bosch Stiftung) that has no voting power. Most of the voting rights in Robert Bosch GmbH are held by another entity, Robert Bosch Industrietreuhand KG: Robert Bosch (2019): 21.

63 Destatis (2020): 49 tbl. 4.2. Only entities with turnover of over EUR 17,500 are included: ibid. tbl. 4.2 note 1. GmbH figures exclude the 150,967 GmbH & Co KGs with a total turnover of EUR 1,254.9 billion or the 451 GmbH & Co OHGs with a total turnover of EUR 35.769 billion.

64 Although expulsion is not the focus of this Book, the history of expulsion and withdrawal in German GmbH law are intricately connected, and references are made to expulsion where necessary to advance the narrative.

As the GmbH was originally conceived, it was not intended that a GmbH member would have withdrawal rights. Unilateral withdrawal rights were expressly rejected in the drafter's commentary to the 1891 draft GmbHG,[65] and to this day, the text of the GmbHG still does not reflect the availability of withdrawal.[66] Initially resistant to forms of exit that are not specifically provided for in the GmbHG, the courts also refused to draw on withdrawal and expulsion provisions applicable to commercial partnerships (OHG) in the Commercial Code when resolving cases involving GmbHs.[67] An example of this is a 1920 judgment in which the Imperial Court of Justice, on the basis that concepts from one business form should not be applied to another distinct form, declined to apply by analogy the Commercial Code provision on expulsion of OHG partners.[68]

Later, however, the Imperial Court of Justice in 1930[69] carved out an[70] exception to the principle against withdrawal for GmbHs that imposed additional obligations on its members (*Nebenleistungs-GmbH*).[71] The GmbH at issue was founded, among other things, to produce sugar. Transfer of membership interests was restricted and required approval of the members in general meeting. Further, as a condition of maintaining their membership, members were obligated to supply sugar beets to the company. A member had a falling out with the company and refused to supply sugar beets, upon which the company sued for breach of obligation, and the member sought withdrawal. In a groundbreaking judgment, the Court demonstrated a readiness to apply general principles such as the principle of good faith to the GmbH:

> Permeating the whole of today's private law is the idea that in all relationships featuring a continuing obligation, it should be possible for the obligor to unilaterally terminate the relationship.[72] It ... applies particularly to corporate law, which is especially subject to the principles of good faith.[73] ... The member's right to terminate his[74] firm bond to the GmbH is provided only as the final and ultimate legal remedy, when other ways of severing the bond to the company are impossible due to the financial sacrifice involved,

65 Entwurf (1891): 86.

66 This was notwithstanding two attempts at extensively reforming GmbH law, once under the Nazi regime and once in postwar Germany. See IV.C.1.ii below.

67 HGB, § 132 (withdrawal) and § 140 (expulsion).

68 RG, 07.12.1920, RGZ 101, 55, 55–8. For a summary of the judgment in English, see Scogin (1993): 136–8.

69 RG 07.02.1930, RGZ 128, 1, 16ff.

70 Another early exception recognised by the Imperial Court of Justice was not applicable to GmbHs in general, but only to cartels, in which members had cartel obligations. RG 02.07.1926, RGZ 114, 213.

71 These are GmbHs in which maintenance of member status required not only an initial capital contribution, but also the performance of ongoing obligations to the GmbH. Personal service obligations may be stipulated for in the constitutional document of the GmbH, the *Satzung*. GmbHG, § 3, Paragraph 2. I shall refer to the *Satzung* as 'corporate constitution'.

72 RG 07.02.1930, RGZ 128, 1, 16.

73 RG 07.02.1930, RGZ 128, 1, 16.

74 The non-gender neutral term 'his' is used here as it is a direct translation from the original German.

> and when the continuation of regularly recurring additional obligations of indefinite duration would seriously jeopardise the member's economic advancement.[75]

The judgment was warmly received by Franz Scholz,[76] who argued in an influential 1930 lecture that availability of withdrawal should be extended beyond the *Nebenleistungs-GmbH*.[77] To him, the failure of the GmbHG to provide for a unilateral right of exit was 'perhaps its greatest flaw'.[78] Central to Scholz's argument for the availability of withdrawal was the concept of *wichtiger Grund*, variously translated as 'good cause'[79] or 'substantial basis'.[80] He argued that this concept is recognised across many areas of law as the basis for a party's unilateral right to terminate a long-term relationship,[81] and should also apply to the GmbH.[82] *Wichtiger Grund* remains until today the key, operative concept in withdrawal and expulsion from the GmbH.

ii Abortive Law Reform Efforts

Before long, GmbH member exit became an issue for law reform under the National Socialist regime.[83] Included in the Ministry of Justice's 1939 unpublished draft of a reformed GmbHG (1939 Ministry Draft) were provisions for member withdrawal (section 137) and expulsion (section 136) by court order on the condition that *wichtiger Grund* is established.[84] The official reason for introducing a statutory right of withdrawal was as follows:

> the individual shareholder may also be desirous of exit from the company. Although the [1939 Ministry] Draft accepts, in principle, that the relationship between members should be held together by particularly strong bonds and protected against self-seeking attempts to dissolve it, the Draft must from a minority protection standpoint provide a withdrawal right for the individual member when the majority, abusing its position of power, grossly violates the

75 RG 07.02.1930, RGZ 128, 1, 17.

76 A senior administrative law judge in pre-World War II Prussia, Scholz was an influential legal writer who founded a leading commentary on the GmbHG that still bears his name.

77 Scholz (1930): 21–2.

78 Scholz (1930): 7 (quoting from the 1928 edition of his eponymous GmbHG commentary: 'Es ist vielleicht der großte Mangel im GmbH-G, daß es den einseitigen Austritt nicht geregelt hat').

79 Schmolke adopts this terminology: Schmolke (2012): 385. Compare 'Good cause' in Garner (2014): 'A legally sufficient reason. • Good cause is often the burden placed on a litigant (usu. by court rule or order) to show why a request should be granted or an action excused'.

80 Scogin (1993): 134.

81 Scholz (1930): 4–5 and passim.

82 Scholz (1930): 22.

83 For background on corporate law reform efforts made under the National Socialist regime and their ideological bases, see in German Fleischer (2018b): Rdn 89–98, and in English Scogin (1993): 148–52.

84 For the text of the draft provisions, see Schubert (1985a): 133.

> member's protected interests (section 137). The detriment caused to the individual member by the majority can even be found in circumstances where a course of action is beneficial to the interests of the company as such. For example, accumulation of excessive profits in the reserves may 'starve out'[85] some minority members because they are dependent on returns from their membership interests. However, if it were possible for the minority to bring an action to set aside a majority resolution that oppresses the minority, the minority would in general first need to make use of this means of defence, and can avail itself of the possibility of withdrawal only in extreme cases.[86]

Before long, however, the GmbH reform effort was abandoned in late November 1939 with the start of World War II.[87]

A further attempt at codifying the judicially developed and increasingly accepted exit solutions was made from the 1950s through early 1970s as part of a massive project for the revision of GmbH law. Again, legislative reform efforts would fail to come to fruition. As with the 1939 Ministry Draft, the Ministry of Justice draft bill of 1969 (1969 Ministry Draft) would have introduced a statutory right of withdrawal predicated on *wichtiger Grund*.[88] In terms of both structure and content, the 1969 Ministry Draft was quite similar to the Nazi-era 1939 Ministry Draft.[89] After public consultation and minor changes to the 1969 Ministry Draft, the federal government submitted its draft bill of 1971 (1971 Government Draft) to the 6th Bundestag,[90] but the bill did not secure passage before the legislative session ended prematurely.[91] The version resubmitted after the 1972 West German federal elections (as the 1973 Government Draft) to the 7th Bundestag[92] also did not become law for reasons including the then-raging debate over co-determination, which diverted considerable legislative attention.[93] The first major postwar reform attempt of the GmbH

85 In the original German, *aushungern*.

86 Translated from Schubert (1985a): 192. In contrast to the relatively politically neutral, shareholder protection-oriented tone of the reason for introducing withdrawal, the expulsion right as it was proposed by the Ministry was geared directly at a key political agenda: the expulsion of Jewish persons from the national economy: Schubert (1985a): 192. For an English translation, see Scogin (1993): 152.

87 By order of Reich Ministry of Justice State Secretary Franz Schlegelberger: Schubert (1985b): 90.

88 BMJ (1969): 98–9 (text of proposed section 215), 355–6, 364–5 (official commentary). Expulsion (draft sections 211–14) was also provided for: ibid. 96–8.

89 Fleischer (2018b): Rdn 99. Among the criticisms levelled at the 1969 Ministry Draft was that 'as compared to the 1939 Ministry Draft, it introduced virtually no new ideas and has consequently no claim to originality in content': translated from Schubert (1985b): 91.

90 Entwürfe (1972). The federal government first submitted the draft bill to the Bundesrat in 1971. The withdrawal provision (draft section 211) is at ibid. 58–9.

91 Fleischer (2018b): Rdn 107. Although not elaborated upon by Fleischer, the legislative session ended early because Chancellor Willy Brandt called for snap elections in September 1972 after his Social Democrat-Free Democrat coalition lost its majority in the Bundestag.

92 Enwürfe (1973).

93 Fleischer (2018b): Rdn 107.

thus ended in failure,[94] along with the last serious attempt to introduce withdrawal and expulsion into the law of the GmbH by statute.[95]

iii Maturation by Judicial Effort

With the legislature (both pre- and postwar) consistently and conspicuously unable to act on the subject of member exit, it is not surprising that the German courts stepped up to fill the vacuum. Expulsion for *wichtiger Grund* not restricted to *Nebenleistungs-GmbH* was first recognised in 1942 by the Imperial Court of Justice in a controversial decision[96] that drew heavily on Scholz's writings.[97] The postwar Federal Court of Justice of West Germany also recognised expulsion in its landmark 1953 judgment.[98] Although mentioned only in passing in the 1953 judgment,[99] withdrawal came to be generally known and accepted in the scholarly literature,[100] and was ultimately expressly recognised by the Federal Court of Justice of unified Germany in 1991.[101]

2 *The Concept of* 'wichtiger Grund'

i Doctrinal Bases

Although till present uncodified in legislation,[102] a GmbH member's right to withdraw when a *wichtiger Grund* is established is now settled in the jurisprudence

94 Fleischer (2018b): Rdn 107. Karsten Schmidt speculates that the main reason for the ultimate failure of the 1970s GmbH reform attempt lay in the overtly AG-esque features it adopted in its perfectionistic attitude and image of the GmbH as a flawless corporate form: Schmidt (2002): § 33 II 2 b ('Nicht nur in ihrem [i.e. the draft bills'] Perfektionismus, sondern auch in ihrem Bild von der GmbH als einer lupenreinen Kapitalgesellschaft trugen diese Entwürfe ausgeprägt aktienrechtliche Züge. Das mag ein Hauptgrund für ihr Scheitern gewesen sein').

95 Subsequent major GmbHG reforms in 1980 (referred to as 'GmbH-Novelle 1980' in the literature) and 2008 (MoMiG) did not address the matter of exit. Schubert suggests that because the judiciary had resolved many of the issues outstanding at the time of the 1939 Ministry Draft, the Bundestag Committee on Legal Affairs (*Rechtsausschuss*) greatly reduced the scope of what would be included in the GmbH-Novelle 1980: Schubert (1985b): 91. Although Schubert does not specifically enumerate the issues resolved by the judiciary, it is reasonable to say that withdrawal is a problem that is at least partially solved by the BGH in a landmark 1953 judgment. See (n. 99) below and text thereto.

96 RG 13.08.1942, RGZ 169, 330.

97 As advanced in a revised and expanded 1942 version of his 1930 monograph: Scholz (1942): 18–23. For a summary of the Court's reasoning in English, see Scogin (1993): 144–6.

98 BGH 01.04.1953, BGHZ 9, 157. The reasons will, as appropriate, be introduced in the discussion below.

99 BGH 01.04.1953, BGHZ 9, 157, 162–3.

100 Pre-1991 sources include: Balz (1984a): 105ff; Becker (1985): 16 ff; Röhricht (1991): 361; Scholz (1950): 18ff (the final revised edition of his monograph); Wiedemann (1980): § 7 IV 2 b. This non-exhaustive list does not include earlier editions of some commentaries under different authors cited in this Chapter.

101 BGH 16.12.1991, BGHZ 116, 359.

102 Goette (2014): 97.

and legal literature. However, despite consensus on the *existence* of withdrawal, the *doctrinal foundations* of this remedy have been and remain disputed. Positions advanced include:

(1) by analogy with the right to withdraw from an association (*Verein*[103])[104] or a cooperative (*Genossenschaft*[105]);[106]
(2) the right to resign from a partnership;[107]

103 BGB, § 39 Paragraph 1 (providing that members of associations have the *right* to withdraw), Paragraph 2 (providing that the constitution of the association may provide for restrictions on the right to withdraw by permitting withdrawal only at the end of a financial year or only with a notice period, but that such notice period may not exceed two years).

104 Becker (1985): 18–19 (preferring the technique of a purposive extension of the scope of section 39 para. 1 of the Civil Code (BGB) to using the general concept that long-term legal relationships must be terminable on the basis that the latter is a paraphrase of the former), 78–9 (arguing that although section 39 of the Civil Code is primarily tailored for non-*Kapitalkörperschaft* and therefore neither can nor needs to take into account the particularities connected with the loss of membership in a *Kapitalkörperschaft*, there is no obstacle to applying section 39 to the law of the GmbH if compliance with the intended legal consequences can be ensured either by interpretation of section 39 or by supplementing it with appropriate criteria; as a basis for withdrawal (on a *wichtiger Grund* basis) from the GmbH, section 39 is superimposed by capital maintenance rules and therefore constrained to that extent to a GmbH-compliant interpretation).

Author/translator's note: non-*Kapitalkörperschaft* (*Nicht-Kapitalkörperschaft* in the original text), which may be roughly translated as 'bodies corporate that are not based on capital', is very roughly equivalent to the concept of a corporation that is not used as a business vehicle. Examples would include an incorporated association or a company limited by guarantee (UK). *Kapitalkörperschaft* approximates to business corporation (US) or for-profit company limited by shares (UK).

See also Wolany (1964): 99 (although the GmbH must, in the interests of creditor protection, restrict the right of exit provided for the purpose of protecting individual freedom by the law of associations, for a member who has discharged their basic obligations but who now finds membership to have become an unreasonable burden, withdrawal can be considered as a stopgap solution).

105 A member of a cooperative has the right to resign: GenG, § 65 Paragraph 1.

106 Reuter (1977): 78 (arguing that both section 39 of the Civil Code (BGB) and section 65 of the Cooperatives Act (GenG) supply the basis for withdrawal of a member from the GmbH *as of right*).

107 Wiedemann argues that in companies or partnerships with *Nebenleistung* (i.e. entities in which maintenance of status as a member required ongoing contributions other than in the form of capital) it is impossible to terminate only the *Nebenleistung* relationship; rather, membership status can only be terminated as a whole because there is doubt whether one is intended without the other. Consequently, GmbH members with personal ancillary obligations (*Nebenverpflichtung*) should not only have an extraordinary (*außerordentliche*) right to withdraw, but rather also a right of withdrawal at will based on the right to resign from (*Kündigungsrecht*; may also be translated as a right to 'withdraw' from or 'terminate') a civil-law (non-commercial) partnership in section 723 of the Civil Code but which is subject to the requirement of reasonable notice in section 132 of the Commercial Code: Wiedemann (1965): 91. See further Wiedemann (1980): § 7 IV 2 b (as in his 1965 work, adding that examples of member's personal service obligations that would provide a basis for an ordinary right of withdrawal include a duty to manage the company or a non-compete duty).

(3) the duty of loyalty that attaches to the relationship between a company and its members and between the members inter se (*gesellschaftsrechtliche Treuepflicht*[108]);[109] and
(4) the principle, supported by a leading case[110] and by the plurality of academic opinion, that a long-term relationship with legal obligations (*Dauerschuldverhältnis*) should be terminable.[111]

These doctrinal disagreements did not stop withdrawal on *wichtiger Grund* from developing into a readily identifiable, largely coherent, and generally functional legal institution with a substantial body of jurisprudence and legal literature. It is to the inner, practical workings of this institution that we now turn.

ii General Principles

For the purposes of the non-German or otherwise comparative law-oriented reader, I propose that the concept of '*wichtiger Grund*' in the GmbH withdrawal context be understood as essentially a multifactorial, judicially developed and administered test of 'unreasonableness' or 'unbearableness'.[112] This interpretation is consistent with the highest authorities. According to the Federal Court of Justice:

> A GmbH member is in general allowed the right to exit the GmbH when a good cause (*wichtiger Grund*) exists. This right, as a fundamental principle of the law of associations, is a mandatory, inalienable right of membership.[113]

Prevailing opinion requires that the unilateral withdrawal of a member without the company's consent[114] be possible only if *wichtiger Grund* exists, with no

108 Generally, the positive formulation of a member's duty of loyalty requires that they affirmatively advance the company's interests, and the negative formulation requires that they refrain from anything that would harm the company's interests: Hueck (1947): 18–19; Lutter (1980): 102–20 (with in-depth analysis); Raiser & Veil (2015): § 38 Rdn 33.

A ccording to prevailing opinion, the duty of loyalty does not only exist in relationships with the company, but also as between individual members: BGH 05.06.1975 ('ITT'), BGHZ 65, 15, 18; Merkt (2018): Rdn 98 (describing the ' 'triangle' of the corporate law duty of loyalty', comprising duties of members to the company, the company to its members, and between members inter se) and 101 (although contested for a long time, the existence of a duty of loyalty as between members inter se is now accepted by prevailing opinion); see also Winter (1988): 88ff.

109 Müller (1996): 33.

110 BGH 01.04.1953, BGHZ 9, 157, 162–3.

111 Balz (1984a): 106; Fastrich (2013b): Rdn 1; Röhricht (1991): 371; Schindler (1999): 47; Seibt (2012): Rdn 4; Strohn (2018): Rdn 102; Scholz (1930): 4–6; Teichmann (1970): 238–9; Wiedemann (1965): 89; Winkler (1967): 75.

112 As *wichtiger Grund* is not a concept that applies only to GmbH law, I express no opinion on the concept meaning except as it applies to the GmbH, and specifically in the comparative corporate law context. For another take by a foreign observer, see Scogin (1993): 139ff (contextualising *wichtiger Grund* as a 'general clause' and describing the role of general clauses in German legal history).

113 BGH 16.12.1991, BGHZ 116, 359, 369 (quotations omitted); see also Strohn (2018): Rdn 194.

114 Of course, if the company consents to the member's withdrawal, the situation is different; no *wichtiger Grund* is necessary in such a situation: BGH 18.02.2014, NZG 2014, 541, 542.

exceptions.[115] A *wichtiger Grund* in this context is anything that makes it unbearable (*unzumutbar*) for the member to remain in the GmbH.[116] Whether a *wichtiger Grund* is recognised in any particular case would depend on an overall assessment (*Gesamtabwägung*) of the respective circumstances and interests of the parties involved.[117]

Three general factors are relevant to the overall assessment. The first is the structure of the GmbH at issue. With its structural flexibility, the GmbH form has lent itself as a corporate vehicle suitable for intimate, closely held enterprises characterised by strong personal ties between members despite its design and classification as a capital- (as opposed to person-) based company (*Kapitalgesellschaft*[118]).[119] As discussed above at IV.C.1, it was in the *Nebenleistungs-GmbH*, which incorporates personal obligations other than capital contributions as an integral part of membership and therefore has a strong personalistic character, that withdrawal was first recognised.[120] Although at one time disputed,[121] the majority opinion today is that neither *Nebenleistungs*-obligations nor a personalistic structure in the GmbH are necessary preconditions to the availability of withdrawal.[122] In general, however, the more capital-centric the GmbH, the less likely for a *wichtiger Grund* to be recognised,[123] or the narrower the range of situations recognised as *wichtiger Grund*.[124]

The second general factor is the difficulty in disposing of the membership interest in question. Although the mere legal or factual impossibility of disposing of one's

115 See sources cited in Strohn (2018): Rdn 178 fn. 897. For scholarly attempts to develop a right to withdraw without *wichtiger Grund* see below IV.C.6.

116 Ulmer & Habersack (2014a): Rdn 51; BGH 16.12.1991, BGHZ 116, 359, 369. An alternative way of phrasing the test is '*unreasonable to expect or require* the member to remain in the GmbH'.

117 Balz (1984a): 106–7 (with examples); Fastrich (2013b): Rdn 19–20 (with examples); Müller (1996): 52; Röhricht (1991): 378; Schindler (1999): 52–60 (with examples); Seibt (2012): Rdn 10–13 (with examples); Strohn (2018): Rdn 180; Wiedemann (1965): 91; Sosnitza (2010): Rdn 50.

118 See (nn. 51–52) above and text thereto.

119 Indeed, the GmbH is often called *die personalistiche Kapitalgesellschaft*, a term popularised by Immenga in his *Habilitationsschrift*: Immenga (1970).

120 RG 07.02.1930, RGZ 128, 1 (the seminal sugar company case).

121 Compare Fichtner (1967): 18 (dismissing the possibility that there could be *wichtiger Grund* for withdrawing from a purely capital-based company (*reine Kapitalgesellschaft*); *ie*, a company without *Nebenleistung*) with Immenga (1970): 305 (arguing that since a GmbH member's ability to realise the value of their membership interest is as a practical matter severely limited irrespective of the GmbH's structure, the members' bond must be terminable on *wichtiger Grund*).

122 But see Seibt (2012): Rdn 11 (*Nebenleistung* obligations could be possibly decisive [in favour of permitting withdrawal]).

123 Balz (1984a): 112 (withdrawal for cause is available to all members regardless of the GmbH's structure; GmbH structure is of significance in assessing whether *wichtiger Grund* exists, as it would be more frequently reasonable for a member to remain in a capital-centric GmbH, withdrawal from a personalistic GmbH is by comparison more easily available); Ulmer & Habersack (2014a): Rdn 49 (the capital-centric structure of a GmbH or the lack of *Nebenleistung* does not exclude possibility of withdrawal, but would be taken into consideration).

124 Fastrich (2013b): Rdn 18 (the fact that a member contributes only capital does not exclude the possibility of withdrawal, but could narrow the grounds).

membership interest does not by itself constitute *wichtiger Grund*, they are relevant to the interest-weighing exercise.[125]

A third general factor is fault[126] on the part of the member seeking withdrawal. If fault rests primarily or solely with the member seeking withdrawal, their demand to withdraw can appear unmeritorious or even deemed an abuse of right.[127] It is important to note that, at least according to the prevailing opinion, none of these general factors are in and of themselves determinative of the *wichtiger Grund* issue.

Conversely, an action of the GmbH, on which the member desirous of withdrawal had voluntarily given consent or elected abstention, must be excluded from the overall assessment when determining the existence of *wichtiger Grund*.[128] The right to withdraw, if it arises in the circumstances, should be exercised without delay; the member is not permitted to adopt a 'wait-and-see' approach in response to an act of the company and only take steps to withdraw upon its failure.[129]

We next move onto the factual situations that give rise to *wichtiger Grund*. For ease and clarity of discussion, I organise them into three categories based on classification practices found in the German legal literature.[130]

iii Category I: Behaviour of Other Members (*Verhalten der Mitgesellschafter*)

This is the category where withdrawal most clearly serves as a form of minority protection.[131] Repeated abuse of majority power is a classic example under this

125 Compare Strohn (2018): Rdn 178 (legal or factual impossibility of disposing of membership interest taken into consideration as a factor in favour of allowing withdrawal); with Schindler (1999): 42 (to legal impossibility of transfer or obstruction by the company must be added other circumstances lying with the person of the member or with the company); Ulmer & Habersack (2014a): Rdn 48 (in individual cases of unreasonable hardship, the impossibility in law or in fact of disposing of one's membership interest could be recognised as a *wichtiger Grund* in the person of the member); and Sosnitza (2010): Rdn 49 (the *wichtiger Grund* criterion is flexible enough to acknowledge the particularities of a specific case through its intrinsic balancing requirement; the key question is whether the transfer of one's membership interest is, because of legal or factual reasons, so difficult that it would be unreasonable for the member to remain in the company).

126 Fault is addressed in greater detail below at IV.C.2.iii.

127 Fastrich (2013b): Rdn 19; Ulmer & Habersack (2014a): Rdn 51; Strohn (2018): Rdn 180 (if fault rests primarily or solely with the member seeking withdrawal, their wish to withdraw can appear unmeritorious); Seibt (2012): Rdn 10 (if fault rests primarily or solely with the member seeking withdrawal, their demand to withdraw is generally considered to be an abuse of right).

128 Ulmer & Habersack (2014a): Rdn 51. This exclusion does not apply if the consent or abstention was not voluntary; if the member was compelled to consent or abstain by their duty of loyalty (*Treuepflicht*), withdrawal may still be possible provided that the declaration of intention to withdraw is made without delay: Fastrich (2013b): Rdn 19; see also Seibt (2012): Rdn 13 fn. 2; Müller (1996): 56; Röhricht (1991): 380.

129 Strohn (2018): Rdn 180; Fastrich (2013b): Rdn 19.

130 Authors who broadly adopt this classification include Maximilian Goette, Müller, Strohn, and Ulmer & Habersack. As a preliminary note, the boundaries of these three categories are not set in stone, and my classification – as with those of different German authors – may differ.

131 See Strohn (2018): Rdn 186; Ulmer & Habersack (2014a): Rdn 54 (referring to withdrawal as '*Notbremse*', which translates to 'emergency brake'). Gross violation of the interests of the aggrieved member by other members abusing their majority power would have been the basis for a statutory

category of *wichtiger Grund*.[132] Although individual instances of abuse of majority power may be addressed with alternative legal remedies such as actions to invalidate members' resolutions[133] or a derivative action-equivalent against a wrongdoing member,[134] when the majority's abuses of power are not one-off or isolated events, but rather part of a long-term strategy, it would not be reasonable for the minority member to continuously defend its own interests using these alternatives to withdrawal. In such situations, therefore, notwithstanding the (technical) availability of legal alternatives to the minority member, withdrawal on *wichtiger Grund* may be available.[135] A concrete example would be a freeze-out (*Aushungern*[136]) of the minority. This can take the form of the majority's consistent refusal to distribute profits,[137] or the majority's decision to adopt an earnings retention policy that is unreasonable in the context of the GmbH's financial situation.[138] Another example would be the repeated refusal of the majority to permit the member to transfer or sell their membership interest, although opinion is divided on this point as well.[139]

withdrawal right, as envisioned by legislative reformers and codified as Draft § 137, Paragraph 1 in the 1939 Ministry Draft: Schubert (1985a): 133.

132 Lutter (2012): Rdn 72; Seibt (2012): Rdn 13; Ulmer & Habersack (2014a): Rdn 54; Balz (1984a): 107; Schindler (1999): 57–9; Müller (1996): 63–4; see also Immenga (1970): 305–6.

133 Although the GmbHG does not provide expressly for it, it has been long recognised that this remedy is also available in the GmbH. See RG 09.10.1914, RGZ 85, 311, 313ff; Kübler & Assmann (2006): § 18 V 3d; Fleischer (2014): 63–4.

134 This is known in the German GmbH context as *actio pro socio*. See BGH 14.05.1990, NJW 1990, 2627, 2628; Merkt (2018): Rdn 318ff; Mock (2015): 595–6. For a very general introduction in English, see Roth & Kindler (2013): 129–30.

135 Seibt (2012): Rdn 14; Sosnitza (2010): Rdn 55; Strohn (2018): Rdn 187; Ulmer & Habersack (2014a): Rdn 54; Balz (1984a): 107; Eschenlohr (2000): 139; Röhricht (1991): 382.

136 Note that *Aushungern* is narrower than 'freeze out' in the American sense, as the former refers only to the exclusion of members from financial benefits of membership in the GmbH.

137 By default, disposition of GmbH profits is made pursuant to a resolution of the members: GmbHG, § 29, Paragraph 2.

138 OLG Köln 26.03.1999, NZG 1999, 1222, 1223; Seibt (2012): Rdn 13; Sosnitza (2010): Rdn 52; Becker (1985): 99–107; Müller (1996): 63–4. For a more cautious view, see Fastrich (2013b): Rdn 20 (accepting withdrawal only in the case of a freeze out perpetrated in gross breach of duty); Sosnitza (2010): Rdn 52 (mere fact of insufficient return on the membership interest does not constitute *wichtiger Grund* if the distributions were themselves lawful); Röhricht (1991): 382–3 (ultimately accepting the necessity of the withdrawal remedy in extreme cases). But see OLG München 09.06.1989, GmbHR 1990, 221, 222 (holding that the plaintiff's perception that dividends were too low did not justify withdrawal, and in any event did not cause her unbearable hardship, and had the option of bringing an action to challenge the members' resolution that determined how profits were to be used). Note that it is also open to the aggrieved member to challenge the dividend and reinvestment policy of the GmbH in court; for a discussion on this point in English see Brinkman (2002): 75–6.

139 A GmbH may by its constitution (*Satzung*) provide for transfer restrictions of membership interests: GmbHG, § 15, Paragraph 5. In favour of withdrawal: Lutter (2012): Rdn 72; Strohn (2018): Rdn 188 (on the basis that without good justification, such refusal would be in breach of the majority's duty of loyalty); Wiedemann (1965): 91 (on the basis that no one may undertake to commit one's property to the disposal of the enterprise for an indefinite period of time). For opinions against making withdrawal available in cases of refusal of consent to transfer without more, compare Seibt (2012):

Other wrongful acts of co-members that cause prejudice or harm to a member may also provide the prejudiced member the right to withdraw.[140]

The acquiescence of co-members forming the majority in a shareholders meeting in the face of a member's serious breaches of the duty of loyalty also satisfies the *wichtiger Grund* requirement.[141] Where a GmbH member is confronted with a situation in which another member has behaved in a way liable to expulsion from the GmbH, the member (who is not at fault) has a choice: they can either attempt an action to expel the wrongdoing co-member, or they can withdraw of their own accord. The member has the option to withdraw as it may not be reasonable to expect them to undertake the inconvenience of bringing an expulsion action, and if successful, to continue running the GmbH without the expelled member.[142]

Finally, a serious breakdown in the relationship between the members that makes it unreasonable for the members to continue working together may also give rise to withdrawal rights;[143] this applies even when expulsion or even dissolution of the GmbH are under consideration.[144] Here, fault is an important consideration, although opinion is divided on whether fault on the part of the member desiring withdrawal in causing the breakdown in relations would deny them access to withdrawal outright. One commentator argues that a member responsible for causing the dispute between the members may not resort to withdrawal, although withdrawal and expulsion would be available to the other members.[145] Another commentator takes the view that the difficulty of ascertaining fault in retrospect makes it inappropriate for fault to be the decisive factor in determining the availability of withdrawal, and that it would be sufficient to take fault into consideration as part of the overall assessment.[146]

Rdn 9 (refusal to consent to transfer, even repeated refusals, that are neither arbitrary nor wrongful do not give rise to *wichtiger Grund*); Sosnitza (2010): Rdn 52 (refusal of transfer *per se* not *wichtiger Grund*, but refusal for unrelated reasons, in breach of the principle of equal treatment of members (*Gleichbehandlungsgrundsatz*), significantly disproportionate, or otherwise in bad faith are a different matter), with Müller (1996): 46–51 (providing in-depth analysis of the issues and arguing that the general rule should be that mere refusal to consent to transfer of membership interests does not suffice as *wichtiger Grund*, but an exception would lie where the refusal is wrongful). But see also Eschenlohr (2000): 141 (in the family GmbH context, aggrieved member must bring a legal challenge against a wrongful refusal of permission to transfer, and may not fall back on withdrawal even in the case of failure).

140 Strohn (2018): Rdn 186, 188; see also Goette (2014): 125–8, 130.

141 Lutter (2012): Rdn 72; Sosnitza (2010): Rdn 52; Ulmer & Habersack (2014a): Rdn 54.

142 Strohn (2018): Rdn 186; see also Röhricht (1991): 382.

143 Seibt (2012): Rdn 13; Strohn (2018): Rdn 188; Wolany (1964): 100. See also Sosnitza (2010): Rdn 52 (adding the condition of the non-existence of a requisite majority of the members for the expulsion of disruptive member). Contra Goette (2014): 111 (arguing that where all members contributed to the strife equally and acted in bad faith in a similar way, dissolution is the only appropriate solution).

144 Strohn (2018): Rdn 188.

145 Goette (2014): 111.

146 Müller (1996): 65. See also (n. 127) above and text thereto.

iv Category II: Circumstances of the GmbH (*Verhältnisse der Gesellschaft*)

As a starting point, circumstances of the GmbH that justify dissolution would simultaneously suffice as grounds for withdrawal. This is particularly useful when the member desirous of exit in the circumstances does not meet the 10 per cent ownership threshold required to trigger judicial dissolution.[147] Even if the member in question satisfies the standing requirements for judicial dissolution, there is no reason why they should be denied the option of withdrawal, given that the other members would suffer no prejudice either way the member chooses.[148]

One particular situation that might justify both dissolution and withdrawal would be a complete breakdown in the relationship between members that threatens the viability of the GmbH as a going concern.[149] Similarly, sustained unprofitability of the GmbH over a long period of time may also constitute *wichtiger Grund*,[150] albeit with restrictions. Possible additional requirements include failure of all efforts to salvage the situation and that dissolution of the GmbH is under consideration;[151] that the member desiring withdrawal suffers special hardship due to personal circumstances under conditions that other members are better able to weather;[152] or where there was an element of wrongfulness or bad faith in the majority members' decision not to dissolve the non-performing and commercially unsustainable GmbH, thereby unreasonably locking in the aggrieved member.[153]

Changes in the GmbH's circumstances may have the effect of altering the member's legal or economic position to their detriment. A capital increase conducted without the member's voluntary consent[154] and which subjects the member

147 Strohn (2018): Rdn 182; Ulmer & Habersack (2014a): Rdn 53. The 10 per cent threshold for judicial dissolution is set out in statute: GmbHG, § 61, Paragraph 2.

148 This is a logical inference from a point made by Strohn: see Strohn (2018): Rdn 182 (pointing out that the other members may either continue running the GmbH, or decide to dissolve and liquidate the GmbH with the withdrawn member participating pro rata).

149 Ulmer & Habersack (2014a): Rdn 56. Ulmer & Habersack acknowledge that there is a slight doctrinal difficulty with regards to the overlap. Technically, the *wichtiger Grund* assessment made in the context of judicial dissolution is from the perspective of the GmbH, whereas in withdrawal the perspective taken is the member's: Ulmer & Habersack (2014a): Rdn 56. Although personal circumstances of the member cannot justify dissolution of the GmbH (BGH 01.04.1953, BGHZ 9, 157), a relationship breakdown that threatens the viability of the enterprise, on the other hand, is grounds for dissolution (BGH 23.02.1981, BGHZ 80, 346). Ulmer & Habersack therefore suggest the latter as an example that would bridge the gap: Ulmer & Habersack (2014a): Rdn 56.

150 Görner (2013): Rdn 102; Seibt (2012): Rdn 13; Strohn (2018): Rdn 182.

151 Strohn (2018): Rdn 182.

152 Röhricht (1991): 386 (although in principle circumstances of the GmbH that affect all members equally do not constitute *wichtiger Grund*, the member's special hardship may be taken into consideration in the overall interest weighing exercise).

153 Goette (2014): 115–16 (arguing that the basis for permitting withdrawal in this situation is in the majority's wrongful refusal to dissolve the GmbH). Whether withdrawal is in practice a viable remedy for the member in this situation is in doubt; for a discussion see ibid.

154 A member may be compelled to 'consent' to a capital increase by virtue of their duty of loyalty: BGH 25.09.1986, BGHZ 98, 276, 279ff.

to the risk of pro rata liability to make up any unpaid shortfall,[155] is grounds for withdrawal[156] provided that the prejudiced member takes immediate steps to withdraw.[157] Changes in the basis on which the GmbH is run, such as the purpose of the GmbH,[158] would also give rise to withdrawal rights.[159] Changes need not be in a proper legal form such as a members' resolution to be actionable; any act attributable to the GmbH would suffice.[160] The rationale for withdrawal on such grounds is that a member cannot be expected to continue an investment when the basis upon which the member joined the GmbH, or the GmbH itself was founded, no longer holds.[161] This holds especially true where the GmbH changes its business so as to place itself in competition with the member in question.[162] In similar vein, significant expansion in the GmbH's scope of business or investment with the effect of significantly increasing business risk may also qualify as *wichtiger Grund*.[163] Withdrawal or expulsion of another member,[164] change in the identity of the controlling majority,[165] or shift of the GmbH's administrative seat to a foreign jurisdiction,[166] may also suffice. However, less serious matters such as late presentation of financial statements,[167] errors in the contents of the financial

155 GmbHG, § 24.

156 Fastrich (2013b): Rdn 20; Görner (2013): Rdn 102; Seibt (2012): Rdn 13; Strohn (2018): Rdn 183; Müller (1996): 55–6.

157 LG Mönchengladbach 23.10.1985, NJW-RR 1986, 837, 838; Fastrich (2013b): Rdn 19; Strohn (2018): Rdn 183; Müller (1996): 56.

158 Sosnitza (2010): Rdn 53; Strohn (2018): Rdn 183. The constitution of the GmbH (*Satzung*) must contain the company's objects: GmbHG § 3, Paragraph 1, Number 2.

159 Strohn (2018): Rdn 183; Ulmer & Habersack (2014a): Rdn 53.

160 Strohn (2018): Rdn 183; Röhricht (1991): 380.

161 This is a principle that was developed in the law of the publicly held limited partnership (*Publikums-Kommanditgesellschaft*), but various authors have argued that the same principle should apply to the GmbH: Strohn (2018): Rdn 183; Müller (1996): 53; Röhricht (1991): 379. The 1971 Government Draft's proposed § 211, Paragraph 1, Sentence 2 similarly captures the idea that where a member's 'legal and economic circumstances are altered in an unreasonable way by the company' the member should be entitled to withdraw: Entwürfe (1972): 58.

162 Seibt (2012): Rdn 13; Sosnitza (2010): Rdn 53; Strohn (2018): Rdn 183; Ulmer & Habersack (2014a): Rdn 53; Müller (1996): 54.

163 Lutter (2012): Rdn 73; Strohn (2018): Rdn 183.

164 Strohn (2018): Rdn 183. Although Strohn does not elaborate, he cites Altmeppen, who points out that when a co-member is expelled, the remaining members are personally liable to the expelled co-member for the quantum of their compensation: Altmeppen (2012): 1691. The BGH's landmark 2012 judgment, which held that co-members are liable to a member whose membership interest is involuntarily cancelled (*Zwangseinziehung*), is consistent with Altmeppen's position; see BGH 24.01.2012, BGHZ 192, 236. For details see Strohn (2018): Rdn 174. It stands to reason that the personal liability of the remaining member would be to their detriment and therefore in turn justifies their withdrawal.

165 Seibt (2012): Rdn 13; Sosnitza (2010): Rdn 53; Strohn (2018): Rdn 184; Ulmer & Habersack (2014a): Rdn 53. This concerns the German law on corporate groups (*Konzernrecht*), an extremely complex and well-developed area of corporate law the detailed discussion of which is beyond the scope of this Chapter.

166 Goette (2014): 123.

167 OLG Hamm 28.09.1992, GmbHR 1993, 656, 657; Lutter (2012): Rdn 74; Seibt (2012): Rdn 13; Sosnitza (2010): Rdn 53; Strohn (2018): Rdn 188. The *Geschäftsführer* are required to present annual financial

statements,[168] or disputes between the member and the GmbH over the member's employment relationship with the GmbH, do not, without more, justify withdrawal.[169]

v Category III: Personal Grounds (*Persönliche Gründe*)

In exceptional situations, circumstances that are personal to the member desirous of withdrawal can constitute *wichtiger Grund*. Personal circumstances that are so closely connected to the GmbH that are for all intents and purposes equivalent to the GmbH's own circumstances,[170] or otherwise at least materially connected to the member's continued participation in the GmbH,[171] would seem to suffice. Situations making it extremely difficult for the member to exercise their membership rights or to discharge their membership obligations include a change in residence[172] and severe illness over an extended period.[173]

By contrast, there is controversy over whether circumstances purely within the personal sphere of the member and that are completely irrelevant to the GmbH may constitute *wichtiger Grund*. There is consensus that the member's personal insolvency does not constitute *wichtiger Grund*.[174] However, the authorities are starkly divided on the example most raised in the literature: an urgent need of money that can be met only by liquidating one's membership interest. While some commentators categorically reject this,[175] others are generally in favour,[176] and still others adopt a nuanced approach that hinges on the GmbH's own financial situation.[177] The prevailing uncertainty has led one commentator to conclude that, in general, withdrawal offers hardly any assistance to the minority member in urgent need of

statements to the members without undue delay, and the members must decide by resolution whether to approve the accounts: GmbHG, § 42a, Paragraphs 1 and 2.

168 Lutter (2012): Rdn 74; Seibt (2012): Rdn 13; Sosnitza (2010): Rdn 53; Strohn (2018): Rdn 188.

169 Strohn (2018): Rdn 188.

170 Mäusl (2001): 270–1.

171 Goette (2014): 101; Müller (1996): 65; Seibt (2012): Rdn 10 and 12; Sosnitza (2010): Rdn 50; Wolany (1964): 100.

172 Strohn (2018): Rdn 181; Sosnitza (2010): Rdn 51; Ulmer & Habersack (2014a): Rdn 52 (raising the example of moving one's residence to a non-European foreign country).

173 Müller (1996): 66; Seibt (2012): Rdn 12; Strohn (2018): Rdn 181.

174 Heckschen (2010): 526 (arguing that the risk of the member's personal insolvency should be borne solely by the member's personal creditors); Seibt (2012): Rdn 12; Goette (2014): 106 (arguing that since the right of withdrawal is possibly based on the duty of loyalty applicable only in the intracorporate context, it does not cover third parties such as members' creditors).

175 Fastrich (2013b): Rdn 20; Seibt (2012): Rdn 12; Sosnitza (2010): Rdn 51.

176 Görner (2013): Rdn 102; Lutter (2012): Rdn 72; Ulmer & Habersack (2014a): Rdn 52; Balz (1984a): 107; Schindler (1999): 60.

177 Müller (1996): 66, (provided the payout to the withdrawing member would not breach capital maintenance rules, and there is no other way for the member in question to secure their livelihood but to withdraw, the duty of loyalty owed to the member in question may demand that the company save the member from financial ruin by letting them withdraw); see also Röhricht (1991): 386–7; Strohn (2018): Rdn 181.

money.[178] Finally, opinion on whether divorce between two co-members in a family-owned GmbH could constitute *wichtiger Grund* is divided.[179]

vi Last Resort

Withdrawal on *wichtiger Grund* is accepted by consensus to be the remedy of last resort.[180] Withdrawal is permitted only when no alternative and less drastic method of conflict resolution is available, reasonable, or likely to succeed. Less drastic avenues that should be explored in preference to withdrawal include:

(1) voluntary sale or transfer of membership interests, even at a financial loss; unless the sale price is so low as to be unreasonable, or the GmbH membership interests are subject to transfer restrictions, and it is generally unlikely for the GmbH to approve the transfer to any new third-party transferee;[181]
(2) resorting to contractual rights to withdrawal (at will); unless it is unreasonable to expect the member to comply with contractually stipulated requirements such as a notice period (if any);[182]
(3) commencing legal proceedings to set aside defective members' resolutions;[183] unless the need for recourse to judicial relief arises so many times as to exceed the threshold of reasonableness;[184]

178 Goette (2014): 105.

179 Cf Strohn (2018): Rdn 181 (for) with Goette (2014): 110 (against).

180 BGH 18.02.2014, NZG 2014, 541, 542; OLG München 09.06.1989, GmbHR 1990, 221, 222. Different commentators use different phrases to capture the last resort idea: Fastrich (2013b): Rdn 22 ('*Äußerstes Mittel*'); Görner (2013): Rdn 101 ('*äußerste Mittel*'); Seibt (2012): Rdn 14 ('*Ultima Ratio-Prinzip*'); Sosnitza (2010): Rdn 54–6 ('*Ultima Ratio*'), Strohn (2018): Rdn 109 ('*ultima ratio*') and 189–90 ('*Subsidiarität*'); Ulmer & Habersack (2014a): Rdn 55 ('*letztes und äußerstes Mittel*').

181 Fastrich (2013b): Rdn 22 (financial risk shall be borne by the member when withdrawal is due to the member's personal circumstances, but not when the GmbH's circumstances cause the withdrawal); Seibt (2012): Rdn 14 (a sale price significantly below the purchase price is a question of reasonableness that may be considered in the overall weighing exercise); Sosnitza (2010): Rdn 54 (a member denied permission to transfer membership interest to a particular third party need not seek out another transferee if denial of permission by the members' meeting is based on past practice or other facts and if that attitude is inconceivable); Ulmer & Habersack (2014a): Rdn 55 (the member need not find a transferee if the GmbH's circumstances caused a sale on the free market to fail); Strohn (2018): Rdn 190 (similar to Sosnitza and Ulmer & Habersack, and adding that where co-members deter prospective buyers with their reckless behaviour, this should not be allowed to work in their favour); in similar vein and in greater detail, Röhricht (1991): 383–5 (adding that it may be appropriate in certain circumstances to require the GmbH, not the withdrawing member, to find a buyer and thereby avoid paying the compensation). Contrast Eschenlohr (2000): 141 (for family GmbHs, there should be no resort to withdrawal even in the face of repeated refusals of permission to transfer).

182 Strohn (2018): Rdn 189; Ulmer & Habersack (2014a): Rdn 55.

183 Fastrich (2013b): Rdn 22; Görner (2013): Rdn 101; Seibt (2012): Rdn 14; Sosnitza (2010): Rdn 55; Strohn (2018): Rdn 189.

184 See IV.C.2.ii.

(4) dismissing a *Geschäftsführer* acting in breach of duty;[185] and
(5) terminating,[186] or, where termination is impossible, modifying[187] the personal ancillary obligation (*Nebenleistung*) that has become unreasonably onerous to perform.

However, dissolution and expulsion of a co-member are not considered measures less extreme than withdrawal;[188] their availability as alternatives does not deprive the aggrieved member of their option to withdraw.[189]

vii Modification by Agreement

On the issue of withdrawal, GmbH members may include provisions in the corporate constitution (*Satzung*) that deviate from the default rules.[190] However, there are limits to their ability to do so, as withdrawal on *wichtiger Grund* is a fundamental, mandatory right.[191] Although it may be possible to provide that certain factual circumstances would not suffice as *wichtiger Grund*,[192] withdrawal cannot be entirely excluded[193] or otherwise practically and substantially curtailed, or its exercise made more difficult.[194]

On the other hand, it is open to GmbH members to provide for additional grounds for withdrawal in the corporate constitution beyond those recognised as *wichtiger Grund* in the jurisprudence and literature.[195] They may even include a general right to withdraw at will (*ordentliches Austrittsrecht*) – notwithstanding that it

185 Görner (2013): Rdn 101; Seibt (2012): Rdn 14; Sosnitza (2010): Rdn 55; Strohn (2018): Rdn 189.

186 Fastrich (2013b): Rdn 22; Görner (2013): Rdn 101; Sosnitza (2010): Rdn 55.

187 Prevailing opinion holds there is no right to terminate only the personal ancillary obligation and not the overall relationship between the GmbH member and the GmbH: Strohn (2018): Rdn 181. However, even if the personal ancillary obligation cannot be lawfully terminated, the member must nonetheless attempt to seek amendment or waiver of the obligation: Strohn (2018): Rdn 189.

188 Görner (2013): Rdn 101; Sosnitza (2010): Rdn 56; Strohn (2018): Rdn 189; Ulmer & Habersack (2014a): Rdn 56.

189 Fastrich (2013b): Rdn 22; Sosnitza (2010): Rdn 56; Müller (1996): 84 (withdrawal should generally take priority over dissolution); Ulmer & Habersack (2014a): Rdn 56 (withdrawal should take priority over dissolution, except when the financial consequences of withdrawal threaten the withdrawing member's ability to enforce their entitlement to their compensation, or when the other members expressly choose to dissolve the GmbH).

190 This follows from the general freedom of members to regulate matters of the GmbH by provision in the corporate constitution; see GmbHG, § 45, Paragraph 1 and § 53.

191 BGH 16.12.1991, BGHZ 116, 359, 369; Strohn (2018): Rdn 194; Ulmer & Habersack (2014a): Rdn 46.

192 Seibt (2012): Rdn 24; Strohn (2018): Rdn 194; see also Sosnitza (2010): Rdn 67.

193 Fastrich (2013b): Rdn 27; Sosnitza (2010): Rdn 66; Strohn (2018): Rdn 194; Ulmer & Habersack (2014a): Rdn 68.

194 Fastrich (2013b): Rdn 27; Sosnitza (2010): Rdn 66; Strohn (2018): Rdn 194 (no unjustifiable restrictions); Ulmer & Habersack (2014a): Rdn 68.

195 Fastrich (2013b): Rdn 27; Seibt (2012): Rdn 24; see also Sosnitza (2010): Rdn 67.

is not a recognised right in the general law of GmbH[196] – plus attending restrictions in the corporate constitution.[197]

3 *Effect of Withdrawal*

The withdrawal process comprises two steps: the declaration of withdrawal (*Austrittserklärung*), and the payment of compensation (*Abfindung*). To begin the process, a unilateral,[198] unconditional,[199] declaration of withdrawal addressed to the GmbH[200] by the member will suffice. For this declaration, there is neither a prescribed form[201] nor a need to commence a formal action in court.[202] The declaration becomes effective the moment it is received[203] by the GmbH,[204] or more specifically, the *Geschäftsführer* representing the GmbH.[205] Once the declaration takes effect, it becomes irrevocable[206] except with consent of the GmbH.[207] The declaration in and of itself does not complete the member's exit from the GmbH.[208] It merely creates for the member – provided *wichtiger Grund* is present – the right to claim compensation (*Abfindung*) against the GmbH in exchange for either the cancellation (*Einziehung*) of the member's membership interest, or its assignment

196 At least according to prevailing opinion: Lutter (2012): Rdn 70; Strohn (2018): Rdn 178, 230. See IV. C.6 for more discussion.

197 Lutter (2012): Rdn 70 and 81 (restriction in compensation quantum); Seibt (2012): Rdn 24 (suggesting restrictions in the form of a notice period or suspension of membership rights immediately upon the member's declaration of withdrawal); Sosnitza (2010): Rdn 68 (prescriptions as to form of valuation techniques) Strohn (2018): Rdn 195 (restrictions on when withdrawal can be exercised) and 230 (restriction on compensation quantum). Specific possible contractual modifications to the default rules are discussed below; on membership rights and obligations, see IV.C.3; on valuation of compensation, see IV.C.4; on enforcement, see IV.C.5.

198 '*einseitige*': Ulmer & Habersack (2014a): Rdn 57; Immenga (1970): 312; Müller (1996): 87.

199 '*bedingungsfeindliche*': Seibt (2012): Rdn 16; Sosnitza (2010): Rdn 58; Strohn (2018): Rdn 197; Ulmer & Habersack (2014a): Rdn 57; Müller (1996): 87.

200 Fastrich (2013b): Rdn 24; Ulmer & Habersack (2014a): Rdn 57; Müller (1996): 87.

201 Lutter (2012): Rdn 75; Seibt (2012): Rdn 16; Müller (1996): 87; Görner (2013): Rdn 108 (adding that declaration can be oral, but recommends it to be in writing and bundled with the GmbH's acknowledgment of receipt); Sosnitza (2010): Rdn 58 (similar to Görner, pointing out that the withdrawing member bears the burden of proof); Strohn (2018): Rdn 197 (declaration should be in writing for evidential purposes).

202 Strohn (2018): Rdn 197; Ulmer & Habersack (2014a): Rdn 57; Immenga (1970): 312; Müller (1996): 87. Contra Schwerdtner (1976): 106; Wiedemann (1965): 92.

203 There is no need for the declaration to be formally 'accepted': Görner (2013): Rdn 108.

204 Schmidt (2002): § 35 IV 3 c (using the term '*empfangsbedürftige*', which is used to refer to declarations of intent (*Willenserklärungen*) that must be received by the addressee to become effective); Müller (1996): 87 (same).

205 Görner (2013): Rdn 108; Sosnitza (2010): Rdn 58; Strohn (2018): Rdn 197; Müller (1996): 87.

206 OLG Köln 21.05.1996, GmbHR 1996, 609, 610; Seibt (2012): Rdn 16; Ulmer & Habersack (2014a): Rdn 57; Bacher & von Blumenthal (2008): 406. The declaration, however, can be set aside for mistake under general Civil Code principles: Seibt (2012): Rdn 16; Sosnitza (2010): Rdn 58; see BGB, § 119ff.

207 Görner (2013): Rdn 108; Sosnitza (2010): Rdn 58; Strohn (2018): Rdn 197.

208 Strohn (2018): Rdn 198; Ulmer & Habersack (2014a): Rdn 56.

(*Abtretung*) to another party[209] at the GmbH's choice.[210] The member's exit is completed upon the cancellation or assignment of their membership interest.[211] The GmbH is required either to pay compensation to the withdrawing member directly or arrange for a third party assignee of the membership interest to pay.[212]

Given that the member cannot complete the withdrawal process without the GmbH's cooperation, issues arise as to the status of the member's rights and duties during the 'limbo' period between the declaration of withdrawal and completion of exit. In principle, until their membership interest is lost by cancellation or assignment, the member in question remains a full member of the GmbH,[213] albeit with some restrictions. Exercise of withdrawing members' voting rights is restricted to the extent necessary to secure their economic interests: the right to compensation from the GmbH.[214] As to income rights, opinion is divided on whether the member may share in profit distributions declared after the declaration of withdrawal was received.[215]

Duties of the member connected with the status of membership in the GmbH remain generally applicable,[216] although there are exceptions relating to *Nebenleistungen*. Where the member has elected to withdraw from the GmbH because of *Nebenleistungen* that have become an unreasonable burden, it may be

209 Sosnitza (2010): Rdn 59; Strohn (2018): Rdn 198; Ulmer & Habersack (2014a): Rdn 56.

210 Fastrich (2013b): Rdn 24; Seibt (2012): Rdn 19; Sosnitza (2010): Rdn 59 and 63; Strohn (2018): Rdn 198; Ulmer & Habersack (2014a): Rdn 59.

211 Strohn (2018): Rdn 201.

212 Strohn (2018): Rdn 202.

213 BGH 26.10.1983, BGHZ 88, 320, 325; BGH 30.11.2009, NJW 2010, 1206, Rdn 17; Fastrich (2013b): Rdn 26; Lutter (2012): Rdn 75; Seibt (2012): Rdn 17; Strohn (2018): Rdn 198 and 200; Müller (1996): 94–5; Balz (1984b): 1866; Heidinger & Blath (2007): 1188; Wellhöfer (1994): 216–17. Contra Immenga (1970): 312; Esch (1981): 27–8; Fichtner (1967): 18.

214 BGH 26.10.1983, BGHZ 88, 320, 325–6; BGH 30.11.2009, NJW 2010, 1206, Rdn 17; Fastrich (2013b): Rdn 26; Görner (2013): Rdn 111; Lutter (2012): Rdn 75; Seibt (2012): Rdn 17; Strohn (2018): Rdn 198; Ulmer & Habersack (2014a): Rdn 60. See also Blath (2012): 663 (opining that the 2009 BGH judgment [NJW 2010, 1206] had, insofar as voice rights are concerned, the effect of reversing the rule and the exception, such that post-declaration of withdrawal, voice rights may be (exceptionally) exercised only when the member's interest in their compensation claim is concerned). Information rights (GmbHG, § 51a) are relevant to the member's ability to protect their interest in the compensation claim, and are therefore left untouched: Ulmer & Habersack (2014a): Rdn 61.

215 For: Seibt (2012): Rdn 17; Sosnitza (2010): Rdn 65; Strohn (2018): Rdn 199 (but offsetting interest on the compensation claim against profits received); Müller (1996): 95–6; Balz (1984b): 1867. Against: Ulmer & Habersack (2014a): Rdn 61 and 65; Becker (1985): 187–8. See also Görner (2013): Rdn 111 (no claim to profits if share of profits is already taken into consideration in the compensation).

216 Strohn (2018): Rdn 200. This is especially true of claims of the GmbH against the member that are ultimately for the purpose of creditor protection and therefore mandatory: Ulmer & Habersack (2014a): Rdn 62; see also Strohn (2018): Rdn 200 (making special mention of the duty of every member to contribute pro rata to make up any shortfall from the sale of the membership interest of another member who failed to fulfil their capital contribution obligation pursuant to GmbHG, § 24 and the duty of members under GmbH, § 31, Paragraph 3 to make pro rata reimbursement to creditors of sums distributed in breach of capital maintenance rules to the extent necessary for the creditors' satisfaction).

necessary, having regard to all the circumstances, to release the member from those obligations.[217] A non-competition clause intended to be effective so long as membership status is maintained may cease to have effect if exit would have been completed but for a dispute over the compensation quantum.[218] In such cases, the non-competition clause will take effect from the time of the declaration of withdrawal and not the time of completed exit.[219]

Absent specific constitutional provisions to the contrary, the member's overall legal position until payment of compensation is a 'floating' one subject to a condition subsequent: the member's membership rights would revive and their power to dissolve the GmbH would arise, when the compensation cannot be lawfully paid[220] and no other members are willing to acquire the membership interest.[221] However, as with *wichtiger Grund*,[222] members are free to depart from the default legal position by provision in the corporate constitution,[223] so long as such arrangements do not constitute an unreasonable restriction of the withdrawal right.[224] Examples of permissible alternative arrangements include making the exit legally effective and suspending or restricting membership rights and obligations immediately upon receipt of the declaration to withdraw, and stipulations as to the method by which the membership interest would be surrendered to the GmbH.[225]

As the responsibility for paying the compensation lies with the GmbH[226] or upon the party undertaking to acquire the membership interest,[227] the members remaining in the GmbH are not personally liable to the withdrawing member.[228] This creates enforcement difficulties which I discuss in greater depth below.[229] For now, we turn to the issue of money: how much compensation should be paid?

[217] Strohn (2018): Rdn 200; Ulmer & Habersack (2014a): Rdn 62; see also Sosnitza (2010): Rdn 65; Balz (1984a): 117; Müller (1996): 97–8.

[218] Strohn (2018): Rdn 200; Ulmer & Habersack (2014a): Rdn 62 (observing that to reason otherwise would conflict with the mandatory nature of the withdrawal regime); see also BGH 30.11.2009, NJW 2010, 1206, Rdn 12–6.

[219] Strohn (2018): Rdn 200.

[220] On capital maintenance see IV.C.5.

[221] Ulmer & Habersack (2014a): Rdn 62.

[222] See IV.C.2.vii.

[223] Fastrich (2013b): Rdn 27; Strohn (2018): Rdn 203; Ulmer & Habersack (2014a): Rdn 68.

[224] Fastrich (2013b): Rdn 27; Strohn (2018): Rdn 203.

[225] Fastrich (2013b): Rdn 27; Strohn (2018): Rdn 203; Ulmer & Habersack (2014a): Rdn 68.

[226] See (n. 212) above and text thereto.

[227] Strohn (2018): Rdn 206 (adding that in this situation, the GmbH retains secondary liability).

[228] Fastrich (2013b): Rdn 24; Lutter (2012): Rdn 77; Seibt (2012): Rdn 22; Ulmer & Habersack (2014a): Rdn 49. But see Strohn (2018): Rdn 207 (suggesting that the remaining members are in fact indirectly liable, insofar as the compensation claim becomes a liability on the balance sheet of the GmbH and therefore impacts the extent to which profits may be legally distributed to the remaining members).

[229] At IV.C.5.

4 Valuation

i Default Position

As a starting point, the compensation is valued at the full market value (*Verkehrswert*) of the membership interest surrendered.[230] Although there are no precise rules laid out in statute, several general principles on valuation have emerged from the literature and judicial precedent, including the Federal Court of Justice's landmark 1991 decision confirming the existence of the withdrawal remedy.

First, the valuation of the membership interest should not be based on the interest itself, but rather on the GmbH as a whole, specifically on the actual value of the GmbH as a going concern, which would include hidden reserves and possibly goodwill.[231] This is generally the price that a third party would pay to acquire the enterprise as a whole,[232] and must in principle be proved by expert evidence.[233] The court has discretion on which valuation standard to apply.[234] As a general default, the (then-) prevailing earnings method (*Ertragswertmethode*) would apply,[235] but in exceptional cases, the net asset value method (*Substanzwertmethode*) may also be used where necessary.[236] The well-established *Ertragswert* method is similar to, but differs slightly from the internationally recognised discounted cash flow method.[237]

Exceptional cases in which the net asset value approach would apply include: (1) a business with weak earnings and in which the break-up value of the enterprise surpasses its *Ertragswert*; (2) a holding company whose activities are limited to the management of equity investments; and (3) a business involved in activities such as freelancing, in which the earnings potential depends on the participation of specific members and would evaporate with the departure of such members.[238] Opinion is divided[239] on whether the liquidation value (*Liquidationswert*), which is the sum of

230 This is uncontroversial: BGH 01.04.1953, BGHZ 9, 157, 168; OLG Köln 26.03.1999, Neue Zeitschrift für Gesellschaftsrecht [NZG] 1999, 1222, 1224; BGH 16.12.1991, BGHZ 116, 359, 370; Fastrich (2013b): Rdn 25; Lutter (2012): Rdn 78; Sosnitza (2010): Rdn 61; Ulmer & Habersack (2014a): Rdn 64.

231 BGHZ 116, 359, 370.

232 BGHZ 116, 359, 370; see also Ulmer & Habersack (2014b): Rdn 77.

233 BGHZ 116, 359, 371; Lutter (2012): Rdn 79.

234 BGHZ 116, 359, 371.

235 BGHZ 116, 359, 371; Strohn (2018): Rdn 209; Ulmer & Habersack (2014b): Rdn 77.

236 BGHZ 116, 359, 371; Ulmer & Habersack (2014b): Rdn 77.

237 On the *Ertragswertmethode*, see Strohn (2018): Rdn 210. On differences between the two methodologies, see sources cited in Ulmer & Habersack (2014b): Rdn 77 fns 263–264. Until 2000, the Institute of Public Auditors in Germany (*Institut der Wirtschaftsprüfer in Deutschland*) (IDW) recognised only the *Ertragswert* methodology, but they have since 2000 included DCF on an equal footing with *Ertragswert*: Nestler & Kupke (2003): 163.

238 Ulmer & Habersack (2014b): Rdn 77; see also Strohn (2018): Rdn 212 (adopting a narrower position with respect to the applicability of this valuation method).

239 Compare Strohn (2018): Rdn 214 (liquidation value should be the floor only when either the member has, by virtue of the size of their membership interest, the power to compel liquidation, or when a liquidation is in fact planned but foiled by the remaining members acting wrongfully in refusing to consent to it) with Lutter (2012): Rdn 79 (liquidation value of relevance only when a corporate asset is

the realisable value of individual assets less the cost of liquidation,[240] should be the floor for valuation.

The membership interest's value is the enterprise value multiplied by the percentage represented by the membership interest of the total.[241] Transfer restrictions on GmbH membership interests affecting all members equally should not result in any valuation discount,[242] but if necessary, particularities attached to a particular member's membership interest may be taken into consideration via an individual premium or discount.[243] The valuation date (*Bewertungsstichtag*) is the date of receipt of the member's declaration of withdrawal.[244]

ii The Limits of Provision by Agreement

GmbH members may in principle include in the corporate constitution (*Satzung*) provisions deviating from the default position on valuation matters.[245] Valuation methods generally regarded as less suitable for business valuation may nonetheless be provided for by agreement; examples include asset value (*Substanzwert*)[246] and book value (*Buchwert*).[247] Contractual provisions reducing the compensation (*Abfindung*) quantum are permissible on bases such as ensuring the GmbH's continued existence after member withdrawal by reducing outflow of capital and simplification of the valuation process.[248]

However, this freedom to contract is not without its limits. Given withdrawal on *wichtiger Grund*'s mandatory nature,[249] valuation clauses are subject to the general Civil Code rule[250] that legal transactions contrary to public policy are unenforceable.[251] In general, no contractual provision with the effect of eliminating or unduly restricting withdrawal is permissible.[252] Withdrawal is unjustifiably restricted when the compensation quantum, as calculated pursuant to contractual provisions designed to

in fact liquidated or there is an obligation, owed to the party entitled to compensation, to liquidate assets). For details see sources cited in Strohn (2018): Rdn 214.

240 Strohn (2018): Rdn 214.

241 Ibid. Rdn 208.

242 Ibid.

243 Ibid. (citing the possibility that a 'Package Premium' (*Paketzuschlag*), or in Anglo-American terms, a control premium, may be justified for a majority stake).

244 Fastrich (2013b): Rdn 25; Seibt (2012): Rdn 22; Sosnitza (2010): Rdn 61; Strohn (2018): Rdn 215; Ulmer & Habersack (2014a): Rdn 65; Müller (1996): 106.

245 This follows from the general freedom of members to regulate matters of the GmbH by provision in the corporate constitution; see GmbHG, § 45, Paragraph 1 and § 53.

246 Strohn (2018): Rdn 212.

247 Ibid. Rdn 213.

248 BGH 16.12.1991, BGHZ 116, 359, 368.

249 Ulmer & Habersack (2014a): Rdn 66.

250 BGB, § 138.

251 BGH 16.12.1991, BGHZ 116, 359, 368. For detailed analysis of this topic in English, see Schmolke (2012).

252 Strohn (2018): Rdn 227; Ulmer & Habersack (2014a): Rdn 66.

limit the quantum, is significantly disproportionate (i.e. much less) as compared to the full market value (*Verkehrswert*) of the membership interest in question.[253]

There are no bright line rules in judicial review of valuation provisions; the assessment considers all the circumstances.[254] A valuation clause providing for book value as the basis for valuation is generally unproblematic.[255] However, only under exceptional circumstances will the complete exclusion,[256] or the reduction in the compensation quantum by half of the book value of the GmbH,[257] be justified. An example of exceptional circumstances would be where the membership interest is granted to the member as an employee's or manager's incentive. In such a situation, it is permissible to restrict the compensation quantum to the amount paid by the member for their membership interest; where the membership interest is awarded gratis, compensation may be eliminated entirely.[258]

It is contested as to whether a valuation provision governing compensation quantum is subject to the same degree of judicial scrutiny when invoked in a case of withdrawal on *wichtiger Grund* when the provision does not expressly refer to such a scenario. Some prefer to apply valuation clauses broadly to all types of member exit;[259] others make distinctions based on the type of exit – such as withdrawal on *wichtiger Grund* versus involuntary cancellation (*Einziehung*)[260] – or even between different categories of *wichtiger Grund*.[261] A contractual provision found to be unlawful is unenforceable, and the withdrawing member is entitled to the full market value of their membership interest.[262]

5 *Enforcement*

Three issues arise in enforcement. First is where the GmbH disputes the existence of *wichtiger Grund*. In such cases, it falls upon the member desirous of withdrawal to

253 BGH 16.12.1991, BGHZ 116, 359, 369; Strohn (2018): Rdn 227.

254 Strohn (2018): Rdn 227 (also adding that the assessment is based on the circumstances at the time of the agreement's (*Satzung*) formation).

255 Ibid. Rdn 227.

256 Ibid. Rdn 227–228; BGH 29.04.2014, NZG 2014, 820, 822 (holding that a contractual provision that excludes all compensation in a situation where a member's interest is involuntarily cancelled on the ground of (gross) breach of duty is wrongful, and is in principle not permitted as a contractual penalty).

257 Ibid. Rdn 227.

258 Ibid. Rdn 228.

259 Ulmer & Habersack (2014a): Rdn 64 (arguing that the valuation clause should govern withdrawal on *wichtiger Grund* when in doubt).

260 OLG Köln 26.03.1999, NZG 1999, 1222, 1224 (on the basis that the regulation of valuation clauses is oriented towards the interests of the GmbH in the involuntary cancellation context, but towards the interests of the withdrawing member in the withdrawal on *wichtiger Grund* scenario).

261 Schindler (1999): 75 (arguing that a valuation clause with the effect of restricting compensation should not have effect where the *wichtiger Grund* lies in the behaviour of other members [Category I in this Chapter] or the circumstances of the company [Category II]).

262 Lutter (2012): Rdn 86; Ulmer & Habersack (2014b): Rdn 110.

commence an action for payment of the compensation (*Zahlungsklage*), and in connection with that, seek a judicial finding on the *wichtiger Grund* issue.[263]

Second is where the GmbH is, because of a legal obstacle, unable to pay the compensation quantum lawfully, even if it might otherwise be willing to. Although withdrawal can be an informal process that can be initiated and concluded entirely without judicial intervention,[264] one primary obstacle stands in the way of private resolution of withdrawal matters without judicial involvement and of effective enforcement of withdrawal: capital maintenance.

Capital maintenance is a critically relevant GmbHG mandatory regime because it is the GmbH that is liable to pay compensation to the departing member.[265] Essentially, distributions to members may only be lawfully made from GmbH assets that are in excess of its registered capital (*Stammkapital*).[266] Although the mandatory minimum registered capital for the GmbH is EUR 25,000,[267] it is up to the members to decide any amount above the statutory minimum. Consequently, a withdrawing member with a sizeable membership interest in a GmbH with a registered capital significantly above the statutory minimum faces the non-negligible risk that the compensation quantum may exceed the distributable limit.[268] In such cases, the member's attempt at withdrawal cannot be lawfully executed.[269]

When the GmbH cannot lawfully pay the compensation from its own funds, it may arrange for a remaining member or a third party to purchase the withdrawing member's interest.[270] This theoretical possibility may nonetheless be cold comfort for the withdrawing member if no one steps up. The withdrawing member has no right to compel the purchase of their membership interest by any particular member or third party.[271] Nor do they have a right to claim the compensation quantum from the remaining members.[272] Instead, the withdrawing member has recourse only to remedies against the GmbH, namely judicial dissolution,[273] albeit exempt from the 10 per cent ownership share requirement[274] and the GmbHG's statutory dissolution grounds.[275] Opinion is divided on whether judicial dissolution is also available if the GmbH can lawfully pay the compensation, but fails to do so within a reasonable

263 Sosnitza (2010): Rdn 60; Strohn (2018): Rdn 204; Ulmer & Habersack (2014a): Rdn 57.

264 Strohn (2018): Rdn 204.

265 See (nn. 209–210, 212) above and text thereto.

266 See GmbHG, § 30, Paragraph 1.

267 GmbHG, § 5, Paragraph 1.

268 This is regardless of the GmbH's actual financial position. Even an asset-rich GmbH would not be able to distribute much to the members if the registered capital is also very high.

269 Sosnitza (2010): Rdn 57; Ulmer & Habersack (2014a): Rdn 49.

270 Seibt (2012): Rdn 20.

271 Ibid.; Strohn (2018): Rdn 206; Ulmer & Habersack (2014a): Rdn 49.

272 Fastrich (2013b): Rdn 24; Lutter (2012): Rdn 77; Seibt (2012): Rdn 22; Ulmer & Habersack (2014a): Rdn 49. But see Strohn (2018): Rdn 207 (suggesting that the remaining members are indirectly liable).

273 Fastrich (2013b): Rdn 23; Sosnitza (2010): Rdn 60; Strohn (2018): Rdn 204; Grunewald (1991): 187.

274 GmbHG, § 61, Paragraph 2, Sentence 2.

275 GmbHG, § 61, Paragraph 1; Seibt (2012): Rdn 21; Strohn (2018): Rdn 204; Ulmer & Habersack (2014a): Rdn 56; Müller (1996): 121.

time. Some favour enforcement by dissolution;[276] others insist that the action for payment takes precedence over dissolution.[277]

The third issue concerns the limits of ex ante contracting in the withdrawal enforcement context. The members may, by appropriate constitutional provisions, impose a duty on specific members to purchase the membership interests of withdrawing members,[278] or require the GmbH to dispose of the withdrawing member's interest by a specific method.[279] There are suggestions that disputes over the requirements and consequences of withdrawal may, by agreement, be made subject to arbitration.[280]

6 *The Debate over Withdrawal: General At-Will Right or Extraordinary Remedy upon Grounds?*

The wide availability of withdrawal – of even the at-will variant – in German business entities may surprise the foreign observer. All corporate forms except capital-based companies[281] have withdrawal at will;[282] the AG has no withdrawal remedy whatsoever.[283] With its institution of withdrawal but only for good cause, the GmbH now straddles the gulf between these two positions. Yet in GmbH law's long history, arguments have been advanced from time to time in favour of withdrawal at will for the GmbH,[284] including at the premier forum of the German legal world, the German Jurists Forum (*Deutscher Juristentag*).[285]

i The Case for and against Withdrawal at Will

The arguments for withdrawal *at will* are classifiable into the following three doctrinal bases. First, the general principle in the law of obligations that all legal relationships of long-term or indefinite duration, regardless of the specific corporate form at issue, should be terminable. This view draws support from the law of silent

276 BGH 26.10.1983, BGHZ 88, 320, 326; Fastrich (2013b): Rdn 24; Lutter (2012): Rdn 77; Ulmer & Habersack (2014a): Rdn 59.
277 Seibt (2012): Rdn 21; Sosnitza (2010): Rdn 60; Müller (1996): 122; Grunewald (1991): 187 fn. 24.
278 Ulmer & Habersack (2014a): Rdn 68.
279 Fastrich (2013b): Rdn 27; Strohn (2018): Rdn 203; Ulmer & Habersack (2014a): Rdn 68.
280 Strohn (2018): Rdn 204 (by analogy with expulsion).
281 Namely GmbH, AG, and *Kommanditgesellschaft auf Aktien* (KGaA): Schmidt (2002): § 3 I 2 b. As of 1 January 2015 there were only 294 registered KGaA in Germany: Kornblum (2015): 688 tbl. 1. The KGaA is therefore for practical purposes mostly irrelevant.
282 Roitzsch (1981): 92 (observing that all corporate forms except capital-based companies have withdrawal at will); Hofmann (2011): 500 (observing that all person-based companies (*Personengesellschaften*) have withdrawal at will that cannot be completely excluded).
283 Hofmann (2011): 484. See also ibid. 525–9 (arguing for expansion of AG shareholder exit rights). Other forms of 'exit' rights such as appraisal in certain defined situations exist for AGs, are beyond this Book's scope.
284 See Goette (2014): 248–56 (offering concise summaries).
285 Reuter (1984): B66. On the German Jurists Forum, see (n. 23) above.

partnerships (*stille Gesellschaft*) and commercial partnerships (OHG),[286] the Civil Code, and the law of cooperatives.[287]

The second basis supporting withdrawal at will applies only to GmbHs where transfer of membership interests is not as of right, but rather subject to GmbH approval. This position finds sympathy in judicial precedent.[288] Making the case for withdrawal at will requires circumventing the historic legislator's intention that termination of membership status – and corresponding withdrawal of one's investment – must be exclusively by transfer of membership interest. One line of argument goes that this circumvention is permissible because the legislator's basic premise – that GmbH membership interests are transferable – simply does not apply in GmbHs with transfer restrictions.[289] The argument for withdrawal at will may be further extended to situations in which the member's attempts to transfer their membership interest fail due to factual, as opposed to legal, circumstances.[290]

The third type of argument for withdrawal at will is specifically limited to GmbH members subject to personal ancillary obligations (*Nebenleistungen*[291]). The reasoning is as follows.[292] Since there is doubt whether either the membership status or the personal ancillary obligation is intended to stand without the other, it is impossible for the member to terminate only the personal ancillary obligation part of the relationship; instead, membership and all its attached obligations can only be terminated together as a whole. Consequently, GmbH members with personal ancillary obligations should, in addition to an extraordinary (*außerordentliche*) right to withdraw, also have a right of withdrawal at will. This second right has its basis in the right to resign[293] from a civil law (non-commercial) partnership as provided in the Civil Code,[294] but to which the Commercial Code requirement of reasonable notice[295] is added.

In addition to doctrinal arguments, there are also arguments for withdrawal at will based on more overtly political considerations. Vollmer, for example, advocates for a right of withdrawal at will only for minority members given their lack of influence on

286 See Teichmann (1970): 242.

287 Reuter (1977): 78 (arguing from § 39 BGB and § 65 GenG).

288 See OLG Karlsruhe 25.04.1984, BB 1984, 2015, 2016.

289 Teichmann (1970): 245–7; see also Reuter (1973): 390–7 (developing the argument at length). See also Roitzsch (1981): 90, 92.

290 Reuter (1984): B66.

291 i.e. entities in which maintenance of status as a member required ongoing contributions other than in the form of capital; see also (n. 71).

292 The rest of the paragraph follows Wiedemann (1965): 91. In later work Wiedemann names the duty to manage the company and the duty not to compete with the company as examples of member's personal service obligations that would provide a basis for an ordinary right of withdrawal. The withdrawing member's compensation payout, however, must be made in compliance with capital maintenance rules: Wiedemann (1980): § 7 IV 2 b.

293 '*Kündigungsrecht*', which may also be translated as a right to 'withdraw' or 'terminate'.

294 BGB, § 723.

295 HGB, § 132.

the GmbH's business policy.[296] Reuter, who saw the individual person (as opposed to the collective) as the primary subject of law,[297] argues that without a right to withdraw at will, the resulting continued reduced mobility of corporate assets risks obstructing the dissolution of 'feudal structures in the economy and society';[298] his solution was to argue for the development of a market for equity interests in businesses.[299]

These arguments drew a range of critical responses. A contemporary criticism was that withdrawal at will, being premised on the primacy of the withdrawing member's interests over all other interests, could in some situations lead to the unnecessary destruction of economic value at the expense of other members, employees, and by extension, society generally.[300] Another response, which rejected the application of rules governing commercial partnerships to the GmbH,[301] pointed out that the interests involved in the GmbH are different given that GmbH members have limited liability but not those of OHGs.[302] This second response itself drew a further critical response, which is as follows.[303] The dominant *Personengesellschaft* is the hybrid GmbH & Co KG,[304] which is similar to the GmbH in that all natural persons in a GmbH & Co KG, including GmbH-unlimited partner's own members, have limited liability. Given that the Commercial Code provides KG limited partners with the right to withdraw at will,[305] the argument that members of the GmbH should be denied the right to withdraw at will solely on the basis that they have limited liability is unpersuasive.

ii Prevailing Opinion

Prevailing opinion offers three reasons against withdrawal at will. First, a right to withdraw at will, even if limited to certain types of GmbH, would run counter to the value judgement embodied in statute that the GmbH's legal basis lies in the GmbH membership interests (*Geschäftsanteile*), and not in the contractually bound members as might be the case for person-based companies (*Personengesellschaften*).[306] A

296 Vollmer (1979): 170–2 (arguing that their lack of influence creates a need to be able to decide how to apply their capital at any time).
297 Reuter (1973): 395 (criticising the shift of the economic initiative from the individual to the collective).
298 Ibid. 396 ('feudaler Strukturen in Wirtschaft und Gesellschaft').
299 Reuter (1977): 79.
300 Schwerdtner (1976): 104 (responding to Reuter's argument).
301 Responding to Wiedemann (1965): 91.
302 Winkler (1967): 77; see also Röhricht (1991): 374–8.
303 The rest of the paragraph follows Müller (1996): 42.
304 This is a commercial limited partnership (KG) in which the general partner with unlimited liability (*Komplementär*) is a GmbH, and any other members is a limited partner with limited liability (*Kommanditist*).
305 HGB, § 161, Paragraph 2.
306 Schmidt (2002): § 35 IV 1; Strohn (2018): Rdn 178.

practical implication of this distinction lies in the different legal consequences that withdrawal creates for person-based companies and GmbHs. In the former, membership status simply expires upon withdrawal, with the remaining members automatically acquiring the withdrawing member's property interests in the company. However, in the GmbH, where there is no equivalent straightforward mechanism, the legal consequences are more complicated.[307]

A second reason, applicable to the transfer-restricted GmbH context, is that recognising the right to withdraw at will would circumvent the statutory rule expressly providing that restrictions on transfer of GmbH membership interests are permissible. It would also render majority members susceptible to threats of withdrawal.[308]

The third reason is that there is no compelling, irrefutable need for an unrestricted right of withdrawal. Even without withdrawal at will, situations where the personal ancillary obligations attaching to membership in a GmbH (such as the duty to manage the GmbH or the duty not to compete) becomes unbearable to the member may be addressed by recognising such circumstances as *wichtiger Grund*.[309] In similar vein, even if the mere factual or legal impossibility of disposing of one's GmbH interests does not by itself constitute *wichtiger Grund*, it may nonetheless be taken into account in the overall assessment as a factor in favour of the withdrawal seeker.[310] Finally, a member who seeks to transfer their membership interest, but who is aggrieved by the majority members' wrongful refusal to approve the transfer, may enforce their claim to the GmbH's approval of the transfer in court.[311]

Despite the weight of 'prevailing opinion' having ultimately settled on the necessity of *wichtiger Grund*,[312] it is interesting to observe that arguments for withdrawal at will were not condemned to *damnatio memoriae*; they remain on the books and commentaries edition after edition,[313] neither fully rebutted nor completely forgotten.

iii Implications for Comparative Corporate Law

Three points of interest to comparative corporate law emerge from the German debate. First, it is possible to make serious doctrinal arguments not just for

307 Schmidt (2002): § 35 IV 1; see also Strohn (2018): Rdn 178.

308 Schmidt (2002): § 35 IV 3 a; Strohn (2018): Rdn 178.

309 Strohn (2018): Rdn 178.

310 Ibid.; see also IV.C.2.ii above.

311 Strohn (2018): Rdn 178. However, some commentators take the view that repeated wrongful refusal to approve a transfer constitutes *wichtiger Grund* for withdrawal's purposes: see IV.C.2.iii above.

312 Lutter (2012): Rdn 70; Fastrich (2013b): Rdn 21; Seibt (2012): Rdn 9; Sosnitza (2010): Rdn 49; Strohn (2018): Rdn 178; Röhricht (1991): 374; Schmidt (2002): § 35 IV 3 a; see further sources cited in Strohn (2018): Rdn 178 fn897.

313 See Fastrich (2013b): Rdn 21; Seibt (2012): Rdn 9; Sosnitza (2010): Rdn 48; Strohn (2018): Rdn 178; Ulmer & Habersack (2014a): Rdn 48; Schmidt (2002): § 35 IV 3 a.

withdrawal on *wichtiger Grund*, but also withdrawal at will, by drawing on the body of ideas and concepts contained in or developed from the civil and commercial codes.[314] German legal thought may be contrasted in this respect with other jurisdictions, where the tendency is to view corporate law and doctrine less as a part of a highly integrated legal system that includes other business entities such as partnerships, and more as a separate field of its own. For jurists from such jurisdictions, the German-style mode of argumentation, which is based heavily on fundamental legal concepts permeating the whole of civil and commercial law such as 'long-term relationships', may understandably feel alien and difficult to apply.[315] Even so, foreign observers may take heart from the fact that arguments in favour of withdrawal at will – or at least, withdrawal for a wider range of situations and corporations – may be supported not only by functional or policy-based arguments, but also in conservative, doctrinal terms. Short of legislative fiat, doctrinal arguments are indispensable to developing a scholarly or judicial consensus in favour of withdrawal rights where there might previously have been none – as was the case in Germany.

The second point: notwithstanding the protracted nature of the dogmatic doctrinal debates, the stakes are low – at least with the benefit of hindsight. From a practical standpoint, the versatility and flexibility of the *wichtiger Grund* concept addresses a wide range of situations in which withdrawal would be the necessary or desirable solution. With few serious gaps remaining,[316] recognising a right of withdrawal at will *at present* arguably goes against the weight of prevailing opinion to little practical profit.

The third and final point: who won the debate? While the *wichtiger Grund* faction seemingly carried the day in law, the facts are more equivocal. Wedemann's study of GmbH corporate constitutions registered with four Bavarian local courts conducted in 2011[317] reveals that 67 per cent of constitutions of multi-member GmbHs provided for rights to withdraw at will.[318] Compared to a corresponding figure of not more than 33 per cent from a study conducted from 1961 to 1963, the evidence suggests that withdrawal at will has gained considerable popularity over the past few decades.[319] Although impossible to determine with certainty, it is at least plausible that the widely publicised debate over the merits of withdrawal at will has permeated the legal sphere and contributed to the shift in preferences decisively in favour of withdrawal at will.

The overall result of the debate over withdrawal is better characterised as a draw, if not an overall victory to the at will faction. Admittedly, the widespread preference for withdrawal at will does not directly undermine the prevailing opinion's insistence for *wichtiger Grund* as a matter of mandatory (and default) law. Prevailing opinion has always conceded that broader withdrawal rights than that provided under the

314 Compare IV.C.2.i.

315 England (and perhaps also the UK) is an example of a jurisdiction where corporate law and private law have been considered separate and distinct. An example of an attempt to bridge this gap is Lim (2015).

316 Breakup of a marriage between core members of a GmbH is an exception: see IV.C.2.v above.

317 Augsburg, Bayreuth, Regensburg, and Würzburg.

318 Wedemann (2013): 80.

319 Ibid.

mandatory law on *wichtiger Grund* may be contractually provided for. Nonetheless, the fact that the 'market' has spoken in favour of withdrawal at will suggests that reversing the default rule is far from a fanciful way forward.

D THE ALCHEMY OF LEGISLATIVE NEGLECT, SCHOLARLY PERSISTENCE, AND JUDICIAL COURAGE

An overarching external narrative (or caricature[320]) of the civil law tradition – of which Germany is an undisputed member[321] – of legislators fashioning elegant and comprehensive codes[322] that are faithfully applied by faceless judge-bureaucrats[323] persists to an extent among common law jurists. Such a narrative is emphatically untrue for either German law generally[324] or German *corporate law* specifically.[325] In fact, the history of *German GmbH law* has been famously characterised by leading corporate law scholars as a story of judicial development of the law.[326]

The true heroes in the story of GmbH withdrawal are the judges who shaped the law, and the scholars who developed the legal concepts and doctrines over generations. They are the now-forgotten judges of the Imperial Court of Justice who laid the earliest foundations;[327] Scholz, who popularised the *wichtiger Grund* concept and maintained momentum with his scholarship for two decades and through Germany's and Europe's greatest catastrophe;[328] the generations of contributors to

320 This is a composite picture derived from my personal experience over the course of my own early legal education, and work experience as a scholar and teacher in predominantly common law environments. I do not suggest that the authors of the sources cited in the next few footnotes are guilty of this; on the contrary, the sources are only selected for general, broad-brush statements written by well-informed comparativists that may or may not be applicable to the German context, but which may be misconstrued by casual readers or students schooled only in the common law tradition without specific knowledge of the German legal system.

321 See Siems (2018b): 89 tbl. 4.1 (summarising in one table the major comparative works of the past 100 years and their classifications of important jurisdictions, including Germany).

322 See e.g. Merryman & Pérez-Perdomo (2007): 27–33.

323 Siems (2018b): 56 ('Overall, the method of civil law judges may therefore criticised as positivist, mechanical and uncreative. More sympathetically, it may be described as seeking to respect the decisions of the legislator, and applying the law in a rational and predictable matter [*sic*].'); Merryman & Pérez-Perdomo (2007): 36–7.

324 See e.g. Siems (2018b): 56–7 (on the influence of legal scholars on judges and judging in Germany), 65–6 (German judges write judgments in an 'academic style' and take academic opinions seriously); see also Rodger (2010): 32, 36.

325 Siems & Cabrelli (2013): 372–3 (observing that both case law and legal scholarship are highly relevant sources of corporate law in Germany). But see Hopt (1997): 270 (observing that company law judges are given much more power in Britain than in Germany). Note that Hopt was writing (primarily) in the context of public companies, not the GmbH.

326 Schmidt (2002): § 33 II 2 a (987–8); Raiser & Veil (2015): § 2 Rdn 7 (also observing that GmbH law 'politisch im Windschatten des Aktienrechts bleibend' [remains politically in the wake of AG law]).

327 RG 07.02.1930, RGZ 128, 1.

328 For Scholz' contribution, see IV.C.1.i above. Notwithstanding the Second World War, between 1931 and 1950 Scholz produced four editions (in 1931, 1942, 1947, and 1950) of his short monograph, as well as several articles on withdrawal.

commentaries[329] and other scholarly works[330] who kept the subject alive and made incremental contributions; the judges of the Federal Court of Justice who boldly and firmly established withdrawal as a legal institution[331] in spite of the nineteenth-century-legislator's misgivings;[332] and last but not least, the judges of the Regional Courts and Higher Regional Courts who resolve withdrawal disputes on a daily basis, and who occasionally make their mark on the development of this institution.[333]

Even if events of a purely political nature had not derailed legislative attempts at codification,[334] what such attempts, even if successful, would have added to the mass of jurisprudence and literature on withdrawal is debatable. Arguably, none of the proposed legislative formulations would have added anything to the understanding or practical workings of this legal institution.[335] The fact is that withdrawal has gradually developed into a recognisable legal institution with an accepted core – the concept of *wichtiger Grund*[336] – and a penumbra in which debate in jurisprudence and literature still continues.[337] Given the sheer variety of situations that a withdrawal regime must address, having areas of persistent disagreement is not a failure calling for legislative intervention. Rather, the debates reflect the complexity of close corporations and the dynamism of German legal thought. Any codification attempt, as both pre- and postwar German law reformers discovered, may well be doomed to failure by political circumstances beyond their control. Alternatively, the legislative formulation could be either so heavily circumscribed in the interests of clarity that it fails to respond to the demands of reality, or so vague as to be practically useless.

The tale of withdrawal's travails in Germany thus gives the lie to any notion that withdrawal is – or should be – within the legislator's exclusive domain; it is proof of the capacity of a vibrant legal culture to shape, over time, a solution to the close corporation problem despite – or perhaps because of – legislative neglect.

329 Including Fastrich, Görner, Habersack, Lutter, Seibt, Sosnitza, Strohn (who served as a judge of the Federal Court of Justice's Second Civil Senate in charge of corporate law cases), Ulmer, as well as their predecessors. Presumably, countless unnamed *Doktorand*innen* and *Habilitand*innen* also assisted.

330 Including Eschenlohr, Wulf Goette (onetime presiding judge of the Second Civil Senate), Reuter, Röhricht (also onetime presiding judge of the Second Civil Senate), Schwerdtner, and Wiedemann. Doctoral dissertations on the subject include works by Balz, Becker, Maximilian Goette, Mäusl, Müller, Roitzsch, and Schindler.

331 BGH 01.04.1953, BGHZ 9, 157; BGH 16.12.1991, BGHZ 116, 359.

332 See (n. 65) above and text thereto.

333 Including OLG Köln 26.03.1999, NZG 1999, 1222; OLG Köln 21.05.1996, GmbHR 1996, 609; OLG Hamm 28.09.1992, GmbHR 1993, 656; OLG München 09.06.1989, GmbHR 1990, 221.

334 See IV.C.1.ii.

335 Goette (2014): 137–8 (1939 Ministry Draft), 139 (1971/73 Government Draft).

336 Extensively discussed above at IV.C.2.

337 Among the more contested issues include the precise theoretical basis for the withdrawal regime; the range of circumstances recognised as *wichtiger Grund* under the 'personal circumstances' category; and the degree to which contractual freedom to deviate from the default rule especially as to compensation quantum should be circumscribed. These are discussed above at IV.C.2.i, IV.C.2.v, IV.C.2.vii, and IV.C.4.ii respectively.

E CONCLUSION

The product of a decades-long discourse between judges and scholars within a serious, well-established tradition of close corporation scholarship and legal thought, Germany's withdrawal regime for its popular and influential quintessential close corporation form, the GmbH, has remained to date in the realm of unwritten law. Regrettably, this sophisticated shareholder remedy is also – at least in the English language literature – a relatively unknown feature of the GmbH.

Withdrawal in Germany, as in other target jurisdictions, is not without its weaknesses. Enforcement of the withdrawing member's right to compensation, which may conflict with a strong commitment to creditor protection, stands out as a particularly vexed issue. Nonetheless, *wichtiger Grund* is not only a flexible legal standard that responds to the need for shareholder exit in a wide variety of situations; it is also a legal concept that can always be further developed through the work of the courts and scholars. It would be remiss of any serious comparative corporate law scholar to disregard the wisdom (and mistakes) of the world's oldest body of close corporation law.

If Germany's experience shows what a jurisdiction with scholars and judges serious about close corporation law and legal scholarship can accomplish despite – or perhaps precisely because of – the legislator's absence, what about the reverse? To that, we now turn to the other major corporate law jurisdiction of Europe: the United Kingdom.

V

The United Kingdom

The Meteoric Rise and Gradual Fall of Unfair Prejudice

A INTRODUCTION

The UK has been for centuries – and notwithstanding Brexit, remains – a major world economy and legal heavyweight. UK company law,[1] as well as related jurisprudence and scholarship, has always had impact beyond British shores. When the UK was part of the EU, the English/British 'limited company' (abbreviated '**Ltd**') for some years occupied a particular niche as a popular choice of corporate vehicle for businesses operating in other EU jurisdictions.[2] Globally, UK law and scholarship continue to serve as shared points of reference for jurists of Commonwealth jurisdictions. These attributes make the UK a natural choice as a target jurisdiction for serious multi-jurisdiction comparative corporate law analysis and necessitate its inclusion in the present work.

Despite its oft-repeated characterisation (or caricature) as a 'common law' or 'case law' jurisdiction, UK close corporation law has been primarily driven by statutory

1 This Chapter uses 'corporate law' and 'company law' interchangeably. 'Companies Act' without further modifiers means the Companies Act 2006 (c 46) (UK), as amended.

2 See V.B.3 below; for Germany's response to competition from the Ltd, see IV.B.1.

reform. This is particularly true for withdrawal, which was introduced twice as part of broader statutory remedies designed to be of great versatility and flexibility. Yet the UK's experience with the law of close corporation withdrawal stands as a cautionary tale of the respective limits of legislative reform and judicial responses in close corporation law matters. After a lacklustre first legislative attempt, withdrawal's second incarnation – as the 'unfair prejudice' remedy – gained overwhelming popularity, but also evoked such strong responses from the courts, the legislature, and the academic world that concerted efforts were made to tame this phenomenon. Chronic dissension amongst the appointed law reformers, practitioners, and academics resulted in paralysis that was ultimately broken in 1999 by one judge on the nation's highest court. The cost: restrictions on access to justice, and neutralisation of unfair prejudice's capacity to grow and respond to changing problems.

V.B introduces the UK Ltd, highlighting its history, legal characteristics, and enduring popularity in (and outside) the UK. V.C examines the origins and evolution of the unfair prejudice remedy – the mechanism by which members may withdraw from the Ltd. To offer a comprehensive yet concise account of the voluminous case law on the subject, I depart from the usual Anglo-Commonwealth style of exposition by refraining from detailed discussion of individual cases. Instead, I classify existing cases using a functional framework that aims to be accessible to foreign jurists, drawing attention to the complete absence of withdrawal at will, or even withdrawal on non-fault grounds. V.D critically and briefly recounts the events, forces, and personalities that shaped member withdrawal in the UK. V.E concludes.

B THE PRIVATE LIMITED COMPANY (LTD)

1 *History*

The emergence of the English 'private limited company' (or 'private company') as a business vehicle for closely held businesses was unexpected by the legislature, jurists, or economists.[3] Until the mid-nineteenth century, business ventures run by small groups of people fell within the realm of the partnership, whereas the company was traditionally reserved for large-scale ventures who relied on equity financing from members of the public.[4] Incorporation was a privilege conferred only by an Act of Parliament or Royal Charter or both.[5]

3 See generally Harris (2013).

4 Harris (2013): 342; Davies & Worthington (2016): para. [1–3]. The attempt to segregate the two in written law resulted in the Joint Stock Companies Act 1844's requirement that any association of twenty-five or more persons carrying on a business for profit must incorporate as a company instead of operating as a partnership: Gower (1953): 536.

5 Harris (2013): 342.

General incorporation as of right was only introduced in 1844[6] and limited liability for members from 1855 to 1856.[7]

For a time, no formal legal distinction existed between companies recognisable today as close corporations ('quasi-partnerships') and those seen as stereotypically 'public'.[8] What came to be christened 'private companies' in the press and legal literature would thrive in the several decades leading up to formal statutory recognition.[9] Notwithstanding the seven-member statutory requirement, smaller companies of one to six members could be formed simply by recruiting nominal members to hold shares for and on behalf of the true owners.[10] The seven-member requirement was reduced to two in 1907 when the private company was finally statutorily recognised as legally distinct from the public company.[11] Although tacitly permitted by judicial precedent since 1896,[12] single-member companies would be expressly permitted by legislation only nearly one century later.[13]

In its modern incarnation, the UK 'private company limited by shares' (Ltd)[14] remains by far the most popular corporate form in the UK,[15] and continues to be regulated together with its public cousin (plc) primarily by the Companies Act 2006.[16]

2 *Legal Aspects*

In contrast with other jurisdictions, a single organic statute regulates both Ltds and plcs. Reflecting its common ancestry with the plc, the Ltd possesses by default all five core features of the paradigmatic business corporation.[17] Save for separate legal personality and limited liability, the remaining three features – transferability of shares, centralised management, and investor ownership – can be deviated from in

6 The Joint Stock Companies Act 1844 permitted incorporation by registration with a government office (now Companies House): Harris (2013): 342–3.

7 The Companies Acts of 1855–56 granted opt-in limited liability: Gower (1953): 536; Harris (2013): 343. The Limited Liability Act 1855 did not apply to companies in Scotland (s. 18), but the Joint Stock Companies Act 1856 made limited liability available to all UK.

8 The Acts of 1844, 1855, 1856, and 1862 (the consolidated Companies Act 1862) did not make distinctions based on number of members, share capital, or share transferability: Harris (2013): 343.

9 Harris (2013): 351–2, 378.

10 Harris (2013): 364.

11 Companies Act 1907 (7 Edw 7 c 50), s. 37(1) (stating the private company's three defining features as share transfer restrictions, maximum of fifty members, and no public offering of securities), s. 37(4) (two-member requirement).

12 *Salomon* v. *A Salomon & Co Ltd* [1897] AC 22 (HL) (decided 16 November 1896).

13 Companies Act 1985, s. 1(3A), inserted by Companies (Single Member Private Limited Companies) Regulations 1992, SI 1992/1699, reg. 2, Sch. Para. 1, implementing the Twelfth Council Company Law Directive 89/667/EEC of 21 December 1989 on single-member private limited-liability companies [1993] OJ L395/40. Cf Companies Act, s. 7(1).

14 On nomenclature see Davies & Worthington (2016): para. [1–11].

15 As of 31 March 2020, the 4,183,970 Ltds comprise 92.8 per cent of the total register (4,507,901): Companies House (2020): tbl. C1.

16 Companies Act, ss. 1, 4(1)–(2).

17 See Armour & Enriques et al (2017): 5.

practice. Ltd members enjoy much freedom to regulate the company's affairs and the relationship between members through provision in the corporate constitution[18] and, if desired, by shareholder agreement or another form of contract.[19] Ltds may not market their shares or other securities to the public;[20] share transfer restrictions that practically negate transferability are often imposed through the corporate constitution or shareholder agreement.[21] Centralised management is only mandatory in a formal sense: while every Ltd must appoint at least one director,[22] in close corporation practice directors are often drawn from the members.[23] Investor ownership – the default rules of 'one share, one vote'[24] and equal income rights per share[25] – can be deviated from by agreement.

The outsize impact of the law of the UK Ltd on former colonies is a result of centuries of British imperialism. In former British colonies (excluding the United States[26]) – so-called 'Commonwealth' or 'Anglo-Commonwealth' jurisdictions – courts continue to look to British judgments as persuasive authority to varying degrees.[27] Although decisions from former colonies are seldom directly invoked as authority in the UK courts,[28] they nonetheless form part of the body of common law learning.[29] Consequently, this Chapter discusses selected Commonwealth decisions as well.

3 *The Ltd's Enduring Popularity and Dominance*

Within ten years of receiving statutory recognition in 1907, private companies accounted for more than 90 per cent of new incorporations each year. During the

18 Davies & Worthington (2016): paras. [3–13], [3–15]. The 'company's constitution' includes both the articles of association and certain shareholder resolutions or agreements: Companies Act, ss. 17, 29. Shareholder agreements in the ordinary sense are not included: Davies & Worthington (2016): para. [3–17]. On the 'memorandum of association', see Davies & Worthington (2016): para. [4–5] and fn. 11; Companies Act, s. 28.

19 Holllington (2017): para. [3–15]; Davies & Worthington (2016): para. [3–33].

20 Companies Act, s. 755.

21 Restrictions on share transfers were previously statutorily mandated for private companies, but not today: Davies & Worthington (2016): para. [2–26].

22 Companies Act, s. 154(1).

23 Particularly in 'quasi-partnerships': Hollington (2017): paras. [7–138]–[7–139]. On the member's expectation of involvement in management as a director, see V.C.4.iii.d below.

24 Modifiable by constitutional provision: Companies Act, s. 284(4).

25 See Davies & Worthington (2016): paras. [23–4]–[23–10].

26 Since World War I American legal precedents are rarely cited as formal persuasive legal authority in UK courts and almost never in the corporate law context: see Gower (1956): 1401.

27 Postwar, former British colonies (and later, Commonwealth jurisdictions) gradually severed their judicial systems from the UK by abolishing final appeals to the Judicial Committee of the Privy Council in London. Canada did so in 1949; Australia 1986; Singapore 1993; Hong Kong 1997 (superseded by the Hong Kong Court of Final Appeal), and New Zealand 2003 (superseded by the modern Supreme Court of New Zealand). See Koh (2018): 687.

28 A rare exception being *Re Wondoflex Textiles Pty Ltd* [1951] VLR 458 (Supreme Court of Victoria), an Australian winding-up case that was cited with approval in *O'Neill* v. *Phillips* [1999] 1 WLR 1092 (HL) 1100.

29 Commonwealth decisions – especially from Hong Kong – are discussed in British treatises such as Joffe et al. (2015) and Hollington (2017).

1910s an estimated 145,000 existing companies, representing a majority of all active companies in the UK, converted into private companies.[30] The Ltd's popularity saw another surge in the 1940s and 1950s as many sole proprietors and family businesses incorporated for the sole purpose of reducing the tax burden.[31] By 1961, more than 90 per cent of the over 400,000 companies on the register were Ltds;[32] by 1970 it was estimated that there were 200,000 operating Ltds reasonably classifiable as close corporations.[33] The growth in Ltds would continue to outpace that of public companies, with Ltds comprising just under 99 per cent of the 960,600 companies on the register as of 1993,[34] and over 99 per cent through the late 1990s.[35] A study conducted around this period also reported that 90 per cent of all companies have fewer than five members.[36]

Except for a sharp drop during the Great Recession, the Ltd has shown consistent growth over the last decade until the Brexit era, as shown by Table 5.1.

TABLE 5.1 *Growth of Ltds in Great Britain and the United Kingdom 2006–20*

Year (Great Britain 2006–09; United Kingdom 2010–20)[1]	Effective number[2] (in thousands)*	Increase from previous year[3] (in thousands)	Growth (%)
2006	2,113.4	150.2	7.65
2007	2,324.7	211.3	10.00
2008	2,407.3	82.6	3.55
2009	2,255.5	151.8	6.31
2010	2,345.1	see note 1	
2011	2,441.4	96.3	4.11
2012	2,599.1	157.7	6.46
2013	2,766.6	166.3	6.40
2014	2,956.7	190.1	6.87

30 Harris (2013): 378.

31 Hadden (1977): 216.

32 See Freedman (1994): 570 (observing that only about 16,000 of the 403,000 companies on the register were public companies). Accounting for the unlimited companies and companies limited by guarantee included in the remaining 96.03 per cent, 90 per cent is a conservative estimate for Ltds.

33 Hadden (1977): 44–5 (estimating that there were about 300,000 companies with five or fewer members, of which two thirds are 'partnership companies' in 1969), 42 (just under half a million companies on the register). See also Chesterman (1973): 130 (estimating that 'quasi-partnership' companies numbered in the 'many thousands').

34 See Freedman (1994): 571.

35 See Freedman (2000): 320 fn. 19; CLRSG (2000a): para. 6.7.

36 CLRSG (2000a): para. 6.9 (noting that a survey of company auditors suggests that companies where all members are simultaneously directors comprise 'a significant proportion' of the total).

TABLE 5.1 *(continued)*

Year (Great Britain 2006–09; United Kingdom 2010–20)	Effective number (in thousands)	Increase from previous year (in thousands)	Growth (%)
2015	3,192.5	235.9	7.98
2016	3,423.1	230.6	7.22
2017	3,638.1	215.0	6.28
2018	3,759.9	121.8	3.35
2019	3,916.6	156.7	4.17
2020	4,054.6	138.1	3.53

Source: Department of Trade and Industry and Companies House Statistics, 2006–20.[37]
Note 1: The figures are as of 31 March of each year. The figures from 2006 to 2009 are for Great Britain (comprising England and Wales, and Scotland but excluding Northern Ireland), and for the United Kingdom (comprising all three) from 2010 onwards.[38]
Note 2: 'effective number on register' excludes companies in the process of liquidation or dissolution.[39]
Note 3: Contains rounding errors.[40]
* The numbers are computed by subtracting the number of unlimited companies from the number of 'effective' private companies for each year. From 2013 onwards, the raw data figures are exact (i.e. not rounded off to the nearest thousand).

The Ltd has also enjoyed success in other jurisdictions as an inexpensive and flexible alternative to native corporate forms. Part of the Ltd's success can be attributed to the line of Court of Justice cases cementing the freedom of establishment within the European Union.[41] From 1997 to 2006, around 145,000 Ltds were incorporated for the purpose of doing business outside the UK, with Germany hosting the plurality.[42] As of 2011, an estimated 103,305 UK companies were operated by entrepreneurs in eight major EU member states, with 61,485 in Germany alone.[43]

37 Official statistics (as Microsoft Excel files) from 2013/2014 to 2019/2020 are available at Gov.uk at www.gov.uk/search/research-and-statistics?keywords=Companies+Register+Activities%3A+Statistical+Release&content_store_document_type=published_statistics&organisations%5B%5D=companies-house&order=relevance; for 2006/2007 to 2012/2013, statistics are available in Adobe PDF format at the National Archives website at https://webarchive.nationalarchives.gov.uk/20141104110623/http://www.companieshouse.gov.uk/about/companiesRegActivities.shtml.
38 The Northern Ireland Register was merged with the Register for Great Britain in October 2009: Companies House (2015): 7 fn. 1.
39 But includes dormant companies and companies in receivership: Companies House (2016).
40 Computations for pre-2013 figures contain rounding errors because the official raw statistics contained varying numbers of significant figures.
41 See IV.B.1.
42 Becht et al. (2008) 244–7, 247 tbl. 2; see also IV.B.1.
43 Armour et al. (2017): 231 tbl. 2. Most of these may be safely assumed to be Ltds.

C WITHDRAWAL ON GROUNDS UNDER THE UNFAIR PREJUDICE REMEDY

1 *History and Development*

i From Dissolution to 'Oppression', and Then to 'Unfair Prejudice'

Historically, the only form of protection for minority members of Ltds was statutory: the right to petition for 'just and equitable winding-up'[44] (i.e. judicial dissolution). Despite dissolution's serious core deficiency,[45] the courts did not organically develop the superior alternative of withdrawal. Instead, it would take a reformist British Parliament two attempts and over four decades to implement a workable solution over resistance from the judicial establishment.

The first attempt resulted in the 'oppression' remedy in section 210 of the Companies Act 1948. Proposed by the Cohen Committee in its milestone 1945 Report,[46] the oppression remedy was intended to strengthen protection of minority members in private companies vulnerable to opportunistic behaviour by majority members. As a welcome alternative to the inherently problematic judicial dissolution,[47] the oppression jurisdiction would grant the English courts:[48]

> ... *the power to impose upon the parties to a dispute whatever settlement the Court considers just and equitable*. This discretion must be unfettered, for it is impossible to lay down a general guide to the solution of what are essentially individual cases.

Parliament did not specifically set out to create a withdrawal remedy as such; withdrawal was only one of the possible reliefs for oppression that a judge is free to select at their discretion.[49]

The Cohen Committee's good sense would be thwarted by an uncooperative judiciary. Despite a promising beginning for the new remedy, where petitioners achieved a measure of success,[50] judges refused relief in the all-too-common situation where a minority member is removed from their position as director by an

44 First enacted as Joint Stock Companies Winding-up Act 1848, s. 5(8); now Insolvency Act 1986 (UK), s. 122(1)(g). See also Davies & Worthington (2016): para. [20–21].

45 'If the company was prospering, presenting a "just and equitable" petition was tantamount to killing the goose that might lay the golden egg': Davies & Worthington (2016): para. [20–21].

46 Cohen (1945).

47 Even if dissolution were granted, the minority member's position would not improve if there were little realistic prospect of realising much in the way of proceeds from liquidation: Cohen (1945): para. 60.

48 Cohen (1945): para. 60 (emphasis added).

49 See Companies Act 1948 (c 38), s. 210(2) (repealed).

50 *Scottish Co-operative Wholesale Society Ltd* v. *Meyer* [1959] AC 324 (HL); *Re H R Harmer Ltd* [1959] 1 WLR 62 (CA); *Re Jermyn Street Turkish Baths Ltd* [1970] 1 WLR 1194 (ChD), reversed [1971] 1 WLR 1042 (CA).

oppressive majority exercising their voting power.[51] Additional discouragement for would-be petitioners followed as courts declined to grant relief in cases featuring sustained mismanagement,[52] excessive directors' remuneration,[53] or a single instance (as opposed to a continuing course) of oppressive conduct.[54] Judges also seemed to prefer the familiar option of winding up the company.[55] It was clear by the 1970s that the oppression remedy far from a success.[56]

To their credit, law reformers persevered. In response to restrictive judicial interpretations of 'oppression', the Jenkins Committee in 1962 proposed replacing 'oppression' with the broader concept of 'unfair prejudice' as the basis on which relief would be granted.[57] Under this new ground of 'unfair prejudice', a member could seek relief for a wide array of unfair acts committed to their detriment.[58] Eighteen years passed before the proposal saw fruition as the modern 'unfair prejudice' remedy, as introduced by section 75 of the Companies Act 1980.

In line with the Jenkins Committee's intentions, the courts swiftly abandoned the restrictions that had previously hamstrung the oppression remedy.[59] By the late 1980s, unfair prejudice had become the remedy of choice for members of UK Ltds, with dozens of reported cases and far more petitions successfully settled.[60]

ii The Crisis of Unfair Prejudice and Further Reform Attempts

Unfair prejudice soon became a 'victim of its own success'.[61] By the mid-1990s, unfair prejudice petitions had become popular, protracted, and pricey.[62] The

51 *Elder* v. *Elder & Watson Ltd* 1952 SC 49 (IH, 1st Div) 57, 58, followed by *Harmer* [1959] 1 WLR 62, 77–8, in turn followed and applied by *Re Lundie Brothers Ltd* [1965] 1 WLR 1051 (ChD) 1057–8. For academic criticism, see Prentice (1972):131; Lowry & Reisberg (2012): 285.

52 *Re Five Minute Car Wash Services Ltd* [1966] 1 WLR 745 (ChD) 751–2.

53 *Jermyn* [1971] 1 WLR 1042, 1059–60, reversing [1970] 1 WLR 1194 (ChD).

54 *Re Westbourne Galleries Ltd* [1970] 1 WLR 1378 (ChD) 1390 (requiring 'a course of oppressive conduct [that] continued up to the date of the petition').

55 Lowry & Reisberg (2012): 285; *Lundie* [1965] 1 WLR 1051, 1058–9 and *Westbourne* [1970] 1 WLR 1378 (both decided by Plowman J). *Westbourne* would ultimately be appealed to the House of Lords and achieve lasting fame as *Ebrahimi* v. *Westbourne Galleries Ltd* [1973] AC 360 (HL).

56 Rajak (1972): 169; Prentice (1972): 148.

57 Jenkins (1962): para. 204.

58 Ibid. para. 205.

59 See *Re a Company (No 00477 of 1986)* [1986] BCLC 376 (ChD) 378–9; *Re a Company (No 008699 of 1985)* [1986] BCLC 382 (ChD) 387–8; *Re a Company (No 002567 of 1982)* [1983] 1 WLR 927 (ChD) 933; Lowry & Reisberg (2012): 288; Davies & Worthington (2016): para. [20–4].

60 Lowry & Reisberg (2012): 286.

61 Sugarman (1997): 239.

62 *Re Unisoft Group Ltd (No 3)* [1994] 1 BCLC 609 (ChD) 611; *Latimer Holdings Ltd* v. *SEA Holdings NZ Ltd* [2005] 2 NZLR 328 (NZCA) [83]. Notorious examples include *Re Freudiana Music Co Ltd* (High Court of England and Wales, 24 March 1993, Jonathan Parker J), cited in LawComm (1997): para. 1.6 fn. 13 (hearings lasted over a year and took 165 court days, costs of GBP two million were awarded); *Re Elgindata*

Law Commission responded with reform proposals in its 1996 *Consultation Paper*. One was to grant courts greater case management powers, such as the power to dismiss any claim or part thereof without realistic prospect of success.[63] The objective was to reduce costs and complications in shareholder litigation.[64] 'Self-help' options in the form of additional provisions in the statutory model constitutional documents[65] – a standard form article referring disputes to arbitration, a share valuation procedure, and an exit article for smaller private companies[66] – were also proposed. To encourage settlement,[67] the Law Commission recommended a series of presumptions to facilitate purchase of the minority's shares for situations where the minority had been unfairly excluded from management.[68]

iii *O'Neill* v. *Phillips* and the End of Reform

In parallel with law reform efforts, attempts by appellate courts to give greater guidance on the unfair prejudice remedy culminated in the seminal *O'Neill* v. *Phillips*,[69] a decision of the UK's then-apex court, the House of Lords.

In *O'Neill*, the petitioning minority member alleged that the majority member had reneged on the unspoken understanding that they would share the company's profits equally, and that the minority member would be allotted additional shares in the company.[70] The House of Lords allowed the majority member's appeal and restored the trial judge's order dismissing the petition. In the sole reasoned speech of the House, Lord Hoffmann seized the opportunity to clarify the ambit of unfair prejudice. His Lordship first considered the meaning of 'fairness' in the context of the unfair prejudice remedy, emphasising its fundamentally 'promissory'[71] nature.[72] Exceptionally, where 'equitable considerations' exist, unfairness may result from exercise of strict legal powers by persons conducting the company's affairs.[73] Lord Hoffmann also provided guidelines

Ltd (No 1) [1991] BCLC 959 (ChD) (as noted in LawComm (1997): para. 1.6 fn. 14) (hearing lasted 43 days, GBP 320,000 in costs incurred in a dispute over shares ultimately valued at GBP 24,600).

63 LawComm (1996): para. 17.16.

64 Ibid. para. 14.13.

65 The former 'Table A' was superseded by the 'Model Articles for Private Companies Limited by Shares' in Companies (Model Articles) Regulations 2008, SI 2008/3229, sched. 1; Companies Act, s. 20 (1) (model articles apply to newly incorporated Ltds except where excluded or modified).

66 The proposed articles would only bind a company if adopted by special resolution of the members: LawComm (1996): para. 15.6.

67 LawComm (1997): para. 3.32.

68 Ibid. para. 3.30 (for elaboration, see paras. 3.26–3.62).

69 *O'Neill* [1999] 1 WLR 1092.

70 Ibid. 1092, 1097.

71 Boyle (2002): 97; see also V.C.4.iii.b below.

72 *O'Neill* [1999] 1 WLR 1092, 1098–9 ('a member of a company will not ordinarily be entitled to complain of unfairness unless there has been some breach of the terms on which he agreed that the affairs of the company should be conducted').

73 *O'Neill* [1999] 1 WLR 1092, 1098–9. On 'equitable considerations' see V.C.4.iii.a–b below.

on how unfair prejudice may be negated with a fair offer to buy out the petitioner's shares.[74]

Ultimately, *O'Neill* pre-empted and terminated serious reform efforts. The Company Law Review initiated in March 1998[75] by the then-Department of Trade and Industry (DTI)[76] resulted in a series of consultation papers and reports.[77] Although the Company Law Review Steering Group (CLRSG)[78] accepted[79] the Law Commission's proposal for stronger case management powers,[80] it opposed and ultimately rejected the proposed 'exit article'[81] and presumptions.[82] The CLRSG put the final nail in the coffin of unfair prejudice reform in June 2001, indicating its agreement with *O'Neill* 'in the interests of certainty and the containment of the scope of [unfair prejudice] actions' and recommending against legislative reversal.[83]

With substantive reform abandoned, the structure and substance of the unfair prejudice regime established by the Companies Act 1980 remained unchanged (save for one clarificatory amendment)[84] throughout its iterations as sections 459 to 461 of the Companies Act 1985 and sections 994 to 996 of the Companies Act 2006.

2 *The Relationship between 'Withdrawal' and the Unfair Prejudice Remedy*

The unfair prejudice remedy and withdrawal (usually called 'share purchase order'[85]) are not strictly synonymous in the UK context. Withdrawal – as defined for this Book – is just one of many possible reliefs under the unfair prejudice remedy,[86] albeit the most frequently sought and granted[87] and unavailable outside the unfair prejudice remedy.[88] Accordingly, the unfair

74 The fair buyout offer is discussed at V.C.5.ii below.

75 DTI (1998).

76 As of writing the Department of Business, Energy & Industrial Strategy (BEIS).

77 BIS (2012).

78 Charged with management of the Review, the CLRSG comprised representatives from DTI, the judiciary, academics, legal practitioners, and industry. For a list of members, see CLRSG (1999): 159 (Annex A).

79 CLRSG (2000a): para. 4.103.

80 LawComm (1997): paras. 2.1–2.38.

81 Ibid. paras. 5.4–5.33 and pp. 133–6 (Appendix C).

82 CLRSG (2000b): para. 5.76 (opposing the presumptions and calling for further feedback); CLRSG (2001): para. 7.41 (concluding that the proposed presumptions should be rejected).

83 CLRSG (2001): para. 7.41.

84 Companies Act 1989, Schedule 19, para. 11, reversing *Re a Company (No 00370 of 1987), ex p Glossop* [1988] 1 WLR 1068 (ChD) 1075.

85 See e.g. Hollington (2017): para. [8–44].

86 Companies Act, s. 996(2)(e). The Act also specifically provides for five other reliefs (s. 996(2)(a)–(d)), plus a general judicial discretion to fashion others (s. 996(1)).

87 Neuberger (2002): 69; Hollington (2017): para. [8–44]; *Grace* v. *Biagioli* [2005] EWCA Civ 1222; [2006] 2 BCLC 70 [75].

88 Insolvency Act 1986, s. 111(2) is not really comparable.

prejudice regime is the appropriate subject of a comparative study of withdrawal.

As the statute confers an extremely wide discretion to fashion any relief it deems fit,[89] the court would not necessarily grant withdrawal even where the substantive elements of unfair prejudice have been established and the desired relief is withdrawal. In rare and 'exceptional' cases,[90] the court may also order the expulsion of the wrongdoer;[91] in this sense, unfair prejudice is also the appropriate UK analogue to expulsion[92] in other jurisdictions.

3 *'Unfair Prejudice': The Constituent Elements*

i Statutory Basis

Today's unfair prejudice remedy has its basis in the Companies Act 2006. Section 994(1) of the Act provides:

> **Petition by company member**
>
> A member of a company may apply to the court by petition for an order under [Part 30; sections 994 to 999] on the ground –
>
> (a) that the company's affairs are being or have been conducted in a manner that is unfairly prejudicial to the interests of members generally or of some part of its members (including at least himself), or
>
> (b) that an actual or proposed act or omission of the company (including an act or omission on its behalf) is or would be so prejudicial. …

The member applying to court for relief under this statutory regime is the 'petitioner', and the opposing party the 'respondent'.

For ease of exposition, the statute may be broken down into four requirements, namely (1) conduct of the company's affairs; (2) interests of the member; (3) prejudice; and (4) unfairness.[93] The first two may be understood as requirements of *standing*; prejudice as proof of *loss or damage*; and unfairness as the core concept and the *substantive legal basis* for relief. This subsection analyses the first three statutory elements, and the next examines unfairness.

89 Companies Act, s. 996(1).

90 *Re a Company (No 00836 of 1995)* [1996] 2 BCLC 192 (ChD) 205.

91 *Re a Company (No 00789 of 1987), ex p Shooter* [1990] BCLC 384 (ChD); *Re Brenfield Squash Racquets Club Ltd* [1996] 2 BCLC 184 (ChD).

92 *Ausschließung/Ausschluss* (Germany); *jomei* (Japan).

93 *Re a Company (No 005685 of 1988), ex p Schwarcz (No 2)* [1989] BCLC 427 (ChD) 437 (in different order); Hollington (2017): para. [7–42]; cf Dignam & Lowry (2016): paras. [11.23]–[11.43] (combining 'prejudice' and 'unfairness' for a total of three).

ii Conduct of the Company's Affairs

The words 'affairs of the company' are given a wide interpretation.[94] As a starting point, they encompass all business matters within the board's competence.[95] The court will adopt a practical approach grounded in business realities, and not a technical or legalistic one.[96] A subsidiary's affairs can also be the parent's affairs[97] or vice versa,[98] provided that there is a relationship of control between parent and subsidiary.[99] Not all acts of the board or individual directors constitute 'conduct of the company's affairs'. Board deliberations prior to a board decision count, but unsuccessful attempts by a minority to swing the collective decision in favour of their stance do not.[100] A director who steals money from the company safe may be breaching their fiduciary duties to the company, but the theft is arguably not 'conduct of the company's affairs'.[101]

This statutory requirement also aims to draw a distinction between matters that have a connection to the company and matters solely within the personal sphere of the members themselves. Matters such as a member's exercise of individual membership rights that do not constitute an 'act' of the company[102] itself appear to fall within the latter sphere, and thus cannot be basis for an unfair prejudice claim.[103]

Ultimately, the distinction between the affairs of the 'company', and of the 'director' or 'members', may be illusory. In one case with three members each holding equal

94 *Re Neath Rugby Ltd, Hawkes* v. *Cuddy* [2009] EWCA Civ 291; [2010] BCC 597 [48].

95 *Rackind* v. *Gross* [2004] EWCA Civ 815; [2005] 1 WLR 3505 [29]; *Neath Rugby* [2010] BCC 597 [50].

96 *Re Coroin Ltd (No 2), McKillen* v. *Misland (Cyprus) Investments Ltd* [2012] EWHC 2343 (Ch); [2013] 2 BCLC 583 [628].

97 Especially when both parent and subsidiary have the same directors: *Rackind* [2005] 1 WLR 3505 [26].

98 *Nicholas* v. *Soundcraft Electronics Ltd* [1993] BCLC 360 (CA) 364, 370–1; see also *Meyer* [1959] AC 324, 367.

99 *Re Grandactual Ltd, Hough* v. *Hardcastle* [2005] EWHC 1415 (Ch); [2006] BCC 73 [29]; *Hawkes* v. *Cuddy (No 2)* [2007] EWHC 2999 (Ch); [2008] BCC 390 [213] ('[c]ommonality of directors is also an important feature'). Affairs of other companies in the same corporate group may also count: *Oak Investment Partners XII Ltd Partnership* v. *Boughtwood* [2009] EWHC 176 (Ch); [2009] 1 BCLC 453 [9], affirmed on other grounds [2010] EWCA Civ 23; *Re Woven Rugs Ltd, Sharafi* v. *Woven Rugs Ltd* [2010] EWHC 230 (Ch) [161]. See also Tan (2014).

100 *Re Astec (BSR) plc* [1998] 2 BCLC 556 (Ch) 570.

101 *Re a Company (No 001761 of 1986)* [1987] BCLC 141 (ChD) 148; *Lloyd* v. *Casey* [2002] 1 BCLC 454 [73]. But see *Oak Investment* [2009] 1 BCLC 453 [15] (depends on the facts).

102 For members' acts to be deemed 'acts' of the company, members must act as an organ of the company, i.e. collectively at general meeting by passing members' resolutions. A member's act of voting that causes a members' resolution to be passed can therefore ground an unfair prejudice claim: *Unisoft (No 3)* [1994] l BCLC 609, 611, 623.

103 In one case where the company was incorporated by four persons holding equal shares and serving as directors and employees, relations broke down between one member and the others. Dismissed as an employee, the member then resigned from the board shortly before formal removal and refused to sell his shares. The other three members applied to court to expel him as member. The Court of Appeal denied the three petitioners relief on the basis that the excluded member's decision to remain in the company, being 'conduct of a member of his own affairs', did not constitute 'affairs of the company' or 'an act or omission of the company': *Re Legal Costs Negotiators Ltd* [1999] BCC 547 (CA) 551. Other examples of member's conduct irrelevant to the issue of unfair prejudice raised by the judge include 'requesting a general meeting of the company' and 'seeking answers to an excessive number of questions': ibid.

shares in a company, the act of two out of three members in selling their shares to a third party behind the remaining member's back was found to be conduct of the company's affairs.[104] In another case, physical assault with a hammer by one member-director against another member-director due to unhappiness over reduced remuneration was recognised as unfairly prejudicial conduct.[105] Had the attack not been precipitated by a remuneration dispute, the unfair prejudice claim might have failed on the basis that the 'affairs of the company' requirement was not met.[106]

iii Interests of the Member

Under an older line of cases, it is a requirement that the petitioner show that it is their interests *qua* member that have been unfairly prejudiced.[107] Subsequent cases have adopted a broader approach,[108] and now it is sufficient for the petitioner to establish that the prejudice was to their interests 'in some capacity connected with [their] shareholding',[109] such as the interest *qua* creditor of a joint venture investor who also provided a loan to the company on top of subscribing for shares.[110] Depending on the specific facts, what may also be recognised as interests of the member may include status as a director or other forms of participation in the management of the company.[111]

iv Prejudice

The UK courts 'take a wide view of prejudice suffered' by members,[112] the most obvious of which would be serious jeopardy to or diminishment in the value of the petitioner's shares.[113] An extension to this would be where the shares were themselves

104 *Richardson* v. *Blackmore, Capital Cabs Ltd* v. *Blackmore* (unreported, 1 November 2004) (ChD) (Wyn Williams QC), affirmed and reversed in part [2005] EWCA Civ 1356; [2006] BCC 276. The trial judge's holdings are summarised in the Court of Appeal judgment (at [24]) and this point was left undisturbed on appeal (at [58], [65]).

105 *Re Home & Office Fire Extinguishers Ltd, Rodliffe* v. *Rodliffe* [2012] EWHC 917 (Ch) [72]. The hammer-wielding attacker was ordered to sell his shares to the other member: ibid. [73].

106 This was a factor in the judge's decision: ibid. [72].

107 *No 00477 of 1986* [1986] BCLC 376, 378; *Re J E Cade & Son Ltd* [1992] BCLC 213 (ChD) 228; *Re a Company (No 00314 of 1989)* [1991] BCLC 154 (ChD) 160.

108 *R & H Electric Ltd* v. *Haden Bill Electrical Ltd* [1995] 2 BCLC 280 (ChD) 292–3; *O'Neill* [1999] 1 WLR 1092, 1105.

109 *Re Tobian Properties Ltd, Maidment* v. *Attwood* [2012] EWCA Civ 998; [2013] 2 BCLC 567 [12]. See also *Coroin (No 2)* [2013] 2 BCLC 583 [630].

110 *Gamlestaden Fastigheter AB* v. *Baltic Partners Ltd* [2007] UKPC 26; [2007] 4 All ER 164 [36]–[37]. Although a Privy Council decision on appeal from Jersey, *Gamlestaden* was cited with approval in *Tobian Properties* [2013] 2 BCLC 567 [12].

111 These will be discussed in V.C.4.iii.d below.

112 *Tobian Properties* [2013] 2 BCLC 567 [12].

113 *Re Bovey Hotel Ventures Ltd* (31 July 1981, unreported) (ChD) (Slade J), quoted and cited with approval in *Re R A Noble & Sons (Clothing) Ltd* [1983] BCLC 273 (ChD) 290–1; for an older example, see *Scottish Co-operative* [1959] AC 324.

rendered valueless but the petitioner could nonetheless gain 'real financial benefit' should relief be granted.[114]

Prejudice need not be to the member's financial interest,[115] although it may be more difficult to establish the prejudicial nature of an act or conduct that did not cause financial detriment.[116] In one case, the company's unreasonable delay in responding to the lawful exercise of membership rights such as the requisitioning of an extraordinary general meeting of the members was held to be prejudice.[117] Failure of other directors to consult a member-director petitioner on policy decisions may also suffice,[118] as might intentionally inflicted physical injury.[119]

The general permissive approach to prejudice has limits. For example, the weight of authority suggests that there is no prejudice if the petitioner suffered no financial detriment from otherwise wrongful conduct such as breaches of directors' duties,[120] although there is also authority to the contrary.[121] Another example is failure to comply with Companies Act requirements on annual general meetings (AGMs) and the laying of accounts for members' approval.[122] A threat of expropriation of shares and dismissal as employee and director addressed to the petitioner is not prejudicial if the threat did not ultimately materialise due to the petitioner's self-help.[123] Finally, mere hurt feelings would not suffice, as the prejudice must be in the 'commercial', not 'emotional' sense.[124]

v Unfairness

'Unfairness' is conceptually distinct from 'prejudice'; conduct that may be prejudicial is not necessarily unfair, and unfair conduct is not always prejudicial. To succeed, the petitioner must establish both prejudice and unfairness.[125] Next up is an in-depth examination of unfairness as a concept, and of factual scenarios frequently encountered in practice.

114 *Gamlestaden* [2007] 4 All ER 164 [36].
115 *Jaber* v. *Science and Information Technology Ltd* [1992] BCLC 764 (ChD) 783–4.
116 *Coroin (No 2)* [2013] 2 BCLC 583 [631].
117 *McGuinness* v. *Bremner plc* 1988 SLT 891 (OH) 895, 898.
118 *RA Noble* [1983] BCLC 273, 289, 291–2 (recognising the possibility, but holding that on the facts of the case the prejudice was not unfair due to the petitioner's own fault); *Elgindata (No 1)* [1991] BCLC 959, 1004.
119 *Rodliffe* v. *Rodliffe* [2012] EWHC 917 (Ch) [72].
120 *No 001761 of 1986* [1987] BCLC 141, 147; *Re Blackwood Hodge plc* [1997] 2 BCLC 650 (ChD) 684; *Rock Nominees Ltd* v. *RCO (Holdings) plc (in liquidation)* [2004] EWCA Civ 118; [2004] 1 BCLC 439 [79].
121 *Elgindata (No 1)* [1991] BCLC 959, 1004 (director's misapplication of assets for benefit of family and friends is inherently unfairly prejudicial).
122 *Irvine* v. *Irvine (No 1)* [2006] EWHC 406 (Ch); [2007] 1 BCLC 349 [341]–[347].
123 *Re John Reid & Sons (Strucsteel) Ltd, Reid* v. *Reid* [2003] EWHC 2329 (Ch); [2003] 2 BCLC 319 [44].
124 *Unisoft (No 3)* [1994] 1 BCLC 609, 611.
125 *Re Saul D Harrison & Sons plc* [1995] 1 BCLC 14 (CA) 31; *Re Sunrise Radio Ltd, Kohli* v. *Lit* [2009] EWHC 2893 (Ch); [2010] 1 BCLC 367 [4]; *Schwarcz (No 2)* [1989] BCLC 427, 437.

4 'Unfairness'

i Introduction

A CATEGORIES OF UNFAIRNESS. Generally, unfairness arises from acts or conduct that contravene what I call 'protected expectations'. I adopt this terminology as a jurisdiction-neutral category applicable to analysis of unfair prejudice remedies across the Commonwealth. Protected expectations mostly fall into two categories.

Expectations in the first category are independently rooted in or protected by the formal, 'written' *rules* governing the company's affairs. Binding on the participants in the corporate enterprise,[126] these rules may stem from formal contractual documents such as the corporate constitution and shareholders' agreements, or Companies Act provisions forming part of 'the terms on which … the affairs of the company should be conducted'.[127] Breach of expectations in this category is per se unlawful and may result in other legal consequences and remedies, and includes what some commentators have termed the 'independent illegality' subtype of unfair prejudice.[128]

The second category comprises a petitioner's informal, '*unwritten*' expectations concerning the application of the formal, 'written' rules, and are known variously as 'equitable considerations' (UK today), 'legitimate expectations (previously), or 'reasonable expectations' (Commonwealth). These expectations arise in *quasi-partnerships*,[129] a company subtype in which the relationship between the members is more than just a purely commercial association. Such expectations comprise mostly understandings between the parties that control – through constraining, restraining, or otherwise qualifying – the exercise of powers under the formal rules. By contrast with the first category, breach of the second category of expectations has no remedy except via the unfair prejudice remedy.

I round off this section by grouping together other protected expectations recognised in judicial precedent. This nascent category includes *norms* that do not squarely fit within the contractual paradigm, as their legal effect is not conditioned on the parties' agreement or consent to be specifically bound by these norms.[130] Expectations classified under this category may be characterised as quasi-regulatory in nature.

126 Although legally *binding*, they are not necessarily always privately *enforceable* by the parties. On non-compliance with directors' duties, see V.C.4.ii.b below.

127 Quotation from *O'Neill* [1999] 1 WLR 1092, 1099. Although Lord Hoffmann did not expressly refer to Companies Act provisions in that context, it is uncontroversial that Companies Act provisions form part of the 'terms'; see Hannigan (2018): paras. [19–44]–[19–52].

128 E.g. Davies & Worthington (2016): para. [20–6].

129 See V.C.4.iii.c below.

130 However, it is also possible to think of this category as 'terms implied in (common) law'; cf Chen-Wishart (2018): 409–14.

B GENERAL PRINCIPLES. There are three general principles on unfairness relating to the petitioner themselves, which are consistent with the contractual paradigm[131] of unfair prejudice.

First is the role of intention.[132] The petitioner need not establish that the respondent acted in bad faith[133] or had subjectively intended to cause unfair prejudice to the petitioner,[134] although proof of such intent would increase the petitioner's chances of success.[135]

The second concerns the petitioner's consent or acquiescence: a petitioner may not base their complaint on matters to which they have consented.[136] Consent precludes unfairness[137] unless there are good reasons why the respondent should not rely upon the petitioner's consent.[138] However, consent or acquiescence to a presumptively unfairly prejudicial course of conduct may be revoked with reasonable notice.[139] Unjustified delay in the commencement of proceedings by the petitioner that causes 'prejudice or an irretrievable change of position' to the respondents would be a significant factor for the court's consideration in exercising its discretion as to whether to grant or refuse relief.[140]

The third general principle concerns the petitioner's behaviour or 'fault', broadly construed. Although not a bright-line rule, the petitioner's poor behaviour is a factor considered by the court, and possible adverse consequences range from costs consequences[141] to complete refusal of relief.[142] Examples of poor behaviour include disinterest in management,[143] creating and sending a forged letter to induce the respondents to sell their shares at lower prices,[144] and a director's attempt to negotiate the purchase of a competing business without disclosure to the company.[145] Similar

131 The contractual paradigm in this context is based on English contract law.

132 In English contract law, it is unnecessary to prove intent or fault to establish a culpable breach of contract because contractual liability is strict. See *Raineri* v. *Miles* [1981] AC 1050 (HL) 1086; Smith (2004): ch. 10.

133 *Shooter* [1990] BCLC 384, 395.

134 *Re Jayflex Construction Ltd, McKee* v. *O'Reilly* [2003] EWHC 2008 (Ch); [2004] 2 BCLC 145 [56]; *Re Sam Weller & Sons Ltd* [1990] Ch 682 (ChD) 690.

135 *Sunrise Radio* [2010] 1 BCLC 367 [11].

136 *Re Batesons Hotels (1958) Ltd, Bateson* v. *Bateson* [2013] EWHC 2530 (Ch); [2014] 1 BCLC 507 [53]; *Croly* v. *Good* [2010] EWHC 1 (Ch); [2010] 2 BCLC 569 [94]; *Neath Rugby* [2010] BCC 597 [72].

137 *Batesons Hotels* [2014] 1 BCLC 507 [53].

138 Ibid. [54] ('any express agreement or understanding giving rise to some equitable consideration preventing reliance being placed upon such shareholder consent').

139 *Fisher* v. *Cadman* [2005] EWHC 377 (Ch); [2006] 1 BCLC 499 [93]–[94].

140 *Re Edwardian Group Ltd, Estera Trust (Jersey) Ltd* v. *Singh* [2018] EWHC 1715 (Ch), [2019] 1 BCLC 171 [571].

141 *Richardson* v. *Blackmore, Capital Cabs Ltd v Blackmore* [2005] EWCA Civ 1356; [2006] BCC 276 [62].

142 *Richardson* v. *Blackmore* [2006] BCC 276 [53]; *Grace* v. *Biagioli* [2006] 2 BCLC 70 [68]–[70]; *Re London School of Electronics Ltd* [1986] Ch 211 (ChD) 221–2; *R A Noble* [1983] BCLC 273, 290–2.

143 *R A Noble* [1983] BCLC 273, 292.

144 *Richardson* v. *Blackmore* [2006] BCC 276, [11], [27]. On the facts the forged letter did not preclude the petitioner from relief: ibid [61].

145 *Grace* v. *Biagioli* [2006] 2 BCLC 70 [65]. The Court of Appeal affirmed the trial judge's holding that the petitioner's dismissal as director was justified, but allowed the petitioner's appeal and ordered relief on other grounds: ibid. [70], [83]–[85].

to the case of consent, relief may be denied on the basis that the prejudice incurred by the petitioner was not unfair in the circumstances.[146]

ii Category I: Formal, Written Rules

Conceptually the most straightforward category, it is also the oldest. Even under the former oppression regime, conduct that was wrongful in and of itself[147] – that is, in breach of legally binding rules – was a recognised basis for relief.[148] Rules are classified by source below.

A CORPORATE CONSTITUTION AND SHAREHOLDER AGREEMENT. The contractual[149] terms on which a company's affairs are conducted are usually contained in the corporate constitution and shareholder agreements.[150] The two are closely related but distinct.[151] Breaches of the corporate constitution (to which the member has not consented or acquiesced) generally constitute unfair prejudice,[152] subject to one limitation: mere 'trivial or technical infringements of [the corporate constitution]' do not suffice.[153] As for shareholder agreements, a breach may in principle give rise to an unfair prejudice petition,[154] but there are no well-known (if any) examples of relief actually being granted on this basis. In any event, breach of a shareholder agreement usually gives rise to relief in contract; resort by the aggrieved member to unfair prejudice may be unnecessary.[155] Things are different if the aggrieved member intends to withdraw, and the shareholder agreement does not specifically provide for exit options. Here, the aggrieved member would have the incentive to invoke the unfair prejudice remedy. Whether withdrawal would be permitted on this basis remains an open question.

146 *London School of Electronics* [1986] Ch 211, 222–3; *R A Noble* [1983] BCLC 273, 292.

147 This is distinguished from conduct that may not be 'wrongful', but which is still considered unfairly prejudicial. See V.C.4.iii below.

148 *Scottish Co-operative* [1959] AC 324 (HL) 342 ('burdensome, harsh, and wrongful').

149 I use 'contractual' here in the narrow and strict sense, meaning terms arising from clearly contractual, as opposed to mandatory or regulatory sources.

150 *O'Neill* [1999] 1 WLR 1092, 1098.

151 The corporate constitution is governed by company law, whereas the shareholder agreement is regulated by contract law: Muth & FitzGerald (2012): para. [1–03]. For further differences see ibid. ch 1.

152 *Fisher* v. *Cadman* [2006] 1 BCLC 499 [90]–[93]; see also *Anderson* v. *Hogg* 2000 SLT 634 (OH) 639.

153 *Saul D Harrison* [1995] 1 BCLC 14, 18; see also *O'Neill* [1999] 1 WLR 1092, 1098 (observing that the unfair prejudice provision was intended to 'free the court from technical considerations of legal right and to confer a wide power to do what appeared just and equitable'); *Parkinson* v. *Eurofinance Group Ltd* [2001] 1 BCLC 720 (Ch) [85].

154 *Re Coroin Ltd (No 2), McKillen* v. *Misland (Cyprus) Investments Ltd* [2013] EWCA Civ 781; [2013] 2 BCLC 583 [17]; Hollington (2017): para. [7–82].

155 Remedies for breach of shareholder agreement are limited to those provided for in the agreement itself or in contract law (termination and/or damages); unfair prejudice relief is theoretically limited only by imagination.

B STATUTORY AND COMMON LAW. The *law* – whether the Companies Act, other primary or subsidiary legislation, or the common law – is also a source of the precise terms on which the members associate.[156] These terms apply to all companies and their members as a sort of 'universal expectation'.[157] Non-compliance with the law would appear on its face to be a ground for relief under unfair prejudice.[158] Examples of actionable non-compliance with Companies Act regulatory requirements include the failure to hold AGMs when the law so required[159] and the removal of auditors '(a) on grounds of divergence of opinions on accounting treatments or audit procedures, or (b) on any other improper grounds'.[160]

The most important class of cases under this category feature breaches of directors' duties. Previously composed primarily of duties at common (not statutory) law, directors' duties have since been codified in the Companies Act.[161] A significant number of cases in which the courts have granted relief[162] were pre-codification cases featuring misapplication of corporate assets,[163] self-dealing,[164] diversion of business opportunities,[165] or secret profits[166] – situations that would today fall under the codified duty to avoid conflicts of interest.[167] By contrast, for petitions founded on breaches of directors' duties of skill and care[168] (an area of law traditionally receiving less judicial attention[169]) there is greater judicial reluctance to grant

156 *Tobian Properties* [2013] 2 BCLC 567 [22].

157 Boros (1995): 137 ('Universal expectations are (by definition) common to all companies and can be equated with external standards of fair dealing'). See also Goddard (1999a): 74–5 ('highly generalised hypothetical bargain').

158 *Tobian Properties* [2013] 2 BCLC 567 [22]; Hollington (2017): para. [7–122].

159 *Fisher* v. *Cadman* [2006] 1 BCLC 499 [97]. This case was decided under old law; currently, AGMs are mandatory for only public companies and traded companies, and public companies are required to lay accounts before AGMs: Companies Act, ss. 336, 437. Previously, all companies were subject to these requirements: Companies Act 1985, s. 366 (repealed).

160 Companies Act, s. 994(1A). See also *Sunrise Radio* [2010] 1 BCLC 367 [10].

161 Companies Act, ss. 170–177. Although statutorily codified duties replace pre-existing general law duties, the latter remain relevant to the interpretation of the former: Companies Act, s. 170(3)–(4); Langford (2015): 637.

162 Cited below (nn. 163–166) are cases in which relief was actually granted; in many other cases, the issue arose during interlocutory proceedings. See also Dignam & Lowry (2016): para. [11.55].

163 *London School of Electronics* [1986] Ch 211 (diversion of existing customers); *Elgindata (No 1)* [1991] BCLC 959, 1004 (unfairly prejudicial to misapply assets for benefit of family and friends).

164 *Lloyd* v. *Casey* [2002] 1 BCLC 454 [102]–[103]; *Dalby* v. *Bodilly* [2004] EWHC 3078 (Ch); [2005] BCC 627.

165 *Allmark* v. *Burnham* [2005] EWHC 2717 (Ch); [2006] 2 BCLC 437.

166 *Re Baumler (UK) Ltd, Gerrard* v. *Koby* [2004] EWHC 7673 (Ch); [2005] 1 BCLC 92.

167 Companies Act, s. 175. See generally Lim (2013) (on the duty under English law) and Langford (2019): 408–17 (on unfair prejudice as a remedy for breaches of the duty in the UK, Australia, Canada, Hong Kong, and New Zealand).

168 Now codified as Companies Act, s. 174.

169 No precise empirical data exists on the frequency with which director's duty of care and skill is litigated in the UK. Given the rarity of private enforcement of directors' duties in general, it is likely to be extremely low. See Armour (2009): 83 tbl. 3.2 (reporting that the number of decided derivative action cases is consistently low); Armour et al. (2009b): 699 (reporting that in public limited companies (plcs) the number of claims filed naming directors as defendants (i.e. attempts at private enforcement of

relief,[170] and petitioners have succeeded on this ground only infrequently and in exceptional cases.[171] In a 2019 case, relief was ordered on the basis that the respondent directors' failure to adopt a dividend policy constituted failures to act fairly as between members and to exercise reasonable care, skill, and diligence.[172] A workable distinction would be between mere negligent mismanagement, which without more is unlikely to result in relief, and more serious forms of mismanagement, which would suffice.[173]

C OTHER RULES OF QUASI-LEGAL AND PUBLIC CHARACTER. Finally, the UK position is unclear as to breaches of norms with quasi-legal character such as corporate governance codes. Breaches of the London Stock Exchange Listing Rules, the City Code on Takeovers and Mergers, or the Cadbury Code (forerunner of the UK Corporate Governance Code) did not entitle listed company shareholders to relief.[174] More recently, Arden LJ (later Lady Arden JSC) opined that directors' remuneration issues in unfair prejudice cases should be judicially decided with reference to 'objective commercial criteria' such as non-binding guidelines issued by various bodies, citing as the reason the remedy's importance in building investor confidence in smaller companies.[175] How the UK position will evolve going forward remains to be seen.

iii Category II: Informal, Unwritten Expectations

A CONCEPT AND TERMINOLOGY. Practically, affairs of companies are often not governed exclusively by exhaustive, formal, written rules.[176] From a 'contractual' perspective, the 'full bargain'[177] between the members in relation to the company includes not just the formal written contractual documents, but also any informal 'agreements' or 'understandings' that do not by themselves satisfy the formal requirements of an independently legally enforceable contract.[178] If proved to the court's

directors' duties) is very low). See also Gerner-Beuerle & Schuster (2014): 199 (observing that the duty of care is generally poorly defined and enforced across Europe).

170 *Oak Investment* [2010] 2 BCLC 459 [8] (court slow to 'second guess' business decisions); *Saul D Harrison* [1995] 1 BCLC 14, 31; *Elgindata (No 1)* [1991] BCLC 959, 993–994; *Sam Weller* [1990] Ch 682, 694.

171 See e.g. *Re Macro (Ipswich) Ltd* [1994] 2 BCLC 354 (ChD) 406 (granting relief in view of 'specific acts of mismanagement' of which 'several … were repeated over many years').

172 *Routledge* v. *Skerritt* [2019] EWHC 573 (Ch) [142], [144]. The former is a statutory duty (Companies Act, s. 172(1)(f)), and the latter is non-statutory. See also *Re McCarthy Surfacing Ltd, Hequet* v. *McCarthy* [2008] EWHC 2279 (Ch); [2009] 1 BCLC 622 [84] ('[this] is a case where the board has consistently failed to consider whether or not to declare dividends, and that must be a breach of duty').

173 A coup by one quasi-partner member against another is more than mere 'mismanagement': *Oak Investment* [2010] 2 BCLC 459 [114] ('coup … was of the utmost gravity and was admittedly unfairly prejudicial'), [120] ('disgraceful, and inexcusable, conduct'), [121] ('serious piece of misconduct'); see also Riley (1992): 795 (distinguishing between 'competent' and 'honest' management); Goddard (1999a): 74–5.

174 *Astec* [1998] 2 BCLC 556, 589–90.

175 *Tobian Properties* [2013] 2 BCLC 567 [28], [36] (Arden LJ).

176 Davies & Worthington (2016): para. [20–7].

177 Riley (2003): 388.

178 *O'Neill* [1999] 1 WLR 1092, 1101('A promise may be binding as a matter of justice and equity although for one reason or another … it would not be enforceable in law').

satisfaction, informal unwritten expectations constrain or otherwise qualify the exercise of legal rights and powers as provided for in the formal, written rules, making otherwise rule-compliant, lawful conduct unfair and accordingly actionable.[179] Protected expectations falling within the 'informal, unwritten' category have since *O'Neill* (1999) been called 'equitable considerations' in the UK.[180]

A brief note on 'equity' is in order, as Anglo-Commonwealth unfair prejudice literature is peppered with references to 'equity', and two highly salient and authoritative cases of the House of Lords – *Ebrahimi* and *O'Neill* – were ostensibly[181] decided using principles of 'equity'. However, in keeping with this Book's functional approach, a typology based on 'informal, unwritten expectations' is adopted, with references to 'equitable considerations' and other doctrinal formulations only where clarity so requires.

B UK 'EQUITABLE CONSIDERATIONS' VERSUS COMMONWEALTH 'REASONABLE EXPECTATIONS'. Notwithstanding the invocation of 'equity', which might suggest notions of 'fairness' broader than the narrow bounds of contract, UK unfair prejudice law fits the 'contractual' paradigm perfectly.[182] In a memorable, oft-quoted portion of Lord Hoffmann's speech in *O'Neill*, judges are exhorted to use the so-called 'cross-check':

> I think that one useful cross-check in a case [involving 'equitable considerations'] is to ask whether the exercise of the power in question would be contrary to what the parties, by words or conduct, have actually agreed. Would it conflict with the promises which they appear to have exchanged?[183]

This statement clearly frames the judicial inquiry as a fundamentally contractual one. It is undisputed that informal expectations – even those that add to, rather than merely qualify the express rules of the corporate constitution[184] – are protected by the law of unfair prejudice where they are based on a clear promise to the petitioner by words or conduct. Conversely, relief seems unlikely where the words or conduct relied on by the petitioner fall short of a promise.[185]

179 *Saul D Harrison* [1995] 1 BCLC 14, 19–20.
180 Cf *O'Neill* [1999] 1 WLR 1092, 1099, 1102 with *Saul D Harrison* [1995] 1 BCLC 14, 19–20.
181 'Equity', 'equitable', 'inequitable' or variations thereof appear forty-four times (including citations) in *O'Neill* but Lord Hoffmann never identified the specific principle of equity he was relying on. Although *Blisset* v. *Daniel* (1853) 10 Hare 493 was cited by Lord Hoffmann in *O'Neill* and by Lord Wilberforce in *Ebrahimi*, *Blisset* also appears to be distinguishable from or otherwise inconsistent with the two modern cases. See discussion in Hollington (2007): 23, 25–7 (arguing that *Ebrahimi* and *O'Neill* did not represent well-established positions in equity).
182 *O'Neill* [1999] 1 WLR 1092, 1101 ('equity could give effect to what it considered to have been the true intentions of the parties by preventing or restraining the exercise of legal rights').
183 Ibid.
184 *Fisher* v. *Cadman* [2006] 1 BCLC 499 [90].
185 *O'Neill* [1999] 1 WLR 1092, 1103 (respondent held to have made no promise on the facts as he withdrew from negotiations); *Khoshkou* v. *Cooper* [2014] EWHC 1087 (Ch) [24] ('the members must have reached a sufficient degree of agreement that it can be said that there has been a breach of good faith in departing from it').

The 'equitable considerations' (or former 'legitimate expectations') approach prevailing in the UK may be contrasted with the 'reasonable expectations' model followed by New Zealand and Canada at the Commonwealth's other end. Under the 'reasonable expectations' model, the court may grant unfair prejudice relief if it finds the petitioner's expectations reasonable;[186] the expectation need not strictly have a quasi-contractual basis such as an informal agreement or shared understanding.[187] The reasonable expectations model may be described as 'fairness-based', as opposed to contractual.[188] Consequently, relief may be possible even if the expectation's basis was less than a clear promise.

The 'unimaginative[ness]'[189] and circularity of the Canada and New Zealand approaches may understandably frustrate seekers of a clear and elegant solution. Being a concept relatively open to external norms, 'reasonable expectations' boasts one critical advantage: it retains the capacity for growth. By contrast, *O'Neill* left the UK's substantive law of unfair prejudice in the contractual paradigm's conceptual straitjacket.[190]

C THE 'QUASI-PARTNERSHIP' AS A DE FACTO REQUIREMENT FOR 'EQUITABLE CONSIDERATIONS'. As a starting point, in most companies large or small, the Companies Act and the corporate constitution are the exclusive sources of rules and expectations as between the company and the members themselves.[191] Consequently, members generally cannot claim to have been unfairly treated unless there is a breach of the rules (in the Category I sense) to which they have consented to be bound.[192] It is only when certain circumstances exist that the otherwise lawful exercise of legal rights may be constrained by 'equitable considerations'.[193]

For equitable considerations to arise, it is insufficient for the company to be small or private; the underlying distinction is between a purely commercial relationship in which formal documents exhaustively document the terms of the relationship, and

186 See (for New Zealand) *Latimer* [2005] 2 NZLR 328 [96]; (for Canada) *BCE Inc v 1976 Debentureholders* 2008 SCC 69; [2008] 3 SCR 560.

187 Given the absence of unequivocal judicial authority on this point, the position is open.

188 Paterson (2006): 215.

189 Ibid. 214.

190 *O'Neill* quickly received considerable public backlash: CLRSG (2001): para. [7.41] (reporting that 'the majority of views expressed in responses to *Developing the Framework* [CLRSG (2000a) – an earlier consultation document] were in favour of reversing *O'Neill* and thereby extending the scope of the [unfair prejudice] remedy'). Scholars have noted the judgment's fundamentally conservative tone and its potential to constrain further expansion of situations eligible for unfair prejudice relief. See e.g. Davies & Worthington (2016): para. [20–8]; Goddard (1999c): 335; Lowry (2002): 246 (questioning the appropriateness of restricting the scope of unfair prejudice). Contrast Boyle (2002): 98 ('[*O'Neill*] neither extends nor restricts the range of circumstances which may amount to unfair prejudice.'). The devastating and incisive criticism of *O'Neill* in Shapira (2000) is worth reading in full.

191 *Ebrahimi* [1973] AC 360 (HL) 379, quoted with approval in *O'Neill* [1999] 1 WLR 1092, 1099.

192 *O'Neill* [1999] 1 WLR 1092, 1098–9; *Saul D Harrison* [1995] 1 BCLC 14, 17–18.

193 Although originating in just and equitable winding-up, 'equitable considerations' have been equally applicable to unfair prejudice since before *O'Neill*; see *Re Bird Precision Bellows Ltd* [1984] Ch 419 (ChD) 429–30.

'something more' than just that.[194] That determination is based on a multi-factorial test. Although non-exhaustive,[195] according to *Ebrahimi* the most well-known three factors are:[196]

> (i) an association formed or continued on the basis of a personal relationship, involving mutual confidence … ;
> (ii) an agreement, or understanding, that all, or some … of the shareholders shall participate in the conduct of the business;
> (iii) restriction upon the transfer of the members' interest in the company – so that if confidence is lost, or one member is removed from management, he cannot take out his stake and go elsewhere.

Whether the company is a family company may be a fourth factor.[197] A company that exhibits one or more of the above factors is often called a *quasi-partnership*.

The existence of a quasi-partnership is a necessary but not sufficient condition for invoking equitable considerations.[198] Under the 'contractual' paradigm prevailing post-*O'Neill*, the onus is still on the petitioner to establish the exact protected expectations ('equitable considerations') existing in the quasi-partnership, and how such expectations have been breached by the respondents. The practical implication of the quasi-partnership requirement is to significantly restrict the scope of companies in which members may rely upon 'equitable considerations' in pursuing unfair prejudice petitions. For now, it appears that public, listed companies are firmly excluded in the UK.[199] Typical expectations of members in quasi-partnerships protected by the law of unfair prejudice are discussed next.

D EXPECTATIONS AS TO PARTICIPATION IN MANAGEMENT. Exclusion from management is by far the most commonly invoked ground in unfair prejudice petitions.[200] A classic and oft-encountered example of exclusion is removal of the petitioner from their position as director.[201] As a matter of strict legal powers, this is not difficult for two reasons. First, formal written rules of UK company law permit removal of directors without cause by simple majority vote of the members.[202] Second, members do not by

[194] *Ebrahimi* [1973] AC 360, 379.
[195] Ibid. ('It would be impossible, and wholly undesirable, to define the circumstances in which these considerations may arise.').
[196] Ibid.
[197] *Kam Leung Sui Kwan* v. *Kam Kwan Lai* [2015] HKCFA 79; [2015] 6 HKC 644 [46]. Although a winding-up case, the family company point is equally applicable to unfair prejudice.
[198] *Coroin (No 2)* [2013] 2 BCLC 583 [635]; *Fisher* v. *Cadman* [2006] 1 BCLC 499 [84].
[199] *Astec* [1998] 2 BCLC 556, 588–9.
[200] LawComm (1997): para. 3.13 fn. 18 (64 per cent of petitions contained allegations of this type).
[201] See Joffe et al. (2015): para. [6.152] note 370.
[202] Companies Act, s. 168(1). Although seemingly a mandatory rule, by case law small, private companies may entrench member-directors by granting them, for the purpose of any resolution aimed at their removal, extra voting rights sufficient to block the resolution: *Bushell* v. *Faith* [1970] AC 1099 (HL)

mere fact of their shareholding status have any entitlement or expectation to be appointed, or protected from removal, as director.[203] However, members in quasi-partnerships often expect to become, and are indeed appointed as directors pursuant to informal agreements or understandings amounting to protected expectations.[204] Removing them as directors in such cases,[205] or where the petitioner is removed in breach of formal, written rules such as the convening of a meeting and quorum requirements,[206] would be presumptively unfairly prejudicial. However, a member who held office as a director but did not actually participate in management has no protected expectation to retain their position.[207] Exclusion of the petitioner in their capacity as member or employee may also suffice under this ground.

Examples of exclusion include a situation where the results of board meetings are pre-determined and the meeting itself has become a 'charade',[208] withholding from the petitioner the company's financial information[209] or important matters concerning the company's survival,[210] failure to call shareholder meetings and to present accounts,[211] changing the locks to limit[212] or exclude outright the petitioner's access to the company's premises,[213] denial of access to the company's banking facilities or corporate records,[214] suspending the petitioner's use of a company mobile phone or car, denying the petitioner contact with customers,[215] or instituting rigged disciplinary

1109. Unless legislatively reversed, this case means that section 168(1) is effectively a default rule in small, private companies: see Davies & Worthington (2016): para. [14–51].

203 Hannigan (2018): para. [19–63]. This applies even where the member holds half the shares: *Baker v Potter* [2004] EWHC 1422 (Ch); [2005] BCC 855 [90].

204 One classic factor weighing in favour of quasi-partnership classification is an agreement that some or all of the members participate in management. See text to (n. 196) above. See also Riley (2003): 392 (suggesting that 'a shareholder in a company in which substantially all the shareholders were directors would have an expectation of remaining a director thereof, or of being bought out on fair terms if the directorship were terminated' as a matter of default, and not just restricted to 'cases where there was some actual, albeit informal, understanding to that effect') (citing Lord Hoffmann in *O'Neill*).

205 See e.g. *00477 of 1986* [1986] BCLC 376, 379.

206 *Re J&S Insurance & Financial Consultants Ltd, Judge* v. *Bahd* [2014] EWHC 2206 (Ch) [20], [117]. This situation can be considered an example of Category I unfairness; see V.C.4.ii.

207 *Re Estate Acquisition & Development Ltd* [1995] BCC 338 (ChD) 350 (petitioner did not attend board meetings).

208 *Re LCM Wealth Management Ltd, Moxon* v. *Litchfield* [2013] EWHC 3957 (Ch) [118].

209 *Re Abbington Hotel Ltd, DiGrado* v. *D'Angelo* [2011] EWHC 635 (Ch); [2012] 1 BCLC 410 [91], [118]; *Fowler* v. *Gruber* [2009] CSOH 36; [2010] 1 BCLC 563 [129].

210 *Whillock* v. *Henderson* [2007] CSOH 175; [2009] BCC 314 [6], [14] (interlocutory proceedings; respondent caused the company to cease trading and set up a competing company without informing the petitioner). Unusually, what would otherwise appear to be a Category I breach of director's duty case is pleaded as an exclusion from management case, but it supports the broader proposition that exclusion from management may have a wide meaning.

211 *Fowler* [2010] 1 BCLC 563 [129].

212 *Re Phoenix Contracts (Leicester) Ltd, Shepherd* v. *Williamson* [2010] EWHC 2375 (Ch) [115].

213 *Abbington Hotel* [2012] 1 BCLC 410 [91], [118].

214 Ibid.

215 *Phoenix Contracts* [2010] EWHC 2375 (Ch) [115].

proceedings against the petitioner.[216] Conversely, exclusion may also be recognised if the petitioner is, in breach of an agreement, *not* appointed director.[217]

Exclusion from management precedents appear generous to petitioners, but respondents may invoke three powerful 'defences' to deprive petitioners of judicial relief. First is the role of consent:[218] for exclusion to be unfairly prejudicial it must be against the will of the excluded petitioner. A director-employee who resigned their position as employee voluntarily is unlikely to be granted relief.[219] It is not unfairly prejudicial to remove a director who had expressed the intention to 'withdraw' from the business of the company (albeit without resigning their position formally) and did not exercise their powers or perform their duties as a director.[220]

The second is that fault of the petitioner may adversely affect their chances of success.[221] Depending on the seriousness of the petitioner's conduct,[222] the court may consider exclusion to be justified and therefore not unfair, and deny relief to the petitioner.[223] A buyout at a discounted valuation may be ordered notwithstanding that the petitioner's exclusion itself was justified by the petitioner's own conduct.[224] Even if temporary exclusion is justified, continuing and complete exclusion might not.[225] Whether exclusion is justified is to be determined based on the facts known to the respondent at the time of exclusion; the respondent may not invoke the petitioner's problematic conduct that became known only later as an ex post facto justification for the exclusion.[226] However, once the exclusion is found to be justified by the petitioner's own fault, the petitioner would be hard pressed to show that the exclusion is unfair based on other circumstances. The courts are unsympathetic even if the petitioner would have been excluded regardless of their conduct,[227] or if the petitioner were treated

216 Ibid. [115]–[116].

217 *Rahman* v. *Malik* [2008] EWHC 959 (Ch); [2008] 2 BCLC 403 [82]–[85].

218 See V.C.4.i.c above.

219 *Re Phoenix Office Supplies Ltd, Phoenix Office Supplies Ltd* v. *Larvin* [2002] EWCA Civ 1740; [2003] 1 BCLC 76 [33]. The court hinted that if the petitioner's demand had been for a buyout at 'an appropriately discounted value', refusal of the respondents to agree could perhaps be unfairly prejudicial: ibid. [34]. The parties seem to have informally agreed on an arrangement where any party wishing to leave the business could do so at will and receive an undiscounted share of the company's net asset value, but failed to formalise the arrangement: ibid. [8]. The petitioner sought to leave for personal reasons and resigned as an employee, but retained office as a director pending resolution of buyout arrangements: ibid. [9]–[11]. The relationship deteriorated and the respondents would have excluded the petitioner from management had he sought to resume involvement: ibid. [14].

220 *Maresca* v. *Brookfield Development and Construction* [2013] EWHC 3151 (Ch) [38].

221 See V.C.4.i.c above.

222 Not every degree of misbehavior justifies exclusion: *Shah* v. *Shah* [2010] EWHC 313 (Ch) [115]; *R & H Electric* [1995] 2 BCLC 280, 295; *London School of Electronics* [1986] Ch 211, 222–3.

223 *Grace* v. *Biagioli* [2006] 2 BCLC 70 [64], [69]–[70] .

224 *Re Lloyds Autobody Ringway Ltd, Davies* v. *Lynch-Smith* [2018] EWHC 2336 (Ch) [130]–[131].

225 *Rahman* v. *Malik* [2008] 2 BCLC 403 [94]–[95].

226 *Judge* v. *Bahd* [2014] EWHC 2206 (Ch) [19], [119].

227 Ibid. [19]; *Mears* v. *R Mears & Co (Holdings) Ltd* [2002] 2 BCLC 1 (ChD) [34].

disproportionately harshly compared to other misbehaving participants in the corporate enterprise.[228]

The third and most helpful 'defence' of the respondent is a fair buyout offer.[229] As Lord Hoffmann famously declared in *O'Neill*, 'the unfairness does not lie in the exclusion alone but in exclusion without a reasonable offer'.[230] The fair buyout offer's requirements are discussed later.[231]

E EXPECTATIONS AS TO RETURNS ON INVESTMENT. Returns on investment in a Ltd take two forms: dividends paid to members, and remuneration or salary for services rendered as director or employee. Although conceptually distinct, the line between the two forms of investment returns may be blur, as it is common for small companies to structure the balance between the two around tax considerations.[232]

Dividends. As a general principle, mere non-payment of dividends, even over a period of years, is not by itself unfairly prejudicial, as members have no general legal right to dividends,[233] although some members may have stronger entitlements to dividends than others depending on the circumstances. Once declared, dividends must be paid to the member entitled to them; no dispute or grievance with the petitioner justifies withholding of dividends.[234] Where the members have an express agreement,[235] or by a course of dealing come to an informal agreement on dividends,[236] breach of the agreement may be unfairly prejudicial.

On the other hand, the company is 'a vehicle for carrying on a business for the benefit of all members',[237] and profits 'ought to be distributed by way of dividends'.[238] Consequently, for directors to exercise their powers to retain profits in the company in disregard of 'the [interest[239]] of members to have profits distributed so far as [is] commercially possible'[240] may be unfairly prejudicial,[241] especially when the company has accumulated substantial

228 Ibid. [35]; *Schwarcz (No 2)* [1989] BCLC 427, 441.
229 For contexts other than exclusion from management, see V.C.5.ii below.
230 *O'Neill* [1999] 1 WLR 1092, 1107.
231 See V.C.5.ii below.
232 See *Baker* v. *Potter* [2005] BCC 855 [117]; see also *Glossop* [1988] 1 WLR 1068, 1075 (observing that the UK tax system was once 'extremely discriminatory against dividends').
233 *Hequet* v. *McCarthy* [2009] 1 BCLC 622 [69].
234 *Grace* v. *Biagioli* [2006] 2 BCLC 70 [72].
235 *Croly* v. *Good* [2010] 2 BCLC 569 [97].
236 *Rahman* v. *Malik* [2008] 2 BCLC 403 [99]–[109], [119].
237 *Glossop* [1988] 1 WLR 1068, 1075.
238 Ibid. 1076.
239 The original quotation used 'right', but it is misleading to say that members have a legal 'right' to dividends.
240 *Glossop* [1988] 1 WLR 1068, 1077.
241 With the basis for the holding in *Glossop* [1988] 1 WLR 1068, 1074–5, 1077 (dividend-type complaints could be basis for just and equitable winding-up, but not unfair prejudice relief because these did not

reserves.[242] Failure of the directors to even consider the issue of dividends – which is itself a breach of duty – is also unfairly prejudicial,[243] as is the respondent directors' consistent disregard of the petitioner's interests by failing to adopt a dividend policy.[244]

'Defences' available to respondents include commercial justification. Executing a growth policy requiring the application of otherwise distributable profits toward acquiring and financing subsidiaries and leaving no cash for dividends is not unfairly prejudicial.[245] Further, the petitioner's consent[246] or acquiescence[247] to a policy of profit retention renders judicial relief unavailable.

Remuneration. Breach of an informal understanding that work would be remunerated could amount to unfair prejudice.[248] However, the mere fact of working for the company without an employment contract or pay does not create a protected expectation to be remunerated, and non-payment of remuneration is accordingly not unfairly prejudicial.[249] More frequently, remuneration-type complaints concern improper or excessive remuneration of directors or employees *other than* the petitioner. A case for relief is difficult to make, as the general principle is that remuneration matters are questions of commercial judgment[250] in which the courts are reluctant to interfere.[251] In addition to breaches of clear legal rules[252] or breaches of formal contractual terms[253] (except those that cannot be cured with the company's internal processes[254]) more properly falling within Category I

constitute discrimination between members) legislatively eliminated (Dignam & Lowry (2016): para. [11.58]), *Glossop* no longer poses an obstacle.

242 *Quinlan* v. *Essex Hinge Co Ltd* [1996] 2 BCLC 417 (ChD) 427; see also *Sam Weller* [1990] Ch 682, 687, 693.

243 *Hequet* v. *McCarthy* [2009] 1 BCLC 622 [84].

244 *Routledge* v. *Skerritt* [2019] EWHC 573 (Ch) [139]–[144].

245 *Sunrise Radio* [2010] 1 BCLC 367 [137]–[142].

246 *Richards* v. *Lundy* [2000] 1 BCLC 376 (ChD) 395 (on the facts, no consent was given by the petitioner).

247 *Sunrise Radio* [2010] 1 BCLC 367 [142].

248 Joffe et al. (2015): para. [6.194].

249 *Amin* v. *Amin* [2009] EWHC 3356 (Ch) [559]–[564].

250 To avoid evoking the American concept of the 'business judgment rule', the term 'business judgment' is deliberately avoided.

251 *Re Halt Garage (1964) Ltd* [1982] 3 All ER 1016 (ChD) 1039 (not an unfair prejudice case). But see V. C.4.iv below on remuneration-type unfair prejudice precedents.

252 Such as the directors' failure to review accounts with care and to investigate accounting irregularities concerning the proper documentation of directors' remuneration (as required by Companies Act, s. 1295 and Sch. 16), even if the remuneration itself was reasonable and properly authorised, is unfairly prejudicial: *Sunrise Radio* [2010] 1 BCLC 367 [220]–[224]. See V.C.4.iv below on *O'Neill*'s impact on this category of unfair prejudice.

253 *Fisher* v. *Cadman* [2006] 1 BCLC 499 [98]–[99].

254 No remedy is available solely on the ground that remuneration arrangements with member-directors controlling over 50 per cent of the company were made without approval at a shareholder meeting as required by the corporate constitution; this is because the non-compliance could have been remedied at the shareholder meeting by the member-directors themselves and accordingly caused no prejudice: *Hequet* v. *McCarthy* [2009] 1 BCLC 622 [80].

unfairness subtypes,[255] breach of informal agreements or understandings on remuneration matters would also constitute unfair prejudice.[256] The issue of excessive remuneration will be addressed in greater detail below.[257]

The primary defence against a remuneration complaint appears to be petitioner's acquiescence or consent.[258] The mere fact that the remuneration quantum is disclosed in the annual accounts filed with the authorities but went unnoticed by the petitioner does not suffice as acquiescence.[259] It may also be possible for the respondent to counter the petition with a fair buyout offer.[260]

F EXPECTATIONS AS TO THE BASIS OF THE RELATIONSHIP OR BUSINESS. A wide variety of agreements or understandings may theoretically be recognised as protected expectations under this residual subtype. There is however scant UK precedent directly on point.[261] It is recognised in other Commonwealth jurisdictions that change in the identity of the corporate participants can be unfairly prejudicial. In a leading Singapore oppression case,[262] the original majority member, a private company, demanded that the minority member waive the company's pre-emption provisions so that the original majority member could sell its shares in the company to a related listed company. The original members had dealt with each other on the basis that the company was a collaboration exclusively between two families through their respective privately owned corporate vehicles. The Singapore Court of Appeal held that it was unfairly prejudicial for the original majority member to insist that the minority member continue in the business with the listed company as it was 'a radically different entity' from the original privately held majority member.[263] The Hong Kong Court of Appeal held in another case that it was unfairly prejudicial for the majority member to appoint a replacement for the deceased managing director with whom the petitioner had a sixteen-year working relationship as fellow directors.[264]

The minority member's acquiescence to the change in the company's participants does not constitute a defence if the minority member had no reasonable alternative.[265]

255 See V.C.4.ii above.

256 *Fisher* v. *Cadman* [2006] 1 BCLC 499 [98]–[99]; *Croly* v. *Good* [2010] 2 BCLC 569 [96].

257 See V.C.4.iv below.

258 *Tobian Properties* [2013] 2 BCLC 567 [42] (no finding that the petitioner 'knowingly acquiesced'; respondent's defence unsuccessful); *Croly* v. *Good* [2010] 2 BCLC 569 [94], [96] (partial defence).

259 See *Tobian Properties* [2013] 2 BCLC 567 [31]–[32] (petitioners have no duty to check the company's accounts).

260 See V.C.5.ii below.

261 *O'Neill* [1999] 1 WLR 1092, 1101–1102; *Re Metropolis Motorcycles Ltd, Hale* v. *Waldock* [2006] EWHC 364 (Ch); [2007] 1 BCLC 520 [89]–[91] (citing *O'Neill* but holding on the facts that circumstances have not changed sufficiently for relief to be granted). See also Hollington (2017): paras. [7-185]–[7-188].

262 Singapore's 'oppression remedy' is materially similar to the UK unfair prejudice remedy.

263 *Over & Over Ltd* v. *Bonvests Holdings Ltd* [2010] SGCA 7; [2010] 2 SLR 776 [102]–[105] (adding that the majority member pursued this course of action so as to liquidate its stake in the company while the minority member remained locked in).

264 *Re Silver Bell Uniform Ltd* [2011] HKCA 481; [2012] 1 HKLRD 719 [50].

265 *Over & Over Ltd* v. *Bonvests Holdings Ltd* [2010] SGCA 7; [2010] 2 SLR 776 [102] (VK Rajah JA).

iv Beyond Category II: Room for Judicially Imposed Expectations Post-*O'Neill*?

While academics' concerns that *O'Neill* would narrow the scope of unfair prejudice would appear to have been partially vindicated by the test of time,[266] there was also optimism. One commentator writing shortly after *O'Neill* remarked that:

> [Lord Hoffmann's] observations do not amount to a restatement of the pre-existing body of case law. Earlier decisions are not overruled. It neither extends nor restricts the range of circumstances which may amount to unfair prejudice.[267]

Some lower court judges similarly downplay *O'Neill*'s impact by maintaining that the law of unfair prejudice is not confined to pre-existing precedent and remains capable of adapting to new cases and challenges.[268] Remnants of pre-*O'Neill* law persist in remuneration-type cases.

A well-established line of cases holds that excessive remuneration to directors in and of itself constitutes unfair prejudice. In a 1985 case, the trial judge held that '[t]he remuneration paid to [the respondent director] in 1984 was plainly in excess of anything he had earned and was so large as to be unfairly prejudicial to [the petitioner]'.[269] In a 1997 case, the judge, dismissing the respondents' application to strike out the petition, held that:

> If the respondents are unable to justify by *objective commercial criteria* that … the remuneration the [respondent] directors were paid by the companies was within the bracket that executives carrying the sort of responsibility and discharging the sort of duties that they were carrying and discharging would expect to receive, the petitioners will, in my opinion, have succeeded in establishing their [unfair prejudice] case.[270]

Interestingly, this judicial attitude seems undampened by *O'Neill*. Courts post-*O'Neill* continue to accept that unfair prejudice could be established if the respondent was responsible for the payment of unreasonably high remuneration.[271] Although judges in post-*O'Neill* remuneration-type cases not uncommonly further justify their findings of unfair prejudice on related grounds such as breach of corporate formalities in the corporate constitution or breach of directors' duties,[272] this is not strictly

266 See Davies & Worthington (2016): para. [20–8]; Kershaw (2012): 689.

267 Boyle (2002): 98; see similarly Hollington (2017): paras. [7–36]–[7–37].

268 See e.g. *Sunrise Radio* [2010] 1 BCLC 367 [12]–[14], citing *Re BSB Holdings Ltd (No 2)* [1996] 1 BCLC 155 (ChD) 243 and *Saul D Harrison* [1995] 1 BCLC 14, 30. Lady Arden JSC, who tried prominent unfair prejudice cases as a High Court judge, emphasised the flexibility of the concept of 'unfair prejudice' and thereby indirectly downplayed *O'Neill*'s restrictive impact. See e.g. *Tobian Properties* [2013] 2 BCLC 567 [28].

269 *Re a Company (No 002612 of 1984)* (1986) 2 BCC 99453 (ChD) 99482, affirmed by *Re Cumana Ltd* [1986] BCLC 430 (CA) 435.

270 *Re a Company (No 004415 of 1996)* [1997] 1 BCLC 479 (ChD) 492 (emphasis added).

271 *Anderson* v. *Hogg* 2000 SLT 634 (OH) 640; *Fisher* v. *Cadman* [2006] 1 BCLC 499 [98]; *Croly* v. *Good* [2010] 2 BCLC 569 [99].

272 See the discussion in V.C.4.iii.e above.

necessary.[273] Accordingly, some judicially implied expectation against unreasonable remuneration may continue to be part of unfair prejudice law.

Two different standards of unreasonableness have emerged. The first is gross unreasonableness; to fall foul of it, the remuneration must be so excessive on its face that it simply cannot be justified.[274] The second is a more moderate standard of unreasonableness, which may be breached by remuneration not justifiable by 'objective commercial criteria'.[275] The test is whether the respondent's remuneration falls 'within the bracket that executives carrying the sort of responsibility and discharging the sort of duties that [the respondent was] carrying and discharging would expect to receive'.[276] In making its assessment, the court would typically rely on expert evidence.[277] Publicly available guidelines on directors' remuneration published by industry groups may also be 'useful background material'.[278]

Judicial scrutiny of commercial matters applying standards of reasonableness has little place within a contractual paradigm. The continued vitality of such standards demonstrates *O'Neill*'s limits and the continued vigilance of the courts in enforcing minimum standards of commercial behaviour.

5 *Unfair Prejudice As a 'Second' Resort*

i The Statutory Remedy's Gap-Filling Function

The unfair prejudice remedy serves 'an essentially "gap-filling" role', and is available only when the petitioner cannot remedy the situation with their own means.[279] The courts are much less ready to entertain petitions from majority members, as they are expected to resolve their own difficulties using their majority voting power.[280] When the conduct complained of is successfully remedied by the majority, it cannot provide any basis for judicial relief under the unfair prejudice remedy.[281] The exception is where the petitioner, notwithstanding their majority shareholding, either lacked the power or ability, or was otherwise obstructed in their lawful attempts to use their

273 *Hurd* v. *TPL Holdings Ltd* (25 March 2014) [2014] Lexis Citation 40 [71] (ChD) (AG Bompas QC).

274 *Allmark* v. *Burnham* [2006] 2 BCLC 437 [96]; *No 002612 of 1984* (1986) 2 BCC 99453 (ChD) 99459–61, 99482.

275 *Tobian Properties* [2013] 2 BCLC 567 [36]; see also *No 004415 of 1996* [1997] 1 BCLC 479, 492–3; *Irvine (No 1)* [2007] 1 BCLC 349 [267]–[270]; *Fowler* v. *Gruber* [2010] 1 BCLC 563 [132].

276 *No 004415 of 1996* [1997] 1 BCLC 479 (ChD) 492, followed in *Irvine (No 1)* [2007] 1 BCLC 349 [267]–[268].

277 *Lloyd* v. *Casey* [2002] 1 BCLC 454 [61]; *Irvine (No 1)* [2007] 1 BCLC 349 [277]–[297]; *Sunrise Radio* [2010] 1 BCLC 367 [186]. But see *Tobian Properties* [2013] 2 BCLC 567 [44]–[49] (given particular facts such as the company's insolvency, the court granted the petitioner leeway regarding expert evidence).

278 *Tobian Properties* [2013] 2 BCLC 567 [36].

279 Goddard (1999b): 241.

280 Tan (2015): 127.

281 *Legal Costs Negotiators* [1999] BCC 547, 554.

power to resolve the situation.[282] Cases where majority member petitioners successfully obtained court-ordered relief fall into this exception.[283]

ii Alternatives to Unfair Prejudice Petitions

Judicial dissolution is not considered a preferable alternative to unfair prejudice. Legally, the grounds for dissolution differ from unfair prejudice.[284] The courts' discouragement of concurrent proceedings under both regimes by petitioners[285] suggest this was not an uncommon practice.

The courts' willingness to let an unfair prejudice petition proceed to full trial depends on the relief sought. Where the desired remedy is the withdrawal of the petitioner from the company facilitated by an order that the respondent purchase the petitioner's shares, *O'Neill* forcefully articulates the judicial preference for out-of-court settlement. The respondent who makes a reasonable offer considered satisfactory by the court would be entitled to have the petition dismissed in a procedural hearing without a full trial,[286] as providing the petitioner the opportunity to exit from the company ameliorates the unfairness.[287] A reasonable offer must, in principle, be for the purchase of the petitioner's shares at fair value on an undiscounted, pro-rata basis.[288] If parties fail to agree on the price, the valuation should be conducted by a competent expert[289] without the need for a formal arbitration procedure or reasons to be given.[290] Parties must be given equal access to corporate information that affects the value of the shares, and granted the right to present oral or written arguments to the valuer.[291] Finally, if the offer is not made within a reasonable time after the relationship between the parties had broken down, the offer should cover the petitioner's costs.[292]

Beyond exclusion from management scenarios,[293] there is uncertainty as to the categories of unfairness in which this 'fair buyout offer' doctrine would deny petitioners their day in court. While the *O'Neill* discussion was in the exclusion from management context,[294] Lord Hoffmann's vague reference to 'breakdown in relations

282 On this theme see generally Tan (2015).

283 *Re H R Harmer Ltd* [1959] 1 WLR 62 (CA) 85 (minority beneficial interest exercised voting control); *Parkinson* [2001] BCLC 720 [51], [88]–[89]; *Abbington Hotel* [2012] 1 BCLC 410 [111]–[112] (two members with equal shareholdings).

284 *Neath Rugby* [2010] BCC 597 [104], [107], overruling *Re Guidezone Ltd* [2000] 2 BCLC 321 (ChD).

285 Civil Procedure Rules Practice Direction 49B, para. 1.

286 'Striking out' or 'summary judgment': Civil Procedure Rules 1998, SI 1998/3132, rr. 3.4(2), 24.2.

287 At least in the exclusion from management context (see also V.C.4.iii.d above): *O'Neill* [1999] 1 WLR 1092, 1107.

288 Ibid. (adding that discounted valuation may be possible in special circumstances); on valuation see also Hollington (2017): paras. [8–91]–[8–94] and V.C.7 below.

289 *O'Neill* [1999] 1 WLR 1092, 1107.

290 Ibid.

291 Ibid.

292 Ibid. 1108.

293 See V.C.4.iii.d above.

294 *O'Neill* [1999] 1 WLR 1092, 1107–8.

between the parties'[295] left room to extend the doctrine to other unfairness scenarios. Post-*O'Neill*, the Court of Appeal on one occasion declined to dismiss summarily a petition alleging breaches of directors' fiduciary duties notwithstanding the existence of a buyout offer,[296] but the High Court in a later case ruled differently.[297]

The courts are unwilling to dismiss petitions without a proper hearing notwithstanding the existence of a buyout offer in situations raising issues of fact and law relevant to valuation that are appropriately heard by a court. As a trial judge cautioned, 'Lord Hoffmann's remarks [in *O'Neill*] were not intended to have the effect of establishing a mechanism for seizure and exclusion'.[298] Examples include where the petitioner is denied access to information about the company and possible wrongdoing,[299] and where the petitioner seeks a remedy other than withdrawal such as winding up[300] or expulsion of the respondent by forcing the respondent to sell.[301]

As a tentative categorisation, I suggest that a fair buyout offer may suffice to have petitions founded on Category II unfairness (such as exclusion from management or deprivation from returns on investment) disposed of without a full hearing for two reasons. First, unlike other categories, Category II unfairness scenarios do not often raise complex legal issues concerning directors' duties or other judicially developed doctrines which should be reserved for a judicial forum. Second, income and dividend issues are particularly well-suited for expeditious determination by expert valuers without the hassle of expensive court proceedings. It bears repeating that a fair buyout offer must meet the stringent guidelines laid down in *O'Neill* if it is to withstand judicial scrutiny.

6 *Effect and Procedure of Invoking Unfair Prejudice*

A member cannot unilaterally withdraw from the company unless there is an express contractual right to that effect. Even where grounds establishing unfair prejudice exist, without a legally enforceable contract, legally effective withdrawal may be facilitated only by the court in the exercise of its powers.[302] Consequently, until and unless the court makes a ruling on liability finding some party to be at fault in a given case and further makes an order that the respondent must buy out the petitioner's shares, the petitioner remains a member.[303]

295 Ibid. 1108.

296 *North Holdings Ltd* v. *Southern Tropics Ltd* [1999] 2 BCLC 625 (CA) 637; see also *Harborne Road Nominees Ltd* v. *Karvaski* [2011] EWHC 2214 (Ch); [2012] 2 BCLC 420 [30].

297 *Wilkinson* v. *West Coast Capital* [2005] EWHC 3009 (Ch); [2007] BCC 717 [329]–[331].

298 *Harborne Road Nominees* [2012] 2 BCLC 420 [27].

299 Ibid. [31].

300 *Re Copeland & Craddock Ltd* [1997] BCC 294 (CA) 299–300.

301 Ibid.

302 The court has no jurisdiction to *order* a share buyout unless it is satisfied that there was indeed unfair prejudice: Hollington (2017): paras. [8–01], [8–06], [8–75].

303 The judicial preference for maintaining status quo is evident in *Re a Company (No 002612 of 1984)* [1985] BCLC 80 (ChD) 82–3.

To commence unfair prejudice proceedings, a petitioner must follow specific court procedures.[304] The company is always a nominal party to the proceedings,[305] with its involvement generally restricted to matters such as discovery or disclosure of documents[306] unless special circumstances exist.[307] The petitioner should, at a minimum, make every person against whom relief is sought or whose interests would otherwise be affected by the proceedings a respondent.[308]

Owing to the broad nature of the unfair prejudice jurisdiction, there is no hard limit to who may be made party to – and if grounds are established, against whom relief can be granted – in unfair prejudice proceedings.[309] The test of liability, stated generally, is 'whether what was done involved unfairness in which the relevant [respondent] was sufficiently implicated to warrant relief being granted against him'.[310] It is possible for the court to order non-members[311] or a member who did not directly perpetrate the unfairly prejudicial conduct[312] to purchase the petitioner's shares.

How the petitioner's rights would be affected while proceedings are underway would depend on their source. In exclusion from management cases,[313] the court will be reluctant to order that the petitioner be retained – even temporarily – as a director.[314] However, contractual rights (such as directors' service contracts) or rights or expectations connected with the shares themselves (such as the company's shareholding structure[315] and the petitioner's indirect veto rights[316]) are likely to be preserved pending resolution of the proceedings.

304 Companies (Unfair Prejudice Applications) Proceedings Rules 2009, SI 2009/2469.

305 Ibid. rr. 3(3), 4(1); *Re Crossmore Electrical and Civil Engineering Ltd* [1989] BCLC 137 (ChD) 138.

306 The company is generally so obligated unless the documents are covered by legal privilege: *Arrow Trading and Investments Est 1920* v. *Edwardian Group Ltd* [2004] EWHC 1319 (Ch); [2005] 1 BCLC 696 [24].

307 *Crossmore* [1989] BCLC 137, 138; *Re Hydrosan Ltd* [1991] BCLC 418 (ChD) 420 (defending respondents using company funds is itself unfair prejudice); *Re a Company (No 004502 of 1988), ex p Johnson* [1992] BCLC 701 (ChD) 708 (company's participation or expenditure should be 'necessary or expedient in the interest of the company as a whole'); *Re a Company (No 1126 of 1992)* [1994] 2 BCLC 146 (ChD) 155–6.

308 Compare *Re a Company (No 007281 of 1986)* [1987] BCLC 593 (ChD) 599 with *Re Ravenhart Service (Holdings) Ltd, Reiner* v. *Gershinson* [2004] EWHC 76 (Ch); [2004] 2 BCLC 376 [101].

309 *Re Little Olympian Each-Ways Ltd* [1994] 2 BCLC 420 (ChD) 424–5; *Apex Global Management Ltd* v. *FI Call Ltd* [2013] EWHC 1652 (Ch); [2014] BCC 286 [125].

310 *F & C Alternative Investments (Holdings) Ltd* v. *Barthelemy (No 2)* [2011] EWHC 1731 (Ch); [2012] Ch 613 [1096].

311 *Apex Global Management* [2014] BCC 286 [125].

312 *Re Dinglis Properties Ltd, Dinglis* v. *Dinglis* [2019] EWHC 1664 (Ch); [2019] Bus LR 3100 [353] (ordering the respondent member, a corporate entity under the sole ownership and control of the respondent former director-member (Andreas) and to which Andreas had transferred shares of the company, to buy out the petitioner's shares).

313 See V.C.4.iii.d above.

314 *Pringle* v. *Callard* [2007] EWCA Civ 1075; [2008] 2 BCLC 505 [33]. An exception may lie where the petitioner seeks not withdrawal, but rather expulsion of the respondent: see *Re R S M Industries Ltd, Williams* v. *Brinkmann* [2004] EWHC 601 (Ch).

315 *No 002612 of 1984* [1985] BCLC 80, 82–83.

316 See *Re Sticky Fingers Restaurant Ltd* [1992] BCLC 84 (ChD) 89–90.

When in doubt, the petitioner may also give notice of the petition, without making them parties, to other persons who may be interested in the proceedings to give them the opportunity to be heard.[317]

7 *Valuation*

i General Principles

The court has wide discretion in determining the price the purchaser should pay for the seller's shares: 'the "proper" price is the price which the court in its discretion determines to be proper having regard to all the circumstances of the case'.[318] As a starting point:[319]

> There are essentially three possible bases on which a minority holding of shares in an unquoted [i.e. unlisted] company can be valued. In descending order these are:
>
> (i) as a rateable proportion of the total value of the company as a going concern without any discount for the fact that the holding in question is a minority holding;
> (ii) as before but with such a discount; and
> (iii) as a rateable proportion of the net assets of the company at their break up or liquidation value.

If the party forced to purchase the petitioner's shares intends to continue operating the company as a going concern, the general approach is to value the company as a going concern, and not on the basis of its liquidation or break-up value, so as to avoiding giving 'the purchaser a windfall at the expense of the seller'.[320]

It is impossible, beyond these general principles, to state with any certainty precisely which valuation methodology, be it on an earnings or income basis or net asset valuation or some combination thereof,[321] would be adopted on the facts of any particular case. Much would depend on the expert evidence,[322] although the

[317] Hollington (2017): paras. [9–43]–[9–44]; Joffe et al. (2015): para. [7.12].

[318] *Re Bird Precision Bellows* [1986] Ch 658 (CA) 669.

[319] *CVC/Opportunity Equity Partners Ltd* v. *Demarco Almeida* [2002] UKPC 16; [2002] 2 BCLC 108 [37]. This is a judicial dissolution (just and equitable winding up) case appealed to the Privy Council from the Cayman Islands Court of Appeal. Although the Cayman Islands does not have a UK-style unfair prejudice remedy, since 2009 a Cayman court has 'the same wide range of powers' 'as an English court would have in an unfair prejudice petition' if the court is satisfied that there are sufficient grounds to order a just and equitable winding up: Hollington (2013): 173. Privy Council decisions are not strictly binding on UK courts the same way House of Lords or Supreme Court of the United Kingdom decisions are, but as they are often decided by the same judges sitting in the House of Lords or the Supreme Court, Privy Council decisions are frequently applied by lower court judges in the UK.

[320] *CVC/Opportunity Equity* [2002] 2 BCLC 108 [38].

[321] For a brief overview, see Hollington (2017): paras. [8–134]–[8–145].

[322] See Joffe et al. (2015): 590–2 (explaining valuation methodologies).

court retains the discretion to choose between the evidence of competing experts[323] or to appoint its own expert.[324]

ii Minority Discounts and Majority Premiums

For quasi-partnerships, it is reasonably settled that the starting point is a pro-rata valuation that does not include a minority discount where the petitioner is not at fault and the respondent is ordered to buy out the petitioner.[325] A 50 per cent shareholder would not be ordered to sell to the other shareholder at a discount if the former's unfairly prejudicial conduct did not cause the company loss.[326] Refusing to apply minority discounts avoids creating perverse incentives for majorities to oppress minorities,[327] and encourages settlement in lieu of protracted and expensive litigation.[328] However, where the petitioner in a quasi-partnership 'deserves' their exclusion or contributes to the majority's unfairly prejudicial conduct, a discount would be appropriate.[329]

In non-quasi-partnership scenarios where the petitioner acquired their shares as a minority shareholder without any expectation or entitlement to participate in management of the company, a number of older authorities suggest that a minority discount is applicable.[330] The trend appears to have reversed in recent cases, with the court declining to impose a discount, citing the effect of a minority discount in unjustly enriching wrongdoing majority members[331] – which would have defeated the purpose of the unfair prejudice remedy.[332] At present, it would be more accurate to summarise the position

323 See e.g. *Re Blue Index Ltd, Murrell* v. *Swallow* [2014] EWHC 2680 (Ch) [58]–[68].

324 Civil Procedure Rules 1998, SI 1998/3132, r. 35.7 (single joint expert) and r. 35.15 (assessor).

325 *Bird Precision Bellows* [1986] Ch 658 (CA) 667–9; *Profinance Trust SA* v. *Gladstone* [2001] EWCA Civ 1031; [2002] 1 BCLC 141 [18]; *O'Neill* [1999] 1 WLR 1092, 1107; *CVC/Opportunity Equity* [2002] 2 BCLC 108 [40]; *Strahan* v. *Wilcock* [2006] EWCA Civ 13; [2006] 2 BCLC 555 [1], [17]; *Re BC&G Care Homes Ltd, Crowley* v. *Bessell* [2015] EWHC 1518 (Ch), [2016] BCC 615 [141] (although not completely innocent, petitioner's conduct did not warrant exclusion without fair buyout offer). Conversely, a majority member ordered to sell its shares to the minority should not receive a control premium: Hollington (2017): para. [8–152].

326 *Rodliffe* v. *Rodliffe* [2012] EWHC 917 (Ch) [77]. The unfairly prejudicial conduct was one member attacking the other with a hammer.

327 Prentice (1988): 83–5; Prentice (1986): 180.

328 Prentice (1988): 83; Prentice (1986): 182–4.

329 *Bird Precision Bellows* [1984] Ch 419 (ChD) 431; *Hequet* v. *McCarthy* [2009] 1 BCLC 622 [98]–[99].

330 *Bird Precision Bellows* [1984] Ch 419 (ChD) 431; *Elgindata (No 1)* [1991] BCLC 959, 1007; *Re Planet Organic Ltd* [2000] 1 BCLC 366 (ChD) 371 (preference shareholders contributing to unfairly prejudicial conduct ordered to sell their shares to petitioner at a discount); *Irvine* v. *Irvine (No 2)* [2006] EWHC 583 (Ch); [2007] 1 BCLC 445 [11].

331 *Sunrise Radio Ltd* [2010] 1 BCLC 367 [305] (although no longer quasi-partner, petitioner's shares should be valued without discount because otherwise wrongdoing majority member would be unjustly enriched); *Blue Index* [2014] EWHC 2680 (Ch) [36] (declining to follow *Irvine (No 2)*), [51]–[52] (ordering respondent to buy out petitioner ('sleeping partner' with no right to participate in management) without minority discount).

332 *Blue Index* [2014] EWHC 2680 (Ch) [26] ('It would substantially defeat the purpose of the [unfair prejudice] remedy if the oppressing majority were routinely rewarded by the application of a discount

for non-quasi-partnerships as a judicial preference for a pro-rata valuation without discount unless the shares were acquired initially at a discount.[333] Where the exclusion is justified by the petitioner's own conduct, a minority discount is also appropriate.[334]

The court is not forced to choose between a pro-rata valuation and a 'full' minority discount; it may in its discretion apply an intermediate discount.[335]

iii Judicial Adjustments

The court generally values the shares on the basis that the unfairly prejudicial conduct did not occur.[336] To achieve this, 'actual share values can be adjusted [by the court] to reflect the effect on the company of all or any wrongs which the wrongdoer respondents have committed against it'.[337] 'Losses' suffered by the company due to unfairly prejudicial conduct such as transactions at undervalue,[338] improper[339] or unnecessary[340] litigation costs, excessive payments made by the company in the form of remuneration,[341] management charges,[342] or rent,[343] as well as outstanding loans and other claims owed by shareholders to the company[344] may be taken into account in valuation. A similar judicial adjustment may also apply where the petitioner has been unfairly deprived of dividends for many years.[345]

Another way courts account for the respondent's fault is by adjusting the valuation date to reflect the true value of the shares had the unfairly prejudicial conduct not occurred.[346] Although the starting point for the valuation date appears to be the date of the share purchase order by the court,[347] fairness is the overriding consideration for the court in choosing the valuation date,[348] and the date which best remedies the unfair

for a minority shareholding'); in similar vein, *Re Annacott Holdings Ltd, Attwood* v. *Maidment* [2013] EWCA Civ 119; [2013] 2 BCLC 46 [11].

333 *Blue Index* [2014] EWHC 2680 (Ch) [51].

334 *Davies* v. *Lynch-Smith* [2018] EWHC 2336 (Ch) [130]–[131].

335 *Richards* v. *Lundy* [2000] 1 BCLC 376, 398; *Planet Organic* [2000] 1 BCLC 366, 371–372; see also *Fowler* v. *Gruber* [2010] 1 BCLC 563 [187].

336 *Scottish Co-operative* [1959] AC 324, 364, 369; *Profinance* [2002] 1 BCLC 141 [31].

337 *Tobian Properties* [2013] 2 BCLC 567 [26].

338 *Richards* v. *Lundy* [2000] 1 BCLC 376, 400.

339 *Elgindata (No 1)* [1991] BCLC 959, 1008.

340 *Macro* [1994] 2 BCLC 354, 409.

341 *Irvine (No 1)* [2007] 1 BCLC 349 [357]; *Lloyd* v. *Casey* [2002] 1 BCLC 454 [107].

342 *Macro* [1994] 2 BCLC 354, 409.

343 *Re Scitec Group Ltd, Sethi* v. *Patel* [2010] EWHC 1830 (Ch); [2011] 1 BCLC 277 [48].

344 *Scitec* [2011] 1 BCLC 277 [56], [70]; *Richards* v. *Lundy* [2000] 1 BCLC 376, 400.

345 *Hequet* v. *McCarthy* [2009] 1 BCLC 622 [100]–[101] (petitioners received no dividends for the twelve years between their exclusion from management and their petition).

346 I discuss the rule against reflective loss in Koh (2016), where I defend the English practice of applying judicial adjustments to achieve recovery for what might otherwise appear to be non-recoverable reflective loss.

347 *London School of Electronics* [1986] Ch 211, 224.

348 *Profinance* [2002] 1 BCLC 141 [60]; *London School of Electronics* [1986] Ch 211, 224.

prejudice in each case is favoured.[349] In particular, where the unfairly prejudicial conduct was especially reprehensible, an early valuation date may apply so that a general decline in market conditions after unfair prejudice proceedings began would not result in a decreased valuation.[350] Similarly, an earlier valuation date may also apply when the evidence is unclear on whether or to what extent changes in market conditions are responsible for the decline in the company's fortunes and valuation, on the basis that the petitioner should not bear the risk in situations where there is reasonable suspicion that the company's decline in the interim may have been caused by the respondent.[351]

A further tool in the judicial arsenal is 'quasi-interest'. Quasi-interest can be ordered to accrue from the selected valuation date, which can be much earlier than the date of the share purchase order.[352] Generally, a share purchase order with an early valuation date may only be supplemented by an award of 'quasi-interest' when that is the best, if not the only way to achieve a fair result.[353] Quasi-interest was ordered in a quasi-partnership case where the respondents, having excluded the petitioner and deprived the petitioner of any salary or dividends, indicated interest in buying out the petitioner but did not follow through, and instead resisted the unfair prejudice petition.[354] The court has discretion over the rate of interest awarded, though interest rates applied in damages awards may be a useful benchmark.[355]

8 *Enforcement*

Enforcement of withdrawal is theoretically straightforward: the party or parties against whom a share purchase order is made are legally bound to purchase the shares and pay the sum assessed or agreed upon. The usual rules of personal civil liability apply. Impecuniosity of the respondent is not a defence to a share purchase order.[356] Conversely, the specifics of how the purchaser may be compelled to pay is a matter for the petitioner, and not the court deciding the unfair prejudice case.[357] The court may, however, consider ordering payment on deferred terms.[358]

349 *Abbington Hotel* [2012] 1 BCLC 410 [123], [141].

350 *Cumana* [1986] BCLC 430, 435–6, 444.

351 *Croly* v. *Good* [2010] 2 BCLC 569 [113], [117]; *Phoenix Contracts* [2010] EWHC 2375 (Ch) [150]–[154] (both cases set the valuation date as date of the petitioner's exclusion from the company).

352 *Profinance* [2002] 1 BCLC 141 [30]–[31]. This is equivalent to, but different from regular interest, which can only accrue from the date of the court's share purchase order. See *Re Bird Precision Bellows Ltd* [1984] Ch 419 (ChD) 437, affirmed [1986] Ch 658, 677, 679.

353 *Profinance* [2002] 1 BCLC 141 [32].

354 *BC&G Care Homes* [2016] BCC 615 [143].

355 *Annacott Holdings* [2013] 2 BCLC 46 [31]–[36] (upholding trial judge's decision to award quasi-interest at similar rates as section 35A of the Senior Courts Act 1981).

356 *Cumana* [1986] BCLC 430, 436–7, 439, 443–4; *Re Ghyll Beck Driving Range Ltd* [1993] BCLC 1126 (ChD) 1134.

357 *Cumana* [1986] BCLC 430, 437.

358 *Re Phoenix Office Supplies Ltd* [2002] EWHC 591 (Ch); [2002] 2 BCLC 556 [121]–[122], reversed on unrelated grounds [2002] EWCA Civ 1740; [2003] 1 BCLC 76.

In the extremely rare case in which the court orders the company to purchase the petitioner's shares,[359] the court order may provide for the necessary capital reduction.[360]

9 *Avoiding the Unfair Prejudice Regime Ex Ante by Contract*

The unfair prejudice remedy in the limited company is a mandatory remedy that members may not exclude entirely by contract.[361] However, there are two common methods by which would-be petitioners can be denied access to their opportunity to present their case before a court, which we examine below.

i Contractual Exit and Valuation Mechanisms

Not infrequently, members agree to terms governing exit from the company, which can take the form of provisions stipulating circumstances under which one member can buy out another, as well as valuation mechanisms that would be used to determine the price. Common variations include delegating the valuation to auditors or an external, independent expert. If the valuation mechanism breaks down because of disagreement over critical issues such as the appointment of the valuer, the court may step in to perform the valuation itself.[362]

Judicial attitudes towards enforcing contractual valuation mechanisms change over time. Early first instance judgments suggested a willingness to enforce 'rough and ready' contractual exit mechanisms that imposed on the withdrawing member the risk of a minority discount.[363] A turning point in the jurisprudence[364] came when the Court of Appeal reversed Hoffmann J's summary dismissal of a petition, stating that depending on the facts, it might not be unreasonable for a petitioner to refuse an offer carrying the risk of having a minority discount applied.[365] For a time it seemed, similarly to the 'fair buyout offer' doctrine,[366] that the judicial stance would be of proactive case management, where specific issues of law

359 The sole example thus far appears to be *Re Edwardian Group Ltd* [2019] 1 BCLC 171 [630]–[631] (making share purchase order against both the defendant CEO and the company).

360 Companies Act, s. 996(2)(e).

361 This appears to be so taken for granted that to my knowledge, no British author has ever commented on the possibility of excluding the substantive right by contract. By contrast, the unfair prejudice remedy also applies to the limited liability partnership (LLP), but may be excluded indefinitely or for a specified period by unanimous agreement of the LLP members: Limited Liability Partnerships (Application of Companies Act 2006) Regulations 2009, SI 2009/1804, reg. 48.

362 *Cream Holdings Ltd* v. *Davenport* [2010] EWHC 3096 (Ch) [134]–[136], appeal dismissed [2011] EWCA Civ 1287; [2012] 1 BCLC 365.

363 *Re a Company (No 004377 of 1986)* [1987] 1 WLR 102 (ChD); *Re a Company (No 006834 of 1989), ex p Kremer* [1989] BCLC 365 (ChD); *Re Castleburn Ltd* [1991] BCLC 89 (ChD).

364 *Re a Company (No 00330 of 1991), ex p Holden* [1991] BCLC 597 (ChD) 603–4. But see *North Holdings* [1999] 2 BCLC 625, 638 (opining that *Virdi* v. *Abbey Leisure* was decided on the facts).

365 *Virdi* v. *Abbey Leisure Ltd, Re Abbey Leisure Ltd* [1990] BCLC 342 (CA) 350, reversing *Re Abbey Leisure Ltd* [1989] BCLC 619 (ChD).

366 See V.C.5.ii above.

are resolved separately in court in preliminary proceedings, while the rest of the valuation process is delegated to an independent valuer.[367] The unfair prejudice remedy remained available as an avenue for petitioners seeking to challenge the valuer's independence.[368]

Recent Court of Appeal decisions suggest reversion to a more contractarian, less interventionist stance. The court declined in a 2015 case to permit a financially sophisticated investor from circumventing a valuation mechanism to which they had agreed even if the mechanism may act to their disadvantage.[369] In 2014, the court adopted a set of principles governing judicial review of expert determination pursuant to which only errors of non-compliance with mandated procedure or errors on points of law beyond the expert's mandate may be challenged in court.[370] Valuers may decide on issues of law falling within the scope of their mandate; valuers' errors on issues of fact and law within their mandate are unreviewable; and the risk of such errors must be borne by the parties.[371] Where the valuer's mandate is framed in broad terms, interpretation and application of valuation principles are likely to be treated as within the scope of the valuer's mandate and accordingly judicially unreviewable.[372] Going forward, members who consent to ex ante contractual exit and valuation mechanisms may well be denied access to the benefits of the unfair prejudice remedy.

ii Ousting Jurisdiction by Arbitration

Members may agree to exclude the courts' unfair prejudice jurisdiction outright with a properly drafted arbitration clause.[373] This is consistent with an emerging trend across the Commonwealth.[374] Although arbitrators may not grant relief that would affect non-parties to the arbitration agreement such as dissolution,[375] this does not apply to a share purchase order made against a party to the agreement. Therefore, withdrawal can conceivably be litigated and facilitated entirely by binding arbitration.

367 *North Holdings* [1999] 2 BCLC 625, 639.

368 *Re Benfield Greig Group plc, Nugent* v. *Benfield Greig Group plc* [2001] EWCA Civ 397; [2002] 1 BCLC 65 [37]–[41].

369 *Re Charterhouse Capital Ltd, Arbuthnott* v. *Bonnyman* [2015] EWCA Civ 536; [2015] BCC 574 [121], [126] (drag-along clause).

370 *Premier Telecom Communications Group Ltd* v. *Webb* [2014] EWCA Civ 994 [8].

371 Ibid. [9], [12].

372 Ibid. [18], [23]–[26].

373 *Fulham Football Club (1987) Ltd* v. *Richards* [2011] EWCA Civ 855; [2012] Ch 333 [78], [88] overruling *Exeter City Association Football Club Ltd* v. *Football Conference Ltd* [2004] EWHC 831 (Ch); [2004] 1 WLR 2910.

374 See *Tomolugen Holdings Ltd* v. *Silica Investors Ltd* [2015] SGCA 57; [2016] 1 SLR 373 and cases cited therein at [94].

375 *Fulham* [2012] Ch 333 [83].

10 No Withdrawal At Will – Or Even on Non-Fault Grounds

The UK stands alone amongst leading corporate law jurisdictions in lacking substantive 'debate' over withdrawal at will.[376] Take for example the Law Commission's statement in its 1997 Report: 'In our view there are strong economic arguments against allowing shareholders to exit at will'.[377] Without any citation or elaboration, the 'economic' arguments that prompted the Commission to make such a bold, unsupported, and unreasoned declaration remain a mystery. The following sentence is, however, revealing:[378]

> … as a matter of principle, such a right [to exit at will] would fundamentally contravene the sanctity of the contract binding the members and the company which we considered should guide our approach to shareholder remedies.

Accordingly, the true underlying motivation appears to be a unilateral ideological commitment to a contractarian vision of company law[379] rather than a reasoned or balanced policy stance or opinion. Note, that while the Law Commission cites the support of 'a large majority of respondents' for its contractarian 'guiding principle',[380] it was conspicuously silent on whether and to what extent these 'respondents' *specifically* opposed the concept of withdrawal at will *on this ground*. Despite serious yet strangely unnoticed and unarticulated flaws and questionable support (if any) from the legal community, the Law Commission's stance against withdrawal at will and its contractarian ideology would soon be imposed on the land by Lord Hoffmann, who granted the Commission's remarks the House of Lords' imprimatur in *O'Neill*.[381]

While voices expressly articulating and advancing the case for withdrawal *at will* were practically non-existent in the UK, the same is not true for withdrawal upon *non-fault* grounds. At least a segment of the practising Bar sees value in applying the unfair prejudice remedy in a way not entirely fixated on fault, although strong advocacy for applying the unfair prejudice remedy in non-fault situations is infrequently recorded in decided cases.[382] Amongst scholars, withdrawal on grounds broader than what would have been accepted under a contractarian vision of unfair prejudice (if not exactly non-fault grounds) drew some support.[383] Even the Law Commission, which had rejected

[376] Even smaller jurisdictions had their own debates; see de Kluiver (2007) (the Netherlands); Neville (2010) (Denmark).

[377] LawComm (1997): para. 3.66.

[378] Ibid., citing LawComm (1996): para. 14.11.

[379] LawComm (1996): para. 14.11.

[380] LawComm (1997): para. 3.66.

[381] *O'Neill* [1999] 1 WLR 1092, 1105.

[382] The Law Commission's proposal to introduce statutory presumptions into the unfair prejudice remedy is based on the proposal of two Queen's Counsel; per the proposal, raising the presumption would not have required fault of the respondent to be shown. See LawComm (1997): para. 3.26ff. Robin Hollington QC, who acted for the unsuccessful petitioner in *O'Neill*, advocated for non-fault withdrawal on at least one other occasion, albeit unsuccessfully: *Neath Rugby* [2010] BCC 597 [102], [107]–[108].

[383] E.g. Lowry (1996):72 (arguing that the requirement of 'unfairly prejudicial' should be removed and relief should be granted whenever it is 'just and equitable'); Copp (2000) (arguing that a restrictive

withdrawal at will without a full hearing, recognised the value of providing some avenue for withdrawal in non-fault situations and attempted to formulate workable proposals,[384] even if such efforts ultimately did not see fruition in *O'Neill*'s aftermath.[385]

The judiciary would be another matter. Without any strongly articulated judicial statement in support of non-fault withdrawal, it is little surprise that Lord Hoffmann's uncompromising stance against the concept was quickly echoed by the academic establishment.[386] Post-*O'Neill*, the only judicial attempt at articulating reasons for not granting withdrawal on non-fault grounds could cite only the sudden financial burden that a share purchase order would impose on the forced purchaser.[387] Ultimately, the window of opportunity for implementing non-fault withdrawal has closed; all that is left is the contractarian, fault-based system cemented by *O'Neill*.

D THE METEORIC RISE AND GRADUAL FALL OF UNFAIR PREJUDICE

This Chapter thus far has shown how the level of protection offered to minority shareholders as provided by the law of withdrawal in the UK has undergone rather dramatic changes within a few short decades. What then are the factors driving these changes, and what lessons do they offer those interested in comparative corporate law?

1 *How One Judge Successfully Shaped Unfair Prejudice Law …*

That judges have historically had – and arguably continue to have – the leading role in shaping the contours of unwritten, 'common' law in the UK is relatively uncontroversial.[388] UK corporate law, however, is dominated by statute, now mostly consolidated under the interminable Companies Act 2006.[389] The example of withdrawal (manifesting as the unfair prejudice remedy) thus exhibits a unique duality: the remedy itself has formal legal basis in an extremely vaguely worded statute, but for all intents and purposes, its substance is a product of judicial interpretation if not creation.[390]

approach to unfair prejudice might deter investment in small companies due to fears of lock-in); Shapira (2000): 271–2 (arguing that quasi-partners should be provided with a default right to withdraw at will but subject to the court's power to relieve the controlling member of the obligation to purchase the withdrawing member's shares where 'just and equitable').

384 LawComm (1996): para. 18.10; LawComm (1997): para. 3.67.

385 See V.C.1.ii–iii above.

386 Exemplified by Prentice & Payne (1999).

387 *Phoenix Office* [2002] EWCA Civ 1740; [2003] 1 BCLC 76 [30].

388 See e.g. Bell (2006): 334–7 (describing the lawmaking role of the English judiciary and its changes over time).

389 Until very recently, large parts of corporate law including the law of directors' duty remained judge-made law, but much of that body of law has been 'codified' in the Companies Act. See generally Langford (2015); Davies & Worthington (2016): para. [3–10]. Insolvency law, of course, has its own monster statute in the Insolvency Act 1986.

390 Davies & Worthington (2016): para. [20–4]. In this regard the law of unfair prejudice may be distinguished from the law on directors' duties.

In its formative years, with little common law baggage to tie the hands of judges charged with its application, the unfair prejudice remedy might have seemed to be a legislative remedy of unprecedented potential and scope. Unfortunately, its inherent flexibility was simultaneously its greatest strength and its fatal weakness: the unfair prejudice remedy was the sole legal outlet (or 'one-stop-shop') through which all the ills of the UK's close corporations (as the quasi-partnership Ltd) might seek cure. What doomed the remedy was a confluence of several unfortunate factors: seemingly overwhelming litigation costs exactly when litigation costs were drawing high-level attention in England and Wales; and the *perception* by a judicial faction exemplified by Lord Hoffmann that unfair prejudice petitions had become a burden to the legal system.[391]

The timing could not have been worse. The 1990s backlash against unfair prejudice can be partly attributed to the general dissatisfaction with the astronomical costs of civil litigation in the UK.[392] Under Lord Woolf's leadership,[393] a reform attempt aimed at addressing the endemic problems of civil litigation in England and Wales was well underway.[394] Unfortunately, those reforms – which included new case management powers for the courts – only saw fruition in 1998 with the Civil Procedure Rules (CPR).[395] The Court of Appeal disposed of its first post-CPR unfair prejudice appeal[396] on 17 June 1999, shortly after *O'Neill* was decided on 20 May. Given that the Law Commission's 1997 Report saw case management as the critical limb to solving unfair prejudice's problems,[397] it is unfortunate that neither the Chancery Division[398] nor the Chancery Bar were given time or opportunity to adapt to the new case management regime before Lord Hoffmann seized the opportunity to settle the unfair prejudice question permanently in 1999.

For all the faults of English civil litigation, the courts pre-*O'Neill* did right by the substantive law of unfair prejudice. Actively engaged in examining the details of the relationships between members, English judges did more than give effect to the 'contractual' (both formal and informal) terms, rules, and expectations. They developed 'a set of legitimate expectations – particularly in relation to "quasi partnerships" – that are often seen as legitimate by virtue of their conventionalism'.[399] These 'legitimate expectations'

391 See V.C.1.ii–iii above.

392 See Zuckerman (1996) (comparing the costs of civil litigation in England and in Germany).

393 As Master of the Rolls (head of the civil justice system of England and Wales), Lord Woolf was the third-most senior judge (after the Lord Chief Justice and Lord Chancellor) in the judiciary of England and Wales.

394 Woolf (1996).

395 Civil Procedure Rules 1998, SI 1998/3132.

396 *North Holdings* [1999] 2 BCLC 625, 639.

397 LawComm (1997): para. 2.38. This was also accepted by the Department of Trade and Industry: CLRSG (2000a): para. 4.103.

398 The Chancery Division (and specifically, the Companies Court) of the High Court of England and Wales was almost exclusively responsible for unfair prejudice petitions; now the function is performed by the Insolvency and Companies List of the Business & Property Courts.

399 Riley (2003): 392.

became a 'code of conduct'[400] – a concept that draws on objective standards of conduct and was therefore by definition a poor fit with a strictly 'contractual' paradigm. It was unfairness 'suffered' by the minority, and not 'inflicted' by the majority, that was the court's main concern.[401] All this received wisdom was cast out when *O'Neill* retroactively imposed a contractarian framework onto a rich body of law painstakingly built up over nearly two decades.[402]

Both Lord Hoffmann (through his speech in *O'Neill*) and other persons involved in the Law Commission and CLRSG-led reform process contemporaneously voiced similar concerns about the cost and length of unfair prejudice litigation.[403] Yet today it is only Lord Hoffmann's words that are remembered and quoted, while the reformers' failures gradually fade into history. One man's clear, unyielding, and authoritative voice at a strategic juncture changed the course of unfair prejudice's history, whereas a multitude of voices within a drawn-out and contentious law reform process did not.

2 … *When Law Reformers Failed: Internal Dissension and the Role of Academics*

The convoluted reform and reform attempt history of oppression/unfair prejudice in the UK is a stark demonstration of how inefficient and ineffectual *legislative* reform can be. The groups involved in the process simply could not reach agreement. The Law Commission favoured the introduction of statutory presumptions and was willing to consider a standalone additional remedy to address the exclusion from management claims featuring in the bulk of unfair prejudice cases.[404] These were at the very least a good faith attempt drawing on the expertise of practising barristers,[405] and expressly intended to address a practical problem discovered through a laborious empirical study of the unfair prejudice petitions filed with the Companies Court.[406] Even if its suggestions ultimately failed to materialise into implemented reform, there can be no doubt as to the fact that the Commission made a serious, good-faith effort at its job.

By contrast, the CLRSG succeeded more in undermining the Law Commission's work than steering the reform towards success. Not only did the CLRSG quickly

400 Hannigan (1988): 80 ('[The unfair prejudice remedy] has called into question many of the accepted rules of company regulation and has replaced them with what essentially is a code of conduct for the quasi-partnership which requires fairness and evenhandedness in the running of the company').

401 Shapira (2000): 268.

402 Contemporary commentary on *O'Neill*'s disruptive impact include Shapira (2000): 271 ('*O'Neill* retroactively invalidates many former decisions without saying so'); Goddard (1999c): 335 (*O'Neill* closed the door on developing 'legitimate expectations' not supported by 'equitable principles' but much would still depend on 'the extent to which future courts approach the remedy purposively'); Lowry (2002): 246 (questioning the appropriateness of restricting the scope of unfair prejudice).

403 *O'Neill* [1999] 1 WLR 1092, 1099; for reformers' concerns, see V.C.1.ii–iii above.

404 See V.C.1.ii above.

405 LawComm (1997): paras. 3.26–3.62, 3.26 fn. 24 (naming three Queen's Counsel).

406 LawComm (1996): paras. 18.1–18.6. Exclusion of the petitioner from management of the company is the most frequently pleaded allegation: LawComm (1996): para. 15.5, 235–8.

dispose of Law Commission's exit article proposal, it also demonstrated reluctance towards accepting any suggestion or feedback that would expand withdrawal remedies for aggrieved shareholders. In successive consultations, the CLRSG consistently downplayed or disregarded all feedback supportive of the Law Commission's proposals, responses critical of *O'Neill*, and suggestions for either broadening the scope of unfair prejudice or introducing alternative remedies. Given the CLRSG's decision to ultimately abandon all substantive reform and to invoke *O'Neill* to justify the status quo of injustice,[407] one may reasonably doubt if the CLRSG ever had either the capacity or will to execute its mission of reforming the unfair prejudice remedy.

Prominent academics arguably only added fuel to the bonfire of dissent by attacking the Law Commission's proposals for failing to address practical concerns[408] and having a 'fundamentally flawed' conceptual framework.[409] Such harsh (if justified[410]) criticism may have had the unintended if unfortunate and ironic effect of undermining the authority and legitimacy of the Law Commission's efforts even before the CLRSG killed the reform.

Without a strong thought leader amongst the law reformers or academics around whom others could rally, or any workable consensus between the interest groups involved, the reformers quickly lost the initiative. A reform movement divided against itself could not stand against one man with one voice backed by a united House (of Lords). Unfair prejudice has never been the same since.

E CONCLUSION

Responding to the common law's recalcitrant failure to develop solutions to the demands of close corporation conflicts, the unfair prejudice remedy was the boldest legislative measure – and indeed, experiment – in UK company law since the advent of general incorporation in the nineteenth century. It could have been UK company law's finest hour; indeed, for a brief time, it was. And then it wasn't – a victim of its own phenomenal popularity amongst the newly empowered members of UK Ltds. On that sobering note, it is now time to hop across the pond to The Other 'common law' giant: the United States.

407 See V.C.1.iii above. A sitting judge (later Master of the Rolls and President of the Supreme Court) contemporaneously (albeit extra-judicially) observed: 'Interestingly, the [CLRSG] has recommended that the *O'Neill* [approach] be maintained … despite the fact that the majority of respondents to earlier consultations thought that *O'Neill* … might lead to cases of injustice': Neuberger (2002): 68, citing CLRSG (2001): para. 7.41.

408 Sugarman (1997): 244.

409 See e.g. Lowry (1997): 255–6.

410 Lowry's criticism is consistent with his stated position favouring a far more expansive approach to unfair prejudice than the Law Commission's: Lowry (1997): 255; Lowry (1996): 72.

VI

The United States

The Divergent Lives of Withdrawal in Two Close Corporation Forms across One Hundred Corporation Laws

A INTRODUCTION AND PRELIMINARY NOTES

Rarely is the presence of US law and legal scholarship greater felt than in comparative corporate law. As the world's single largest national economy for well over a century,[1] the US's economic significance is beyond question. However, in contrast to the two preceding Chapters on Germany and the UK, strictly speaking this Chapter is not about a single jurisdiction named 'the US'. Unusually even among federal polities,[2] virtually all business entities in the US are organised under the laws of a single state (state of incorporation), and all corporate governance matters are governed by the *lex incorporationis* pursuant to the internal affairs doctrine.[3] To further complicate matters, firms organising as close corporations in the US may choose not only the state of incorporation,[4] but also between two rather different business entities that are each created by separate statutes in each state: the business corporation and the limited liability company (LLC).[5]

[1] In nominal terms; since 2017 the US has been surpassed by China in purchasing power parity terms: World Bank (2021a).

[2] Canada offers both federal incorporation (under the federal Canada Business Corporations Act, RSC 1985, c C-44) and incorporation under provincial corporation statutes. Historically a State matter in Australia, powers over corporation law were transferred by State legislatures to the Commonwealth (federal) legislature in 2001; Australia has had a single corporation statute ever since (Corporations Act 2001 (Cth)).

[3] Bainbridge (2020): 8; *Santa Fe Industries, Inc* v. *Green* (1977) 430 US 462, 479 (US).

[4] O'Neal & Thompson (2020a): § 2:13.

[5] Ibid. § 2:3.

In other words, strictly speaking 'US' or 'American' corporate law – especially close corporation law – does not exist. What does exist is over one hundred business corporation and LLC *statutes* (plural) and bodies of case law spread across the fifty states, the District of Columbia (DC), and five inhabited territories offering incorporation.[6] Even with some degree of convergence and harmonisation amongst different state laws, they are hardly identical.[7] While defying easy classification, the US nonetheless offers an exceptionally rich source of law – both written and unwritten – as well as legal scholarship on the subject of this Book: shareholder withdrawal.

The US's exceptional size and complexity calls for extensive clarifications on terminology and approach. For this Book's purposes, references to the 'United States' or 'US' or to US law are usually to the fifty states and their laws, excluding DC and the territories. Further, model laws and uniform acts[8] – that are not themselves the statutes of any state, but which may be enacted in whole or part – also play significant roles in business organisation law.[9] Although state corporate law matters may be adjudicated by federal courts in some circumstances,[10] this Chapter focuses on decisions of state courts interpreting or applying their own corporation laws.

For practical reasons, this Chapter departs from the in-depth and comprehensive analysis of legal sources executed in the other three jurisdictional chapters. Although federal law is relatively uniform and important to corporate practice,[11] it has less to say about core corporate law issues such as shareholder oppression and withdrawal in close corporations, which remain state law matters.[12] Without 'unity' in the

6 By 'territories' I mean the five unincorporated territories with substantial populations: Puerto Rico, Guam, US Virgin Islands, American Samoa, and Northern Mariana Islands. Wake Island is inhabited and administered by US Air Force personnel but excluded for corporate law purposes.

7 How uniform corporate law is across states is debated. Cf Carney (1998) (finding 'substantial uniformity' based on a study including neither withdrawal remedies nor oppression more broadly) with Karjala (1989) (criticising close corporation law's non-uniformity). Conversely, it has been observed that many states have some version of oppression and withdrawal remedy: Thompson (1993) (close corporations in the narrow sense (US-CCs)); Thompson (2011) (both US-CCs and to a lesser extent, LLCs). On harmonisation via the Model Business Corporation Act and the Uniform Limited Liability Company Acts, see VI.B.2 and VI.D.2 below. In any event, the case that *withdrawal* law specifically is uniform *de lege lata* has never been made out.

8 See generally Clark (2011).

9 See VI.B.2 and VI.D.2.

10 O'Neal & Thompson (2020b): § 7:27; Fletcher (2020). More rarely, one state court can decide a matter of another state's corporate law; see e.g. *Ex parte Bentley* (2010) 50 So3d 1063, 1074 (Ala).

11 Although individual states have their own securities regulation ('blue sky laws'), securities regulation is centered primarily on the Securities Act of 1933, Securities Exchange Act of 1934, and the Securities and Exchange Commission's Rule 10b-5 (17 CFR § 240.10b-5); see Bainbridge (2020): 11–12. On federal tax law's role, see VI.B.3, VI.D.1, VI.D.3, VI.F.3.

12 Although the leading treatise by O'Neal and Thompson devote a chapter to remedies under federal securities laws (O'Neal & Thompson (2020b): ch. 8 (titled 'Resisting Squeeze-outs and Oppression: Remedies Under Federal Law'), § 7:28), the scenarios covered usually involve corporations with traded securities, and only involve close corporations exceptionally.

corporate law of the misnamed 'United States', a truly rigorous study of withdrawal in US close corporation law would require going through all fifty-plus states' statutes and jurisprudence for each state's two major business entities – an exercise far beyond this Book's scope. Picking a single dominant state or model to focus on – most notably Delaware in public corporation jurisprudence and discourse[13] – would be poor strategy for the close corporation context. This is because no single state or model dominates outright, notwithstanding the relative legal and/or economic importance of certain states (e.g. Delaware, New York, and California) and of model and uniform acts. When the goal is to offer a sufficiently rich and representative account of withdrawal in the US, there is no good substitute for engaging directly with the laws of a wide range of other states. Accordingly, this Chapter applies a broad-brush approach in categorising various state laws and doctrinal approaches; decided cases are examined less for what courts *say* and more on what they *do*: whether withdrawal is ordered or not, and on what grounds.

As to general legal terminology, 'close corporation' without modifiers is, except where the context strongly suggests otherwise, used in the broad sense and refers to both distinct legal entities used in organising business in the US. These are: (1) a business corporation that is either legally or functionally a '**US Close Corporation**' (**US-CC**) (i.e. a close corporation in the narrow sense); and 2) a **Limited Liability Company** (**LLC**).[14] 'Incorporation' and 'formation' refer to the creation of business corporations (including US-CCs) and LLCs respectively.

Citations to statutory provisions indicate in parentheses the year the provision went into force; if the source is unclear, the year of enactment or last amendment is provided. Court names are omitted for cases decided by state supreme courts.

VI.B introduces the US Close Corporation (US-CC). VI.C examines the law of withdrawal as a subset of oppression law and doctrine, focusing on the states that do offer withdrawal but also touching on those that do not. The debate over whether withdrawal at will should be available for US-CC shareholders is also discussed in this Section. After introducing the LLC in VI.D, VI.E examines the two types of withdrawal regimes available to LLC members: at will (by dissociation etc), and on oppression and other grounds. VI.F summarises the trends identified from the analyses of the withdrawal regimes of US-CCs and LLCs and contextualises them within the broader US corporate law environment – in particular, the influence of contractarianism on US corporate law. VI.G concludes.

[13] See e.g. Bainbridge (2020): 10 (on Delaware's dominance in public corporation law). Delaware, however, is relatively unusual in rejecting withdrawal for close corporations (business corporations) entirely; see VI.C.2.iv below.

[14] For detailed definitions see VI.B.2 (US-CCs) and VI.D.2 (LLCs).

B THE CLOSE CORPORATION (US-CC)

1 *History*

US business corporation law was not initially designed with the needs of close corporations in mind. The first American corporations[15] were created by special charters issued by colonial or state legislatures, primarily engaged in activities of public character.[16] The incorporation of business corporations in the early years of the independent American Republic[17] was justified on the basis that they served the public interest,[18] and were subject to the overriding powers of the incorporating legislature to police the corporation,[19] including the power to revoke the charter should the corporate purpose fail to be achieved.[20] Later, Joseph Story's conception of the corporation as a 'private' entity[21] made its way into mainstream legal discourse[22] and paved the way for the transformation of early US corporate law into recognisably modern business corporation law.[23]

Despite the inconvenience of procuring state charters, business corporations flourished, with the New England states alone chartering almost 1,900 by 1830.[24] A substantial body of American court decisions also developed during this time.[25] Nonetheless, it was not until well into the nineteenth century, when followers of President Andrew Jackson attacked the special privileges conferred by state charters,[26] that state incorporation laws underwent

15 The first *business* corporation chartered in America – and the only one pre-Revolution – is The Philadelphia Contributionship for Insuring Houses from Loss by Fire, a mutual insurance company founded in 1752 but chartered in 1768: Williston (1888): 165. In total, seven corporations were chartered during the colonial period: Davis (1917): 26 tbl. II.

16 They were mostly local government bodies, religious institutions, educational institutions, or quasi-monopolies with state backing, rather than private for-profit firms. See Davis (1917): 49–74 (on public (government or quasi-government) corporations), 75–81 (religious institutions), 82–6 (educational institutions), 87–103 (private for-profit corporations).

17 Post-Revolution, of the more than 300 charters issued by 1800, over 90 per cent were granted after 1789; see Davis (1917): 26 tbl. II.

18 *Currie's Administrators* v. *Mutual Assurance Society* (1809) 14 Va (4 Hen & M) 315, 347–8 (Virginia Supreme Court of Appeals).

19 See e.g. *Head & Amory v Providence Insurance Co* (1804) 6 US (2 Cranch) 127, 167 (US) (Marshall CJ); Davis (1917): 227–30 (describing the regulation of corporations established to construct bridges, highways, and canals).

20 *Terrett* v. *Taylor* (1815) 13 US (9 Cranch) 43, 51 (US) (Story J).

21 *Trustees of Dartmouth College* v. *Woodward* (1819) 17 US (4 Wheat) 518, 668–9 (US); see generally Newmyer (1976).

22 See e.g. Kent (1826): 391–2; Kent (1827): 245; Angell & Ames (1832): 8–9.

23 Newmyer (1976): 838. See also Arner (2002): 56–7.

24 Kessler (1948): 46 tbl. 1(reporting that Connecticut, Maine, Massachusetts, New Hampshire, Rhode Island, and Vermont chartered a total of 1,893 business corporations (all by special charter) by 1830), 47 tbl. 2 (providing a breakdown by industry).

25 See Dodd (1954): 13.

26 See Hurst (1970): 120; Schlesinger (1945): 188–9; Hovenkamp (1991): 37.

liberalisation, beginning with the enactment of general incorporation statutes by Pennsylvania (1836) and Connecticut (1837).[27] By 1852, over half the Union's states and territories possessed general incorporation statutes,[28] and the business corporation had begun taking on a recognisably modern character, including limited liability.[29]

In the immediate decades following the advent of general incorporation,[30] the number of incorporations skyrocketed and many industries came to be dominated by incorporated firms.[31] During this period, general incorporation laws were less concerned with the creation of public corporations with nation-wide reach, and more with conferring limited liability – combined with various restrictions – on local, closely held firms.[32] With the rise of large public corporations towards the end of the nineteenth century,[33] however, states attempted to cater to the particular needs of such corporations in a bid to attract out-of-state incorporations for the associated tax and other revenues.[34] The resulting legislative changes, which included the concomitant weakening of shareholder power and strengthening of managerial power,[35] were never designed with close corporations in mind.[36] Unsurprisingly, corporation laws of the early twentieth century customised for large public corporations failed to benefit close corporations.[37]

Nonetheless, by the second half of the twentieth century, there was 'a definite, albeit inarticulate, trend' leading toward eventual judicial[38] and later statutory treatment of the close corporation as *sui generis*. We discuss some of the specifics next.

27 Hamill (1999): 101. New York's (1811) statute came earlier but differed materially from Jacksonian-era enactments: ibid.

28 The sixteen out of the thirty-five then-states and territories that enacted general incorporation statutes after 1837 and by 1852 were Michigan, New Jersey, and Ohio (1846), Iowa (1847), Louisiana (1848), Wisconsin (1849), California and Tennessee (1850), Massachusetts and Vermont (1850), Alabama, Florida, Illinois, Indiana, Maryland, and North Carolina (1852): Hamill (1999): 178.

29 See Hovenkamp (1991): 2, 49; but see Horwitz (1985): 208.

30 Even after the advent of general incorporation, special charters remained available and continued to be issued in large numbers in a number of states well into the twentieth century: Hamill (1999): 122–37.

31 Wells (2008): 279–80; see also Navin & Sears (1955): 109.

32 Rutledge (1937): 306–7; Skeel (2005): 52–3; see also *Louis K Liggett Co* v. *Lee* (1933) 288 US 517, 548–56.

33 America would not see the rise of large, widely held public industrial corporations until the late nineteenth century, when the 'Great Merger Movement' caused widespread consolidation of smaller firms: Navin & Sears (1955): 127, 136; Nelson (1959): 71–105.

34 For a succinct account, see Wells (2008): 281–5.

35 Ibid.; Wells (2015): 19–20.

36 Rutledge (1937): 311–12, 312 fn. 21, 337.

37 See Wells (2008): 285–9; *Jackson* v. *Hooper* (1910) 75 A 568, 571, 573 (NJ Court of Errors and Appeals).

38 *Galler* v. *Galler* (1964) 32 Ill2d 16, 28, 203 NE2d 577, 584 (Ill); see also *Helms* v. *Duckworth* (1957) 249 F2d 482, 486–7 (DCCir). See also generally Ayres (1992): 388–98.

2 *Legal Aspects*

US-CCs are ultimately created pursuant to state incorporation statutes, but the American Bar Association's (ABA) Model Business Corporation Act (MBCA),[39] which is adopted by a substantial number of states in whole or part,[40] is a highly influential instrument in corporate law. References to 'MBCA' in this Chapter are to the 2016 revision. Although eclipsed by more 'modern' statutes including more recent versions of the MBCA, the ABA's Model Statutory Close Corporation Supplement ('Model Supplement') will also be referred to.[41]

US-CCs – in contrast with LLCs – are a subset of business corporations.[42] Of the business corporation's 'five core structural characteristics',[43] those other than legal personality and limited liability are negotiable to some extent in the US-CC. Share transfer restrictions are permissible,[44] and in fact indispensable to maintaining favourable tax treatment (S-Corporation status) under federal tax law.[45] Deviations from board governance, such as shareholder agreements restricting the discretion of the directors, were historically frowned upon by the courts,[46] but became increasingly permitted under statute.[47] The modern approach, as encapsulated in the Model Supplement[48] and the MBCA,[49] would expressly permit board governance – including the existence of a board itself – to be abolished or restricted by shareholder agreement. Financial contributions, returns, and voting control may be customised for equityholding participants by using different classes of shares.[50]

The US-CC can be defined using either formal-legalistic or functional criteria. A definition according to the former – 'statutory close corporation' – covers business corporations that are subject to special close corporation legislation (such as the Model Supplement or narrower, targeted provisions) available in some states governing statutorily defined close corporations differently from other corporations.[51] Functionally, a US-CC (sometimes 'closed' or 'closely held'[52]) is usually characterised by one or more of the following: few shareholders, no open market for shares

39 For an early history, see Eisenberg (1974): 1407–8.
40 See ABA (2016): v, v fn. 1.
41 Although officially discontinued as of 2008, the Model Supplement was adopted by South Carolina and Georgia (among other states) in 1988 and remains as of 2021 on the books as SCCodeAnn, §§ 33–18–101 to 33–18–500 and GaCodeAnn, §§ 14–2–901 to 14–2–950.
42 See O'Neal & Thompson (2020a): §§ 1:3–1:4.
43 Namely legal personality, limited liability, transferable shares, 'centralized management under a board structure', and 'shared ownership by contributors of equity capital': Armour & Enriques et al. (2017): 5.
44 See generally Moll & Ragazzo (2017): §§ 2.01[A][4] (2–19 to 2–20), 4.01 (4–2 to 4–19).
45 O'Neal & Thompson (2020a): § 2:6 text to fns. 33–35, § 7:2 text to fn. 9.
46 Moll & Ragazzo (2017): § 3.05 (3–30 to 3–35).
47 See O'Neal & Thompson (2020a): § 4:6.
48 Model Supplement, §§ 20 to 21.
49 MBCA, §§ 7.32, 8.01.
50 See generally O'Neal & Thompson (2020a): §§ 3:22 to 3:34.
51 Karjala (1989): 668–71; O'Neal & Thompson (2020a): § 1:25.
52 O'Neal & Thompson (2020a): § 1:4.

(i.e. not traded on a securities exchange), a relationship between shareholders akin to partners in a partnership, and substantial overlap between share ownership and management.[53] This Chapter's focus is on the absence of a market for shares[54] as this is the single most proximate (even if not exclusive) reason why *withdrawal* specifically is the essential shareholder remedy.

3 *Economic Aspects*

Difficult to define, the US-CC is even harder to quantify. Even the most unambiguous subset of US-CCs, statutory close corporations, cannot be counted because states frequently do not keep the necessary records.[55] In any event, statutory close corporations most likely make up an extremely small minority of all business corporations in the US,[56] at least in part due to resistance from legal practitioners.[57] However, US-CCs – including those that are functionally US-CCs but not statutory close corporations – likely make up a 'great',[58] if not 'vast', majority of all US business corporations.

In addition, most US-CCs would 'find it advantageous' to elect to be taxed as 'S-Corporations'[59] under the federal Internal Revenue Code (IRC).[60] Thus, although precise statistics do not exist on the number of *incorporated* US-CCs, S-Corporation statistics and data capture the economic realities of US-CCs quite well. As compared to the regular multi-member C-Corporation tax treatment, the key advantage of S-Corporation status is 'pass-through taxation' that, similarly but not identical to partnerships, levies no federal income tax on the corporation, treats the corporation's income and losses as those of the shareholders, and avoids the double taxation problem in C-Corporations.[61] Research has also shown S-Corporation tax treatment benefits not just owners, but also employees,[62] although pass-through taxation makes minority shareholders particularly susceptible to oppression when dividends or compensation are withheld because the minority shareholder is nonetheless liable to pay tax on their unreceived 'share' of the corporation's profits.[63]

53 Ibid. § 1:3.
54 Following ibid. § 1:3 text after fn. 24.
55 Ibid. § 1:26.
56 Ibid.
57 *Nixon* v. *Blackwell* (1993) 626 A2d 1366, 1380 fn. 19 (Del) (citing a practitioner treatise).
58 O'Neal & Thompson (2020a): §§ 1:3, 1:26.
59 So-named for Subchapter S of the tax code: IRC, §§ 1361 to 1379.
60 See generally O'Neal & Thompson (2020a): § 2:6.
61 See ibid.; ibid. § 2:5 (on double taxation).
62 Donohoe et al. (2015): 975, 993–4.
63 See O'Neal & Thompson (2020b): § 6:34; see also ibid. §§ 6:33, 6:35; *Litle* v. *Waters*, No CIV A 12155, Chandler VC, 11 February 1992, 1992 WL 25758, at *8, (1993) 18 Delaware Journal of Corporate Law 315, 328–9 (DelCh).

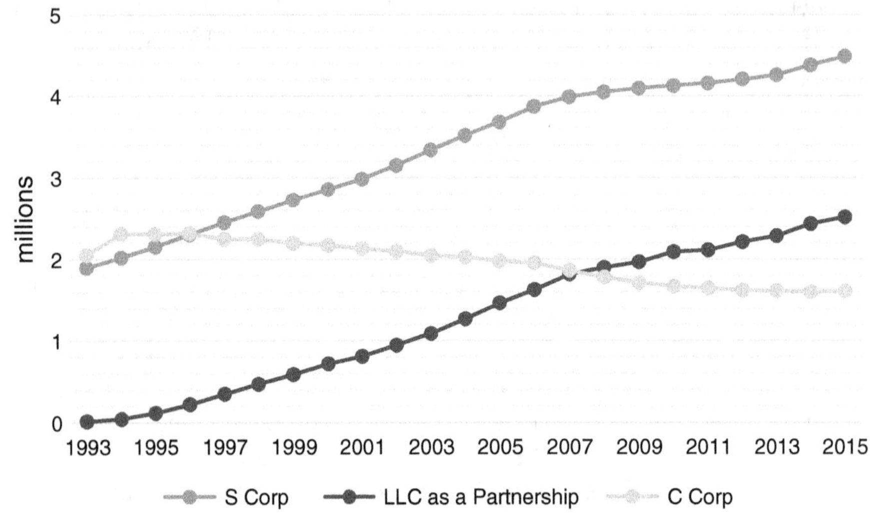

FIGURE 6.1 Tax returns by entity classification, tax years (1993–2015)

Although historically subject to numerous limitations (such as number of shareholders), restrictions on S-Corporations have since been liberalised in large part.[64] As Figure 6.1[65] shows, S-Corporation tax filings exceeded C-Corporation filings in 1997 and never looked back; since the turn of the century, the S-Corporation has maintained its position as the most popular classification by far. In tax year 2013, S-Corporations also make up a substantial share of total business receipts (US$ 6,745 billion and 20.28 per cent of all businesses) and total net income (US$ 515.9 billion, 13.48 per cent).[66] Although dwarfed by C-Corporations (at US$ 20,104 billion and 60.45 per cent; US$ 1,480 billion and

64 O'Neal & Thompson (2020a): § 2:6.

65 Source: IRS (2020).

66 Percentages calculated based on IRS (2020), according to which the estimated figures for business receipts and net income by form of business (in thousands of US dollars) are as follows:

Total business receipts: 33,260,092,484
Total net income: 3,826,792,224
S-Corp business receipts: 6,745,095,028
S-Corp net income: 515,948,187
C-Corp business receipts: 20,104,450,974
C-Corp net income: 1,479,670,755
LLC business receipts: 2,960,510,637
LLC net income: 452,526,597
Sole prop business receipts: 1,341,571,082
Sole prop net income: 357,417,038
LLC figures are for LLCs taxed as partnerships. S-Corp net income data is only available up to 2013; for all others up to 2015.

38.67 per cent respectively[67]), as some US-CCs are taxed as C-Corporations, the share attributable to S-Corporations alone does not capture the full economic significance of US-CCs.[68]

C WITHDRAWAL AS A REMEDY FOR OPPRESSION IN THE US-CC

1 *The Relationship between Oppression and Withdrawal*

In this Chapter, oppression is used in a broad sense that includes squeeze-outs and other majority shareholder conduct that is harmful to the interests of minority shareholders in the context of a going concern. However, cash-out mergers or other fundamental changes, sales of control, and voluntary dissolution by the majority are not included.[69]

As in the UK,[70] *oppression* in the US-CC context and *withdrawal* as defined in this Book are not synonymous. Rather, withdrawal remedies form only a subset of possible judicial responses falling under the broader framework of oppression-type remedies. Oppression-type remedies include share buyouts (i.e. withdrawal), dissolution, compensation, appointment of custodians, and customised arrangements limited only by the needs of the parties and the corporation, and the creativity of counsel and the judge.[71] However, US jurisprudence and literature distinguish between withdrawal and other oppression remedies only infrequently. This Chapter focuses on buyout remedies and discusses oppression cases concerning other remedies only insofar as they are relevant and helpful towards understanding how withdrawal operates in the US.

2 *Buyout Remedy Variants*

Historically, the closest thing to relief from oppression in corporation statutes was the action for involuntary (judicial) dissolution of the business corporation. The pioneers,[72] Illinois and Pennsylvania, introduced oppression as a basis for dissolution – but not withdrawal – into their respective corporation laws in 1933.[73] Modern approaches, which include a variety of reliefs permitting an oppressed

67 Ibid.

68 LLCs may elect S Corporation treatment. Although precise figures are unavailable, differences in tax treatment make it unlikely that LLCs make up any substantial share of S Corporations. See Ribstein & Kobayashi (2001): 97–8 (explaining subtle differences between S Corporation and LLC-as-partnership pass-through tax treatment).

69 The appraisal remedy, which may be available in fundamental changes, is not withdrawal as it is defined for this Book: II.D.1.iii.

70 See V.C.2.

71 See O'Neal & Thompson (2020b): §§ 7:21 to 7:24; *Baker* v. *Commercial Body Builders, Inc* (1973) 264 Or 614, 632–3, 507 P2d 387, 395–6 (Or).

72 The short-lived (1931–33) attempt in California to allow dissolution on grounds of 'persistent fraud or mismanagement or abuse of authority, or persistent unfairness toward minority shareholders' by directors is outlined in Thompson (1993): 709 fn. 67.

73 *Central Standard Life Insurance Co* v. *Davis* (1957) 10 Ill2d 566, 572, 141 NE2d 45, 49 (Ill); see also Murdock (1990): 452–61; Thompson (1993): 709–13.

shareholder to withdraw from the US-CC, are much more diverse. In this subsection, I describe buyout remedies as they were historically and are currently implemented in a selection of US states, classified into four categories according to the basis of the court's power to order a share buyout.

i Direct Statutory Remedies

Statutes specifically designed both to create a cause of action in oppression and provide the court with the power to order a buyout of the plaintiff's shares are a relatively recent development. South Carolina's[74] enactment is perhaps the first of this type, and fittingly for a possible product of British influence, went on to inspire other (American) states.[75] Other states in which buyout relief for oppression was introduced by legislative enactment include Illinois[76] and Michigan.[77] Another example is Minnesota's statute, which empowers the court to order a buyout in two scenarios: either upon motion by the corporation or any shareholder; or at the court's discretion.[78] North Carolina was, exceptionally, an early adopter of a direct statutory buyout remedy (1973) that subsequently abolished it (1989).[79]

More recently, the power of courts to order buyouts and other reliefs hitherto based solely on their historical powers in equity in states such as Oregon[80] and Montana,[81] or

74 SCCodeAnn, § 12–22.23(a)(4) (1962); currently SCCodeAnn, § 33–14–310(d)(4) (1988); *Kiriakides* v. *Atlas Food Systems & Services, Inc* (2001) 343 SC 587, 607, 541 SE2d 257, 268 (SC).

75 On British influence, see Afterman (1969): 1043; Folk (1966): 954. See also *Meiselman* v. *Meiselman* (1982) 58 NCApp 758, 295 SE2d 249, 254 and 254 fn. 9 (NCApp) (citing the precise source as 'S. C. Code Ann. § 12–22.23 (1962), subsequently recodified as S. C. Code Ann. § 33–21–230 (1976)'), affirmed as modified and remanded (1983) 309 NC 279, 307 SE2d 551 (NC). South Carolina's statutory provision also inspired Montana's: MontCodeAnn, § 35–1–939 Editor's Notes – Official Comments.

76 The first statutory buyout remedy in Illinois was introduced as Illinois Statutes 1983, ch. 32 ¶ 12.55 (1983) (effective 1 July 1984); see *Coduti* v. *Hellwig* (1984) 127 IllApp3d 279, 469 NE2d 220, 231 (IllAppCt). The current codified version is 805 IllCompStatAnn 5/12.56(b)(11) (2007). See generally Quinlan & Kennedy (1998).

77 MichCompLAnn, § 450.1825(2)(d) (1973); now § 450.1489(1)(e) (2006). The court is not limited to ordering the successful plaintiff's shares to be bought out; see *Berger v Katz*, Court of Appeals of Michigan No 291663, 28 July 2011, 2011 WL 3209217, at *6–*7 (offering the plaintiff a choice between being bought out and doing the buying out), appeal denied (2012) 491 Mich 886, 809 NW2d 586 (Mich), reconsideration denied (2012) 491 Mich 947, 815 NW2d 426 (Mich).

78 MinnStatAnn, §§ 302A.751 subdivision 2, 302A.751 subdivision 3a (2011). Minnesota's regime can also be classified as an 'indirect remedy' as discussed at VI.C.2.iii. The Reporter's Notes to § 302A.751 note that this provision 'is derived from a mandatory buy-out provision in the New Jersey law' (§ 302A.751, Reporter's Notes – 1981 – General Comment).

79 The old dissolution section was enacted in 1955 and codified as the old North Carolina General Statutes, § 55–125(a)(4) (1982); in 1973 an alternative remedies provision was enacted and later codified as § 55–125.1(a)(4). For the leading case see *Meiselman* v. *Meiselman* (1983) 309 NC 279, 307 SE2d 551 (NC). The above provisions were substantially modified in 1989 to restrict the availability of buyout relief: McLean (1990): 1120–3.

80 OrRevStatAnn, § 60.952(5) (2001); *Hickey* v. *Hickey* (2015) 269 OrApp 258, 344 P3d 512, 518–520 (OrCtApp), review denied 357 Or 415, 356 P3d 638.

81 MontCodeAnn, § 35–1–939(1)(d) (1991); see also *Kulko* v. *Davail, Inc* (2015) 381 Mont 511, 363 P3d 430, 433–4 (Mont).

on the court's statutorily preserved discretion in equity (as in North Dakota[82]) have since been codified. Recently, Louisiana, a non-common law state,[83] became perhaps the first US jurisdiction to implement an explicitly named oppressed US-CC shareholder's right to 'withdraw' – a buyout remedy conceptually distinct from others such as dissolution, and available only in cases of oppression.[84]

ii Non-Statutory Judicial Remedies

Other state courts have asserted their power to order buyouts notwithstanding the absence of express statutory authorisation. The classic modern example of this is Indiana, whose statute does not permit even judicial dissolution for oppression,[85] but its highest court has asserted that Indiana courts have the power to fashion reliefs for breaches of fiduciary duties in US-CCs, including dissolution and share buyouts.[86] Courts in other states, including those in Missouri,[87] Oregon,[88] Alaska,[89] Iowa,[90] New Jersey,[91] North Dakota,[92] Texas,[93] Maryland,[94] and Montana,[95] have at one time or another claimed the power to order buyouts (among other remedies alternative to dissolution) based on their general powers in equity, whereas the basis of such powers is less clear in New York,[96] New

82 ND Century CodeAnn, § 10–19.1–115(4) (2013). The earliest version of this statute providing expressly for the court's power to order a buyout appears to be 1993 ND Laws Ch 54 (SB 2223), § 50; it assumed its current form with 1995 ND Laws Ch 103 (SB 2343), § 43. Cf the original 1985 version as reproduced in Macdonald (1986): 156 fn. 3.

83 See generally Palmer & Borowski (2012).

84 Codified as LaStatAnn, §§ 12:1–1435, 12:1–1436 (2017), effective retroactively from 1 January 2015. Louisiana became the fortieth state to implement a statutory remedy for oppression: Moll (2014): 462.

85 For the reasoning behind this, see IndCodeAnn, Comment to § 23–1–47–1 (1986).

86 *G & N Aircraft, Inc* v. *Boehm* (2001) 743 NE2d 227, 243–244 (Ind).

87 *Kirtz* v. *Grossman* (1971) 463 SW2d 541, 545 (MoCtApp); *21 West, Inc* v. *Meadowgreen Trails, Inc* (1995) 913 SW2d 858, 867 (MoCtApp).

88 *Baker* v. *Commercial Body Builders, Inc* (1973) 264 Or 614, 507 P2d 387, 395–6 (Or); see also *Delaney* v. *Georgia-Pacific Corp* (1977) 278 Or 305, 564 P2d 277, 288–9 (Or).

89 *Alaska Plastics, Inc* v. *Coppock* (1980) 621 P2d 270, 275 (Alaska); *Stefano* v. *Coppock* (1985) 705 P2d 443, 446 (Alaska).

90 *Sauer* v. *Moffitt* (1984) 363 NW2d 269, 275 (IowaCtApp); *Baur* v. *Baur Farms, Inc* (2013) 832 NW2d 663, 677–8 (Iowa).

91 *Brenner* v. *Berkowitz* (1993) 134 NJ 488, 513, 634 A2d 1019, 1031 (NJ); *Musto* v. *Vidas* (1995) 281 NJSuper 548, 560–1, 658 A2d 1305, 1312 (NJAppDiv).

92 *Balvik* v. *Sylvester* (1987) 411 NW2d 383, 388–9 (ND) (quoting *Baker* at length).

93 *Davis* v. *Sheerin* (1988) 754 SW2d 375, 380 (TexApp); overruled by *Ritchie* v. *Rupe* (2014) 443 SW3d 856 (Tex).

94 *Edenbaum* v. *Schwarcz-Osztreicherne* (2005) 165 MdApp 233, 885 A2d 365, 380 (MdSpecApp); *Boland* v. *Boland* (2011) 423 Md 296, 31 A3d 529, 574 (Md); *Bontempo* v. *Lare* (2015) 444 Md 344, 119 A3d 791, 807 (Md).

95 *Maddox* v. *Norman* (1983) 206 Mont 1, 669 P2d 230, 238 (Mont) (citing the Oregon cases of *Baker* and *Delaney*).

96 *Matter of Wiedy's Furniture Clearance Center Co, Inc* (1985) 108 AD2d 81, 84–5, 487 NYS2d 901, 904 (NYAppDiv). This is in addition to the statutory indirect (election) remedy discussed below (n 126).

Mexico,[97] or Nevada.[98] Rhode Island seems to have read into its election-type statute[99] a broad discretion of the court to order alternative relief – including a buyout – even in the absence of an election.[100] A federal court in Pennsylvania applying Pennsylvania law also ordered a buyout in lieu of dissolution despite the Pennsylvania statute lacking statutory language expressly permitting this.[101]

In Massachusetts, the court's power to order a buyout for a controlling shareholder's breach of fiduciary duty to a minority shareholder was recognised in the celebrated *Donahue* decision,[102] although this seemingly expansive basis for judicial intervention was quickly limited in *Wilkes*.[103] More recently, in *Brodie* v. *Jordan*,[104] the Massachusetts Supreme Judicial Court cast doubt on the appropriateness of the buyout as judicial relief for breach of fiduciary duty,[105] although it stopped short of renouncing the power to order buyouts outright.[106]

The power to order buyouts in the absence of express statutory authorisation was once asserted and exercised in Texas, but was since largely renounced by its supreme court.[107] Although there is no decision directly on point, it is likely that Virginia has neither a direct statutory nor non-statutory judicial buyout remedy.[108] Interestingly,

97 *McCauley* v. *Tom McCauley & Son, Inc* (1986) 104 NM 523, 724 P2d 232, 236 (NMCtApp).

98 *Bedore* v. *Familian* (2006) 122 Nev 5, 11–12, 125 P3d 1168, 1172 (Nev).

99 See VI.C.2.iii below.

100 See *Teixeira & Co* v. *Teixeira* (1994) No PC 84–0152, Superior Court of Rhode Island, Providence County, Gibney J, 21 Jul 1994, 1994 WL 930950, *8, affirmed sub nomine A *Teixeira & Co* v. *Teixeira* (1996) 674 A2d 407 (RI); see also *Hendrick* v. *Hendrick* (2000) 755 A2d 784, 792 (RI).

101 *Orchard* v. *Covelli* (1984) 590 F Supp 1548, 1560 (WD Pa), affirmed without published grounds (1986) 802 F2d 448 (3d Cir). There appears to be no Pennsylvania state court decision in which a buyout was specifically ordered for oppression. See also Bugay (2013): 132–4 (appointing a custodian seems to be the usual order in oppression/deadlock cases).

102 *Donahue* v. *Rodd Electrotype Co* (1975) 367 Mass 578, 603–4, 328 NE2d 505, 520–1 (Mass) (ordering a buyout of the minority by the corporation as one of two alternative reliefs). But see *Brodie* v. *Jordan* (2006) 447 Mass 866, 872 fn. 5, 857 NE2d 1076, 1081 fn5 (Mass) (characterising the relief ordered in *Donahue* not as withdrawal but rather a minority's tag-along right in a majority shareholder's sale of shares at a favourable price).

103 See VI.C.3.i below.

104 *Brodie* v. *Jordan* (2006) 447 Mass 866, 857 NE2d 1076 (Mass), reversing (2006) 66 MassAppCt 371, 847 NE2d 1125 (MassAppCt) (which affirmed No 98–518-E, 13 June 2002, Elizabeth Fahey J, 2002 WL 34077196 (MassSuper)).

105 *Brodie* v. *Jordan* (2006) 447 Mass 866, 872–873, 857 NE2d 1076, 1081–2 (criticising the buyout and preferring alternative, more 'proportional' remedies such as monetary damages and injunctions).

106 See *Brodie* v. *Jordan* (2006) 447 Mass 866, 867, 870, 857 NE2d 1076, 1078, 1080 (Mass) (declining to order a buyout 'on this record').

107 See VI.C.2.iv below.

108 Authorities holding that statutory remedies (which include dissolution but not share buyouts) are the sole available remedies are *White* v. *Perkins* (1972) 213 Va 129, 135, 189 SE2d 315, 320 (Va) and *Giannotti* v. *Hamway* (1990) 239 Va 14, 28–29, 387 SE2d 725, 733–4 (Va). These cases do not address other shareholder remedies such as derivative actions; see *Cattano* v. *Bragg* (2012) 283 Va 638, 727 SE2d 625, 630 (Va); *Baylor* v. *Beverly Book Co, Inc* (1975) 216 Va 22, 216 SE2d 18, 19 (Va). See also Martinez (2014); see also discussion at VI.C.2.iii below.

in Washington state,[109] although there is yet to be any written judgment of a court exercising its discretion to order a defendant to buy out the plaintiff's shares, a reverse example exists.[110] A California provision authorising the court to 'make such orders … as justice and equity require'[111] does not seem to have been used to order a buyout during its more than eighty years of existence.[112]

iii Indirect Remedies

The typical indirect remedy statute permits a shareholder to seek judicial dissolution, but also allows the US-CC to avoid dissolution if the corporation or another shareholder offers to purchase the aggrieved shareholder's shares at fair value.[113] Also known as 'election statutes',[114] the MBCA is an example of this type.[115] As it requires a party (the US-CC itself or another shareholder) to make an affirmative election, conceptually this family of remedies is not strictly speaking 'judicial' in the sense that the buyout may be ordered by the court against an involuntary purchaser. However, there are often provisions that govern how the court may manage proceedings arising from a buyout offer such as valuation disputes, and how the court could eventually enforce the buyout.[116]

States[117] implementing this 'dissolution unless buyout'[118] type of remedy include West Virginia,[119] Virginia,[120] Alaska,[121] Minnesota,[122] New Jersey,[123] North

109 Washington RevCodeAnn, § 23B.14.330(1) (1995); *Scott* v. *Trans-System, Inc* (2003) 148 Wash2d 701, 718, 64 P3d 1, 9 (Wash) (dissolutions under the Washington statute are equitable in nature and the court may order alternative reliefs less severe than dissolution). Although citing *Baker* (Oregon) and *Sauer* (Iowa), the court did not expressly refer to the buyout as an alternative remedy.

110 *Skarbo v. Skarbo Scandinavian Furniture Import, Inc* (2005) 128 WashApp 1072, 2005 WL 1950599 (WashCtApp).

111 AnnCalCorpCode, § 1804 (1977). Its immediate predecessor provision (California Corporations Code, § 4657) was enacted in 1947, but the provision can be traced to at least 1931 (Civil Code, § 404).

112 Quite the reverse: a trial court declined to order a minority shareholder – who had initially requested a sale of his shares to the majority 'at an acceptable price' but later changed his mind after trial – to follow through on the sale. Upon appeal by the majority shareholder (who sought an order that the minority sell) the judgment was affirmed: *Pacific Sun Distributing* v. *Martin*, No B221716, 15 February 2011, 2011 WL 522040 (CalCtApp).

113 O'Neal & Thompson (2020b): § 7:18.

114 See generally Moll & Ragazzo (2017): § 8.02[B][2] (8–20 to 8–25).

115 MBCA, § 14.34. It was first introduced in 1990; see ABA (1990): 310–18.

116 MBCA, §14.34(b)–(h).

117 For a partial list, see *Dawkins* v. *Hickman Family Corp*, No 1:09–CV–164, US District Ct, Northern District of Mississippi, Sharion Aycock J, 13 June 2011, 2011 WL 243653, *2.

118 Terminology by Moll (2014): 491.

119 WVaCode, § 31–1–81 (1931); WVa Code, §31–1–134 (1974); § 31D–14–1434(a) (2002). See *Masinter* v. *WEBCO Co* (1980) 164 WVa 241, 262 SE2d 433 (WVa).

120 VaCodeAnn, § 13.1–749.1(A) (2015), most recently amended by 2019 Virginia Laws ch 734 (HB 2478).

121 Alaska StatAnn, § 10.06.630(a) (1989).

122 MinnStatAnn, § 302A.751, subdivision 2 (2011).

123 NJStatAnn, § 14A:12–7(8) (1988); *Bostock* v. *High Tech Elevator Industries, Inc* (1992) 260 NJSuper 432, 445, 616 A2d 1314, 1321 (NJAppDiv).

Carolina,[124] Arizona,[125] New York,[126] California,[127] and Louisiana (albeit for director or shareholder deadlock, but not oppression).[128]

Although they fit only very imperfectly into the withdrawal paradigm that is the subject of this Book, the MBCA and a considerable number of economically significant states – including New York and California – offer primarily if not exclusively indirect remedies. Election statutes also tend to address important technical issues such as valuation and give rise to useful case law. Hence, indirect remedies will be discussed as if they are 'withdrawal remedies' within the meaning of this Book.

iv No Buyout Remedy

Some state courts have expressly disclaimed the power to order buyouts. In *Nixon* v. *Blackwell*, the Delaware Supreme Court adopted a strictly contractarian stance in rejecting judicial withdrawal remedies:

> The tools of good corporate practice are designed to give a purchasing minority stockholder the opportunity to bargain for protection before parting with consideration. It would do violence to normal corporate practice and our corporation law to fashion an ad hoc ruling which would result in a court-imposed stockholder buy-out for which the parties had not contracted. …
>
> One cannot read into the situation presented in the case at bar any special relief for the minority stockholders in this closely-held, but not statutory 'close corporation' because [Delaware's statutory close corporation provisions][129] and other statutory schemes preempt the field in their respective areas. It would run counter to the spirit of the doctrine of independent legal significance,[130] and would be inappropriate judicial legislation for this Court to fashion a special judicially-created rule for minority investors when the entity does not fall within those statutes, or when there are no negotiated special provisions in the certificate of incorporation, by-laws, or stockholder agreements.[131]

124 NC General StatAnn, § 55–14–30 (1989).

125 Arizona RevStatAnn, § 10–1434(A) (1996).

126 NYBCL, § 1118(a) (1990). Although § 1118 only applies to a petition under § 1104-a, which may be presented only by a shareholder holding 20 per cent or more of the voting power of the company (§1104-a(a)), it is possible for a shareholder with less than the required shareholding to bring an oppression petition in equity and for the corporation to elect to buy out the petitioner's shares: *In re Davis* (1991) 174 AD2d 449, 571 NYS2d 234, 235–6 (NYAppDiv).

127 AnnCalCorpCode, § 2000 (2018).

128 LaStatAnn, §§ 12:1–1430(A)(2)(a), 12:1–1430(A)(2)(c), 12:1–1434 (A), 12:1–1431(D) (2015).

129 Even for statutory close corporations, DGCL's Subchapter XIV provides no withdrawal right or remedy.

130 This Delaware corporate law doctrine provides that 'action taken under one section of that law is legally independent, and its validity is not dependent upon, nor to be tested by the requirements of other unrelated sections under which the same final result might be attained by different means': *Orzeck* v. *Englehart* (1963) 195 A2d 375, 378 (Del).

131 *Nixon* v. *Blackwell* (1993) 626 A2d 1366, 1380–1 (Del).

Nixon was enthusiastically followed in Kansas.[132]

Overturning a longstanding lower court decision,[133] Texas' highest court recently declined categorically in *Ritchie* v. *Rupe* to allow any relief – including the buyout – for oppression that is not specifically provided for in the corporation statute.[134] The impact of this decision was not lost on the dissenting justice:

> The ultimate effect of this holding is to negate the very foundations of protection the legislatures and U.S. courts have long afforded to minority shareholders in closely held corporations.[135]

For the avoidance of doubt, states that have expressly disclaimed the buyout as a remedy will not be characterised as having 'withdrawal remedies' for minority oppression within the meaning of this Book.

3 *Grounds*

Even in states offering statutory oppression relief, critical questions such as what constituted oppression and what remedies (in addition to or in lieu of dissolution) can or should be granted were left to judicial interpretation.[136] Interestingly, early UK jurisprudence on what constituted oppression[137] was cited and applied in early key cases from Illinois,[138] Virginia,[139] and Oregon.[140] Over time, however, statutory provisions and jurisprudence on oppression developed along different trajectories in different states.

The diversity in approaches and the immense quantity of jurisprudence in the American states make a finely textured analysis based on fact patterns[141] or black letter doctrine in this Chapter impossible.[142] In lieu of going into the details, this

132 *Hunt* v. *Data Management Resources, Inc* (1999) 26 KanApp2d 405, 407–8; 985 P2d 730, 732–3 (KanCtApp).

133 *Davis* v. *Sheerin* (1988) 754 SW2d 375 (TexApp).

134 *Ritchie* v. *Rupe* (2014) 443 SW3d 856, 891 (Tex) (majority opinion); *Cardiac Perfusion Services, Inc* v. *Hughes* (2014); 436 SW3d 790, 791, 792 (Tex). Somewhat paradoxically, the *Ritchie* majority opinion does not seem to have categorically foreclosed all possibility of the buyout as relief for breach of fiduciary duty specifically: *Ritchie* v. *Rupe* (2014) 443 SW3d 856, 891–2 (Tex).

135 *Ritchie* v. *Rupe* (2014) 443 SW3d 856, 892 (Tex) (Guzman J dissenting). For other criticism, see Dawson (2014): 90; Bittle & Hinson (2015): 411.

136 Matheson & Maler (2007): 665; Thompson (1993): 711–12.

137 Which was later considered problematic and legislatively reformed; see V.C.1.i–ii.

138 *Central Standard Life Insurance Co* v. *Davis* (1957) 10 Ill2d 566, 574, 141 NE2d 45, 50 (Ill) (citing *Elder* v. *Elder & Watson* 1952 SC 49 (Scot 1st Div) 55).

139 *White* v. *Perkins* (1972) 213 Va 129, 134; 189 SE2d 315, 320 (Va) (citing *Elder* 1952 SC 49, 55 and *Scottish Co-operative Wholesale Society Ltd* v. *Meyer* [1958] 3 All ER 66, 86, [1959] AC 324 (HL) 364).

140 *Baker* v. *Commercial Body Builders, Inc* (1973) 264 Or 614, 629 fn. 9, 507 P2d 387, 393 fn. 9 (Or) (primarily citing Comment (1965):134, but also giving due attribution to *Elder* 1952 SC 49, 55 and *Meyer* [1958] 3 All ER 66, 71, 86).

141 For lists of factual situations in which oppression is recognised in some states, see Moll & Ragazzo (2017): § 7.01[C] and O'Neal & Thompson (2020b): chs. 3, 6.

142 On oppression's interaction with other legal doctrines, see generally Moll & Ragazzo (2017): § 7.01[B] and O'Neal & Thompson (2020b): § 3:3.

subsection introduces two ways – one traditional and doctrinal, one scholarly – of organising the myriad state approaches in the US, before discussing non-fault grounds for withdrawal and the interaction of contract with judicial remedies.

i The Classic Trichotomy: 'Burdensome, Harsh and Wrongful' – Breach of Fiduciary Duty – Breach of Reasonable Expectations

A threefold classification popularised by US close corporation law scholars,[143] the dominant *doctrinal* approach (or approaches) may be sorted into one or more of these categories.[144] Jurisdictions adopting the first 'wrongfulness' (or 'bad faith'[145]) standard[146] can be said to have left (or abandoned) parties to the consequences of private ordering, with the courts unaware of or otherwise insensitive to the context in which US-CCs are established and operated, and where shareholder oppression arises.[147]

The second, 'fiduciary duty' approach is premised on a special duty owed by majority shareholders to minority shareholders of US-CCs that conceptually resembles that between partners in partnerships.[148] Exemplified by Massachusetts' seminal *Donahue* v. *Rodd Electrotype Co*[149] decision, minority shareholders in states adopting this concept of oppression may sue majority shareholders directly in a personal action for breach of this duty.[150] *Donahue*'s seemingly expansive approach to shareholder fiduciary duties was subsequently reined in by *Wilkes* v. *Springside Nursing Home*. Recognising the majority shareholder's interest in 'selfish ownership', under *Wilkes* the majority may justify their breach of fiduciary duty by showing a 'legitimate business purpose' for their action. In turn, the minority may counter this by showing that a 'less harmful alternative' to the majority's action existed. The court then makes the final decision by weighing the majority's legitimate business purpose against the practicability of the minority's suggested alternative.[151]

The third and arguably most popular approach[152] concerns the minority shareholder's 'reasonable expectations'. Its genesis may be traced back to a scholar based in Australia writing about the UK oppression remedy,[153] and to

143 Haynsworth (1987): 36–8; Thompson (1988): 208–9; Thompson (1993): 711–12; Moll (2000): 761–2.
144 See Moll & Ragazzo (2017): fig. 7.1 (7–156 to 7–187). Cf Means (2009): 1220–9, 1221 fn. 60.
145 Means (2009): 1220–3.
146 See cases cited in O'Neal & Thompson (2020b): § 7:11 fn. 20.
147 See Means (2009): 1220–3.
148 O'Neal & Thompson (2020b): §§ 7:4 to 7:5.
149 *Donahue* v. *Rodd Electrotype Co* (1975) 367 Mass 578, 592–3, 328 NE2d 505, 515 (Mass) (setting out the key passage). See also *Helms* v. *Duckworth* (1957) 249 F2d 482, 486–7 (DCCir).
150 I.e. not derivative. See generally Thompson (1993).
151 *Wilkes* v. *Springside Nursing Home, Inc* (1976) 370 Mass 842, 850–2, 353 NE2d 657, 663 (Mass). Damages, not withdrawal, was ordered in *Wilkes* because the corporation was dissolved before the appeal was decided: ibid. 370 Mass 842, 853–4, 353 NE2d 657, 664–5. See also VI.C.3.ii.c below.
152 Moll & Ragazzo (2017): § 7.01[D][1][b][i] text between fns. 199–200 (7–78).
153 Thompson (1988): 211 (crediting Afterman (1969)).

O'Neal's work[154] – which was possibly influenced in part by British law[155] – and popularised in part by a series of New York cases.[156] On one view, the reasonable expectations doctrine performs – and also surpasses – the functions of implied contracts.[157] The 'reasonable expectations' formulation is sensitive not only to how US-CCs differ from public corporations in context and nature,[158] but also to differences within the US-CC category. It also provides the legal basis for a court to 'adjust the parties' relationship after the fact'.[159] However, the reasonable expectations standard is ultimately circular;[160] the degree to which it is useful for an oppressed minority shareholder turns on whether 'reasonable' expectations extend beyond those covered under the other two standards.[161]

The three approaches are neither contradictory nor mutually exclusive. The same act or conduct could support a finding of oppression under more than one approach,[162] and some states combine multiple approaches.[163]

ii The 'Perspective' Framework

An alternative framework for classifying state law approaches (attributed to the work of Douglas Moll) turns on the question of *perspective*.[164] That is, from *whose point of view* does the court approach the issue: majority shareholder, minority, or a mixture of both?

A MAJORITY PERSPECTIVES. This group of approaches focus on the 'propriety of the majority's *conduct*'.[165] At its simplest: the majority will not be liable in oppression unless it was subjectively at fault – which means engaging in conduct that is unlawful or in breach of fiduciary duty.[166] However, a majority perspective in its pure form goes even further: all the majority needs to do to avoid prima facie oppression liability is to raise a 'legitimate business purpose defense'.[167] A legitimate business purpose is likely to be recognised for any majority act that

154 O'Neal & Derwin (1961): 193; Thompson (1988): 213–15; see also O'Neal (1978): 885–8.
155 See O'Neal (1978): 885–7 (discussing mainly British cases).
156 Most notably *Matter of Kemp & Beatley, Inc* (1984) 64 NY2d 63, 72–3, 473 NE2d 1173, 1179 (NY).
157 See generally Moll (2001).
158 Means (2009): 1226–8.
159 Ibid. 1227.
160 See Moll (2003): 844.
161 cf Means (2009): 1227 and 1227 fn. 96 (describing New York's approach).
162 O'Neal & Thompson (2020b): § 7:11 text to fns. 23.50–28.
163 See Moll & Ragazzo (2017): § 7.01[D][1][b][i] fn. 202 (7–79).
164 VI.C.3.ii draws extensively on Moll (2000).
165 Moll (2000): 766.
166 See ibid. 762.
167 Ibid. 762–3; for cases, see e.g. *Wilkes* v. *Springside Nursing Home, Inc* (1976) 370 Mass 842, 851, 353 NE2d 657, 663 (Mass); *Zidell* v. *Zidell, Inc* (1977) 560 P2d 1086, 1089–90 (Or); *Nelson* v. *Martin* (1997) 958 SW2d 643, 650 (Tenn).

benefits the US-CC,[168] regardless of how much the minority suffers.[169] Approaches taking the majority perspective are thus less concerned with – or protective of – minority shareholder interests.[170] The only situation in which oppression would be found under the pure majority perspective is when there is 'majority fault'[171] (i.e. without any legitimate business purpose to justify it) and no 'minority fault'[172].[173]

B MINORITY PERSPECTIVES. As a direct counter to the approach above, approaches taking the minority's perspective focus 'the analysis not on the propriety of the majority's conduct, but on the impact that majority actions have on the minority'.[174] The emphasis is on 'the absolute protection of the minority's interests'.[175] In its purest form, the court adopting a minority perspective considers only whether the minority's reasonable expectations have been disappointed,[176] and is unconcerned with the merits of or justifications for the majority's conduct[177] or how egregious the minority's own conduct was.[178] In other words, any harm to the reasonable expectations of the minority – regardless of the presence or absence of majority or minority fault – is actionable as oppression.[179]

C MIXED APPROACHES. Majority and minority perspectives in their 'pure' form can produce very different results in cases with similar facts.[180] Some courts have adopted mixed approaches – 'modified majority' and 'modified minority' in Moll's terminology – that take into consideration both majority and minority interests.[181]

The 'modified majority' approach[182] can be broken down into a two-step inquiry. First, can the majority's conduct be justified by legitimate business considerations? If the answer is yes, the second question is: can the minority show that the same legitimate business objective 'could have been achieved through an alternative

[168] An act that benefits the majority shareholder but not the corporation is not a legitimate business purpose: *Zimmerman* v. *Bogoff* (1988) 402 Mass 650, 658–9, 524 NE2d 849, 854 (Mass); *AW Chesterton Co* v. *Chesterton* (1997) 128 F3d 1, 7 (1stCir).

[169] Moll (2000): 766–7; Mitchell (1990): 1716.

[170] Moll (2000): 762–3.

[171] According to Moll's terminology, only majority actions without any legitimate business purpose to be 'majority fault': Moll (2000): 756 fn. 31, 778. This does not include exclusion from management or employment per se as part of majority 'fault': see ibid. 779.

[172] 'Minority fault' is defined as 'misconduct or incompetence' of the minority shareholder that 'harms the corporation and brings about the majority's allegedly oppressive actions': Moll (2000): 756 fn. 32.

[173] Moll (2000): 770, 778.

[174] Ibid. 764.

[175] Ibid. 770.

[176] *In re Topper* (1980) 107 Misc2d 25, 28; 433 NYS2d 359, 362 (NYSupCt).

[177] See also *Balvik* v. *Sylvester* (1987) 411 NW2d 383, 388 (ND); *Gunzberg* v. *Art-Lloyd Metal Products Corp* (1985) 492 NYS2d 83, 86 (NYAppDiv).

[178] See Moll (2000): 770, 768 fn. 91.

[179] Ibid. 770–1.

[180] Ibid. 771.

[181] Ibid. 772.

[182] Ibid. 772–5.

course of action less harmful to the minority's interest'?[183] If the answer is 'yes', it is oppression; otherwise, it is not.[184] Put another way, the outcomes flowing from the modified majority approach are largely similar to the pure majority approach (oppression only if majority fault is present and minority fault is not),[185] albeit with the scope of majority fault extended to include situations where the majority's means at achieving the legitimate business purpose is disproportionate to the ends.

The modified minority perspective protects the minority's reasonable expectations, but only to the extent that they remain reasonable in light of the circumstances, taking into consideration changes in business conditions, justification for the majority's conduct, and blameworthy conduct on the minority's part.[186] That is to say, if minority fault is present – regardless of whether the majority is at fault[187] – the oppression action fails[188] insofar as it is based on minority expectations of active participation.[189]

Moll favours[190] the modified minority perspective on the ground that it is compatible with his theory of oppression[191] and hypothetical bargains as to the scope of the oppression doctrine in constraining majority discretion over business decisions.[192]

iii Non-Fault

A non-fault regime is where a court may order a buyout even if majority fault – whether in the form of unlawful conduct, breach of fiduciary duty, or breach of reasonable expectation – is not established.[193] Conceptually, insofar as they arise from bona fide disagreement, deadlock in director or shareholder decision-making may be considered a non-fault ground.[194] Although deadlock is recognised as a basis

183 *Wilkes v. Springside Nursing Home, Inc* (1976) 370 Mass 842, 851–2; 353 NE2d 657 (Mass).

184 Moll (2000): 772–3; for consideration of whether the 'less harmful alternative' must be no more costly or infeasible for the corporation, see ibid. 773–5.

185 See Moll (2000): 778–84.

186 Ibid. 775–7. See also ibid. 809–15 (discussing the use of rebuttable presumptions based on hypothetical bargaining).

187 In the case of mixed majority motives (i.e. partly legitimate business purpose based on minority fault and partly improper freezeout intentions is unjustifiable majority fault), it is possible but unlikely that a modified minority court may grant relief: Moll (2000): 783.

188 Moll (2000): 780–1, 783.

189 Minority fault arising from 'an active participation role (employment, management)' does not justify exclusion of minority from 'passive participation (profit sharing and other status-based shareholder rights)': Moll & Ragazzo (2017): §§ 7.01[D][1][b][ii][A] text to fns. 217–217.1 (7–84), 7.01[D][1][d] text to fn. 285 (7–102).

190 Moll (2000): 806–9.

191 Developed in Moll (1999): 537–47; Moll (2000): 793–7.

192 Moll (2000): 797–806. Hypothetical bargains will be explained below at VI.F.1.

193 Note that the concept of fault used for this Book and used here is not the same as Moll's; for Moll's terminology, see (nn. 171–172).

194 True 'non-fault' deadlock is not easily distinguished from 'both at fault' deadlock.

for judicial dissolution in most states,[195] there are scant examples of deadlock resolution specifically by judicially ordered buyout.[196] There is little if any discussion in the literature of changes in circumstances of the US-CC or of the shareholders on a personal level which affect minority interests – but without a particular action or conduct of the majority – as grounds for judicial relief of the minority.[197]

In jurisdictions adopting indirect remedies (election statutes), even if a proceeding was commenced on fault grounds, an election to buy out the petitioner is enforceable without the need for the court to make a finding of fault.[198] In this sense, election statutes can facilitate no-fault resolution.[199] However, since buyouts pursuant to an election are functionally little different from privately negotiated settlements – which naturally do not require fault – they should not strictly speaking be considered a form of non-fault withdrawal.

Rhode Island has an election statute, but there is precedent in which the court exercised its discretion to order a buyout despite there being no election made by any party.[200] South Carolina is possibly another non-fault jurisdiction.[201]

Notwithstanding the above, it is difficult to point to any US state in which judicially ordered buyouts are expressly made and unequivocally recognised as appropriate relief in situations where neither party is at fault.

iv Effect of Contract

California[202] and New York[203] do not permit judicial dissolution to be contracted out of entirely. More generally, some states give effect to contractual stipulations as to permissible conduct or reasonable expectations such as valuation[204] and stock repurchase provisions,[205] thereby restricting the scope of majority conduct

195 O'Neal & Thompson (2020b): § 7:16 fn1 and text thereto; Moll & Ragazzo (2017): § 7.02 (7–146 to 7–154); MBCA, § 14.30(a)(2)(i) (director deadlock), § 14.30(a)(2)(iii) (shareholder deadlock).

196 Exceptions being *Schaub* v. *Kortgard* (1985) 372 NW2d 427 (MinnCtApp); *Hendley* v. *Lee* (1987) 676 FSupp 1317, 1323, 1325 (DSC).

197 To be distinguished from 'at will'; see VI.C.7.

198 Except Minnesota. See Olson (1985): 646 fn. 118. Olson was the draftsman for the 1983 amendments that introduced Minnesota's modern oppression statute.

199 Moll & Ragazzo (2017): § 8.02[B][2] text to fns. 88–9 (8–24); see also *Go* v. *Pacific Health Services, Inc* (2009) 179 CalApp4th 522, 532–3, 101 CalRptr3d 736, 744 (CalApp).

200 See (n. 100) and text thereto.

201 *Kreischer* v. *Kerrison Dry Goods Co* (1999) 172 F3d 863, 1999 WL 30836, *8 (4th Circuit, unpublished) (interpreting South Carolina's § 33–14–310 as permitting buyout relief even if grounds for dissolution (§ 33–14–300(2)) were not established). Cf *Kiriakides* v. *Atlas Food Systems & Services, Inc* (2001) 343 SC 587, 600–2, 541 SE2d 257, 265–6 (SC) (adopting a majority perspective).

202 AnnCalCorpCode, § 300(c) (1977).

203 *Matter of Validation Review Associates, Inc* (1996) 223 AD2d 134, 136–7, 646 NYS2d 149, 150–1 (NYAppDiv) (referring to NYBCL, §§ 1104 and 1104-a), order reversed as moot (1997) 91 NY2d 840, 690 NE2d 487 (NY), holding affirmed *Schimel* v. *Berkun* (1999) 264 AD2d 725, 728, 696 NYS2d 49, 52 (NYAppDiv).

204 Agreements on valuation are addressed below at VI.C.5.

205 Moll & Ragazzo (2017): §7.01[E][2] (7–124 to 7–131).

actionable by the minority as oppression. Whether a contractual provision could pre-empt an action for withdrawal and supersede the usual judicial relief depends on the provision's scope.[206]

South Carolina (and the Model Supplement) provide that a statutory close corporation shareholder who has agreed in writing to resolve a dispute through non-judicial means must exhaust those means before commencing judicial proceedings for relief.[207]

It is trite that parties may enter into buyout agreements with specific triggers that are judicially enforceable as contracts. However, there is scant authority on whether parties may contractually define specific acts or conduct to be oppressive and actionable under oppression law.[208]

States are divided on whether a buyout exercised by the purchaser opportunistically or on terms disadvantageous to the forced seller pursuant to pre-existing contractual arrangements would survive a challenge by the forced seller on separate breach of fiduciary duty (i.e. oppression) grounds.[209]

4 *Effect of Seeking Oppression Relief*

There is no uniform approach. Under the MBCA, upon the entry of an order for the purchase of the withdrawing shareholder's shares in lieu of dissolution of the corporation, dissolution proceedings are terminated.[210] The withdrawing shareholder loses their status and all rights as a shareholder,[211] including any outstanding claims they might have had in their capacity as a shareholder that is not accounted for in the buyout order itself.[212] In North Dakota, the court may make a buyout order without determining fair value;[213] the withdrawing shareholder loses rights and status as shareholder, director, or officer only if the purchasing shareholder or corporation furnishes adequate security or satisfies the court that the full purchase price plus any additional awards will be paid.[214] California's statute requires the selling shareholder to transfer their shares only after payment is received.[215]

206 *Matter of Pace Photographers, Ltd*, 71 NY2d 737, 747–8, 525 NE2d 713, 718 (1988); *Brent D Redstone* v. *National Amusements, Inc* (2006) No 24-C-06–001493, Circuit Court of Maryland, Baltimore City, Evelyn Omega Cannon J, 7 Aug 2006, 2006 WL 4476415.

207 SCCodeAnn, § 33–18–400(c) (1988); Model Supplement, § 40(c).

208 The closest example is *Bostock* v. *High Tech Elevator Industries, Inc* (1992) 260 NJSuper 432, 616 A2d 1314 (AppDiv). See also O'Neal & Thompson (2020a): § 7:3 text to and after fns. 14–15 (regarding buy-sell agreements).

209 See O'Neal & Thompson (2020a): § 7:12.

210 MBCA, § 14.34(f).

211 Ibid.

212 ABA (2016): 14–28.

213 ND Century CodeAnn, § 10–19.1–115(4)(c) (2013).

214 ND Century CodeAnn, § 10–19.1–115(4)(d) (2013).

215 AnnCalCorpCode, § 2000(d) (2018).

5 Valuation

Valuation date.[216] New York law stipulates the day before the filing date of the petition as the reference date.[217] The MBCA adopts a similar default date but also grants the court discretion to set any other date.[218] In California,[219] New Jersey,[220] and arguably Minnesota,[221] the default valuation date is the day of commencement of the action, but their respective laws also permit a different date to be designated, including a future date.

Valuation principles.[222] There is little consensus over the meaning of 'fair value' in the oppression valuation context.[223] For example, other than using the term 'fair value', the MBCA offers no specific guidance on valuation matters, leaving it to the court's discretion.[224] In assessing fair value, New York considers what a voluntary purchaser would offer for the business as a going concern in a transaction at arm's length.[225] California's statute takes liquidation value as the starting point but would also consider the possibility of sale of the business as a going concern,[226] and case law suggests that the value that would be received by the plaintiff in dissolution is a floor below which the buyout amount cannot fall.[227] Similarly, judicial approaches to minority[228] and marketability[229] discounts[230] differ by state,[231] although courts overall seem to disfavour[232] minority discounts in the oppression context.

Effect of contract. Some statutes direct that agreements between the parties shall be taken into consideration when performing valuation of shares, although such agreements are not binding on the court. Examples include the Model

216 On the possible justifications and weaknesses for each approach, see generally Moll & Ragazzo (2017): § 8.02[B][4] (8–48 to 8–53); Moll (2004): 373–81.

217 NYBCL, § 1118(b) (1990). A valuer may take into consideration evidence of events occurring after the valuation date: *Hall* v. *King* (1998) 177 Misc2d 126, 130, 675 NYS2d 810, 813 (NYSupCt).

218 MBCA, § 14.34(d).

219 AnnCalCorpCode, § 2000(f) (2018); *Trahan* v. *Trahan* (2002) 99 CalApp4th 62, 76–77, 120 CalRptr 2d 814, 825 (CalCtApp) (future date possible).

220 NJStatAnn, § 14A:12–7(8)(a) (1988).

221 MinnStatAnn § 302A.751, subdivision 2 (2011).

222 See generally O'Neal & Thompson (2020b): § 7:20.

223 See generally Moll & Ragazzo (2017): § 8.02[B][3][a] (8–25 to 8–30); Moll (2004).

224 MBCA, § 14.34(e).

225 *Matter of Pace Photographers, Ltd* (1988) 71 NY2d 737, 748, 525 NE2d 713, 718–19 (NY).

226 AnnCalCorpCode, § 2000(a) (2018).

227 *Brown* v. *Allied Corrugated Box Co* (1979) 91 CalApp3d 477, 486–7, 154 CalRptr 170, 176 (CalCtApp).

228 See Moll & Ragazzo (2017): §8.02[B][3][b] (8–30 to 8–31) and O'Neal & Thompson (2020b): § 7:20 fns. 28–32 and text thereto.

229 O'Neal & Thompson (2020b): § 7:20 fns. 39–43; Moll & Ragazzo (2017): §8.02[B][3][c] (8–32 to 8–33).

230 On the arguments for and against discounts, see Moll & Ragazzo (2017): §8.02[B][3][d] (8–34–8–48).

231 For an overview see Moll & Ragazzo (2017): fig. 8.1 (8–65 to 8–75), fig. 8.3 (8–92 to 8–103).

232 Ibid. §8.02[B][3][b] fn. 112 and text thereto; *Murphy* v. *US Dredging Corp* (2010) 74 AD3d 815, 818, 903 NYS2d 434, 437–8 (NYAppDiv) (marketability discounts are permissible but minority discounts are not).

Supplement,[233] South Carolina,[234] and Minnesota.[235] States without similar statutory language but would take shareholder agreements into consideration include New Jersey[236] and New York.[237] In New York, the willingness of defendants to renegotiate buyout agreement terms may bar the plaintiff from oppression relief.[238] States such as Nebraska and Minnesota do not regard valuation agreements crafted for voluntary exit to be necessarily applicable to the oppression setting,[239] whereas North Dakota[240] would apply valuation agreements even to cases of majority shareholder misconduct.

Interest. The MBCA provides that interest may be ordered on the assessed fair value of the shares if the court deems this equitable, but not if the withdrawing shareholder unreasonably refused to accept a settlement offer.[241] New York leaves the award of interest to the court's discretion.[242]

Judicial adjustments for misconduct. The MBCA itself makes no express reference to judicial adjustments for misconduct affecting the value of the corporation or its shares, although the Official Comment seems to suggest that 'any claims that the petitioner may have had in [their] capacity as a shareholder' may be 'asserted as part of the "fair value" of the petitioner's shares'.[243] New York law expressly provides that '[t]he court may order stock valuations be adjusted and may provide for a surcharge upon the directors or those in control of the corporation upon a finding of wilful or reckless dissipation or transfer of assets or corporate property without just or adequate compensation therefor'.[244] Adjustments may be made in the case of excessive compensation to directors or shareholders, and the valuation proceeding is the proper forum for addressing misappropriation by wrongdoers.[245] In California, derivative claims for breach of fiduciary duty against defendants must be taken into account when assessing fair value.[246] In a New Jersey case, defendant shareholders were ordered to purchase the plaintiff's shares, but compensation for denial of

[233] Model Supplement, § 42(b)(1).

[234] SCCodeAnn, § 33–18–420(b)(1) (1988).

[235] MinnStatAnn § 302A.751, subdivision 2 (2011).

[236] *Bostock* v. *High Tech Elevator Industries, Inc* (1992) 260 NJSuper 432, 445–6, 616 A2d 1314, 1321–2 (NJAppDiv).

[237] *Matter of Pace Photographers, Ltd* (1988) 71 NY2d 737, 748, 525 NE2d 713, 719 (NY).

[238] *DiPace* v. *Figueroa* (1996) 223 AD2d 949, 951–2, 637 NYS2d 222, 224 (NYAppDiv).

[239] *Anderson* v. *Clemens Mobile Homes, Inc* (1983) 214 Neb 283, 287, 333 NW2d 900, 903–4 (Neb); *Matter of Villa Maria, Inc* (1981) 312 NW2d 921, 923 (Minn); O'Neal & Thompson (2020b): § 7:25 fn. 6 and text thereto.

[240] *Brandt* v. *Somerville* (2005) 2005 ND 35, 692 NW2d 144 (ND); ND Century CodeAnn, § 10–19.1–115(5) (2013).

[241] MBCA, § 14.34(e).

[242] NYBCL, § 1118(b) (1990).

[243] ABA (2016): 14–28.

[244] NYBCL, § 1104-a(d) (1998).

[245] *Markman* v. *Exterior Delite, Inc* (2006) 14 Misc 3d 910, 915–16, 831 NYS2d 656, 661 (NYSupCt) (citing cases).

[246] *Goles* v. *Sawhney* (2016) 5 CalApp5th 1014, 1019, 210 CalRptr3d 261, 265 (CalCtApp).

minority shareholder's employment was ordered to be paid by the corporation.[247] In Indiana, a defendant majority shareholder/director may be liable to pay the plaintiff minority shareholder punitive damages for breach of fiduciary duty on top of fair market value for the plaintiff's shares.[248]

6 *Enforcement*

In principle, the MBCA considers the buyout order to be enforceable as a regular court judgment.[249] This is straightforward where the purchasers of the withdrawing shareholder's shares are other shareholders of the business corporation; the withdrawing shareholder becomes a judgment creditor of the purchasers.[250] However, where the corporation is the purchaser, the purchase price is considered a distribution and subject to the applicable rules governing distributions to shareholders,[251] which prohibits any distribution that would render the corporation insolvent either on a solvency or balance sheet basis.[252]

It is possible that pursuant to the US-CC's election to purchase the withdrawing shareholder's shares, the ensuing court order provides for the purchase of the shares at a price that cannot be lawfully paid by the corporation without infringing the rules on distributions. Since the question of whether the corporation's purchase of the shares would contravene the distribution rules is determined as of the buyout order's effective date,[253] it is possible that the corporation's financial position would have changed sufficiently during dissolution/buyout proceedings that an initially feasible price would cease to be so by the date of the order. Such an order's effect in this situation is unclear, but the better view[254] would be to treat the buyout order as a judgment enforceable against the corporation, albeit one that the directors of the corporation may not lawfully comply with. Enforcement therefore would mean liquidation of the corporation,[255] with the withdrawn shareholder treated as the corporation's unsecured creditor.[256]

247 *Musto* v. *Vidas* (1995) 281 NJSuper 548, 561–2, 658 A2d 1305, 1312 (NJAppDiv).

248 *G & N Aircraft, Inc* v. *Boehm* (2001) 743 NE2d 227, 245 (Ind).

249 MBCA, § 14.34(f); ABA (2016): 14–28.

250 MBCA, § 14.34(f); ABA (2016): 14–29.

251 ABA (2016): 14–29 (referring to MBCA, § 6.40).

252 MBCA, § 6.40(c); ABA (2016): 6–31 to 6–34.

253 MBCA, § 6.40(c)(1) defines the reference date as the earlier of '(i) the date cash or other property is transferred or debt to a shareholder is incurred by the corporation or (ii) the date the shareholder ceases to be a shareholder with respect to the acquired shares'. Unless the corporation voluntarily pays the shareholder first, the latter date – the date on which the shareholder ceases to be one – is earlier and therefore the effective date of the share buyout order.

254 The alternatives – treating the buyout order as unenforceable or void – would either be unfair to the withdrawing shareholder or create great uncertainty over the withdrawing shareholder's rights and status.

255 MBCA, § 16.30(a)(3) (creditor-initiated judicial dissolution).

256 MBCA, § 6.40(f).

If a California corporation or majority shareholder elects buyout in lieu of dissolution, the corporation will be dissolved automatically without further judicial intervention if the ordered purchase price is not paid, and the purchasing parties and their sureties will be liable for the plaintiff's expenses, including attorney's fees.[257] The MBCA[258] and New York statute[259] empower the court to order security to be furnished to the withdrawing shareholder. Payment by instalment is permitted under the MBCA and New York jurisprudence.[260]

7 *The Withdrawal at Will Debate*

As described above, the US approach to withdrawal in US-CCs is predominantly based on a judicial assessment of whether the majority shareholder's acts or conduct amounts to oppression of the minority. This contrasts with the concept of withdrawal at will, which is not premised on satisfying legal grounds with facts provable in court. At the time of writing, no business corporation statute in the US implements withdrawal at will,[261] although a serious but unsuccessful attempt was made in Oregon by a local attorney who was personally embroiled in a notorious oppression case as co-owner of a prominent local family business.[262]

By contrast, withdrawal at will has long had its share of scholarly advocates, of whom Hetherington and Dooley are arguably the most famous and influential. They observe that majority shareholders in close corporations (i.e. US-CCs) have the power to transfer wealth from minority shareholders to themselves by virtue of their control over managerial power, whereas the latter have no liquidity.[263] Subject to the dual hazards of indefinite exclusion from economic benefits and illiquidity, the minority is thus in a uniquely precarious position.[264] Involuntary dissolution, a legal response to majority exploitation and minority illiquidity, is however unfortunately ineffectual.[265] The authors report that involuntary dissolution is used mostly tactically: viable firms are never liquidated for good, and a buyout of one party by another

257 AnnCalCorpCode, § 2000(c) (2018); *Go* v. *Pacific Health Services, Inc* (2009) 179 CalApp4th 522, 531–2, 101 CalRptr3d 736, 742–3 (CalCtApp); *In re Orange City Nursery, Inc* (2010) 439 BR 144, 151 (CDCal).

258 MBCA, § 14.34(e).

259 NYBCL, § 1118(c)(2) (1990).

260 MBCA, § 14.34(e); *Elniski* v. *Niagara Falls Coach Lines, Inc* (2012) 101 AD3d 1722, 957 NYS2d 544 (NYAppDiv).

261 For the avoidance of doubt, provisions permitting 50 per cent shareholders in 50–50 joint ventures to petition for judicial dissolution (e.g. MoAnnStat, § 351.467 (1999); DGCL, § 273 (2010)) do not fall within this Book's definition of withdrawal at will.

262 See Art (2003): 405–7. The Oregon proposal was inspired by Hetherington and Dooley's: Art (2003): 406 fn. 228.

263 Hetherington & Dooley (1977): 5.

264 Ibid. 6.

265 Ibid.

was by far the most common outcome.[266] The discretionary and fault-based dissolution mechanism is thus reduced to little more than a minority shareholder-unfriendly, costly, and inefficient valuation procedure for an eventual buyout.[267] With liquidity for the minority shareholder entirely within the majority's control, nothing short of legislation will change that.[268]

To that end, Hetherington and Dooley propose a statute that grants a shareholder petitioner holding a minority or 50 per cent shareholding the unconditional right to demand that their shares be bought out by the corporation or other shareholders. Under their proposal, the petitioner would have the right to a court decision on price and other terms if the parties do not reach agreement, and a further right to dissolve the corporation if the purchaser fails to complete.[269] Safeguards are also proposed.[270] Hetherington and Dooley argue that their proposal discourages exploitation and incentivises efficient management by majority shareholders, and subjects the majority to the market forces that discipline business entities other than close corporations.[271] A modernised proposal for withdrawal at will covering both US-CCs and LLCs was made in 2007.[272]

Notwithstanding withdrawal at will's continuing appeal in some quarters, it remains a minority opinion in the face of diverse opponents. The contractarian champions Easterbrook and Fischel claim that fault-based involuntary dissolution and remedies for breach of fiduciary duty available in egregious cases are adequate, and that withdrawal at will is beset by costly valuation difficulties and would encourage minority opportunism and prejudice creditors.[273] They further assert that withdrawal at will is undesirable even to minority shareholders, and that minority shareholders do not usually obtain rights to withdraw at will when they do negotiate buyout provisions.[274] Easterbrook and Fischel conclude that the 'failure of the parties themselves to provide routinely for [withdrawal at will]' suggests that imposing mandatory withdrawal at will is inefficient, and that 'courts should not readily infer a right to withdraw capital from the firm on behalf of minority shareholders'.[275] In similar vein, Hillman opposes dissolution at will on the ground that it would result in buyouts that are costly and difficult to finance for corporations and shareholders,[276] and reduce the corporation's ability to attract debt and equity

266 Ibid. 33; Haynsworth (1987): 51–5 (reporting, based on a study of opinions published in 1984–85, that buyouts (including judicially ordered or those pursuant to election statutes) were the most common relief in dissolution suits).
267 Hetherington & Dooley (1977): 34–5.
268 Ibid. 44, 38.
269 Ibid. 45–6, 50–1.
270 Ibid. 51–2.
271 Ibid. 47–8.
272 Matheson & Maler (2007): 692, 695.
273 Easterbrook & Fischel (1986): 288–90.
274 Ibid. 290.
275 Ibid. 290.
276 Hillman (1982): 70–2.

financing.[277] Thompson criticises the mandatory buyout regime for rewarding minority shareholders – even those at fault for causing the breakdown in the relationship between shareholders – by enabling them to impose on the majority the costs of obtaining substitute capital. Instead, Thompson favours an approach where judges, armed with the discretion to refuse relief and alive to the context of close corporations, serve a gatekeeping function.[278]

D THE LIMITED LIABILITY COMPANY (LLC)

1 *History*

In contrast with the long and storied history of the modern business corporation (of which US-CCs form a large subset), the LLC story is that of a late twentieth-century phenomenon born of interest group lobbying against government regulation. The origin story of the LLC 'boils down to innovative professionals creating solutions when the current legal system fails to meet client needs'.[279] It began with Hamilton Brothers, a Denver oil company that sought an alternative business entity in the US modelled on a foreign entity[280] which combined full limited liability for all participants with partnership taxation.[281] After failing to procure passage of necessary legislation in Alaska in 1975–76,[282] the company ultimately succeeded when Wyoming passed an exact copy of the failed Alaskan bill as the first LLC statute in 1977 with little fuss or fanfare.[283] The second state to adopt an LLC statute, Florida, did so only in 1982.[284]

Reflecting legislative indifference towards the quality of the resulting corporate law, the precise source of the earliest LLC statutes' provisions remain murky.[285]

277 Ibid. 74–5.

278 Thompson (1988): 223–5.

279 Hamill (1998): 1463.

280 The Panamanian *limitada* was frequently used by the Hamilton Brothers Oil Company for its foreign oil and gas exploration activities as the entity type had received partnership taxation status in the US under federal tax rulings: Hamill (1998): 1483 and fn. 14.

281 Hamill (1998): 1464.

282 Alaskan legislators were keenly aware of the proposed legislation's revolutionary nature, but the bills failed to pass for unrelated political reasons: Hamill (1998): 1464–5 and fn. 21.

283 Hamill (1998): 1465 (describing the Wyoming bill as 'identical' to the Alaskan and the enactment as 'without any struggle'); Carney (1995): 857 (noting the lack of publicity surrounding the act's passage).

284 On the Florida act, see generally Johnson (1983).

285 Cf Carney (1995): 857–8 (tracing the 1977 Wyoming Act's provisions to the state's general corporation and limited partnership statutes), 860–1 (debunking the theory that the LLC's antecedent was the *limitada*) with ibid. 857 and fn. 7 (citing a practitioner text attributing the Wyoming Act's basis to the German GmbHG) and with Johnson (1983): 387 ('The LLC is similar to a business organization called a *limitada* which exists in [Central and South America]'), and Geu (1992): 49–50. Even if the LLC did trace its ancestry to the *limitadas*, the ultimate ancestor is arguably the German GmbH; see Lutter (1992): 52–3 (describing the spread of GmbH-equivalents across South America, albeit without mentioning Panama specifically).

With the federal tax authority, the Internal Revenue Service (IRS), reluctant to allow the new entities to be taxed as partnerships,[286] and with businesses suffering little or no disadvantage when taxed as a corporation until 1986,[287] the LLC remained a fringe curiosity[288] until tectonic changes in corporate taxation occurred in the late 1980s. That 'the sole attraction of this new business form was the desire to obtain statutory limited liability and flow-through taxation under the partnership regime'[289] was thus amply illustrated by the fact that states did not rush to enact LLC statutes and users did not create LLCs in large numbers until the tax question was resolved.

The turning point was IRS Revenue Ruling 88–76, which classified Wyoming LLCs as partnerships;[290] rulings for other states' LLCs followed.[291] By 1994, all states (including DC) except three had enacted their own statutes; by the end of 1996, all US jurisdictions had done so.[292] In 1997, IRS put an end to any remaining uncertainty by adopting 'check-the-box' regulations that permitted entities to elect their own taxation status, whether as C- or S-Corporations, or as partnerships.[293] The LLC revolution swept the nation, and the number of LLCs grew explosively to dominate the universe of entities by the 2000s.[294]

What has drawn less attention in the literature – but which is especially germane to the context of withdrawal – is how LLC statutes and LLCs themselves have evolved during this process. Under the Kintner Regulations formally in force until superseded in 1997, the IRS would not grant partnership status to an entity that possessed more than two of the following corporate characteristics: continuity of life, centralised management, limited liability, and free transferability of interests.[295] The earliest LLC, Wyoming's, received partnership taxation classification in 1980[296] because it did not offer continuity of life or free transferability of interests.[297] Other early LLC statutes were also designed to comply, in varying ways, with the Kintner criteria,[298] but most importantly for our purposes, most provided that LLC members had the right to withdraw at will from the LLC and demand payment for

286 Hamill (1996): 401.

287 Hamill (1998): 1509–12.

288 Hamill (1996): 402 fn. 46 (reporting that fewer than 100 LLCs were formed before the IRS changed its stance in 1988).

289 Ibid. 398.

290 IRS Revenue Ruling 88–76,1988–2 CB 360, declared obsolete by Revenue Ruling 98–37, 1998–2 CB 133.

291 Hamill (1995): 590 fn. 116.

292 Hamill (1998): 1460, 1475–7.

293 Treasury Regulations § 301.7701; 61 Federal Register 66584, effective 1 January 1997.

294 Compare figures reported in Lee (2000) with Friedman (2004) and Chrisman (2009).

295 O'Neal & Thompson (2020b): § 6:2 fn. 7; Moll (2005): 928–30; Hamill (1995): 573, citing Treasury Regulations § 301.7701–2 (as amended in 1993).

296 IRS Private Letter Ruling 81–06–082 (18 November 1980).

297 Field (2009): 461.

298 See generally Keatinge et al. (1992): 424–30.

the value of their interest.[299] How modern LLC statutes have since deviated from that standard[300] and the role played by federal tax rules in driving such changes[301] will be discussed below.

2 *Legal Aspects: Concepts, Features, and the Uniform Acts*

Although LLCs are creatures of state statutes, the Uniform Limited Liability Company Acts ('Uniform Acts') drafted by the National Conference of Commissioners on Uniform State Laws (NCCUSL) (now also known as 'Uniform Law Commission') are indispensable subjects of any study of LLCs. Although the Uniform Acts are frequently updated with minor revisions, this Chapter refers only to the following versions:[302]

- 1996 (original ULLCA) – 'ULLCA 1996' for this Book;[303]
- 2006 (often called the 'Revised Uniform Limited Liability Act' or 'RULLCA');[304] and
- 2013 (also known as the 'Harmonized Act' or 'Uniform Limited Liability Company Act (2006) (Last Amended 2013)') – 'ULLCA 2013' or simply 'ULLCA' for this Book.[305]

As states are increasingly harmonising[306] their LLC statutes by adopting one of the Uniform Act versions, this Chapter refers most frequently to the Uniform Acts,[307] and to individual state statutes primarily to illustrate differences from the Uniform Acts.

A relatively recent entrant into the universe of closely held business entities, the LLC blends characteristics of partnerships and business corporations,[308] and has been famously dubbed an 'uncorporation' by Ribstein, a leading figure in LLC

299 Moll (2005): 926–7, 926 fn. 148, 927 fn. 149; Miller (2001): 426–7; Bishop (1995): 297–8.

300 See VI.E.2.

301 See VI.F.3.

302 Before the ULLCA's earliest version was adopted by the NCCUSL, the PULLCA was drafted under a working group of the ABA's Section of Business Law (reporter Larry E. Ribstein).

303 Adopted by Hawaii, Montana, South Carolina, US Virgin Islands, and West Virginia. A bill to replace South Carolina's current LLC statute with a RULLCA-based one was introduced in 2019 but not yet passed as of early 2021: see 2019 South Carolina SB No 265. Although ULLCA 1996-type statutes are gradually being superseded, they are nonetheless worth some attention because they are among the few regimes that make express provisions governing various technical and procedural issues arising in withdrawal.

304 Adopted by Alabama, California, DC, Florida, Iowa, Minnesota, Nebraska, New Jersey, South Dakota, and Wyoming.

305 Adopted by Connecticut, Idaho, Illinois, North Dakota, Pennsylvania, Vermont, and Washington.

306 On harmonisation see Ribstein & Keatinge (2020): § 1:8.

307 There is the Uniform Commercial Code-inspired Uniform Business Organizations Code (UBOC), which includes an Article on LLCs that is similar to the ULLCA (2013), but it will not be discussed.

308 See O'Neal & Thompson (2020a): § 1:14 tbl. 14–1.

law.[309] Even more than in US-CCs, the fundamental principle of LLC governance is freedom of contract: the operating agreement containing rules as agreed upon by the parties is the lynchpin, and LLC statutes play a mostly supplemental role by providing 'default' rules that govern only in the absence of contrary agreement.[310]

Modern LLC statutes are considerably diverse compared to corporation or partnership statutes.[311] Of the business corporation's 'five core structural characteristics',[312] only separate legal personality[313] and limited liability[314] are standard features; others are entirely optional. Management of the entity can be by members or delegated to managers who need not be members.[315] There are no 'shares' or 'ownership' by equity contributors to speak of, only 'membership' and 'transferable interests' (in Uniform Act terminology[316]) which are connected but separate concepts.[317]

Transferable interests (or distributional interests) are essentially economic rights to receive distributions either in the course of the business or upon dissolution[318] in LLCs. As the name suggests, transferable interests are transferable,[319] but acquisition of a transferrable interest does not by itself confer on the transferee the rights and duties (in other words, the *status*) of membership.[320] Membership, which usually – but not necessarily – includes a transferable interest,[321] may be gained only according to the operating agreement or unanimous vote or consent of all members.[322] For ease of discussion, this Book uses the term 'membership interest' without distinguishing between 'membership interest', 'transferable interest', or 'distributional interest'.[323]

3 *Economic Aspects*

There are no national-level statistics on LLC formations, which is the responsibility of individual states. Data assembled by commentators show that LLC formations

309 Ribstein (2010):1 (defining 'uncorporation' in contradistinction with 'corporation').
310 Moll & Ragazzo (2017): § 2.01[C][1] (2–33 to 2–34); see also Ribstein & Keatinge (2020): § 3:2. On mandatory statutory provisions in LLCs, see Ribstein & Keatinge (2020): §§ 3:3, 5:7.
311 Moll & Ragazzo (2017): § 2.01[C][1] (2–32).
312 Namely legal personality, limited liability, transferable shares, 'centralized management under a board structure', and 'shared ownership by contributors of equity capital': Armour & Enriques et al. (2017): 5.
313 Moll & Ragazzo (2017): § 2.01[C][1] text to fns. 182–3 (2–35).
314 Ibid. § 2.01[C][3] (2–38); Ribstein & Keatinge (2020): § 1:5.
315 Moll & Ragazzo (2017): § 2.01[C][2] (2–37 to 2–38); Ribstein & Keatinge (2020): §§ 1:6, 2:3.
316 ULLCA 1996 uses 'distributional interest': ULLCA 1996, § 101(6).
317 See generally Moll & Ragazzo (2017): § 2.01[C][4] (2–39), Ribstein & Keatinge (2020): § 7:2, 9:1 to 9:3.
318 ULLCA, §§ 102(4), 102(24), 404, and Comments thereto.
319 ULLCA, §§ 502(a)(1), 502(b).
320 ULLCA, §§ 502(a)(3), 502(b), 502(g), 401(c).
321 ULLCA, § 401(d) and Comment thereto.
322 ULLCA, § 401(c).
323 Cf NYLLCL, § 102(r) (2006).

appear to have overtaken incorporations of corporations by the early 2000s,[324] with the gap between new LLC formations and new incorporations generally widening in favour of LLCs throughout the mid-2000s.[325]

An alternative useful source is data collected by the federal tax authorities, the Internal Revenue Service (IRS). By default, multi-member LLCs are taxed as partnerships, and wholly owned LLCs are entirely disregarded for taxation purposes,[326] although LLCs can elect their own tax classification (partnership, S-Corporation, C-Corporation, or disregarded) and therefore appear in tax statistics under each of these different categories.[327] IRS data on LLC tax filings show the clear attraction of partnership tax treatment and also (indirectly) its impact on LLC formations. After a period of double-digit percentage annual growth in LLCs filing as partnerships (the LLC's unique selling point) in the 1990s,[328] as Figure 6.1 above shows, LLC growth continued to be strong well into the twenty-first century. This contrasts with a steady decline in C-Corporations and steady but slower growth in S-Corporations (which roughly corresponds to US-CCs[329]) although the S-Corporation is likely to remain the dominant classification in at least the near future. According to IRS statistics, LLCs taxed as partnerships have become a substantial presence in the economy. As of tax year 2013, they accounted for USD 2.961 trillion in business receipts, or 8.90 per cent of all businesses; and USD 452.5 billion in net income, or 11.83 per cent of the total for all businesses.[330]

The role of federal tax rules in driving changes in LLC statutes' withdrawal regimes will be discussed below.[331]

E WITHDRAWAL IN THE LLC

1 *Terminology*

A frequently encountered term in LLC law is 'dissociation', which is defined in the ULLCA 1996 as the 'change in the relationships among the dissociated member, the company and the other members caused by a member's ceasing to be associated in the carrying on of the company's business'.[332] Conceptually, dissociation[333] is broader than voluntary exit at will or on terms and grounds

[324] Friedman (2004): 36, 92–6.
[325] See Chrisman (2009): 476–8.
[326] Treasury Regulations, § 301.7701–3(b)(1)(i)–(ii).
[327] LLCs that are disregarded do not appear at all in the tax statistics.
[328] See Petska et al. (2005): 47 fig. B.
[329] See VI.B.3 above.
[330] Percentages calculated based on data from (nn. 65–66).
[331] VI.F.3.
[332] ULLCA 1996, Comment to § 601. Cf the Japanese concept of *taisha* at VII.D.1.
[333] Depending on the state, 'dissociate' may be substituted with 'withdraw', 'resign', or 'retire'.

provided by the operating agreement ('withdrawal' in the broader sense).[334] In light of the distinction between 'membership' and 'transferable interest' discussed above,[335] whether a member has the right to dissociate or otherwise exit (e.g. via a dissolution action), and whether a dissociating or otherwise exiting member has a right to receive payment in respect of their interest in the LLC are completely separate issues.

For the avoidance of doubt, 'withdrawal at will', following this Book's definition,[336] means dissociation at will that is coupled with a right to payment. Mirroring the US-CC discussion,[337] this is distinct from withdrawal for 'grounds', which includes buyout remedies available in proceedings commenced on both oppression-type and other (e.g. 'not reasonably practicable to carry on' business) grounds.

2 *Withdrawal at Will (Dissociation etc.)*

This section provides a brief overview of both dissociation as withdrawal at will (i.e. a dissociation right bundled with a monetary claim) and mere dissociation (i.e. without a right to payment). For the avoidance of doubt, a reference to 'dissociation' does not mean 'withdrawal' unless the context clearly specifies otherwise.

i Rights to Dissociate etc.

In the 1990s, most states offered at least a default, if not a mandatory right for a member to dissociate at will, with or without notice periods of varying lengths.[338] All ULLCA versions offered a default right to dissociate at any time,[339] as do Uniform Act states such as California, New Jersey, and Pennsylvania.[340]

Non-Uniform Act states such as Delaware until 1996 offered members the default right to dissociate with six months' written notice,[341] as did New York until 1999.[342] Delaware and New York today permit dissociation at will only if the operating agreement so provides.[343] Today, several non-ULLCA states still retain the classic dissociation at will with notice mostly as a default, including Missouri (ninety days),[344]

334 Cf PULLCA, Comment to § 802 ('Note that this section refers to member 'dissociation', which is a broad term that includes the voluntary act of "withdrawal"').

335 VI.D.2.

336 II.C.

337 VI.C.2.i–iii.

338 Gevurtz (1995): 514 fn. 95.

339 ULLCA 1996, §§ 601(1), 602(a); RULLCA, § 601(a); ULLCA, § 601(a) and Comment thereto (albeit frowning on eliminating dissociation rights entirely).

340 AnnCalCorpCode, § 17706.01(a), § 17706.01(b)(2)(A) (2014), § 17701.10 (2016); NJStatAnn, § 42:2C-45(a) (2012), § 42:2C-11 (2014); 15 Pa Consolidated StatAnn, §§ 8862(a), 8815 (2017).

341 DLLCA, § 18-603 (pre-amendment by 1996 Delaware Laws Ch 360 (HB 528), § 13).

342 NYLLCL, § 606 (repealed by 1999 Session Laws of New York Ch 420, § 3), § 509 (1994).

343 DLLCA, § 18-603 (2015); NYLLCL, § 606(a) (1999).

344 Missouri AnnStat, §§ 347.121(1) (1997), 347.081 (2004).

Louisiana (thirty days),[345] New Mexico (thirty days),[346] Ohio (no notice period),[347] and Wisconsin (no notice period).[348] Massachusetts' dissociation at will with thirty days' notice appears to be a mandatory rule,[349] and Illinois[350] quite unusually makes the member's power to dissociate at will – any time – a clearly mandatory rule.

ii Rights to Payment

The other effects of dissociation per se notwithstanding,[351] a mere dissociation right – even at will – *without* a corresponding right to receive payment is largely worthless as self-help against oppression or dissension. In the era before check-the-box tax classification,[352] most LLC statutes granted dissociating members rights to receive payment.[353] A remnant of this is the ULLCA 1996 model adopted and retained by Hawaii, Montana, South Carolina, and West Virginia, which provide by default that the LLC shall buy out the dissociated member's interest.[354]

More recently, so-called 'Hotel California' provisions whereby 'the Member may check out at any time but may never leave'[355] have proliferated. By default, a dissociated member under the ULLCA 2013 or RULLCA receives no payment in connection with dissociation.[356] Increasingly, the right to payment in exchange for the dissociating member's membership interest is no longer the default feature in states[357] adopting near-copies or relevant parts of more recent ULLCA versions such as California,[358] New Jersey,[359] North Dakota, Pennsylvania, and

345 LaStatAnn, § 12:1325(B) (1995); *It's Golden, LLC v. Watercolors Unit 6, LLC* (2017) 223 So3d 545 (LaApp1Cir).
346 NMStatAnn, § 53–19–37 (1993).
347 Ohio RevCodeAnn, §§ 1705.15(A), 1705.16(A) (1994).
348 WisStatAnn, § 183.0802(3) (2002).
349 See MassGenLAnn ch 156C, § 36 (1995); see also Ribstein & Keatinge (2020): Appendix 14–2.
350 805 IllCompStatAnn, 180/35–50(a) (2001) (member-managed LLCs only), 180/15–5(b)(5) (2018).
351 Discussed below at VI.E.2.iii.
352 For dissociation's consequences then, see generally Bishop (1995): 297–8.
353 Albeit with differing valuation standards; see Gevurtz (1995): 514 fn. 95.
354 ULLCA 1996, §§ 603(a)(1), 701(a)(1); Hawaii RevStatAnn, §§ 428–603(a)(1), 428–701(a)(1) (1999); MontCodeAnn, §§ 35–8–805(1)(a), 35–8–808(1)(a) (1999); WVaCodeAnn, §§ 31B-6–603(a)(1), 31B-7–701(a)(1) (1996); SCCodeAnn, §§ 33–44–603(1), 33–44–701(a)(1) (1998). Cf proposed § 33–44–404(b) in 2019 South Carolina SB No 265 (no default right of payment).
355 Ribstein & Keatinge (2020): § 14:4 fn. 10.
356 ULLCA, §§ 603(a)(3), 404(b) and Comments thereto; RULLCA, §§ 603(a)(3), 404(b) and Comments thereto.
357 See Ribstein & Keatinge (2020): Appendix 14–2.
358 AnnCalCorpCode, § 17706.03(a) (2016), § 17704.04(b) (2016). Cf AnnCalCorpCode, § 17252(c) (fair market value of interest) (1994) (repealed by Statutes 1996, Ch 57 (SB 141)). It should be noted that California adopted only parts of the ULLCA.
359 Cf NJStatAnn, § 42:2C-47(a)(3) (2012), § 42:2C-34(b) (2014) (similar wording to ULLCA, §§ 603(a)(3), 404(b)) with § 42:2B-39(a) (1998) (repealed by Laws 2012 c 50 (Assembly 1543)).

Utah.[360] Non-ULLCA states such as Ohio[361] and more recently Illinois[362] also abolished the default right to payment. Delaware,[363] New York,[364] Massachusetts,[365] Missouri,[366] Louisiana,[367] and Wisconsin[368] continue to offer payouts as a default.

For the avoidance of doubt, withdrawal at will – combining rights to dissociate and to receive payment – has been supplanted by mere dissociation as the dominant position in US LLC law.

iii Legal Consequences of Dissociation etc.

Under the Uniform Acts, dissociation takes effect when the LLC 'knows or has express notice' of the member's intent to withdraw,[369] whereupon the dissociated member loses their status and rights as a member[370] and ceases to be bound by obligations as a member with respect to matters arising after dissociation.[371] However, there is no relief for the dissociating member from their personal obligations to the LLC or other members.[372]

Although many statutes provide that a member may dissociate at will, such dissociation may be wrongful[373] and carry negative consequences.[374] Statutes then[375] and now[376] often provide that damages resulting from wrongful dissociation – by analogy

360 ND Century CodeAnn, §§ 10–32.1–49 (2015), § 10–32.1–30(2) (2017); 15 Pa Consolidated StatAnn, § 8863 and Committee Comment to § 8863(a)(3), § 8844 (2017); Utah CodeAnn, §§ 48-3a-603, 48-3a-404(2) (2014). See also Ribstein & Keatinge (2020): Appendix 14–2.

361 Ohio RevCodeAnn, § 1705.12 (1999), amended by 1999 Ohio Laws 102 (HB 312), § 1.

362 Cf 805 IllCompStatAnn 180/35–55 (a) (1998) with 180/35–55(a)(4) (2017), as amended by PA 99–637 (HB 4361), § 5, effective 1 July 2017.

363 DLLCA, § 18–604 (1999).

364 NYLLCL, § 509 (1994).

365 MassGenLAnn ch 156C, § 32 (1995).

366 MoAnnStat, § 347.103(2) (1997) (within 180 days of withdrawal).

367 LaStatAnn, § 12–1325(C) (1995).

368 WisStatAnn, § 183.0604 (1994).

369 ULLCA, § 602(1) (unless dissociating member specifies later withdrawal date); RULLCA, § 602(1) (same). ULLCA 1996 has no equivalent provision.

370 ULLCA, § 603(a)(1); RULLCA, § 603(a)(1); ULLCA 1996, § 603(b)(1).

371 ULLCA, § 603(a)(2); RULLCA, § 603(a)(2); ULLCA 1996, § 603(b)(2)–(3).

372 ULLCA, § 603(b); RULLCA, § 603(b). ULLCA 1996 has no equivalent provision.

373 See ULLCA, §§ 601(b)(1), 601(b)(2)(A); RULLCA, §§ 601(b)(1), 601(b)(2)(A); ULLCA 1996, § 602(b)(1).

374 The language of 'power' but not 'right' to dissociate is used to express this; see explanation to code '2' in Ribstein & Keatinge (2020): Appendix 14–2.

375 RULLCA, § 601(c); ULLCA 1996, § 602(c); Bishop (1995): 297 (noting fair value less wrongful dissociation damages is the most common payout), 304 tbl. III (under row '(2) Fair Value (D) (dmgs if wrongful)').

376 ULLCA, § 601(c); Ribstein & Keatinge (2020): Appendix 14–5 (on 'Penalty for Wrongful Withdrawal').

with breach of contract[377] – must be either paid by the withdrawing member or offset against the withdrawing member's payout. Other state statutes have no provision on the consequences of wrongful dissociation.[378]

3 *Withdrawal on Grounds*

There are two types of withdrawal grounds from the LLC: oppression, and 'not reasonably practicable to carry on' business/deadlock. In almost all states, the specific relief of withdrawal (i.e. buyout of the member's membership interest) is positioned as an alternative to judicial dissolution, and only rarely as a standalone direct statutory remedy. Several states offer dissolution, but not withdrawal, on grounds. This subsection explores each in turn.

i Oppression: Buyout As Dissolution Alternative

In stark contrast with the decline of withdrawal at will by dissociation, the remedy of judicial dissolution for oppression-type[379] grounds has become an increasingly common feature in LLC statutes.[380] All three ULLCA versions offer dissolution as a remedy for oppression on a mandatory basis.[381] The Uniform Acts' respective Official Comments say little about the scenarios covered by oppression, but suggest that US-CC oppression doctrine (with some caveats) would be relevant.[382] This was borne out in a recent South Carolina decision applying US-CC oppression doctrine to the LLC.[383] Arizona's statute includes 'wilfully or persistently breached the operating agreement or the duty of loyalty' and 'wasted, misapplied or diverted substantial assets' of the LLC by managers or controlling members as judicial dissolution grounds.[384]

377 Made express in ULLCA, Comment to § 601(c).

378 Ribstein & Keatinge (2020): Appendix 14–5 (states marked '3').

379 Used in the same sense as for the US-CC; cf VI.C.1. For the non-fault 'not reasonably practicable to carry on' business or deadlock grounds, see VI.E.3.iii below.

380 See Moll (2017): 87, 100, 100 fn. 56, 107, Appendix 1; see also O'Neal & Thompson (2020b): § 6:25.

381 ULLCA 1996, § 801(4) (especially § 801(4)(v): managers/controlling members 'have acted, are acting, or will act in a manner that is illegal, oppressive, fraudulent, or unfairly prejudicial to the petitioner'), § 103(b)(6) & Comment to § 801 (mandatory); RULLCA, § 701(a)(4)–(5) (especially § 701(a)(5): managers/controlling members' past, ongoing, or future actions are illegal/fraudulent or past or ongoing actions are 'oppressive' and 'was, is, or will be directly harmful to the applicant'), § 110(c)(7) & Comment to § 701(a)(5) (mandatory); ULLCA, § 701(a)(4) (especially § 701(a)(4)(C)), *in pari materia* with RULLCA, § 701(a)(5)), § 105(c)(9) & Comment to § 701 (mandatory).

382 See ULLCA, Comment to § 701(a)(4)(C); RULLCA, Comment to § 701(a)(5) (observing that '[e]ven in non-ULLCA states, courts have begun to apply close corporation "oppression" doctrine to LLCs'). See also Ribstein & Keatinge (2020): § 14:41 ('under LLC statutes that limit the default power of members to dissociate from the firm, the corporate "oppression" standard may be appropriate. As in close corporations, the members may not have anticipated being locked in and may need a judicial exit mechanism').

383 *Wilson* v. *Gandis* (2020) 430 SC 282, 303–306, 844 SE2d 631, 642–4 (SC).

384 Arizona RevStatAnn, § 29-3701(A)(4)(d)(ii)–(iii) (2019).

A dissolution mechanism only counts as a form of withdrawal remedy if the buyout of the plaintiff member's interest can be judicially facilitated. Uniform Act states such as Illinois,[385] Minnesota,[386] and North Dakota[387] expressly provide for the buyout as an alternative judicial remedy to dissolution. The RULLCA and current ULLCA texts provide as a default that 'the court may order a remedy other than dissolution' and also refer to buyouts in their respective Official Comments.[388] In South Carolina, where buyouts are not expressly authorised in the dissolution provision but mentioned in the official comment, the state supreme court in a recent decision ordered that the LLC purchase the minority member's interest, and that the oppressing members be secondarily liable for the purchase in proportion to their respective membership interests if the LLC defaults.[389] States may mix and match grounds and remedies.[390]

Other states combine oppression-type triggers for dissolution proceedings with US-CC-style election statutes.[391] Utah's latest statute[392] adopts RULLCA-type oppression grounds, whereas Florida[393] adopts modified grounds. California[394] and North Carolina[395] are election statute states with even more generous dissolution triggers. In a parallel to non-statutory judicial remedies for US-CC oppression,[396] Wisconsin's judicial dissolution provision does not expressly provide for alternative remedies, but a trial court judgment ordering the defendant member to purchase the plaintiff member's interest was upheld on appeal.[397]

385 805 IllCompStatAnn 180/35–1(b) (2017).

386 MinnStatAnn, §§ 322C.0701 Subdivision 1(5) (grounds), 322C.0701 Subdivision 2 (alternative remedies including sale of interest at fair value) (2015).

387 ND Century CodeAnn, §§ 10–32.1–50(1)(e), 10–32.1–50(2) (2015). But see *Jundt* v. *Jurassic Resources Development* (2003) 2003 ND 9, ¶¶ 16–17, 656 NW2d 15, 21 (ND).

388 RULLCA, § 701(b) & Comment to § 701(b) (court's power to order alternative remedy can be restricted or eliminated by operating agreement); ULLCA, § 701(b) & Comment to § 701(b) (same as RULLCA). Cf ULLCA 1996, Comment to § 801 (recommending against dissolution where member had power to withdraw (and receive payment) via dissociation).

389 SCCodeAnn, Comment to § 33–44–801 (2004); *Wilson* v. *Gandis* (2020) 430 SC 282, 310–11, 844 SE2d 631, 646 (SC).

390 See e.g. 31 Maine RevStatAnn, §§ 1595(1)(E), 1595(2) (2011).

391 Typically, an election statute offers the LLC or other members the right to terminate the dissolution proceeding by making an irrevocable offer to purchase the plaintiff's interest. For the US-CC context, see VI.C.2.iii (indirect remedies).

392 Utah CodeAnn, §§ § 48-3a-702 (election provision), 48-3a-701(5) (grounds) (2014).

393 FlaStatAnn, §§ 605.0706 (election provision) (2020), 605.0702(1)(b) (grounds) (2020).

394 AnnCalCorpCode, §§ 17707.03(c) (election provision, members only), 17707.03(b)(2), 17707.03(b)(5) (2016).

395 NC General StatAnn, §§ 57D-6–03(d), 57D-6–02(2)(ii) (2014).

396 VI.C.2.ii.

397 WisStatAnn, § 183.0902(3)–(4) (1994); *Decker* v. *Decker* (2006) 2006 WI App 247, ¶¶ 17–18, 298 Wis2d 141, 153–154, 726 NW2d 664, 671 (WisCtApp).

ii Oppression: Buyout As Direct Statutory Remedy

Michigan exceptionally offers a true oppression-type judicially facilitated withdrawal remedy not parasitic on a dissolution provision. There, where acts of managers or controlling members are 'illegal or fraudulent or constitute willfully unfair and oppressive conduct', the court may order that either the LLC, or any members who have acted wrongfully, shall purchase the aggrieved member's interest at fair value.[398] It is unclear whether the provision can be contracted out of entirely, but 'conduct or actions that are permitted by the articles of organisation, an operating agreement, another agreement to which the member is a party, or a consistently applied written company policy or procedure' may be excluded from the scope.[399] No case of precedential value appears to have ever been decided pursuant to the withdrawal sub-provisions as of early 2021.

iii 'Not Reasonably Practicable to Carry on' the Business of the LLC/Deadlock

Judicial dissolution in all ULLCA versions[400] and most state LLC statutes[401] is available on the ground that it is 'not reasonably practicable to carry on' the LLC's business or affairs according to its constitutional documents (i.e. the certificate/articles of organisation and/or the operating agreement). This ground may include member deadlocks.[402] Withdrawal as an alternative to dissolution in ULLCA-type statutes (discussed above in the oppression context[403]) is arguably also available for the 'not reasonably practicable' ground.

Although New York's dissolution provision does not expressly authorise the court to order a buyout in lieu,[404] the court has asserted and exercised the power to order the defendant to buy out the plaintiff's membership interest.[405] A New York court may also order an auction of the LLC between the members.[406]

Separately, Arizona, California, Florida, Kansas, and New Hampshire[407] specify member or manager deadlock resulting in or threatening irreparable harm to the

398 MichCompLAnn, § 450.4515(1)(d) (2010). Dissolution is separately provided for and under more limited grounds: §§ 450.4801(d) (2010), 450.4802 (1993).

399 MichCompLAnn, § 450.4515(2) (2010).

400 ULLCA, § 701(a)(4)(B); RULLCA, § 701(a)(4)(B); ULLCA 1996, § 801(4)(iii).

401 See e.g. Moll (2017):84, Appendix 2, 111–12 (classifying LLC statutes).

402 *Kirksey* v. *Grohmann* (2008) 2008 SD 76, ¶¶ 26–30, ¶34, 754 NW2d 825, 830–831, 832 (SD) (ULLCA-type provision); see also Moll (2017): 89–98, 111–12 (on interpretation of this ground).

403 VI.E.3.i.

404 NYLLCL, § 702 (1994).

405 *In re Superior Vending, LLC* (2010) 71 AD3d 1153, 1154, 898 NYS2d 191, 192 (NYAppDiv).

406 *Lyons* v. *Salamone* (2006) 32 AD3d 757, 758, 821 NYS2d 188, 189 (NYAppDiv).

407 Arizona RevStatAnn, § 29–3701(A)(4)(c), 29–3701(B) (2019); AnnCalCorpCode, § 17707.03(b)(4) (no irreparable harm statutory requirement), 17707.03(d) (2016); FlaStatAnn, §§ 605.0702(1)(b)(5) (2020), 605.0703(4)(b)–(c) (alternative remedies) (2014), 605.0706 (election statute) (2020);

LLC as grounds for dissolution and alternative remedies – which may include withdrawal.

iv States With Dissolution But No Withdrawal

Delaware,[408] Ohio,[409] Mississippi,[410] South Dakota,[411] and Washington[412] are characterised as offering judicial dissolution but not withdrawal as they make no reference either in statute or case law to buyouts or alternative remedies generally. Tennessee courts seem to have a broad power to order equitable relief or dissolution, but as the grounds for judicial relief are unclear,[413] it is not prudent to classify Tennessee as a state offering withdrawal for its LLCs.

4 *Valuation*

Valuation issues are seldom addressed in LLC statutes or treatises. Unsurprisingly, the RULLCA and ULLCA 2013 – which adopt 'Hotel California' dissociation provisions (*ie* no withdrawal at will) and offer withdrawal for oppression only as a dissolution alternative – contain no valuation provision whatsoever; the operating agreement thus becomes absolutely crucial.[414] The default valuation date is the date of dissociation for the ULLCA 1996, Louisiana, and New York.[415] In a recent New York decision, the day before commencement of the dissolution action was adopted as the valuation date for an agreed buyout in lieu of dissolution.[416]

KanStatAnn, § 17–76,117(b) (at least 25 per cent interest in LLC required for standing) (2014); NHRevStatAnn, § 304-C:134(I)(b), 304-C:134(II) (2013).

408 DLLCA, § 18–802 (1995); *In re Carlisle Etcetera LLC* (2015) 114 A3d 592, 601–606 (DelCh).

409 Ohio RevCodeAnn, § 1705.47(B)(2) (2012).

410 Mississippi CodeAnn, § 79–29–803(1)(b) (2013). Mississippi also offers a default right to payment upon withdrawal but not a default right to withdraw: §§ 79–29–603, 79–29–303 (2011).

411 South Dakota Codified Laws § 47-34A-801(4) (2009). The 'Hotel California'-type (see VI.E.2.ii) dissociation provisions (§ 47-34A-603(b)(1) (1998), § 47-34A-503 (2009)) are the result of Session Laws 2009, ch 234 (HB 1103), §§ 1, 3.

412 Although counted by the ULC as a ULLCA 2013 state, Washington does not follow the ULLCA model on dissolution and simply provides that the court has the mandatory power to dissolve the LLC upon application by a member or manager where the 'circumstances render dissolution equitable': WashRevCodeAnn, §§ 25.15.265(5), 25.15.274, 25.15.018(3)(k) (mandatory) (2016). Note that Washington does not even offer a default right to dissociate or to receive payment upon dissociation: §§ 25.15.131(2), 25.15.216 (2016).

413 See TennCodeAnn, §§ 48–245–901 (1994), 48–245–902(a) (2010). Cf O'Neal & Thompson (2020a): § 9:50 fn. 4 and text thereto (classifying Tennessee as a state with 'broad generic equitable grounds' as dissolution triggers).

414 On how courts have addressed operating agreement provisions relevant to valuation and other issues in buyouts, see generally O'Neal & Thompson (2020b): §6:16.

415 ULLCA 1996, § 701(a)(1); Hawaii RevStatAnn, § 428–701(a)(1) (1999); MontCodeAnn, § 35–8–808(1)(a) (1999); WVaCodeAnn, § 31B-7–701(a)(1) (1996); SCCodeAnn, § 33–44–701(a)(1) (1998); LaStatAnn, § 12:1325(C) (1995); NYLLCL, § 509 (1994).

416 *PFT Technology, LLC* v. *Wieser* (2020) 181 AD3d 836, 122 NYS3d 313 (NYAppDiv).

While the ULLCA 1996,[417] Minnesota,[418] and New York[419] provide that a buyout shall be at 'fair value', California[420] and Louisiana[421] use 'fair market value'. Operating agreement provisions on valuation are effective in New York and under the ULLCA 1996.[422] Minority and marketability discounts are permitted under Louisiana law.[423]

Express provisions on interest are uncommon. ULLCA 1996-type statutes are exceptional in this regard in specifying that interest 'must' be awarded on the amount ordered from the date of withdrawal to the date of payment.[424]

5 *Enforcement*

Most LLC statutes including RULLCA and ULLCA 2013, where withdrawal is but a possible alternative remedy to judicial dissolution,[425] are unhelpfully silent on the enforcement aspects if and when withdrawal is ordered. By contrast, the ULLCA 1996 is noteworthy for its elaborate set of enforcement-related provisions. First, it governed the withdrawing (i.e. dissociating) member and the LLC's respective obligations upon dissociation. It also offered a procedural framework (including timelines) by which the membership interest's purchase price would be either negotiated between the dissociating member and the LLC, or judicially determined. Additionally, the ULLCA 1996 facilitated flexible payment arrangements (including instalments), specified the priority of the dissociated member's monetary claim, structured enforcement proceedings in event of the LLC's default, and granted the court discretion to order payment of attorneys' and experts' reasonable expenses.[426]

417 ULLCA 1996, § 702(a)(1) (directing the court to consider the LLC's 'going concern value', pre-existing agreements on valuation, experts' recommendations, 'any legal constraints on the company's ability to purchase the interest', and other relevant evidence), Comment to § 702 (elaborating that 'fair market, liquidation, or any other method deemed appropriate under the circumstances' may be used by the court, but not 'fair market value' 'because it is too narrow, often inappropriate, and assumes a fact not contemplated by this section – a willing buyer and a willing seller').

418 MinnStatAnn, § 322C.0701 Subdivision 2 (2015).

419 NYLLCL, § 509 (1994).

420 AnnCalCorpCode, §§ 17707.03(c)(2)–(3) (2016).

421 LaStatAnn, § 12:1325(C) (1995); *Fancher* v. *Prudhome* (2013) 112 So3d 909, 912 (LaApp2Cir) (defining 'fair market value' as 'the price a willing buyer would pay to a willing seller . . . in an arm's length transaction').

422 NYLLCL, § 509 (1994); *Jacobs* v. *Cartalemi* (2017) 156 AD3d 635, 66 NYS3d 503 (NYAppDiv), leave to appeal denied (2018) 32 NY3d 903, 109 NE3d 1157 (NY); ULLCA 1996, § 701(c).

423 *Wall* v. *Bryan* (2018) 251 So3d 650, 659–660 (LaApp2Cir) (interpreting LaStatAnn, § 12–1325(C) (1995)), writ denied (2018) 255 So3d 1047 and 255 So3d 1051.

424 ULLCA 1996, § 702(e); Hawaii RevStatAnn, § 428–702(f) (1999); MontCodeAnn, § 35–8–809(5) (1999); SCCodeAnn, § 33–44–702(e) (1996); WVaCodeAnn, §31B-7–702(e) (1996) and *Marrara* v. *Ripley Associates, LLC* (2014) 233 WVa 102, 106–7, 755 SE2d 120, 124–5 (WVa).

425 See VI.E.3.i, VI.E.3.iii.

426 ULLCA 1996, §§ 701, 702, 801(4)(iv).

In New York, the withdrawn member's claim to payment for their interest is statutorily subordinated to the creditors if the LLC is dissolved.[427]

F LETTING A HUNDRED CORPORATION LAWS BLOSSOM: SITUATING WITHDRAWAL IN THE AMERICAN FLOWERING OF CLOSE CORPORATION LAW

Without exclusive federal incorporation or formal unification of state laws, US close corporation law will continue to comprise over one hundred state statutes and bodies of jurisprudence for two distinct sets of entities: US-CCs and LLCs. Keeping track of the applicable laws and doctrine and their changes over time is a daunting task for all but the most committed and well-resourced jurists. Regardless of the merits or weaknesses of individual states' laws or doctrine, the overall complexity of the US close corporation law landscape poses the single greatest practical obstacle to meaningful understanding and application – especially to comparatively oriented, non-insider scholars.

The same challenges apply equally to shareholder withdrawal as an important part of US close corporation law. Nevertheless, the task of understanding and appreciating withdrawal in the US becomes easier when the law and legal developments are placed into their intellectual- and legal-historical context. This section takes stock of forces driving the evolution of withdrawal legislation and jurisprudence in the US-CC and LLC.

1 *Contractarianism's Shadow over US Close Corporation Law*

US corporate law scholarship is often driven by broad ideas and grand ideologies. The great American debate in corporate law – whether public or close corporations – has since the 1980s revolved around the respective roles of 'contract' (itself an imprecise concept[428]) and statutory law in corporate law.[429] On the offensive were the 'contractarians'[430] expounding the vision that everything or close to everything in corporate law should be left to the 'private ordering' of the 'parties' (usually shareholders and managers).[431] They further believe that agreements, regardless of whether a bargaining process ever took place, should be enforced by the courts without question,[432] even if such agreements deprive shareholders of protections

427 Albeit unclear whether default or mandatory: NYLLCL, § 704(b) (1995).

428 Gordon (1989): 1549–50 (contrasting the meanings of 'contract' as used by jurists and economists).

429 See e.g. the papers for the symposium 'Contractual Freedom and Corporate Law', published at (1989) 89 Columbia Law Review 1395–74.

430 See Klausner (2018): 84 fn. 2 (citing Easterbrook & Fischel (1991) and other pioneering work).

431 See Coffee (1989): 1619. In fairness, opponents of contractarians do concede that close corporation participants must have room to make their own enforceable arrangements: Callison & Vestal (2009): 498–9.

432 Bainbridge (1997): 864–71.

against other shareholders or managers otherwise available at law.[433] Issues not actually addressed by a legally binding contract should be dealt with according to 'hypothetical bargaining': in other words, the court should decide according to how the parties would have contracted if they had thought about the issue.[434] Lamenting the pervasiveness and continuing existence of mandatory rules in corporate law, contractarians have waged campaigns against them in key areas of corporate law – including oppression in close corporation law.[435]

The contractarians' heyday may be over,[436] yet their publications – many of which are highly cited – remain. A non-American reader exposed to easily accessible contractarian writing would be forgiven for walking away with the distinct impression that US close corporation law *should be* – if not in reality already *is* – contractarian. The modern law on LLCs would appear, at first blush, to reinforce the conclusion that US close corporation law as a whole is unabashedly contractarian. However, as VI.C reveals, the contractarians never achieved ultimate victory in the arena of close corporations in the narrow sense (US-CCs). Case law on the US-CC is far from uniformly contractarian. There is neither consensus nor a clear majority opinion among US states on whether the contractarian approach is in fact the law on the ground. Approaches are diverse and fall across the contractarian/anti-contractarian spectrum.[437] There is also a significant body of US scholarship that takes US case law seriously, but without adopting a pro-contractarian ideology.[438] Nonetheless, even without an overwhelming and lasting victory, contractarianism looks set to continue casting a long shadow on withdrawal in US close corporation law.

2 *Oppression Jurisprudence in US-CCs: Holding the Line on Hard-Won Gains*

As VI.C shows, oppression statutes and jurisprudence have undergone a long process of piecemeal, gradual development in the US. The judicially ordered buyout – the most practical relief and which delivers lasting resolution of close corporation disputes – began as piecemeal and cautious initiatives by courts under the shadow of dissolution or colour of equitable power, but has since been crystalised into statute in a respectable number of states. Many others offer indirect withdrawal remedies in the form of MBCA-style dissolution-unless-buyout election statutes that offer the opportunity to – or perhaps exert some pressure on – the US-CC or co-shareholders to avoid dissolution by electing to buy out the petitioning shareholder. A handful of

433 See e.g. Butler & Ribstein (1990).
434 Coffee (1989): 1622; Ribstein (2010): 37–8.
435 See e.g. Bainbridge (2020): 548–56.
436 I thank Robert Thompson for his characterisation that contractarianism reached its peak in the 1980s to 1990s.
437 For an example falling somewhere in the middle, see Means (2010).
438 Compare the tone of the O'Neal and Thompson treatises (not contractarian), in contrast with Ribstein and Keatinge (contractarian).

states – including Minnesota, New York, Oregon, Pennsylvania, and Rhode Island – combine the best of both worlds by not only offering the corporation/co-shareholders the opportunity to put an end to the dispute on fair terms, but also providing an additional safeguard for the aggrieved minority shareholder by vesting the court with ultimate discretion to do right by them by making a judicial buyout order. With some exceptions, shareholders of US-CCs are thus not completely dependent on ex ante bargaining – limited as it is by indeterminacy, unforeseeability, poor legal advice, lack of economic power, or even an optimistic or trusting disposition[439] – to protect their own interests.

The anti-oppression campaign did face its share of setbacks. Most prominently, Delaware's Supreme Court would rather let its contractarian ideology tie its own hands – and the Court of Chancery's – in the face of the demands of reality and justice.[440] Even in states where buyouts are technically available, it is not all smooth sailing; in most states the courts made buyout orders in only a few cases. Judicial readiness to take the minority's perspective matters:[441] if the courts are at once too ready to accept invocations of 'legitimate purpose' by majority shareholders attempting to justify their oppression of minorities, and too sceptical of minority arguments, the utility of any oppression/withdrawal regime would be easily undermined.

Empirical research sheds little light on whether stronger withdrawal regimes are more 'efficient' or preferable to business owners. A study by Dammann and Schüdeln looks at whether firms choose to incorporate in the state where they have their primary place of business ('PPB state'). Their findings suggest that states offering less generous minority shareholder protection in their corporation law appear to have a greater share of corporations incorporating in the PPB state instead of in another state.[442] However, the authors refrain from concluding that weaker minority protection is more efficient or that there is a 'race to the bottom', acknowledging that the tendency of corporations to incorporate outside of PPB states with strong minority protection may be attributable to factors such as controlling shareholder opportunism.[443] Crucially, as Dammann and Schüdeln did not code specifically for withdrawal *relief*,[444] the relevance of their findings to the US-CC withdrawal context is debatable.

As in other aspects of American life, the nation is and looks to be for the foreseeable future intractably divided across state and ideological lines on withdrawal in the US-CC. Whether the twentieth-century's hard-won gains against majority oppression can be defended against future contractarian or formalist resurgence remains to be seen.

439 See II.E.3.
440 VI.C.2.iv.
441 See VI.C.3.ii.
442 Dammann & Schündeln (2011): 82, 107.
443 Ibid. 95–6.
444 See ibid. 91–2 (coding only for oppression statute [NB: without distinguishing between withdrawal and other reliefs such as dissolution] versus Massachusetts-style fiduciary duty).

3 *Withdrawal Remedies in LLCs: Going (Almost) Full Circle – in Reverse?*

In contrast with US-CCs, contractarians may more easily claim LLCs as proof of victory.[445] Almost uniquely among close corporation statutes across the developed world,[446] LLC statutes initially offered rights to withdraw at will. In retrospect, early LLC law seems extraordinarily generous to LLC members especially when compared to US-CC shareholders. The spirit of the pre-check-the-box era was captured by the ULLCA 1996, which offered withdrawal at will as a default.

Despite certain advantages of a clear unambiguous default right to withdraw over oppression-based withdrawal in the US-CC and the Uniform Acts' dissolution for oppression regime,[447] minority protection was hardly the first thing on the minds of American legislators when withdrawal at will was written into early LLC statutes. The surest motivation for withdrawal rights – and indeed, the LLC revolution itself – was much more immediate and prosaic: avoiding the taxman. Withdrawal rights – and other non-corporate features such as unilateral dissolution rights – were put in place to ensure entity impermanence and qualify for pass-through tax treatment for LLCs formed thereunder.[448] Any benefits accruing to minorities were – depending on whether one took the minority's or majority's perspective – merely a happy bonus or an unavoidable cost. Nevertheless, by offering withdrawal at will through dissociation, early LLC statutes also provided relatively good protection against oppression.[449]

But what federal taxation policy giveth, it can also taketh away. After the IRS decided to leave income tax treatment to taxpayer choice with 'check-the-box' regulations, the incentive for LLC statutes to maintain default withdrawal rights is lost.[450] The pressure now acted in the opposite direction: estate and gift tax valuation rules that impose higher tax burdens on members of family LLCs formed under statutes offering withdrawal at will (dissociation at will plus payment) as a mandatory or default rule.[451] In response, states gradually eliminated default withdrawal rights,[452] increasingly treating 'dissociated LLC members as guests who have overstayed their welcome: mere assignees of their own interests, with financial but no management rights'.[453] An initially promising minority protection landscape was gradually overrun by provisions offering free (mandatory) 'dissociation' but without

445 See e.g. Callison & Vestal (2009): 496. Contracting in LLCs is perceived as being taken more seriously than was the case for US-CCs: Ribstein (2011): 548 (observing that judges adjudicating LLC cases focus more on figuring out what the specific parties in fact wanted based on the contractual arrangements they entered into, in contrast to the more generalised hypothetical bargaining approach adopted in US-CC cases).

446 Until Japan in the twenty-first century: VII.D.

447 See Ribstein (1995b): 367–8, 378–9.

448 See VI.D.1.

449 Moll (2005): 887, 926–8, 931.

450 Ibid. 928–31.

451 See generally Ribstein & Keatinge (2020): § 21:13. On these tax rules' origins and logic, see Miller (2003): 362 fn. 36; Ribstein (1995a): 427–8, 427 fn. 224.

452 Moll (2005): 931–40; Miller (2001): 429–31; Ribstein (2010): 179–80.

453 Ribstein (2010): 180.

payment. Like Hotel California, a minority LLC member can check in, but they can never leave[454] – at least not with their money.

Even though changes in LLC statutes are driven by the imperative to maximise tax advantages under federal tax rules[455] rather than any anti-minority agenda, the legislative retreat on withdrawal rights had the consequence of increasing the vulnerability of minority members to oppression by majorities.[456] It should not surprise that history has repeated itself: squeeze out techniques first developed in US-CCs have re-emerged in the LLCs.[457] Despite an environment perceived as highly supportive of private ordering, a survey of legal practitioners reveals that LLCs are not infrequently formed based on un-negotiated or insufficiently negotiated standard form agreements.[458] Of particular note is the finding that only a minority of LLCs make provision for withdrawal at will[459] or dissolution for oppression[460] in their operating agreements. Regardless of the precise reasons, when left to their own devices, minority LLC members seldom contract for withdrawal-type remedies.

Still, sometimes when a door closes, a window opens somewhere. Withdrawal is making a fledgling comeback in the LLC in a fashion reminiscent of the US-CC: as an alternative to dissolution for oppression and other grounds. Although yet to be codified into a provision of the ULLCA, buyouts are expressly mentioned in the Official Comment, and a handful of states have codified withdrawal as oppression relief into their LLC statutes.[461] Other states have gradually made judicial dissolution available for oppression,[462] and most LLC statutes offer dissolution for deadlock-type (including the 'not reasonably practicable') grounds.[463] It does remain to be seen whether the courts would develop and use withdrawal remedies to the same extent as they have in US-CCs. It seems fair to say that withdrawal for grounds has superseded withdrawal at will as the plurality approach for LLCs, albeit with none of the structural clarity or comprehensiveness ULLCA 1996-type statutes offered.

Relatively free from the vicissitudes and spectre of federal tax policy, withdrawal via the oppression route may finally be guided by proper corporate law concerns: the demands and realities of life and oppression in close corporations. It could be that legislatures are, in introducing judicial dissolution-for-oppression and statutory remedies, consciously or subconsciously responding to the failure or unwillingness

454 See Ribstein & Keatinge (2020): § 14:4 fn. 10.
455 See also Ribstein (1995a): 384–90 (describing the 'tax/regulation hypothesis' by which tax and regulatory rules either drive the evolution of close corporation statutes towards rules offering greater tax and regulatory advantages to firms, or constrain such evolution).
456 Moll (2005): 939–40; Farrar & Hamill (1998): 937, 939; Miller (2001): 433, 436–8.
457 Miller (2004): 1612.
458 See Miller (2003): 399, 422.
459 Ibid. 391, 416.
460 Ibid. 356, 421.
461 VI.E.3.i–ii.
462 Moll (2017): 107.
463 VI.E.3.iii.

of minorities to protect themselves against oppression by agreement. Regardless, there is hope that judges would be mindful of their past role and successes in developing oppression and withdrawal into a staple of US-CC law, and act accordingly in the LLC context as well. The story of withdrawal in LLC law – which mirrors to an extent US-CC law in experiencing shifts between contractual ordering and judicial intervention[464] – is not yet over.

G CONCLUSION

Close corporation law has come a long way, although it might still be premature to say that the arc of withdrawal law is always bending towards justice for the minority shareholder.[465] Withdrawal exists in the US primarily as a form of relief for shareholder oppression, the legal bases for which developed through a mix of judicial innovation and legislative advancements over the second half of the twentieth century. Oppression law has not fully held onto its gains in US-CCs against contractarianism's ascendance in *fin de millénaire*, but it is making inroads into LLCs in the twenty-first century. Other variants of withdrawal, including withdrawal at will in connection with dissociation, continue to be part of LLC law albeit to differing degrees. Boasting over one hundred bodies of corporation statutes and jurisprudence across more than fifty jurisdictional units each with two distinct close corporation forms, plus a rich tradition of insightful and provocative scholarship on close corporation and withdrawal law, the US has always been and will continue to be an unparalleled treasure trove of lessons both encouraging and cautionary.

Yet, as we shall see in the next Chapter, US close corporation laws' heterogeneity posed no obstacle to exerting influence in unexpected places. Whether unperturbed by or unaware of the US LLC's chequered past on minority protection, jurists in another highly developed and economically powerful nation with a proud legal and scholarly tradition – and not one but two existing and thriving close corporation forms – took to the LLC with fervour. So enamoured they were with the LLC that they abolished one of their own close corporation forms just to adopt a simulacrum of the US LLC, and with unexpected results for close corporation withdrawal law. We now complete the circle by heading west and across the Pacific to our final jurisdiction: Japan.

464 Thompson (2011): 403.

465 In homage to the memorable phrase first used by abolitionist Theodore Parker and popularised later in modified form by Martin Luther King, Jr ('the arc of the moral universe, although long, is bending toward justice').

VII

Japan

The Curious Case of Withdrawal by Semi-Accidental Legislation

A INTRODUCTION

Japan[1] presents an intriguing puzzle: alone among the jurisdictions under study, for the longest time it did not have any form of withdrawal remedy for its then-dominant close corporation forms. The period prior to 2005 saw problematic partial functional substitutes emerging in response to close corporation conflict, and an ultimately unsuccessful legislative reform to introduce withdrawal remedies.

A new chapter in Japan's history opened with the introduction of a new close corporation form, the ***Gōdō Kaisha*** (abbreviated '**GK**') by the monumental *Kaishahō* (Companies Act of 2005).[2] Among the close corporation forms examined in this Book, the GK is the newest form, and the only one that offers both withdrawal at will and withdrawal on grounds (on 'unavoidable grounds'). By virtue of a semi-accident in the law reform process, Japanese corporate law now has, for the first time in its long and turbulent history, a close corporation form offering full limited liability that is just beginning to gain momentum – and which offers a legal framework for withdrawal at least on the books. The future of GK withdrawal remains open as debate continues raging on the entity's proper role, and on the fundamental issues of withdrawal's scope and enforcement.

VII.B sets the historical context to Japan's close corporation law, and answers an unnoticed (in Western literature) but critical puzzle: if withdrawal is essential for close corporations, how did Japanese companies and shareholders survive without it for so long? VII.C follows with a concise introduction to Japan's new close corporation form, the GK, that highlights its features and legal significance. Some clarifications as to terminology will also be made. VII.D is an in-depth, critical examination of Japan's withdrawal regime, drawing on historical doctrine and jurisprudence, as well as the latest academic debates. The discussion will include the scope of withdrawal for cause in the Japanese context, the mandatory versus default tension that is the subject of much recent literature, valuation issues, enforcement problems, as well as my observations and critique. VII.E identifies trends in business practice and scholarship that will impact the GK and the withdrawal regime for the foreseeable future.VII.F concludes.

B THE HISTORICAL CONTEXT OF JAPAN'S CLOSE CORPORATION LAW

1 *The* Kabushiki Kaisha *and* Yūgen Kaisha

Before 2005, the two corporate forms used most often for close corporations were the ***Kabushiki Kaisha*** ('Stock Corporation', abbreviated '**KK**') and the ***Yūgen Kaisha***

[1] Parts of this Chapter draw on material previously published as Koh (2020) in the Vanderbilt Journal of Transnational Law (VJTL). I am grateful to the VJTL editors for granting me permission to incorporate the published material here.

[2] *Kaisha Hō* [*Companies Act], Act No 86 of 26 July 2005 ('*Kaishahō*'). The GK is regulated under its own Part of the Act: *Kaishahō*, Pt III (Articles 575–675).

('Limited Liability Corporation', abbreviated 'YK'). Although the KK was originally intended to be the vehicle for large, publicly traded corporations and pre-dates even the *Shōhō* (Commercial Code) itself,[3] the KK came to be widely used by small, even de facto single-owner, businesses in the post-war era.[4] Although there was for a number of years a legal prohibition on share transfer restrictions in KKs, that did not pose a practical obstacle to the use of the KK as a close corporation form; even before legalisation in 1966, a significant proportion of small KKs had some form of share transfer restrictions.[5] With the introduction of a simplified management structure option for KKs,[6] the *Kaishahō* has made it possible for close corporations adopting the KK to reduce their compliance burden.[7] Taking into account the KK's consistent dominance in new incorporations year after year,[8] the available evidence suggests that it remains a popular choice for close corporations.[9]

The YK, Japan's 'representative' close corporation form before 2005, was introduced in 1938 by the *Yūgen Kaisha-hō* ('Limited Liability Corporations Act') (*YK-hō*),[10] a special, separate law that was not intended to be codified into

[3] Although formally and legally named *Kabushiki Kaisha* only after the enactment of the first Commercial Code of 1890, entities that were in substance KKs were incorporated under specific legislation or charters granted by government ministries even before that: Egashira (2017): 1. Japan's first KK was also the first bank of Japan, first founded as *Dai'ichi Kokuritsu Ginkō* ('First National Bank') on 20 July 1873 by Shibusawa Ei'ichi, the father of Japanese capitalism. Through several name changes and mergers, the bank survives today as Mizuho Bank, one of the largest in Japan.

[4] Takahashi (2010): 5.

[5] ibid. (citing a survey conducted between 1961 and 1963 that reported share transfer restrictions in 33.0 per cent of surveyed KKs with a capitalisation of under JPY 1,000,000).

[6] Oda (2005): 98; see also Takahashi & Shimizu (2005): 40–5.

[7] The notion that businesses should be given the option of choosing the internal governance structures most suitable for their 'state of development' (see Aizawa & Kōriya (2006a): 9) suggests room for optimisation, although not officially stated as such in the Drafters' Commentary (i.e. Aizawa (2006)).

[8] Based on my calculations using Ministry of Justice statistics hosted on the e-stat portal of the Statistics Bureau, Ministry of Internal Affairs and Communications, the cumulative number of incorporations of the four *Kaishahō* corporate forms for the period 2006–19 are as follows:

Stock corporation (KK) :	1,306,596
New US LLC-inspired form (*Gōdō Kaisha*) (GK) :	216,951
Limited partnership (*Gōshi Kaisha*) :	3,469
Commercial partnership (*Gōmei Kaisha*) :	1,390

All above figures include new incorporations and incorporations via merger or entity conversion, but figures for the KK and GK exclude incorporations by company splits; this was done because incorporated partnerships and limited partnerships cannot be incorporated by company splits. For the source statistics with breakdowns by year, see Sōmu-shō (2016, 2020) (all tables).

[9] As of 2014 there were approximately 1.776 million KKs excluding ex-YKs: Baum & Goto (2016): 97 tbl. 1. Note that this figure includes dormant or otherwise economically inactive KKs. By way of comparison, NTA's statistics for assessment year 2014 report 2,477,769 KKs, a figure that includes an unspecified number of ex-YKs: Kokuzei-chō (2016): 14 tbl. 4. For assessment year 2018 (the latest available as of March 2021), NTA reports 2,554,582 KKs: Kokuzei-chō (2020): 14 tbl. 4.

[10] Act No 74 of 5 April 1938, repealed by Act No 87 of 26 July 2005.

the *Shōhō*.[11] The YK was modelled primarily on the German GmbH because of the GmbH's success and influence across the world, and the fact that Japan's commercial law was based on Germany's, but other foreign influences were also taken into account.[12] Despite greater suitability as the corporate form for small businesses as a matter of design,[13] and marked growth in numbers over the decades,[14] the YK did not achieve dominance over the KK during its lifetime for a number of reasons. First was the *YK-hō*'s poor drafting and structure. Containing dozens of provisions that merely applied *Shōhō* provisions *mutatis mutandis*, the Act was excessively long: it would total over 200 provisions if all the cross-referenced *Shōhō* provisions were counted.[15]

Another reason was the YK's negative signalling among businesspeople. This was borne out by survey data from the 1960s, where a clear majority of respondents reported that the YK's weaker reputation was the primary reason for their decision not to adopt the YK.[16] This finding would be largely confirmed by a later survey conducted in 1982.[17] The YK's nomenclature itself was part of the problem: the word *yūgen* has a dictionary meaning of 'limited', but as part of the compound word *Yūgen Kaisha* it is not clear as to *what* exactly is being 'limited'.[18] Ordinary citizens would time and again come under the mistaken impression that it was the YK's scale,[19] duration of existence, or capacity to act that was 'limited'.[20] A further difficulty faced by businesses incorporated as YKs lay in the recruitment of new employees from the pool of fresh university graduates.[21]

11 This was to prevent the YK regime, which was experimental in nature, from destroying the Commercial Code's structure, and to make subsequent amendments easier: Sakamaki (1973): 240–1.

12 Such as England, France, and Austria: Sakamaki (1973): 238–9.

13 Suzuki (1994): 361, 363 n. 1.

14 For a useful graph showing how KKs continued to outnumber YKs until the 1980s despite steady growth of both in the postwar era, see Hamada (1986b): 4 fig. 2. As an example of a more precise figure at a specific point in time, in 1980, KKs (791,300) outnumbered YKs (606,500) by a comfortable margin: Baum & Goto (2016): 97 tbl. 1. By 1996, YKs (1,219,215) would outnumber KKs (1,123,034): Takahashi (1998): 215 (citing NTA statistics and suggesting a connection between the introduction of minimum capital in 1990 and the YK's surpassing of the KK in numbers). Finally, according to NTA's survey for assessment year 2005, the last year before the *Kaishahō* entered into force, there were 1,453,540 YKs comprising 56.3 per cent of active corporate business entities, and 1,036,664 KKs comprising 40.2 per cent. Figures exclude parents and subsidiaries. See Kokuzei-chō (2006): 157 tbl. 12.

15 Sakamaki (1973): 240.

16 Takahashi (2010): 5 (70.9 per cent of respondents raised reputational concerns as their number one reason).

17 Kitazawa &Hamada (1983): 30 tbl. 13 (58.9 per cent of KK respondents reported choosing the KK for its superior credibility vis-à-vis trading partners, versus 34.7 per cent for YK respondents) and 31 tbl. 14 (32.1 per cent of KK respondents expressly rejected the YK in favour of the KK because the YK was low on social credibility).

18 Sakamaki (1973): 240–1.

19 Kitazawa & Hamada (1983): 31 tbl. 14 (24.3 per cent of KK respondents chose not to incorporate as a YK because 'YKs tend to be perceived as small-scale').

20 Takahashi (2010): 5.

21 Egashira (2005b): 5 n. 3. For context, it is important to note that Japanese businesses have traditionally preferred to hire fresh graduates from elite universities and to keep them until retirement, although this employment model has been under pressure. See e.g. Economist (2008); Shimoda (2016): 770–8.

Together with other reasons,[22] the negative image of the YK as a 'limited' company ultimately led to the repeal of the *YK-hō*[23] in conjunction with the enactment of the *Kaishahō*. Since then, no new YKs can be incorporated. All YKs existing at the time of the *Kaishahō*'s entry into force are formally and involuntarily converted into KKs, albeit with special transitionary governing provisions.[24] A significant number of ex-YKs still remain, and as of 2020, number about 1.5 million.[25]

2 *Japan's Puzzle: Close Corporations without (Formal) Withdrawal*

At this juncture, Japan before the *Kaishahō* may seem like an outlier to the casual observer. After all, Japan was for many decades the world's fastest growing major economy even though neither of its major forms of business organisation – the KK and the YK – offered any withdrawal remedies. The regime governing restricted-transfer shares is an exit mechanism, but not withdrawal.[26] A preliminary question arises: did they generally remedy the statute's shortcomings by making contractual or constitutional arrangements that provided for withdrawal? For better or for worse, the Japanese, as shareholders or members of Japanese close corporations, generally do not make adequate ex ante contractual arrangements with a view to forestalling or resolving possible future disputes[27] – an attitude that most likely extends to withdrawal arrangements. Without withdrawal either at general law or in contract, Japan would appear to have been the glaring exception to the argument in Chapter II[28] that withdrawal remedies are essential to close corporation law in general. But was Japan an outlier at all?

22 See Koh (2020): 1222 fn. 78; Aizawa (2009): 12.

23 Takahashi (2010): 6.

24 Although the *Kaishahō* would deregulate the KK to some extent and thereby narrow the gap between the old YK and the new KK, transitionary arrangements were still necessary to maintain, as far as possible, the old *YK-hō* regime for the forcibly converted ex-YKs. See Yamamoto (2006): 230–8 (detailing the differences between the old YK and the deregulated KK preserved by the transitionary arrangements). For an English overview on the changes to the KK, see Takahashi & Shimizu (2005): 41, 45–6.

25 Kanda (2021): 7 n. 1 (citing the figure of 1.508 million as of October 2020); see also Baum & Goto (2016): 97 tbl. 1 (citing the figure of 1.64 million as of 2014). Note also that NTA statistics on ex-YKs are unavailable post-2005 as there is no separate breakdown of KKs into ex-YKs and other KKs.

26 On this regime, see Koh (2020): 1223–7.

27 Ueyanagi et al. (1984): 140 (Statement by Hámada Michiyo). One apparent exception to the general failure of shareholders in Japanese KK close corporations to use contract to customise corporate internal ordering arrangements is share transfer restrictions, which appear to have been adopted almost universally in all KKs incorporated from 1975: Kitazawa & Hamada (1983): 30 tbl. 12 (reporting that share transfer restrictions were present in over 90 per cent of KKs incorporated from 1975). Express share transfer restrictions were not necessary in the YK, as any transfer of membership interests to persons who were not existing members of the YK required the approval of the members in general meeting: *YK-hō*, Article 19 Paragraph 2 (repealed). The approval requirement did not apply to transfers between members; see *YK-hō*, Article 19 Paragraph 1 (repealed).

28 II.C–D.

i Partial, Functional Substitutes to Withdrawal

A much closer look would reveal that all was not well. Without any specific statutory provision entitling them to relief by withdrawal, aggrieved shareholders – and their lawyers – had to get creative. From time to time shareholders would resort to threatening the company and its controlling shareholders with disclosure of illegal activities such as tax evasion,[29] a method that, while presumably effective, nonetheless amounts to borderline or actual extortion.[30] Attorneys representing aggrieved minority shareholders often adopted a more legal – and legalistic – solution. This took the form of lawsuits challenging corporate procedures on the basis of non-compliance with necessary legal formalities.[31] Such lawsuits could be actions seeking invalidation of a shareholder resolution or a declaration of the non-existence thereof,[32] or a declaration of nullity of a board resolution.[33] Other techniques include combining a challenge to the validity of a shareholder resolution appointing a director[34] or an application to remove a director for cause[35] with an application for provisional court orders (*kari-shobun*) suspending the director in question and appointing an acting director in place.[36]

29 Hamada (1983):63.

30 Although Hamada does not characterise these matters as such in her article (ibid.), it takes no leap of logic to arrive at this conclusion.

31 For a more recent study, see generally Baum & Takahashi (2011). The existence of such legal avenues is not restricted to Japan; many European jurisdictions contain similar avenues for shareholder challenges, although not the UK: Fleischer (2014): 63–4. For a brief comparative survey see Koh & Tang (2021): 445–7.

32 In the context of KKs, provided for, respectively, under the pre-*Kaishahō Shōhō* (Commercial Code): *Shōhō* [*Commercial Code], Act No 48 of 9 March 1899, Articles 247, Paragraph 1, Item (i) and 252 (repealed). These provisions, among others, were applied *mutatis mutandis* to the YK: *YK-hō*, Article 41 (repealed). They are also under available under current law with minor modifications: *Kaishahō*, Articles 831 and 830.

There is no statutory equivalent for the GK, as there is no mandatory requirement that the members, each and every one of whom have executive powers by default (Article 590, Paragraph 1), to pass formal 'resolutions' (*ketsugi*) at a 'meeting' (*sōkai*). The default rules applicable where there are multiple members in a membership company is that decisions on day-to-day business (*jōmu*) may be taken by members individually unless objected to by another member (Article 590, Paragraph 3), and in the case of ordinary business decisions with objections and management decisions (*gyōmu*) to be made by simple majority (Article 590, Paragraph 2). See generally Shishido (2014b): 134–5.

33 Unlike for shareholder resolutions, there was no specific *Shōhō* provision regulating this regime, but it is recognised in judicial precedent at the highest level. See Saikō Saibansho [Supreme Court] 08.11.1972, 26(9) Minshū 1489, also available at https://perma.cc/3ACE-Z627; Egashira (2005): 359, 360 n. 16. This regime remains applicable under the *Kaishahō*, which similarly has no applicable statutory provision: Egashira (2017): 425. Note that there appears to be no equivalent to this regime in the YK or the GK, where there is no 'board' as such.

34 See (n. 32) above.

35 *Shōhō*, Articles 257, Paragraph 3 and 257-3, Paragraph 4 (repealed) (for the KK); *YK-hō*, Article 31-3 (repealed). For current law, see *Kaishahō*, Articles 854 (in KKs, removal of directors and other officers) and 860 (in membership companies including the GK, termination of executive members' rights to manage or represent the company).

36 Hamada cites Articles 270 and 271 of the *Shōhō* as the basis for this type of action: Hamada (1983): 63. Article 270's current equivalent is *Minji Hozen Hō* [*Civil Provisional Remedies Act], Act No 91 of 22 December 1989, Article 23, Paragraph 2. Current equivalents of Article 271 (prescribing restrictions on

These lawsuits in and of themselves did nothing to resolve the underlying issues in dispute[37] even if the aggrieved shareholder won the lawsuit itself.[38] After all, if the aggrieved shareholder's complaint was, on its face, that a shareholder resolution was not passed at a properly convened shareholder meeting, all the controlling majority shareholders had to do was to convene a meeting properly and pass the resolution correctly the next time. Why, then, did attorneys commence such lawsuits when their clients hardly cared – or even knew – about corporate law formalities?[39] Quite simply, these lawsuits worked, albeit indirectly. First, given that non-compliance with corporate formalities in small, closely held corporations was an endemic problem,[40] it was easy to find some basis to commence such lawsuits, and even win.[41] Second, neither the attorneys nor the shareholders needed or even necessarily wanted to succeed in these lawsuits per se. Instead, it was the shock – especially to a small company – caused by the commencement of legal proceedings that brought the relevant parties to the negotiating table.[42] Ultimately, the dispute would be almost invariably be resolved with withdrawal of one or the other of the parties in conflict, with the settlement facilitated, with great effort, by the parties' attorneys and even the judges hearing the lawsuits.[43]

The fact that this phenomenon went largely unnoticed by foreign observers is unsurprising.[44] Without adequate knowledge of Japan's somewhat peculiar context, even careful analysis of the reported cases on actions challenging corporate procedures would have yielded little insight. Constrained by doctrine as to the scope of the facts and issues that can be addressed, in cases where only peripheral issues could be litigated, Japanese court judgments could have said little to shed light on the real, underlying core issues.[45] Within Japan, however, the practice appeared to be

the acting director's authority) are *Kaishahō*, Articles 352 (for KKs) and 603 (for membership companies, including the GK) as read with *Minji Hozen Hō*, Article 56.

37 Shishido (1984b): 237.

38 Hamada (1983): 63; Shishido (1990): 341–4.

39 Hamada (1983): 63 (observing that minority shareholders had little awareness that non-compliance with corporate formalities is unlawful, and that clients were often surprised when their attorneys suggested bringing procedural challenges as a means of resolving shareholder disputes).

40 Hamada (1983): 63; Aotake (1979): 318–19 (observing that many small-scale KKs have neither the inclination nor ability to comply with the law governing KKs); Hamada (1986b): 15 (pointing out that small businesses can only 'remain stock corporations by disregarding the stock corporation law' and that there was 'prevailing disregard of corporation law'). For an example of an observation directly from practice experience, in this case by a practising attorney (and adjunct lecturer in law), see Ueyanagi et al. (1984): 119 (Statement by Imanaka Toshiaki) (observing that Japan lacked a spirit of legal compliance).

41 Shishido (1984a): 541 (reporting that in a majority of over 100 reported decisions from 1950 to 1982 on shareholder challenges to shareholder resolutions, the shareholder plaintiff won).

42 Hamada (1983): 63.

43 ibid. 63–4; Ueyanagi et al. (1984): 129, 141 (Statements by Hamada Michiyo).

44 To the best of my knowledge, there is only one published English source that discusses this phenomenon, and it is by Shishido, the consummate inside observer; see Shishido (1990): 341–4. Hamada's 1986 Harvard Law School paper (Hamada (1986b)) while insightful and powerfully written, is unfortunately unpublished and appears to be available only at the Harvard Law Library or as a photocopy at the library of the Max Planck Institute for Comparative and International Private Law in Hamburg, Germany.

45 Shishido (1984b): 237–8; Shishido (1990): 341–4.

established and well-known within the practitioner community and to astute academic commentators such as Hamada Michiyo,[46] so much so that its existence was later expressly acknowledged by the Ministry of Justice's law reform officers.[47]

Even though the practical workarounds arguably achieved a measure of success by prompting settlement leading to withdrawal in most cases, they were not without their shortcomings. For example, cooperation from understanding judges, whether tacit or active, was key. Yet not all judges were sufficiently sensitive to the context, as there was a string of Japanese judgments in which shareholder applications challenging corporate formalities were dismissed by judges in the exercise of their discretion on grounds of abuse.[48] The second shortcoming is more obvious: compelling aggrieved shareholders and their attorneys to bring lawsuits unrelated to the underlying dispute to force settlements imposed unnecessary burdens on the justice system.[49] Even if the indirect means by which the desired outcome may be procured is testament to the resourcefulness of Japanese attorneys, the very fact that shareholders were forced to resort to such practices – which might well be construed as abusive even in other legal systems[50] – did little credit to Japanese corporate law or the legal system as a whole. By the 1980s, a consensus had emerged: it was necessary to reform the law of KKs, and to a lesser extent, the law of YKs.

ii Reform Attempt of the 1980s

The need to implement some form of withdrawal remedy for the KK was identified at least as early as 1951.[51] As the problems of close corporations came to be better understood over the 1970s, many Japanese academics came to the view that reform was necessary.[52] The emerging consensus culminated in one serious attempt at introducing a withdrawal regime for the KK and the YK, which took place during

46 Hamada (1983): 63.

47 Inaba & Ōtani (1986b): 64.

48 See the cases cited in Egashira (2005a): 323 n. 1. They have not escaped criticism by academics more sympathetic to the plight of these shareholders, such as Egashira himself, who criticised the courts for being excessively moralistic: ibid.

49 See Hamada (1986b): 16 (reporting that overburdened judges have called for reform).

50 For example, under English law, bringing a lawsuit purely for a collateral purpose is an abuse of process and the suit may be struck out or stayed. See Civil Procedure Rules 1998, SI 1998/3132 (L17), r 3.4; *Re Majory (A Debtor)* [1955] Ch 600 (CA) 623–4 (Lord Evershed MR); *Goldsmith* v. *Sperrings Ltd* [1977] 1 WLR 478 (CA), 498–9 (Scarman LJ), 503 (Bridge LJ); *JSC BTA Bank* v. *Ablyazov (No 6)* [2011] EWHC 1136 (Comm), [2011] 1 WLR 2996 [22] (Teare J).

51 Komachiya (1951): 404 (albeit as a substitute for the then-newly introduced shareholder right to apply to court for judicial dissolution).

52 Among the earliest to take up the cause of reform is Hamada Michiyo, who began advocating for a withdrawal right *at will* based on her research on the law of close corporations in the United States in a 1974 book: Hamada (1974): 340–5. Converts to the notion that a withdrawal remedy is necessary included Takeuchi Akio, a leading corporate law scholar at the University of Tokyo: Yazawa et al. (1977): 119–20 (Statement by Takeuchi Akio). Younger scholars also added to the call for reform; see e.g. Mori (1984): 25–7.

the 1980s as part of a comprehensive reform primarily of KK law.[53] Consultations in 1984[54] culminated in the 1986 Commercial Code and Limited Liability Corporation Act Reform Proposal ('1986 Reform Proposal') by the Ministry of Justice.[55] Clause 3–8-a of the 1986 Reform Proposal provides:

> In stock corporations [KKs] without marketable share certificates and limited liability corporations [YKs], if the interests of a part of the shareholders or members are dealt with in a significantly unfair manner, the affected shareholders or members shall have a claim against the corporation for the designation of a purchaser for their shares or membership interests.

Under the proposed regime, the corporation may purchase its own shares but only up to the limit that may be distributed as dividends (Clause 3–8-c). If the person designated as purchaser fails to perform their obligation, or the corporation fails to make a designation within a specified time frame, the representative director or directors[56] would be respectively deemed the designated purchaser or purchasers with joint and severable liability (Clause 3–8-d and explanatory note).[57]

Amidst incessant debate and criticism over the 1986 Reform Proposal's lack of clarity on important issues,[58] the one and only attempt at reforming close corporation law by introducing a withdrawal mechanism ultimately ended in failure.[59] The reasons are not completely clear, although there are suggestions that the lack of judicial support over concerns about the difficulty of making a decision as to

53 The best summaries of this issue in English are Shishido (1990) and Hamada (1986b).

54 For the original consultation document, see Hōmushō (1984): 190–208.

55 For the full text of the Reform Proposal, see Hōmushō (1986): 125–42.

56 Under Japanese company law not all directors *ipso facto* have the power to 'represent' (*daihyō*) the company, i.e. to act as its legal agent with power to bind the company. Directors so empowered are called 'representative directors' and are functionally equivalent to the managing director, president, or CEO.

57 Three weeks was suggested as an example of the timeframe.

58 Hamada observed that the 1986 Reform Proposal lacked clarity as to precisely which organ of the company, the board of directors or the shareholder meeting, should appoint the designated purchaser, and also noted the increased complexity of the issue in the situation where the company itself is the designated purchaser: Hamada (1986a): 7 (pointing out that where the company re-purchases its own shares, decisions as to the proper disposition of the shares and payment for them out of the company's distributable profits should be decided by the shareholder meeting, but that to do so may involve the hassle of calling an extraordinary meeting).

59 Toward the end of 1989, the Commercial Law Subcommittee (*Shōhō-bukai*) (forerunner of today's Corporate Law Subcommittee (*Kaishahō-bukai*)) of the Legislative Council of the Ministry of Justice (*Hōsei Shingikai*) determined that it would be too difficult to resolve all the issues covered by the extensive 1986 Reform Proposal together. Subsequently, the Legislative Council prepared a much-reduced reform outline in March 1990 that was later submitted, with a few amendments, as the reform bill by the government to the Diet in April 1990. The bill was passed without amendment by both Houses in June 1990. The proposed withdrawal reforms were dropped in their entirety. See Hamada (1993): 30–1. Although Hamada did not specify at specifically which stage withdrawal was dropped, it is likely that it was during the Legislative Council stage of the proceedings. For a concise introduction to the function of the Legislative Council in corporate law reform prior to 1997, see Morita (2014): 27–8.

whether the grounds for withdrawal are met,[60] as well as concerns over the procedural aspects[61] and on enforcement mechanisms,[62] are responsible. As such, the Japanese legislator failed to act notwithstanding the academic consensus on the salience of the issue of shareholder conflict and oppression.[63]

iii Why Did Japanese Businesses Choose Corporate Forms without Withdrawal?

If withdrawal is essential to the resolution of close corporation disputes, and neither the KK nor YK expressly offered this solution, why did the Japanese consistently choose to incorporate millions of KKs and YKs, but not other corporate forms that offered withdrawal such as the commercial partnership (*gōmei kaisha*) or limited partnership (*gōshi kaisha*)?

Withdrawal's availability or value aside, there were compelling strategic reasons to incorporate as KKs or YKs. The first is limited liability. In contrast to the commercial partnership and limited partnership, only KKs and YKs offered limited liability for all shareholders/members.[64] The choice for Japanese businesspeople was not between limited liability without withdrawal versus limited liability plus withdrawal; it was *either* limited liability *or* withdrawal.[65] It is clear that corporate forms with full limited liability were consistently preferred, as evidenced by the fact that the two incorporated partnership forms were greatly outnumbered by KKs as early as 1950, and by YKs by 1955.[66] From the perspective of the vast majority of businesses in Japan's post-war era, the only practical choice was between the KK and the YK.

60 See Hōmushō (1987): 55 (reporting that support for the reform proposal was not overwhelming among the fifty-two court organisations surveyed, and even those in support took the position that the criteria on which a buyout is to be ordered should be made as clear as possible); Egashira et al. (1990): 63 (Statement by Yamashita Tomonobu) ('As to the fact that [the proposed statutory buyout provision] was not included [in the final reform], it was said that the courts seem to be extremely troubled by [the prospect of] having to make findings of fact [as part of assessing] whether the grounds are satisfied').

61 ibid. ('I am also under the impression that corporate law scholars did not fully think through … relevant issues in procedural law').

62 Kawamoto made a very brief observation, without citing any source, that the reforms on withdrawal were dropped over problems with the proposed enforcement mechanism, by which the designated purchaser's failure to pay would result in dissolution of company: Kawamoto (1990): 14. As a member of the Commercial Law Subcommittee (Nakahigashi & Matsui (2010): 1175 (including Kawamoto Ichirō on list of *i'in*))) involved in refining the 1986 Reform Proposal into a workable legislative agenda, Kawamoto was well-placed to comment. For further analysis and critique of the proposed enforcement mechanism, see Hamada (1986a): 3–5; Ōga (1988).

63 Hamada (1990): 53.

64 Using a German-style GmbH & Co KG hybrid such as a YK & Co limited partnership was also out of the question, as prior to the *Kaishahō* only unlimited members may manage a commercial/limited partnership, and companies were not permitted to become unlimited members: see (n. 171) below.

65 For reasons already set out above at text to (n. 27), it was highly unlikely that businesspeople would have even considered the question framed as such.

66 Hamada (1986b): 4 fig. 2 (based on NTA data). The unpopularity of the incorporated partnership forms did not change with the *Kaishahō*: see (n. 8) above, (n. 110) below.

Japanese commentators have offered other reasons for the popularity of KKs and YKs. It was well-accepted that tax advantages[67] likely played a major role in the 'corporatisation' (*hōjin-nari*) of businesses in the post-war years, in which businesses previously run as sole proprietorships incorporated *en masse* as close corporations, and almost invariably as KKs or YKs.[68] Another related advantage was the impression of size and social credibility that trading as a KK conveyed.[69] Hamada, however, challenged this received wisdom. Drawing on new survey data revealing a decline in emphasis on the tax factor among respondents especially amongst KK users,[70] she argued that tax considerations no longer dominated the decision to incorporate, and in any event did not explain the strong preference for KKs, and to a lesser extent YKs, when the incorporated partnership forms offered the same tax benefits.[71] She also cast doubt on the argument that the mere fact of incorporating as a KK or YK boosted social credibility with two points. First, creditors and suppliers were not so naïve as to be swayed by the mere fact that a counterparty was a KK. Second, the social credibility argument did not explain the small business owners' perception that the YK brand, which did not by itself convey the impression of a large business, would also confer social credibility.[72]

Hamada offered a more sophisticated account for the popularity of the KK and YK: accounting standards. Surveys she conducted in 1982 revealed that the most common reason for incorporating as a KK or YK, cited by almost two-thirds of KK and over half of YK respondents, was that 'clearer accounting contributes to the optimization of corporate management'[73].[74] The connection between the KK and YK and accounting lay in Japan's post-war corporate compliance environment. As businesses began incorporating as KKs or YKs *en masse* for tax advantages after the war, they became subject to more exacting mandatory accounting requirements.[75] Without any expertise in accounting, they came to rely heavily on accounting professionals,[76] with many companies retaining them as corporate advisors.[77] Over

67 Different rates for corporate income tax and personal income tax, double taxation, and tax deductions for small and medium enterprises were among the factors that contributed to significant tax advantages for incorporated small businesses over their unincorporated counterparts. For details see Ishi (2001): 171–82.

68 Hamada (1986b): 6 (pointing out that the KK's overwhelming popularity astonished observers); Egashira (2005a): 4 n. 7 (noting the role of tax accountants in encouraging incorporations).

69 Hamada (1986b): 6 (summarising earlier literature and survey findings).

70 Kitazawa & Hamada (1983): 30 tbl. 13 (reporting that tax advantages were a reason for only 8.0 per cent of KK respondents, compared to 24.8 per cent of YK respondents).

71 Hamada (1986b): 6, 10.

72 ibid. 10.

73 Cf Hamada's own translation in Hamada (1986b): 8 tbl. 2 ('better accounting techniques are employed and it promotes the rationalisation of our management').

74 Kitazawa & Hamada (1983): 30 tbl. 13 (64.3 per cent for KKs and 52.5 per cent for YKs). The second most popular reason was 'increased credibility when dealing with trading partners': ibid.

75 Hamada (1986b): 10–11.

76 ibid. 11.

77 Hamada (1983): 69 fig. 4 (78.3 per cent of KKs and 73.6 per cent of YKs with stated capital of under JPY 100 million retained certified tax accountants (*zeirishi*) or other accounting professionals such as certified public accountants (*kōnin kaikeishi*) in an advisory capacity).

time, businesses gradually came to realise that good accounting practices contributed towards business optimisation, and gave greater consideration to this factor when making incorporation decisions.[78] Over time, optimisation led to greater business success in KKs and YKs that in turn generated social credibility. Businesspeople who chose the KK, with the strictest applicable accounting standards, benefited from being perceived as 'businesspeople who are determined to manage a modern enterprise systematically rather than small businesspeople who only wish to support their families'.[79] Hamada's account suggests that initial unintentional commitment to higher accounting standards by incorporating as KKs and YKs led to better business outcomes that in turn reinforced the logically fallacious[80] but nonetheless popular perception of KKs and YKs as successful businesses, which in turn led to voluntary and intentional commitment to higher accounting standards.

The best explanation for the longstanding popularity of KKs and YKs as close corporation vehicles, notwithstanding their other limitations, lies in the combination of factors. First is the 'halo signalling'[81] effect of incorporating as KKs (and to a much lesser extent, YKs). The second is the tangible benefits derived from voluntary commitment to better accounting. I further suggest that an additional contributor to the superior social credibility offered by the KK and the YK could lie in the titles that owners and managers could avail themselves of. KK and YK managers are legally permitted to style themselves as 'director' (*torishimariyaku*), and the CEO or managing director-equivalent could and usually did call themself 'representative director' (*daihyō torishimariyaku*).[82] These titles are universally recognised in Japan and carry an instant measure of familiarity and credibility. By contrast, the title of 'director' is unavailable to owners of incorporated partnerships, who must content themselves with less reputable titles.[83]

Although the preceding discussion proceeds from a historical perspective, there is little to suggest that matters have changed significantly since then. The *Kaishahō* still contains no withdrawal provisions applicable to KKs, including the ex-YKs. However, the *Kaishahō* was also a silent revolution in withdrawal, introducing a new corporate form offering limited liability for all members *and* withdrawal almost as an afterthought. What is this new corporate form, and how did it come to offer withdrawal? This is the subject of the next section.

[78] Hamada (1986b): 11, 14.

[79] ibid. 14.

[80] It is fallacious because stricter accounting standards may be adopted voluntarily and the resulting benefits from business optimisation enjoyed regardless of corporate form. See Hamada (1986b): 10 (observing that while KKs and YKs were required by law to adopt proper accounting, other businesses were free to opt into such standards).

[81] The term is coined by Puchniak & Lan (2017). On 'signaling' as it is used in the management literature, see generally Connelly et al. (2011).

[82] A variation is 'representative director-cum-president' (*daihyō torishimariyaku-shachō*).

[83] Compare the similar current situation where GKs are disadvantaged compared to KKs: see (nn. 242–244) below and text thereto.

C GŌDŌ KAISHA (GK)

1 *The GK As 'Membership Company': Origins and Features*

The archetypical close corporation form in Japan today is the relatively new GK,[84] a creature of the *Kaishahō*. It is crucial to note that the GK is not a renamed or modernised version of the YK. Rather, it was a legislative invention modelled upon the American limited liability company (LLC)[85] as part of a plan to create a Japanese version of the LLC that would serve as an entity with pass-through taxation following the precedent set by the US LLC. However, this original concept fell through due to opposition from the Ministry of Finance; what was ultimately enacted was the GK, a corporation subject to corporation tax.[86] In contrast to the YK, which was governed by its own statute supplemented by *mutatis mutandis* application of mainly *Shōhō* provisions governing KKs, the GK is situated as part of a family of corporate forms known as 'membership companies'.

Under the *Kaishahō*, the GK, together with two historic corporate forms, namely the incorporated 'commercial partnership' with unlimited liability[87] (*gōmei kaisha*) and the incorporated 'limited partnership' (*gōshi kaisha*), now comprise a new category of corporation, the 'membership companies' (*mochibun kaisha*).[88] As a category, the membership companies are distinguished from the KK, and are regulated primarily by their own separate Part within the Companies Act.[89]

As a category, 'membership companies' were conceptualised purely for convenience. During the *Shōhō* era, incorporated partnerships and limited partnerships were regulated under separate divisions, but the Code did not set out the provisions governing limited partnerships comprehensively. Instead, provisions governing incorporated partnerships were simply applied *mutatis mutandis* to limited partnerships, which led to difficulties in interpretation. A further difficulty lay with the application *mutatis mutandis* of Civil Code provisions relating to (unincorporated) partnerships. The *Kaishahō*'s legislative drafters sought to

84 Although the modern KK, which includes ex-YKs that have yet to change corporate forms or dissolve, still make up a large share of close corporations in Japan, I do not focus on them going forward as the *Kaishahō* does not offer withdrawal for KK shareholders.

85 Shishido (2014a): 21. The critical difference, however, is that the GK did not have the pass-through taxation that was characteristic of the American LLCs on which the GK was based: ibid.

Because the *gōdō kaisha* did not receive pass-through taxation, the Diet enacted legislation for the *yūgen sekinin jigyō kumiai*, which roughly translates to limited liability enterprise partnership, but is also sometimes confusingly called the limited liability partnership (J-LLP): Shishido, ibid. For the statute see *Yūgen Sekinin Jigyō Kumiai Keiyaku ni kansuru Hōritsu* [*Limited Liability Partnership Act] [more literally and accurately, 'Act on Limited Liability Enterprise Partnership Agreements'], Act No 40 of 6 May 2005. The J-LLP terminology is adopted in McCahery & Vermeulen (2008):29. See also (n. 116).

86 Baum & Goto (2016): 93; Sekiguchi & Nishigaki (2008): 18–19.

87 In Anglo-Commonwealth terms, a comparison with the unlimited company is also appropriate.

88 'Membership Company' (in the singular) is the semi-official translation as per JLTC (2019): 276.

89 See *Kaishahō*, Pt III (Articles 575–675).

increase the user-friendliness of the new statute by creating an umbrella category for the two historic and one new (GK) corporate forms and organising the applicable rules into those of general application across the three corporate forms, and those specific to each form.[90] The category was thus created entirely by legislative fiat without regard for each individual corporate form's distinct historical and doctrinal origins.[91]

Nevertheless, under the current regime, membership companies are distinguished from KKs in three aspects. First, they are permitted a larger degree of freedom in contractual ordering in their corporate constitutions.[92] On the practical side, this is facilitated by lower incorporation and related costs: there is no need for notarisation (*ninshō*; 'certification'[93]) of the constitution,[94] and the registration licence fees are also much lower.[95]

Second, the members are not conceptually separated from the corporate organs; in principle they *are* the corporate organ.[96] There are no directors (*torishimariyaku*) or board of directors (*torishimariyaku-kai*) as such; membership company members by default are 'executive members' who have executive (*gyōmu wo shikkō suru*) powers, and are also by default 'representative members' (*daihyō sha'in*) who each have the authority to bind the company.[97] The membership company also has the option of limiting representative powers to specific executive members through the corporate constitution by either designating specific individual(s) as, or by stipulating procedures for the appointment of, representative member(s).[98]

Third, membership companies are close corporations,[99] optimised for small organisations or joint ventures.[100] The personalistic element (*jinteki yōso*) is stronger

90 Aizawa & Kōriya (2016b): 153.

91 For criticisms, see e.g. Uemura (2006): 95–6 (observing that while the incorporated partnership and limited partnership are concepts of 'ancient and honorable origin (*yuishotadashii*)' with their roots in the [Roman] *societas* and the [medieval Italian] *commenda* respectively, the GK as a startup-oriented corporate form lacked such ancient and honorable origins, and that the legislator acted 'arbitrarily' and 'without reason' in combining the three). For more general information on the historical origins of modern corporate forms in English see Hansmann et al. (2006).

92 Shishido (2014a): 9–11. It should be noted that the modern *Kaishahō* KK has also been deregulated to a such an extent that the difference may not be as large as it once was; see (n. 24) above.

93 JLTC (2019): 232.

94 Article 30 Paragraph 1 (requiring notarisation for KKs); Sekiguchi & Nishigaki (2008): 19 (expressly stating that GKs do not need notarisation). The cost of notarisation is JPY 50,000: *Kōshōnin Tesū-ryō Rei* [*Order for Notary Fees], Cabinet Order No 224 of 25 June 1993, Article 35. There is no notarisation requirement for GKs or other membership companies: Hayashi (2012): 365.

95 *Tōroku Menkyo-zei Hō* [*Registration and License Tax Act], Act No 35 of 2 June 1967, Beppyō [Annexed Table] 1, Heading 24 (Kaisha mata wa Gaikoku Kaisha no Shōgyō Tōki [Business Registration of Companies or Foreign Companies]), No 1, Item (i) (KKs: the higher of 0.7 per cent of registered capital or JPY 150,000); Item (ro) (incorporated partnerships and limited partnerships: JPY 60,000); Item (ha) (GKs: the higher of 0.7 per cent of registered capital or JPY 60,000).

96 Takahashi (2014): 281.

97 Articles 590 and 599.

98 Article 599 Paragraph 3.

99 Takahashi (2014): 281.

100 Shishido (2014a): 8.

in membership companies than in the KK.[101] Membership companies are premised on personal trust between the members, and as a concept stand in opposition to the KK.[102] It is also difficult in practice to implement hierarchical structures within membership companies, rendering them unsuitable vehicles for large organisations other than as wholly owned subsidiaries.[103] The transfer of a membership interest in principle requires unanimous consent of the other members,[104] which is diametrically opposed to the KK in which shares are fully transferable unless express transfer restrictions are provided for.[105] The personalistic nature of membership companies is stronger than in analogous organisational forms in other jurisdictions: in contrast with the US limited partnership or LLC,[106] membership interests in membership companies may not be publicly traded.[107]

It should be noted that none of the three membership companies offers the critical tax advantage of pass-through taxation.[108] Two of the three membership company forms, offering no or only partial limited liability, are likely to be of limited legal or practical significance going forward, whether alone or in hybrid forms,[109] due to their unpopularity and impracticability.[110] That leaves us with the GK, the newest but also the only viable membership company.

101 Koide (2014a): 213–15 (explaining how this difference influences the design of the members' withdrawal regime).

102 Shishido (2014a): 6; see also Koide (2014a): 213–14.

103 Shishido (2014a): 6.

104 Article 585 (but which permits deviation by provision in the corporate constitution); Takahashi (2014): 281.

105 Article 127 (basic principle of free transferability) read with Article 2, Item 17; Article 107, Paragraph 1, Item 1; Article 108, Paragraph 1, Item 4 (defining limited transferability as an optional feature of a share, but excluding this option for public companies (*kōkai kaisha*) or companies with three committees (a form adopted almost exclusively in listed companies; *shimei i'inkai-tō secchi kaisha*)).

106 For a study of the operating agreements of publicly traded LLCs and LPs in Delaware, see Manesh (2012). However, a publicly traded LLC would lose the preferential tax treatment granted to LLCs unless passive income makes up 90 per cent or more of its income: ibid 573; IRC, § 7704, as amended by PL 110-343 (3 October 2008) (US).

107 In the GK context: Shishido (2015): 374.

108 Both the commercial partnership and limited partnerships are also subject to corporation tax: Baum & Goto (2016): 91–2.

109 Hybrid forms in which a corporation offering limited liability for members (*i.e.* the KK, YK or GK) serves as the unlimited partner(s) in a limited partnership (or commercial partnership) were impossible before the *Kaishahō*: see (n. 171) below. They are today rare enough that they do not merit mention in the mainstream texts. Unlike in Germany, in Japan pass-through taxation was never an option for commercial partnerships or limited partnerships. Without pass-through taxation, a hybrid form today offers no tax advantages over the GK.

110 These two forms today comprise only minuscule proportions of business corporate entities. As of assessment year 2018 (the latest available as of March 2021), there were just 3,371 incorporated partnerships and 14,170 limited partnerships, respectively comprising a mere 0.1 per cent and 0.5 per cent of total business corporate entities. By comparison, the 98,652 GKs comprised 3.6 per cent and 2,554,582 KKs 93.3 per cent. See Kokuzei-chō (2020): 14 tbl. 4. See (n. 8) above; see also Shishido (2015): 376 fn. 10 (pointing out that it is 'not realistic' for newly incorporated businesses to adopt the incorporated partnership or limited partnership forms because of the requirement that at least one member shall bear unlimited liability).

2 *Legal Significance and Terminological Clarifications*

With the passage of the *Kaishahō*, Japan now has a new close corporation form in the GK, which offers withdrawal *at will* (VII.D.2 below) and withdrawal on grounds (VII.D.3 below). As Japan's GK has received relatively little attention in the Western language literature, to avoid inappropriate confusion with the more prominent KK, some clarification on terminology and nomenclature is in order. The word *mochibun*, which is adopted by the *Kaishahō* legislator as the name of the new category that is membership companies, is the Japanese word used for 'membership interests' in the three entities. They are not shares or stock (*kabu*), which is the term used for interests in the KK.[111] The correct term for equity investors of *mochibun kaisha* is not 'shareholder' (*kabu'nushi*), but rather 'member' (*sha'in*). In this Chapter, therefore, 'member' is not used interchangeably with 'shareholder', and other membership company-specific terminology such as 'executive member' instead of 'director' are used accordingly.

In the interests of clarity, I deviate from the semi-official or otherwise not infrequently used translations in two cases. Instead of using 'articles of incorporation' when referring to *teikan*, I prefer the functional term 'corporate constitution' in the interests of maintaining consistency with the other chapters.[112] Also, despite the fact that the initial impetus came from the US LLC, the GK exhibits significant differences from the US LLC,[113] not least in the idiosyncratic native Japanese nomenclature that was ultimately adopted.[114] Therefore, in the interests of rigour and to avoid any possible confusion, in referring to the Japanese *Gōdō Kaisha* I use the term 'GK', which is adopted by a number of prominent companies in their English corporate names,[115] exclusively.[116]

111 Aizawa & Kōriya (2006b): 153 n. 1.

112 See I.B.5.

113 See (n. 85) above.

114 A direct translation of 'limited liability company' was not chosen as the name for the new corporate form. The term *gōdō kaisha* was not based on any existing word or meaning, but was a term constructed primarily for the convenience of making the new entity – together with the existing *gōmei kaisha* (commercial partnership incorporated with unlimited liability) and *gōshi kaisha* (limited partnership) – conform to a *gō*___ *kaisha* naming formula. Aizawa & Kōriya (2006b): 153 n. 1.

115 Examples include Seiyu GK, Cisco Systems GK, and Amazon Japan GK. Seiyu became a wholly owned subsidiary of Walmart in 2008 and was reorganised as a GK in 2009: Walmart (2019). Cisco Systems GK is a wholly owned subsidiary of Cisco Systems Netherlands Holdings BV, which is in turn a subsidiary of Cisco Systems Inc: Cisco (2019). Amazon Japan GK was formed from the merger of Amazon Japan KK and Amazon Japan Logistics GK, and is officially styled 'Amazon Japan GK' in English: Nikkei (2016).

116 In this regard, this Book is in the minority in the English language literature; other authors prefer to use less distinctly local abbreviations or terms, especially when making cross-jurisdictional comparisons. For a prominent Western example, see McCahery & Vermeulen (2008): 29 (using the term 'J-LLC'). The best Japanese example is Shishido (2015) (using simply 'LLC').

D WITHDRAWAL (*TAISHA*)

1 *History and Concept*

For our purposes, the most important feature common to the three membership company types is the availability of withdrawal. All three types of membership companies are subject to the same basic withdrawal regime set out at Articles 606 to 613 of the current *Kaishahō*.[117] The basic framework had existed for over a century by the time the GK came into existence. Under the *Shōhō* of 1899, the core of Japan's companies legislation until it was superseded by the *Kaishahō*, members of commercial partnerships and limited partnerships had withdrawal rights.[118] By consolidating the *Shōhō* withdrawal provisions and making them applicable to membership companies in general, the *Kaishahō* extended the withdrawal regime to cover the GK. Thus, as a membership company, the GK offers both withdrawal *at will* (VII. D.2 below) and withdrawal on grounds (VII.D.3 below).

In contrast with the reform efforts of the 1980s to introduce withdrawal into the KK and YK,[119] key documents from the reform period reveal only the most cursory concern with *why* precisely the GK should be equipped with withdrawal remedies. In the *Preliminary Draft Principles for the Modernization of the Corporate Law Regime* approved on 22 October 2003[120] (*Preliminary Draft Principles*), it was taken for granted that the proposed new corporate form (that became the GK) would incorporate features of the legacy incorporated partnership form, including withdrawal.[121] The rationale given for withdrawal is to provide the means by which a member could withdraw their investment, and which takes the place of transfer of shares or membership interests as would otherwise be the case in KKs or YKs.[122] The only policy question related to the withdrawal regime that was opened for public consultation and feedback was on the relatively technical issue of creditor protection.[123] In other words, even from a relatively early stage of the reform

117 Supplemented by special provisions applicable only to the GK in *Kaishahō* (Articles 635 to 636); see VII.D.6.

118 *Shōhō*, Articles 84 and 147 (repealed).

119 Discussed above at VII.B.2.ii.

120 Approved at the 15th Meeting of the Corporate Law (Modernization) Subcommittee (*Kaishahō (Gendaika Kankei) Bukai*) of the Legislative Council of the Ministry of Justice (*Hōsei Shingikai*). This document, which offers up to three options for each important point of reform (called 'Proposal A', 'Proposal B', and 'Proposal C' and so on), was later opened for public consultation and feedback. Based on the feedback received, a reworked version would be submitted for approval by the full Legislative Council, the final version of which would be the basis for the Ministry of Justice's legislative drafters' work on the actual draft statutory provisions for the bill.

121 Hōsei-Shingikai (2003): 49 (Dai-6-bu, 1 chū 1(1)–(2)).

122 ibid. (Dai-6-bu, 1 chū 1(2) chū) ('The regime shall not guarantee the recovery of investment via transfer [of ownership interests]') (translated); Hōmushō (2003): 98 (drawing the connection between the new corporate form's emphasis on the relationship between members with the decision to specify withdrawal (*taisha*) as the means of recovery of investment as opposed to transfer).

123 There were two options offered for public feedback, with Proposal A being a procedure akin to capital reduction, and Proposal B being akin to liquidation; see Hōsei-Shingikai (2003): 49 (Dai-6-bu, 1 chū 2 (5)); Hōmushō (2003): 99.

process, the subject of *whether* the GK should have withdrawal was never up for debate, only the *how*.[124]

The exclusive focus on 'how' instead of 'why' was maintained in subsequent documents. The finalised *Principles for the Modernization of the Corporate Law Regime* adopted on 9 February 2005[125] (*Principles*) did not touch on the specific rationale, but stated plainly that 'notwithstanding the provisions of the corporate constitution, members of GKs shall have the right to withdraw if there are unavoidable grounds'.[126] The *Principles* also provided that the withdrawing member shall have the right to a refund, albeit subject to creditor protection rules and procedures where the GK has insufficient distributable surplus to pay the refund.[127] In his authoritative commentary on the *Principles*,[128] Egashira Kenjirō mentioned only that the GK member's right to withdraw where unavoidable grounds exist follows from restrictions on the recovery of investment via transfer of membership interests, and that the issue was already addressed in the *Preliminary Draft Principles*.[129] In similar vein, the official drafters' commentary on the *Kaishahō* provided a wealth of detail on the 'how', but was completely silent on the 'why'.[130]

From the law reform documents, it appears that once the decision was made to create the GK in the image of the Meiji-era incorporated partnership, that the GK would come packaged with mandatory withdrawal rights was a foregone conclusion. Ultimately, the advent of Japan's first withdrawal regime for close corporations offering full limited liability would be the semi-accidental – but profound – consequence of the conceptualisation and creation of the GK as a member of the 'membership company' family.

Going forward, the story of withdrawal in Japan is the story of withdrawal *in the* GK. The GK is not without its challenges; with former YKs converted automatically into KKs post-*Kaishahō*,[131] the stable rate of new KK

124 The 'how' question was answered by special additional rules specific to the GK that apply on top of the general rules for membership companies. The fact that the GK, unlike the other two membership companies, has limited liability for all its members, is a reason for the additional rules: Aizawa & Kōriya (2006b): 165 (also pointing out that the special creditor protection procedures are similar to those found in liquidation). The GK is treated differently as it has, similarly to the KK, a need for capital maintenance: Koide (2014a): 213–14. See discussion below at VII.D.6.

125 At the plenary meeting of the Legislative Council of the Ministry of Justice. For the full text as adopted, see Hōsei-Shingikai (2005).

126 ibid. dai-3-bu, dai-2, 5(1).

127 ibid. dai-3-bu, dai-2, 5(2).

128 Technically, the commentary was on the draft *Principles* (i.e. pre-formal adoption by the Legislative Council), but for our purposes the contents are the same.

129 Egashira (2005b): 91 (making a reference to the *Preliminary Draft Principles*, Dai-6-bu, 1 chū 1(2)). Egashira went on to note (at 92) that the (draft) *Principles* adopted Proposal B in the *Preliminary Draft Principles* on the matter of creditor protection procedures.

130 See Aizawa & Kōriya (2006b): 162, 164–5.

131 Technically, the conversion of YKs into KKs is not provided for in the *Kaishahō* itself, but a companion act that, amongst other things, also repealed the *YK-hō* and other companies legislation that accumulated over the decades. The conversion is made pursuant to *Kaisha Hō no Shikō ni tomonau Kanren Hōritsu no Seibi-tō ni kansuru Hōritsu* [*Act on Arrangement of Relevant Acts Incidental to Enforcement of the Companies Act], Act No 87 of 26 July 2005, Article 2.

incorporations,[132] and slow start in GK incorporations, the status quo in which the overwhelming majority of closely held businesses remain KKs is likely to continue for some time yet. But that is not the end of the story. If history and recent trends are any guide, the GK, like the YK before it during the latter's early years, may well grow substantially in popularity over time.[133] The role played by the two legacy membership companies also offering withdrawal in Japanese business life has steadily diminished since the end of World War II,[134] and has been minimal since the *Kaishahō* went into force.[135] In this context, the *legal* significance of the GK is clear – it is the sole close corporation form with growth potential that provides a legal framework for withdrawal. It is therefore imperative that we investigate the GK's withdrawal remedies rigorously on its own terms and in its own right as a distinct legal regime of comparative corporate law significance.

In the discussion that follows, I focus on the *Kaishahō* regime currently in force, but I also make frequent references to *Shōhō*-era (i.e. pre-*Kaishahō*) doctrine and jurisprudence as there is yet to be substantial *Kaishahō*-era jurisprudential developments on membership companies.

As a preliminary terminological point, the term *taisha* is sometimes used in the Japanese literature for the (broader) concept of 'exit' and its variants.[136] For clarity and consistency with the rest of the Book, I do not adopt direct translations of Japanese terminology in this Chapter; instead, I refer to withdrawal *without cause* as 'withdrawal at will', and withdrawal *for cause* as 'withdrawal on unavoidable grounds'.[137]

2 *Withdrawal at Will*

i General

Article 606, Paragraph 1 provides:

> Each member may withdraw from the membership company at the end of the fiscal year if the membership company's duration of corporate existence is not specified in

[132] See (n. 247) below and text thereto. However, it is impossible to determine what percentage of new incorporations are by closely held businesses given the lack of detailed breakdowns in the government data.

[133] See Table 7.1 below and (n. 14) above.

[134] Hamada (1986b): 4 fig. 2 (based on NTA data).

[135] Based on government business registration figures (see (n. 8)), the two legacy forms comprise a mere 0.3347 per cent (4,708 out of 1,406,468) of cumulative incorporations from 2006–18.

[136] See for example the discussion on terminology in Koide (2014a): 212–13.

[137] Somewhat confusingly, the term *nin'i taisha* (literally 'withdrawal at will') appearing as the heading to *Kaishahō*, Article 606 means withdrawal that *initiated voluntarily and unilaterally by the member*, which includes both withdrawal for cause and without cause, as opposed to only withdrawal *without cause*. See Koide (2014a): 211; Ōta (2008): 352. By contrast, Article 607 provides for member's automatic *exit* (not withdrawal) upon occurrence of specific events as defined by law (*hōtei taisha*) which includes expulsion, death, and unanimous consent of the members. The automatic consequence of exit here differentiates Article 607 from 606 on both substantive and procedural grounds. For the avoidance of doubt, where *taisha* in the original Japanese is used in the broader sense, I use 'exit'; I use 'withdraw' only when it is in the narrower context of withdrawal at will or on unavoidable grounds.

the corporate constitution, or is specified in the corporate constitution as the lifetime of a particular member. In such cases, each member [who seeks withdrawal] must give notice of intention to withdraw at least six months in advance.

The *raison d'être* for withdrawal at will – also described as withdrawal by advance notice (*yokoku ni yoru taisha*) – is that in companies with neither a defined duration of existence nor withdrawal, there is a risk that it would be against the public interest to bind members so harshly, that is, semi-permanently.[138] Similarly, companies that would exist for the lifetime of a particular member can be thought of as unduly restrictive for the members. In such companies, both the member whose lifetime is defined as the company's duration of existence as well as other members may have recourse to withdrawal under Article 606, Paragraph 1.[139]

A member does not need any reason to invoke withdrawal under this Paragraph.[140] According to prevailing opinion, the notice of intent to withdraw should be addressed to the representative member.[141] The purpose of the six months' minimum advance notice requirement is twofold: to simplify accounting, and to give due regard to the interests of the company.[142]

ii Deviation by Contract

Withdrawal at will is a default rule that membership companies are free to deviate from by express provision in their corporate constitutions (Article 606, Paragraph 2).[143] The precise scope of permissible deviations under this Paragraph is currently an open question. One unresolved issue is whether, in the absence of contrary provision in the constitution, the six months' minimum notice requirement can be waived by the company.[144] Another issue is whether withdrawal at will can be excluded completely for a set period of time, but here at least the legislative drafter provides a tentative answer in the affirmative.[145]

Finally, and most importantly for our purposes, deviation from the default rule of withdrawal at will by constitutional provision is ultimately subject to the mandatory rule that withdrawal on 'unavoidable grounds' cannot be eliminated (Article 606, Paragraph 3), and it is this to which we now turn.

138 Matsumoto (1929): 556.
139 Koide (2014a): 216–17.
140 By contrast with Article 606, Paragraph 3; Kosemura (1985): 306–7; Koide (2014a): 216.
141 Ōsumi & Imai (1991): 94; Koide (2014a): 217.
142 Koide (2014a): 217–18 (also noting that the six months' requirement may also be construed as a creditor protection measure); Kosemura (1985): 306.
143 There is, however, an influential strand of academic opinion that considers it to be a semi-mandatory rule. See text and sources cited at Koide (2014a): 219.
144 Koide (2014a): 218–19 (summarising both the arguments for and against, and preferring the position that does not permit the company to waive the notice requirement).
145 Aizawa & Kōriya (2006b): 162.

3 *Withdrawal on 'Unavoidable Grounds'* (yamu wo enai jiyū)

i The Statute

Article 606, Paragraph 3 provides:

> Notwithstanding the two Paragraphs above, each member may withdraw at any time if an unavoidable ground[146] exists.

The significance of this withdrawal variant is twofold. First, unlike withdrawal at will, withdrawal on unavoidable grounds requires no advance notice, and takes effect immediately upon communication of the exiting member's intent to withdraw.[147] The scope of this remedy delimits the range of situations under which a member may seek immediate relief.

Second, Paragraph 3 circumscribes the degree of freedom of the company to restrict withdrawal rights. There is general consensus that there may be no provision in the corporate constitution that would hinder the freedom of the member to trigger withdrawal for unavoidable grounds at any time, making Article 606, Paragraph 3 a mandatory provision.[148] Therefore, the extent to which the member's right to withdraw is guaranteed is determined by the scope of 'unavoidable grounds'.

As the operative concept, 'unavoidable grounds' requires elaboration. The first port of call, the legislative drafters' commentary on the *Kaishahō* is, unfortunately, unhelpful on this point:

> As to 'unavoidable grounds', it is not sufficient that the member in question has changed their mind. The circumstances on which the creation of the corporate constitution, the entry of the specific member, or the initial formation of the company were premised must have changed so significantly that it has become impossible to continue on as a member according to the original agreement.[149]

There is only one published judgment since the *Kaishahō* went into force that touches on 'unavoidable grounds'. This case was not strictly in the context of a GK, but rather a special corporate form for judicial scriveners[150] that applies provisions of the *Kaishahō* relevant to membership companies (including Article 606) *mutatis*

146 Alternative translations are 'compelling reason' and 'unavoidable circumstances': JLTC (2019): 277. I depart from the practice in Chapter IV (Germany) by using the translated term 'unavoidable grounds' consistently in this Chapter as the Romanised Japanese term is simply too unwieldy.

147 Kosemura (1985): 307; Koide (2014a): 221; Ōsumi & Imai (1991): 95.

148 Kosemura (1985): 309–10; Wada (2012): 444; Ōta (2008): 354; Koide (2014a): 219, 225. However, the precise extent to which the scope of 'unavoidable grounds' can be narrowed by contract is debatable. See discussion below at VII.D.3.ii.

149 Aizawa & Kōriya (2006b): 162.

150 *Shihō shoshi* are legal professionals separate and distinct from *bengoshi*, and have no direct equivalent in the US or Anglo-Commonwealth world. They perform some of the functions (such as small civil claims, preparation of legal documents, and registration of land and corporate matters) that might be exclusively performed in other jurisdictions by attorneys-at-law or, in jurisdictions with split legal professions, solicitors. See e.g. JFSA (2021). *Shihō shoshi* may incorporate using a special legal

mutandis to the corporate form and its members.[151] The company commenced expulsion proceedings against the plaintiff,[152] whereupon the plaintiff gave notice of their intention to withdraw on unavoidable grounds. In a decision upheld by the Tokyo High Court,[153] the Tokyo District Court held that a *shihō shoshi hōjin* is founded on a 'relationship of mutual trust between its members', and at the point in time the plaintiff gave notice of intent to withdraw, the 'relationship of trust between the plaintiff and the other members had already been lost', and hence the notice of intent to withdraw was properly founded on unavoidable grounds.[154]

ii Historical Precedent and Doctrine

With only vague guidance from the drafter and scant modern case precedent directly on point,[155] old, pre-*Kaishahō* doctrine from the *Shōhō* era, as well as old pre–World War II jurisprudence, remain instructive. For clarity of exposition, they may be classified into two competing theories of 'unavoidable grounds'.[156] The first considers only the personal circumstances of the withdrawing member in determining whether unavoidable grounds exist. Circumstances that are of the company itself or otherwise external to the member are not taken into consideration at all, which excludes situations such as a slump in business without prospect for eventual success.[157]

The second theory would similarly determine the existence of unavoidable grounds by evaluating the personal circumstances of the member, but would also take into account the overall circumstances surrounding the member in question. The second approach is broader than the first, and recognises a wider range of situations as unavoidable grounds. The leading case on the interpretation of 'unavoidable grounds' decided by the precursor to the modern Supreme Court for civil and criminal matters, the Great Court of Cassation (*Daishin'in*), lends support to the second approach. The case concerned withdrawal of four limited members from a limited partnership. Amongst other things, the sole unlimited member had died without a successor capable of running the business, the members sued each other over management and accounting disputes, the relationship between the members had broken down, and voluntary dissolution was impossible because of disagreement over the disposal of corporate assets. The court held that the

form (*shihō shoshi hōjin*) but it does not come with limited liability; see *Shihō shoshi-hō* [*Judicial Scriveners Act] (Act No 197 of 1950), Article 38.

151 *Shihō shoshi-hō*, Article 46(2).

152 A membership company may commence court proceedings to expel a member with a resolution of a majority of the members (excluding the member subject to the expulsion): *Kaishahō*, Article 859.

153 Tokyo High Court 24.02.2010, 591 Tōki Jōhō 125, 125–6.

154 Tokyo District Court 05.10.2009, 591 Tōki Jōhō 126, 128.

155 Writing in 2014, Shishido observes that, to his knowledge, there are no post-World War II cases interpreting 'unavoidable grounds': Shishido (2014c): 435 fn. 33.

156 This following discussion tracks the framework adopted in Koide (2014a): 221–3.

157 Ōsumi & Imai (1991): 95; Tokyo District Court 30.06.1925, cited in Koide (2014a): 221.

circumstances as a whole constituted unavoidable grounds for the purposes of withdrawal.[158]

Finally, there are also cases that are consistent with either of the two competing theories. In one such case, the company had its head office and operations entirely in the city of Osaka. A member's move from Osaka to Tokyo that prevented him from continuing his involvement in the company's affairs as a member was recognised as an unavoidable ground.[159]

Old doctrine and the few decided cases consistently demonstrate that the member's personal circumstances are at least highly relevant to the issue of whether 'unavoidable grounds' exist. There is, however, one problem: *Shōhō*-era jurisprudence is premised on organisational forms in which all members are natural persons, and with at least one member bearing unlimited liability. The situation has since changed.[160]

iii Modern Doctrine

Given that the *Kaishahō*, in contrast with the *Shōhō*, permits legal persons to be members, and provides for the GK form in which every member has full limited liability, old precedents and doctrine based on premises no longer valid may be of doubtful applicability to the current *Kaishahō* regime. Therefore, in light of legal changes and modern business practice, commentators have begun revisiting the concept of 'unavoidable grounds' in more recent writings.[161]

The modern commentator's concern is primarily with the extent to which 'unavoidable grounds' may be narrowed by contract; in other words, the concept's absolute mandatory minimum content. Influenced by the US experience with LLCs, multiple commentators have stressed the importance of contractual freedom in internal corporate ordering.[162] As a constraint on that freedom, the scope of unavoidable grounds is therefore of great concern and practical relevance.

Commentators appear to agree on a minimum core for the concept of 'unavoidable grounds'. At a bare minimum, severe conflict over corporate management resulting in deadlock and improper squeeze-out of members[163] must be recognised

158 Daishin'in [Great Court of Cassation] 01.06.1931, 3301 Hōritsu Shimbun 14, discussed at Koide (2014a): 222 and Wada (2012): 445. See also Tokyo District Court 29.08.1941 (limited member permitted to withdraw from a limited partnership in which trust between the members had broken down due to discord), discussed at Koide (2014a): 222 (arguing that this second case from the Tokyo District Court is more consistent with the second theory) and Wada (2012): 445.

159 Ōsaka Kōso'in [Osaka Court of Appeal] 20.12.1932, 3509 Hōritsu Shimbun 9, discussed at Koide (2014a): 222–3.

160 Koide (2014a): 223.

161 ibid.

162 Ōsugi (2004): 206–9; Shishido (2013): 220ff.

163 This ground is never elaborated upon in the literature on withdrawal.

as 'unavoidable grounds'.[164] Beyond this very narrow consensus on deadlock and squeeze-outs, the legal position remains uncertain as to the types of situations that fall within the scope of 'unavoidable grounds'. In contrast with the situation pre-*Kaishahō*, modern commentators seem to agree that the scope of 'unavoidable grounds' should take into consideration matters beyond the member's personal circumstances.[165] What is at dispute is whether such additional considerations narrow or broaden the scope of 'unavoidable grounds'.

In support of their position that the scope of 'unavoidable grounds' should be narrower in the GK context, commentators have made the following arguments: (1) personal circumstances of the members should not be recognised as 'unavoidable grounds', or at least have limited applicability; (2) negotiated agreement on withdrawal grounds and procedures should prevail over the 'unavoidable grounds' mechanism; and (3) withdrawal on unavoidable grounds should only be used as a last resort.

The first argument is a response to the limitations of pre-*Kaishahō* doctrine. Historically, some personal circumstances of the member desirous of withdrawal recognised under pre-*Kaishahō* jurisprudence or theories as unavoidable grounds are founded on one premise: the member in question is a natural person.[166] However, GK joint ventures are different from membership companies in the pre-*Kaishahō* era: they have or may have only legal persons as members,[167] and all members have limited liability.[168] The question arises: to what extent is pre-*Kaishahō* jurisprudence applicable to the GK joint venture context? In particular, Shishido and Ōsugi argue that since historical doctrine on members' personal circumstances is premised on members being natural persons, such doctrine should not apply to the modern GK joint venture, which does not share that premise.[169] Consequently, it follows that personal circumstances such as an urgent need for money therefore have limited relevance in a GK with members that are legal, not natural, persons.[170]

Although not without its attractions, this argument has its share of difficulties. The now-repealed Article 55 of the *Shōhō* did not bar all legal persons from becoming members in the incorporated unlimited partnership or limited partnership; it only barred *companies* (a species of legal person) from becoming members *with*

164 Shishido (2013): 235; Egashira et al. (2011): 17–18 (Statement by Ōsugi Ken'ichi). Both sources point out that the situations contemplated may also suffice as grounds for judicial dissolution (on unavoidable grounds).

165 See e.g. Egashira et al. (2011): 17 (Statement by Ōsugi Ken'ichi) (arguing that when determining if unavoidable grounds are present, not only should the circumstances of the member be considered, but also those of the company, which would after all be affected by the member's withdrawal).

166 See VII.D.3.i above.

167 Egashira et al. (2011): 17 (Statement by Ōsugi Ken'ichi).

168 Shishido (2013): 235.

169 Egashira et al. (2011):17 (Statement by Ōsugi Ken'ichi); Shishido (2013): 235 (also noting that under old law there had to be at least one member with unlimited liability).

170 Egashira et al (2011): 17 (Statement by Ōsugi Ken'ichi); Koide (2014a): 223.

unlimited liability.[171] As a starting point, circumstances that would permit a *limited* member to withdraw under old doctrine would still apply with equal force to current law, as it would not matter whether the member is a legal or natural person. Therefore, it is not entirely clear where Ōsugi's or Shishido's objection to the reception of old doctrine precisely lies. One possible explanation might be that personal circumstances applicable to natural person members such as illness or change of residence would not translate well to legal persons. Even so, financial hardship can be analogised to serious financial difficulties amounting to insolvency,[172] and other circumstances recognised in old jurisprudence such as change of residence and the corresponding loss of ability to contribute to the company[173] could be, in the corporate context, a change in real seat or state of incorporation. With a little creative thinking, therefore, the above doctrinal difficulty largely disappears.

Arguments such as those by Ōsugi and Shishido, therefore, require context; they only make sense if they are integrated into the broader idea that the *structure* of the company is relevant to the scope of unavoidable grounds for withdrawal.[174] The line between personal and corporate circumstances can be thin. Being the only common ground between the two competing schools of thought briefly described above, the unusual focus of historical Japanese jurisprudence on personal circumstances may be doctrinal baggage that continues to plague the modern scholar.[175] This baggage may have been what prompted commentators to use the language of 'personal' circumstances of the member rather than the circumstances of the company. So what they could have meant (or perhaps should have said) is simply this: for a highly negotiated, commercial relationship at arms' length – which correlates strongly with

171 *Shōhō*, Article 55 (repealed): 'Companies may not become members with unlimited liability of other companies'. While the precise technical classification of entities under Japanese civil, commercial, and corporate law is complex, a distinction was drawn between 'legal persons' (*hōjin*) in general and 'companies' (*kaisha*). The old *Shōhō* defined *kaisha* as '*shadan* ['association'] established with a motive towards profit' (repealed Article 52, Paragraph 1), and also as a species of *hōjin* (repealed Article 54, Paragraph 1).

172 Note that Article 607 includes, as statutory default grounds for member exit (but not withdrawal), the following: commencement of insolvency proceedings (but not the state of insolvency per se) of a member, whether a natural or legal person (Paragraph 1, Item 5); and dissolution for reasons other than through insolvency proceedings, applicable only to members that are legal persons (Paragraph 1, Item 6). These grounds, amongst others, may be excluded by the company: Article 607, Paragraph 2. See generally Koide (2014b): 234–6.

173 Ōsaka Kōso'in [Osaka Court of Appeal] 20.12.1932, 3509 Hōritsu Shimbun 9, discussed at Koide (2014a): 222–3.

174 Compare with IV.C.2.ii (Germany), V.C.4.iii.c. (UK), and VI.C.3.iv (US). Note, that apart from the few instances where the close corporation is a 'statutory close corporation', the US focuses more on contract and less with structure per se, although structure can and is often created by contractual or corporate-constitutional arrangements (an example of the latter being election as a statutory close corporation).

175 Problems caused by doctrinal baggage are not uncommon in Japanese corporate law; for another example of pre-*Kaishahō*, *Shōhō*-era debate casting shadows on matters of more contemporary import recently taken up in the English-language literature, see Koh (2014): 438–9 (on the interpretation of the concept of fair value in appraisal proceedings).

limited liability of the member and the likelihood of the member being a legal person – the scope for withdrawal is more limited than a personalistically structured, trust-based company comprising natural persons who may, under the old regime, have had unlimited liability. This (re-)interpretation is bolstered by the fact that Shishido, arguably the most prominent commentator on GKs, has primarily focused on a narrow subset of GKs: joint ventures.[176] Consequently, Shishido's position – that old doctrine (which most decidedly did not contemplate joint ventures) should not be followed – does have persuasive power, but primarily within the very specific and limited GK joint venture context.

In any event, Shishido concedes that the *default* position for companies without contrary provision by contract must be a broad withdrawal right that recognises a wide range of 'unavoidable grounds', as well as withdrawal at will. Given that the purpose of Article 606, Paragraph 3, a mandatory provision, is to safeguard the members' freedom to withdraw,[177] Shishido's concession is rightly made. A wide interpretation of 'unavoidable grounds' as a starting point would cohere better with legislative intention, and would cover most GKs not employed as joint venture vehicles.

Beyond the joint venture context, negotiated arrangements are of critical importance to the scope of unavoidable grounds. Tanahashi, writing as a practising attorney, stresses the importance of making ex ante contractual arrangements to govern member withdrawal as far as possible, including deferred payment terms that would enable the enterprise to continue operations in the immediate aftermath of a withdrawal. He recommends that such agreements provide that withdrawal should be a last resort applicable only where alternatives, including transfer to another member, are unavailable. If withdrawal by agreement is sought, the member must follow the relevant provisions governing withdrawal agreed to ex ante and contained in the corporate constitution. A member who fails to do so and instead invokes the statutory right of withdrawal under Article 606, Paragraph 3 should not be permitted to succeed on the basis that the 'unavoidable grounds' requirement is not satisfied.[178]

The final argument narrows 'unavoidable grounds' by placing an additional hurdle: withdrawal on this basis must be a last resort in the GK, so as to differentiate the newly introduced GK from the other two traditional membership companies. Citing the detriment to creditors that ensues from the GK paying the refund to the member upon withdrawal, Takahashi argues that the grounds for withdrawal from the GK should be more narrowly construed than for incorporated partnerships and limited partnerships. He further argues, drawing on the German experience with

176 In the background of Shishido's writings on GKs, there appears to be a strong concern with the extent to which joint ventures adopt the GK: see e.g. Shishido (2014c): 434 (pointing out the that the scope of the mandatory provision on withdrawal has implications for the extent to which the GK is adopted for joint ventures).

177 As Shishido would readily concede: Shishido (2014a): 15; see also Shishido (2014c): 435.

178 Tanahashi (2013): 644.

commercial partnerships and the GmbH, that withdrawal should be recognised only as a last resort in the absence of any other appropriate means of member protection.[179]

Takahashi's argument for reading into 'unavoidable grounds' an express 'last resort' requirement may seem consistent with heightened creditor protection concerns in the GK context. However, such a gloss is unnecessary considering the additional rules applicable only to the GK that already impose harsh and rigid limitations on the member's entitlement to a refund upon withdrawal.[180] Also, characterising withdrawal as a last resort fails to account for dissolution, which should logically be the true, if unsatisfactory, last resort.[181] As a line of inquiry, drawing fine distinctions between 'withdrawal on unavoidable grounds-last resort' and 'dissolution-last resort' hardly seems promising.

By contrast, voices against the movement to limit 'unavoidable grounds' in the GK are in the minority. One rare example is Kobayashi, who argues that, considering that the internal relationship between members is in substance one of partnership, the freedom to terminate the relationship should not be unduly narrowly construed.[182]

4 *Effect of Withdrawal*

A member who exercised the right to withdrawal at will ceases to be a member at the end of the fiscal year.[183] For withdrawal on unavoidable grounds, withdrawal takes effect immediately upon the member's communication of intent to withdraw to a representative member of the company.[184] With the termination of status as a member of a GK, any rights and obligations pertaining to membership or management of the GK as between the now ex-member and the GK are also dissolved[185] – save one. Article 611, Paragraph 1 provides that the withdrawn member is entitled to the 'refund' of their membership interest (*mochibun no haraimodoshi*). Note that despite the *functional* similarity between refund and buyout, the word for 'refund' (*haraimodoshi*) is specific to the membership company context,[186] and is not used

179 Takahashi (2012a): 7–8. Compare IV.C.2.iv (discussing the nature of withdrawal in Germany as the 'last resort').

180 I discuss these below in VII.D.6.

181 Takahashi's position makes sense provided one accepts the premise that dissolution, unlike withdrawal, does not protect members' interests, and is therefore not a true last resort. On dissolution see II.D.1.ii.

182 Kobayashi (2008): 97.

183 Implicit in Article 606, Paragraph 1.

184 Koide (2014a): 221.

185 The situation is different for the other two membership companies, where withdrawn members continue to be liable in some respects for a period of two years: Article 612, Paragraphs 1 and 2; Aizawa et al. (2006): 590 (explaining why Article 612 does not apply to ex-GK members).

186 The term only appears in the *Kaishahō* provisions governing membership companies, and not in the general or KK-specific provisions.

interchangeably with 'buyout' (*kaitori*) in Japanese legal language. Therefore, in this Chapter, I use the word 'refund' exclusively when writing in the Japanese membership company context.

Regardless of the form of the member's capital contribution, the member is entitled to a monetary refund.[187] As monetary sums are involved, next up is the subject of valuation.

5 *Valuation*

To calculate the refund quantum corresponding to the withdrawing member's membership interest, a valuation of the company must be performed.[188]

i Default Position

On the critical subject of valuation, the *Kaishahō* offers little concrete guidance. Article 611, Paragraph 2 provides:

> 'Accounting as between the member who has exited[189] and the membership company shall be conducted on the basis of the company's asset situation as at the time of exit.'

According to the legislative drafters, the valuation should be based on 'the mark-to-market valuation of the assets and liabilities of the company on a going concern basis, with future earnings and other factors taken into consideration'.[190] However, this short statement does not settle the longstanding debate in academic literature. The prevailing opinion favours valuing the company as a going concern.[191] A sub-strand of this takes the position that this should not be on a book value basis as in a profit and loss statement; rather, without undervaluing assets or overvaluing liabilities, revaluation of fixed assets (within appropriate boundaries) is permitted, as is the inclusion of intangibles.[192] More recently, support has emerged for an approach that disregards book value in favour of using, in principle, only discounted cash flow (DCF).[193]

In opposition to DCF, Shishido advocates for a default standard based on the 'hypothetical sale value of the business as a whole to a third party, not based on the presence of any particular set of management'.[194] His reasoning is as follows. If the parties

187 Article 611, Paragraph 3.

188 Article 611, Paragraph 1 read with Paragraph 2; Aizawa et al. (2006): 589.

189 I use 'exited' in lieu of 'withdrawn' because the original Japanese term *taisha* is broader than withdrawal as I define and use in this Chapter and the Book more generally. See (n. 137) above for terminological clarifications.

190 Aizawa et al. (2006): 589.

191 See Matsumoto (2014): 263 and references cited therein.

192 Matsumoto (2014): 263; Ōsumi & Imai (1991): 100–1 n. 2.

193 Summarised in Shishido (2014a): 13 and Matsumoto (2013): 263.

194 Shishido (2014c): 436. In earlier works, Shishido used the somewhat confusing terminology of 'liquidation value': Shishido (2013): 236; Shishido (2009): 188.

to a venture were to contract ex ante over the issue, neither party would, as the remaining party in the event of the other's exit, agree to pay the exiting party a refund based on a DCF valuation of the company. This is because a DCF valuation would be based on the remaining party's future human capital contribution to the company. A default standard based on DCF would have interfered with the parties' ex ante incentives to participate in the joint venture. Hence, a standard less favourable to the exiting party, such as the standard proposed by Shishido, should be adopted as the default.[195]

Again, it must be noted that Shishido's position is, as usual, premised on the GK joint venture context, and that he has articulated no clear opinion as to the appropriate valuation standards in non-joint venture GKs or the other two membership companies. A further flaw in Shishido's creative formulation is that it merely begs the question: on what basis would the hypothetical third party purchaser value the company in question? A meta-valuation standard such as Shishido's suggestion may have merits, but it would have to be carefully defined, and Shishido has not yet done so in his existing, popular works. Therefore, Shishido's proposed valuation standard should also be treated with caution in the GK joint venture context.

Judicial precedents are generally consistent with a going concern approach to valuation. The leading case,[196] which was decided by the Supreme Court in 1969, concerned not a company, but rather a cooperative enterprise regulated under a specific law on cooperatives[197] with a provision similar to the *Kaishahō*'s Article 611, Paragraph 2.[198] The Supreme Court held that

> In general, the valuation of the cooperative's assets, on which accounting of the exiting cooperative member's membership interest would be based, should not be performed based on the so-called book value that is used for purpose of calculating the cooperative's profit and loss. Instead, the valuation should be performed on the premise that (1) the cooperative would operate the business as a going concern, and (2) the business would be sold in its entirety on the most advantageous terms.[199]

195 Shishido (2014c): 435–6; Shishido (2013): 236 (arguing that since the 'liquidation value' measure is less generous than a going concern valuation, the former is more in line with the intentions of the businesses that are party to the [GK] joint venture, as the joint venture partners are likely to prefer restricting freedom of withdrawal at a stage where it is not clear which party is going to withdraw). Shishido also adds that his idiosyncratic formulation may in certain circumstances approximate more established valuation standards. For example, a company that would have stable cash flows regardless of who the management is would have a valuation similar to a DCF valuation, whereas a company that would suffer heavily in earnings if the existing management were replaced would have a valuation that would be the same as its net asset value: Shishido (2014c): 436.

196 Saikō Saibansho [Supreme Court] 11.12.1969, 23(12) Minshū 2447, also available at https://perma.cc/Q33D-9Y76.

197 Specifically, the *Chūshō Kigyō-tō Kyōdō Kumiai Hō* [*Small and Medium-Sized Enterprise Cooperatives Act], Act No 181 of 1 June 1949. There is no consolidated cooperatives legislation as such, and different types of cooperatives have their own governing laws. For an overview of cooperative laws in Japan, see Kurimoto (2013).

198 Chūshō Kigyō-tō Kyōdō Kumiai Hō, Article 20, Paragraph 2.

199 Supreme Court 11.12.1969, 1–2 (cited to https://perma.cc/Q33D-9Y76) (numbering added for clarity). See also Matsumoto (2014): 264 for analysis of the decision.

Subsequent reported decisions in the lower courts from the 1980s have generally followed the Supreme Court's lead.[200]

The going concern approach generally adopted by the courts should not be conflated with DCF valuation.[201] At this juncture, it is helpful to recall that Japan experienced an economic bubble which resulted in extremely high land prices especially towards the end of the 1980s.[202] Inflated land prices played an important role in the reported cases, as the main point of dispute was over the valuation of land forming part of the assets of the cooperative or company.[203] Without exception, the net asset value of the entity in question was greater than its DCF valuation.[204] In fact, in one exceptional case from 1995, to avoid an asset bubble-influenced valuation that was disproportionately large compared to the company's earnings, the Tokyo District Court adopted a weighted average of the DCF and net asset value figures.[205]

Taking the historical context into consideration, Shishido argues that the going concern approach laid down in the 1969 Supreme Court decision should not be construed as a general requirement for DCF valuation; instead, the valuation can be on either DCF or net asset value basis, whichever is the higher. Further, he posits that when performing valuation on the net asset value basis, it should be based on the market value of the business sold as a whole and on the most advantageous terms possible, and not the book value or liquidation value.[206]

ii Provision in Corporate Constitution

Opinion is divided on whether Article 611, Paragraph 2 is a mandatory provision, and if so, the scope of mandatory regulation. The legislative drafters appear to contradict themselves on this point. On one hand, they take the position that the *Kaishahō*'s provisions on membership companies are generally mandatory unless the Act itself expressly permits deviation by provision in the corporate constitution.[207] Yet on the other, the drafters also appear to accept without elaboration that where the company has included provisions on valuation in the corporate constitution those provisions should be followed[208] – despite the absence of any *Kaishahō* provision within Article 611 permitting deviation. Academic commentators have also expressed uncertainty

200 Kōbe Chihō Saibansho [Kobe District Court] 29.08.1986, 1222 Hanrei Jihō 135; Nagoya Chihō Saibansho [Nagoya District Court] 29.09.1987, 1264 Hanrei Jihō 128. Both were commercial partnership (*gōmei kaisha*) cases.

201 Shishido (2014a): 14.

202 See Cutts (1990): 168–9 (describing the impact of inflated land values on corporations).

203 Shishido (2014c): 428 fn. 3.

204 Shishido (2014a): 14.

205 Tokyo District Court 27.04.1995, 1541 Hanrei Jihō 130 (weighting DCF and net asset value 6:4).

206 Shishido (2014c): 428 fn. 3. Indeed, in its 1969 judgment the Supreme Court held that the lower court did not err in valuing the land at issue on a market value basis rather than book value: Supreme Court 11.12.1969, 2 (cited to https://perma.cc/Q33D-9Y76).

207 Aizawa et al. (2006): 563.

208 ibid. 590.

on the subject,[209] although Shishido stands firm in his position that Article 611 is a default that may be modified by the constitution.[210]

Amidst this uncertainty and the absence of any definitive case precedent, most commentators have been content to proceed on the assumption that the company may specify a valuation mechanism in its constitution. From a practical standpoint, the important questions are whether there are limits to the company's freedom to do so, and the content of those limits, if any. A strand of pre-*Kaishahō* doctrine suggests that the company's discretion is unfettered in this respect, and even a constitutional provision specifying that an exited member should receive no refund would be enforceable.[211]

Countering this is another doctrinal strand arguing that extreme provisions in a corporate constitution, such as those denying outright or severely restricting the exiting member's refund, may be at odds with the fundamental for-profit nature of the membership company. In particular, constitutional provisions denying refunds outright may, on this basis, be invalid.[212] In similar vein, Ōsugi raises the possibility that, without at least some minimum level of justification by the company, a constitutional provision denying refunds outright may be struck down as against public order and good morals.[213]

Although the arguments based on the for-profit nature of companies and on general civil code provisions have their theoretical attractions, I prefer an approach that is not only practical, but also based on a holistic reading of the *Kaishahō*. My position on the valuation issue is that the enforceability of any valuation mechanism depends on its impact on Article 606, Paragraph 3, which provides that members may withdraw on unavoidable grounds at any time. Notwithstanding uncertainty over whether Article 611, Paragraph 2 is mandatory, it is clear that withdrawal on unavoidable grounds is mandatory.[214] Any valuation mechanism specified in the corporate constitution that functionally interferes with the member's statutorily protected right to withdraw on unavoidable grounds should be deemed invalid. To strike the appropriate balance between the interests of the parties to order their affairs ex ante via the corporate constitution and the legally protected withdrawal rights of members, valuation mechanisms deviating substantially from any of the established valuation bases (going concern value based on discounted cash flow, liquidation value, etc.) should be subject to review on a

[209] Egashira et al. (2011):18 (Statements by Egashira Kenjirō (expressing doubt); Ōsugi Ken'ichi (arguing that Article 611, Paragraph 2 is a default rule but conceding the plausibility of an alternative interpretation) and Niinomi Hiroshi (acknowledging the possibility that the provision is a mandatory rule and also hinting at tax implications)).

[210] Shishido (2013): 238 fn. 54 (arguing that an interpretation of Article 611 as a mandatory rule would be at odds with the general legislative intent to reserve to the parties the broadest possible contractual freedom).

[211] Matsumoto (2014): 264.

[212] ibid. 265.

[213] Ōsugi (2013): 79.

[214] See (n. 148) above and text thereto.

reasonableness basis.[215] As a matter of prudence, the parties should be slow to deviate from established valuation practices in the absence of compelling reasons.[216]

6 *Enforcement*

Enforcement of the withdrawn member's claim to the refund is fraught with difficulties in the GK. The only party against whom the refund claim can be enforced is the company, not any of its (remaining) members.[217] Unlike the other two membership company forms featuring at least one member with unlimited liability, creditor protection is given special consideration in the GK.[218] The involvement of creditor interests has real consequences for the withdrawn member: the withdrawn member's ability to legally enforce their claim to a refund depends on the refund quantum. Let us look at the three possible situations in turn.

Situation one is where the refund quantum is less than the 'distributable surplus' (*jōyokin-gaku*). The *Kaisha Keisan Kisoku* (Regulation on Corporate Accounting) defines the distributable surplus for the purpose of withdrawal from the GK as the sum of capital surplus (*shihon jōyokin*) and retained earnings (*rieki jōyokin*).[219] In this situation, from the creditors' perspective, the GK's payment of a refund is functionally no different from an ordinary distribution; therefore, no special creditor proceedings are necessary.[220]

Situation two is where the refund quantum lies between the distributable surplus and the company's net asset book value (*boka junshisan*). Functionally speaking, to convert situation two into situation one such that creditors are not prejudiced, what the company needs to do is to increase the distributable surplus such that it equals or exceeds the refund quantum. It can do so by undergoing a capital reduction procedure that increases the capital surplus component of the distributable surplus. While the company is not required to actually execute a capital reduction under

215 Compare the approach taken by the German courts: see IV.C.4.ii.

216 My suggested approach finds support in the balanced and cautious approach of Tanahashi, a practising attorney. He advocates that, in the interests of certainty, parties should agree on either the quantum or valuation mechanism of the refund and reflect their agreement in the corporate constitution. Albeit without citing Article 606, Paragraph 3, he also implied that a constitutional provision that has the effect of making withdrawal on unavoidable grounds difficult in reality – such as one that sets the refund quantum extremely low – might not be enforceable. See Tanahashi (2013): 645.

217 This is implicit; there is nothing in the literature that even suggests that any person other than the company may – or should – be liable to pay the refund. There is also a functional similarity between stock repurchases by a KK and the payment of a refund of a withdrawn member's membership interest by a membership company: Kōriya & Hosokawa (2006): 165. This further supports the position that only the company is liable to the withdrawn member in respect of the refund.

218 Aizawa & Kōriya (2006b): 164–5.

219 *Kaisha Keisan Kisoku* [*Regulation on Corporate Accounting], Ministry of Justice Order No 13 of 7 February 2006, as amended and in force as of 15 October 2018, Article 164, Item 3 (ho).

220 Aizawa & Kōriya (2006b): 165.

Article 627 to pay the refund, a functionally similar procedure is required under Article 635.[221] The company must provide information on the refund that is in excess of distributable surplus, and inform creditors of their right to object[222] and that such right may be exercised within a certain period that may not be less than one month.[223] Where a creditor objects within the specified period, unless there is no risk of harm to the creditor's interests, the company must either satisfy the debt, furnish appropriate security, or deposit into escrow appropriate sums for the purpose of satisfying the debt.[224]

In situation three, the refund quantum exceeds the company's net asset book value. This can occur if the company's net present value, based on mark-to-market valuation of corporate assets, goodwill, and future earnings, is greater than its net asset book value.[225] From the creditors' perspective, however, there is no way to ascertain the accuracy of the valuation or whether the refund is a fraudulent distribution.[226] To address these concerns, in situation three a procedure resembling that applying in liquidation is required by the *Kaishahō*. There are key differences from the procedure applicable in situation two. First is the minimum period for creditor objections: in situation three it must not be less than two months (compared to one month for situation two).[227] Second, if a creditor raises an objection, the company must without exception satisfy the claim or furnish appropriate security.[228] The situation three procedure is therefore stricter than that for situation two.[229]

The consequences for failure to follow the necessary creditor protection procedures are severe. The executive member responsible for paying the refund in violation of the legal requirements and the member who received the refund are jointly and severally (*rentai*) liable in unjust enrichment to the GK for a sum equivalent to the refund.[230] However, responsible executive members may avoid or limit liability in two ways. First, they may invoke an affirmative, complete defence to liability by

221 This explanation is an expansion and clarification of the legislative drafters' extremely terse explanation. See Aizawa & Kōriya (2006b): 165.

222 Article 635, Paragraph 1 (creditors have the right to object to the payment of a refund in excess of distributable surplus).

223 Article 635, Paragraph 2. By default, the companies must publish the information in the Official Gazette, and notify known creditors individually: Article 635, Paragraph 2. However, by provision in the corporate constitution, the company may specify publication in a daily newspaper or electronic notification as alternatives to publication in the Official Gazette: Article 939, Paragraph 1. If the company provides, in addition to publication in the Official Gazette, for either of the two alternative notification methods, individual creditor notification is not necessary: Article 635, Paragraph 3.

224 Article 635, Paragraph 5 read with the Proviso.

225 Aizawa & Kōriya (2006b): 165.

226 Aizawa et al. (2006): 603.

227 Article 635, Paragraph 2.

228 Article 635, Paragraph 5.

229 A further difference is that regardless of any alternative notification methods that may be specified in the corporate constitution, the requirement that known creditors be individually notified applies without exception. Article 635, Paragraph 3 read with the Proviso and Paragraph 2.

230 Article 636, Paragraph 1; Aizawa et al. (2006): 604 (citing Article 703 of the Civil Code, which is the provision forming the basis for unjust enrichment liability).

proving that they did not act negligently in paying the refund.[231] Second, the responsible executive member's liability may also be limited, by unanimous consent of the members, to a sum not less than the difference between the refund quantum and the GK's distributable surplus.[232] The liability of the withdrawn member receiving the refund may also be waived by the company in accordance with civil law principles.[233]

Given that the withdrawn member may only lawfully receive the refund in situations two and three provided the necessary creditor protection procedures are followed, what remedy does the withdrawn member have if the company – or more realistically, the executive member(s) of the company – refuses to perform the required procedures? The legislative drafters suggest that the ex-member bring suit for judicial dissolution in this situation.[234] Not only is the drafters' suggestion at odds with the Japanese cultural preference for the maintenance of the enterprise,[235] it also ignores the problem that the ex-member may very well simply have no legal standing to bring a dissolution action.[236] In practice, therefore, as a leading commentator has observed, the only feasible solution for a member desirous of exit would be to forgo withdrawal and to bring a dissolution action directly.[237] It is difficult to escape the impression that withdrawal from the GK is either intentionally or negligently hamstrung from the outset by rigid creditor protection rules that severely diminish the member's likelihood of enforcing what is ultimately a *legal* entitlement to a refund against the company.

E THE FUTURE OF *GŌDŌ KAISHA* AND WITHDRAWAL: A BRAVE NEW WORLD?

1 *The GK's Growing Popularity and Legal Significance*

Member's withdrawal may be a legal institution that applies to the three types of membership companies in general, including two legacy corporate forms under which much of the existing doctrine and all the jurisprudence were developed. Going forward and on a practical level, however, subject to yet another major

231 Article 636, Proviso to Paragraph 1.

232 Article 636, Proviso to Paragraph 2.

233 Aizawa et al (2006): 604 (also cautioning that executive members responsible for waiving the liability of withdrawn members might themselves be liable under Article 597). Article 597 provides that executive members acted with knowledge or gross negligence in the discharge of their duties are directly liable for any loss suffered by the third parties. In this context, the third parties would be the company's creditors.

234 Aizawa & Kōriya (2006b): 165. In context, the drafters appear to refer only to situation three, but given that situations two and three both involve procedures that must and can only be performed by the company but not the withdrawing member, the point applies just as well to situation two.

235 Wada (2012): 443.

236 Egashira (2011): 253 fn. 23.

237 ibid.

legislative reform to the KK introducing withdrawal remedies,[238] withdrawal's importance to Japanese corporate law is entirely dependent on the GK's popularity as a corporate form. The critical question is: what are the GK's prospects?

It is true that the GK has not lived up to the high hopes surrounding its birth. Subject to corporation tax and denied the pass-through tax advantages that were a key motivation behind the GK's US LLC-inspired design, the GK's greatest merit as originally conceived never materialised.[239] As a legal transplant of the US LLC, the GK has not exactly been a raging success[240] – if even a bona fide transplant at all. Ten years on, the GK remains something of a novelty to the Japanese people[241] and at a disadvantage in terms of brand name recognition compared to the KK.[242] Website articles by legal, accounting, and tax professionals targeted at people interested in incorporating companies point out differences between the KK and GK that might seem banal to the uninitiated outsider, but which are of a practical nature and carry weight in the Japanese business context, right down to the titles that may be used by business owners on their business cards. Those who prize the time-honoured and universally recognised 'representative director' (*daihyō torishimariyaku*) title have no choice but to use a KK, whereas those who would be satisfied with 'representative member' (*daihyō sha'in*) may find the GK adequate.[243] Due to a linguistic quirk, however, representative members run the risk of being mistaken as mere company employees – the Japanese word for member (*sha'in*) in the non-legal context nearly always means 'company employee'. The perceived gap in status between the 'high-ranking' KK representative director and the 'mere employee' GK representative member should not be underestimated in Japan's status-conscious society. However, there are exceptions to the GK's branding weaknesses; the importance of choice of corporate form to the business' brand value varies by industry.[244]

238 Despite some academic interest within Japan for introducing withdrawal remedies modelled on foreign regimes (for a proposal drawing inspiration from UK and Canadian law, see Hirota (2013): 465–7), it is unlikely to make its way into the legislative agenda, and almost certainly not soon after the last major revamp of 2014.

239 Sekiguchi & Nishigaki (2008): 18–19.

240 The appropriate standard by which the 'success' of a legal transplant is judged is an issue of some difficulty. As two renowned commentators put it (Kanda & Milhaupt (2003): 890): 'we take success to mean simply use of the imported legal rule in the same way that it is used in the home country, subject to adaptations to local conditions. Conversely, failure occurs when the imported rule is ignored by relevant actors in the host country, or the application and enforcement of the rule lead to unintended consequences'.

The GK has by this narrow standard arguably 'failed', as it plays a relatively minor role in Japan and has been deprived from its inception of pass through taxation advantages that are an integral component of the LLC and its success in the US.

241 Setsuyaku-Shachō (2015).

242 Uchida (2016).

243 See e.g. Subaru-Juku (2015).

244 freee (2013) (listing the respective merits of setting up GKs in the care, construction, food and beverage, aesthetics and beauty, property leasing, IT, consulting, and foreign exchange investment industries).

Despite obstacles and teething troubles, the tide appears to be turning in favour of the GK. Since the GK became available in 2006,[245] incorporation numbers have risen steadily, according to business registration records from the Ministry of Justice. The figures with separate breakdowns for new incorporations and incorporations via mergers or entity conversions are as follows:

The doubling of new incorporations over the 2012–15 period suggests that the GK might finally be coming into its own as a recognised, viable corporate form. By comparison, KK incorporations (new and by merger or entity conversion) never regained their post-*Kaishahō* peak at 114,928 in 2007; from 2009 to 2019 they have fluctuated between 85,000 and 95,000 each year.[246] Although the GK is likely to continue playing catch-up to the KK for the foreseeable future, the narrowing gap augurs well for the GK.

As GKs become an increasingly valued part of the economic landscape of the world's third-largest economy, growth in their broader significance to Japanese and comparative corporate law will follow. This applies to withdrawal. As GK businesses

TABLE 7.1 *Growth of GKs 2006–19*

Year	New Incorporations	Mergers & Conversions	Total[1]
2006[2]	3,392	58	3,450
2007	6,076	110	6,186
2008	5,413	90	5,503
2009	5,771	109	5,880
2010	7,153	114	7,267
2011	9,130	115	9,245
2012	10,889	138	11,027
2013	14,581	144	14,725
2014	19,808	158	19,966
2015	22,223	158	22,381
2016	23,787	148	23,935
2017	27,270	160	27,430
2018	29,076	159	29,235
2019	30,566	155	30,721

Source: Business Registration Statistics, Ministry of Justice (as of 29 May 2020).[247]
Note 1: Computed from the Business Registration Statistics.
Note 2: As the *Kaishahō* went into force only on 1 May 2006, the figures for 2006 do not capture a full typical year.

245 The *Kaishahō* went into force on 1 May 2006.

246 Sōmu-shō (2016, 2020): tbls. 19-00-16, 15-00-16.

247 Sōmu-shō (2016, 2020): tbls. 19-00-20, 15-00-20. Not included in these figures are incorporations by company splits, which range from 1 to 12 cases per year. ibid.

gradually increase, it is likely that incidents of members withdrawing will correspondingly arise. The salience of the withdrawal regime to GKs will also grow correspondingly as more withdrawal cases will appear in court and in the law reports, providing valuable raw material for scholars and commentators to chew on. It is possible that the weaknesses of the GK's withdrawal regime, particularly in enforcement, may impede the regime's legal development. On the other hand, there is hope that attorneys and judges would devise creative solutions that would address these difficulties, although preferably of a less problematic variety than that which evolved as a response to the absence of withdrawal in KKs and YKs.[248] Scholars and practitioners working on close corporations may find future developments in Japan to be enlightening.

2 *Influence of Foreign Law and Scholarship*

As it stands, the bulk of scholarship on the GK draws on the body of literature inherited from the pre-*Kaishahō* era.[249] However, what little influence there is from foreign law appears to be primarily American. Two of the most prominent key players, Shishido Zen'ichi and Ōsugi Ken'ichi, draw predominantly on US LLC law and literature to the exclusion of every other foreign law.[250] By contrast, save for Takahashi Eiji, the German influence appears to be on the wane.[251] In light of the clear US influence on the GK at least as it was originally conceived, and the abolishment of the German GmbH-inspired YK, it may be unsurprising that the German-inspired scholarship in this area has been eclipsed by its US-inspired counterpart.

Be that as it may, this is an unfortunate development. With no significant body of new cases under the *Kaishahō* regime immediately at hand, it is more important than ever for scholars and commentators to draw on foreign law for insight. Yet those sources are becoming increasingly impoverished. Notwithstanding the efforts of a vocal minority in keeping German corporate law scholarship alive in Japan, the wealth of experience and knowledge on the GmbH – and for our purposes, its withdrawal regime – may very well be forgotten. No quantity, no matter how high

[248] As detailed above at VII.B.2.i.

[249] This is especially true for the law on withdrawal: see e.g. Shishido (2014a): 13–14.

[250] For examples, see Shishido (2014a): 18–19 (citing German law only for historical context and to show the irrelevance of the GmbH & Co KG model to Japanese practice); Shishido (2014c) (citing US law exclusively); Ōsugi (2004): 212 n. 12 (mentioning the UK LLP only once and tangentially). Egashira Kenjirō, the driving force behind the *Kaishahō*, does the same: Egashira (2011) (citing only US sources for foreign law except one tangential reference to a Japanese source on a point of German law not relevant to GKs or membership companies as such).

[251] Takahashi Eiji is one of the few scholars who continue to draw inspiration from German law when writing on the GK; see also Masuda & Urakawa (2010). Even then, there is no direct exchange of ideas between Japanese and German corporate law: Takahashi (2015) (observing that Japanese and German corporate law are 'converging' in terms of substantive content due to influence from US law). See further Takahashi (2016).

quality, of scholarship drawing exclusively on the US, if any foreign jurisdiction at all, can overcome the limitations inherent in the monoculture of scholarly ideas. It is time for other perspectives – including, but not limited to, Germany, and perhaps the UK – to be introduced into the Japanese mainstream discourse on the GK.

3 *The Battle for the Soul of the GK*

Ultimately, one thing remains unclear: for whom is the GK? Insofar as scholars are concerned, the target 'consumer' for the GK form is surprisingly narrow. Spearheaded by Shishido, a joint ventures specialist with an international scholarly presence, academic attention is overwhelmingly directed to the use of the GK as a corporate joint venture vehicle – and the encouragement thereof.[252] By comparison, scant academic attention is dedicated to GKs as a general SME vehicle, and even less to the other two membership company forms.[253] It would be a pity for observers to be misled into typecasting the GK solely as a vehicle for joint ventures with bespoke contractual arrangements when the GK's growing popularity cannot be completely attributed to use in corporate joint ventures.[254] The GK's untapped potential as the YK's functional successor, or even as a worthy competitor to the KK, should not be underestimated.

Just as there is no reason to limit the GK to joint ventures, discourse on the withdrawal regime should not be dictated by joint venture advocates. Withdrawal law must be sensitive to different sets of needs by different types of GK users. Going forward, in developing the law of withdrawal on 'unavoidable grounds' for the GK, one should be slow to overgeneralise arguments that apply best, or even exclusively to GK joint ventures.[255] Instead, care must be taken to contextualise those arguments. As argued above,[256] the scope of unavoidable grounds for GKs *in general* should be broader than just deadlock or improper squeeze-outs. How withdrawal fits into other contexts in which the GK's potential may be usefully harnessed, such as

[252] In his Japanese works, Shishido focuses heavily on GK joint ventures. See e.g. Shishido (2014c): 439–40 (concluding the chapter with a discussion of the impact of withdrawal on joint ventures); Shishido (2013) (the title says it all); Shishido (2014a): 24 ('By all rights, it is as the vehicle for joint undertakings such as corporate joint ventures that is GK is most suited for'). For a (rarer) example of a work on GKs more generally and in English, see Shishido (2015).

[253] Although Koide does not confine his commentary to GK joint ventures as such, he frequently relies on Ōsugi and Shishido, whose arguments are almost always based on the joint venture premise. See Koide (2014a): 223–4. To the best of my knowledge, except Shishido (2015), there is no English language source purporting to be a general introduction to GKs (or membership companies more generally) that is anything more than extremely cursory.

[254] Registration statistics offer no detailed breakdowns, but it is highly unlikely that the growth in joint ventures is quite as dramatic as the growth in GK numbers.

[255] Most notably, those by Shishido and Ōsugi on the minimum scope of 'unavoidable grounds'; see VII. D.3.ii.

[256] At the end of VII.D.3.ii.

the less trendy – but no less economically and legally significant – SME sector, is a subject worthy of further research.

F CONCLUSION

Japan's close corporation landscape was and still is complicated by co-existence of multiple corporate forms. While KKs – including former YKs – still dominate in absolute numbers, the new GK is on the ascendant. Among other differences, the GK is, at least one paper, the only viable Japanese close corporation form with a member's withdrawal regime.

Japan is not without its problems, especially regarding the withdrawn member's ability to enforce their entitlement to refund of their membership interest. Driven primarily by advocates and specialists in joint venture law, contemporary discourse on the withdrawal regime, whether on the scope of 'unavoidable grounds' or on valuation standards, is dominated by the debate on whether the *Kaishahō* provisions are default or mandatory, and if default, the extent to which they may be modified by the corporate constitution. With only limited jurisprudence of considerable vintage and no post-*Kaishahō* judicial precedent, little is settled. Lack of attention to the use of GKs and its withdrawal regime in non-joint venture contexts further hampers understanding and development of the law.

Whether and how much the GK's popularity and importance would be impeded by the current legal uncertainty is an open question, although recent growth trends give reason for optimism. The story of withdrawal in the GK illuminates the many pitfalls one may encounter while developing a viable withdrawal remedy for close corporations.

PART 3

Application

VIII

A Model Withdrawal Remedy

A INTRODUCTION

This Chapter sets out a model instrument ('Model Remedy') that builds on the conceptual framework in Chapter II and integrates the findings from the comparative analysis of target jurisdiction withdrawal regimes in Chapter III. Specifically, the Model Remedy strikes a balance between mandatory and default norms in withdrawal design and implements both the corrective and insurance models of withdrawal.

The Model Remedy applies the findings of this Book in a non-jurisdiction-specific setting and, as such, may be useful to various audiences. First, corporate law scholars should find the Model Remedy to be an elaborate but structured and clear framework that organises issues arising in the resolution of shareholder conflict by withdrawal, and which offers a set of answers *de lege ferenda*. Regardless of whether one agrees with the positions I have taken, my goal is to make it easier for scholars to articulate clearly what precisely it is they are arguing about.

For law reformers, the Model Remedy is drafted as a generalised model for jurisdictions across the common/civil law divide. Substantial adaptation of the Model Remedy would be required to fit the legal terminology and pre-existing written law and doctrinal frameworks of implementing jurisdictions.

For litigators and judges, the Model Remedy offers near-comprehensive coverage of practical issues arising in withdrawal. It may serve as a checklist that guides litigators and judges in resolving issues, especially novel ones, as they arise. It is also possible for a court to adopt the Model Remedy in whole or part as a judicial decision-making framework.

The contract-like style of the Model Remedy may be helpful as a checklist to transactional lawyers planning exit mechanisms. The Model Remedy's core – open-textured 'fault' and 'non-fault' grounds – would likely call for decision by a third-party arbiter. Depending on the prevailing contract drafting philosophy,[1] the Model Remedy may or may not be a good fit. Even then, it may serve as

[1] For example, in a common law setting where exit mechanisms are rarely based on 'fault' type considerations, the heavy reliance placed on 'fault' and 'non-fault' grounds – which are standards rather than rules – might be less comfortable to lawyers.

a compromise alternative in non-common law jurisdictions, or in situations where neither rule-based exit mechanisms nor leaving matters entirely to extra-contractual regulation would be acceptable to the parties.

VIII.B sets out the Model Remedy's three guiding principles. VIII.C contains the Model Remedy text. In VIII.D, I provide commentary on selected individual provisions of the Model Remedy. VIII.E closes.

B GUIDING PRINCIPLES

Finality. Withdrawal must be the *solution*, not the *cause* of further problems. Shareholder conflict so serious that a minority shareholder would decide to call it quits with the close corporation entirely must be ended, not prolonged, by corporate law. Withdrawal under the Model Remedy is therefore a right of any shareholder satisfying prescribed requirements as to standing.[2] The member seeking withdrawal does not need to 'justify' to the court that withdrawal relief is (the most) appropriate in the circumstances, nor does the court have discretion over whether to grant or withhold relief. Withdrawal is as of right so long as the member can plead facts falling within the various grounds and bases for withdrawal. Conversely, it is the other parties (i.e. those who oppose withdrawal) who must justify why withdrawal should be denied and why this would be fair to the member desiring withdrawal. This principle undergirds the Provisions on enforcement proceedings and challenges against withdrawal.[3]

Structured flexibility. To cater to a wide range of close corporations with different needs and goals, the Model Remedy combines not only 'simple' default and mandatory provisions,[4] but also 'sticky defaults'. Sticky defaults facilitate deliberate, informed customisation[5] by parties who need something different from what the Model Remedy offers – provided that 'enhanced requirements' governing how parties may contract around the Model Remedy default are satisfied.[6]

Comprehensive functionality. Withdrawal in the target jurisdictions may be classified into two ideal-types: corrective and insurance models of withdrawal.[7] A synthesis[8] of both models, the Model Remedy offers comprehensive protection for minority shareholders from the predictable vicissitudes of close corporation life. Both fault and non-fault grounds[9] give rise to withdrawal rights which are enforceable against different liable parties.[10] The election-to-purchase mechanism by which any other member may

2 This follows the German and Japanese withdrawal regimes.
3 VIII.D.3, especially VIII.D.3.iv.
4 VIII.D.3.ii.
5 See II.E.3.i, II.E.3.iii, II.E.4.i.
6 VIII.D.7.iii.
7 III.G.3.i–ii.
8 III.G.3.iii.
9 VIII.D.3.i–ii.
10 VIII.D.4.

voluntarily opt to buy the withdrawing member out (i.e. pay the monetary claim in exchange for acquiring the equity)[11] further strengthens the withdrawal regime's minority protection function.

C THE MODEL REMEDY

The Model Remedy is structured as one Part comprising thirty-six Provisions. Jurisdiction-neutral terminology – which may be unfamiliar to many readers – are marked on first mention with asterisks (*); alternative terminology more familiar to some jurisdictions or further explanations are provided in the footnotes. Some Provisions are italicised to indicate their purely procedural nature; these are not critical to the exposition below and are included mainly for structural completeness.

Definitions and Interpretation

§ 1 In this Part,[12]

'agreement' means any *corporate constitution, contract, agreement, or understanding, whether written or unwritten, formal or informal.

'*close corporation' means either

(i) a *recognised close corporation form[13]; or
(ii) a *limited liability entity[14] offering limited liability for all *members[15] that is not traded on a *securities market or over-the-counter

that is *organised[16] under the laws of this *Jurisdiction.[17]

'*complainant' means any member who:

(i) owns 50 per cent or less of the close corporation's issued *equity;[18] or
(ii) owns more than 50 per cent of the close corporation's issued equity and controls 50 per cent of the voting rights or less; or
(iii) has no voting rights.

'controller' means any person who exercises de jure or de facto control over the affairs of the close corporation.'court' means any court properly seized of jurisdiction or, except where inconsistent with other law, any arbitral tribunal impanelled according to law or a valid arbitration agreement.'

11 VIII.D.4.iv.
12 Article/Section/Chapter/*Abschnitt/setsu* etc.
13 GmbH/Ltd/statutory close corporation/ LLC/GK etc.
14 Corporation/KK/AG/plc etc.
15 *Gesellschafter/Aktionär*/shareholder/stockholder/member/*sha'in/kabunushi* etc.
16 To cover both incorporations (of corporations) and formations/filings of entities not universally considered to be corporations (uncorporations etc).
17 Country/State/Territory etc.
18 Shares/stock/membership interest etc.

*respondent' means the close corporation or any member, director, or controller that is a liable party under § 9 against whom the complainant commences enforcement proceedings under § 13.

Scope of Application

§ 2 This Part applies to any close corporation.

Withdrawal Grounds: At Will, Fault, Non-Fault

§ 3 The complainant may *withdraw from the close corporation:

(i) if one or more grounds specified in § 4 are established; or
(ii) at will.

§ 4 Grounds for withdrawal exist:

(i) on a fault basis, if, in respect of the affairs of the close corporation,
  (a) an act, omission, or course of conduct by one or more directors, members, or controllers was, is, or is likely to be:
    (A) illegal or fraudulent, or wrongful to the close corporation or one or more members (including the complainant); or
    (B) unfairly prejudicial to one or more members (including the complainant)

and was, is, or will be performed intentionally or in bad faith; or

  (b) an act, omission, or course of conduct by one or more directors, members, or controllers was, is, or is likely to be:
    (A) illegal, or wrongful to the close corporation or one or more members (including the complainant); or
    (B) unfairly prejudicial to one or more members (including the complainant); or
(ii) on a non-fault basis, if
  (a) the directors or members are deadlocked on the management, supervision, or administration of the close corporation and there is no reasonable prospect that the situation would change within a reasonable time;
  (b) there is an irretrievable loss of trust and confidence between the complainant and any director or other member;
  (c) the original circumstances under which the complainant consented to acquiring or maintaining status as a member in the close corporation have changed substantially and there is no reasonable prospect that the original circumstances would be restored within a reasonable time; or

(d) it is otherwise unreasonable to expect the complainant to remain as a member of the close corporation.

Withdrawal Procedure

§ 5 The complainant must serve a notice of intent to withdraw in writing, stating:

(i) *in the case of withdrawal on fault grounds under § 4(i), the ground or grounds of withdrawal, the one or more directors, members, or controllers whose one or more acts or omissions or course of conduct form the basis of the ground or grounds of withdrawal, and brief supporting facts that are within the knowledge of the complainant;*
(ii) *in the case of withdrawal on non-fault grounds under § 4(ii), the ground or grounds of withdrawal and brief supporting facts that are within the knowledge of the complainant; or*
(iii) *in the case of withdrawal at will under § 3(ii), that the withdrawal is at will.*

§ 6 The notice of intent must be served:

(i) *in the case of withdrawal on fault grounds under § 4(i), on the close corporation at its registered office or principal place of business and every director, member, or controller whose one or more acts or omissions or course of conduct form the basis of the ground or grounds of withdrawal;*
(ii) *in the case of withdrawal on non-fault grounds under § 4(ii), on the close corporation at its registered office or principal place of business; or*
(iii) *in the case of withdrawal at will under § 3(ii), on the close corporation at its registered office or principal place of business.*

Effect of Withdrawal

§ 7 Withdrawal becomes effective:

(i) in the case of withdrawal on fault grounds under § 4(i), immediately upon receipt by the close corporation or any director, member, or controller on whom service is required under § 6(i), whichever is earliest;
(ii) in the case of withdrawal on non-fault grounds under § 4(ii), one month from the close corporation's receipt of the notice of intent;
(iii) in the case of withdrawal at will under § 3(ii), three months from the close corporation's receipt of the notice of intent; and
(iv) in the case where more than one period of time under (i) to (iii) above apply, when the longest applicable period has elapsed.

§ 8 When withdrawal becomes effective, the complainant:

(i) except as provided in (ii) below, ceases to have the status, rights, powers, or duties in their capacity as a member, director, or in any other related capacity as against the close corporation or any other member, director, or controller;
(ii) gains a *monetary claim[19] for:
  (a) the value of their equity; and
  (b) in the case of withdrawal on fault grounds under § 4(i):
    (A) the loss caused to the complainant personally by the liable party or parties specified by § 9, if any; and
    (B) the proportion of the loss caused, if any, by the liable party or parties as specified by § 9 to the close corporation corresponding to the proportion of the close corporation's total equity that is held by the complainant prior to withdrawal;

and

(iii) unless otherwise ordered by the court pursuant to § 27(v), must, after receipt of the full amount of the monetary claim under (ii)(b) above, transfer their equity to the liable party or parties specified by § 9, the member or members making the election to purchase under § 19, or both, in such proportions as is applicable.

§ 9 The following party ('liable party') or parties ('liable parties') (collectively 'liable party or parties') are liable to pay the complainant the monetary claim under § 8(ii):

(i) in the case of withdrawal on fault grounds under § 4(i), each of the directors, members, or controllers whose one or more acts or omissions or course of conduct form the basis of the ground or grounds of withdrawal, on a joint and several basis;
(ii) in the case of withdrawal on non-fault grounds under § 4(ii), the close corporation; and
(iii) in the case of withdrawal at will under § 3(ii), the close corporation.

§ 10 The complainant must, to the fullest extent permitted by law, be released from any personal obligation arising from or in connection with their status or duties as a member to a party other than the close corporation or its members, directors, or controllers that is not released pursuant to § 8(i), and must, to the fullest extent permitted by law, be indemnified by the liable party or parties specified by § 9 in respect of any outstanding obligation.

19 *Abfindungsanspruch*/purchase price/compensation/*haraimodoshi* etc.

§ 11 The monetary claim accruing under § 8(ii):

(i) may not be offset by any sums owed by the complainant to the liable party or parties specified in § 9; and
(ii) in the case of withdrawal on fault grounds under § 4(i), may be enforced against the close corporation in respect of the unpaid balance in the case of default by the liable party or all liable parties.

§ 12 A monetary claim of the complainant accruing under § 8(ii) that is enforceable against the close corporation under § 9(ii) and § 9(iii) or as a consequence of default by the liable party or parties under § 11(ii) must:

(i) rank equally with claims of unsecured creditors of the close corporation against the close corporation; and
(ii) notwithstanding any inconsistent or contrary law or agreement, entitle the complainant to dissolve the close corporation as of right.

Enforcement Proceedings

§ 13 The complainant may commence an enforcement proceeding in court at any time after the withdrawal becomes effective under § 7 to enforce their monetary claim accruing under § 8(ii) against the liable party or parties specified by § 9 who will be party to the proceeding as the respondent or respondents.

§ 14 A respondent may, in an enforcement proceeding, challenge their liability to pay the complainant's monetary claim accruing under § 8(ii) during a period of three months commencing on the day of the respondent's receipt of the notice of intent to withdraw required by § 5.

§ 15 Unless at least one respondent challenges their liability to pay within the time period specified by § 14, the court must without delay issue an order confirming the validity of the complainant's withdrawal, and:

(i) if the complainant, respondent, and any other party to the proceeding (including any member making an election to purchase under § 19, any other person agreeing to be the transferee of the complainant's equity in whole or part, and any party joined under § 27(iii)) reach agreement on:
  (a) the quantum and terms of payment of the complainant's monetary claim accruing under § 8(ii);
  (b) the terms of the transfer of the complainant's equity required by § 8(iii); and
  (c) any other relevant term,

record the terms as agreed in the same order; or

(ii) if agreement is not reached on any of the items in (i)(a) to (c) above:
  (a) immediately commence a valuation proceeding under § 23 below; or

(b) if requested by the complainant and one respondent, order that a valuation proceeding under § 23 will commence unless agreement is reached on all items in (i)(a) to (c) above within two months, or such longer period as may be agreed to by the complainant or one respondent.

§ 16 The court must not make any order other than those specified under § 15 (including an order declaring the complainant's withdrawal to be invalid or ineffective or an order terminating the enforcement proceeding) unless:

(i) the respondent satisfies the court that:
   (a) none of the withdrawal grounds relied upon by the complainant are established on the facts; or
   (b) the facts and circumstances supporting the withdrawal grounds relied upon by the complainant are solely caused by or attributable to the complainant and without good reason;
(ii) in the case of withdrawal on fault grounds under § 4(i), the respondent undertakes to restore to, cause to be restored to, or secure for the complainant any advantage that would have accrued but for the complainant's withdrawal attempt or would accrue to the complainant in the complainant's right as member or any related capacity (including but not limited to *distributions,[20] the office and *remuneration as a director,[21] or the status, salary, and other benefits as an employee, as applicable);
(iii) the respondent undertakes any and all actions necessary:
   (a) to remedy past detriment incurred by the complainant arising from; and
   (b) to resolve prospectively

the matters complained of by the complainant; and

(iv) the respondent satisfies the court that the final result:
   (a) is fair and reasonable to the complainant in light of the totality of the circumstances; and
   (b) will put an end to the matters complained of.

§ 17 If the respondent breaches any undertaking under § 16(ii) or (iii), § 15 will apply.

Election to Purchase

§ 18 Upon receipt of the notice of intent to withdraw under § 6, the close corporation must at its own expense:

(i) inform all members of the contents of the notice of intent to withdraw; and
(ii) furnish all members a copy of this Part.

[20] Dividends/*Gewinn*/*haitō* etc.
[21] By virtue of office as a director; alternatives: fees/ *Geschäftsführergehalt*/ *hōshū* etc.

§ 19 Any member or members other than the complainant may voluntarily elect to purchase the complainant's equity in whole, and:

(i) any member or members making the election will become party to any enforcement or valuation proceeding; and
(ii) if more than one member makes such a voluntary election, all members making the election will:
    (a) become parties to any enforcement and valuation proceeding; and
    (b) unless otherwise agreed among themselves, each have the right to purchase the complainant's equity in proportion to their respective equity holdings as of the date on which a member first made the election.

§ 20 A member who has made the election under § 19 may not revoke the election without the complainant's written consent.

§ 21 The complainant or any member making the election under § 19 may commence a valuation proceeding under § 23 at any time after one month from the date on which a member first made the election unless:

(i) the complainant and the member or all members making the election under § 19 reach agreement on the terms specified in § 15(i)(a) to (c); or
(ii) the complainant and the member or all members making the election under § 19 agree to an extension or extensions of time that may not be longer than two months at a time.

§ 22 Upon default of the member or any of the members who have made the election under § 19 to complete the purchase, the complainant may commence an enforcement proceeding under § 13 against:

(i) the defaulting member or members as if they are the liable party or parties specified in § 9;
(ii) the liable party or parties specified in § 9; or
(iii) both parties specified in (i) and (ii) above jointly and severally.

Valuation Proceedings

§ 23 The court must determine or decide,[22] in a valuation proceeding to which the complainant and the liable party or parties specified in § 9 will be party, any matter that is not agreed between the parties, including but not limited to:

(i) the quantum of the monetary claim accruing under § 8(ii)(a);
(ii) in the case of withdrawal on fault grounds under § 4(i):

[22] 'Determine' for technical issues such as quantum in valuation; 'decide' for issues of contested fact, law, or both.

(a) whether a monetary claim accruing under § 8(ii)(b) is supported by the facts;
(b) if the court is satisfied that a monetary claim accruing under § 8(ii)(b) is supported by the facts:
   (A) the quantum of the monetary claim; or
   (B) if there is more than one liable party, the apportionment of the liability to pay the monetary claim accruing under § 8(ii) between the liable parties;

or

(ii) terms of payment of the monetary claim accruing under § 8(ii) and of the transfer of the complainant's equity required by § 8(iii).

§ 24 The complainant's monetary claim accruing under § 8(ii)(a) must be valued, without any discount, as the proportion of the total value of the close corporation corresponding to the proportion of the close corporation's total equity that is held by the complainant as of the date on which the notice of intent to withdraw is first served by the complainant under § 6.

§ 25 The following will apply in a valuation proceeding unless otherwise agreed between the parties:

(i) the total value of the close corporation must be determined as of the date on which the notice of intent to withdraw is first served by the complainant under § 6; and
(ii) in the case of withdrawal on fault grounds under § 4(i), if the court is satisfied that a monetary claim accruing under § 8(ii)(b) is supported by the facts, the quantum of the claim will be the sum proposed by the complainant, unless:
   (a) the liable party or parties under § 9 satisfy the court otherwise; or
   (b) the court decides that the proposed quantum is manifestly unreasonable.

§ 26 The court may in a valuation proceeding do any one or more of the following unless otherwise agreed between the parties:

(i) in determining the total value of the close corporation, use any generally accepted valuation methodology, having regard to the nature of the business, structure of the assets, and any other aspect of the close corporation the court considers relevant;
(ii) *in respect of the complainant's monetary claim accruing under § 8(ii), if the court decides that it fair and reasonable to do so, order the liable parties to do any or all of the following:*
   (a) *to pay the monetary claim on deferred terms or in instalments;*
   (b) *to pay an additional sum to account for any financial loss or other detriment incurred by the complainant; or*
   (c) *to furnish security to guarantee payment of the monetary claim;*

(iii) if the court does not make any order declaring the complainant's withdrawal attempt invalid or ineffective or any order terminating the enforcement proceeding, make reasonable adjustments to the quantum of the complainant's monetary claim accruing under § 8(ii); or
(iv) order the liable party or parties to pay interest on the monetary claim at the standard rate or any other lawful rate accruing from the date on which the complainant first serves the notice of intent to withdraw under § 5 or any other date the court considers appropriate.

Power to Cure Irregularities, Join Parties, etc.

§ 27 *In any enforcement or valuation proceeding, if the court decides that it is fair and reasonable to do so, it may do any one or more of the following:*

(i) *at the court's own initiative or upon request by the complainant or any respondent, order the close corporation or any member, director, or controller, regardless of whether they are party to the proceeding, to disclose any information or permit the inspection of any document relevant to the proceeding, including but not limited to anything relating to the business or affairs of the close corporation, or any act, omission, or conduct of any member, director, or controller relevant to the basis of the ground or grounds of withdrawal;*
(ii) *order that any past or prospective failure to comply with the notice and service requirements under § 5 and § 6 will be waived or excused;*
(iii) *order any person with a reasonable connection to the facts or the proceeding, or with a financial interest in the proceeding, to be joined as a party;*
(iv) *order costs and expenses of the proceeding to be paid by any party or parties in any apportionment it decides; or*
(v) *order any party to do anything necessary to the fair, just, and efficient operation of any proceeding or enforcement of any outcome.*

Deviation by Contract

§ 28 § 29 to § 35 apply to any agreement made before the notice of intent to withdraw is first served under § 6 ('pre-existing agreement') to which any member, director, controller, or the close corporation is party.

§ 29 No term in any pre-existing agreement may be inconsistent with or contrary to the following Provisions: § 1, § 2, § 3(i), § 4(i)(a), § 5, § 6, § 7(i), § 7(iv), § 8(ii), § 9(i), § 11(ii), § 12(i), § 13, § 15, § 16, § 17, § 18, § 19, § 20, § 21, § 22, § 23, § 26,[23] § 27, § 28, § 29, § 30, § 31, § 32, § 33, § 34, § 35, § 36.

[23] To be precise, only § 26(ii) is classified 'procedural'.

§ 30 Any pre-existing agreement with any term inconsistent with or contrary to the following Provisions in this Part must be made in writing signed by all parties and in compliance with at least two enhanced requirements under § 32: § 4(i)(b), § 4(ii), § 7(ii), § 8(i) and (iii), § 9(ii), § 10, § 11(i), § 12(ii), § 14, § 24, and § 25.

§ 31 Any pre-existing agreement with any term inconsistent with or contrary to the following Provisions in this Part must be made in writing signed by all parties: § 3(ii), § 7(iii), and § 9(iii).

§ 32 The following enhanced requirements apply to any pre-existing agreement subject to § 30:

(i) the complainant must receive competent and independent legal advice, and all members, directors, and controllers must make all disclosures reasonably relevant to the complainant's consent to the term, having regard to the impact of the term on the complainant's ability to access and enforce withdrawal;

(ii) in respect of any term inconsistent with or contrary to the Provisions of this Part: the pre-existing agreement must contain:

  (a) an explanation in writing forming part of the text of the pre-existing agreement or as an attachment thereto as to the purpose of and the factual bases or assumptions underlying that specific term; and

  (b) one or more *conditions upon which the term would cease to have effect[24] other than (iii) below; and

(iii) any term deviating from the relevant Provisions of this Part will be effective for not longer than two years from the effective date of the pre-existing agreement, and may be extended in writing signed by all parties for not more than two years each time.

§ 33 If any term in a pre-existing agreement is inconsistent with or contrary to any Provision listed in § 29:

(i) the term is invalid and unenforceable by any person; and

(ii) any resulting gap must be filled by the Provisions of this Part or by the court in favour of the complainant.

§ 34 If a pre-existing agreement containing a term inconsistent with or contrary to any Provision listed in § 30 fails to comply with § 30:

(i) the term is invalid and unenforceable by any person; and

(ii) any resulting gap must be filled by the Provisions of this Part or by the court with what the court decides is fair and reasonable to the parties in the totality of the circumstances.

[24] Condition subsequent/*auflösenden Bedingung*/*kaijo jōken* etc.

§ 35 If a pre-existing agreement containing a term inconsistent with or contrary to any Provision listed in § 31 fails to comply with § 31:

(i) the term is, to the extent of the inconsistency, invalid and unenforceable by any person; and
(ii) any resulting gap must be filled by the Provisions of this Part or by the court with what the court decides is necessary to avoid gross injustice to the complainant.

§ 36 Nothing in this Part will affect the validity or enforceability of any agreement, settlement, or compromise made by the parties in writing signed by the parties if:

(i) the agreement, settlement, or compromise is concluded after the notice of intent to withdraw is served under § 6; and
(ii) the agreement, settlement, or compromise satisfies the enhanced requirement under § 32(i).

D COMMENTARY ON SELECTED INDIVIDUAL PROVISIONS

1 *Definitions and Scope of Application (§ 1, § 2)*

'Agreement' is defined broadly. The critical distinction is between 'pre-existing' agreements (see § 28; also referred to as 'ex ante') and those that are not (referred to as 'ex post' in this Commentary). Validity and enforceability of an agreement deviating from a Provision of the Model Remedy turn on different rules and standards depending on whether the agreement is pre-existing/ex ante or ex post. The critical date is the date on which the notice of intent to withdraw is first served as required by § 5 and § 6; an agreement entered into prior to that date is an ex ante or pre-existing agreement, whereas one entered into on or after that date is ex post. For the avoidance of doubt, any use of 'agree', 'agreed', or 'reach agreement' in the Model Remedy without the 'pre-existing' modifier means ex post agreement. On ex post agreements, see also VIII.D.7.v below.

'Close corporation' is defined broadly, prioritising factual characteristics – the lack of a market for equity interests – over legal form.

Majority or controlling shareholders may cause conflict not only by exercising their shareholder power directly, but also in other ways such as in their capacity as directors, or indirectly through pliable directors, employees, or other (minor) shareholders. Persons who are not formally shareholders may exercise substantial factual control over the close corporation and make life intolerable for complainants. The concept of 'controller' covers these circumstances.

The Model Remedy is designed on the premise that a court of law would be the third-party arbiter and enforcement organ, but arbitration may also be acceptable. Definitions are mandatory (§ 29) to preserve the structure of the Model Remedy.

2 *Standing and Procedure (§ 1, § 5 to § 7, § 18)*

Only a shareholder ('member') who is a 'complainant' has the right to withdraw and the standing to enforce that right. As withdrawal is a *right* rather than a mere remedy or a form of judicially ordered relief under the Model Remedy, its existence is confirmed, but not created, by a court decision.

§ 5 and § 6[25] are structured around a formal notice of intent to withdraw[26] that communicates essential information to affected parties; these Provisions together with § 7[27] establish critical dates and timelines that in turn structure subsequent judicial proceedings.

§ 18 facilitates dissemination to all close corporation members of information relevant to a decision on whether to make an election to purchase the complainant's equity.[28]

Although envisioned as mandatory provisions[29] (except subdivisions relating to non-fault or at will withdrawal[30]) to prevent tinkering by parties that would render the Model Remedy as a whole inoperable, § 1, § 5, § 6, and § 7 are procedural in nature and subject to the civil procedure system of the implementing jurisdiction. § 18 is an integral part of the election-to-purchase feature and therefore mandatory as well.

3 *Withdrawal: At Will, Fault Grounds, Non-Fault Grounds, and Challenges Thereto: § 3, § 4, § 16*

The distinction between withdrawal 'at will' and 'on grounds' is central to the analysis in this Book[31] and is reflected in § 3. The substantive core of the Model Remedy, § 4, further distinguishes between and defines types of 'grounds', which are further subdivided into 'bases'.

i Fault: § 4(i)

Withdrawal on fault grounds under § 4(i) is based on the 'corrective model'.[32] Compared to non-fault and at will withdrawal, withdrawal on fault grounds results in the most favourable treatment for the complainant and the harshest consequences for the perpetrator in the form of personal liability (§ 9(i)).

25 They are italicised in the Model Remedy text to indicate their purely procedural nature.
26 Cf IV.C.3 (on the *Austrittserklärung*).
27 Not italicised as the effective date of withdrawal has substantive consequences.
28 See VIII.D.4.iv below.
29 § 29.
30 § 7(ii), § 7(iii); see § 30, § 31 and VIII.D.3.ii and VIII.D.3.iii below.
31 II.C, III.C.
32 III.G.3.ii.

Both fault bases (under § 4(i)(a)–(b)) share two elements: (i) some concrete misconduct or misbehaviour in respect of the 'affairs' of the close corporation that is (ii) attributable to an identifiable actor, who can be a member, director, controller, or some combination thereof. Both are standards rather than rules.[33] The overarching principle is to focus on the factual detriment caused by the misconduct, regardless of form or means, on the complainant's interests instead of being constrained by pre-existing dogma.

The phrase 'an act, omission, or course of conduct' means that an omission or series of acts or omissions forming a 'course of conduct' would suffice to establish fault. The 'affairs'[34] requirement circumscribes the types of misconduct for fault grounds by excluding conduct of a purely personal nature. It matters not whether the actor personally acted or caused inaction by using their own rights or powers directly;[35] indirectly through their associates;[36] indirectly through control of the close corporation's organs or agents;[37] or even more indirectly through other sources of influence.[38] For example, obstructing withdrawal proceedings by not cooperating with any creditor protection or capital reduction procedure would itself be conduct justifying withdrawal separately on fault grounds.[39]

The terms 'illegal' and 'wrongful' refer to more serious forms of misconduct, but the misconduct need not be independently[40] legally impermissible to be considered fault. Any form of detriment reasonably connected to participation in a close corporation business would suffice as 'prejudice'.[41]

The distinction within fault grounds is between 'bad faith' (§ 4(i)(a)) and 'non-bad faith' (§ 4(i)(b)) bases. Bad faith covers intentional or malicious misconduct and is meant as a catch-all for misconduct short of 'intentional' acts such as recklessness or callous disregard of the consequences, but not as a legal term of art in any particular jurisdiction.[42] It is meant to capture the most egregious forms of majority shareholder or controller misbehaviour. Bad faith misconduct is the absolute minimum 'mandatory core'[43] and cannot be excluded as a basis for withdrawal by ex ante agreement.[44]

33 Cf II.C; III.C.1.
34 Drawn from UK Companies Act 2006, s 994(1)(a).
35 E.g. not re-electing the complainant as director despite having agreed to.
36 E.g. by abstaining formally from a vote but coordinating the votes of other members to achieve the desired result.
37 E.g. causing no dividends to be declared or the complainant's salary as an employee to be reduced.
38 E.g. threatening to have an associate call in a loan to the close corporation at an inopportune time unless the complainant complied with a demand or acquiesced to a change of circumstances detrimental to the complainant's interests.
39 See VIII.D.4.ii below.
40 I.e. under some law beyond the law of withdrawal itself.
41 Cf V.C.3.v.
42 Concepts of intention, recklessness, etc. are highly jurisdiction-specific and must be left to the implementing jurisdiction.
43 II.E.4.
44 See § 29 and commentary at VIII.D.7 below.

As to non-bad faith, § 4(i)(b) mirrors § 4(i)(a) except that intention or bad faith is not required. Contractual exclusion of non-bad faith (as opposed to bad faith) misconduct is not nearly as objectionable. However, given the severe consequences it would have for the complainant, the non-bad faith basis in the Model Remedy is a sticky default.[45]

ii Non-Fault: § 4(ii)

The 'insurance model'[46] manifests as 'non-fault' withdrawal under § 4(ii). 'Non-fault' captures scenarios ranging from unbearable consequences resulting from voluntary action taken with care and in good faith, to major changes in circumstances not attributable to voluntary action of either majority or minority shareholders.[47] Since there is no actor to whom fault can be definitively attributed and who can be justifiably made personally liable to buy out the complainant, in non-fault cases the party responsible for paying the complainant is the close corporation (§ 9(ii)). The Provisions on non-fault withdrawal are sticky defaults that can be modified subject to two enhanced requirements.[48]

Non-fault grounds include chronic deadlock (§ 4(ii)(a)); irretrievable loss of trust and confidence (§ 4(ii)(b));[49] irreversible change of circumstances (§ 4(ii)(c));[50] and where continued membership would be unreasonable (§ 4(ii)(d)). As a catch-all residual category, § 4(ii)(d) ('otherwise unreasonable to expect the complainant to remain as a member of the close corporation') is the jurisdiction-neutral rendering of the relatively open-ended general concepts of Germany's *wichtiger Grund* and Japan's *yamu wo enai jiyū*.[51] Situations covered could include purely personal circumstances[52] such as severe illness, divorce between two co-shareholders in a family-owned close corporation,[53] or change of residence.[54] It also provides a basis for courts to continue developing the law in the future.

45 § 30; § 32; VIII.D.7.iii.
46 V.C.3.i.
47 III.C.3.
48 See § 30, § 32, and Commentary thereto at VIII.D.7.iii below.
49 This is widely recognised as legitimate grounds for withdrawal save in the UK (where it only supports judicial dissolution): see III.C.3. It is not necessary for the loss of trust and confidence to be mutual: see French (2015): paras. [8.388]–[8.389].
50 Withdrawal on this ground would be available for changes in the greater business environment can turn an initially profitable business model obsolete (cf IV.C.2.iv; Koide (2014a): 221–2), and for investors who could have invested specifically on the basis that a party they trust would be running the business (cf V.C.4.iii.f).
51 IV.C.2; VII.D.3.
52 VII.D.3.
53 VII.D.3; IV.C.2.v.
54 VII.D.3.ii.

iii At Will (§ 3(ii))

Withdrawal at will under § 3(ii) is the simplest of all: no reasons are necessary, and there is no room to challenge the validity of the withdrawal on substantive grounds. The corporation itself is liable to pay (§ 9(iii)). It is a simple default; contracting out of it requires only signed agreement in writing (§ 31).

iv Challenges against Withdrawal: § 14, § 16

The respondent (i.e. a party who is potentially financially liable to pay the complainant under § 9[55]) should be allowed to challenge their own liability to pay. If the challenge is not to liability but purely to quantum, that is a matter for valuation (§ 23 to § 26[56]).

To challenge liability, there are theoretically two ways. The first is to challenge the validity of the complainant's withdrawal itself. The second is to concede that the complainant's withdrawal is itself valid, but that for some other reason, the respondent personally should not have to pay anything. The Model Remedy would permit both types of challenges (through § 14), subject to the caveat that only in specific and narrow circumstances would no one (respondent or otherwise) be liable to pay the complainant (§ 16).

§ 14 and § 16 facilitate information exchange and communication between the complainant and respondent parties under the watchful eye of a third-party arbiter. Provided that the respondents had not acted in bad faith, conflicts could be resolved through a judicial forum. Although not the primary function of the Model Remedy, the communication-facilitating and information-forcing function of § 16 – strengthened and supported by the sanction of withdrawal[57] – is useful.

§ 14 is not mandatory (§ 30), but rather a sticky default subject to enhanced requirements for contracting around (§ 32). § 16 is mandatory (§ 29) to prevent majority circumvention of pro-complainant safeguards.

4 *Financially Liable Parties:* § 9, § 11(*ii*), § 12(*i*), § 19, § 22

i General Principle

The 'golden thread' of withdrawal design – protecting shareholders desirous and deserving of exit, but not at the expense of imposing on innocent constituencies financial liability for the consequences of shareholder withdrawal[58] – runs through the Model Remedy. Careful balancing of the interests of various participants and

55 See VIII.D.4. below.
56 See VIII.D.6.i, VIII.D.3.iv, VIII.D.6.v below.
57 See II.D.2.ii.
58 III.G.3.iii.

stakeholders is called for. To decide who will be *legally* liable to pay the complainant's monetary claim, the question is: who is *not* innocent for the circumstances causing the complainant to withdraw?

ii Persons (Co-Members, Directors, Controllers) at Fault: § 9(i)

For withdrawal on fault grounds, the persons responsible for the circumstances behind the complainant's withdrawal are the most clearly non-innocent party or parties. The corrective model imposes the liability to pay on parties at fault.[59] All liable parties under this provision are liable jointly and severally to maximise the chance that the complainant can successfully enforce their claim. Responsibility is interpreted widely: complicity in another party's misconduct or obstruction of the complainant's withdrawal effort in any way would suffice for personal liability. That any person at fault will be personally liable to pay the complainant is part of the mandatory core of withdrawal and may not be contracted out of ex ante (§ 29).

iii Close Corporation Itself: § 9(ii), § 9(iii), § 11(ii), § 12(i)

A NON-FAULT GROUND: § 9(II). When there is no person at fault, the close corporation is the only party capable of paying the complainant. This is consistent with the insurance model of withdrawal.[60] In certain settings – such as a Silicon Valley start-up or other businesses heavy on match assets and investments – a rigid rule that the close corporation must be liable may not necessarily be appropriate.[61] Mirroring the approach taken for withdrawal on non-fault grounds generally,[62] ex ante agreements deviating from the rule that the close corporation must pay the complainant are permissible subject to two or more enhanced requirements (sticky default).[63]

If, in a non-fault setting (or any other setting), the close corporation fails to undertake the necessary steps to pay due to interference or obstruction by any person, in principle that person will themselves be personally liable under § 9(i). The close corporation may also be liable here, but only upon default of the newly liable party or parties.[64] This strikes a balance between the interests of the close corporation (and its creditors) and the complainant.

59 III.G.3.ii.
60 III.G.3.i.
61 See II.E.3.i.
62 VIII.D.3.ii above.
63 § 30, § 32; VIII.D.7 below.
64 § 11(ii); VIII.D.4.iii.c below.

B AT WILL: § 9(III). For similar reasons as non-fault grounds,[65] the close corporation is liable to pay upon withdrawal at will. As with other provisions concerning withdrawal at will,[66] this is a simple default requiring only signed writing (§ 31).

C ON DEFAULT OF PERSONS AT FAULT: § 11(II). The close corporation is a fallback for a complainant who, in a withdrawal on fault grounds situation, has attempted and failed to enforce their claim against the (principal) liable party or parties. This provision's justification lies in the insurance model of withdrawal,[67] and it is mandatory.[68] Nonetheless, enforcement against the close corporation based on default of others should be regarded as a last resort. Ideally, the prospect of enforcement against the close corporation would encourage a member to make an election to purchase (under § 19).

D PRIORITY OF COMPLAINANT'S CLAIM: § 12(I). The complainant's claim against the close corporation is ranked *pari passu* with other unsecured creditors. The provision is mandatory (§ 29) to prevent agreements that reduce the priority of the complainant's claim so as to render it meaningless, or that increase the claim's priority over third parties not subject to ex ante contracting between members and other insiders.

iv Other Members Electing to Purchase: § 19, § 22

The Model Remedy provides that members other than the complainant may elect to purchase the complainant's equity. Inspired by US election statutes,[69] this is a mandatory provision (§ 29). By opening the opportunity to buy out the complainant to other members, the election Provision facilitates non-contentious dispute resolution, increases the probability that the complainant's monetary claim will be paid somehow by facilitating a bidding process among interested purchasers. This also reduces the burden of payment on the close corporation and the corresponding risk of prejudice to corporate creditors.

5 *Enforcement: § 8(iii), § 12(ii), § 13 to § 17, § 21, § 23, § 27*

i Transfer of Complainant's Equity: § 8(iii)

The default position is that the complainant is obligated to transfer their equity only upon receipt of full payment. Flexibility is injected in two ways: first by express

65 Discussed above at VIII.D.4.iii.a.
66 VIII.D.3.iii.
67 III.G.3.i.
68 § 29. It is made mandatory to support the partially mandatory regime of withdrawal on fault grounds (bad-faith basis; see VIII.D.3.i above). If, for example, close corporation liability could be excluded, a bad-faith liable party may abscond or declare bankruptcy to circumvent the strict bad-faith regime.
69 VI.C.2.iii, VI.E.3.i.

reference to the judicial discretion to make an order to the contrary;[70] and second by making this provision a sticky default requiring enhanced requirements to be met.[71]

ii Enforcement by Dissolution: § 12(ii)

Capital maintenance and creditor protection regimes pose formidable obstacles to the enforcement of monetary claims against the close corporation.[72] They can further be strategically used by majority shareholders to render withdrawal on non-fault grounds a dead letter.[73] This Provision, a manifestation of the insurance function of withdrawal,[74] eliminates any doubt[75] that a monetary claim properly payable by the close corporation is enforceable by the ultimate sanction of dissolution.

Dissolution is a sticky default that can be contracted out of ex ante provided enhanced requirements are met,[76] and in any event may be averted ex post in many ways. For example, members have an absolute right to elect to purchase the complainant's equity and thereby free the close corporation from enforcement.[77] In such a case the close corporation is only on the hook if the electing member defaults.[78]

iii Enforcement and Valuation Proceedings: § 13 to § 17, § 21, § 23, § 27

The three Guiding Principles of finality, structured flexibility, and comprehensive functionality[79] apply with special force to the Provisions on enforcement and valuation proceedings. First, permanent resolution of shareholder conflict must always be achieved; whenever in doubt, this must be the completion of withdrawal. Second, parties are encouraged to reach agreement at any stage of proceedings and on any matter, but that any issue not agreed on will be decided by the court according to the norms set out in the Model Remedy. Third, the court is empowered to do anything it considers necessary to ensure that proceedings are carried out smoothly and fairly.

70 The judicial discretion to 'order any party to do anything necessary to the fair, just, and efficient operation of any proceeding or enforcement of any outcome' (§ 27(v)) may not be compatible with all civil procedure systems; insofar as § 8(iii) is concerned, it is worth incorporating a specific judicial discretion to deviate from the default ex post (on top of ex ante alternative arrangements by contract).

71 § 30.

72 III.E.3; IV.C.6; VII.D.6.

73 E.g. by setting an extremely high registered capital. Cf IV.C.5 (registered capital as an enforcement obstacle in Germany).

74 III.G.3.i.

75 Cf VII.D.6 (enforceability by dissolution unclear for Japanese GK).

76 § 30.

77 § 19; VIII.D.4.iv.

78 § 22; VIII.D.4.iv.

79 VIII.B.

Except for § 14 (on challenges),[80] the intricate provisions on court proceedings are all mandatory (§ 29) and may not be deviated from ex ante. Any problems in actual operation may be ameliorated by the court's discretionary powers (§ 27) or by ex post agreement of the parties (§ 36).

6 *Scope of Protection: § 8(i) and (ii), § 10, § 11(i), § 24 to § 26*

i Valuation – The Equity Portion: § 8(ii)(a), § 24, § 25(i), § 26(i)

Arguably the most technical and non-legal aspect of a withdrawal regime, valuation relies heavily on experts with accounting expertise. The Model Remedy provisions on valuation and accompanying commentary establish a legal framework, but do not engage in detailed exposition of valuation methodologies or other technical aspects.

A NO DISCOUNTS: § 24. § 24 takes an enterprise value approach based on the pro rata 'fair value' of the business as a whole, and in which the complainant's equity interest is not subject to discounts for minority interests or illiquidity. § 24 is a sticky default subject to enhanced requirements.[81]

B VALUATION DATE AND METHODOLOGY: § 25(I), § 26(I). Valuation dates adopted by the target jurisdictions include the effective date of withdrawal and the date on which the complainant takes the decisive step to withdraw.[82] The Model Remedy adopts the latter: the date on which the notice of intent to withdraw is served.[83] This choice offers clarity and reduces any incentive of the respondents to reduce the business' valuation opportunistically after receipt of the complainant's notice of intent to withdraw.[84] The valuation date is a sticky default (§ 32) to avoid careless tampering. The court is in any event empowered to ameliorate any injustice arising from rigid application of the valuation date.[85] § 25 itself also makes it clear that it applies 'unless otherwise agreed between the parties' ex post.

Valuation methodology is left open by § 26(i) because different types of businesses at different stages of the business life cycle are best valued using different methods. Any generally accepted method for valuing unlisted businesses, whether based on

80 VIII.D.3.iv.

81 § 30, § 32.

82 IV.C.4.i (Germany: date of receipt of declaration of withdrawal – i.e. both dates); V.C.7.iii (UK: date of share purchase order, i.e. date of withdrawal); VI.C.5 (US-CC: various but often the date of filing of an oppression action – i.e. date of decisive step); VI.E.4 (US-LLC: date of withdrawal, i.e. both dates); VII.D.5.i (Japan: date of *taisha* (withdrawal), i.e. both dates in the case of unavoidable grounds).

83 In the case of withdrawal on fault grounds, this is also very close to the effective date: see § 7(i).

84 Loss to the close corporation due to opportunistic behaviour of the respondents before the date of the notice of intent to withdraw could be accounted for through the compensatory component (§ 8(ii)(b)).

85 § 26(ii)(b), § 26(iii).

dividend yield, net asset value, cash flow, any other method, or any combination thereof may be used. Judicial discretion is essential as businesses can – and not infrequently – change substantially and rapidly over time; a contractually agreed valuation methodology may become grossly unfair to one party or another when the nature and structure of the business change. § 26(i) is therefore classified as mandatory (§ 29). This prohibition applies to ex ante agreements on valuation methodology purporting to bind the court, but agreements that provide the court helpful information for the purposes of valuation may be taken into consideration[86] even if they are not binding on the court.

ii Valuation – The Compensatory Component: § 8(ii)(b), § 25(ii)

A cornerstone of the corrective model[87] is for a member withdrawing on fault grounds to be compensated for their share of any loss incurred by the close corporation in connection with the misconduct.[88] § 25(ii) creates a presumption to ease the complainant's burden of proof in establishing the precise quantum of loss caused by the liable party or parties, but with safeguards in § 25(ii)(a) and (b) to counter any temptation of complainants to propose any quantum without reasonable basis.

The complainant's entitlement to a compensatory component (§ 8(ii)(b)) is itself mandatory (§ 29). § 25(ii) protects complainants by resolving difficult questions of evidence and proof in their favour but is not an absolute necessity; it is therefore a sticky default (§ 30, § 32).

iii Adjustments, Structuring Payments, Interest etc.: § 26(ii) to (iv)

§ 26 (ii) to (iv) grant the court powers to make orders necessary to accomplish a comprehensive withdrawal solution suitable for the parties' needs. The Provisions may also be used to facilitate and enforce any ex post agreement of the parties. To prevent parties from fettering the court's discretion, § 26(ii), (iii), and (iv) are mandatory.[89]

iv Release of Obligations and Indemnification: § 8(i), § 10

A withdrawal regime would be substantially undermined if the complainant remains tied to the close corporation through legal obligations such as personal guarantees for business debt. § 8(i) and § 10 permanently and completely sever any

86 For example, if the parties have reached an informal agreement that the close corporation will liquidate the business by sale of business assets piecemeal in three years, this fact may be relied upon by the court to decide that the liquidation basis would be appropriate in lieu of going concern basis.

87 III.G.3.ii.

88 III.E.2; V.C.7.iii; VI.C.5.

89 § 29.

lingering ties of the complainant to the close corporation as far as possible.[90] To account for situations where this is impossible, especially where external creditors with strong bargaining power do not consent,[91] the complainant is also granted the protection of indemnification under § 10, which shifts the risk post-withdrawal onto the liable party or parties.

To account for situations where a withdrawing member may wish to retain rights and duties post-withdrawal, or where the capital structure or other features of the close corporation may not permit indemnification, both Provisions are sticky defaults.[92]

v No Set Offs: § 11(i)

The rule against setting off any claims against the complainant aims to prevent withdrawal proceedings from metastasising into a free-for-all in which respondents hurl any and all allegations against the complainant. The only issues of fault or responsibility of the complainant that may be litigated in the withdrawal context must be in relation to the withdrawal grounds themselves. These should be addressed under respondent challenges,[93] and may be accounted for in the final result by judicial adjustments to the monetary claim quantum.[94] § 11(i) is a sticky default that can be altered.[95]

7 *Contracting Around the Model Remedy: § 28 to § 36*

i Introduction

Different types of close corporations and shareholders may desire arrangements deviating from those provided by the Model Remedy.[96] To balance demands for both ex ante private ordering and robust minority protection, the Model Remedy offers not only a mix of mandatory and (simple) default rules, but also applies the 'sticky default' concept first introduced and explored in Chapter II.[97]

§ 28 to § 36 implement a three-tier classification – mandatory core, sticky default, and (simple) default – of Model Remedy Provisions. Each tier is subject to altering norms of varying strictness; in other words, the permissibility and ease of opting out ex ante (through 'pre-existing agreements') depends on the tier. Each Model

90 § 8(i) is not intended to address non-financial obligations such as duties of confidentiality, where there are good policy reasons for such duties to survive withdrawal.

91 Any such creditor may be joined as a party to the proceedings: § 27(iii).

92 § 30, § 32.

93 § 16(i); VIII.D.3.iv.

94 § 26(iii).

95 § 30, § 32.

96 For example, technology start-ups or joint ventures between corporates may very well wish to do away with any extracontractual mechanism for withdrawal outright; see II.E.3.i.

97 II.E.4.i.

Remedy Provision is classified under only one tier to make it clear whether it can be deviated from, and if so, how.

ii Mandatory Core: § 29, § 33

No target jurisdiction regards withdrawal in all its forms and aspects as a purely default affair.[98] Much of the Model Remedy is classified as mandatory (§ 29) norms from which no deviation ex ante will be enforceable (§ 33(i)). Despite this, it is foreseeable that majorities may be tempted to include sneakily or force upon the minority terms contrary to or inconsistent with mandatory Provisions. Thus, § 33(ii) directs the court to fill any gap in a way that will be advantageous to the complainant so as to leave a respondent who has attempted to contract around a mandatory core Provision at the risk of being worse off than they would have been had they worked with the unmodified Model Remedy.[99]

Mandatory Provisions include Provisions applicable to bad-faith fault withdrawal[100] because of its centrality to the corrective model of withdrawal. Other mandatory Provisions have a structural function as they constitute the Model Remedy's enforcement and valuation framework, and others establish the court's extensive powers to administer withdrawal proceedings. They are mandatory to prevent ill-advised or inadvertent modifications to the mechanism's structure. This prohibition only applies to ex ante ('pre-existing') agreements entered into before the date on which the notice of intent to withdraw is first served (§ 28). There is flexibility to deviate from the Model Remedy so long as they are made ex post – and subject to basic safeguards in the form of legal advice and disclosure.[101]

iii Sticky Defaults and Enhanced Requirements: § 30, § 32, § 34

Sticky defaults occupy a position in between mandatory norms and 'simple' defaults.[102] Provisions that are not structurally essential, do not pertain to judicial case management and gap-filling powers, and do not relate to bad-faith fault grounds are usually classified as sticky defaults under § 30. Sticky defaults may be displaced by the parties, but if and only if the applicable altering norms[103] – 'enhanced requirements' under § 32 – are complied with.

The enhanced requirements comprise debiasing/information-forcing[104] strategies and insulating strategies.[105] The § 32(i) and (ii) requirements of competent and

98 Save the US with regards to the LLC: II.F.
99 On 'altering penalties' see II.E.4.i.
100 § 4(i)(a) and any Provision applicable to § 4(i) (fault grounds, which includes bad-faith fault).
101 § 36, § 32(i) and (ii).
102 See II.E.4.i.
103 Altering norms are introduced in II.E.4.i.
104 On information-forcing defaults, see Ayres (2012): 2098–9.
105 On debiasing and insulating strategies see II.E.3.iii.

independent[106] legal advice and full disclosure are common-sensical safeguards essential to the integrity of the bargaining process which are relatively easy to meet.[107] Designed to compel parties to agree on a purpose (§ 32(iii)(a)) and clearly defined limits (§ 32(iii)(b)) for any term in derogation of sticky default Model Remedy Provisions, this Provision reduces party error and alleviates evidential difficulties by making an authoritative statement of content and scope of the parties' intentions available to the court. The auto-limitation compelled by § 32(iii)(b) restricts the derogating contractual term from overreaching its purposes and factual premises.[108] § 32(iv) imposes a time limit on any derogating provision;[109] this insulating strategy limits the detriment from a disadvantageous arrangement. Parties are offered the flexibility of choosing any two (or more) enhanced requirements to comply with.

Derogating terms that do not satisfy the necessary number of enhanced requirements (or none) are invalid and unenforceable (§ 34(i)), and any gaps that may arise are to be filled by the court in a way that is fair and reasonable to the parties (§34(ii)). This is less punitive than the position for terms deviating from mandatory Provisions.[110] The enhanced requirements themselves are mandatory (§ 29) to prevent circumvention.

iv Simple Defaults: § 31, § 35

Provisions on withdrawal at will are simple defaults that can be contracted out of ex ante with signed writing. Failure to comply with the most basic requirements of reasonable contracting practice will render the term invalid and unenforceable (§ 35(i)); the court will fill any gap arising from this.[111]

v Ex Post Agreements: § 36

Regulation of pre-existing (ex ante) agreements is stricter under the Model Remedy because of concerns with majority shareholder opportunism. Once the notice of intent to withdraw is served and the withdrawal process commenced, the monetary

106 Independent here means a legal practitioner free from any conflicts of interest or influence from any contracting party or their related parties.

107 For example, independent advice from a notary in some civil law jurisdictions when forming a close corporation would ordinarily suffice to satisfy § 32(i).

108 For example, in an 'omelette' close corporation (see II.E.3.i), there is good reason to eliminate withdrawal outright, but the moment it ceases to be in that stage, the withdrawal restriction's *raison d'être* ceases, and the restriction should accordingly lapse.

109 Cf II.E.4.i.

110 § 33, VIII.D.7.ii.

111 See II.E.4.i. For example, an oral agreement that the complainant must not withdraw at will would be invalid and unenforceable, but the court may order that complainant's monetary claim be based on a heavily discounted valuation of their equity that is seriously disadvantageous, but not grossly unjust, to the complainant.

claim quantum is fixed (§ 25(i)), and the main consideration shifts from majority opportunism to putting an end to the conflict or dispute. Ex post agreements, which are indispensable to both settlement and narrowing issues for judicial resolution, should be permissible and even encouraged. § 36 provides a 'safe harbour' by which no agreement that satisfies the enhanced requirements of competent, independent legal advice and full disclosure may be challenged.

E CLOSING REMARKS

The Model Remedy is long and detailed by comparison with currently existing withdrawal regimes in the target jurisdictions for three reasons. The first is scope: whereas the Model Remedy directly addresses matters that have arisen in practice, statutes in force have been content to leave them to unwritten law or judge-made precedent. A jurisdiction new to withdrawal should find the Model Remedy more useful than any other existing statute for the purposes of understanding the problem, context, and solutions to close corporation shareholder conflict.

The second reason is gap-filling. This builds on Chapter II's findings that it is neither practically feasible,[112] nor (in the unlikely event that it were possible) in the interests of fully informed rational parties[113] to make an exhaustive bargain on all possible exit scenarios and options.

Finally, the Model Remedy aims to provide flexibility for shareholders and judges to make informed choices. To educate shareholders and their legal advisers on their options (e.g. how to contract around certain elements of the Model Remedy) and judges on their role in resolving close corporation disputes (e.g. on what they should consider doing if they have the necessary powers), there is no substitute for careful textual exposition. Only with nuance and complexity – as encapsulated in the Model Remedy – may a course be steered between the Scylla and Charybdis of unbounded judicial discretion and unlimited contractual freedom.

[112] II.E.3.iii.

[113] II.E.2.ii.

PART 4

Conclusion

IX

Conclusions, Contributions, and Applications

Even a longish book deserves a shortish conclusion.[1] IX.A summarises the key findings of this Book and explains their scholarly contributions. IX.B proposes practical applications in law reform, judicial practice, and extra-judicial dispute resolution for the concepts analysed and models developed in this Book. Accordingly, practice-oriented jurists and policymakers may wish to focus here. For comparative law-oriented readers, IX.C briefly explores future extensions of the methods and concepts in this Book.

A PRINCIPAL FINDINGS AND THEIR CONTRIBUTIONS

1 *Theory*

Shareholder conflict between majority/controlling and minority shareholders is the cardinal problem of close corporation law. Minority shareholders lack the majority's formal powers and are – in the absence of an easy exit option – 'locked-in'. In

[1] Cf Armour & Enriques et al. (2017): 267.

majority-minority conflict, the minority is structurally vulnerable to majority opportunism. The minority can count on neither the ability to impose its own will on nor to defend itself against majority power using lawful means, nor have the option of extricating themselves from the situation through exit. To address shareholder conflict and its resulting problems, some form of legal mechanism minority shareholder protection is essential.[2]

'Withdrawal' is this Book's term for a category of solutions responding to the problem of shareholder conflict in close corporations. Withdrawal regimes exist in jurisdictions including Germany, US, UK, and Japan (collectively 'target jurisdictions') for their close corporation forms (German GmbH, UK Ltd, US Close Corporation (US-CC), US-LLC, Japanese GK). I define withdrawal as voluntary exit from a close corporation by a shareholder desirous of exit resulting in a monetary claim payable to the withdrawing shareholder in exchange for the latter's loss of status, rights, duties, and other interests in the close corporation. Withdrawal is classified into two major variants: 'at will' and 'on grounds',[3] comprises both standards and rules,[4] and must be conceptually distinguished from other forms of 'exit' and other institutions relating to shareholder rights.[5]

Despite withdrawal's utility to minority shareholders, leaving it entirely to private ordering of the parties based only on enabling or simple default mechanisms is unsatisfactory. This is due to incomplete contracting, complexities of human behaviour, and other considerations. Neither is completely mandatory provision of withdrawal acceptable or desirable; needs and considerations vary between different users of close corporation forms. Concepts from behavioural law and economics, such as 'sticky defaults' and 'mandatory core', offer tools for striking a balance between default and mandatory extremes and goals such as vindicating socially beneficial behaviours (particularly trust and trustworthiness) of shareholders and deterring majority shareholder opportunism against minorities.[6]

Chapter II makes two scholarly contributions. The first is establishing a coherent, jurisdiction-neutral set of corporate law concepts and terminology on shareholder exit. In particular, the concept of shareholder 'withdrawal' is defined, explained, and distinguished from related yet distinct shareholder rights and remedies such as appraisal. The second contribution is to expand, through application of concepts and insights from behavioural law and economics, both our understanding of the close corporation problem and the range of potential solutions.

2 II.B.
3 II.C.
4 II.C.
5 II.D.
6 II.E.

2 *Operation*

A jurisdiction-neutral framework for the analysis and comparison of withdrawal remedies should comprise five main aspects: (1) legal bases (sources of law); (2) types of grounds for withdrawal ('when can I withdraw?'); (3) financially liable parties ('who pays when I withdraw?'); (4) scope of protection ('how much does withdrawal protect me?'); and (5) the default/mandatory balance.[7]

Withdrawal remedies in the four target jurisdictions have different legal bases. In two target jurisdictions (UK, Japan), withdrawal is entirely statutory in origin. Despite two codification attempts, Germany's withdrawal regime today remains without textual basis in the GmbH's organic statute. US-CC withdrawal may be either expressly and directly provided for by statute; direct and judicial in origin; available only indirectly; or completely unavailable depending on the relevant state. US-LLC withdrawal at will is based exclusively on clear statutory provision, whereas withdrawal on oppression or other grounds may either be specifically provided for by statute or exist as a possible option for a court statutorily vested with discretion to order alternatives to dissolution.[8]

Courts played a crucial role in withdrawal's development in all four target jurisdictions. Although legislators can and do in the UK, some US states, and Japan play an important role in placing withdrawal on a firm footing in written law, the most they can do is to offer – but not compel – judicial flexibility and progressiveness. It is acceptable and legitimate for judges to take the lead in creating or advancing withdrawal regimes, regardless of legal tradition or other considerations.[9]

The scope of the grounds for withdrawal differs across target jurisdictions. All target jurisdictions offer withdrawal on the ground that other close corporation participants – primarily co-members/co-shareholders – are at fault.[10] In all target jurisdictions, fault is a standard, not a rule. Germany, Japan, and the US permit withdrawal on no-fault grounds, but not the UK.[11] Withdrawal at will is not available in the Ltd, GmbH, or US-CC, and is only available as a default in the US-LLC and GK. Withdrawal at will regimes are artefacts of other considerations and cannot be said to have been introduced consciously by legislators on shareholder protection grounds.[12]

The target jurisdictions generally regulate access to withdrawal through a mandatory core approach: access to withdrawal per se cannot be completely excluded by contract,[13] but material aspects are otherwise largely modifiable by contract ex ante. Contractual arrangements on the valuation of a withdrawing/

7 III.B–F.
8 III.B.
9 III.G.1.
10 III.C.1–2.
11 III.C.3.
12 III.C.4.
13 III.F.1.

exiting shareholder's monetary claim deviating from the general position at law are permitted in all target jurisdictions.[14]

Each target jurisdiction developed their own respective withdrawal regimes mostly independently, drawing primarily if not exclusively on *domestic* legal sources and inspirations. In so doing, the four target jurisdictions demonstrate a level of spontaneous functional convergence that points to withdrawal as an evolutionary milestone for close corporation law.[15] Beneath *broad* spontaneous functional convergence towards withdrawal as shareholder protection in each of the four target jurisdictions, *narrow(er)* spontaneous convergence has also taken place within two pairs of two target jurisdictions each: Germany/Japan and the UK/US.[16]

Germany and Japan have adopted what I call the 'insurance' model of withdrawal, providing inclusive but weaker and contingent forms of member protection. In terms of breadth of withdrawal grounds, Germany is the most liberal by far, closely followed by Japan. Withdrawal is permitted not only when fault of other participants is present, but also when the attribution of fault is unclear, when both the member seeking withdrawal and other participants are at fault, as well as non-fault scenarios.[17] The withdrawing member is not compensated for harm caused by the fault of others.[18] As only the close corporation is liable to pay the withdrawing member's monetary claim, the withdrawing member's claim is balanced against creditor protection considerations, and capital maintenance poses a major obstacle in enforcement,[19] The close corporation thus acts as a limited, quasi-'insurance fund' for members wishing to withdraw.[20]

In contrast, what I call the 'corrective' model of withdrawal is the model adopted in the US and the UK. The corrective model serves a compensatory function for minority shareholders. Shareholders successful in withdrawing on fault grounds may claim the value of their membership interest from the very parties at fault,[21] and also stand a chance of being compensated for their 'share' of the loss caused to the close corporation by the party responsible for the grounds of withdrawal.[22] With the close corporation not usually liable to pay,[23] business creditors' interests are not affected as a matter of corporate law, and thus pose no obstacle to the withdrawing shareholder's ability to enforce their monetary claim.[24] However, as non-fault withdrawal is not available in the UK,[25] and is

14 III.F.2.
15 III.G.2.
16 III.G.3.
17 III.G.3.i.
18 III.E.2.
19 III.E.3.
20 III.G.3.i.
21 III.G.3.ii.
22 III.E.2.
23 III.D.3.
24 III.E.3.
25 III.C.3.

largely limited to deadlock in some US states,[26] the scope of protection is narrower under the corrective model.

Both models are built around the same meta-principle or 'golden thread' of withdrawal design: protecting shareholders desirous of and deserving of withdrawal, but not at the expense of making innocent constituencies financially liable for the consequences. The two models, in making different constituencies their subjects on the two ends of the golden thread, do not contradict, but rather complement each other. The Model Remedy in this Book aims to achieve synthesis of both models of withdrawal.[27]

Taken together, Chapters III to VII make two contributions. First, they clarify and expand our understanding of how some of corporate law's most fundamental and intractable problems manifest across diverse jurisdictions, how they are addressed, and what the remaining challenges are. Chapters IV to VII do so through richly textured jurisdictional studies using the jurisdictionally neutral and theoretically informed comparative framework laid down in Chapter III.

Second, Chapter III contributes to comparative corporate law by identifying and analysing a phenomenon, which I call 'spontaneous functional convergence', in withdrawal law. This subtype of convergence occurs where jurisdictions appear to have – largely independently of other jurisdictions – developed legal regimes that are functionally similar but formally different using mostly, if not exclusively, *domestic* legal sources and inspirations. The spontaneous convergence observed in the withdrawal regimes of the target jurisdictions point to withdrawal as – if not quite the end of history – then at least a critical evolutionary milestone for close corporation law.

3 *Model*

The long and elaborate Model Remedy[28] drafted applies, within a non-jurisdiction -specific setting, findings from close corporation theory and comparative analysis of the target jurisdictions' withdrawal regimes. The Model Remedy's structure and key features of the Model Remedy flow from three guiding principles.[29]

The first is finality: withdrawal must bring intractable shareholder conflict to an end. For any shareholder meeting the standing criteria, withdrawal is a right that is exercisable by the withdrawal seeker in the circumstances prescribed by the Model Remedy without further justification.[30] Rather, it is the parties opposing withdrawal (e.g. other members or the close corporation) who are required to justify why withdrawal should be denied and how this would be fair to the withdrawal

26 III.C.3.
27 III.G.3.iii.
28 VIII.C.
29 VIII.B.
30 VIII.D.2, VIII.D.3.i–iii.

seeker.[31] Enforcement proceedings[32] and challenges against withdrawal[33] are accordingly structured to implement these features.

The second principle is structured flexibility. To cater to a wide range of close corporations with different needs and goals, the Model Remedy combines not only 'simple' default and mandatory provisions,[34] but also 'sticky defaults' that facilitate deliberate, informed customisation by parties so long as enhanced requirements[35] governing how parties may contract around the Model Remedy default are satisfied.

The third and final principle is functionality. A synthesis of both the corrective and insurance models, the Model Remedy offers comprehensive protection for minority shareholders from the vicissitudes of close corporation life that are not knowingly and expressly undertaken. Both fault and non-fault grounds[36] give rise to withdrawal rights that are enforceable against different liable parties.[37] The election to purchase mechanism, which permits any other member to choose to pay the withdrawing member's monetary claim in exchange for their equity,[38] further strengthens the Model Remedy's protective function at no cost to the close corporation.

The Model Remedy in Chapter IX makes two contributions. First, it offers a solution transcending the conceptual straitjackets that have long hampered close corporation law and scholarship. By applying insights from behavioural law and economics such as 'sticky defaults' in drafting, the Model Remedy offers a third way through the tired mandatory/default tension that has long driven and divided close corporation law scholarship.

Second, the Model Remedy offers a robust mechanism for shareholder protection that is potentially generalisable and applicable across diverse jurisdictions.[39] Incorporating a wide range of micro-solutions from different jurisdictions into a single, organised remedial framework, the Model Remedy is unconstrained by the jurisdiction-specific intellectual silos shaping and hampering the development of each individual jurisdiction's withdrawal regime. By integrating both corrective and insurance conceptual models of withdrawal, the Model Remedy aims to achieve the best of both worlds in the pursuit of extending corporate law's protection to the deserving.

31 VIII.D.3.iv.
32 VIII.D.5.
33 VIII.D.3.iv.
34 VIII.D.3.ii.
35 VIII.D.7.iii.
36 VIII.D.3.i–ii.
37 VIII.D.4.
38 VII.D.4.iv.
39 Subject to fundamental assumptions such as reasonably functioning legal dispute resolution systems (where corruption, cost, and delay are not insurmountable) and the existence of a lawful private sector organised as legal entities.

B APPLICATIONS

1 Legislation

Although scholarship and legislative agendas have historically given close corporations and their legal problems short shrift,[40] recent developments hint at increased awareness of the importance of close corporation legislation and of withdrawal specifically. Take for example UNCITRAL's Working Group I (Micro, Small and Medium-sized Enterprises)'s draft 'legislative guide' on a 'UNCITRAL Limited Liability Organization' ('UNLLO').[41] The 30 November 2020 version proposes a form of withdrawal based on 'reasonable cause' that seems to comprise both fault and non-fault grounds[42] and is premised on the entity being the party liable to pay the withdrawing member's claim.[43] The completed scholar-led proposal for a European Model Companies Act ('EMCA') also provides for withdrawal ('redemption' in the text), albeit apparently restricted to serious fault.[44] These cross-jurisdictional efforts and existing jurisdiction-specific legislative regimes reinforce withdrawal's importance within a system of corporate law; reformers would do well to include withdrawal on the agenda of any close corporation or SME law reform.

At this point, it may be tempting to conclude that legislation is the obvious, if not best, way of making withdrawal law. The devil, however, is in the details: if withdrawal legislation were to be crafted, how should reformers decide which model is best? Neither UNCITRAL's proposal nor the EMCA delves into specifics on technical aspects of withdrawal such as valuation, enforcement, and the precise extent to which parties may contract around each aspect.[45] Review of existing law and practice, including that of foreign jurisdictions, would be essential in any rigorous reform process.

This is precisely where this Book comes in handy. Its critical analysis of several existing statutory regimes (in the UK, US, and Japan) illuminates the pros and cons of each within a relatively jurisdiction-neutral framework. This offers legislators and other law reform participants the opportunity to look beyond their respective legal families, former colonisers/imperialists, or the 'prestigious' 'United' States, for

40 Albeit with exceptions in jurisdictions such as Germany, and on issues such as minimum capital (resulting in entities such as the UG (haftungsbeschränkt)), ease of incorporation, and taxation (e.g. LLC reform). The attempt to create a European *societas Privata Europaea* Regulation was also abandoned.

41 Available at https://uncitral.un.org/en/working_groups/1/msmes.

42 See UNICTRAL (2020b): 35 para. 122.

43 Ibid. 35 para. 124 ('it will be the UNLLO itself and not its members to bear the burden of the withdrawal payment').

44 See EMCA (2017): § 11.37 ('If any shareholder has, intentionally or by gross negligence, caused a loss'). The EMCA is a 'one law model' encompassing private, public, and traded companies: EMCA (2017): 14–16.

45 But see UNCITRAL (2020b): 35 para. 124 (briefly commenting on 'fair value' and suggesting pro-rata liquidation or going concern value as a starting point)

inspiration.[46] For jurisdictions dissatisfied with all four existing regimes examined on political, policy, or even aesthetic grounds, this Book further proposes a Model Remedy that addresses many of the limitations of existing legislative withdrawal regimes, and which is also more concrete, structured, rigorous, and comprehensive than any existing or proposed legislative regime. To give a statutory withdrawal remedy structure and substance and provide protection to weaker minorities while preserving room for private ordering by sophisticated parties, adoption or adaptation of the Model Remedy would be a logical and time-saving first step.

Lest one be carried away by faith in the legislature's power to write problems out of existence with the figurative pen, here is a reminder that creating or codifying withdrawal regimes by legislation has its limits. First is the issue of political will and circumstance. Withdrawal's success rate on the legislative agenda leaves something to be desired. Germany tried and failed at least twice to make withdrawal part of statute.[47] Japan tried once seriously and failed;[48] it arguably succeeded later *because* no one paid withdrawal much attention![49] The UK's attempt at statutory reform of unfair prejudice got bogged down in dissension and collective action problems.[50] As in most things in life (except perhaps academia), the perfect is the enemy of the good; better a flawed but *enacted* statutory withdrawal regime than the perfect unenacted one.

Second is the risk that judges, despite being entrusted with wide-ranging discretion in discharging the responsibility of interpreting and applying withdrawal legislation, may act in a manner that hinders rather than furthers the legislative objective. In the UK, two separate legislative withdrawal regimes separated by decades were respectively undermined by judicial intransigence[51] and the ambivalence of both reformers and a top judge.[52] The US picture is, as with most things, one of variety or chaos depending on one's point of view.[53] These (at best) mixed experiences with withdrawal legislation in the courts reinforce one fundamental if obvious point: legislators can make withdrawal part of written *law*, but judges make or break a withdrawal as a legal *remedy*.

We next turn to the challenges of implementing withdrawal as part of judicial dispute resolution.

46 This Book's choice of four former (and many might say current) imperialist powers for comparative analysis is at least partly attributable to an untenured academic's need to survive in today's international scholarly marketplace.
47 IV.C.1.ii.
48 VII.B.2.ii.
49 VII.D.1.
50 V.C.1; V.D.2.
51 V.C.1.i.
52 V.C.1.ii–iii, V.D.
53 VI.F.

2 Judicial Dispute Resolution

Two jurisdictional chapters (Germany, US) in this Book show that judges across the common-civil law divide have, despite only tenuous or no direct basis in written law, nonetheless fashioned withdrawal remedies.[54] Creating withdrawal by means of judicial lawmaking cannot be summarily dismissed as illegitimate.[55] With or without legislation,[56] for withdrawal to be truly part of a close corporation law premised on rule of law and effectively administered through judicial dispute resolution, there is no substitute for judicial acceptance of this mechanism.[57]

Yet so long as withdrawal is implemented by judges,[58] challenges are foreseeable. First, to be effective, withdrawal should ideally be judicially developed in a manner not inconsistent with that jurisdiction's existing written law, judicial precedent, and what might be loosely termed legal and judicial culture. Within these constraints, courts will need to show some level of creativity and decisiveness for withdrawal to grow into its own.[59] The precise doctrinal tools and legal arguments at hand differ by jurisdiction; the Book offers a sampling[60] that may be helpful. In any event, convergence on function (models of withdrawal) can occur without convergence in form (doctrine/statutory text).[61] This Book cannot speak to or resolve the idiosyncrasies or doctrinal problems of every jurisdiction considering judicial development of withdrawal, but the individual jurisdictional analyses, theoretical and comparative frameworks, and Model Remedy should nonetheless be useful from a broader policy and troubleshooting perspective.

Second, what is made by judges can also be unmade by them. A withdrawal remedy that exists only as unwritten law may be destroyed by a single judgment of the highest court, as setbacks in some US states have shown. However, this weakness is not unique to purely judicial withdrawal regimes. As the history of legislative withdrawal regimes in the UK and some US states also show, even a statutory regime can be largely neutralised by judges inclined to do so. To make judicial progress less

54 IV.C.1–2; VI.C.2.ii–iii.

55 Appeals to the superior ability of legislatures in making law, or invocation of legislation's democratic legitimacy in contrast with the bogeyman of 'gouvernement des juges' as grounds to exclude judicial lawmaking fall especially flat in corporate law. Although not without exceptions (e.g. Republic of Korea where derivative action reform in a presidential election campaign; see Chun (2018)), since when has corporate law ever been of broad interest to the voting public? Further, in authoritarian democracies or non-democracies, some of which are economically prosperous and here to stay, corporate law's legitimacy will not be determined by who makes it.

56 See IX.B.1.

57 See III.G.1.

58 Largely applicable also to arbitrators; cf IX.B.3.

59 For example, even if it is generally deemed illegitimate in a particular jurisdiction to refer expressly to scholarly writing or foreign law, there is nothing to stop intelligent and dedicated judges from reproducing aspects of a foreign withdrawal regime or the Model Remedy without public attribution. Having said that, citation would still be preferable – if only to make my bosses happier.

60 IV.C.1–2; VI.C.2.ii–iii.

61 III.G.2–3.

easily undone and missteps more likely corrected, robust engagement from practitioners and scholarly jurists through published analysis and critique[62] and other feedback mechanisms would be necessary.

A third obstacle for judges administering withdrawal law (whether of legislative or judicial creation) is valuation. It should be noted that this issue would remain relevant even if withdrawal legislation is enacted. Depending on jurisdiction, judges have varying levels of involvement, expertise, and experience in technical questions such as valuation. It is not impossible that judicial reluctance to order or recognise withdrawal may originate less from an anti-withdrawal or anti-minority protection attitude, but more from a lack of comfort or familiarity with the judicial role in minutiae such as valuation standards and discounts.[63] *Ceteris paribus*, a jurisdiction's withdrawal regime is more likely to operate effectively with a substantial corps of accounting and finance professionals supporting judges either directly as court experts/assessors or indirectly as parties' experts.

3 *Alternative/Informal Dispute Resolution*

This Book makes no claim that withdrawal as facilitated by judicial processes must be a mandatory component of any close corporation legal regime. It is always possible for some shareholder disputes to be resolved out of court effectively and cheaply in appropriate circumstances. In formalised alternative dispute resolution settings such as arbitration, the Model Remedy's fault/non-fault analysis and suggested outcomes may be helpful – especially in complex cases[64] – to arbitrators, adjudicators, and counsel, to the extent that neither the *lex causae* nor *lex fori* compels an inconsistent result.[65] Similarly, where withdrawal is the goal of a negotiation, the Model Remedy would assist parties and lawyers in identifying and prioritising issues for settlement negotiations and agreement drafting. This applies regardless of whether the parties' desired outcome is the same as or different from the result following from applying the Model Remedy directly.

Even where the oppressed or aggrieved minority shareholder's goal is not withdrawal, legal advisers may find the fault/non-fault categorisation explored in this Book[66] helpful when advising parties. Depending on the specific subtype of alternative dispute resolution adopted, it may be possible for the third party (mediator, conciliator, expert etc.) to offer an impartial if non-binding assessment of the parties' positions. Complaints reminiscent of non-fault scenarios may be more amenable to amicable resolution not ending in withdrawal, whereas intractable disputes over

62 In reasonably accessible forms recognised by that jurisdiction as forming part of the legal corpus.
63 I thank Kim Kon-Sik for this point.
64 Although many (if not most) close corporation disputes can throw up complex factual issues if parties or counsel were so minded.
65 *Quaere* if withdrawal must necessarily be governed by *lex societatis* or contractual choice of law.
66 III.C, III.G.3.i–ii.

unlawful or other fault-type conduct are more likely to be beyond non-contentious resolution.

4. *Ex Ante Contractual Arrangements*

For reasons discussed earlier,[67] it is not necessarily in the interests of the parties to try negotiating exhaustively for withdrawal remedies. The inherent flexibility of the 'fault' and 'non-fault' standards is advantageous when determining ex post liability in a wide range of factual scenarios, but that same quality may be unacceptable to parties seeking high levels of contractual certainty ex ante. Nevertheless, for parties ready and willing to engage in high levels of ex ante private ordering by contract, participants may find the Model Remedy helpful as either a template for drafting a contractual withdrawal mechanism, a checklist of issues to address in negotiations or the final agreement, or both. The safer approach – at least for minorities with some bargaining power – may be to agree to contract away withdrawal rights but with specific limits on the scope of that concession. In other words, it is better to have clarity on when exactly withdrawal would be *unavailable*, rather than attempt to stipulate exhaustively the circumstances where withdrawal would be *available*.

5 *Global Indices and Studies of Corporate Law and Governance*

Studies, assessments, or rankings of corporate law and governance regimes purporting to cover many jurisdictions have hitherto been conducted by scholars[68] and bodies such as the World Bank[69] without reference to or even awareness of withdrawal's existence.[70] This Book has identified withdrawal as a category of legal solutions distinct from other shareholder remedies and made a case for why withdrawal is the best – if not the only – solution to close corporation shareholder oppression and conflict. The time is ripe for revision of existing global (or multi-jurisdictional) indices and ranking methodologies to incorporate withdrawal as a vital component of any investor protection or corporate law and governance system.

To execute any large-N study, index, or ranking, careful input from local jurisdictional experts is helpful if not essential. Yet as the omission of withdrawal from earlier works suggests and the analysis in this Book reveals, identifying whether any given jurisdiction has a withdrawal regime or assessing the extent of its regime's effectiveness can be challenging. The concepts, definitions, and examples in this

67 II.E.3.iii.

68 See e.g. Djankov et al. (2008): 434 tbl. 1 (assessing world economies for regulation of related party transactions but failing to include withdrawal as a variable); Katelouzou & Siems (2015) (looking at the derivative action but not withdrawal as part of shareholder protection).

69 Which produces the highly influential *Doing Business Reports*.

70 On the World Bank's failure to account for 'direct suits' including withdrawal in its 'Protecting Minority Investors' indicators, see Koh (forthcoming 2022).

Book would go far in guiding jurisdiction corporate law experts in gathering and reporting the necessary information.

C EXTENSIONS

1 *Geographical/Jurisdictional*

For methodological and practical reasons,[71] this Book defines and develops withdrawal as a distinct concept by analysing a sample of four target jurisdictions drawn from the world's largest developed economies. This may and should be taken further by scholars who are, either individually or (more realistically) in teams, armed with in-depth knowledge and critical understanding of local law and context in jurisdictions not covered in this Book. Jurisdictions with both legislation and judicial precedent on withdrawal-type regimes are easier places to start. Singapore, for example, deserves a close look as it appears to offer two separate statutory withdrawal regimes, one corresponding to fault grounds and the other non-fault grounds.[72] Other candidates amenable to comparative investigation include Anglo-Commonwealth jurisdictions such as Canada (federal and some provinces), the Cayman Islands,[73] Malaysia, Australia, Hong Kong, and New Zealand,[74] and (non-Commonwealth) Israel.[75]

Where directly relevant legislation is lacking, analysing the legal basis and examples of withdrawal poses a greater challenge. Nevertheless, as the analysis of Germany and parts of the US has revealed, withdrawal can, in the absence of targeted legislation,[76] develop and subsist as judicial precedent, scholarly opinion, or both.[77] Studies of European jurisdictions[78] can be relatively easily arranged and would undoubtedly reveal interesting results, but the other continents – Asia, Africa, Latin America, and Oceania – also deserve a look. Scholarly bodies (e.g. International Academy of Comparative Law), professional associations (e.g. Inter-Pacific Bar Association), as well as international and regional organisations (e.g. UNCITRAL) could do much to raise awareness

71 I.B.2–3.

72 Companies Act 1967 (Singapore), s. 216 (oppression remedy); Insolvency, Restructuring and Dissolution Act 2018 (Singapore), s. 125(1)(i) (just and equitable winding up), s. 125(3) (share buyout order in lieu of winding up). See Koh & Tang (2017).

73 See Koh & Tang (2017): 377.

74 Albeit with the caveat that the larger jurisdictions may have bodies of judicial precedent no less substantial than the UK and hence similarly challenging.

75 Companies Law 1999, ss. 191, 192(b)–(c) (Israel).

76 I accept that in Germany's case selected provisions of the Civil Code (BGB) and Commercial Code (HGB) can be interpreted as supplying the textual basis for withdrawal – but they are most definitely not targeted at *GmbH* withdrawal specifically.

77 IV.C.1–2; VI.C.2.ii–iii; IX.B.2.

78 Cf Fleischer (2014).

of withdrawal as a distinct topic of investigation within broader contexts of corporate and commercial law or small-and-medium enterprise regulation.

2 *Applying the Tripartite Method to Comparative Corporate Law and Beyond*

It should be uncontroversial that whether a methodology is suitable largely turns on the nature of the endeavour. This Book is about solving a problem – shareholder conflicts in close corporations – through law. The 'tripartite method'[79] executed in this Book – comprising a theoretical and comparative framework; several in-depth and critical jurisdictional studies; and a concrete generalised model solution – is designed for precisely that purpose. A refinement and synthesis of methods used in books on comparative corporate law, the tripartite method is consciously and unabashedly rooted in the tradition of using comparative legal analysis to understand and solve real problems.[80] No method old or new is above criticism from comparativists.[81] In any event, the tripartite method aspires to be merely good, not perfect, and only for specific purposes. Accordingly, it is likely unnecessary or unsuitable for non-jurists and a subset of jurists.[82]

Who might benefit from adopting (or adapting) the tripartite method? First would be jurists working in comparative corporate law. Both established academic jurists collaborating with foreign counterparts in joint projects (scholarly or policy-oriented) and resourceful, disciplined graduate student jurists working solo are likely to find the tripartite method relatable and handy. Comparative law-oriented academic jurists working to solve concrete problems in areas of substantive law other than corporate law, but who find limited workable guidance from methodological debates applicable to their respective fields,

79 A name is a necessary (though insufficient) condition for a method to be recognised as such.

80 The tripartite method has no pretensions to being a new Grand Theory of comparative law or herald of a scientific revolution. While no comparative law scholar is, regardless of whether they are self-aware, is truly without 'theory' or 'method', it should not surprise that the great debates over comparative law Theory or Method are waged mostly by senior scholars with tenure or its equivalent. *Quaere* if any scholar can ever live up to the idealised standards set by the 'Masters' of comparative law old and new.

81 In particular, the tripartite method's 'model solution' may well suffer from the same problems plaguing 'legal transplants', albeit as one from a fictitious legal system. On the challenges and value of studying legal transplants, see e.g. Siems (2018a); Siems (2018b): 255–9; Graziadei (2019). I thank Tobias Tröger for this insight. For a critical view of 'tracks of comparison', see Frankenberg (2016): ch. 4. The tripartite method most closely fits Frankenberg's 'cognitive control' track; on this see ibid. 85–96.

82 Including: non-jurists approaching law from an disciplinarily external perspective (e.g. social sciences); researchers (jurists or otherwise) working with large-N designs; legal theorists and philosophers; persons working in established law-and-something interdisciplinary fields; jurists interested in making comparative observations but not in adapting or creating a solution (i.e. the traditional 'bipartite' method); single-jurisdiction jurists; severely time- and resource-strapped jurists, especially from under-resourced jurisdictions and institutions; and anyone (jurist or not) uninterested in tackling problems with legal tools (juntas, despots, organised crime elements, terrorists etc.).

may also benefit from the tripartite method.[83] Finally, legal policymakers, law reform bodies, or perhaps even appellate courts[84] – presumptively legal problem solvers *par excellence* – who are patient, well-resourced, and sincere in doing something other than mere signalling may find in the tripartite method a rigorous tool suitable for crafting solutions to complex and technical areas of law.[85]

3 *Models and Convergence in Corporate Law Beyond Withdrawal*

This Book's basic contribution to substantive corporate law is in defining, demarcating, and analysing a category of legal solutions to the close corporation problem of shareholder conflict as 'withdrawal remedies'.[86] Another contribution of the Book is to the comparative corporate law and governance literature on convergence and divergence. This Book identifies a modality of convergence – 'spontaneous functional convergence' – through analysis of four withdrawal regimes. This convergence is not towards a single point, but two distinct 'models' or 'ideal-types' named 'corrective' and 'insurance' models. The two models are not based on abstract scholarly theories, but rather built from the ground-up based on critical understanding and synthesis of legal concepts as understood and applied in the analysed jurisdictions, and the facts of decided cases. When juxtaposed, the two models reveal themselves to be different and partial expressions of the same broader function: protecting shareholders desirous and deserving of exit without financially prejudicing innocent constituencies.[87]

By identifying in corporate *law* not *convergence* (singular), but *convergences* (plural) towards *models* (plural), with each model representing a different approach to a single, broader *function* (singular) in the *absence* of strong external forces, this Book contributes to convergence literature in two ways. First, this Book is one of the rare studies (if not the first) to show functional convergence despite the absence of foreign influence[88] or external forces such as unification or har-

[83] This may be more helpful for emerging areas of substantive law, whereas scholars working in established sub-fields should prioritise engagement with the canon of comparatively oriented literature of their specific fields.

[84] Albeit only to the extent that judges are not constrained by rules or practice from publicly taking into consideration foreign and comparative law in justifying their decisions – which varies greatly by jurisdiction. Private international law cases, however, are a good place for courts to start doing comparative law.

[85] Depending on jurisdiction, using foreign/comparative law may be more controversial in comparatively politically sensitive areas such as constitutional, administrative, or criminal law, or economic regulation.

[86] II.C–D.

[87] III.G.3.

[88] III.G.2.i.

monisation of law,[89] regulatory competition,[90] or incentives to signal compliance with some single assumed desirable standard of Western (specifically Anglo-American) origin.[91] Second, this Book has highlighted the importance of not only identifying similarities and differences, but also seeing patterns (i.e. models) where possible within these similarities and differences in multi-jurisdictional studies.[92]

Although beyond the scope of this Book, there might very well be areas of corporate law other than withdrawal where spontaneous functional convergence has occurred or is in progress. The promise of identifying models and synthesising from different models a grand solution forming the best of all worlds should excite problem-solving-oriented comparative corporate law scholars. To use an extended analogy: when great minds seemingly think alike in corporate law or governance, this might be attributable to a loud, pushy actor dominating the room and depriving the great minds of the opportunity to form and exchange their views freely. What if great minds were (as in withdrawal law) left in peace to think things through mostly on their own? If they were to meet later and exchange their views as equals, should we be surprised to find that these great minds spontaneously came to conclusions that could be organised as schools of thought, with each school capturing a different aspect of the greater whole? There is never a better time for global discourse to progress towards a more egalitarian and multipolar footing than now.

89 À la Europe.

90 À la US state corporate laws; European reforms in the wake of the Court of Justice's cases on freedom of establishment.

91 See Puchniak & Lan (2017): 272, 332 and Puchniak & Kim (2017): 127, 131 (characterising Asia's seeming 'convergence' on independent directors as misleading and attributing it to 'halo signalling' of compliance with '(Anglo)American-cum-global norms of "good" corporate governance'); Goto, Koh & Puchniak (2020) (on 'faux convergence' in shareholder stewardship).

92 For an example identifying 'principal factors' to explain the evolution of independent directors in target jurisdictions and using these to classify jurisdictions under a 'loose taxonomy' for future comparison, albeit without developing 'models' as in this Book, see Puchniak & Kim (2017): 118–31.

Bibliography

ABA (1990)	Committee on Corporate Laws, 'Changes in the Revised Model Business Corporation Act – Amendments Pertaining to Closely Held Corporations' (1990) 46 Business Lawyer 297
ABA (2016)	American Bar Association Business Law Section Corporate Laws Committee, *Model Business Corporation Act (2016 Revision): Official Text with Official Comment & Statutory Cross-References* (American Bar Association 2016)
ADB (2015)	Asian Development Bank, *Asia SME Finance Monitor 2014* (Mandaluyong, Philippines, Asian Development Bank 2015)
Afterman (1969)	Afterman, Allen B., 'Statutory Protection for Oppressed Minority Shareholders: A Model for Reform' (1969) 55 Virginia LRev 1043
Aizawa (2006)	Aizawa, Tetsu (ed.), *Ritsuan Tantōsha ni yoru Shin-Kaisha Hō no Kaisetsu* [*The Drafters' Commentary on the New Companies Act*] (Bessatsu Shōji Hōmu vol. 295, Tokyo, Shōjihōmu 2006)
Aizawa (2009)	Aizawa, Tetsu (ed.), *Ichimon Ittō: Shin-Kaisha Hō* [*Q&A: The New Companies Act*] (rev ed., Tokyo, Shōjihōmu 2009)
Aizawa & Kōriya (2006a)	Aizawa, Tetsu & Kōriya Daisuke, 'Kaisha Hōsei no Gendaika ni tomonau Jisshitsu Kaisei no Gaiyō to Kihonteki na Kangaekata [The Substantive Reforms Accompanying the Modernization of the Corporate Law System: Overview and Fundamental Approaches]' in Aizawa (2006)
Aizawa & Kōriya (2006b)	Aizawa, Tetsu & Kōriya Daisuke, 'Mochibun-Kaisha [Membership Companies]' in Aizawa (2006)
Aizawa et al. (2006)	Aizawa, Tetsu, Hadama Masami & Kōriya Daisuke (eds.), *Ronten Kaisetsu Shin-Kaisha*

Hō: Senmon no Michishirube [*Commentary on the New Companies Act: A Thousand-Question Guide*] (Tokyo, Shōjihōmu 2006)

ALI (1994) — American Law Institute, *Principles of Corporate Governance: Analysis and Recommendations*, vol. 2 (St Paul, MN, American Law Institute Publishers 1994)

Altmeppen (2012) — Altmeppen, Holger, 'Die Dogmatik des Abfindungsanspruchs und die offenen Fragen zum Ausscheiden aus der GmbH [The Doctrine on Membership Interest Compensation Claims and Open Questions on Exit from the GmbH]' [2012] Zeitschrift für Wirtschaftsrecht 1685

AmJur2d (2019) — *American Jurisprudence, Second Edition*, vol. 37 (West 2019) *Fraud and Deceit* § 17

Andersson (2010) — Andersson, Jan, 'Minority Shareholder Protection in SMEs: A Question of Information Ex Post and Bargaining Power Ex Ante?' in Neville & Sørensen (2010)

Angell & Ames (1832) — Angell, Joseph K. & Samuel Ames, *Treatise on the Law of Private Corporations Aggregate* (1st ed., Boston, MA, Hilliard, Gray, Little & Wilkins 1832)

Aotake (1979) — Aotake, Shōichi, *Shō-Kibo Heisa Kaisha no Hōkisei* [*Legal Regulation of Small-Scale Closed Corporations*] (Tokyo, Bunshindō 1979)

Armour (2009) — Armour, John, 'Enforcement Strategies in UK Corporate Governance: A Roadmap and Empirical Assessment' in John Armour & Jennifer Payne (eds.), *Rationality in Company Law: Essays in Honour of DD Prentice* (Oxford, Hart Publishing 2009)

Armour et al. (2009a) — Armour, John, Simon Deakin, Priya Lele & Mathias Siems, 'How Do Legal Rules Evolve? Evidence from a Cross-Country Comparison of Shareholder, Creditor and Worker Protection' (2009) 57 AJCL 579

Armour et al. (2009b) — Armour, John, Bernard Black, Brian Cheffins & Richard Nolan, 'Private Enforcement of Corporate Law: An Empirical Comparison of the United Kingdom and the United States' (2009) 6 Journal of Empirical Legal Studies 687

Armour et al. (2017) — Armour, John, Holger Fleischer, Vanessa Knapp & Martin Winner, 'Brexit and Corporate Citizenship' (2017) 18 EBOR 225

Armour & Enriques et al. (2017) — Reinier Kraakman, John Armour, Paul Davies, Luca Enriques, Henry Hansmann, Gerard Hertig, Klaus Hopt, Hideki Kanda, Mariana

	Pargendler, Wolf-Georg Ringe, Edward Rock, Sofie Cools & Gen Goto, *The Anatomy of Corporate Law: A Comparative and Functional Approach* (3rd ed., Oxford University Press 2017)
Arner (2002)	Arner, Douglas, 'Development of the American Law of Corporations to 1832' (2002) 55 Southern Methodist University LRev 23
Art (2003)	Art, Robert C., 'Shareholder Rights and Remedies in Close Corporations: Oppression, Fiduciary Duties, and Reasonable Expectations' (2003) 28 Journal of Corporation Law 371
Ayres (1992)	Ayres, Ian, 'Judging Close Corporations in the Age of Statutes' (1992) 70 Washington University LQ 365
Ayres (1999)	Ayres, Ian, 'Empire or Residue: Competing Visions of the Contractual Canon' (1999) 26 Florida State University LRev 897
Ayres (2003)	Ayres, Ian, 'Response: Valuing Modern Contract Scholarship' (2003) 112 Yale LJ 881
Ayres (2012)	Ayres, Ian, 'Regulating Opt-Out: An Economic Theory of Altering Rules' (2012) 121 Yale LJ 2032
Bacher & von Blumenthal (2008)	Bacher, Philipp & Wolfram von Blumenthal, 'Die Verwertung von GmbH-Geschäftsanteilen bei Ausscheiden eines Gesellschafters [The Valuation of GmbH Membership Interests in the Case of a Member's Exit]' [2008] *Neue Zeitschrift für Gesellschaftsrecht* 406
Bachmann (2008)	Bachmann, Gregor, 'Introductory Editorial: Renovating the German Private Limited Company – Special Issue on the Reform of the GmbH' (2008) 9 German LJ 1063
Bachmann et al. (2014)	Bachmann, Gregor, Horst Eidenmüller, Andreas Engert, Holger Fleischer & Wolfgang Schön, *Regulating the Closed Corporation* (Berlin, De Gruyter 2014)
Bachner (2009)	Bachner, Thomas, *Creditor Protection in Private Companies: Anglo-German Perspectives for a European Legal Discourse* (Cambridge, Cambridge University Press 2009)
Bainbridge (1997)	Bainbridge, Stephen M., 'Community and Statism: A Conservative Contractarian Critique of Progressive Corporate Law Scholarship' (1997) 82 Cornell LRev 856
Bainbridge (2002)	Bainbridge, Stephen M., *Corporation Law and Economics* (New York, Foundation Press 2002)
Bahls (1990)	Bahls, Steven C., 'Resolving Shareholder Dissension: Selection of the Appropriate Equitable Remedy' (1990) 15 Journal of Corporation Law 285

Bainbridge (2020) Bainbridge, Stephen M., *Corporate Law* (4th ed., St Paul, MN, Foundation Press 2020)

Balz (1984a) Balz, Gerhard K., *Die Beendigung der Mitgliedschaft in der GmbH: Eine empirische und dogmatische Untersuchung zur Ausschließung und zum Austritt von Gesellschaftern* [*The Termination of Membership in the GmbH: An Empirical and Doctrinal Study of Expulsion and Withdrawal of Members*] (Berlin, Duncker & Humblot 1984)

Balz (1984b) Balz, Gerhard K., 'Rechte und Pflichten des Gesellschafters nach Austritt aus der GmbH [Rights and Duties of the Member After Withdrawal from the GmbH]' [1984] *Der Betrieb* 1865

Barnert (2003) Barnert, Thomas, *Die Gesellschafterklage im dualistischen System des Gesellschaftsrechts* [*The Shareholder Suit in the Dualistic Corporate Law System*] (Tübingen, Mohr Siebeck 2003)

Baum & Goto (2016) Baum, Harald & Gen Goto, 'Die japanische LLP im gesellschaftsrechtlichen Kontext [The J-LLP in the Corporate Law Context]' (2016) No. 41 ZJapanR/JJapanL 89

Baum & Puchniak (2012) Baum, Harald & Dan W Puchniak, 'The Derivative Action: An Economic, Historical and Practice-Oriented Approach' in Puchniak et al. (2012)

Baum & Takahashi (2011) Baum, Harald & Eiji Takahashi, 'Klagen gegen fehlerhafte Hauptversammlungsbeschlüsse im japanischen Aktienrecht [Legal Challenges against Flawed Shareholder Meeting Resolutions in Japanese KK Law]' (2011) No. 32 ZJapanR/JJapanL 153

Baumbach & Hueck (2013) Baumbach, Adolf & Alfred Hueck (eds.), *GmbHG: Gesetz betreffend die Gesellschaften mit beschränkter Haftung* [*GmbH Law*] (20th ed., Munich, C. H. Beck 2013)

Becht et al. (2008) Becht, Marco, Colin Mayer & Hannes F. Wagner, 'Where Do Firms Incorporate? Deregulation and the Cost of Entry' (2008) 14 Journal of Corporate Finance 241

Becker (1985) Becker, Michael, *Der Austritt aus der GmbH: Durchsetzung eines unentziehbaren Individualrechts im Interesse effektiven Minderheitenschutzes* [*Withdrawal from the GmbH: Implementation of an Inalienable Individual Right in the Interests of Effective Minority Protection*] (Kehl am Rhein, N. P. Engel 1985)

BEIS (2020) Department for Business, Energy & Industrial Strategy (UK), *Statistical Release: Business Population Estimates for the UK and Regions 2020* (Department for Business, Energy & Industrial Strategy, 8 October 2020), archived 7 March 2021 at https://perma.cc/P83Q-BRRD

Belcredi & Ferrarini (2013) Belcredi, Massimo, & Guido Ferrarini (eds.), *Boards and Shareholders in European Listed Companies: Facts, Context and Post-Crisis Reforms* (Cambridge, Cambridge University Press 2013)

Bell (2006) Bell, John, *Judiciaries Within Europe: A Comparative Review* (Cambridge, Cambridge University Press 2006)

Bell (2011) Bell, John, 'Legal Research and the Distinctiveness of Comparative Law' in Mark Van Hoecke (ed.), *Methodologies of Legal Research: Which Kind of Method for What Kind of Discipline?* (Oxford, Hart 2011)

Ben-Shahar (2011) Ben-Shahar, Omri, 'Fixing Unfair Contracts' (2011) 63 Stanford LRev 869

Ben-Shahar & Pottow (2006) Ben-Shahar, Omri, & John A. E. Pottow, 'On the Stickiness of Default Rules' (2006) 33 Florida State University LRev 651

Bennedsen (2014) Bennedsen, Morten, 'Centuries-Old Japanese Family-Owned Inn a Model for Succession', *South China Morning Post* (28 February 2014) www.scmp.com/business/companies/article/1436947/centuries-old-japanese-family-owned-inn-model-successionaccessed 4 June 2019

Berghof (2006) Berghoff, Hartmut, 'The End of Family Business? The Mittelstand and German Capitalism in Transition, 1949–2000' (2006) 80 Business History Review 263

Beurskens & Noack (2008) Beurskens, Michael & Ulrich Noack, 'The Reform of German Private Limited Company: Is the GmbH Ready for the 21st Century?' (2008) 9 German LJ 1069

BIS (2012) Department for Business, Innovation & Skills, 'Archived Documents: Company Law Review' (*UK Government Web Archive*, 1 November 2012) http://webarchive.nationalarchives.gov.uk/20121029131934/http:/www.bis.gov.uk/policies/business-law/company-and-partnership-law/company-law/publications-archive

Bishop (1995) Bishop, Carter G., 'Treatment of Members Upon Their Death and Withdrawal from a Limited Liability Company: The Case for a Uniform Paradigm' (1995) 25 Stetson LRev 255

Bittle & Hinson (2015)	Bittle, Lyndon & Kelli Hinson, 'Texas Turns A Corner: Resolving Shareholder Disputes in Closely Held Businesses After *Ritchie v Rupe*' (2015) 67 Baylor LRev 339
Black & Kraakman (1996)	Black, Bernard, & Reinier Kraakman, 'A Self-Enforcing Model of Corporate Law' (1996) 109 Harvard LRev 1911
Blair & Stout (2001)	Blair, Margaret M., & Lynn A Stout, 'Trust, Trustworthiness, and the Behavioral Foundations of Corporate Law' (2001) 149 University of Pennsylvania LRev 1735
Blath (2012)	Blath, Simon, 'Der Vollzug des Ausscheidens aus der GmbH – dogmatische und praktische Fragen [Executing Exit from the GmbH: Doctrinal and Practical Issues]' [2012] *GmbH-Rundschau* 657
Bloomberg (2019)	Bloomberg, 'Company Overview of Cisco Systems Netherlands Holdings B.V.' (*Bloomberg LP*, 1 June 2019), archived 1 June 2019 at https://web.archive.org/web/20190601170934/https://www.bloomberg.com/research/stocks/private/snapshot.asp?privcapId=8175804
BMJ (1969)	Bundesministerium der Justiz [Federal Ministry of Justice] (ed.), *Referentenentwurf eines Gesetzes über Gesellschaften mit beschränkter Haftung* [*Ministry of Justice Draft on an Act on Companies with Limited Liability*] (Cologne, Dr Otto Schmidt 1969)
Borg-Barthet (2013)	Borg-Barthet, Justin, 'Free at Last? Choice of Corporate Law in the EU following the Judgment in *VALE*' (2013) 62 International & Comparative LQ 503
BMWi (2021)	Federal Ministry for Economic Affairs and Energy (Germany), 'The German Mittelstand As a Model for Success' (*BMWi – Federal Ministry for Economic Affairs and Energy*, 2021) archived 7 March 2021 at https://perma.cc/BBW4-QXYY
Boros (1995)	Boros, Elizabeth J., *Minority Shareholders' Remedies* (Oxford, Clarendon Press 1995)
Boyle (2002)	Boyle, A. J., *Minority Shareholders' Remedies* (Cambridge, Cambridge University Press 2002)
Branson (2001)	Branson, Douglas M., 'The Very Uncertain Prospect of "Global" Convergence in Corporate Governance' (2001) 34 Cornell International LJ 321
Brinkman (2002)	Brinkman, Tobias, 'Minority Protection under Section 459 of the Companies Act 1985: A Comparison with the Law of the German GmbH (Private Limited Company)' (2002) 13 European Business LRev 55

Bugay (2013) — Bugay, Arthur L., 'Minority Shareholder Freeze-Out Litigation in Pennsylvania: Remedies Provided at Common Law and by Section 1767 of the Pennsylvania Business Corporation Law' (2013) 84 Pennsylvania Bar Association Quarterly 113

Bussani & Mattei (2012) — Bussani, Mauro, & Ugo Mattei (eds.), *The Cambridge Companion to Comparative Law* (Cambridge, Cambridge University Press 2012)

Butler & Ribstein (1990) — Butler, Henry N., & Larry E. Ribstein, 'Opting Out of Fiduciary Duties: A Response to the Anti-Contractarians' (1990) 65 Washington LRev 1

Cabrelli & Siems (2015) — Cabrelli, David, & Mathias Siems, 'Convergence, Legal Origins, and Transplants in Comparative Corporate Law: A Case-Based and Quantitative Analysis' (2015) 63 AJCL 109

Callison & Vestal (2009) — Callison, J. William, & Allan W. Vestal, 'Contractarianism and Its Discontents: Reflections on Unincorporated Business Organization Law Reform' (2009) 42 Suffolk University LRev 493

Carney (1987) — Carney, William J., 'The Theory of the Firm: Investor Coordination Costs, Control Premiums and Capital Structure' (1987) 65 Washington University LQ 1

Carney (1995) — Carney, William J., 'Limited Liability Companies: Origins and Antecedents' (1995) 66 University of Colorado LRev 855

Carney (1998) — Carney, William J., 'The Production of Corporate Law' (1998) 71 Southern California LRev 715

Charny (1990) — Charny, David, 'Nonlegal Sanctions in Commercial Relationships' (1990) 104 Harvard LRev 375

Charny (1991) — Charny, David, 'Hypothetical Bargains: The Normative Structure of Contract Interpretation' (1991) 89 Michigan LRev 1815

Chayes (1960) — Chayes, Abram, 'Madame Wagner and the Close Corporation' (1960) 73 Harvard LRev 1532

Cheffins (1997) — Cheffins, Brian R., *Company Law: Theory, Structure and Operation* (Oxford, Clarendon Press 1997)

Chen-Wishart (2018) — Chen-Wishart, Mindy, *Contract Law* (6th ed., Oxford, Oxford University Press 2018)

Chesterman (1973) — Chesterman, M. R., 'The "Just and Equitable" Winding Up of Small Private Companies' (1973) 36 MLR 129

Chrisman (2009) — Chrisman, Rodney D., 'LLCs Are the New King of the Hill: An Empirical Study of the Number of New LLCs, Corporations and LPs Formed in the United States Between 2004–2007 and How LLCs Were Taxed for Tax Years 2002–2006' (2009) 15 Fordham Journal of Corporate & Financial Law 459

Chun (2018) Kyung-Hoon Chun, 'Multiple Derivative Actions: Debates in Korea and the Implications for a Comparative Study' (2018) 15 Berkeley Business LJ 306

Cisco (2019) Cisco, 'Kaisha Gaiyō [Company Overview]' (*Cisco*), archived 3 February 2019 at https://web.archive.org/web/20190203043809/https://www.cisco.com/c/ja_jp/about/corporate-profile.html

Clark (1989) Clark, Robert C., 'Contracts, Elites, and Traditions in the Making of Corporate Law' (1989) 89 Columbia LRev 1703

Clark (2011) Clark, Jr, William H., 'The Relationship of the Model Business Corporation Act to Other Entity Laws' (2011) 74(1) Law & Contemporary Problems 56

CLRSG (1999) Company Law Review Steering Group, *Modern Company Law for a Competitive Economy: The Strategic Framework* (URN 99/654, February 1999)

CLRSG (2000a) Company Law Review Steering Group, *Modern Company Law for a Competitive Economy: Developing the Framework* (URN 00/656, London, Department of Trade and Industry, March 2000)

CLRSG (2000b) Company Law Review Steering Group, *Modern Company Law for a Competitive Economy: Completing the Structure*, vol. 1 (URN 00/1335, London, Department of Trade and Industry, November 2000)

CLRSG (2001) Company Law Review Steering Group, *Modern Company Law for a Competitive Economy: Final Report, vol.* 1 (URN 01/942, London, Department of Trade and Industry, June 2001)

Coffee (1988) Coffee, Jr, John C., 'No Exit: Opting Out, the Contractual Theory of the Corporation and the Special Case of Remedies' (1988) 53 Brooklyn LRev 919

Coffee (1989) Coffee, Jr, John C., 'The Mandatory/Enabling Balance in Corporate Law: An Essay on the Judicial Role' (1989) 89 Columbia LRev 1618

Cohen (1945) Cohen Committee, *Report of The Committee on Company Law Amendment* (Cmd 6659, 1945)

Comment (1965) Comment, 'Oppression as a Statutory Ground for Corporate Dissolution' [1965] Duke LJ 128

Companies House (2015)	Companies House, *Statistical Release: Companies Register Activities 2014/15* (August 2015), archived 2 June 2019 at https://web.archive.org/web/20190602093156/https://assets.publishing.service.gov.uk/government/uploads/system/uploads/attachment_data/file/456824/Incorporated_Companies_in_the_UK_2014_15_P1-7.pdf
Companies House (2016)	Companies House, 'Companies House official statistics: definitions to accompany statistical releases' (*Gov.uk*, 24 August 2016), archived 2 June 2019 at https://web.archive.org/web/20190602093034/https://www.gov.uk/government/publications/definitions-to-accompany-our-statistical-releases/companies-house-official-statistics-definitions-to-accompany-statistical-releases
Companies House (2020)	Companies House, 'Companies Register Activity 2019/20' (*Gov.uk*, 25 June 2020), archived 16 March 2021 at https://perma.cc/Z8RX-EJVV
Connelly et al. (2011)	Connelly, Brian L., S. Trevis Certo, R. Duane Ireland & Christopher R. Reutzel, 'Signaling Theory: A Review and Assessment' (2011) 37 Journal of Management 39
Cooter & Ginsburg (2003)	Cooter, Robert, & Tom Ginsburg, 'Leximetrics: Why the Same Laws are Longer in Some Countries than Others' (2003) U Illinois Law & Economics Research Paper No LE03-012 https://ssrn.com/abstract=456520
Copp (2000)	Copp, Stephen, 'Company Law: Individual Shareholder Rights' (2000) 11 International Company & Commercial LRev N6
Cross (2005)	Cross, Frank B., 'Law and Trust' (2005) 93 Georgetown LJ 1457
Cutts (1990)	Cutts, Robert L., 'Power from the Ground Up: Japan's Land Bubble' (1990) 68(3) Harvard Business Review 164
Dalley (2004)	Dalley, Paula J., 'The Misguided Doctrine of Stockholder Fiduciary Duties' (2004) 33 Hofstra LRev 175
Dammann & Schündeln (2011)	Dammann, Jens, & Matthias Schündeln, 'The Incorporation Choices of Privately Held Corporations' (2011) 27 Journal of Law, Economics, & Organization 79
Davies (2020)	Davies, Paul, *Introduction to Company Law* (3rd ed., Oxford, Oxford University Press 2020)
Davies et al. (2013)	Davies, Paul, Klaus J. Hopt, Richard Nowak & Gerard van Solinge (eds.), *Corporate Boards in Law and Practice: A Comparative Analysis in Europe* (Oxford, Oxford University Press 2013)

Davies & Worthington (2016) — Davies, Paul L., & Sarah Worthington, *Gower's Principles of Modern Company Law* (10th ed., London, Sweet & Maxwell 2016)

Davis (1917) — Davis, Joseph Stancliffe, *Essays in the Earlier History of American Corporations*, vol. 2 (Cambridge, Harvard University Press 1917)

Dawson (2014) — Dawson, James, '*Ritchie v Rupe* and the Future of Shareholder Oppression' (2014) 124 Yale LJ Forum 89

Destatis (2020) — Statistisches Bundesamt [Federal Statistical Office], *Finanzen und Steuern: Umsatzsteuerstatistik (Voranmeldungen) 2018* [*Finances and Taxes: Value Added Tax Statistics (Tax Returns) 2018*] (Wiesbaden, Statistisches Bundesamt, 24 March 2020), archived 10 March 2021 at https://perma.cc/9A5C-D5DY

Dignam & Lowry (2016) — Dignam, Alan, & John Lowry, *Company Law* (9th ed., Oxford, Oxford University Press 2016)

Djankov et al. (2008) — Djankov, Simeon, Rafael La Porta, Florencio Lopez-de-Silanes & Andrei Shleifer, 'The Law and Economics of Self-Dealing' (2008) 88 Journal of Financial Economics 430

DJT (2020) — 'djt at a glance' (Deutscher Juristentag eV, 2020) archived 10 March 2021 at https://perma.cc/Z5JZ-GDNQ

Dodd (1954) — Dodd, Edwin Merrick, *American Business Corporations Until 1860, with Special Reference to Massachusetts* (Cambridge, Harvard University Press 1954)

Donald (2005) — Donald, David C., 'Shareholder Voice and Its Opponents' (2005) 5 JCLS 305

Donohoe et al. (2015) — Donohoe, Michael P., Petro Lisowsky & Michael A. Mayberry, 'Who Benefits from the Tax Advantages of Organizational Form Choice?' (2015) 68 National Tax Journal 975

DTI (1998) — Department of Trade and Industry, *Modern Company Law for a Competitive Economy* (London, Department of Trade and Industry, March 1998)

Easterbrook & Fischel (1986) — Easterbrook, Frank H., & Daniel R. Fischel, 'Close Corporations and Agency Costs' (1986) 38 Stanford LRev 271

Easterbrook & Fischel (1989) — Easterbrook, Frank H., & Daniel R. Fischel, 'The Corporate Contract' (1989) 89 Columbia LRev 1416

Easterbrook & Fischel (1991) — Easterbrook, Frank H., & Daniel R. Fischel, *The Economic Structure of Corporate Law* (Cambridge, Harvard University Press 1991)

EC (2019) European Commission, '2019 SBA Fact Sheet: United Kingdom' (2019), archived 1 February 2021 at https://perma.cc/GQP3-VYDT

ECMA (2017) Paul Krüger Andersen et al., 'European Model Companies Act (EMCA) 2017 1st Edition' (2 November 2017) https://papers.ssrn.com/sol3/papers.cfm?abstract_id=2929348 accessed 1 July 2020.

Economist (2004) Economist, The, 'The Business of Survival – The World's Oldest Companies', *The Economist* (16 December 2004) www.economist.com/christmas-specials/2004/12/16/the-business-of-survival accessed 4 June 2019

Economist (2008) Economist, The, 'Sayonara, Salaryman – Employment in Japan' *The Economist* (3 January 2008) www.economist.com/briefing/2008/01/03/sayonara-salaryman accessed 4 June 2019

Egashira (2005a) Egashira, Kenjirō, *Kabushiki Kaisha Hō, Yūgen Kaisha Hō* [**Laws of Stock Corporations and Limited Liability Companies*] (4th ed., Tokyo, Yūhikaku 2005)

Egashira (2005b) Egashira, Kenjirō, '"Kaisha Hōsei no Gendaika ni kansuru Yōkō-an" no Kaisetsu [Commentary on the 'Draft Principles for the Modernization of the Corporate Law Regime']' in Bessatsu Shōji Hōmu Henshūbu (ed.), *Kaisha Hōsei Gendaika no Gaiyō* [*Outline of the Modernization of Corporate Law*] (Bessatsu Shōji Hōmu vol. 288, Tokyo, Shōjihōmu 2005)

Egashira (2011) Egashira, Kenjirō, 'Gōdō-Kaisha Seido no MERITTO: Shimedashi Bōshi-saku no Sokumen [The Merits of the GK Regime: The Aspect of Squeeze-out Prevention Measures]' in Matsushima Hideki, Itō Makoto & Fukuda Takahisa (eds.), *Monguchi Masahito Saibankan Taikan Kinen: Atarashii Jidai no Minji Shihō* [*Festschrift in Celebration of Judge Monguchi Masahito's Retirement: Civil Justice in a New Age*] (Tokyo, Shōjihōmu 2011)

Egashira (2017) Egashira, Kenjirō, *Kabushiki Kaisha Hō* [**The Laws of Stock Corporations*] (7th ed., Tokyo, Yūhikaku 2017)

Egashira & Monguchi (2008) Egashira Kenjirō & Monguchi Masahito (eds.), *Kaisha Hō Taikei: Kaisha Hōsei, Kaisha Gairon, Setsuritsu* [*Compendium on Corporate Law: The Corporate Law System, Corporate Law Theory, Formation*], vol. 1 (Tokyo, Seirinshoin 2008)

Egashira & Nakamura (2012) Egashira, Kenjirō & Nakamura Naoto (eds.), *Ronten Taikei Kaisha Hō: Kabushiki Kaisha IV, Mochibun Kaisha* [*A Systematic Exposition of Issues in Corporate Law: Stock Corporations IV and Membership Companies*], vol. 4 (Tokyo, Dai'ichihōki 2012)

Egashira et al. (1990) Egashira, Kenjirō, Morimoto Shigeru, Iwahara Shinsaku, Yamashita Tomonobu & Kanda Hideki, 'Zadankai: Shōhō Kaisei-jikō ni tsuite no Ronten [Panel Discussion: Issues on Commercial Code Reform]' (1990) 1215 Shōji Hōmu 48

Egashira et al. (2011) Egashira, Kenjirō, Ōsugi Ken'ichi, Niinomi Hiroshi, Itō Tsuyoshi & Kuroda Yutaka, 'Zadankai: Gōdō Kaisha-tō no Jittai to Kadai (jō) [Panel Discussion: The Reality and Issues of GKs, etc]' (2011) 1944 Shōji Hōmu 6

Eidenmüller (2014) Eidenmüller, Horst, 'Analytical Framework' in Bachmann et al. (2014)

Eisenberg (1974) Eisenberg, Melvin Aron, 'The Model Business Corporation Act and the Model Business Corporation Act Annotated' (1974) 29 Business Lawyer 1407

Eisenberg (1989) Eisenberg, Melvin Aron, 'The Structure of Corporation Law' (1989) 89 Columbia LRev 1461

Eisenberg (1995) Eisenberg, Melvin Aron, 'The Limits of Cognition and the Limits of Contract' (1995) 47 Stanford LRev 211

Enriques & Tröger (2019) Enriques, Luca, & Tobias Tröger (eds.), *The Law and Finance of Related Party Transactions* (Cambridge, Cambridge University Press 2019)

Entwurf (1891) *Entwurf eines Gesetzes betreffend die Gesellschaften mit beschränkter Haftung nebst Begründung und Anlagen, mtliche Ausgabe* [*Draft Act on Companies with Limited Liability with Explanatory Statement and Annexes, Official Version*] (Berlin, Franz Dahlen 1891)

Entwürfe (1972) *Entwürfe a) eines Gesetzes über Gesellschaften mit beschränkter Haftung (GmbHG), b) eines Einführungsgesetzes zum Gesetz über Gesellschaften mit beschränkter Haftung*, BT-Drs VI/3088 (31 January 1972)

Entwürfe (1973) *Entwurf eines Gesetzes über Gesellschaften mit beschränkter Haftung (GmbHG), Entwurf eines Einführungsgesetzes zum Gesetz über Gesellschaften mit beschränkter Haftung*, BT-Drs 7/253 (26 February 1973)

Esch (1981) Esch, Günter, 'Die mitgliedschafts- und steuerrechtlichen Wirkungen der Ausschließung oder des Austritts aus einer GmbH aus wichtigem Grund [Consequences for Membership Rights and Tax Law Implications of Expulsion or Withdrawal on wichtiger Grund from the GmbH]' [1981] GmbH-Rundschau 25

Eschenlohr (2000) — Eschenlohr, Harald, 'Beschränkungen der Austritts- und Kündigungsmöglichkeiten des Gesellschafters einer Familien-GmbH [Restrictions on Possibility of Withdrawal and Resignation of the Member of a Family-GmbH]' in Peter Hommelhoff, Rolf Schmidt-Diemitz & Axel Sigle (eds.), *Familiengesellschaften: Festschrift für Walter Sigle zum 70. Geburtstag* (Cologne, Otto Schmidt 2000)

Farrar & Hamill (1998) — Farrar, Laurel Wheeling, & Susan Pace Hamill, 'Dissociation from Alabama Limited Liability Companies in the Post Check-The-Box Era' (1998) 49 Alabama LRev 909

Fastrich (2013a) — Fastrich, Lorenz, 'Einleitung [Introduction]' in Baumbach & Hueck (2013)

Fastrich (2013b) — Fastrich, Lorenz, 'Anhang nach § 34 Ausschluss und Austritt von Gesellschaftern [Appendix to Section 34: Expulsion and Withdrawal of Members]' in Baumbach & Hueck (2013)

Fichtner (1967) — Fichtner, Dieter, 'Austritt und Kündigung bei der GmbH [Withdrawal and Resignation in the GmbH]' [1967] Betriebs-Berater 17

Field (2009) — Field, Heather M., 'Checking in on Check-the-Box' (2009) 42 Loyola of Los Angeles LRev 45

Fleckner & Hopt (2013) — Fleckner, Andreas M., & Klaus J. Hopt (eds.), *Comparative Corporate Governance: A Functional and International Analysis* (Cambridge, Cambridge University Press 2013)

Fleischer (2001) — Fleischer, Holger, 'Grundfragen der ökonomischen Theorie im Gesellschafts- und Kapitalmarktrecht [Fundamental Issues of Economic Theory in Corporate and Capital Market Law]' [2001] Zeitschrift für Unternehmens- und Gesellschaftsrecht 1

Fleischer (2014) — Fleischer, Holger, 'Shareholder Conflicts in Closed Corporations' in Bachmann et al. (2014)

Fleischer (2016) — Fleischer, Holger, 'A Guide to German Company Law for International Lawyers – Distinctive Features, Particularities, Idiosyncrasies' in Fleischer et al. (2016)

Fleischer (2018a) — Fleischer, Holger, 'Comparative Corporate Governance in Closely Held Corporations' in Gordon & Ringe (2018)

Fleischer (2018b)	Fleischer, Holger, 'Einleitung [Introduction]' in Fleischer & Goette (2018)
Fleischer & Goette (2016)	Fleischer, Holger, & Wulf Goette (eds.), *Münchener Kommentar zum Gesetz betreffend die Gesellschaften mit beschränkter Haftung – GmbHG* [*Munich Commentary on the Law on Limited Liability Corporations*], vol. 2 (2nd ed., Munich, C. H. Beck 2016)
Fleischer & Goette (2018)	Fleischer, Holger, & Wulf Goette (eds.), *Münchener Kommentar zum Gesetz betreffend die Gesellschaften mit beschränkter Haftung – GmbHG* [*Munich Commentary on the Law on Limited Liability Corporations*] (3rd ed., Munich, C. H. Beck 2018)
Fleischer et al. (2016)	Fleischer, Holger, Hideki Kanda, Kon Sik Kim & Peter Mülbert (eds.), *German and Asian Perspectives on Company Law: Law and Policy Perspectives* (Tübingen, Mohr Siebeck 2016)
Fletcher (2020)	*Fletcher Cyclopedia of the Law of Corporations*, vol 16A, § 8099 (September 2020)
Folk (1966)	Folk, III, Ernest L., 'Corporation Statutes: 1959–1966' [1966] Duke LJ 875
Frankenberg (2016)	Frankenberg, Günter, *Comparative Law as Critique* (Cheltenham, Elgar 2016)
Freedman (1994)	Freedman, Judith, 'Small Businesses and the Corporate Form: Burden or Privilege?' (1994) 57 MLR 555
Freedman (2000)	Freedman, Judith, 'Limited Liability: Large Company Theory and Small Firms' (2000) 63 (3) MLR 317
freee (2013)	freee KK, 'Shiranai to son suru? Gōdō Kaisha no MERITTO, DEMERITTO [At a Disadvantage If You Don't Know? Pros and Cons of GKs]' (*Keiei HAKKĀ* [Management Hacker], 27 September 2013), archived 28 October 2017 https://web.archive.org/web/20171028160912/https://keiei.freee.co.jp/2013/09/27/goudougaisya/
French (2015)	French, Derek, *Applications to Wind Up Companies* (3rd ed., Oxford University Press 2015)
Friedman (2004)	Friedman, Howard M., 'The Silent LLC Revolution: The Social Cost of Academic Neglect' (2004) 38 Creighton LRev 35
Garner (2014)	Garner, Bryan A. (ed.), *Black's Law Dictionary* (10th ed., St Paul, Thomson West 2014)
Geis (2019)	Geis, George S., 'Information Litigation in Corporate Law' (2019) 71 Alabama LRev 407
Gerner-Beuerle & Schuster (2014)	Gerner-Beuerle, Carsten, & Edmund-Philipp Schuster, 'The Evolving Structure of Directors' Duties in Europe' (2014) 15 EBOR 191

Geu (1992)	Geu, Thomas Earl, 'Understanding the Limited Liability Company: A Basic Comparative Primer (Part One)' (1992) 37 South Dakota LRev 44
Gevurtz (1995)	Gevurtz, Franklin A., 'Squeeze-Outs and Freeze-Outs in Limited Liability Companies' (1995) 73 Washington University LQ 497
Gigerenzer (2007)	Gigerenzer, Gerd, *Gut Feelings: The Intelligence of the Subconscious* (New York, Viking 2007)
Gillette (1985)	Gillette, Clayton P., 'Commercial Rationality and the Duty to Adjust Long-Term Contracts' (1985) 69 Minnesota LRev 521
Gilson (2001)	Gilson, Ronald J., 'Globalizing Corporate Governance: Convergence of Form or Function' (2001) 49 AJCL 329
Goddard (1999a)	Goddard, Robert, 'Enforcing the Hypothetical Bargain: Sections 459–461 of the Companies Act 1985' (1999) 20(3) Company Lawyer 66
Goddard (1999b)	Goddard, Robert, '*Re Legal Costs Negotiators Ltd*: An Oppressed Majority?' (1999) 20(7) Company Lawyer 241
Goddard (1999c)	Goddard, Robert, 'Closing the Categories of Unfair Prejudice' (1999) 20(10) Company Lawyer 333
Goette (2014)	Goette, Maximilian, *Der Exit der Minderheit aus der GmbH* [*Exit of the Minority from the GmbH*] (Cologne, Carl Heymanns 2014)
Gordon (1989)	Gordon, Jeffrey N., 'The Mandatory Structure of Corporate Law' (1989) 89 Columbia LRev 1549
Gordon & Ringe (2018)	Gordon, Jeffrey N., & Wolf-Georg Ringe (eds.), *Oxford Handbook of Corporate Law and Governance* (Oxford University Press 2018)
Gordon & Roe (2004a)	Gordon, Jeffrey N., & Mark J. Roe (eds.), *Convergence and Persistence in Corporate Governance* (Cambridge University Press 2004)
Gordon & Roe (2004b)	Gordon, Jeffrey N., & Mark J. Roe, 'Introduction' in Gordon & Roe (2004a)
Görner (2013)	Görner, André, '§ 34 Einziehung von Geschäftsanteilen [Section 34: Redemption of Membership Interests]' in Heinz Rowedder & Christian Schmidt-Leithoff (eds.), *Gesetz betreffend die Gesellschaften mit beschränkter Haftung (GmbHG): Kommentar* [*The Law on Limited Liability Corporations: A Commentary*] (5th ed., Munich, Franz Vahlen 2013)
Goto, Koh & Puchniak (2020)	Goto, Gen, Alan K. Koh & Dan W. Puchniak, 'Diversity of Shareholder Stewardship in Asia: Faux Convergence' (2020) 53 Vanderbilt Journal of Transnational Law 829

Gower (1953) Gower, L. C. B. (Laurence Cecil Bartlett) , 'The English Private Company' (1953) 18 Law & Contemporary Problems 535

Gower (1956) Gower, L. C. B. (Laurence Cecil Bartlett), 'Some Contrasts Between British and American Corporation Law' (1956) 69 Harvard LRev 1369

Graziadei (2019) Graziadei, Michele, 'Comparative Law, Transplants, and Receptions' in Reimann & Zimmermann (2019)

Grunewald (1991) Grunewald, Barbara, 'Probleme bei der Aufbringung der Abfindung für ausgetretene GmbH-Gesellschafter [Problems in the Funding of Compensation to Withdrawing Members]' [1991] GmbH-Rundschau 185

Hadden (1977) Hadden, Tom, *Company Law and Capitalism* (2nd ed., London, Weidenfeld & Nicolson 1977)

Hamada (1974) Hamada, Michiyo, *AMERIKA Heisa Kaisha Hō: Sono Genjō oyobi Nihon Hō e no Teigen [American Close Corporation Law: Its Current State and Its Suggestions for Japanese Law]* (Tokyo, Shōji Hōmu Kenkyū-kai 1974)

Hamada (1983) Hamada, Michiyo, 'Kabunushi no Mujōken Kabushiki Kaitori Seikyū-ken (ichi) [The Shareholder's Right to Demand a Share Buyout at Will (Part 1)]' (1983) 982 Shōji Hōmu 59

Hamada (1986a) Hamada, Michiyo, 'Kabushiki, Mochibun no Kaitori Seikyū-ken: Kaisha-hō Kaisei Shi'an ni okeru sono Kōsō ni tsuite [The Right to Demand Repurchase of Shares and Membership Interests: On their Conception in the Corporate Law Reform Proposal]' (1986) 1093 Shōji Hōmu 2

Hamada (1986b) Hamada, Michiyo, 'Forthcoming Legislative Reform of Japanese Corporation Law: Comparative Study of Japanese and American Close Corporation Law' (research paper, Harvard Law School 1986)

Hamada (1990) Hamada, Michiyo, 'Heisa-kaisha ni okeru Kabushiki Seido no Kaisei [Reform of the Share System in Closed Corporations]' (1990) 963 Jurisuto 48

Hamada (1993) Hamada, Michiyo, 'Shō-kibo Kaisha ni kansuru Rippō-jō no Mondaiten [Issues in Legislating for Small-scale Corporations]' in Kitazawa & Hamada (1993)

Hamill (1995) Hamill, Susan Pace, 'The Taxation of Domestic Limited Liability Companies and Limited Partnerships: A Case for Eliminating the

Partnership Classification Regulations' (1995) 73 Washington University LQ 565

Hamill (1996) — Hamill, Susan Pace, 'The Limited Liability Company: A Catalyst Exposing the Corporate Integration Question' (1996) 95 Michigan LRev 393

Hamill (1998) — Hamill, Susan Pace, 'The Origins Behind the Limited Liability Company' (1998) 59 Ohio State LJ 1459

Hamill (1999) — Hamill, Susan Pace, 'From Special Privilege to General Utility: A Continuation of Willard Hurst's Study of Corporations' (1999) 49 American University LRev 81

Hannigan (1988) — Hannigan, Brenda, 'Section 459 of the Companies Act – A Code of Conduct for the Quasi-Partnership?' [1988] LMCLQ 60

Hannigan (2018) — Hannigan, Brenda, *Company Law* (5th ed., Oxford, Oxford University Press 2018)

Hansen (2018) — Hansen, Hans, 'Fallacies' in Edward N. Zalta (ed.), *The Stanford Encyclopedia of Philosophy* (Summer 2018 Edition), archived 18 March 2019 at https://web.archive.org/web/20190318072821/https://plato.stanford.edu/archives/sum2018/entries/fallacies/

Hansmann & Kraakman (2001) — Hansmann, Henry, & Reinier Kraakman, 'The End of History for Corporate Law' (2001) 89 Georgetown LJ 439

Hansmann et al. (2006) — Hansmann, Henry, Reinier Kraakman & Richard Squire, 'Law and the Rise of the Firm' (2006) 119 Harvard LRev 1333

Harris (2013) — Harris, Ron, 'The Private Origins of the Private Company: Britain 1862–1907' (2013) 33(2) Oxford Journal of Legal Studies 339

Hart (1988) — Hart, Oliver D., 'Incomplete Contracts and the Theory of the Firm' (1988) 4 Journal of Law, Economics & Organization 119

Hart (1995) — Hart, Oliver, *Firms, Contracts, and Financial Structure* (Oxford, Clarendon Press 1995)

Hayashi (2012) — Hayashi, Hirokazu, 'Dai-575-jō [Article 575]' in Egashira & Nakamura (2012)

Haynsworth (1986) — Haynsworth, Harry J., 'The Effectiveness of Involuntary Dissolution as a Remedy for Close Corporation Dissension' (1986) 35 Cleveland State LRev 25

Heckschen (2010) — Heckschen, Heribert, 'Einziehung, Zwangsabtretung und Ausschluss in der Insolvenz eines GmbH-Gesellschafters [Cancellation, Forced Transfer, and Expulsion in the Insolvency of a

	GmbH Member]' [2010] Neue Zeitschrift für Gesellschaftsrecht 521
Heidinger & Blath (2007)	Heidinger, Andreas & Simon Blath, 'Das Ausscheiden eines Gesellschafters aus der GmbH [The Exit of a Member from the GmbH]' [2007] GmbH-Rundschau 1184
Hertig (2004)	Hertig, Gerard, 'Convergence of Substantive Law and Convergence of Enforcement: A Comparison' in Gordon & Roe (2004a)
Hetherington (1969)	Hetherington, J. A. C., 'Special Characteristics, Problems, and Needs of the Close Corporation' [1969] University of Illinois Law Forum 1
Hetherington & Dooley (1977)	Hetherington, J. A. C. & Michael P. Dooley, 'Illiquidity and Exploitation: A Proposed Statutory Solution to the Remaining Close Corporation Problem' (1977) 63 Virginia LRev 1
Hewitt et al. (2016)	Hewitt, Ian, Simon Howley & James Parkes (eds.), *Hewitt on Joint Ventures* (6th ed., Sweet & Maxwell 2016)
Hillman (1982)	Hillman, Robert W., 'The Dissatisfied Participant in the Solvent Business Venture: A Consideration of the Relative Permanence of Partnerships and Close Corporations' (1982) 67 Minnesota LRev 1
Hirota (2013)	Hirota, Tetsuji, *Shōsū Kabunushi no Hogo to Kyūsai* [*Minority Shareholder Protection and Remedies*] (Tokyo, Dai'ichihōki 2013)
Hirschman (1970)	Hirschman, Albert O, *Exit, Voice, and Loyalty: Responses to Decline in Firms, Organizations, and States* (Cambridge, MA, Harvard University Press 1970)
Hofmann (2011)	Hofmann, Christian, *Der Minderheitsschutz im Gesellschaftsrecht* [*Minority Protection in Corporate Law*] (Berlin, De Gruyter 2011)
Hollington (2007)	Hollington, Robin, 'Oppression of Minority Shareholders – Reflections on *Blisset v Daniel*' (2007) 19 Denning LJ 5
Hollington (2013)	Hollington, Robin, 'Recent Cases on the Winding-Up of Hedge Funds on Treasure Islands' in Joan Loughrey (ed.), *Directors' Duties and Shareholder Litigation in the Wake of the Financial Crisis* (Cheltenham, Edward Elgar 2013)
Hollington (2017)	Hollington, Robin, *Hollington on Shareholders' Rights* (8th ed., London, Sweet and Maxwell 2017)
Hōmushō (1984)	Hōmushō Minji-kyoku Sanjikan-shitsu [Counsellors' Office, Civil Affairs Bureau, Ministry of Justice], 'Daishō (Kōkai, Hi-Kōkai)

Kaisha Kubun Rippō oyobi Gappei ni kansuru Mondaiten – Shōwa 59-nen 5-gatsu 9-nichi (Shiryō) [Issues on Legislating Separately for Companies Based on Size Distinctions (Open, Closed) and Mergers–9 May 1984 (Materials)]' in Inaba Takeo, Ōtsuka Saburō & Kawamoto Ichirō et al. (eds.), *Daishō Kaisha Kubun Rippō-tō no Ronten – Hōmushō no "Mondaiten" no Kaisetsu to Bunken Kaidai [Issues on Legislating Separately for Companies Based on Size Distinctions, etc.– Commentary on the Ministry of Justice's "Issues" and Literature Review*] (Bessatsu Shōji Hōmu No. 75, Tokyo, Shōji Hōmu Kenkyū-kai 1984)

Hōmushō (1986) Hōmushō Minji-kyoku Sanjikan-shitsu [Counsellors' Office, Civil Affairs Bureau, Ministry of Justice], 'Shōhō, yūgen-gaisha-hō kai-sei shi'an (Shōwa 61-nen 5-gatsu 15-nichi) [Commercial Code and Limited Liability Corporation Act Reform Proposal (15.05.1986)]' in Inaba & Ōtani (1986a)

Hōmushō (1987) Hōmushō Minji-kyoku Sanjikan-shitsu [Counsellors' Office, Civil Affairs Bureau, Ministry of Justice] (ed.), *Shōhō, Yūgen-kaisha-hō Kaisei Shi'an: Kakkai Iken no Bunseki [Analysis of Feedback from Various Sectors on the Commercial Code and Limited Liability Corporation Act Reform Proposal*] (Bessatsu Shōji Hōmu No 93, Tokyo, Shōji Hōmu Kenkyū-kai 1987)

Hōmushō (2003) Hōmushō Minji-kyoku Sanjikan-shitsu [Counsellors' Office, Civil Affairs Bureau, Ministry of Justice], 'Kaisha Hōsei no Gendaika ni kansuru Yōkō Shi'an Hosoku Setsumei [Supplementary Explanations to the Preliminary Draft Principles for the Modernization of the Corporate Law Regime]' (October 2003), archived 6 February 2013 at https://web.archive.org/web/20130206135523/http://www.moj.go.jp/content/000071773.pdf

Hopt (1997) Hopt, Klaus J., 'Shareholder Rights and Remedies: A View from Germany and the Continent' [1997] Company, Financial and Insolvency LRev 261

Hopt (2019) Hopt, Klaus J., 'Comparative Company Law' in Reimann & Zimmermann (2019)

Horwitz (1985) Horwitz, Morton J., '*Santa Clara* Revisited: The Development of Corporate Theory' (1985) 88 West Virginia LRev 173

Hōsei-Shingikai (2003) Hōsei Shingikai Kaishahō (Gendaika Kankei) Bukai [Corporate Law (Modernization) Subcommittee,

Legislative Council, Ministry of Justice], 'Kaisha Hōsei no Gendaika ni kansuru Yōkō Shi'an [Preliminary Draft Principles for the Modernization of the Corporate Law Regime]' (22 October 2003), archived 6 February 2013 at https://web.archive.org/web/20130206135536/http://www.moj.go.jp/content/000071772.pdf

Hōsei-Shingikai (2005) Hōsei Shingikai [Legislative Council, Ministry of Justice], 'Kaisha Hōsei no Gendaika ni kansuru Yōkō-an [Draft Principles for the Modernization of the Corporate Law Regime]' (9 February 2005), archived 24 August 2017 at https://web.archive.org/web/20170824222332/http://www.moj.go.jp/shingi1/shingi_050209-1-1.html

Hovenkamp (1991) Hovenkamp, Herbert, *Enterprise and American Law, 1836–1937* (Cambridge, Harvard University Press 1991)

Hueck (1947) Hueck, Alfred, *Der Treuegedanke im modernen Privatrecht* [*The Concept of Loyalty in Modern Private Law*] (Munich, Bavarian Academy of Sciences and Humanities 1947)

Hurst (1970) Hurst, James Willard, *The Legitimacy of the Business Corporation in the Law of the United States, 1780–1970* (Charlottesville, University Press of Virginia 1970)

IfM (2021a) IfM Bonn, 'KMU-Definition des IfM Bonn [IfM Bonn's Definition of SMEs]' (*IfM Bonn: Institut für Mittelstandsforschung* [Institute for Mittelstand Research], 2021), archived 7 March 2021 at https://perma.cc/V2RZ-JRVH

IfM (2021b) IfM Bonn, 'Mittelstand im Überblick [SMEs in Overview]' (*IfM Bonn: Institut für Mittelstandsforschung* [Institute for Mittelstand Research], 2021), archived 7 March 2021 at https://perma.cc/U48B-E3BE

IfM (2021c) IfM Bonn, 'Mittelstandsdefinition des IfM Bonn [IfM Bonn's Definition of Mittelstand]' (*IfM Bonn: Institut für Mittelstandsforschung* [Institute for Mittelstand Research], 2021), archived 7 March 2021 at https://perma.cc/6LM6-S3LS

Iida (2013) Iida, Hidefusa, *Kabushiki Kaitori Seikyū-ken no Kōzō to Kaitori Kakaku Santei no Kōryo Yōso* [*The Structure of Appraisal and Considerations in the Determination of the Purchase Price*] (Tokyo, Shōjihōmu 2013)

Illig (2006) Illig, Robert C., 'Minority Investor Protections as Default Norms: Using Price to Illuminate the Deal in Close Corporations' (2006) 56 American University LRev 275

Immenga (1970) Immenga, Ulrich, *Die personalistiche Kapitalgesellschaft: Eine rechtsvergleichende Untersuchung nach deutschem GmbH-Recht und dem Recht der Corporations in den Vereinigten Staaten* [*The Personalistic Capital-based Company: A Comparative Study of German GmbH Law and the Law of Corporations in the United States*] (Bad Homburg vor der Höhe, Athenäum 1970)

Inaba & Ōtani (1986a) Inaba, Takeo, & Ōtani Yoshio, *Shōhō, Yūgen-kaisha-hō Kaisei Shi'an no Kaisetsu* [*Commentary on the Commercial Code and Limited Liability Corporation Act Reform Proposal*] (Bessatsu Shōji Hōmu No. 89, Tokyo, Shōji Hōmu Kenkyū-kai 1986)

Inaba & Ōtani (1986b) Inaba, Takeo, & Ōtani Sadao, 'Shōhō, Yūgen-kaisha-hō Kaisei Shi'an no Kaisetsu [Commentary on the Commercial Code and Limited Liability Corporation Act Reform Proposal]' in Inaba & Ōtani (1986a)

IRS (2020) Internal Revenue Service, SOI [Statistics of Income] Tax Stats – Integrated Business Data, tbl. 1 (Tax Years 1980–2015), archived 7 March 2021 at https://perma.cc/7WBH-CEEE

Ishi (2001) Ishi, Hiromitsu, *The Japanese Tax System* (3rd ed., Oxford, Oxford University Press 2001)

Jamrisko et al. (2021) Jamrisko, Michelle, Wei Lu & Alexandre Tanzi, 'South Korea Leads World in Innovation as US Exits Top Ten' (*Bloomberg*, 3 February 2021), archived 7 March 2021 https://perma.cc/HU5P-T95Z

Jenkins (1962) Jenkins Committee, *Report of the Company Law Committee* (Cmnd 1749, London, Stationery Office 1962)

Jensen & Meckling (1976) Jensen, Michael C., & William H. Meckling, 'Theory of the Firm: Managerial Behavior, Agency Costs and Ownership Structure' (1976) 3 Journal of Financial Economics 305

JFSA (2021) Japan Federation of Shiho-shoshi's Associations, 'Shiho-shoshi Profile' (*Nihon Shihō Shoshi-kai Rengōkai*), archived 7 March 2021 at https://perma.cc/4UFB-HG9E

JLTC (2019) Japanese Law Translation Council, *Standard Legal Terms Dictionary* (version 14.0, March 2019), available at www.japaneselawtranslation.go.jp/dict/download?re=02 accessed 4 June 2019

Joffe et al. (2015) Joffe, Victor, David Drake, Giles Richardson, Daniel Lightman & Timothy Collingwood, *Minority Shareholders: Law, Practice, and*

Procedure (5th ed, Oxford, Oxford University Press 2015)

Johnson (1983) Johnson, Richard, 'Comments: The Limited Liability Company Act' (1983) 11 Florida State University LRev 387

Jolls (1998) Jolls, Christine, 'Behavioral Economics Analysis of Redistributive Legal Rules' (1998) 51 Vanderbilt LRev 1653

Jolls & Sunstein (2006) Jolls, Christine, & Cass R. Sunstein, 'Debiasing Through Law' (2006) 35 Journal of Legal Studies 199

Jolls et al. (1998) Jolls, Christine, Cass R. Sunstein & Richard Thaler, 'A Behavioral Approach to Law and Economics' (1998) 50 Stanford LRev 1471

Karjala (1989) Karjala, Dennis S., 'An Analysis of Close Corporation Legislation in the United States' (1989) 21 Arizona State LJ 663

Kanda (2014) Kanda, Hideki (ed.), *Kaisha Hō KONMENTAARU: Mochibun Kaisha (1)* [*Commentary on the Companies Act: Membership Companies (1)*], vol. 14 (Tokyo, Shōjihōmu 2014)

Kanda (2021) Kanda Hideki, *Kaisha Hō* [*Corporate Law*] (23rd ed., Tokyo, Yūhikaku 2021)

Kanda & Levmore (1985) Kanda, Hideki, & Saul Levmore, 'The Appraisal Remedy and the Goals of Corporate Law' (1985) 32 UCLA LRev 429

Kanda & Milhaupt (2003) Kanda, Hideki, & Curtis J. Milhaupt, 'Re-examining Legal Transplants: The Director's Fiduciary Duty in Japanese Corporate Law' (2003) 51 AJCL 887

Kaplow (1992) Kaplow, Louis, 'Rules Versus Standards' (1992) 42 Duke LJ 557

Katelouzou & Siems (2015) Katelouzou, Dionysia, & Mathias Siems, 'Disappearing Paradigms in Shareholder Protection: Leximetric Evidence for 30 Countries, 1990–2013' (2015) 15 JCLS 127

Kawamoto (1990) Kawamoto, Ichirō, 'Shōhō, Yūgen-kaisha-hō Kaisei ni tsuite no Kei'i [A Chronology of the Reform of the Commercial Code and Limited Liability Corporation Act]' (1990) 856 Kin'yū Shōji Hanrei 12

Keatinge et al. (1992) Keatinge, Robert R., Larry E. Ribstein, Susan Pace Hamill, Michael L. Gravelle & Sharon Connaughton, 'The Limited Liability Company: A Study of the Emerging Entity' (1992) 47 Business Lawyer 375

Keay (2016) Keay, Andrew, 'Assessing and Rethinking the Statutory Scheme for Derivative Actions under the Companies Act 2006' (2016) 16 JCLS 39

Kent (1826)	Kent, James, *Commentaries on American Law*, vol. 1 (1st ed., New York, O. Halsted 1826)
Kent (1827)	Kent, James, *Commentaries on American Law*, vol. 2 (1st ed., New York, O. Halsted 1827)
Kershaw (2012)	Kershaw, David, *Company Law in Context: Text and Materials* (2nd ed., Oxford, Oxford University Press 2012)
Kessler (1948)	Kessler, William C., 'Incorporation in New England: A Statistical Study, 1800–1875' (1948) 8 Journal of Economic History 43
Kessler (1985)	Kessler, Robert A., 'The ABA Close Corporation Statute' (1985) 36 Mercer LRev 661
Kitazawa & Hamada (1983)	Kitazawa, Masahiro, & Hamada Michiyo, 'Shō-Kibo Kabushiki Kaisha oyobi Yūgen Kaisha ni kansuru Jittai, Iken Chōsa: Chūkan Hōkoku [Surveys on the Realities and Opinions Concerning Small-Scale KKs and YKs: Interim Report]' (1983) 962 Shōji Hōmu 21
Kitazawa & Hamada (1993)	Kitazawa, Masahiro, & Hamada Michiyo (eds.), *Shōhō no Sōten I: Sōsoku, Kaisha* [*Contested Issues in Commercial Law I: General Part, Corporations*] (Tokyo, Yūhikaku 1993)
Klausner (1995)	Klausner, Michael, 'Corporations, Corporate Law, and Networks of Contracts' (1995) 81 Virginia LRev 757
Klausner (2006)	Klausner, Michael, 'The Contractarian Theory of Corporate Law: A Generation Later' (2006) 31 Journal of Corporation Law 779
Klausner (2018)	Klausner, Michael, 'The "Corporate Contract" Today' in Gordon & Ringe (2018)
de Kluiver (2007)	de Kluiver, Harm-Jan 'Private Ordering and Buy-Out Remedies Within Private Company Law: Towards a New Balance Between Fairness and Welfare?' (2007) 8 EBOR 103
Kobayashi (2008)	Kobayashi, Toshiaki, 'Kakushu Kaisha ni okeru Tōka Shihon no Kaishū Shudan [Means of Recovering Invested Capital in Different Types of Companies]' in Egashira & Monguchi (2008)
Kobayashi & Ribstein (2011)	Kobayashi, Bruce H., & Larry E. Ribstein, 'Delaware for Small Fry: Jurisdictional Competition for Limited Liability Companies' [2011] University of Illinois LRev 91
Kobe (2012)	Kobe, Kathryn, *Small Business GDP: Update 2002–2010* (*Small Business Administration Office of Advocacy*, January 2012), archived 19 July 2018 at https://web.archive.org/web/20180719111452/https://www.sba.gov/sites/default/files/rs390tot_1.pdf

Koehnen (2004)	Koehnen, Markus, *Oppression and Related Remedies* (Toronto, Thomson Carswell 2004)
Koh (2014)	Koh, Alan K., 'Appraising Japan's Appraisal Remedy' (2014) 62 AJCL 417
Koh (2016)	Koh, Alan K., 'Reconstructing the Reflective Loss Principle' (2016) 16 JCLS 373
Koh (2018)	Koh, Alan K., '(Non-)Enforcement of Directors' Duties in Corporate Groups' (2018) 81 MLR 673
Koh (2020)	Koh, Alan K., 'Shareholder Protection and the Curious Case of Japan: The Enigmatic Past and Present of Withdrawal in a Leading Economy' (2020) 53 Vanderbilt Journal of Transnational Law 1207
Koh (forthcoming 2022)	Koh, Alan K., 'Direct Suits and Derivative Actions: Rethinking Shareholder Protection in Comparative Corporate Law' Washington University Global Studies LRev (forthcoming 2022)
Koh & Takahashi (2015)	Koh, Alan K. & Eiji Takahashi, 'Of Activist Mayors and Nuclear Reactors: The *Ōsaka v Kansai Electric* Saga and Japan's Curious Regime Governing Shareholder Access to Minutes of Board Meetings' (2015) No. 40 ZJapanR/JJapanL 99
Koh & Tang (2017)	Koh, Alan K., & Samantha S. Tang, 'Towards a "Just and Equitable Remedy" for Companies' (2017) 133 LQR 372
Koh & Tang (2021)	Koh, Alan K. & Samantha S. Tang, 'Direct and Derivative Shareholder Suits: Towards a Functional and Practical Taxonomy' in Afra Afsharipour & Martin Gelter (eds.), *Comparative Corporate Governance* (Cheltenham, Edward Elgar 2021)
Koide (2014a)	Koide, Atsushi, 'Dai-606-jō [Article 606]' in Kanda (2014)
Koide (2014b)	Koide, Atsushi, 'Dai-607-jō [Article 607]' in Kanda (2014)
Kokuzei-chō (2006)	Kokuzei-chō Chōkan-kanbō Kikaku-ka [Planning Section, Director's Secretariat, National Tax Agency], *Heisei-17-nendo-bun Zeimu Tōkei kara Mita Hōjin Kigyō no Jittai – Kaisha Hyōhon Chōsa: Chōsa Kekka Hōkoku* [Assessment Year 2005 *The Reality of Corporate Business Entities Based on Tax Statistics: Sampling Study of Companies: Report*] (National Tax Agency, December 2006), archived 9 March 2021 at https://perma.cc/WH5J-C4N6
Kokuzei-chō (2016)	Kokuzei-chō Chōkan-kanbō Kikaku-ka [Planning Section, Director's Secretariat, National Tax Agency], *Heisei-26-nendo-bun Kaisha Hyōhon Chōsa: Chōsa Kekka Hōkoku: Zeimu Tōkei kara*

Mita Hōjin Kigyō no Jittai [*Assessment Year 2014 Sampling Study of Companies: Report: The Reality of Corporate Business Entities Based on Tax Statistics*] (*National Tax Agency*, March 2016), archived 9 March 2021 at https://perma.cc/LH6V-8ASC

Kokuzei-chō (2020) — Kokuzei-chō Chōkan-kanbō Kikaku-ka [Planning Section, Director's Secretariat, National Tax Agency], *Heisei-30-nendo-bun Kaisha Hyōhon Chōsa: Chōsa Kekka Hōkoku: Zeimu Tōkei kara Mita Hōjin Kigyō no Jittai* [*Assessment Year 2018 Sampling Study of Companies: Report: The Reality of Corporate Business Entities Based on Tax Statistics*] (*National Tax Agency*, May 2020), archived 9 March 2021 at https://perma.cc/T4XM-GLG5

Komachiya (1951) — Komachiya, Sōzō, 'Kaisei Kabushiki Kaisha Hō Kanken [Submissions on the Reforms to the Law on the KK]' (1951) 15 Tōhoku Hōgaku 369

Kōriya & Hosokawa (2006) — Kōriya, Daisuke, & Hosokawa Mitsuru, 'Mochibun Kaisha no Keisan [Membership Company Accounting Matters]' in Aizawa Tetsu (ed.), *Ritsuan Tantōsha ni yoru Shin-Kaisha Hō Kankei Hōmushō-rei no Kaisetsu* [*The Drafters' Commentary on the Ministry of Justice Ordinances Relating to the New Companies Act*] (Bessatsu Shōji Hōmu vol. 300, Tokyo, Shōjihōmu 2006)

Kornblum (2015) — Kornblum, Udo, 'Bundesweite Rechtstatsachen zum Unternehmens- und Gesellschaftsrecht (Stand 1. 1.2015) [The State of Enterprise and Corporate Law in Germany (as of 1 January 2015)]' [2015] GmbH-Rundschau 687

Kosemura (1985) — Kosemura, Kunio, '§ 84' in Ueyanagi Katsurō, Ōtori Tsuneo & Takeuchi Akio (eds.), *Shin-pan Chūshaku Kaisha Hō: Kaisha Sōsoku, Gōmei-Kaisha, Gōshi-Kaisha* [*Corporate Law Commentary, New Edition: General Principles, Incorporated Commercial Partnerships, Limited Partnerships*], vol. 1 (Tokyo, Yūhikaku 1985)

Kraakman et al. (2004) — Kraakman, Reinier, Paul Davies, Henry Hansmann, Gerard Hertig, Klaus Hopt, Hideki Kanda & Edward Rock, *The Anatomy of Corporate Law: A Comparative and Functional Approach* (1st ed, Oxford, Oxford University Press 2004)

Kraus & Scott (2009) — Kraus, Jody S., & Robert E. Scott, 'Contract Design and the Structure of Contractual Intent' (2009) 84 New York University LRev 1023

Kübler & Assmann (2006) Kübler, Friedrich, & Heinz-Dieter Assmann, Gesellschaftsrecht: *Die privatrechtlichen Ordnungsstrukturen und Regelungsprobleme von Verbänden und Unternehmen [Corporate Law: The Structural Ordering and Regulatory Problems of Organizations and Enterprises in Private Law]* (6th ed., Heidelberg, C. F. Müller 2006)

Kurimoto (2013) Kurimoto, Akira, 'Japan' in Dante Cracogna, Antonio Fici & Hagen Henrÿ (eds.), *International Handbook of Cooperative Law* (Heidelberg, Springer 2013)

La Porta et al. (1997) La Porta, Rafael, Florencio Lopez-De-Silanes, Andrei Shleifer & Robert W. Vishny, 'Legal Determinants of External Finance' (1997) 52 Journal of Finance 1131

La Porta et al. (1998) La Porta, Rafael, Florencio Lopez-de-Silanes, Andrei Shleifer & Robert W. Vishny, 'Law and Finance' (1998) 106 Journal of Political Economy 1113

La Porta et al. (1999) La Porta, Rafael, Florencio Lopez-De-Silanes & Andrei Shleifer, 'Corporate Ownership around the World' (1999) 54 Journal of Finance 471

La Porta et al. (2000) La Porta, Rafael, Florencio Lopez-de-Silanes, Andrei Shleifer & Robert Vishny, 'Investor Protection and Corporate Governance' (2000) 58 Journal of Financial Economics 3

de Lacy (2002) de Lacy, John (ed.), *The Reform of United Kingdom Company Law* (London, Cavendish Publishing 2002)

Langevoort & Rasmussen (1997) Langevoort, Donald C., & Robert K. Rasmussen, 'Skewing the Results: The Role of Lawyers in Transmitting Legal Rules' (1997) 5 Southern California Interdisciplinary LJ 375

Langford (2015) Langford, Rosemary Teele, 'General Law and Statutory Directors' Duties: "Unmixed Oil and Water" or "Integrated Parts of the Whole Law"?' (2015) 131 LQR 635

Langford (2019) Langford, Rosemary Teele, *Company Directors' Duties and Conflicts of Interest* (Oxford, Oxford University Press 2019)

Laredo (2008) Laredo, Marc C., 'Shareholder Duties and Disputes in Closely-Held Corporations in Massachusetts' (2008) 91 Massachusetts LRev 138

LawComm (1996) Law Commission, *Shareholder Remedies: A Consultation Paper* (Law Commission Consultation Paper No. 142, London, Stationery Office 1996)

LawComm (1997) Law Commission, *Shareholder Remedies* (Law Commission Report No. 246, Cm 3769, London, Stationery Office 1997)

Lee (2000) Lee, John W., 'A Populist Political Perspective of the Business Tax Entities Universe: "Hey the Stars Might Lie But the Numbers Never Do"' (2000) 78 Texas LRev 885

Legrand (1996) Legrand, Pierre, 'European Legal Systems Are Not Converging' (1996) 45 International & Comparative LQ 52

Lele & Siems (2007) Lele, Priya P., & Mathias M. Siems, 'Shareholder Protection: A Leximetric Approach' (2007) 7 JCLS 17

Levmore (2000) Levmore, Saul, 'Norms as Supplements' (2000) 86 Virginia LRev 1989

Licht (2003) Licht, Amir N., 'Cross-Listing and Corporate Governance: Bonding or Avoiding?' (2003) 4 Chicago Journal of International Law 141

Lim (2013) Lim, Ernest, 'Directors' Fiduciary Duties: A New Analytical Framework' (2013) 129 LQR 242

Lim (2015) Lim, Ernest, 'Corporate Law, Private Law and Instrumentalism' [2015] LMCLQ 541

Lim (2018) Lim, Ernest, 'Controlling Shareholders and Fiduciary Duties in Asia' (2018) 18 JCLS 113

Lim (2019) Lim, Ernest, A *Case for Shareholders' Fiduciary Duties in Common Law Asia* (Cambridge, Cambridge University Press 2019)

LoPucki (2018) LoPucki, Lynn M., 'A Rule-Based Method for Comparing Corporate Laws' (2018) 94 Notre Dame LRev 263

Lowry (1996) Lowry, John, 'The Pursuit of Effective Minority Shareholder Protection – s. 459 of the Companies Act 1985' (1996) 17(3) Company Lawyer 67

Lowry (1997) Lowry, John, 'Reconstructing Shareholder Actions: A Response to the Law Commission's Consultation Paper' (1997) 18(8) Company Lawyer 247

Lowry (2002) Lowry, John, 'Mapping the Boundaries of Unfair Prejudice' in de Lacy (2002)

Lowry & Reisberg (2012) Lowry, John, & Arad Reisberg, *Pettet's Company Law: Company Law and Corporate Finance* (4th ed., Harlow, Pearson 2012)

Lutter (1980) Lutter, Marcus, 'Theorie der Mitgliedschaft: Prolegomena zu einem Allgemeinen Teil des Korporationsrechts [A Theory of Membership: Prologue to a General Part of Corporate Law]' (1980) 180 Archiv für die civilistiche Praxis 84

Lutter (1992)	Lutter, Marcus, 'Die Entwicklung der GmbH in Europa und in der Welt [The Development of the GmbH in Europe and the World]' in Marcus Lutter, Peter Ulmer & Wolfgang Zöllner (eds.), *Festschrift 100 Jahre GmbH-Gesetz [Festschrift 100 Years of the GmbH Law]* (Cologne, Otto Schmidt 1992)
Lutter (2012)	Marcus Lutter, '§ 34 Einziehung von Geschäftsanteilen [Section 34: Redemption of Membership Interests]' in Marcus Lutter & Peter Hommelhoff (eds.), *GmbH-Gesetz: Kommentar [GmbH Law: Commentary]* (18th ed., Cologne, Dr Otto Schmidt 2012)
Macdonald (1986)	Macdonald, D. Charles, 'Corporate Behavior and the Minority Shareholder: Contrasting Interpretations of Section 10–19.1–115 of the North Dakota Century Code' (1986) 62 North Dakota LRev 155
Macneil (1978)	Macneil, Ian R., 'Contracts: Adjustment of Long-Term Economic Relations under Classical, Neoclassical, and Relational Contract Law' (1978) 72 Northwestern University LRev 854
Mahoney (2000)	Mahoney, Paul G., 'Trust and Opportunism in Close Corporations' in Randall K. Morck (ed.), *Concentrated Corporate Ownership* (Chicago, University of Chicago Press 2000)
Manesh (2012)	Manesh, Mohsen, 'Contractual Freedom Under Delaware Alternative Entity Law: Evidence from Publicly-Traded LPs and LLCs' (2012) 37 Journal of Corporation Law 555
Manning (1962)	Manning, Bayless, 'The Shareholder's Appraisal Remedy: An Essay for Frank Coker' (1962) 72 Yale LJ 223
Martinez (2014)	Martinez, Stephanie, 'The Power Paradox: The Need for Alternative Remedies in Virginia Shareholder Oppression Cases' (2014) 49 University of Richmond LRev 287
Masuda & Urakawa (2010)	Masuda, Masaaki & Urakawa Shōji, 'Gōdō-Kaisha kara no Sha'in no Taisha ni kansuru Shomondai [Issues in Member Withdrawal from the GK]' (2010) 58–2/3 Kinki Daigaku Hōgaku 99
Matheson & Maler (2007)	Matheson, John H., & R. Kevin Maler, 'A Simple Statutory Solution to Minority Oppression in the Closely Held Business' (2007) 91 Minnesota LRev 657
Matsumoto (1929)	Matsumoto, Jōji, *Nihon Kaisha Hō Ron [On Japanese Corporate Law]* (Tokyo, Ganshōdō-shoten 1929)

Matsumoto (2014) Matsumoto, Nobuko, 'Dai-611-jō [Article 611]' in Kanda (2014)

Mäusl (2001) Mäusl, Klaus Rudolf, 'Der Austritt eines GmbH-Gesellschafters auf schadensrechtlicher Grundlage: Zugleich ein Beitrag zu den mitgliedschaftlichen Treuepflichten in der GmbH [Withdrawal of a GmbH Member on a Tort Basis: A Contribution towards the Membership Duties of Loyalty in the GmbH]' (Dr iur dissertation, Free University of Berlin 2001)

McCahery & Vermeulen (2004) McCahery, Joseph A., & Erik P. M. Vermeulen, 'The Evolution of Closely Held Business Forms in Europe' in McCahery et al. (2004)

McCahery & Vermeulen (2008) McCahery, Joseph A., & Erik P. M. Vermeulen, *Corporate Governance of Non-Listed Companies* (Oxford, Oxford University Press 2008)

McCahery et al. (2004) McCahery, Joseph A., Theo Raaijmakers & Erik P. M. Vermeulen (eds.), *The Governance of Close Corporations and Partnerships: US and European Perspectives* (Oxford, Oxford University Press 2004)

McLean (1990) McLean, Robert Savage, 'Minority Shareholders' Rights in the Close Corporation under the New North Carolina Business Corporation Act' (1990) 68 North Carolina LRev 1109

Means (2009) Means, Benjamin, 'A Voice-Based Framework for Evaluating Claims of Minority Shareholder Oppression in the Close Corporation' (2009) 97 Georgetown LJ 1207

Means (2010) Means, Benjamin, 'A Contractual Approach to Shareholder Oppression Law' (2010) 79 Fordham LRev 1161

Merkt (2018) Merkt, Hanno, '§ 13 Juristische Person; Handelsgesellschaft [Section 13: Legal Person; Commercial Company]' in Fleischer & Goette (2018)

Merryman (1981) Merryman, John Henry, 'On the Convergence (and Divergence) of the Civil Law and the Common Law' (1981) 17 Stanford Journal of International Law 357

Merryman & Pérez-Perdomo (2007) Merryman, John Henry, & Rogelio Pérez-Perdomo, *The Civil Law Tradition: An Introduction to the Legal Systems of Europe and Latin America* (3rd ed, Palo Alto, Stanford University Press 2007)

METI (2016) Ministry of Economy, Trade and Industry (Japan), 'White Paper on Small and Medium Enterprises in Japan 2016' (28 November 2016), archived 7 March 2021 at https://perma.cc/KG97-SQAX

Michaels (2019) Michaels, Ralf, 'The Functional Method of Comparative Law' in Reimann & Zimmermann (2019)

Miller (1997) Miller, Sandra K., 'Minority Shareholder Oppression in the Private Company in the European Community: A Comparative Analysis of the German, United Kingdom, and French "Close Corporation Problem"' (1997) 30 Cornell International LJ 381

Miller (2001) Miller, Sandra K., 'What Buy-Out Rights, Fiduciary Duties, and Dissolution Remedies Should Apply in the Case of the Minority Owner of a Limited Liability Company?' (2001) 38 Harvard Journal on Legislation 413

Miller (2003) Miller, Sandra K., 'A New Direction for LLC Research in a Contractarian Legal Environment' (2003) 76 Southern California LRev 351

Miller (2004) Miller, Sandra K., 'The Role of the Court in Balancing Contractual Freedom with the Need for Mandatory Constraints on Opportunistic and Abusive Conduct in the LLC' (2004) 152 University of Pennsylvania LRev 1609

Mitchell (1990) Mitchell, Lawrence E., 'The Death of Fiduciary Duty in Close Corporations' (1990) 138 University of Pennsylvania LRev 1675

Mitchell (2002) Mitchell, Gregory, 'Why Law and Economics' Perfect Rationality Should Not Be Traded for Behavioral Law and Economics' Equal Incompetence' (2002) 91 Georgetown LJ 67

Mock (2015) Mock, Sebastian, 'Die Gesellschafterklage (actio pro socio) [The Shareholder Suit (actio pro socio)]' [2015] Juristiche Schulung 590

Molitor (2009) Molitor, Michael K., 'Eat Your Vegetables (Or At Least Understand Why You Should): Can Better Warning and Education of Prospective Minority Owners Reduce Oppression in Closely Held Businesses?' (2009) 14 Fordham Journal of Corporate & Financial Law 491

Moll (1999) Moll, Douglas K., 'Shareholder Oppression v. Employment At Will in the Close Corporation: The Investment Model Solution' [1999] University of Illinois LRev 517

Moll (2000) Moll, Douglas K., 'Shareholder Oppression in Close Corporations: The Unanswered Question of Perspective' (2000) 53 Vanderbilt LRev 749

Moll (2001) Moll, Douglas K., 'Reasonable Expectations v. Implied-in-Fact Contracts: Is the Shareholder

	Oppression Doctrine Needed?' (2001) 42 Boston College LRev 989
Moll (2002)	Moll, Douglas K., 'Shareholder Oppression & Reasonable Expectations: Of Change, Gifts, and Inheritances in Close Corporation Disputes' (2002) 86 Minnesota LRev 717
Moll (2004)	Moll, Douglas K., 'Shareholder Oppression and "Fair Value": Of Discounts, Dates, and Dastardly Deeds in the Close Corporation' (2004) 54 Duke LJ 293
Moll (2005)	Moll, Douglas K., 'Minority Oppression & The Limited Liability Company: Learning (or not) from Close Corporation History' (2005) 40 Wake Forest LRev 883
Moll (2014)	Moll, Douglas K., 'Shareholder Oppression and the New Louisiana Business Corporation Act' (2014) 60 Loyola LRev 461
Moll (2017)	Moll, Douglas K., 'Judicial Dissolution of the Limited Liability Company: A Statutory Analysis' (2017) 19 Transactions: The Tennessee Journal of Business Law 81
Moll & Ragazzo (2017)	Moll, Douglas K., & Robert A. Ragazzo, *Closely Held Corporations* (LexisNexis 2017)
Mori (1984)	Mori, Junjirō, 'Heisa-kaisha ni okeru Shihai no Iji to Tōka-shihon no Kaishū [Maintenance of Control and Recovery of Invested Capital in Closed Corporations]' (1984) 56(11) Hōritsu Jihō 23
Morita (2014)	Morita, Hatsuru, 'Reforms of Japanese Corporate Law and Political Environment' (2014) No. 37 ZJapanR/JJapanL 25
Müller (1996)	Müller, Hans-Friedrich, *Das Austrittsrecht des GmbH-Gesellschafters* [*The GmbH-Member's Withdrawal Right*] (Cologne, Carl Heymanns 1996)
Murdock (1990)	Murdock, Charles W., 'The Evolution of Effective Remedies for Minority Shareholders and Its Impact Upon Valuation of Minority Shares' (1990) 65 Notre Dame LRev 425
Muth & FitzGerald (2012)	Muth, Graham, & Sean FitzGerald, *Shareholders' Agreements* (6th ed., London, Sweet & Maxwell 2012)
Nakahigashi & Matsui (2010)	Nakahigashi, Masafumi, & Matsui Hideyuki, *Kaishahō no Sentaku: Atarashii Shakai no Kaishahō wo Motomete* [*Choices in Corporate Law: The Quest for a Corporate Law for a New Society*] (Tokyo, Shōjihōmu 2010)
Navin & Sears (1955)	Navin, Thomas R., & Marian V. Sears, 'The Rise of a Market for Industrial Securities, 1887–1902' (1955) 29 Business History Review 105

Nelson (1959)	Nelson, Ralph L., *Merger Movements in American Industry, 1895–1956* (Princeton, Princeton University Press 1959)
Nestler & Kupke (2003)	Nestler, Anke & Thomas Kupke, 'Die Bewertung von Unternehmen mit dem Discounted Cash Flow-Verfahren [The Valuation of Enterprise with the Discounted Cash Flow Method]' [2003](6) Betriebswirtschaftliche Mandantenbetreuung 163
Neuberger (2002)	Neuberger, David, 'Company Law Reform: The Role of the Courts' in de Lacy (2002)
Neville (2010)	Neville, Mette, 'A Statutory Buy-out Right in SMEs – An Important Corporate Governance Mechanism and Minority Protection?' in Neville & Sørensen (2010)
Neville (2013)	Neville, Mette, 'Shareholders Conflicts in the European Private Company (SPE)' in Heribert Hirte & Christoph Teichmann (eds.), *The European Private Company – Societas Privata Europaea (SPE)* (Berlin, De Gruyter 2013)
Neville & Sørensen (2010)	Mette Neville & Karsten Engsig Sørensen (eds.), *Company Law and SMEs* (Copenhagen, Thomson Reuters 2010)
Newmyer (1976)	Newmyer, R. Kent, 'Justice Joseph Story's Doctrine of "Public and Private Corporations" and the Rise of the American Business Corporation' (1976) 25 DePaul LRev 825
Nikkei (2016)	'AMAZON JAPAN, "gōdō kaisha" ni ikō; ishi kettei subayaku [Amazon Japan to convert to "gōdō kaisha"; towards faster decision-making]' (*Nihon Keizai Shimbun Denshi-ban* [The Nikkei online edn], 24 March 2016) www.nikkei.com/article/DGXLZO98788460T20C16A3TI5000/ accessed 4 June 2019
Noack & Beurskens (2008)	Noack, Ulrich, & Michael Beurskens, 'Modernising the German GmbH – Mere Window Dressing or Fundamental Redesign?' (2008) 9 EBOR 97
O'Kelley (1992)	O'Kelley, Jr, Charles R., 'Filling Gaps in the Close Corporation Contract: A Transaction Cost Analysis' (1992) 87 Northwestern University LRev 216
O'Neal (1978)	O'Neal, F. Hodge, 'Close Corporations: Existing Legislation and Recommended Reform' (1978) 33 Business Lawyer 873
O'Neal (1987)	O'Neal, F. Hodge, 'Oppression of Minority Shareholders: Protecting Minority Rights' (1987) 35 Cleveland State LRev 121
O'Neal & Derwin (1961)	O'Neal, F. Hodge, & Jordan Derwin, *Expulsion or Oppression of Business*

Associates: "Squeeze-Outs" In Small Enterprises (Duke University Press 1961)

O'Neal & Thompson (2020a) — O'Neal, F. Hodge, & Robert B. Thompson, *O'Neal and Thompson's Close Corporations and LLCs: Law and Practice* (rev. 3rd ed., Clark Boardman Callaghan, looseleaf) (updated Nov 2020)

O'Neal & Thompson (2020b) — O'Neal, F. Hodge, & Robert B. Thompson, *O'Neal and Thompson's Oppression of Minority Shareholders and LLC Members: Protecting Minority Rights in Squeeze-Outs and Other Intracorporate Conflicts* (rev. 2nd ed., Clark Boardman Callaghan, looseleaf) (updated May 2020)

Oda (2005) — Oda, Hiroshi, 'The "Americanisation" of Japanese Corporate Law? – American Freedom, Japanese Discipline' (2005) 69 Rabel Journal of Comparative and International Private Law 47

OECD (2010) — Organisation for Economic Co-operation and Development (OECD), *SMEs, Entrepreneurship and Innovation* (Paris, OECD 2010)

Oesterle & Gazur (1997) — Oesterle, Dale A., & Wayne M. Gazur, 'What's in a Name: An Argument for a Small Business Limited Liability Entity Statute (With Three Subsets of Default Rules)' (1997) 32 Wake Forest LRev 101

Ōga (1988) — Ōga Yoshimitsu, 'Hi-Kōkai Kaisha ni okeru Shōsū-ha Kabunushi, Sha'in no Yokuatsu kara no Kyūsai: Kabushiki, Mochibun no Kaitori Seikyū Seido [Relief from Oppression of Shareholders/Members in Non-Open Corporations: The Share/Membership Interest Buyout Regime]' (1988) 10 Shūdō Hōgaku 275

Olson (1985) — Olson, Joseph Edward, 'A Statutory Elixir for the Oppression Malady' (1985) 36 Mercer LRev 627

Ōsugi (2004) — Ōsugi, Ken'ichi, 'LLC-seido no Dōnyū [Introduction of the LLC Regime]' (2004) 56 Kigyō Kaikei 206

Ōsugi (2013) — Ōsugi Ken'ichi, 'Mochibun Kaisha, Minpō Kumiai no Hōritsu Mondai [Legal Issues in Membership Companies and Civil Law Partnerships]' in Iwahara Shinsaku, Yamashita Tomonobu & Kanda Hideki (eds.), *Kaisha, Kin'yū, Hō (jō-kan) [Corporations, Finance, Law (vol. 1 of 2)]* (Tokyo, Shōjihōmu 2013)

Ōsumi & Imai (1991) — Ōsumi, Ken'ichirō, & Imai Hiroshi, *Kaisha Hō Ron jōkan [On Corporate Law, vol. 1 of 3]* (3rd ed., Tokyo, Yūhikaku 1991)

Ōta (2008) — Ōta, Minoru, 'Mochibun-kaisha no Sha'in no Ka'nyū to Taisha [Joining and Exit of Membership Companies' Members]' in Egashira & Monguchi (2008)

Ozeki (2014) — Ozeki, Yukimi, 'Dai-597-jō [Article 597]' in Kanda (2014)

Palmer & Borowski (2012) — Palmer, Vernon Valentine, & Harry Borowski, 'Louisiana' in Vernon Valentine Palmer (ed.), *Mixed Jurisdictions Worldwide: The Third Legal Family* (2nd ed., Cambridge University Press 2012)

Paredes (2004) — Paredes, Troy A., 'A Systems Approach to Corporate Governance Reform: Why Importing U.S. Corporate Law Isn't the Answer' (2004) 45 William & Mary LRev 1055

Paterson (2006) — Paterson, Paul, 'A Criticism of the Contractual Approach to Unfair Prejudice' (2006) 27 (7) Company Lawyer 204

Petska et al. (2005) — Petska, Thomas, Michael Parisi, Kelly Luttrell, Lucy Altounian & Matt Scoffic, 'An Analysis of Business Organizational Structure and Activity from Tax Data' (2005) 98 Proceedings of the Annual Conference on Taxation and Minutes of the Annual Meeting of the National Tax Association 40

Pistor & Xu (2003) — Pistor, Katharina, & Chenggang Xu, 'Fiduciary Duty in Transitional Civil Law Jurisdictions: Lessons from the Incomplete Law Theory' in Curtis J. Milhaupt (ed.), *Global Markets, Domestic Institutions: Corporate Law and Governance in a New Era of Cross-Border Deals* (New York, Columbia University Press 2003)

Pistor et al. (2002) — Pistor, Katharina, Yoram Keinan, Jan Kleinheisterkamp & Mark D. West, 'The Evolution of Corporate Law: A Cross-Country Comparison' (2002) 23 University of Pennsylvania Journal of International Economic Law 791

Prentice (1972) — Prentice, D., 'Protection of Minority Shareholders: Section 210 of the Companies Act 1948' [1972] Current Legal Problems 124

Prentice (1986) — Prentice, D. D., 'Minority Shareholder Oppression: Valuation of Shares' (1986) 102 LQR 179

Prentice (1988) — Prentice, D. D., 'The Theory of the Firm: Minority Shareholder Oppression: Sections 459–461 of the Companies Act 1985' (1988) 8 Oxford Journal of Legal Studies 55

Prentice & Payne (1999) — Prentice, D. D., & Jennifer Payne, 'Section 459 of the Companies Act 1985 – the House of Lords' View' (1999) 115 LQR 587

Puchniak (2007) Puchniak, Dan W., 'The Japanization of American Corporate Governance? Evidence of the Never-Ending History for Corporate Law' (2007) 9 Asian-Pacific Law & Policy Journal 7

Puchniak (2012) Puchniak, Dan W., 'The Derivative Action in Asia: A Complex Reality' (2012) 9 Berkeley Business LJ 1

Puchniak & Kim (2017) Puchniak, Dan W., & Kon-Sik Kim, 'Varieties of Independent Directors in Asia: A Taxonomy' in Puchniak et al. (2017)

Puchniak & Lan (2017) Puchniak, Dan W. & Luh Luh Lan, 'Independent Directors in Singapore: Puzzling Compliance Requiring Explanation' (2017) 65 AJCL 265

Puchniak et al. (2012) Puchniak, Dan W., Harald Baum & Michael Ewing-Chow (eds.), *The Derivative Action in Asia: A Comparative and Functional Approach* (Cambridge, Cambridge University Press 2012)

Puchniak et al. (2017) Puchniak, Dan W., Harald Baum & Luke Nottage (eds.), *Independent Directors in Asia: A Historical, Contextual and Comparative Approach* (Cambridge, Cambridge University Press 2017)

Quinlan & Kennedy (1998) Quinlan, William R., & John F. Kennedy, 'The Rights and Remedies of Shareholders in Closely Held Corporations Under Illinois Law' (1998) 29 Loyola University of Chicago LJ 585

Rachlinski (2003) Rachlinski, Jeffrey J., 'The Uncertain Psychological Case for Paternalism' (2003) 97 Northwestern University LRev 1165

Raiser & Veil (2015) Raiser, Thomas, & Rüdiger Veil, *Recht der Kapitalgesellschaften: Ein Handbuch für Praxis und Wissenschaft* [*The Law of Capital-based Companies: A Handbook for Practice and Scholarship*] (6th ed., Munich, Franz Vahlen 2015)

Rajak (1972) Rajak, H., 'The Oppression of Minority Shareholders' (1972) 35 MLR 156

Reimann & Zimmermann (2019) Reimann, Mathias & Reinhard Zimmermann (eds.), *Oxford Handbook of Comparative Law* (2nd ed., Oxford University Press 2019)

Reusch (2019) Reusch, Ute (tr.), 'Limited Liability Companies Act' (*Juris BMJ*, 2019), archived 17 June 2019 at https://web.archive.org/web/20190617060654/http://www.gesetze-im-internet.de/englisch_gmbhg/englisch_gmbhg.pdf

Reuter (1973) Reuter, Dieter, *Privatrechtliche Schranken der Perpetuierung von Unternehmen: Ein Beitrag zum Problem der Gestaltungsfreiheit im Recht*

	der Unternehmensformen [*Barriers in Private Law to the Perpetuation of Enterprise: A Contribution on the Problem of Freedom of Design in the Law of Corporate Forms*] (Frankfurt am Main, Athenäum 1973)
Reuter (1977)	Reuter, Dieter, 'Nochmals: Das Kündigungsrecht des GmbH-Gesellschafters [Once Again: The GmbH Member's Right to Resign]' [1977] GmbH-Rundschau 77
Reuter (1984)	Reuter, Dieter, 'Welche Maßnahmen empfehlen sich, insbesondere im Gesellschafts- und Kapitalmarktrecht, um die Eigenkapitalausstattung der Unternehmen langfristig zu verbessern? [What Measures are Recommended, Particularly in Corporate and Securities Law, for the Long-term Improvement of Capital Adequacy of Enterprises?]' in Ständigen Deputation des Deutschen Juristentages [Standing Deputation of the Association of German Jurists] (ed.), *Verhandlungen des fünfundfünfzigsten Deutschen Juristentages Hamburg* 1984, Bd I (Gutachten) Teil B [*Proceedings of the 55th German Jurists Forum*, vol. 1 (Expert Opinions) Part B] (Munich, C. H. Beck 1984)
Ribstein (1995a)	Ribstein, Larry E., 'Statutory Forms for Closely Held Firms: Theories and Evidence from LLCs' (1995) 73 Washington University LQ 369
Ribstein (1995b)	Ribstein, Larry E., 'A Critique of the Uniform Limited Liability Company Act' (1995) 25 Stetson LRev 311
Ribstein (2010)	Ribstein, Larry E., *The Rise of the Uncorporation* (New York, Oxford University Press 2010)
Ribstein (2011)	Ribstein, Larry E., 'Close Corporation Remedies and the Evolution of the Closely Held Firm' (2011) 33 Western New England LRev 531
Ribstein & Keatinge (2020)	Keatinge, Robert R., Larry E. Ribstein & Thomas E. Rutledge, *Ribstein and Keatinge on Limited Liability Companies* (2nd ed., Eagan, West, looseleaf) (updated July 2020)
Ribstein & Kobayashi (2001)	Ribstein, Larry E., & Bruce H. Kobayashi, 'Choice of Form and Network Externalities' (2001) 43 William & Mary LRev 79
Riley (1992)	Riley, Christopher A., 'Contracting Out of Company Law: Section 459 of the Companies Act 1985 and the Role of the Courts' (1992) 55 MLR 782
Riley (2003)	Riley, Christopher, 'Implicit Dimensions of Contract and Oppression of Shareholders' in David Campbell, Hugh Collins & John

	Wightman (eds.), *Implicit Dimensions of Contract: Discrete, Relational and Network Contracts* (Oxford, Hart Publishing 2003)
Ringe (2013)	Ringe, Wolf-Georg, 'Corporate Mobility in the European Union: A Flash in the Pan? An Empirical Study on the Success of Lawmaking and Regulatory Competition' (2013) 10 ECFR 230
Robert Bosch (2019)	Robert Bosch GmbH, 'Bosch Annual Report 2018' (2019), archived 10 May 2019 at https://web.archive.org/web/20190510034048/https://assets.bosch.com/media/global/bosch_group/our_figures/pdf/bosch-annual-report-2018.pdf
Rock (2002)	Rock, Edward, 'Securities Regulation as Lobster Trap: A Credible Commitment Theory of Mandatory Disclosure' (2002) 23 Cardozo LRev 675
Rock & Wachter (1999)	Rock, Edward B., & Michael L. Wachter, 'Waiting for the Omelet to Set: Match-Specific Assets and Minority Oppression in Close Corporations' (1999) 24 Journal of Corporation Law 913
Röder (2014)	Röder, Erik, 'Die Kommanditgesellschaft im Rechtsvergleich: Hintergründe der unterschiedlichen Karriere einer Rechtsform [The KG in Comparative Law: Factors Underlying the Differing Careers of a Legal Form]' (2014) 78 Rabel Journal of Comparative and International Private Law 109
Rodger (2010)	Lord Rodger of Earlsferry, 'Judges and Academics in the United Kingdom' (2010) 29 University of Queensland LJ 29
Röhricht (1991)	Röhricht, Volker, 'Zum Austritt des Gesellschafters aus der GmbH [On the Withdrawal of a Member from the GmbH]' in Reinhard Goerdeler, Peter Hommelhoff, Marcus Lutter, Walter Odersky & Herbert Wiedemann (eds.), *Festschrift für Alfred Kellermann zum 70. Geburtstag am 29. November 1990* (Berlin, Walter de Gruyter 1991)
Roitzsch (1981)	Roitzsch, Frank, *Der Minderheitenschutz im Verbandsrecht [Minority Protection in the Law of Associations]* (Königstein im Taunus, Hanstein 1981)
Roth & Kindler (2013)	Roth, Günter H., & Peter Kindler, *The Spirit of Corporate Law: Core Principles of Corporate Law in Continental Europe* (Munich, C. H. Beck 2013)
Rutledge (1937)	Rutledge, Jr, Wiley B., 'Significant Trends in Modern Incorporation Statutes' (1937) 22 Washington University LQ 305

Sacco (1991) Sacco, Rodolfo, 'Legal Formants: A Dynamic Approach to Comparative Law (Installment I of II)' (1991) 39 AJCL 1

Sakamaki (1973) Sakamaki, Toshio, *Heisa-teki Kaisha no Hōri to Rippō* [*Close Corporations: Doctrine and Legislation*] (Tokyo, Nipponhyōronsha 1973)

Schindler (1999) Schindler, Hendrik, *Das Austrittsrecht in Kapitalgesellschaften: Eine rechtsvergleichende Untersuchung zum Austrittsrecht als Mittel des Individual- und Minderheitenschutzes im deutschen und französischen Kapitalgesellschaftsrecht* [*The Right to Withdraw in Capital-based Companies: A Comparative* Study *on the Right to Withdraw as a Means of Individual and Minority Protection in German and French Capital-based Companies*] (Munich, C. H. Beck 1999)

Schlesinger (1945) Schlesinger, Arthur M., *The Age of Jackson* (Boston, Little, Brown 1945)

Schmidt (2002) Schmidt, Karsten, *Gesellschaftsrecht* [*Corporate Law*] (4th ed., Cologne, Carl Heymanns 2002)

Schmidt (2008) Schmidt, Jessica, 'The New *Unternehmergesellschaft* (Entrepreneurial Company) and the Limited – A Comparison' (2008) 9 German LJ 1093

Schmolke (2012) Schmolke, Klaus Ulrich, 'Expulsion and Valuation Clauses – Freedom of Contract vs. Legal Paternalism in German Partnership and Close Corporation Law' (2012) 9 ECFR 380

Scholz (1930) Scholz, Franz, *Der Austritt aus der GmbH* [*Exit from the GmbH*] (Cologne, Dr Otto Schmidt 1930)

Scholz (1942) Scholz, Franz, *Ausschließung und Austritt eines Gesellschafters aus der GmbH* [*Expulsion and Withdrawal of a Member from the GmbH*] (2nd ed., Cologne, Otto Schmidt 1942)

Scholz (1950) Scholz, Franz, *Ausschließung und Austritt aus der GmbH* [*Expulsion and Withdrawal from the GmbH*] (3rd ed., Cologne, Dr Otto Schmidt 1950)

Schubert (1985a) Schubert, Werner (ed.), *Entwurf des Reichsjustizministeriums zu einem Gesetz über die Gesellschaften mit beschränkter Haftung von* 1939 [*Reich Ministry of Justice Draft on an Act on Companies with Limited Liability of* 1939] (Heidelberg, Recht und Wirtschaft 1985)

Schubert (1985b) Schubert, Werner, 'Einführung [Introduction]' in Schubert (1985a)

Schulz & Wasmeier (2012) Schulz, Martin, & Oliver Wasmeier, *The Law of Business Organizations: A Concise Overview of German Corporate Law* (Berlin, Springer 2012)

Schweitzer et al. (2006) — Schweitzer, Maurice E., John C. Hershey & Eric T. Bradlow, 'Promises and Lies: Restoring Violated Trust' (2006) 101 Organizational Behaviour & Human Decision Processes 1

Schwerdtner (1976) — Schwerdtner, Peter, 'Das Kündigungsrecht des GmbH-Gesellschafters [The Right of Resignation of GmbH-Members]' [1976] GmbH-Rundschau 101

Scogin (1993) — Scogin, Jr, Hugh T., 'Withdrawal and Expulsion in Germany: A Comparative Perspective on the "Close Corporation Problem"' (1993) 15 Michigan Journal of International Law 127

Sealy (1976) — Sealy, L. S., 'Book Review: *Squeeze-outs of Minority Shareholders: Expulsion or Oppression of Business Associates*' (1976) 35 Cambridge LJ 362

Seibt (2012) — Seibt, Christoph H., 'Anhang § 34: Austritt und Ausschließung eines Gesellschafters [Appendix to Section 34: Withdrawal and Expulsion of a Member]' in Franz Scholz (ed.), *Kommentar zum GmbH-Gesetz* [*Commentary on the GmbH Law*], vol. 1 (11th ed., Cologne, Dr Otto Schmidt 2012)

Sekiguchi & Nishigaki (2008) — Sekiguchi, Norihiro, & Nishigaki Kengō, 'Gōdō-Kaisha ya Yūgen-Sekinin-Jigyō-Kumiai no Jitsumu-jō no Riyōrei to Mondaiten [GK and J-LLPs: Practical Examples and Issues]' (2008) 80(11) Hōritsu Jihō 18

Setsuyaku-Shachō (2015) — Setsuyaku Shachō Henshūbu [Thrifty CEO Editorial Board], 'Kabushiki Kaisha wa mō Jidai Okure!? Gōdō Kaisha ga Kyūzō suru Riyū to wa [The KK Is Already Behind the Times!? Reasons for the Rapid Increase in GKs]' (*Setsuyaku Shachō* [Thrifty CEO], 8 July 2015), archived 1 June 2019 https://web.archive.org/web/20190601164132/https://setsuyaku.ceo/post/505/株式会社はもう時代遅れ-合同会社が急増する理

Shapira (2000) — Shapira, Giora, 'The Hand That Giveth Is the Hand That Taketh Away – *O'Neill v Phillips* and Shareholder "Legitimate Expectations"' (2000) 11 Australian Journal of Corporate Law 260

Shapira (2015) — Shapira, Roy, 'A Reputational Theory of Corporate Law' (2015) 26 Stanford Law & Policy Review 1

Shimoda (2016) — Shimoda, Sayuri A, 'Time to Retire: Is Lifetime Employment in Japan Still Viable?' (2016) 39 Fordham International LJ 753

Shishido (1984a) — Shishido, Zen'ichi, 'Heisa Kaisha ni okeru Naibu Funsō no Kaiketsu to Keizai-teki Kōsei (ichi)

[*Ways to Achieve Financial Fairness in Coping with Internal Dissension in the Closely Held Corporation (Part 1)]' (1984) 101 Hōgaku Kyōkai Zasshi 505

Shishido (1984b) Shishido, Zen'ichi, 'Heisa Kaisha ni Okeru Naibu Funsō no Kaiketsu to Keizai-teki Kōsei [*Ways to Achieve Financial Fairness in Coping with Internal Dissension in the Closely-Held Corporation]' (1984) 46 Shihō 237

Shishido (1990) Shishido, Zenichi, 'Problems of the Closely Held Corporation: A Comparative Study of the Japanese and American Legal Systems and a Critique of the Japanese Tentative Draft on Close Corporations' (1990) 38 AJCL 337

Shishido (2009) Shishido, Zen'ichi, 'Gōdō Kaisha Keitai Sōsetsu no Igi to Riyō [The GK Form: Its Usage and the Significance of its Creation]' in Hamada Michiyo & Iwahara Shinsaku (eds.), *Kaisha Hō no Sōten* [*Contested Issues in Corporate Law*] (Tokyo, Yūhikaku 2009)

Shishido (2013) Shishido, Zen'ichi, 'Gōdō Gōben-Kaisha [GK Joint Ventures]' in Koide Atsushi, Kozuka Sōichirō, Gotō Gen & Ban Aken (eds.), *Maeda Shigeyuki-sensei Koki Kinen: Kigyō Hō, Kin'yū Hō no Shin-Chōryū* [*Festschrift in Celebration of Maeda Shigeyuki's 70th Birthday: New Trends in Enterprise Law and Finance Law*] (Tokyo, Shōjihōmu 2013)

Shishido (2014a) Shishido, Zen'ichi, 'Dai 3-ppen Zenchū [Introductory Notes to Part 3]' in Kanda (2014)

Shishido (2014b) Shishido, Zen'ichi, 'Dai-590-jō [Article 590]' in Kanda (2014)

Shishido (2014c) Shishido, Zen'ichi, 'Gōdō-Kaisha no Taisha-in no Mochibun Hyōka: Jōto Seigen Kabushiki no Hyōka to no Hikaku [Valuation of the Membership Interests of Withdrawing Members from the GK: A Comparison with the Valuation of Shares with Transfer Restrictions]' in Deguchi Masayoshi, Yoshimoto Ken'ichi, Nakajima Hiromasa & Tanabe Hiroyasu (eds.), *Kigyō Hō no Genzai: Aotake Shō'ichi-sensei Koki Kinen* [*Enterprise Law's Present: Festschrift in Celebration of Aotake Shōichi's 70th Birthday*] (Tokyo, Shinzansha 2014)

Shishido (2015) Shishido, Zenichi, 'Legislative policy of alternative forms of business organization: the case of Japanese LLCs' in Robert W. Hillman & Mark J. Loewenstein (eds.), *Research Handbook on Partnerships, LLCs and Alternative Forms of*

	Business Organizations (Cheltenham, Edward Elgar 2015)
Shishido et al. (2015)	Shishido, Zenichi, Munetaka Fukuda & Masato Umetani, *Joint Venture Strategies: Design, Bargaining, and the Law* (Cheltenham, Edward Elgar 2015)
Siegel (2011)	Siegel, Mary, 'An Appraisal of the Model Business Corporation Act's Appraisal Rights Provisions' (Winter 2011) 74(1) Law & Contemporary Problems 231
Siems (2005)	Siems, Mathias M., 'Numerical Comparative Law: Do We Need Statistical Evidence in Law in Order to Reduce Complexity?' (2005) 13 Cardozo Journal of International and Comparative Law 521
Siems (2007)	Siems, Mathias M., *Convergence in Shareholder Law* (Cambridge, Cambridge University Press 2007)
Siems (2008)	Siems, Mathias M., 'Shareholder Protection Around the World (Leximetric II)' (2008) 33 Delaware Journal of Corporate Law 111
Siems (2010)	Siems, Mathias M., 'Convergence in Corporate Governance: A Leximetric Approach' (2010) 35 Journal of Corporation Law 729
Siems (2014)	Siems, Mathias M., 'Bringing in Foreign Ideas: The Quest for "Better Law" in Implicit Comparative Law' (2014) 9(2) Journal of Comparative Law 119
Siems (2017)	Siems, Mathias M., 'The Methods of Comparative Corporate Law' in Roman Tomasic (ed.), *Routledge Handbook of Corporate Law* (Abingdon, Routledge 2017)
Siems (2018a)	Siems, Mathias, 'Malicious Legal Transplants' (2018) 38 Legal Studies 103
Siems (2018b)	Siems, Mathias, *Comparative Law* (2nd ed., Cambridge, Cambridge University Press 2018)
Siems & Cabrelli (2013)	Siems, Mathias & David Cabrelli (eds.), *Comparative Company Law: A Case-Based Approach* (Oxford, Hart 2013)
Simon (1957)	Simon, Herbert A., *Models of Man: Social and Rational* (New York, John Wiley & Sons 1957)
Sitkin & Roth (1993)	Sitkin, Sim B., & Nancy L. Roth, 'Explaining the Limited Effectiveness of Legalistic "Remedies" for Trust/Distrust' (1993) 4 Organization Science 367
Skeel (2004)	Skeel, Jr, David A., 'Corporate Anatomy Lessons' (2004) 113 Yale LJ 1519
Skeel (2005)	Skeel, David, *Icarus in the Boardroom: The Fundamental Flaws in Corporate America and*

	Where They Came From (New York, Oxford University Press 2005)
SMEA (2020)	Chūshōkigyōchō [Small and Medium Enterprise Agency] (Japan) (ed.), *Chūshō Kigyō Hakusho 2020-nen-ban* [*2020 White Paper on Small and Medium Enterprises in Japan*] (24 April 2020), archived 7 March 2021 at https://perma.cc/N4AV-2EHE
Smith (2004)	Smith, Stephen A., *Contract Theory* (Oxford, Clarendon Press 2004)
Sneirson (2008)	Sneirson, Judd F., 'Soft Paternalism for Close Corporations: Helping Shareholders Help Themselves' [2008] Wisconsin LRev 899
Solomon & Solomon (1987)	Solomon, Lewis D., & Janet Stern Solomon, 'Using Alternative Dispute Resolution Techniques to Settle Conflicts among Shareholders of Closely Held Corporations' (1987) 22 Wake Forest LRev 105
Sōmu-shō (2016, 2020)	Sōmu-shō Tōkei-kyoku [Statistics Bureau, Ministry of Internal Affairs and Communications], 'Shōgyō, Hōjin Tōki (Nenji-hyō) [Business and Corporation Registrations (Multiyear Statistics with Yearly Breakdowns)]' (*e-stat: Portal Site of Official Statistics of Japan*, 29 May 2020 and 31 May 2016), Tables 19–00–16 https://perma.cc/98N2-MXBH, 19–00–18 https://perma.cc/S7TY-DYUV, 19–00–19 https://perma.cc/UF3X-PE79, 19–00–20 https://perma.cc/QXW5-3TCZ, 15–00–16 https://perma.cc/R6W9-THDY, 15–00–18 https://perma.cc/J4BV-EUZC, 15–00–19 https://perma.cc/2KUK-28SS, 15–00–20 https://perma.cc/45LW-KWNU.
Sosnitza (2010)	Sosnitza, Olaf, 'Anhang § 34 Ausschluss und Austritt von Gesellschaftern [Appendix to Section 34: Expulsion and Withdrawal of Members]' in Lutz Michalski (ed.), *Kommentar zum Gesetz betreffend die Gesellschaften mit beschränkter Haftung (GmbH-Gesetz)* [*Commentary on the Law on Limited Liability Corporations*], vol. 1 (2nd ed., Munich, C. H. Beck 2010)
Spamann (2010)	Spamann, Holger, 'The "Antidirector Rights Index" Revisited' (2010) 23 Review of Financial Studies 467
Storm (2002)	Storm, Timothy J., 'Remedies for Oppression of Non-Controlling Shareholders in Illinois Closely-Held Corporations: An Idea Whose Time Has Gone' (2002) 33 Loyola University of Chicago LJ 379
Strohn (2018)	Strohn, Lutz, '§ 34 Einziehung von Geschäftsanteilen [Section 34 Redemption of

Membership Interests]' in Fleischer & Goette (2018)

Subaru-Juku (2015) — Subaru Juku Un'ei Kanri-nin [Operations Manager, Subaru School], 'Gōdō Kaisha to Kabushiki Kaisha no Chigai wo Osaeru 14 no POINTO [The Differences Between the GK and the KK in 14 Points]' (*Subaru Juku* [Subaru School], 27 May 2015), archived 28 October 2017 https://web.archive.org/web/20171028160612/http://subaru-juku.com/llc-joint%E2%80%90stock-company-difference-867

Sugarman (1997) — Sugarman, David, 'Reconceptualising Company Law: Reflections on the Law Commission's Consultation Paper on Shareholder Remedies: Part 1' (1997) 18(8) Company Lawyer 226

Sunstein (2014) — Sunstein, Cass R., *Why Nudge? The Politics of Libertarian Paternalism* (New Haven, Yale University Press 2014)

Sunstein & Thaler (2003) — Sunstein, Cass R., & Richard H. Thaler, 'Libertarian Paternalism Is Not an Oxymoron' (2003) 70 University of Chicago LRev 1159

Suzuki (1994) — Suzuki, Takeo, *Shin-pan Kaisha Hō* [*Corporate Law: New Edition*] (5th rev. ed., Tokyo, Kōbundō 1994)

Swire (1993) — Swire, Peter P., 'Safe Harbors and a Proposal to Improve the Community Reinvestment Act' (1993) 79 Virginia LRev 349

Takahashi (1998) — Takahashi, Eiji, *Jūzoku Kaisha ni okeru Shōsū Kabu'nushi no Hogo* [*Protection of Minority Shareholders in Dependent Subsidiaries*] (Tokyo, Yūhikaku 1998)

Takahashi (2010) — Takahashi, Eiji, 'Nihon ni okeru Heisa-teki Shihon-kaisha no Hatten to Hō [The Development and the Law of Closed-type Companies of Capital]' (2010) 1914 Shōji Hōmu 4

Takahashi (2012a) — Takahashi, Eiji, 'Mochibun-Kaisha to Kigyō Ketsugō Hōsei (ge) [Membership Companies and the Legal Regime for Corporate Groups (Part 2 of 2)]' (2012) 1969 Shōji Hōmu 4

Takahashi (2012b) — Takahashi, Eiji, *DOITSU Kaisha Hō Gaisetsu* [*Principles of German Corporation Law*] (Tokyo, Yūhikaku 2012)

Takahashi (2014) — Takahashi, Eiji, *Kaisha Hō Gaisetsu* [*Principles of Corporation Law*] (2nd ed., Tokyo, Chūōkeizaisha 2014)

Takahashi (2015) — Takahashi, Eiji, '"Reception" and "Convergence" of Japanese and German Corporate Law' (2015) 12 University of St Thomas LJ 228

Takahashi (2016) — Takahashi, Eiji, *Kaisha Hō no Keiju to Shūren [Reception and Convergence of Corporate Law]* (Tokyo, Yūhikaku 2016)

Takahashi & Shimizu (2005) — Takahashi, Eiji & Madoka Shimizu, 'The Future of Japanese Corporate Governance: The 2005 Reform' (2005) No. 19 ZJapanR/JJapanL 35

Tan (2014) — Tan, Zhong Xing, 'Unfair Prejudice from Beyond, Beyond Unfair Prejudice: Amplifying Minority Protection in Corporate Group Structures' (2014) 14 JCLS 367

Tan (2015) — Tan, Zhong Xing, 'Reverse Oppression and the Residual Nature of the Shareholder's Commercial Unfairness Remedy' (2015) 27 Singapore Academy of LJ 122

Tanahashi (2013) — Tanahashi, Hajime, 'Atarashii Kigyō Keitai: Gōdō-Kaisha, Yūgen Sekinin Jigyō Kumiai, Tōshi Jigyō Yūgen Sekinin Kumiai [New Enterprise Forms: GK, J-LLP, LPS]' in Egashira Kenjirō (ed.), *Kabushiki Kaisha Hō Taikei [Stock Corporation Law Compendium]* (Tokyo, Yūhikaku 2013)

Tang (2018) — Tang, Samantha S., 'Corporate Divorce in Family Companies' [2018] LMCLQ 19

Teichmann (1970) — Teichmann, Arndt, *Gestaltungsfreiheit in Gesellschaftsverträgen [Freedom of Design in Corporate Constitutions]* (Munich, C. H. Beck 1970)

Thaler & Sunstein (2008) — Thaler, Richard H., & Cass R. Sunstein, *Nudge: Improving Decisions About Health, Wealth, and Happiness* (New Haven, Yale University Press 2008)

Thompson (1988) — Thompson, Robert B., 'Corporate Dissolution and Shareholders' Reasonable Expectations' (1988) 66 Washington University LQ 193

Thompson (1993) — Thompson, Robert B., 'The Shareholder's Cause of Action for Oppression' (1993) 48 Business Lawyer 699

Thompson (2011) — Thompson, Robert B., 'Allocating the Roles for Contracts and Judges in the Closely Held Firm' (2011) 33 Western New England LRev 369

Tröger (2005) — Tröger, Tobias H, 'Choice of Jurisdiction in European Corporate Law – Perspectives of European Corporate Governance' (2005) 6 EBOR 3

Tversky & Kahneman (1974) — Tversky, Amos, & Daniel Kahneman, 'Judgment under Uncertainty: Heuristics and Biases' (1974) 185 Science 1124

Tversky & Kahneman (1981) — Tversky, Amos, & Daniel Kahneman, 'The Framing of Decisions and the Psychology of Choice' (1981) 211 Science 453

Uchida (2016) Uchida Atsushi, 'Hōjin-ka (Hōjin Nari) Suru nara Kabushiki Kaisha to Gōdō Kaisha wa Docchi ga Ii? [If I Were to Incorporate, Which Is Better – KK or GK?]' (*Uchida Atsushi Zeirishi Jimusho* [Offices of Uchida Atsushi, Certified Public Tax Accountant], 1 April 2016), archived 28 October 2017 at https://web.archive.org/web/20171028160344/https://www.uchitax.com/2016/04/01/companiy-formation-llc/

Uemura (2006) Uemura, Tatsuo, 'Shin-Kaisha Hō no Seikaku to Kaisha Hōgaku no Arikata [The Character of the New Companies Act and the Way of Corporate Law Scholarship]' in Mori Junjirō & Uemura Tatsuo (eds.), *Kaisha Hō ni okeru Shuyō Ronten no Hyōka* [*An Assessment of the Main Issues in Corporate Law*] (Tokyo, Chuōkeizaisha 2006)

Ueyanagi et al. (1984) Ueyanagi, Katsurō et al., 'SHIMPOJIUMU: Shōkibo, Heisa Kaisha no Rippō [Symposium: Legislating for Small- and Closed Corporations]' (1984) 46 Shihō 117

Ulmer & Habersack (2014a) Ulmer, Peter, & Mathias Habersack, 'Anhang § 34 Ausschließung und Austritt von Gesellschaftern [Appendix to Section 34: Expulsion and Withdrawal of Members]' in Ulmer et al. (2014)

Ulmer & Habersack (2014b) Ulmer, Peter, & Mathias Habersack, '§ 34 Einziehung von Geschäftsanteilen [Section 34 Redemption of Membership Interests]' in Ulmer et al. (2014)

Ulmer et al. (2014) Ulmer, Peter, Mathias Habersack & Marc Löbbe (eds.), *Gesetz betreffend die Gesellschaften mit beschränkter Haftung (GmbHG): Großkommentar* [*Law on Limited Liability Corporations: Grand Commentary*], vol. 2 (2nd ed., Tübingen, Mohr Siebeck 2014)

UNCITRAL (2020a) United Nations Commission on International Trade Law Working Group I (MSMEs), Draft Legislative Guide on an UNCITRAL Limited Liability Organization (15 January 2020), at https://undocs.org/en/A/CN.9/WG.I/WP.118

UNCITRAL (2020b) United Nations Commission on International Trade Law Working Group I (MSMEs), Draft Legislative Guide on an UNCITRAL Limited Liability Organization (30 Nov 2020), at https://undocs.org/en/A/CN.9/WG.I/WP.122

USCB (2020) United States Census Bureau, 'Number of Firms, Number of Establishments, Employment, and Annual Payroll by Legal Form of Organization and Enterprise Employment Size for the United States, NAICS Sectors: 2017' (12 June 2020), archived 7 March 2021 at https://perma.cc/4UET-5DTF

USTR (2019) Office of the United States Trade Representative, 'Small Business' (*United States Trade Representative*), archived 7 March 2021 at https://perma.cc/8Z7Q-7QQC

Utset (2003) Utset, Manuel A., 'A Theory of Self-Control Problems and Incomplete Contracting: The Case of Shareholder Contracts' [2003] Utah LRev 1329

Vagts (2002) Vagts, Detlev F., 'Comparative Company Law – The New Wave' in Rainer J. Schweizer (ed.), *Festschrift für Jean Nicolas Druey zum 65. Geburtstag* (Zurich, Schulthess 2002)

Veziroğlu (2018) Veziroğlu, Cem, 'Buy-Out of the Oppressed Minority's Shares in Joint Stock Companies: A Comparative Analysis of Turkish, Swiss and English Law' (2018) 19 EBOR 527

Vollmer (1979) Vollmer, Lothar, 'Die mitbestimmte GmbH: Gesetzliches Normalstatut, mitbestimmungsrechtliche Satzungsgestaltungen und gesellschaftsrechtlicher Minderheitenschutz [The Co-determined GmbH: Model Corporate Constitution Provided for by Legislation, Corporate Constitution Design under Co-determination Law, and Minority Protection in Corporate Law]' [1979] Zeitschrift für Unternehmens- und Gesellschaftsrecht 135

de Vries (2010) de Vries, Paul P., *Exit Rights of Minority Shareholders in a Private Limited Company* (Deventer, Kluwer 2010)

Wada (2012) Wada, Munehisa, 'Dai-606-jō [Article 606]' in Egashira & Nakamura (2012)

Walmart (2019) 'History of Walmart and SEIYU', archived 1 June 2019 at https://web.archive.org/web/20190601171644/https://cdn.corporate.walmart.com/cf/f1/89162ec04c8890d74eb284b05bfd/walmart-seiyu-history.pdf

Wang (2011) Wang, Qiuju, *Exit Remedies for Minority Shareholders in Close Companies: England, the United States, China* (Deventer, Kluwer 2011)

Wedemann (2013) Wedemann, Frauke, *Gesellschafterkonflikte in geschlossenen Kapitalgesellschaften* [*Shareholder Conflicts in Closed Capital-based Companies*] (Tübingen, Mohr Siebeck 2013)

Wee (2009) Wee, Meng Seng, 'Membership and Members' Rights' in Tan Cheng Han (ed.), *Walter Woon on Company Law* (rev. 3rd ed., Singapore, Sweet & Maxwell 2009)

Weinrib (2012) Weinrib, Ernest, *The Idea of Private Law* (2nd ed., Oxford University Press 2012)

Wellhöfer (1994) Wellhöfer, Werner, 'Ausscheiden eines GmbH-Gesellschafters in der Gesellschaftspraxis [Exit of a GmbH-Member in Corporate Practice]' [1994] GmbH-Rundschau 212

Wells (2008) Wells, Harwell, 'The Rise of the Close Corporation and the Making of Close Corporation Law' (2008) 5 Berkeley Business LJ 263

Wells (2015) Wells, Harwell, 'Shareholder Power in America, 1800–2000: A Short History' in Jennifer G. Hill & Randall S. Thomas (eds.), *Research Handbook on Shareholder Power* (Cheltenham, Edward Elgar 2015)

Wertenbruch (2016) Wertenbruch, Johannes, '§ 47 Anhang Nichtigkeit und Anfechtung von Gesellschafterbeschlüssen [Appendix to Section 47 Nullity and Rescission of Members' Resolutions]' in Fleischer & Goette (2016)

West (1999) West, Mark D, 'Information, Institutions, and Extortion in Japan and the United States: Making Sense of Sokaiya Racketeers' (1999) 93 Northwestern University LRev 767

Whincop (2001) Whincop, Michael J., *An Economic and Jurisprudential Genealogy of Corporate Law* (Aldershot, Hampshire, Ashgate 2001)

Wiedemann (1965) Wiedemann, Herbert, *Die Übertragung und Vererbung von Mitgliedschaftsrechten bei Handelsgesellschaften* [*The Transfer and Inheritance of Membership Rights in Commercial Partnerships and Companies*] (Munich, C. H. Beck 1965)

Wiedemann (1980) Wiedemann, Herbert, *Gesellschaftsrecht: Ein Lehrbuch des Unternehmens- und Verbandsrechts* [*Corporate Law: A Primer on the Law of Enterprise and Organizations*], vol. 1 (Munich, C. H. Beck 1980)

Williamson (1979) Williamson, Oliver E., 'Transaction-Cost Economics: The Governance of Contractual Relations' (1979) 22 Journal of Law & Economics 233

Williamson (1983) Williamson, Oliver, 'Credible Commitments: Using Hostages to Support Exchange' (1983) 73 American Economic Review 519

Williston (1888) Williston, Samuel, 'History of the Law of Business Corporations Before 1800 (Part 2)' (1888) 2 Harvard LRev 149

Windbichler (2013) Windbichler, Christine, *Gesellschaftsrecht: Ein Studienbuch* [*Corporate Law: A Textbook*] (23rd ed., Munich, C. H. Beck 2013)

Winkler (1967) Winkler, Karl, *Die Lückenausfüllung des GmbH-Rechts durch das Recht der Personengesellschaften [Filling Gaps in GmbH Law with the Law of Partnerships]* (Cologne, Dr Otto Schmidt 1967)

Winter (1988) Winter, Martin, *Mitgliedschaftliche Treubindungen im GmbH-Recht: Rechtsformspezifische Aspekte eines allgemeinen gesellschaftsrechtlichen Prinzips [Membership Obligations of Loyalty in GmbH Law: Aspects of a General Corporate Law Principle Specific to the Legal Form]* (Munich, C. H. Beck 1988)

Wiśniewski & Opalski (2009) Wiśniewski, Andrzej W., & Adam Opalski, 'Companies' Freedom of Establishment after the ECJ Cartesio Judgment' (2009) 10 EBOR 595

Wolany (1964) Wolany, Josef, *Rechte und Pflichten des Gesellschafters einer GmbH [Rights and Duties of a GmbH Member]* (Cologne, Dr Otto Schmidt 1964)

Woolf (1996) Lord Woolf M. R., *Access to Justice: Final Report* (London, Stationery Office 1996)

World Bank (2021a) World Bank, International Comparison Program database, 'GDP, PPP (Current International $)' (World Bank Group, 2021) archived 4 March 2021 at https://perma.cc/V86B-H5HB

World Bank (2021b) World Development Indicators Database, 'Gross Domestic Product 2019' (World Bank, 12 February 2021), archived 4 March 2021 at https://perma.cc/BX5J-MJBH

Yamamoto (2006) Yamamoto, Norimitsu, 'Yūgen Kaisha Hō no Haishi ni tomonau Keika Sochi [Transitionary Arrangements Accompanying the Repeal of the YK Act]' in Aizawa (2006)

Yazawa et al. (1977) Yazawa, Makoto et al., 'Shōhō Bukai SHIMPOJIUMU: Kaisha Hō no Konpon Kaisei [Corporate Law Subcommittee Symposium: Fundamental Reform of Corporate Law]' (1977) 39 Shihō 95

Zuckerman (1996) Zuckerman, A. A. S., 'Lord Woolf's Access to Justice: Plus ça change … ' (1996) 59 MLR 773

Cases

GERMANY

BGH 01.04.1953, BGHZ 9, 157
BGH 05.06.1975, BGHZ 65, 15 ('ITT')
BGH 23.02.1981, BGHZ 80, 346
BGH 26.10.1983, BGHZ 88, 320
BGH 25.09.1986, BGHZ 98, 276
BGH 14.05.1990, NJW 1990, 2627
BGH 16.12.1991, BGHZ 116, 359
BGH 30.11.2009, NJW 2010, 1206
BGH 24.01.2012, BGHZ 192, 236
BGH 18.02.2014, NZG 2014, 541
LG Mönchengladbach 23.10.1985, NJW-RR 1986, 837
OLG Hamm 28.09.1992, GmbHR 1993, 656
OLG Karlsruhe 25.04.1984, BB 1984, 2015
OLG Köln 21.05.1996, GmbHR 1996, 609
OLG Köln 26.03.1999, NZG 1999, 1222
OLG München 09.06.1989, GmbHR 1990, 221
RG 09.10.1914, RGZ 85, 311
RG 07.12.1920, RGZ 101, 55
RG 02.07.1926, RGZ 114, 213
RG 07.02.1930, RGZ 128, 1

UNITED KINGDOM

Allmark *v.* Burnham [2005] EWHC 2717 (Ch); [2006] 2 BCLC 437
Amin *v.* Amin [2009] EWHC 3356 (Ch)
Anderson *v.* Hogg 2000 SLT 634 (OH)
Apex Global Management Ltd *v.* FI Call Ltd [2013] EWHC 1652 (Ch); [2014] BCC 286

Arrow Trading and Investments Est 1920 *v.* Edwardian Group Ltd [2004] EWHC 1319 (Ch); [2005] 1 BCLC 696
Baker *v.* Potter [2004] EWHC 1422 (Ch); [2005] BCC 855
Blisset *v.* Daniel (1853) 10 Hare 493 (Vice-Chancellor's Court)
Bushell *v.* Faith [1970] AC 1099 (HL)
Cream Holdings Ltd *v.* Davenport [2010] EWHC 3096 (Ch), appeal dismissed; [2011] EWCA Civ 1287; [2012] 1 BCLC 365
Croly *v.* Good [2010] EWHC 1 (Ch); [2010] 2 BCLC 569
Dalby *v.* Bodilly [2004] EWHC 3078 (Ch); [2005] BCC 627
Ebrahimi *v.* Westbourne Galleries Ltd [1973] AC 360 (HL)
Elder *v.* Elder & Watson 1952 SC 49 (Scot 1st Div)
F & C Alternative Investments (Holdings) Ltd *v.* Barthelemy (No. 2); [2011] EWHC 1731 (Ch); [2012] Ch 613
Fisher *v.* Cadman [2005] EWHC 377 (Ch); [2006] 1 BCLC 499
Fowler *v.* Gruber [2009] CSOH 36; [2010] 1 BCLC 563
Fulham Football Club (1987) Ltd *v.* Richards [2011] EWCA Civ 855; [2012] Ch 333 (Patten LJ), overruling Exeter City Association Football Club Ltd *v.* Football Conference Ltd; [2004] EWHC 831 (Ch); [2004] 1 WLR 2910
Goldsmith *v.* Sperrings Ltd [1977] 1 WLR 478 (CA)
Grace *v.* Biagioli [2005] EWCA Civ 1222; [2006] 2 BCLC 70
Harborne Road Nominees Ltd *v.* Karvaski [2011] EWHC 2214 (Ch); [2012] 2 BCLC 420
Hawkes *v.* Cuddy (No. 2) [2007] EWHC 2999 (Ch); [2008] BCC 390
Hurd *v.* TPL Holdings Ltd (25 March 2014) [2014] Lexis Citation 40 (ChD)
Irvine *v.* Irvine (No. 1) [2006] EWHC 406 (Ch); [2007] 1 BCLC 349
Irvine *v.* Irvine (No. 2) [2006] EWHC 583 (Ch); [2007] 1 BCLC 445
Jaber *v.* Science and Information Technology Ltd [1992] BCLC 764 (ChD)
JSC BTA Bank *v.* Ablyazov (No. 6) [2011] EWHC 1136 (Comm); [2011] 1 WLR 2996
Khoshkou *v.* Cooper [2014] EWHC 1087 (Ch)
Lloyd *v.* Casey [2002] 1 BCLC 454 (ChD)
Maresca *v.* Brookfield Development and Construction [2013] EWHC 3151 (Ch)
McGuinness *v.* Bremner plc 1988 SLT 891 (OH)
Mears *v.* R Mears & Co. (Holdings) Ltd [2002] 2 BCLC 1 (ChD)
Nicholas *v.* Soundcraft Electronics Ltd [1993] BCLC 360 (CA)
North Holdings Ltd *v.* Southern Tropics Ltd [1999] 2 BCLC 625 (CA)
Oak Investment Partners XII Ltd Partnership *v.* Boughtwood [2009] EWHC 176 (Ch); [2009] 1 BCLC 453, reversed in part; [2010] EWCA Civ 23; [2010] 2 BCLC 459
O'Neill *v.* Phillips [1999] 1 WLR 1092 (HL)
Parkinson *v.* Eurofinance Group Ltd [2001] 1 BCLC 720 (Ch)
Premier Telecom Communications Group Ltd *v.* Webb [2014] EWCA Civ 994
Pringle *v.* Callard [2007] EWCA Civ 1075; [2008] 2 BCLC 505

Profinance Trust SA *v.* Gladstone [2001] EWCA Civ 1031; [2002] 1 BCLC 141
Quinlan *v.* Essex Hinge Co. Ltd [1996] 2 BCLC 417 (ChD)
R & H Electric Ltd *v.* Haden Bill Electrical Ltd [1995] 2 BCLC 280 (ChD)
Rackind *v.* Gross [2004] EWCA Civ 815; [2005] 1 WLR 3505
Rahman *v.* Malik [2008] EWHC 959 (Ch); [2008] 2 BCLC 403
Raineri *v.* Miles [1981] AC 1050 (HL)
Re Abbington Hotel Ltd, DiGrado *v.* D'Angelo [2011] EWHC 635 (Ch); [2012] 1 BCLC 410
Re Annacott Holdings Ltd, Attwood *v.* Maidment [2013] EWCA Civ 119; [2013] 2 BCLC 46
Re Astec (BSR) plc [1998] 2 BCLC 556 (Ch)
Re a Company (No. 002567 of 1982) [1983] 1 WLR 927 (ChD)
Re a Company (No. 002612 of 1984) [1985] BCLC 80 (ChD)
Re a Company (No. 00477 of 1986) [1986] BCLC 376 (ChD)
Re a Company (No. 002612 of 1984) (1986) 2 BCC 99453 (ChD)
Re a Company (No. 008699 of 1985) [1986] BCLC 382 (ChD)
Re a Company (No. 004377 of 1986) [1987] 1 WLR 102 (ChD)
Re a Company (No. 001761 of 1986) [1987] BCLC 141 (ChD)
Re a Company (No. 007281 of 1986) [1987] BCLC 593 (ChD)
Re a Company (No. 00370 of 1987), ex p Glossop [1988] 1 WLR 1068 (ChD)
Re a Company (No. 005685 of 1988), ex p Schwarcz (No. 2) [1989] BCLC 427 (ChD)
Re a Company (No. 006834 of 1989), ex p Kremer [1989] BCLC 365 (ChD)
Re a Company (No. 00789 of 1987), ex p Shooter [1990] BCLC 384 (ChD)
Re a Company (No. 00330 of 1991), ex p Holden [1991] BCLC 597 (ChD)
Re a Company (No. 00314 of 1989), ex p Estate Acquisition and Development Ltd [1991] BCLC 154 (ChD)
Re a Company (No. 004502 of 1988), ex p Johnson [1992] BCLC 701 (ChD)
Re a Company (No. 1126 of 1992) [1994] 2 BCLC 146 (ChD)
Re a Company (No. 00836 of 1995) [1996] 2 BCLC 192 (ChD)
Re a Company (No. 004415 of 1996), Re a Company (No. 004416 of 1996), Re a Company (No. 004413 of 1996) [1997] 1 BCLC 479 (ChD)
Re Castleburn Ltd [1991] BCLC 89 (ChD)
Re Crossmore Electrical and Civil Engineering Ltd [1989] BCLC 137 (ChD)
Re Batesons Hotels (1958) Ltd, Bateson *v.* Bateson [2013] EWHC 2530 (Ch); [2014] 1 BCLC 507
Re Baumler (UK) Ltd, Gerrard *v.* Koby [2004] EWHC 7673 (Ch); [2005] 1 BCLC 92
Re BC&G Care Homes Ltd, Crowley *v.* Bessell [2015] EWHC 1518 (Ch); [2016] BCC 615
Re Benfield Greig Group plc, Nugent *v.* Benfield Greig Group plc [2001] EWCA Civ 397; [2002] 1 BCLC 65
Re Bird Precision Bellows Ltd [1984] Ch 419 (ChD), appeals dismissed [1986] Ch 658 (CA)

Re Blackwood Hodge plc [1997] 2 BCLC 650 (ChD)
Re Blue Index Ltd, Murrell *v.* Swallow [2014] EWHC 2680 (Ch)
Re Bovey Hotel Ventures Ltd (31 July 1981, unreported) (ChD)
Re Brenfield Squash Racquets Club Ltd [1996] 2 BCLC 184 (ChD)
Re BSB Holdings Ltd (No. 2) [1996] 1 BCLC 155 (ChD)
Re Charterhouse Capital Ltd, Arbuthnott *v.* Bonnyman [2015] EWCA Civ 536; [2015] BCC 574
Re Copeland & Craddock Ltd [1997] BCC 294 (CA)
Re Coroin Ltd, McKillen *v.* Misland (Cyprus) Investments Ltd [2012] EWHC 521 (Ch)
Re Coroin Ltd (No. 2), McKillen *v.* Misland (Cyprus) Investments Ltd [2012] EWHC 2343 (Ch); [2013] 2 BCLC 583, appeal dismissed; [2013] EWCA Civ 781; [2013] 2 BCLC 583
Re Cumana Ltd [1986] BCLC 430 (CA)
Re Edwardian Group Ltd, Estera Trust (Jersey) Ltd *v.* Singh [2018] EWHC 1715 (Ch); [2019] 1 BCLC 171
Re Elgindata Ltd (No. 1) [1991] BCLC 959 (ChD)
Re Estate Acquisition & Development Ltd [1995] BCC 338 (ChD)
Re Five Minute Car Wash Services Ltd [1966] 1 WLR 745 (ChD)
Re Freudiana Music Co. Ltd (High Court of England and Wales, 24 March 1993, Jonathan Parker J)
Re Ghyll Beck Driving Range Ltd [1993] BCLC 1126 (ChD)
Re Grandactual Ltd, Hough *v.* Hardcastle [2005] EWHC 1415 (Ch); [2006] BCC 73
Re Guidezone Ltd [2000] 2 BCLC 321 (ChD)
Re Halt Garage (1964) Ltd [1982] 3 All ER 1016 (ChD)
Re H R Harmer Ltd [1959] 1 WLR 62 (CA)
Re Home & Office Fire Extinguishers Ltd, Rodliffe *v.* Rodliffe [2012] EWHC 917 (Ch)
Re Hydrosan Ltd [1991] BCLC 418 (ChD)
Re J&S Insurance & Financial Consultants Ltd, Judge *v.* Bahd [2014] EWHC 2206 (Ch)
Re J E Cade & Son Ltd [1992] BCLC 213 (ChD)
Re Jayflex Construction Ltd, McKee *v.* O'Reilly [2003] EWHC 2008 (Ch); [2004] 2 BCLC 145
Re Jermyn Street Turkish Baths Ltd [1970] 1 WLR 1194 (ChD), reversed, [1971] 1 WLR 1042 (CA)
Re John Reid & Sons (Strucsteel) Ltd, Reid *v.* Reid [2003] EWHC 2329 (Ch); [2003] 2 BCLC 319
Re LCM Wealth Management Ltd, Moxon *v.* Litchfield [2013] EWHC 3957 (Ch)
Re Legal Costs Negotiators Ltd [1999] BCC 547 (CA)
Re Little Olympian Each-Ways Ltd [1994] 2 BCLC 420 (ChD)
Re Lloyds Autobody Ringway Ltd, Davies *v.* Lynch-Smith [2018] EWHC 2336 (Ch)

Re London School of Electronics Ltd [1986] Ch 211 (ChD)
Re Lundie Brothers Ltd [1965] 1 WLR 1051
Re Macro (Ipswich) Ltd [1994] 2 BCLC 354 (ChD)
Re Majory (A Debtor) [1955] Ch 600 (CA)
Re McCarthy Surfacing Ltd, Hequet *v.* McCarthy [2008] EWHC 2279 (Ch); [2009] 1 BCLC 622
Re Metropolis Motorcycles Ltd, Hale *v.* Waldock [2006] EWHC 364 (Ch); [2007] 1 BCLC 520
Re Neath Rugby Ltd, Hawkes *v.* Cuddy [2009] EWCA Civ 291; [2010] BCC 597
Re Phoenix Contracts (Leicester) Ltd, Shepherd *v.* Williamson [2010] EWHC 2375 (Ch)
Re Phoenix Office Supplies Ltd [2002] EWHC 591 (Ch); [2002] 2 BCLC 556, reversed by Re Phoenix Office Supplies Ltd, Phoenix Office Supplies Ltd *v.* Larvin [2002] EWCA Civ 1740; [2003] 1 BCLC 76
Re Planet Organic Ltd [2000] 1 BCLC 366 (ChD)
Re R A Noble & Sons (Clothing) Ltd [1983] BCLC 273 (ChD)
Re Ravenhart Service (Holdings) Ltd, Reiner. *v.* Gershinson [2004] EWHC 76 (Ch); [2004] 2 BCLC 376
Re R S M Industries Ltd, Williams *v.* Brinkmann [2004] EWHC 601 (Ch)
Re Sam Weller & Sons Ltd [1990] Ch 682 (ChD)
Re Saul D Harrison & Sons plc [1995] 1 BCLC 14 (CA)
Re Scitec Group Ltd, Sethi *v.* Patel [2010] EWHC 1830 (Ch); [2011] 1 BCLC 277
Re Sticky Fingers Restaurant Ltd [1992] BCLC 84 (ChD)
Re Sunrise Radio Ltd, Kohli *v.* Lit [2009] EWHC 2893 (Ch); [2010] 1 BCLC 367
Re Tobian Properties Ltd, Maidment *v.* Attwood [2012] EWCA Civ 998; [2013] 2 BCLC 567
Re Unisoft Group Ltd (No. 3) [1994] 1 BCLC 609 (ChD)
Re Westbourne Galleries Ltd [1970] 1 WLR 1378 (ChD)
Re Woven Rugs Ltd, Sharafi *v.* Woven Rugs Ltd [2010] EWHC 230 (Ch)
Richards *v.* Lundy [2000] 1 BCLC 376 (ChD)
Richardson *v.* Blackmore, Capital Cabs Ltd *v.* Blackmore (unreported, 1 November 2004) (ChD), affirmed and reversed in part; [2005] EWCA Civ 1356; [2006] BCC 276
Rock Nominees Ltd *v.* RCO (Holdings) plc (in liquidation) [2004] EWCA Civ 118; [2004] 1 BCLC 439
Routledge *v.* Skerritt [2019] EWHC 573 (Ch)
Salomon *v.* A Salomon & Co. Ltd [1897] AC 22 (HL)
Scottish Co-operative Wholesale Society Ltd *v.* Meyer [1958] 3 All ER 66, [1959] AC 324 (HL (Scot))
Shah *v.* Shah [2011] EWHC 313 (Ch)
Shah *v.* Shah [2011] EWHC 1902 (Ch)
Strahan *v.* Wilcock [2006] EWCA Civ 13; [2006] 2 BCLC 555

Virdi *v.* Abbey Leisure Ltd, Re Abbey Leisure Ltd [1990] BCLC 342 (CA), reversing Re Abbey Leisure Ltd [1989] BCLC 619 (ChD)
Wilkinson *v.* West Coast Capital [2005] EWHC 3009 (Ch); [2007] BCC 717
Whillock *v.* Henderson [2007] CSOH 175; [2009] BCC 314

UNITED STATES

* Note that all citations indicating the state/jurisdiction but not the specific court level are to be construed as to referring to that state/jurisdiction's highest court.

21 West, Inc. *v.* Meadowgreen Trails, Inc. (1995) 913 SW2d 858 (MoCtApp)
Alaska Plastics, Inc. *v.* Coppock (1980) 621 P2d 270 (Alaska)
Anderson *v.* Clemens Mobile Homes, Inc. (1983) 214 Neb 283, 333 NW2d 900 (Neb)
AW Chesterton Co. *v.* Chesterton (1997) 128 F3d 1 (1stCir)
Baker *v.* Commercial Body Builders, Inc. (1973) 264 Or 614, 507 P2d 387 (Or)
Balvik *v.* Sylvester (1987) 411 NW2d 383 (ND)
Baur *v.* Baur Farms, Inc. (2013) 832 NW2d 663 (Iowa)
Baylor *v.* Beverly Book Co., Inc. (1975) 216 Va 22, 216 SE2d 18 (Va)
Bedore *v.* Familian (2006) 122 Nev 5, 125 P3d 1168 (Nev)
Berger *v.* Katz, Court of Appeals of Michigan No. 291663, 28 July 2011, 2011 WL 3209217, appeal denied (2012) 491 Mich 886, 809 NW2d 586 (Mich), reconsideration denied (2012) 491 Mich 947, 815 NW2d 426 (Mich)
Boland *v.* Boland (2011) 423 Md 296, 31 A3d 529 (Md)
Bontempo *v.* Lare (2015) 444 Md 344, 119 A3d 791 (Md)
Bostock *v.* High Tech Elevator Industries, Inc. (1992) 260 NJSuper 432, 616 A2d 1314 (NJAppDiv)
Brandt *v.* Somerville (2005) 2005 ND 35, 692 NW2d 144 (ND)
Brenner *v.* Berkowitz (1993) 134 NJ 488, 634 A2d 1019 (NJ)
Brent D. Redstone *v.* National Amusements, Inc. (2006) No. 24-C-06–001493, Circuit Court of Maryland, Baltimore City, Evelyn Omega Cannon J, 7 August 2006, 2006 WL 4476415
Brodie *v.* Jordan (2006) 447 Mass 866, 857 NE2d 1076 (Mass)
Brodie *v.* Jordan (2006) 66 MassAppCt 371, 847 NE2d 1125 (MassAppCt), affirming No. 98–518-E, 13 June 2002, Elizabeth Fahey J, 2002 WL 34077196 (MassSuper)
Cardiac Perfusion Services, Inc. *v.* Hughes (2014); 436 SW3d 790 (Tex)
Cattano *v.* Bragg (2012) 283 Va 638, 727 SE2d 625 (Va)
Central Standard Life Insurance Co. *v.* Davis (1957) 10 Ill2d 566, 141 NE2d 45 (Ill)
Coduti *v.* Hellwig (1984) 127 IllApp3d 279, 469 NE2d 220 (IllAppCt)
Currie's Administrators *v.* Mutual Assurance Society (1809) 14 Va (4 Hen & M) 315 (1809) (Virginia Supreme Court of Appeals)
Davis *v.* Sheerin (1988) 754 SW2d 375 (TexApp)

Dawkins *v.* Hickman Family Corp., No. 1:09–CV–164, US District Court, Northern District of Mississippi, Sharion Aycock J, 13 June 2011, 2011 WL 243653
Delaney *v.* Georgia-Pacific Corp. (1977) 278 Or 305, 564 P2d 277 (Or)
DiPace *v.* Figueroa (1996) 223 AD2d 949, 637 NYS2d 222 (NYAppDiv)
Donahue *v.* Rodd Electrotype Co. (1975) 367 Mass 578, 328 NE2d 505 (Mass)
Edenbaum *v.* Schwarcz-Osztreicherne (2005) 165 Md App 233, 885 A2d 365 (MdSpecApp)
Elniski *v.* Niagara Falls Coach Lines, Inc. (2012) 101 AD3d 1722, 957 NYS2d 544 (NYAppDiv)
Ex parte Bentley (2010) 50 So3d 1063 (Alabama)
Fancher *v.* Prudhome (2013) 112 So3d 909 (LaApp2Cir)
Hall *v.* King (1998) 177 Misc2d 126, 675 NYS2d 810 (NYSupCt)
Hayat *v.* Al-Mazeedi, 10 January 2011, No. 08–1004, 2011 WL 1532109, 28 MassLRptr 243 (MassSuper)
Head & Amory *v.* Providence Insurance Co. (1804) 6 US (2 Cranch) 127
Helms *v.* Duckworth (1957) 249 F2d 482 (DCCir)
Hendrick *v.* Hendrick (2000) 755 A2d 784 (RI)
Hendley *v.* Lee (1987) 676 FSupp 1317 (DSC)
Hickey *v.* Hickey (2015) 269 OrApp 258, 344 P3d 512 (OrCtApp), review denied 357 Or 415, 356 P3d 638
Hunt *v.* Data Management Resources, Inc. (1999) 26 KanApp2d 405, 985 P2d 730 (KanCtApp)
G & N Aircraft, Inc. *v.* Boehm (2001) 743 NE2d 227 (Ind)
Galler *v.* Galler (1964) 32 Ill2d 16, 203 NE2d 577 (Ill)
Giannotti *v.* Hamway (1990) 239 Va 14, 387 SE2d 725 (Va)
Go *v.* Pacific Health Services, Inc. (2009) 179 CalApp4th 522, 101 CalRptr3d 736 (CalCtApp)
Goles *v.* Sawhney (2016) 5 CalApp5th 1014, 210 CalRptr3d 261 (CalCtApp)
Gunzberg *v.* Art-Lloyd Metal Products Corp. (1985) 492 NYS2d 83 (NYAppDiv)
In re Carlisle Etcetera LLC (2015) 114 A3d 592 (DelCh)
In re Davis (1991) 174 AD2d 449, 571 NYS2d 234 (NYAppDiv)
In re Orange City Nursery, Inc. (2010) 439 BR 144 (CDCal)
In re Superior Vending, LLC (2010) 71 AD3d 1153, 898 NYS2d 191 (NYAppDiv)
In re Topper (1980) 107 Misc2d 25, 433 NYS2d 359 (NYSupCt)
IRS Private Letter Ruling 81–06–082 (18 November 1980)
IRS Revenue Ruling 88–76, 1988–2 CB 360, declared obsolete by Revenue Ruling 98–37, 1998–2 CB 133
It's Golden, LLC *v.* Watercolors Unit 6, LLC (2017) 223 So3d 545 (LaApp1Cir)
Jackson *v.* Hooper (1910) 75 A 568 (Court of Errors and Appeals of New Jersey)
Jacobs *v.* Cartalemi (2017) 156 AD3d 635, 66 NYS3d 503 (NYAppDiv), leave to appeal denied (2018) 32 NY3d 903, 109 NE3d 1157 (NY)
Jundt *v.* Jurassic Resources Development (2003) 2003 ND 9, 656 NW2d 15 (ND)

Kiriakides *v.* Atlas Food Systems & Services, Inc. (2001) 343 SC 587, 541 SE2d 257 (SC)
Kirksey *v.* Grohmann (2008) 2008 SD 76, 754 NW2d 825 (SD)
Kirtz *v.* Grossman (1971) 463 SW2d 541 (MoCtApp)
Kreischer *v.* Kerrison Dry Goods Co. (1999) 172 F3d 863, 1999 WL 30836 (4th Circuit, unpublished)
Kulko *v.* Davail, Inc. (2015) 381 Mont 511, 363 P3d 430 (Mont)
Litle *v.* Waters, No. CIV A 12155, Chandler VC, 11 February 1992, 1992 WL 25758, (1993) 18 Delaware Journal of Corporate Law 315 (DelCh)
Louis K. Liggett Co. *v.* Lee (1933) 288 US 517
Lyons *v.* Salamone (2006) 32 AD3d 757, 821 NYS2d 188 (NYAppDiv)
Maddox *v.* Norman (1983) 206 Mont 1, 669 P2d 230 (Mont)
Markman *v.* Exterior Delite, Inc. (2006) 14 Misc 3d 910, 831 NYS2d 656 (NYSupCt)
Masinter *v.* WEBCO Co. (1980) 164 Wva 241, 262 SE2d 433 (Wva)
Matter of Kemp & Beatley, Inc. (1984) 64 NY2d 63, 473 NE2d 1173 (NY)
Matter of Pace Photographers, Ltd, 71 NY2d 737, 525 NE2d 713 (1988)
Matter of Validation Review Associates, Inc. (1996) 223 AD2d 134, 646 NYS2d 149 (NYAppDiv), order reversed as moot (1997) 91 NY2d 840, 690 NE2d 487 (NY), holding affirmed Schimel *v.* Berkun (1999) 264 AD2d 725, 728, 696 NYS2d 49, 52 (NYAppDiv)
Matter of Villa Maria, Inc. (1981) 312 NW2d 921 (Minn)
Matter of Wiedy's Furniture Clearance Center Co., Inc. (1985) 108 AD2d 81, 487 NYS2d 901 (NYAppDiv)
McCauley *v.* Tom McCauley & Son, Inc. (1986) 104 NM 523, 724 P2d 232 (NMCtApp)
Meiselman *v.* Meiselman (1983) 309 NC 279, 307 SE2d 551 (NC)
Meiselman *v.* Meiselman (1982) 58 NCApp 758, 295 SE2d 249 (NCApp)
Miner *v.* Belle Isle Ice Co. (1892) 93 Mich 97, 53 NW 218 (Mich)
Muellenberg *v.* Bikon Corp. (1996) 143 NJ 168, 669 A2d 1382 (NJ)
Murphy *v.* US Dredging Corp. (2010) 74 AD3d 815, 903 NYS2d 434 (NYAppDiv)
Musto *v.* Vidas (1995) 281 NJSuper 548, 658 A2d 1305 (NJAppDiv)
Nelson *v.* Martin (1997) 958 SW2d 643 (Tenn)
Nixon *v.* Blackwell (1993) 626 A2d 1366 (Del)
Orchard *v.* Covelli (1984) 590 Fsupp 1548 (WDPa), affirmed without published grounds (1986) 802 F2d 448 (3d Cir)
Orzeck *v.* Englehart (1963) 195 A2d 375 (Del)
Pacific Sun Distributing *v.* Martin, No. B221716, 15 February 2011, 2011 WL 522040 (CalCtApp)
PFT Technology, LLC *v.* Wieser (2020) 181 AD3d 836, 122 NYS3d 313 (NYAppDiv)
Re Radom & Neidorff, Inc. (1954) 307 NY 1 (NY)
Ritchie *v.* Rupe (2014) 443 SW3d 856 (Tex)
Santa Fe Industries, Inc. *v.* Green (1977) 430 US 462

Sauer *v.* Moffitt (1984) 363 NW2d 269 (IowaCtApp)
Schaub *v.* Kortgard (1985) 372 NW2d 427 (MinnCtApp)
Scott *v.* Trans-System, Inc. (2003) 148 Wash2d 701, 64 P3d 1 (Wash)
Skarbo *v.* Skarbo Scandinavian Furniture Import, Inc. (2005) 128 WashApp 1072, 2005 WL 1950599 (WashCtApp)
Stefano *v.* Coppock (1985) 705 P2d 443 (Alaska)
Terrett *v.* Taylor (1815) 13 US (9 Cranch) 4 (US)
Teixeira & Co. *v.* Teixeira (1994) No. PC 84–0152, Superior Court of Rhode Island, Providence County, Gibney J, 21 July 1994, 1994 WL 930950, affirmed sub nomine A Teixeira & Co. *v.* Teixeira (1996) 674 A2d 407 (RI)
Trahan *v.* Trahan (2002) 99 CalApp4th 62, 120 CalRptr 2d 814 (CalCtApp)
Trustees of Dartmouth College *v.* Woodward (1819) 17 US (4 Wheat) 518 (US)
Wall *v.* Bryan (2018) 251 So3d 650 (LaApp2Cir), writ denied (2018) 255 So3d 1047 and 255 So3d 1051
White *v.* Perkins (1972) 213 Va 129, 189 SE2d 315 (Va)
Wilkes *v.* Springside Nursing Home, Inc. (1976) 353 NE2d 657 (Mass)
Wilson *v.* Gandis (2020) 430 SC 282, 844 SE2d 631 (SC)
Zidell *v.* Zidell, Inc. (1977) 560 P2d 1086 (Or)
Zimmerman *v.* Bogoff (1988) 402 Mass 650, 524 NE2d 849 (Mass)

JAPAN

Daishin'in [Great Court of Cassation] 01.06.1931, 3301 Hōritsu Shimbun 14
Ōsaka Kōso'in [Osaka Court of Appeal] 20.12.1932, 3509 Hōritsu Shimbun 9
Kōbe Chihō Saibansho [Kobe District Court] 29.08.1986, 1222 Hanrei Jihō 135
Nagoya Chihō Saibansho [Nagoya District Court] 29.09.1987, 1264 Hanrei Jihō 128
Saikō Saibansho [Supreme Court] 11.12.1969, 23(12) Minshū 2447, also available at https://perma.cc/Q33D-9Y76
Saikō Saibansho [Supreme Court] 08.11.1972, 26(9) Minshū 1489, also available at https://perma.cc/3ACE-Z627
Tokyo District Court 30.06.1925
Tokyo District Court 29.08.1941
Tokyo District Court 27.04.1995, 1541 Hanrei Jihō 130
Tokyo District Court 05.10.2009, 591 Tōki Jōhō 126
Tokyo High Court 24.02.2010, 591 Tōki Jōhō 125

OTHERS

BCE Inc. *v.* 1976 Debenture Holders 2008 SCC 69; [2008] 3 SCR 560 (Canada)
Case C-212/97 Centros Ltd *v.* Erhvervs- og Selskabsstyrelsen [1999] ECR I-1459 (European Union)

Case C-208/00 Überseering BV *v.* Nordic Construction Company Baumanagement GmbH [2002] ECR I-9919 (European Union)

Case C-167/01 Kamer van Koophandel en Fabrieken voor Amsterdam *v.* Inspire Art Ltd [2003] ECR I-10155 (European Union)

Case C-210/06 Cartesio Oktató és Szolgáltató bt [2008] ECR I-9641 (European Union)

Case C-378/10 VALE Építési kft ECLI:EU:C:2012:440 (European Union)

CVC/Opportunity Equity Partners Ltd *v.* Demarco Almeida [2002] UKPC 16; [2002] 2 BCLC 108 (Cayman Islands)

Gamlestaden Fastigheter AB *v.* Baltic Partners Ltd [2007] UKPC 26; [2007] 4 All ER 164 (Jersey)

Kam Leung Sui Kwan *v.* Kam Kwan Lai [2015] HKCFA 79; [2015] 6 HKC 644 (Hong Kong)

Latimer Holdings Ltd *v.* SEA Holdings NZ Ltd [2005] 2 NZLR 328 (NZCA) (New Zealand)

Over & Over Ltd *v.* Bonvests Holdings Ltd [2010] SGCA 7; [2010] 2 SLR 776 (Singapore)

Re Silver Bell Uniform Ltd [2011] HKCA 481; [2012] 1 HKLRD 719 (Hong Kong)

Sembcorp Marine Ltd *v.* PPL Holdings Pte Ltd [2013] SGCA 43; [2013] 4 SLR 193 (Singapore)

Thio Syn Kym Wendy *v.* Thio Syn Pyn [2018] SGCA 46, [2018] 2 SLR 788 (Singapore)

Thomas *v.* HW Thomas Ltd [1984] 1 NZLR 686 (CA) (New Zealand)

Tomolugen Holdings Ltd *v.* Silica Investors Ltd [2015] SGCA 57; [2016] 1 SLR 373 (Singapore)

Re Wondoflex Textiles Pty Ltd [1951] VLR 458 (Supreme Court of Victoria) (Australia)

Legislation

References to the following statutes in this Book are, unless otherwise indicated, to the original, untranslated versions as amended and in force as of the end of 2020.

GERMANY

Bürgerliches Gesetzbuch [German Civil Code], enacted 18.08.1896, RGBl. S 195 (BGB)

Genossenschaftsgesetz (*Gesetz betreffend die Erwerbs- und Wirtschaftsgenossenschaften*) [Cooperatives Act], first enacted 01.05.1889, RGBl, S 55; recast 16.10.2006, BGBl I, S 2230 (GenG)

Gesetz zur Modernisierung des GmbH-Rechts und zur Bekämpfung von Missbräuchen [Act to Modernise the Law on the GmbH and to Combat Its Abuse], enacted 23.10.2008, BGBl I, S 2026, in force from 01.11.2008 (MoMiG)

Gesetz betreffend die Gesellschaften mit beschränkter Haftung [Limited Liability Companies Act], enacted 20.04.1892, RGBl S 477, in force from 10.05.1892 (GmbHG), English translation in Reusch (2019)

Handelsgesetzbuch [Commercial Code], enacted 10.05.1897, RGBl S 219 (HGB)

Spruchverfahrensgesetz (*Gesetz über das gesellschaftsrechtliche Spruchverfahren*) [Appraisal Proceedings Act], enacted 12.06.2003, in force from 01.09.2003 (SpruchG)

UNITED KINGDOM

Civil Procedure Rules 1998, SI 1998/3132

Companies Act 1862 (25 & 26 Vic c 89)

Companies Act 1907 (7 Edw 7 c 50)

Companies Act 1948 (c 38)

Companies Act 1985 (c 6)

Companies Act 1989 (c 40)
Companies Act 2006 (c 46) (Companies Act)
Companies (Model Articles) Regulations 2008, SI 2008/3229
Companies (Northern Ireland) Order 1986 (SI 1986/1032 (NI 6))
Companies (Single Member Private Limited Companies) Regulations 1992, SI 1992/1699
Companies (Unfair Prejudice Applications) Proceedings Rules 2009, SI 2009/2469
Insolvency Act 1986 (c 45)
Joint Stock Companies Act 1844 (7 & 8 Vic c 110)
Joint Stock Companies Act 1856 (19 & 20 Vic c 47)
Joint Stock Companies Winding-up Act 1848 (7 & 8 Vic c 111)
Limited Liability Act 1855 (18 & 19 Vic c 133)
Limited Liability Partnerships (Application of Companies Act 2006) Regulations 2009, SI 2009/1804
Senior Courts Act 1981 (c 54)

UNITED STATES

Federal Laws

United States Code Annotated (West) (USCA)
Internal Revenue Code of 1986 (26 USCA) (IRC)
Securities Act of 1933 (15 USCA § 77a et seq)
Securities and Exchange Act of 1934 (15 USCA § 78a et seq)
Code of Federal Regulations (CFR)
Treasury Regulations (26 CFR) § 301.7701

State Laws

West's Alaska Statutes Annotated (Alaska StatAnn)
Arizona Revised Statutes Annotated (West) (Arizona RevStatAnn)
West's Annotated California Codes: Corporations Code (AnnCalCorpCode)
West's Delaware Code Annotated (DelCodeAnn):
    Delaware General Corporation Law (8 DelCodeAnn ch 1) (DGCL)
    Delaware Limited Liability Company Act (6 DelCodeAnn ch 18) (DLLCA)
West's Florida Statutes Annotated (FlaStatAnn)
West's Code of Georgia Annotated (GaCodeAnn)
West's Hawaii Revised Statutes Annotated (Hawaii RevStatAnn)
West's Smith-Hurd Illinois Compiled Statutes Annotated (West) (IllCompStatAnn)
West's Annotated Indiana Code (IndCodeAnn)
West's Kansas Statutes Annotated (KanStatAnn)

West's Louisiana Statutes Annotated (LaStatAnn)
Maine Revised Statutes Annotated (West) (Maine RevStatAnn)
Massachusetts General Laws Annotated (West) (MassGenLAnn)
Michigan Compiled Laws Annotated (West) (MichCompLAnn)
Minnesota Statutes Annotated (West) (MinnStatAnn)
West's Annotated Mississippi Code (Mississippi CodeAnn)
Vernon's Missouri Annotated Statutes (West) (MoAnnStat)
West's Montana Code Annotated (MontCodeAnn)
West's North Carolina General Statutes Annotated (NC General StatAnn)
West's North Dakota Century Code Annotated (ND Century CodeAnn)
Revised Statutes Annotated of the State of New Hampshire (West) (NHRevStatAnn)
New Jersey Statutes Annotated (West) (NJStatAnn)
West's New Mexico Statutes Annotated (NMStatAnn)
McKinney's Consolidated Laws of New York Annotated (West):
  Business Corporation Law (NYBCL)
  Limited Liability Company Law (NYLLCL)
Baldwin's Ohio Revised Code Annotated (West) (Ohio RevCodeAnn)
West's Oregon Revised Statutes Annotated (OrRevStatAnn)
Purdon's Pennsylvania Statutes and Consolidated Statutes Annotated, title 15 (West) (15 Pa Consolidated StatAnn)
Code of Laws of South Carolina, 1976 (West) (SCCodeAnn)
West's Tennessee Code Annotated (TennCodeAnn)
West's Utah Code Annotated (Utah CodeAnn)
West's Annotated Code of Virginia (VaCodeAnn)
West's Revised Code of Washington Annotated (WashRevCodeAnn)
West's Wisconsin Statutes Annotated (WisStatAnn)
West Virginia Code (1931, 1974) (WVaCode)
West's Annotated Code of West Virginia (WVaCodeAnn)

State Session Laws

1993 ND Laws Ch 54 (SB 2223)
1995 ND Laws Ch 103 (SB 2343)
2019 SC SB 265
2019 Va Laws Ch 734 (HB 2478)

Model and Uniform Acts

Model Business Corporation Act (2016 Revision) (MBCA)
Model Statutory Close Corporation Supplement (Model Supplement)
Prototype Limited Liability Company Act (1992) (PULLCA)

Revised Uniform Limited Liability Company Act (2006) (RULLCA)
Uniform Limited Liability Company Act (1996) (ULLCA 1996)
Uniform Limited Liability Company Act (2013) (ULLCA)

JAPAN

* indicates that the source of the English translated name of the legislation is the unofficial but Ministry of Justice-supported Japanese Law Translation Database System at www.japaneselawtranslation.go.jp/?re=02. Note that not all of the following legislation have been translated, and that the translated versions usually do not reflect the most recent amendments.

Chūshō Kigyō-tō Kyōdō Kumiai Hō [*Small and Medium-Sized Enterprise Cooperatives Act], Act No. 181 of 1 June 1949, translation at www.japaneselawtranslation.go.jp/law/detail/?id=1942&vm=04&re=02&new=1

Kaisha Hō [*Companies Act], Act No. 86 of 26 July 2005 (Kaishahō), translation at www.japaneselawtranslation.go.jp/law/detail/?id=3206&vm=04&re=02&new=1 and www.japaneselawtranslation.go.jp/law/detail/?id=3207&vm=04&re=02&new=1

Kaisha Hō no Shikō ni tomonau Kanren Hōritsu no Seibi-tō ni kansuru Hōritsu [*Act on Arrangement of Relevant Acts Incidental to Enforcement of the Companies Act], Act No. 87 of 26 July 2005

Kaisha Keisan Kisoku [*Regulation on Corporate Accounting], Ministry of Justice Order No. 13 of 7 February 2006, translation at www.japaneselawtranslation.go.jp/law/detail/?id=3254&vm=04&re=02&new=1

Kōshōnin Tesū-ryō Rei [*Order for Notary Fees], Cabinet Order No. 224 of 25 June 1993, translation at www.japaneselawtranslation.go.jp/law/detail/?id=3096&vm=04&re=02&new=1

Minji Hozen Hō [*Civil Provisional Remedies Act], Act No. 91 of 22 December 1989, translation at www.japaneselawtranslation.go.jp/law/detail/?id=2028&vm=04&re=02&new=1

Shihō shoshi-hō [*Judicial Scriveners Act], Act No. 197 of 22 May 1950

Shōhō [*Commercial Code], Act No. 48 of 9 March 1899 (Shōhō), substantially repealed by Act No. 87 of 26 July 2005, translation at www.japaneselawtranslation.go.jp/law/detail/?id=2735&vm=04&re=02&new=1

Tōroku Menkyo-zei Hō [*Registration and License Tax Act], Act No. 35 of 2 June 1967

Yūgen Kaisha-hō [Limited Liability Corporations Act], Act No. 74 of 5 April 1938, repealed by Act No. 87 of 26 July 2005 (YK-hō)

Yūgen Sekinin Jigyō Kumiai Keiyaku ni kansuru Hōritsu [*Limited Liability Partnership Act] [more literally and accurately, Act on Limited Liability Enterprise Partnership Agreements], Act No. 40 of 6 May 2005, translation at www.japaneselawtranslation.go.jp/law/detail/?id=140&vm=04&re=01&new=1

OTHERS

Canada Business Corporations Act, RSC 1985, c C-44 (Canada)
Companies Act 1967 (Singapore)
Companies Law 1999 (Israel)
Corporations Act 2001 (Cth) (Australia)
Insolvency, Restructuring and Dissolution Act 2018 (Singapore)
Twelfth Council Company Law Directive 89/667/EEC of 21 December 1989 on single-member private limited-liability companies [1993] OJ L395/40 (European Union)

Index

For EU product safety concerns, contact us at Calle de José Abascal, 56–1°,
28003 Madrid, Spain or eugpsr@cambridge.org.

www.ingramcontent.com/pod-product-compliance
Lightning Source LLC
LaVergne TN
LVHW052023200926
848481LV00005B/1569

* 9 7 8 1 0 0 9 5 4 5 7 5 4 *